OREGON FISHING

CRAIG SCHUHMANN

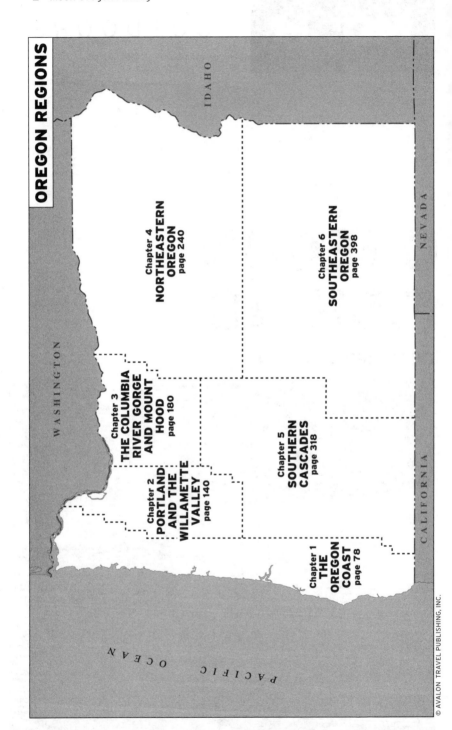

OREGON REGIONS

WASHINGTON

IDAHO

NEVADA

CALIFORNIA

PACIFIC OCEAN

Chapter 1
THE OREGON COAST
page 78

Chapter 2
PORTLAND AND THE WILLAMETTE VALLEY
page 140

Chapter 3
THE COLUMBIA RIVER GORGE AND MOUNT HOOD
page 180

Chapter 4
NORTHEASTERN OREGON
page 240

Chapter 5
SOUTHERN CASCADES
page 318

Chapter 6
SOUTHEASTERN OREGON
page 398

Contents

MAP SYMBOLS

═══ Expressway	🛈 80 Interstate Freeway	✗ Airfield
═══ Primary Road	🛈 101 U.S. Highway	✗ Airport
═══ Secondary Road	29 State Highway	○ City/Town
===== Unpaved Road	66 County Highway	▲ Mountain
········· Ferry	Lake	♠ Park
—·—·— National Border	Dry Lake	ʌ Pass
—··— State Border	Seasonal Lake	◉ State Capital

How to Use This Book

ABOUT THE FISHING PROFILES

The sites are listed in a consistent, easy-to-read format to help you choose the ideal fishing spot. If you already know the name of the specific site you want to visit, or the name of the surrounding geological area or nearby feature (town, national or state park, forest, mountain, lake, river, etc.), look it up in the index and turn to the corresponding page. Here is a sample profile:

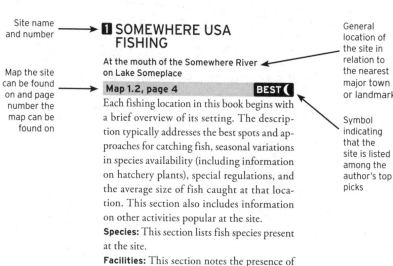

Site name and number →

❶ SOMEWHERE USA FISHING

At the mouth of the Somewhere River on Lake Someplace ←

Map the site can be found on and page number the map can be found on →

Map 1.2, page 4   **BEST (**

General location of the site in relation to the nearest major town or landmark

Symbol indicating that the site is listed among the author's top picks

Each fishing location in this book begins with a brief overview of its setting. The description typically addresses the best spots and approaches for catching fish, seasonal variations in species availability (including information on hatchery plants), special regulations, and the average size of fish caught at that location. This section also includes information on other activities popular at the site.

Species: This section lists fish species present at the site.

Facilities: This section notes the presence of boat ramps and access areas, as well as the facilities available at or near the site, such as restrooms, picnic areas, snack bars, restaurants, lodges, marinas, boat rental outlets, campgrounds, and where to buy supplies, such as groceries and gas. Information on launch and access fees is also noted here.

Directions: This section provides mile-by-mile driving directions to the fishing spot from the nearest major town or highway.

Contact: This section provides contact information for the site as well as nearby boat rentals, bait and tackle shops, and other related services. It also notes whether maps are available for purchase; see *Resources* at the back of the book for additional contact information.

ABOUT THE MAPS

This book is divided into chapters based on major regions in the state; an overview map of these regions precedes the table of contents. Each chapter begins with a map of the region, which is further broken down into detail maps. Sites are noted on the detail maps by number.

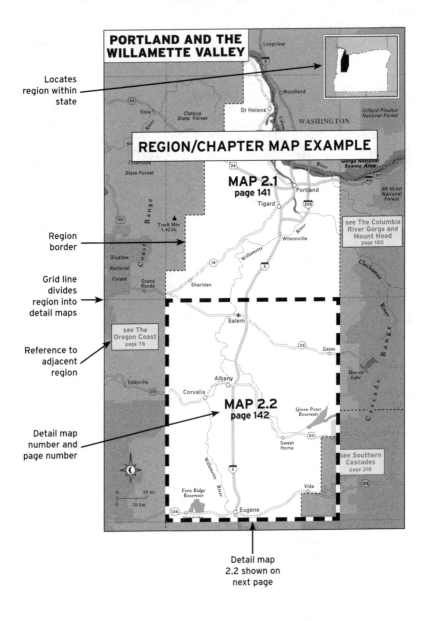

Locates region within state

Region border

Grid line divides region into detail maps

Reference to adjacent region

Detail map number and page number

Detail map 2.2 shown on next page

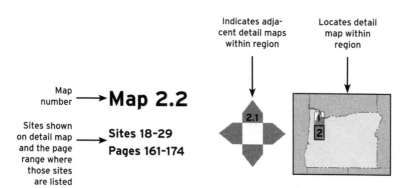

Map number →**Map 2.2**

Sites shown on detail map and the page range where those sites are listed →**Sites 18-29
Pages 161-174**

Indicates adjacent detail maps within region

Locates detail map within region

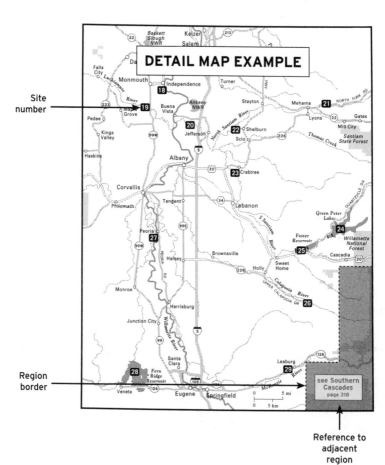

DETAIL MAP EXAMPLE

Site number

Region border

Reference to adjacent region

INTRODUCTION

"Every life has its points of fixity, certain small stillnesses in the incessancy of the world that anchor us with a sense of continuity and location."

—Ted Leeson, *The Habit of Rivers*

Author's Note

My introduction to fishing in Oregon occurred when I was 12 years old. My family had just moved to Oregon from the sun-drenched coast of Southern California and I spent my first months dreaming of the time when I could once again lay on the hot sand of my beloved Laguna Beach, practice surfing and skateboarding, and watch the ocean.

Dark, cold winters, rough mountain rivers, wild fish, and fishing guides were not in my experience—or my plans. So it came as some surprise when I fell in love with winter steelheading, a sport that is bitterly cold, requires bundles of uncomfortable heavy clothing, necessitates waking up prior to sunrise, and generally was the furthest thing from my California beach dreams. My father took me on my first winter steelhead trip; we set out on a wintry January morning at 4 A.M. After an hour of driving, we began our ascent up steep, winding roads, skirting river gorges filled with dense stands of Douglas fir and western red cedars to meet our fishing guide, George Mackie.

Everybody called him "Steelhead George," the "last of the whitewater cowboys," and he was waiting for us in his truck on the side of the road, high above the river. Steelhead George is a Northwest fishing legend, and we were about to find out why. His physique and demeanor reflected the ruggedness of years of winter steelheading on the mountain rivers of the Northwest. His body was short, stout, and solid as a tree trunk, but his personality was as warm as an early morning campfire. I liked him immediately. Not five minutes after we arrived, George began unloading an aluminum drift boat from its trailer onto a steep embankment that plummeted 60 feet to the raging rapids below. Not having a 60-foot guide line, George resorted to a simple solution: Let gravity do its job and hang on. First the boat, and then George, disappeared over the embankment in one fluid motion, leaving my dad and me to wonder what had just happened. We ran to the edge of the cliff and caught the last glimpse of man and boat, two old friends, hurling down the embankment of rock, moss, and trees to the water below. Both finally stopped when George hit the beach and the boat tethered firmly against his rope in the middle of the rapids. The day dawned, and we spent our time drifting through whitewater runs, hooking and landing many bright and feisty winter steelhead, and keeping our minds off the cold weather.

If fishing in Oregon is nothing else, it is diverse and exciting, peopled with characters, towns and landscapes forgotten by progress. From the wide drainages of the Columbia River basin in the north, to the beautiful spring creeks of the Williamson and Wood Rivers in the south, Oregon offers the angler a wonderful diversity of topographies, fish species, and remote challenges: the state boasts much of the same ruggedness of its northern cousins; coastal access and fishing is comparable to the best in the world; remote mountain lakes, desert streams, and rugged coastal rivers emerge from their parent rainforests, offering anglers exciting challenges; anadromous species such as salmon, steelhead, and sea-run trout journey back annually to their birth rivers, while landlocked versions provide unique opportunities in many lakes and rivers; fishing devotees of many warm-water species (bluegill, carp, bass and sunfish) are kept busy year round in natural and manmade ponds, lakes and reservoirs. Each and all of these wonderful watersheds are just waiting to be explored. Armed with this book and your quest for the ultimate fishing experience, I hope to be your guide and friend as you explore Oregon's fishing destinations.

Best Fishing Spots

These lists represent a sampling of the best of the best from around the state. Naturally these lists are highly subjective; the best water is usually whichever water you enjoy fishing. Still, many of these waters are proven producers, and this selection was based equally on my experiences and what tradition has dictated as the best fishing. Places such as Paulina, Henry Hagg, and Wallowa Lakes were chosen because they consistently produce record-book catches. Others because of their proximity to great fishing. Some were chosen because they are underrated—like the Grand Ronde and Wood Rivers—and while some anglers may be upset at the attention drawn to these unsung rivers, there seems little threat in revealing secrets.

Obviously, there are many other equally good rivers, lakes and reservoirs not included here, and these you will have to discover for yourself. A short list of my favorites would include the Ana River, Clackamas River, Trask River, Sandy River, Imnaha River, Wenaha River, North Fork of the Sprague River, and Recreation Creek on Upper Klamath Lake.

◖ Best for Brown Trout

Brown trout—favored by some trout anglers, eschewed by others—enjoys a relatively healthy position among Oregon fisheries. Stocking programs have increased the fish's presence, and in most cases they flourish and grow to great size. If you have any aspiration towards catching trophy fish, or you just like aggressive carnivorous fish, this is a worthwhile species to consider.

Middle Deschutes River, Southern Cascades, page 332. Good populations of naturally reproducing brown trout of average size (12–16 inches), but plentiful and well adapted to taking most offers from an angler.

Wickiup Reservoir, Southern Cascades, page 359. Traditionally the king of brown trout waters, Wickiup is a great producer of these fish and has many devoted anglers.

Paulina Lake, Southern Cascades, page 363. Paulina Lake holds the state record from 2002 (28 lbs., 5 oz.) and as the holder of previous records, it's unlikely to be dethroned as the king of brown trout any time soon.

Wood River, Southern Cascades, page 388. Wood River brown trout fishing is as good as it gets. A challenging river for challenging and big fish; not for the faint of heart or those desiring to catch a lot of trout.

Lower Owyhee River, Southeastern Oregon, page 416. The Owyhee draws anglers from all over the Northwest to catch four- to six-pound browns on streamers and dry flies. Remote for most of Oregon's population centers, but a journey well worth the trip.

◖ Best for Rainbow Trout

These rivers are included without respect to difficulty or access. The best of the best, these are the rivers that push our abilities to their limits; that's why we love them.

Lower Deschutes River: Pelton Dam to Trout Creek, The Columbia River Gorge and Mount Hood, page 227. Deschutes redband trout are the hardest-fighting fish in the state. What these fish lack in size (five-pounders are rare) they more than make up for in fight. A 20-inch Deschutes fish fights like a six-pound steelhead and feels like a trophy fish.

Upper Metolius River, Southern Cascades, page 330. Beauty aside, this is arguably the most challenging trout fishery in Oregon for trophy rainbow and bull trout.

Upper Rogue River, Southern Cascades, page 379. The "Holy Water" between Cole M. Rivers Fish Hatchery and Lost Creek Dam gets crowded at times, but that's the price we pay for catching trout of five pounds or more.

Lower Williamson River, Southern Cascades, page 389. Second only to the fishing in New Zealand, and much closer to home. This is, bar none, the best trophy trout water in the country. Difficult? Yes! Worth the effort? Absolutely! Plus, there is world-class fishing nearby on Upper Klamath Lake, Agency Lake, Wood River, Sprague River and Klamath River—all within an hour's drive. Nothing strikes a fly with the ferocity of an Upper Klamath Lake rainbow.

Klamath River: Keno Dam to Topsy Reservoir, Southern Cascades, page 392. A limited season with extremely challenging access, all in a remote part of Oregon; we would have it no other way! Upper Klamath Lake redband trout average 16–20 inches, but commonly reach 5–10 pounds.

◖ Best for Salmon

As a game fish, salmon is second to no other species in the Northwest. Oregon is blessed to have so many productive fisheries within a short drive of Oregon's major metropolitan areas.

Columbia River Estuary, The Oregon Coast, page 84. Just shy of open-ocean fishing, the Columbia Estuary draws all the fishing world heavy hitters who desire to catch chinook and coho.

Tillamook Bay, The Oregon Coast, page 96. The second-largest bay in Oregon, and the terminus for five Coast Range rivers, provides access to offshore fishing for salmon as well as bay fishing spring and fall chinook.

Sixes River, The Oregon Coast, page 126. Another great river whose superb run of winter steelhead overshadows an equally fine run of fall chinook. Popularity with fishing guides may crowd the river during the peak runs, but it's a fine fishery and well worth the effort.

Chetco River, The Oregon Coast, page 134. Often overshadowed by its superb run of winter steelhead, the Chetco is less-known for its run of fall chinook—one of the strongest and biggest in the state.

Lower Willamette River: Oregon City to Columbia River, Portland and the Willamette Valley, page 150. The area between Willamette Falls and the Columbia River, including the Multnomah Channel, is the most productive and accessible spring chinook and steelhead fishing in the state.

◖ Best for Smallmouth Bass

Once a secret game fish, appreciated by only a small band of devoted anglers, the smallmouth bass has since come into angler consciousness as a spirited, hard-fighting fish, and it is fast becoming one of the most sought-after species next to trout and steelhead. Oregon is lucky in that it has two of the top-rated fisheries in the country, the beautiful Umpqua and the incomparable John Day. The Columbia and Willamette Rivers are not included in this list in order to give a statewide sampling, but both are among the best smallmouth fisheries in the state.

Lower Umpqua River, The Oregon Coast, page 120. The Umpqua, often equated with the John Day as one of the best rivers in the county for smallmouth bass, runs through dense forests of Douglas fir and is often shrouded in the cold mists of the Pacific Ocean.

Henry Hagg Lake, Portland and the Willamette Valley, page 150. The lake holds two consecutive state records for smallmouth bass, the last caught in 2000 (8 lbs., 1.76 oz.).

John Day River: Service Creek to Clarno Rapids, Northeastern Oregon, page 287. Rated as one of the best smallmouth bass rivers in the country, this high desert river is the place to go from March through October.

Brownlee Reservoir, Northeastern Oregon, page 311. Perhaps more popular with Idaho anglers because of its distance from most Oregonians, this reservoir—on par with the best smallmouth fisheries in the country—is worth the trip.

Warm Springs Reservoir, Southeastern Oregon, page 415. Impressive numbers of smallmouth bass—up to four pounds—can be found in Oregon's remote southeast desert.

◖ Best for Steelhead

Steelhead define northwest fishing like no other game fish. There are so many good steelhead rivers in Oregon, it's unlikely that any two anglers could agree on which are the best. That said, I offer, without apology, what I think are the standouts in terms of access, numbers of returning fish, and tradition.

Wilson River, The Oregon Coast, page 97. The Wilson is a proven and consistent producer of year-round steelhead; this is where many new steelhead anglers cut their teeth. River access is excellent, compared to many Oregon coast streams.

Lower Deschutes River: Mack's Canyon to Maupin, The Columbia River Gorge and Mount Hood, page 213. The summer run of Deschutes River steelhead in August and September has captured the imagination of anglers like no other river in Oregon. Great access and easily found holding water make this a great river for both beginners and experts.

Lower Grande Ronde River, Northeastern Oregon, page 269. Beautiful, rugged, and remote country providing excellent winter steelhead fishing in Oregon's far northeast corner.

Middle North Umpqua River, Southern Cascades, page 346. Undoubtedly the jewel of the state for both beauty and fishing, and arguably the most elusive of all steelhead rivers.

Upper Rogue River, Southern Cascades, page 379. This river falls into many categories, and for good reason. Steelhead fishing is no exception, and during October this is one of the best with large numbers of returning fish.

◖ Best Family Fishing

Families with young children require a degree of easy fishing and access. The following sites include convenient facilities, group campsites, cabin rentals, established campgrounds, resorts, boat rentals, and extra-fishing activities such as hiking, biking, wildlife-viewing, and natural and historical attractions.

Lost Lake, The Columbia River Gorge and Mount Hood, page 198. Families will find easy fishing for stocked trout, hiking trails around the lake, scenic camping with stunning views of Mount Hood, resort facilities, and boat rentals—all just a short drive from Portland.

Wallowa Lake, Northeastern Oregon, page 276. This glacier-fed lake at the base of the Wallowa Mountains holds record catches of kokanee and trout, as well as great camping facilities.

Upper Metolius River, Southern Cascades, page 330. Great campgrounds, beautiful surroundings, an eclectic general store and fly shop, excellent accommodations, both easy and world-class fishing, great hiking and biking trails, interesting headwaters, and the fun town of Sisters make this a top pick.

Wickiup Reservoir, Southern Cascades, page 359. This reservoir's central location provides easy access to its neighbors in the Cascades Lakes Basin, nice campgrounds, and a resort.

Upper Klamath Lake, Southern Cascades, page 381. This quiet and remote lake offers fantastic yet relatively easy boat fishing for 6–8-pound trout. There's a wonderful resort with boat and cabin rentals, a restaurant, a general store, and other area attractions.

◖ Best Hike-In Fisheries

These are the playgrounds of anglers who love to explore. I love to pull on my waders or dress in my rugged Filson gear and bushwhack through the forest to discover secret spots hitherto unknown. All these areas are exclusively hike-in fishing, and most are contained in designated wilderness areas.

Salmonberry River, The Oregon Coast, page 94. The emerald forests of the Oregon Coast offers an opportunity to stalk wild steelhead among waterfalls, plunge pools, and old-growth trees.

South Fork Walla Walla River, Northeastern Oregon, page 262. This pristine environment of lush forests and spring-fed waters is home to small trout.

Minam River, Northeastern Oregon, page 273. Great fishing for larger-than-average rainbows and brown trout in Packer County, where the only traffic you're likely to run into are outfitters, mule trains, and a fly-in resort.

Eagle Cap Wilderness, Northeastern Oregon, page 277. An unmarked alpine setting of mountain peaks and wildlife, and more than 75 lakes—some of which have probably never seen an angler.

Donner und Blitzen River, Southeastern Oregon, page 439. A gem of a trout stream with some surprisingly big fish in a wonderful canyon setting.

◖ Best Places to Teach Kids to Fish

The primary criteria here is ease of access and catchable fish, which means stocked trout, panfish and catfish. Oregon offers several opportunities to catch something larger than your average stocked trout, plus a few fisheries suitable for older youth.

Columbia River Estuary, The Oregon Coast, page 84. You haven't lived until you've witnessed the excitement and sheer exhaustion that results from a 14-year-old attempting to land a 30-pound salmon or 50-pound sturgeon. Hire a guide and offer your kids (12 years old and up) the thrill of a lifetime.

Blue Lake, Portland and the Willamette Valley, page 149. Blue Lake offers the perfect opportunity for easy catches of panfish and stocked trout. There are public (and wheelchair-accessible) fishing docks, a swimming beach and play area, boat and canoe rentals, walkways, and bike paths.

North Fork Reservoir, The Columbia River Gorge and Mount Hood, page 190.

Small Fry Lake, within Promontory Park, is a one-acre lake developed exclusively for young anglers. Kids up to 14 years old can fish for their limit of 8–10-inch fish (three per day).

Upper Rogue River, Southern Cascades, page 379. Even though this is more advanced fishing for older youth (10 years old and up), this a great opportunity to catch trout and possibly a steelhead on a big river.

Chickahominy Reservoir, Southeastern Oregon, page 410. The region's most popular fly-fishing reservoir provides excellent fishing from a boat or shore. Larger trout— up to 20 inches—make this a better-than-average fishing opportunity for youth.

◖ Most Accessible for Disabled Anglers

Before selecting these waters I asked myself, "Would I, as a non-disabled angler, want to fish here?" Many accessible fishing areas are not positioned on very productive waters, however the selections below are the standouts in Oregon. And yes, I have fished, or would fish, these places. See you on the river!

Henry Hagg Lake, Portland and the Willamette Valley, page 150. This accessible shoreline features limited obstructions, a wheelchair-accessible fishing dock, and a wheelchair elevator to the floating dock.

Lower Deschutes River: Mack's Canyon to Maupin, The Columbia River Gorge and Mount Hood, page 213. The Blue Hole Recreation Site offers good trout and steelhead fishing from a fishing deck. Amenities include paved parking, wheelchair-accessible restrooms, and handicap priority camping.

Timothy Lake, The Columbia River Gorge and Mount Hood, page 216. Disabled anglers will find extensive facilities—a large T-float by the dam, a hard-packed trail, and an attractive wood deck—as well as good fishing for rainbow and brook trout and early season kokanee.

Upper Rogue River, Southern Cascades, page 379. The Rogue River has highly-developed access points for disabled anglers and offers good opportunities to catch steelhead, salmon and trout.

Wood River, Southern Cascades, page 388. This blue ribbon trout stream includes a recreation site (Kimball State Park) specifically designed for anglers with disabilities.

Fishing Tips

Each fishing profile includes extensive resource information for the sole purpose of planning a trip. Obviously, traveling close to home requires less planning than multi-day or multi-location trips, but every little bit helps. Either way, I have done my best to give you a broad listing of categories, including local chamber of commerce information, tourist centers, regulatory government agencies, special interests, local fishing shops, guides, and areas to camp or find accommodations. Perhaps the best and most-overlooked category for local fishing information is the offices of the Oregon Department of Fish and Wildlife (ODFW) and Bureau of Land Management (BLM). Both agencies have field offices all over the state, staffed with fish biologists just waiting to answer your questions about any stream, lake or reservoir in their jurisdiction. The helpful information these professionals provide cannot be overestimated. Theirs is often the most current, thorough and reliable information you can get anywhere. Many of these biologists are, after all, anglers just like us, and they enjoy talking fishing to the same degree.

PLANNING A SUCCESSFUL FISHING TRIP
Selecting the Best Time and Place

There is no more frustrating phrase in the history of angling than "you should have been here yesterday." I have been on both ends of this statement and it is true more often than not. Knowing when fish are biting is by and large a matter of getting to know your river or lake. This knowledge comes from time spent on the water over many seasons, and it's a good argument for adapting a home water. Understanding variables such as water temperature, water quality, seasonal weather patterns, insect

hatches, food availability, and fish biorhythms is paramount to successful and consistent fishing. For example, if I'm going to drive four hours from Portland to fish the Williamson, I need to know that there will be a couple days of storm-free weather, because nothing kills fishing on the Williamson like a low-pressure system. This is not true for all fisheries, but because I know the Williamson I'm privy to this knowledge (and now so are you).

Timing is particularly paramount with anadromous fish such as salmon and steelhead. Take the variables listed above and double them; the largest variable is the number of returning fish, which fluctuates from year to year depending on ocean conditions, stocking practices, commercial fishing, floods, and logging and forestry uses which can change rivers.

Since many of us have only a few weekends a year to fish, getting in touch with available resources is important. Below are a few suggestions for helping you plan the best times and places to go fishing.

Fishing Shops: Call ahead to local fishing stores to get a basic impression about how the fishing is going in a particular area.

Regulatory Agencies: Call or check the websites of the local field offices of the ODFW, BLM, or Forest Service to get specific and current information from the resident fish biologists.

Internet Angling: The Internet is a great resource for all fishing information and a lot of knowledge can be picked up by reading river reports, contributing to discussion forums, and checking water levels, fish run counts, and fish stocking schedules. Both private and government websites devote a lot of time and energy making sure their sites are kept up to date with the best information. The Internet is also a great way to meet fellow anglers and participate in group outings.

Printed Material: Books, monthly periodicals, and weekly and daily newspapers are all good sources of information. Local newspapers usually provide at least one

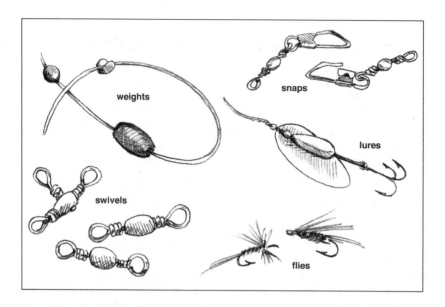

weekly fishing or outdoor column; they may also provide daily reports on river and lake water levels and fish counts over dams. Weekly fishing newspapers such as *Oregon Fishing and Hunting News* are available on newsstands and provide up-to-date fishing reports, fishing tips, and other helpful information. Monthly periodicals such as *Salmon, Trout, Steelheader* and *Northwest Fly-Fishing* offer good in-depth river and lake profiles, fishing techniques, book and gear reviews. Books are useful for general information and in-depth studies of techniques or fish species that can then be applied across all waters (see *Suggested Reading*).

Clubs and Organizations: Entities such as Trout Unlimited, Oregon Trout, and Northwest Steelheaders are great venues for meeting other anglers, attending monthly meetings, hearing presentations by special guests, and learning more about political and environmental concerns important to anglers. These clubs are often run by volunteer members, not professionals, so they are intended for anglers of all levels. Women and children are especially welcome and are encouraged to get involved.

Hire a Fishing Guide: If you really want

the insider information, you're going to have to pay for it. Not all waters in Oregon have guides, but those that do are often worth the expense (see *Hiring a Fishing Guide*).

Tackle Considerations

Tackle choices are highly dependant on your preferred method of angling. Specific tackle details (rods, reels, lures) are discussed under each of the species descriptions as well as in the regional chapters. One thing's for sure: You will never have enough of the right gear for any particular outing; the hot lure, fly or bait that worked one time will probably change the next time. That is fishing! There are two ways to solve this problem, and they usually divide anglers into two camps: the minimalists and the maximalists, also known as the hedgehog and fox. Each have their philosophical basis that seems intrinsic to certain personalities.

The minimalist (or hedgehog) knows one thing, fishes the same lure and gear all the time, and makes it work. They often substitute abstract theories and deductive reasoning for "get the job done." My dad is a great angler and has spent decades catching hundreds of

CHANGING METHODS INSTEAD OF LURES

Next time you're not catching any fish and think a change of lure is in order, consider changing the method with which you fish your spinner or streamer. Changing lures sometimes results in more fish, but 90 percent of the time our lures don't catch fish because we fish them without the proper action or speed. Because many of our lures imitate wounded or vulnerable baitfish, a few things to try are: vary the speed of your retrieves making them either faster or slower (sometimes very slow); make erratic retires with sudden starts and stops; utilize the rod tip by making subtle tugs and twitches; move your whole arm with the rod to impart a pulsing rather than twitching movement to the lure; or troll at different, varying or erratic speeds. These retirinving techniques, combined with the ability to fish at various depths, will quickly make an expert out of any angler.

steelhead on the Deschutes, but to this day he claims he has never used anything other than a Green Butt Skunk or red Wiggle Wort plug. The same holds true for other anglers who only use an Adams as their one dry fly or a yellow Rooster Tail as their only lure. Minimalists will catch fish 70 percent of the time. The only drawback to this approach is that 30 percent of the time they catch nothing.

The maximalists (or foxes), as you can guess, carry enough gear to outfit a small army, and they know many approaches. This is the angler who takes up three-quarters of the available space in the car. They respect the variables involved in fishing and enjoy the challenge of finding the right combination at any particular time. The philosophy here is the old Boy Scout adage, "Be Prepared." This approach also has its pros and cons: Too much gear means too many decisions, and time can be wasted trying to select the right gear rather than fishing. On the other hand, this is usually the first person we look to when our methods of fishing are not working and we want to try something different.

In short, neither approach, that of the hedgehog or fox, is better than the other. Having the right gear is important, as is being armed with fishing theories and knowledge obtained from books, but we can question the effectiveness of any approach when it distracts us from putting lure to water. Nuanced fishing techniques come with experience and experimentation, not from having the right gear. The famous fishing author Gary LaFontaine, renowned for his unorthodox approaches to fishing, has said about fly anglers who false cast too much, "Fish can not be caught in the air." Fish, and more of them, will be caught when our lures, even the wrong ones, are in the water.

What to Bring

Fishing is an outdoor sport, so it requires us to guard against sun, rain or snow. Nothing can ruin a good trip like getting cold and wet or sunburned. The basic rule for time spent in the outdoors is "Be prepared for anything." Don't fail to pack that raincoat or fleece overcoat just because the forecast calls for sun. I have encountered snow storms in the middle of July in both the mountains and deserts of Oregon.

CLOTHING

Avoid cotton at all costs, even if you don't think you're going to get wet. A lot of fishing spots in Oregon require a degree of exertion in remote areas to find fish—and exertion means perspiration which, when combined with cotton, can be deadly even in the middle of summer. There are many great nylon and polyester products on the market, which breathe and provide protection both against wetness and the sun.

Shorts and saddles are great around camp but prove inadequate when it comes to hiking, stomping through tall grass or brush, and boulder hopping. Quick-drying pants, waders, hip boots, solid hiking boots and long- sleeve shirts are far more safe and will prolong your fishing. And include a wide-brimmed hat to the list of items one should never leave home without.

ACCESSORIES

Beyond the usual fleece, rain jacket and hat there are some useful accessories that can help make your fishing experiences more pleasant and productive.

Fishing Vest: Not always necessary and certainly more common among fly anglers, but a very useful item for carrying fishing paraphernalia. A vest also gives anglers the versatility and mobility to move over difficult terrain without worrying about having their hands full with a rod and tackle box. Newer breathable vests made of mesh are a nice option to consider.

Waders and Wading Belt: Waders provide mobility over any terrain and help guard against brush, snakes, and wetness. Waders also encourage exploration when you're not worried about getting wet or stuck by blackberries. Before buying a pair of waders consider your options: Stocking foot waders will give you better options when it comes to boot comfort; Built-in gravel guards, a flap that goes over the wader and top of the boot are a nice comfort feature but can also be bought separately; and the newer breathable Gore-Tex waders are a major improvement over the old neoprene and rubber varieties. If you expect to use waders a lot, more expensive name-brand waders tend to hold up better than cheaper ones, and offer better warranties. Expect to pay anywhere from $150 to $350 for a quality pair of Gore-Tex waders. Always wear a wading belt and/or an inflatable life preserver, especially when fishing rough and dangerous water. Hip boots are a good option only if you're sure there is no possibility of wading in water any deeper than your knees.

Wading Boots: These are required when buying stocking foot waders. The same thought that goes into a good pair of hiking boots should be given to wading boots, especially if you expect to do a lot of hiking. Consider cleated boots or cleat attachments; this seemingly minor asset will prove invaluable on almost any river in Oregon. Some manufactures are producing boots with removable soles, allowing you to switch from studded soles to felt or vibrum soles with a few adjustments.

Wading Staff: Both solid and folding staffs provide a degree of safety and support when wading in moving currents, allowing you to detect whether your next step is safe or leading you into 10 feet of water. Fishing with a staff takes some coordination, and it can be a nuisance when it is dangling at your feet, but that is a small inconvenience for safety.

Landing Nets: This is good for the angler and the fish, and it's the best option for catch-and-release fishing. A necessary tool for boat and float tube anglers, nets help bring the fish to the angler, and fish will take far less abuse than if landed on the shore. Newer nets have a variety of options in fish-friendly materials that limit entanglement problems associated with traditional nets, albeit at a slightly higher cost. Traditional netting is still available, with a choice between rubber netting, which is admittedly heavy, and a fine soft mesh, which is a vast improvement over the traditional coarse netting. Handles and frames are not only a matter of aesthetics and some practicality, but cost: Wood is expensive and elegant; aluminum is light and cost effective; composite fiber materials are the most versatile, the nicest to use, and mid-priced.

Float Tube or Pontoon Boat: These are a luxury in the same way a boat is a luxury, but the versatility of these boats cannot be beat. Pontoon boats, a newer invention, are suitable for rivers and lakes because the angler is not in the water. Accessories include oars, motor transoms, and anchors. Float tubes are designed specifically for lakes and should not be used on rivers. Float tubes are less versatile, kicker fins are often necessary to move around, and the angler often has to sit in the water.

Polarized Sunglasses: Indispensable! Polarized glasses not only give critical eye protection, but allow the angler to see through the glare of the water and identify obstacles and fish. I never leave home without mine, and always carry a back-up in my fishing bag for myself or others.

Assorted Fishing Tools: Tools vary depending on the type of fishing involved and your propensity for buying gadgets. Indispensable items include forceps for removing hooks, scissors or clippers (nail clippers work well) to cut line, pliers, and a folding or fixed-blade knife. Fly anglers will want to add tippet carriers and drying patches to that list.

In addition to lures, files or bait, remember to carry extra weights or split shot, hooks, tippet material, and any extra material you may use including yarn, corkies, floats, and swivels. Fly anglers will want to bring strike indicators and fly floatant. A small first-aid kit is a good idea, as is sunscreen and insect repellent.

ANGLER (MIS)BEHAVIOR

Anglers never tire of reviewing the fundamental principles of fishing—principles that are automatically forgotten by everyone in the presence of a river or lake. Regardless, these are excellent approaches to catching fish which have nothing to do with equipment and tackle and everything to do with our state of mind.

- Avoid the tendency to just walk up to the bank and start fishing. More fish than we realize hangout next to the bank, but we never see them because they're long gone before we get close. To predict where fish may be lying, avoid spooking the bank. Instead stand back, observe, wait for a sign that fish may be present, then stealthily approach the bank or fish from way back on the shore. Beware of walking over undercut banks; this is an especially good way to announce your presence to wary fish.

- Be a naturalist first and an angler second.

Prior to baiting a hook, take the time to walk around and observe your surroundings. Identify likely fish lies and how you might approach them, take note of rising fish, observe hatches of insects, turn over a few rocks to see what is living in the water, consider the time of day and weather, and watch where other anglers are fishing. Bringing binoculars will help you to observe even more. For many of us coming from the work world, this is a good time to slow down and enjoy the process. Rushing up to a river or lake with rod loaded is the best way to get skunked. This is admittedly hard to do, but the payoff here is that you will be able to catch fish when others aren't.

- Avoid wearing red, a color which stands out in the natural world and announces your presence to fish. Instead, wear muted colors like greens, blues, and grays, that conceal your presence.

- Don't rush. A wise man once told me that anything in life worth having is the byproduct of our efforts. Make catching fish a byproduct of your experience and enjoy the process. As ironic as it sounds, the profound truth is that one can not catch a single fish and still have a great day.

- Fishing is best early in the morning and late in the evening, period. I've experimented with many variations to find the best fishing times, and consistently catch more fish on more waters between dawn and the first few hours of light than at any other time of the day. Dusk is the second-best time for me. Some exceptions to this rule include insect hatches in the mid-morning, afternoon or evening, and winter fishing, which is often best in the afternoon.

- Confidence catches fish. We fish better when we think our odds are better, and our odds improve when we think we have the right lure. I once switched a client's fly

USEFUL FISHING KNOTS

Here are the most common fishing knots. These will work much better if they are practiced at home prior to getting on the water. Moistening the knot prior to cinching will help make stronger knots.

Albright Special: Joins two lines of unequal diameter or different materials.

Blood Knot: Joins two sections similar diameter leader.

Surgeons Knot: A fast way to join two sections of unequal diameter leader together.

Improved Clinch: Connects tippet or fishing line to hook.

Nail Knot: Joins fly line and leader.

Egg Loop: Used to attach a cluster of eggs or yarn to a hook.

Perfection Loop: Forms a loop in the end of your tippet.

after he had caught a number of fish. He made a few casts with the new fly and then sat down. He wasn't about to question my judgment, so I finally had to ask him if everything was okay. "I hate this new fly," he said. The problem was one of confidence. I quickly returned the old fly and he was happy as a clam catching fish again.

- Fishing always begins after your lure, bait or fly enters the water. This is the most important fishing tip I can pass along and it is such an important distinction that it may be the only thing that separates an average angler from a great one. Most people think fishing ends after the cast, that it's all up to luck at that point. Nothing could be further from the truth. When we fish, we are trying to lure fish to strike our bait; they have to be enticed, drawn in, and convinced that our offering is something they want. The only way to do that is to understand how your lure is behaving in the water and emphasize its dynamic qualities. This takes imagination and a visualization of the lure's color, size, shape, movement, flash, smell and action in the water. All these elements combine to exploit the fish's natural instincts to feed, flee, or ignore your offerings. Sometimes an orange rooster tail will work, when a purple lure fails; Perhaps the light is not reflecting the right properties of purple to attract fish; Sometimes a jigging or erratic retrieve works better than a smooth retrieve. According to one fishing author, these variables are like the combination that moves the tumblers in a lock; each has to fall into place before the lock springs open or the fish strikes.

- Make a point to fish new water and new lures every time you go out, even if it's on the same river or lake, until all possibilities are exhausted. This habit will turn you into a versatile angler; you can always go back to the sweet spots with your favorite lure.

- When fishing, share advice and support other anglers. I met one of my best fishing buddies, Brian, one day when I invited this seemingly lost soul to come fish a piece of water that I was working. As I would expect from another angler, he was reluctant at first to accept my invitation, not wishing to trespass, but slowly became convinced once I started hooking fish. You never know who you're going to meet on the river, and Brian and I very quickly became good friends.

- Build your own rods, tie your own flies, and make your own lures. Nothing engages the imagination needed to really succeed in this sport like constructing your own gear. Not only does this save a significant amount of money, but it's also a great way to spend a rainy afternoon in winter and can function as a fun engagement for the whole family.

- Adapt a home river close to where you live that is easy to get to and has at least some of the characteristics you're looking for in a fishery. While it is fun to drive to destinations, it is not always practical or necessary. Home rivers can not only teach us a lot about fishing, but they are a great venue to experiment with new techniques and theories without the loss of precious time and money involved in long getaways.

THE ANATOMY OF RIVERS AND LAKES

All species of fish, no matter where they live, require three basic necessities: food, comfort, and cover. Part of the process of scouting unfamiliar waters is to identify areas in which these three components exist together—that is where the fish will be. There are, however, some exceptions to this general rule. Fish will sacrifice one necessity for the others when, for example, the need to feed outweighs the need for protection or comfort. Riffles, while not comfortable places for fish to rest, do provide an abundance of food during insect hatches, and fish will move into these more challenging areas to eat. Another good example is that fish will feed on insects in the middle of the river when the sun is bright and the hawks are flying overhead. This is an example of a trout sacrificing cover and comfort for food. So, while these rules are generally true, they are not hard and fast, and anglers would be well advise to remain flexible in their approaches.

Rivers

Rivers are composed of four parts that repeat themselves over and over: riffle, run, pool, and tail-out. Each of these sections can be either long or short, and each is easily discernable. Fish behave differently in each section and fishing tactics can vary from one to the other.

RIFFLES

Riffles are generally shallow and composed of smaller rock and fast-moving water. They provide good places for people cross the river, and fish generally pass through riffles as quickly as possible to get to the next pool. Fish are sometimes taken in riffles when adequate depths allow them to rest behind rocks and in depressions (pocket water). Broken water will often provide the cover a fish requires to feel safe, and many food forms are found among the rocks. Comfort tends to be in short supply and is the primary reason most fish don't hang out in riffles except as mentioned above. Nymphs, wet flies, spinners and bait will all work in riffle pockets.

RUNS

Runs start at the bottom of riffles and are generally deeper, may have stading waves or rapids and can be quite fast; also, they often contain larger boulders. Here is where comfort and cover can be found in abundance, and this is also where most steelhead, trout and some salmon are caught. Runs often have a sweeping motion, with faster water on the outside. Anglers often fish the seam between this faster, outer water and the slower water inside. If you do find a boulder in this water, fish all around it for a resting steelhead, salmon, or trout. Trout locate food in different places within runs: back eddies, along the banks under brush, slots around rocks or obstructions, suck holes behind rocks, and seams in faster current. Concentrate on seams and pocket water with flies, spinners and bait, and you can't go wrong. Caution: Wading runs can be dangerous and unpredictable because of large rocks, drop-offs and fast-moving water.

POOLS

The pool is where the run peters out into a large, flat area of slow, deep water. Pools are always

The rule of the wild is that wildlife will congregate wherever there is a distinct change in habitat. To find where fish are hiding, look where a riffle pours into a small pond, where a rapid plunges into a deep hole and flattens, and around submerged trees, rock piles, and boulders in the middle of a long riffle.

slower and are the preferred habitat of salmon. The critical area in a pool for catching salmon is its deepest point. If salmon are present you will often see them rolling in this kind of water; it's like a giant salmon bath. This is the preferred water of plunkers and some float anglers who cast bait into the deep pools and wait for a bite. Because the fish often spread out here, pools are of secondary interest to fly and spin anglers, except in the presence of smallmouth bass and sea-run cutthroat which commonly inhabit this water. Pools are a lot like lakes in that they are featureless on the surface, and it's often hard to identify where fish may be holding.

Tail-Outs

The tail-out is the transition between the pool and the next riffle. The very end of the tail-out is obvious on most rivers by the appearance of a V-shaped channel that forms at the top of almost every riffle. Tail-outs are generally shallow with faster currents. Frequently overlooked but often productive, tail-outs may provide good water depending on their length and composition. Short abrupt tail-puts produce a ledge or steep transition between the pool and the next riffle. Fish frequently hang in the deep hole created by this ledge. Longer shallow tail-outs are not very productive, providing little cover or food and fish pass through this water. The exception is trout, which frequently inhabit the sides of these areas especially if there is shade, overhanging trees or brush. Longer tail-outs are most productive at the very end preceding the start of the next riffle. If there are boulders or significant depressions in the river bottom, salmon and steelhead will hold in this water to rest after having come through the previous rapid. Again, look for trout to inhabit the sides of tail-outs near the bank. It always pays to explore tail-outs for their potential to hold fish.

Following these guidelines for reading a river will enable you to find your own productive water and your own secret holes. Remember, fish are everywhere here, even in the most unlikely places. Once you locate a steelhead, salmon or trout, you can be generally certain there will be another one there tomorrow or next week. The trick is finding the good lies and predicting when the fish are present.

Lakes and Reservoirs

Lakes and reservoirs are composed of four areas: shore, shoal, drop-off, and deep water. All four features exist to a greater or lesser degree, depending on the size of the lake. Lakes are difficult to read because there are no telltale signs of these features on the surface. One has to either use a map, in which someone else has gone through the pain of identifying theses areas, use a depth finder, or simply resort to your own observations. On clear lakes where the bottom is visible, identifying the parts of a lake are not difficult. Lakes which have higher turbidity levels will make observation more difficult.

Shorelines

Shorelines, as a point of focus, can divulge a lot about what lies beneath the water, and they are usually the first place anglers begin exploring a lake. Banks create a lot of habitat for fish in the form of protection, cover and food sources. Areas to look for are points of land that jut out into the lake, steep banks and cliffs which drop down into the water, and shoreline debris such as downed logs, brush, and overhanging trees. Shade cast onto the water is another important, and often overlooked, feature.

Shoals

Shoals are shallow areas of a lake and make up the transition points between the shore, shallow areas such sandbars or gravel bars, and the drop-off. Shoals contain most of the water's growth, such as weed beds, grasses and water lilies, and therefore are easily identifiable on some lakes. Shoals also provide an abundance of food, cover and comfort. When, in the profiles, I mention fishing the shorelines of lakes, I'm really saying to fish the shoal areas, but use shoreline as a point of reference. Shoals can also exist in other areas of the lake. I also indicate in the profiles the best times of day or season to fish the shoals. Shoals are seasonal habitat for some species such as trout, smallmouth bass, and kokanee which require deeper, colder water in the summer. Shoals are often the best places to fish year-round warm-water species and panfish.

DROP-OFFS

The drop-off is the transition between the shoal and the deepest parts of the lake. Fish feel especially safe around drop-offs, as they do around shadows, color changes in the lake bottom, or obstructions. Drop-offs are the preferred places to troll flies, spinners and other lures. Stillwater anglers are almost always aiming for the drop-off areas to let their bait hang. Sometimes drop-offs provide some aquatic growth like weed beds which further attracts fish and insects.

DEEP WATER

Deep water is, as it sounds, the lake's lowest areas. Obstructions can be present, but very little plant growth is available, and the deeper the water the less plant growth there is. The deep water offers protection and comfort to many species, and as a result also a lot of food. Depending on the depths this is primary slow trolling water. Fish are often spread out over the lake bottom with little to concentrate their numbers like a shoal or ledge. Deep-water fishing is the most difficult on any lake, but it's also the most rewarding in terms catching bigger fish.

TEACHING OTHERS TO FISH

I learned how to fish from my dad. In all the years we stood side by side, catching trout and steelhead, the times I remember most fondly are the two of us hunched over problems preliminary to fishing: the hours we'd spend at some picnic table by the river, tying knots, building leaders from scratch, constructing weights and rigs, or discussing the merits of certain fishing techniques. My dad is a pragmatist, a firm believer that the best fishing approach is the one that works, so I got schooled from the be-

ginning in everything from fly-fishing to bait fishing. At home, we spent time preparing our fishing equipment, making sure all the camping gear was ready and the cooler was full of all the foods we were never permitted to eat in our health-conscious home: Dinty Moore Beef Stew, Pop-Tarts, Coke, cookies, and donuts. Looking back on that time, I treasure the moments we spent together driving to distant rivers and lakes, talking, listening to music, staying in cheap hotels in the middle of nowhere or pitching a tent by the river at one o'clock in the morning. Catching fish was always a byproduct of the time and energy we had spent together preparing for a successful trip and enjoying each other's company. As a kid I was hooked, even when the fish weren't.

Success in teaching others to fish, whether friend, spouse or child, begins with this exact kind of immersion into the multiple dimensions of our sport: relating, connecting and fellowship. How often has a fishing trip been just about fishing? I would rather take my best friend fishing than the best angler I know, if I thought the "real" angler was no fun. As teachers we will be far more successful if we share the joys of our sport rather than dunk these newcomers, unguided, into the challenges.

As experts we have to set aside expectations when teaching others. My fishing methods, and my challenges, are far more nuanced today than when I started. I'm sure I have surpassed the expectations my father had for me as an angler, having gone so far as to make it my occupation. I still can't out-fish him, but that's another story. Beginners cannot be expected to understand or appreciate my fishing challenges, nor should they have to. My point is that the formative times I spent learning from my father have stuck with me to this day, none more important than the passion he showed me he had for the sport. I am grateful for what he taught me—not just about fishing, but about who he was, the outdoors, nature, and life.

Fishing, in its most nuanced forms, is a difficult skill to acquire, requiring years of trial and error, study, disappointments, and sporadic successes. But most skilled anglers I know have two things in common: great knowledge about their sport and the desire, when opportunity arises, to teach others. Sometimes the desire to find new fishing partners comes at the chagrin of neighbors, friends, and spouses who have to hear yet another story about the big one caught, or lost, or have to politely turn down our insistence that they come with us on our next adventure. Our children have particular potential to become (perhaps unwilling) recipients of our fishing knowledge. And though some may consider fishing an unsophisticated sport, we know that it is a wonderful way to introduce not only a lifetime worth of memories, but also a deep appreciation of our connection with the natural world and, consequently, each other. Sons, daughters, husbands, and wives can all make excellent fishing partners—if we are patient rather than forceful in our desire to teach them.

The seasoned angler is mentally prepared to deal with fishless days, weeks, or even months while maintaining enthusiasm for the sport. Beginners are also resilient, always willing to give it another stab if one or two trips don't pan out, but they are years away from being able to endure the kind of persistence displayed by all real fishing addicts. This is an important thing to keep in mind when teaching others to fish: Beginners will give you the benefit of the doubt, for a while. At some point, if there are no fish caught, or the fishing is too hard, you will lose them. Beginning anglers need to be enticed, and nothing entices like positive reinforcement: in other words, easy fishing. This may require you, as the expert, to set aside your aspirations for a while and trek down to the local pond to catch catfish or bluegill, so that whoever you are teaching can experiment on their own

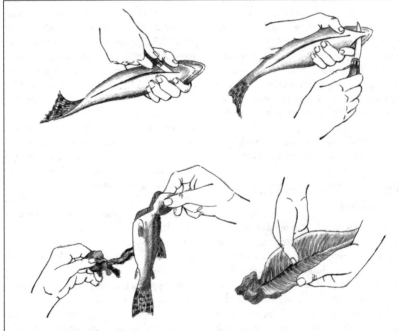

Basic Steps to Cleaning a Fish: First, slit belly from anal vent to gills. Then sever lower junctions of gills. Next, pull out innards and gills. And last but not least, run thumbnail along cavity to clean out dark matter.

without expending the time, effort and expense on what you might consider a "real" fishing trip. Ponds are great places for beginning anglers to experiment and develop their own passion for the sport. Local ponds are also wonderful for working on the practicalities of fishing: casting, baiting hooks, observing fish behavior and feeding patterns, and the subtlest environmental changes that can affect fishing. This is exactly the kind of fishing knowledge that can be applied to bigger areas like the Deschutes, Metolius or Columbia Rivers. This is knowledge which has more to do with feel, intuition and passion than hard scientific theories.

Fishing is a soft science, and success in the sport depends far more on our ability to stay engaged in passionate pursuit rather than implementing some concrete formula. There are few hard and fast rules in fishing, and building a new angler's confidence and interest is the best fishing skill you can pass on.

HIRING A FISHING GUIDE

A guide is a professional whose job it is to lead fishing trips for clients. Guides work on lakes, rivers, reservoirs, oceans, or anywhere fish can be found, and should possess an intimate knowledge of where the fish are and how to catch them. Beyond the fact that a person possess the right to operate as a guide, there are no standards for guides and how they operate. For this reason, hiring a guide should involve a little research in order to ensure you get what you want.

Guide services and expertise varies: most guides accommodate one or two people, while others can take larger groups; some only guide experienced anglers, while some welcome beginners; and others are noted for accommodating handicap anglers and children. (Unfortunately, there are very few female guides—only two in Oregon that I know of.) Guiding style can range from friendly, great teachers who share their knowledge readily to quiet experts

who prefer to avoid questions and explain little about what they do and how they fish.

Hike-in trips are possible, as are those from a car, drift boat, jet boat, raft, horseback, helicopter or plane, and range from multi-day trips to single-, half-day and two-hour trips. Costs vary depending on the location, but expect to pay anywhere between $150 and $225 (plus a 10–20 percent tip) per day, per person; group trips usually cost less per person. Meals, drinks, and snacks; tackle, bait, lures, or flies; shuttles; and fish cleaning and packaging are often included in the price, or these may be seen as extra services requiring an additional fee. While some guides require non-refundable deposits to book a trip, others may wait to receive payment after the trip; advanced notice of any cancellations is appreciated. Confirmation packets, with details such as driving directions, meeting times and places, tackle requirements, and other suggestions about what to bring are sometimes mailed out; or you're lucky to hear from the guide prior to the day of the trip. Catch-and-release fishing might be encouraged, or the day may end once your limit is reached, or at the end of eight hours. Some guides will fish you from sun-up to sundown.

Selecting a Guide
- Clarify your objectives: Why do you want to hire a guide? There are three basic reasons to hire a guide: to catch fish, to learn to catch fish with a particular style, or to learn to catch fish on a particular body of water. While none of these is mutually exclusive, not all guides are well matched for all three—it comes down to whether the guide is a good teacher or not. If you know which of the objectives you want to achieve, then discuss it with a potential guide and decide if they can meet your needs.

- Locate a fishing guide/outfitter: Once you have decided your objective, get referrals from friends, fishing shops, and the Internet, or contact the guides listed these chapters (see also *Resources*). Contact a few guides, using the points covered in this section to ask questions and clarify what is included in the cost and what to expect from a trip. Be honest about your abilities. Most guides expect potential clients to underestimate their abilities, but some water can be extremely demanding—requiring not only physical stamina, but also nuanced fishing techniques in order to be successful. Most guides are honest and won't promise things they can't deliver; repeat business and referrals are the mainstay of building a business and no guide who plans to stay in the industry is going to jeopardize that for a few quick bucks.

• Is your guide registered? According to the Oregon State Marine Board, the regulatory agency overseeing outfitter and fishing guides in the state, "Persons accepting fees for providing outdoor recreational activities must be registered as outfitter/guides with the Oregon State Marine Board. They must show proof of first aid training and insurance coverage. In addition, they must sign an affidavit that all their employees have had first-aid training and are covered under their insurance. Outfitter/guides who use boats are required to display identifying decals on their boats. On a boat with a motor, this decal shows the number of passengers the outfitter/guide is insured to carry. If operating on federally navigable waters, the decal also identifies the type of Coast Guard operator's license and waters where the outfitter/guide can legally operate." Any responsible guide will, upon request, be able to produce a valid outfitter license, proof of insurance, first aid cards, and will have the proper decals on their boat. It's the law and failure to do so should cast suspicion on their legality. To verify outfitter/guide registrations, call the Oregon Marine Board at 503/378-8587. Use the State Police TIP Hotline (800/452-7888) to report any illegal guiding activity.

• Trip preparations: Once you have selected your guide and booked the trip, make all the necessary preparations well ahead of time. Plan your route, make sure you have the correct dates and meeting places, and double-check all your gear. Re-contact the guide if you have any questions prior to the trip.

Making Your Trip Successful

As a fishing guide, I offer a few tips and suggestions from the guide's perspective about what makes a successful trip:

• Be Humble: Even if you have fished your whole life and caught thousands of fish all over the world, that information has little bearing on how a guide is going to treat you. Every fishing trip is different, just as every piece of water is different. The guide's sole objective is to get you into fish, regardless of your experience.

• Prepare for Hard Work: I'm sorry to have to tell you this, but it's true. Perhaps knowing this up front will prepare you for the level of concentration and learning often demanded by fishing guides. You're paying a lot of money and will want to get the most out of your trip; guides know this and will keep you fishing the whole day. Most guides can spend 12 hours on the river, day after day, and not even bat an eye. Although unintentional, guides expect their clients to have the same stamina. A good guide will recognize when someone has reached their limit and not push too hard, but expect to fish the moment you step into the guide's sphere until the end of the trip. You're also going to be learning a lot of new information and the mental concentration required can be exhausting.

• Listen to the Guide: Guides spend hundreds of hours on the water developing nuanced techniques to help clients catch fish. More often than not, a guide will expect you to use their fishing techniques, so prepare to learn new techniques or to have your expectations challenged. Barring ethical concerns, set aside any preconceived notions and do exactly what the guide tells you. If it's unclear what's being asked of you, then ask questions. Ironically, the novice angler often catches more fish with a guide than an experience angler does—beginner anglers follow directions better. As the Buddhists say, "adopt a beginner's mind."

- Respect the Guide's Captain Authority: Guides have to consider more than just fishing; they also have to think about everyone's safety. Boating, wading, casting sharp hooks, and outdoor elements can all be dangerous. Guides are aware of these dangers and are forced to impose safety guidelines. The use of alcohol and drugs on a guided trip are often frowned upon not only because they may be illegal activities, but because they increase the likelihood of accidents.

CONSERVATION ISSUES AND ANGLER ETHICS

The rise of environmental consciousness has forced a re-evaluation of anglers' values and ethics. Though familiar in some circles since the 1960's, today environmental concern is a part of our mainstream consciousness, and directly impacts the sport of angling. Unlimited stocking, nonrestrictive bag limits and year-round seasons are things of the past—and have been for a while. For better or worse, today's fishing environment is highly regulated and arguably more consistent with long-term conservation efforts. Fish management practices are increasingly moving away from the philosophy that the natural world exists strictly for human enjoyment. Instead, crucial decisions are being based on values such as biodiversity, respect for all life, long-term sustainability and consideration of the common good.

Today's anglers must adapt to frequent regulation changes, many of which appear in conflict angler enjoyment. Some rivers and lakes are no longer stocked, and by all indications the trend is towards restoring certain waters back to native and wild fish populations. Fishing seasons are being shortened, lengthened or staggered depending upon a fishery's needs. Some waters are closed alto-

gether and may never allow angling in deference to the needs of fish. Bag limits are always controversial, and there is a heightened emphasis on catch-and-release fishing techniques. Fishing methods, especially the use of bait and tribal hooks, are being limited or eliminated altogether. All this adds up to an increasing need for anglers to consider the heath of our ecosystems. Following are suggestions for all anglers to consider while pursing their favorite pastime.

Angler Code of Ethics

- Read and know all fishing regulations. Regulations often change within the year, and anglers are expected to keep abreast of these changes; ignorance of the changes is not an excuse, and if caught, you will be ticketed. This includes all boating regulations.

- Limit your catch to the number of fish you can use.

- Don't litter, and dispose of all trash properly or carry a small garbage bag with you. This includes bait containers, fishing line, tackle wrappers, broken hooks or lures, food or drink containers and any other trash. Clean up garbage that you see left by others who may not practice the same courtesy.

- Do not trespass. This isn't just a violation of angler ethics; it is also against the law, and property owners can be quite vigilant about calling the authorities.

- Limit your impact on fragile ecosystems such as marshes, river banks, and spawning beds.

- Respect other anglers' rights. Sooner or later you are bound to come in contact with other anglers. These can be opportunities or obstacles, but always treat others the way you expect to be treated. If necessary, make your presence known, but don't be intrusive; allow the other angler sufficient time to respond to your presence if you want to pass through or

GETTING UNCAUGHT

There are two ways to remove a hook embedded in skin. When hooks are imbedded in loose skin, the hook can be backed out with a loop of strong monofilament pulling on the bend of the hook while simultaneously pushing down on the eye of the hook. When hooks are embedded in tight skin such as a finger, feed the hook into the wound, following the natural bend of the hook, until the barb is clear of the skin. Ouch! Then clip off the hook barb with pliers or side cutters and feed the barbless hook back through the wound.

fish the same water. Respect angling methods that may be different from the one you use. Always move behind an angler, never in front, even when fishing from a boat.

• Share fishing information with others and promote the sport of fishing.

• Lead by example and be a part of the solution, not the problem.

• Support local conservation efforts by Oregon Trout and Trout Unlimited.

• Report all angling violations to the proper authorities.

Catch-and-Release Fishing Guidelines

• Use barbless hooks or pinch the barbs on existing hooks.

• Use big enough tackle to land fish quickly.

• Use a net, and avoid removing fish from the water.

• Handle the fish with care using wet hands or special gloves.

• Remove hooks carefully with pliers and back the hook out.

• Cut the line on all hooks that can't be removed because they are set too deeply.

• Revive the fish before letting it go: This is done by moving the fish back and forth in the current until its gills are working and it maintains its balance. Then let the fish swim out of your hands.

REGULATIONS

The Oregon Sportfishing Guide, a free, annual publication by the Oregon Department of Fish and Wildlife (ODFW), contains all the information an angler needs to fish legally in Oregon. The ODFW guide is widely available wherever fishing gear and licenses are sold, and also online at www.dfw.state.or.us. (The ODFW guide was written during the 2006 fishing season. Any regulations discussed here may change in future years.)

The Oregon Sportfishing Guide is broken down into three sections: General (Statewide) Regulations, Zone Regulations and Special Regulations. Sandwiched between these sections is other helpful information, such as fish identification guides, hatchery information, Oregon health advisories, fish measurement guides, and instructions for completing harvest tags.

General Regulations

The General (Statewide) Regulations are straightforward and provide a helpful glossary, defining such terms as artificial fly, fin-clipped fish, non-gamefish, snagging and chumming. This section also discusses general statewide regulations such as licenses, tags, and permits; catch and possession limits; gear, bait and general restrictions; and hook and weight regulations. For instance, all gamefish fishing in Oregon is allowed only between one hour before sunrise and one hour after sunset; all gamefish must be caught by a standard hook and line (sorry, no dynamite, spears, or nets); no more than three hooks can be used on one line when fishing for any species; it is unlawful to hook a fish anywhere but in the mouth (no snagging); and that continuing to fish for the same species after you have retained your limit is illegal. Regulations for non-game fish vary greatly and include the permitted use of such fishing methods as bow and arrows, crossbows, spears, dip nets, and snag hooks. Other important regulations concern licenses and fees: All angers over the age of 14 must have a license, and these can be purchased for the season or various lengths of time (one day, three days and six days); special licenses as well as regulations are provided for youth, disabled anglers, and senior citizens.

Zone Regulations

The Zone Regulations section of the booklet is broken down into nine chapters, each with maps and covering a certain geographical area. There are nine such zones, including separate zones for the coast, Snake River, and Columbia River. Each zone is given a general description and, because every zone is different, a set of general regulations that may differ from the statewide regulations. The general regulations list all species of both gamefish and non-game fish that can be found in the zone along with catch limits, length limits, other specifications, and seasons. For instance, in the Northwest zone, trout fishing is open year-round in lakes, but is seasonal on streams (May 27–Oct. 31); five fish over eight inches may be retained per day on lakes and two fish on rivers; only one fish may be kept over 20 inches; trout over 16 inches in rivers are considered steelhead and salmon under 15 inches are considered trout. Further information can be found for salmon and steelhead, warmwater fish, other fish such as sturgeon, bass

and sucker fish, and any other species such as shellfish, bullfrogs and crayfish. These general regulations will change with each zone, so it is important to know what zone you are fishing prior to catching and keeping any fish.

Special Regulations

The General Regulations for each zone are cross-referenced with a listing of Special Regulations for each zone. It is these special regulations, which list individual waters, that makes up the bulk of the entire Sportfishing Regulation booklet and contain the most important information for anglers. Examples include: limited seasons, protected species, river and lake closures, hatchery and wild fish harvests, and restrictions on angling methods such as bait, lures, flies, external weights and hook sizes. Obviously, these special restrictions can get complex and are too numerous to mention here in detail. Some of the more complicated areas are rivers containing anadromous species (salmon and steelhead), protected species (bull trout) and coastal waters. For instance, the regulations on rivers such as the Columbia, Willamette, Rogue, Snake and Umpqua are revised and changed frequently throughout the season. Anglers can keep up-to-date with these changes through the ODFW website (which features weekly recreation reports, and the latest news releases) or, to a lesser degree, through daily newspapers. The regulations may be complex, but anglers are required to keep abreast of all changes throughout the year; ignorance of the laws is not a defense against penalties.

ODFW regulations require that all retained salmon, steelhead, sturgeon, and halibut must be immediately, and without delay, recorded onto an angler's license with all the proper codes. My advice, if you have never done this before, is to review this procedure in the ODFW Regulation Guide or website prior to going fishing. The procedure is not as straightforward as you might imagine, especially in the excitement of landing a fish.

Sports Fish Overview

Barring specific fishing techniques, anglers often identify themselves with a particular fish species—this defines where they fish. In Oregon, saltwater anglers can choose between oceans, bays and estuaries, and tidewaters; salmon and steelhead anglers are limited to the above, plus coastal and inland river drainages along the Columbia, Snake and Willamette Rivers; warm-water anglers fish lowland lakes and reservoirs and the bottom ends of many rivers; trout anglers are often limited to higher-elevation lakes and rivers. It is easier to fish for salmon, steelhead and warm-water species from most major metropolitan areas in Oregon; trout often require more travel than any other species. Many anglers are adept at fishing for several species, but more often than not, anglers generally stick with what they know or prefer.

Ted Lesson's *The Habit of Rivers* had a profound influence on me as a young budding angler. In the book, Lesson describes in lyrical detail his efforts to catch steelhead when he first arrived in Oregon. After purchasing an old drift boat, he floated as many coastal rivers as he could in pursuit of this elusive fish. His fishless days build into a frustration that finally results in catching one steelhead, at which point Lesson came to the humble realization that he was a trout angler at heart—steelhead would have to remain an elusive species. To an angler like myself, who also struggled trying to catch steelhead, this was a great revelation: Lesson gave me the freedom to choose a species that was most suitable to my methods and styles. I suspect Lesson realized that the pay-off for hours and money invested in fishing gear, traveling, fishing, learning and exploring was most gratifying when he was in pursuit of trout. As a preferred trout angler, I enjoy the comfort of a small river and knowing that I can cast to the far bank to locate

fish easily among the pocket water and pools. By contrast, fishing the Columbia and other larger rivers is fishing on a massive scale, and it's not for everybody. What we can learn from Lesson's account is that fishing is a big world; all we can hope for is to find our niche.

FISHING METHODS

Fishing methods are as varied as anglers themselves. Generally, choices are divided into two categories: fly-fishing and traditional methods, the latter of which encompass a wide variety of bait and spinner options. Advocates for either approach are justified in choosing their particular style—neither is better than the other—and both approaches have practitioners with highly nuanced methods and intricate theories. Deciding which approach to use is partly based upon how we learn to fish and what our influences are. My father is a jack of all trades, and I became well versed in many different methods. It was not until later in life, when I started fishing on my own and money and time became an issue, that I settled on a chosen technique that best reflected my enjoyment of the sport.

Fly-Fishing

At the heart of fly angling is the notion of imitating natural food forms, traditionally mayflies, but also a host of other insects, baitfish, leeches, and terrestrials. Anyone who has seen the meticulous creations which emerge from a fly-tiers vise can't help but have appreciation for this approach. Fly-fishing, and the difficulties it entails, are largely based on the design of its gear and resemble almost nothing of traditional gear. Fly rods, reels, lines, leaders, and flies all work together to create a complex set of relationships that don't always occur with traditional methods of fishing. For instance, at the simplest level, fly-fishing is designed to deliver a small speck of materials, the fly, weighing nothing, long distances without the use of weight. The thick fly line, tapered leaders and rod and reel all work together to facilitate this process. Fly-fishing at its most advanced level takes into consideration a multitude of disciplines sush as entomology, water hydraulics, fish biology, and ecology, not to mention the intricacies of fly tying, fly design and the complicated engineering behind most fly-fishing gear.

There are some drawbacks to fly-fishing: not all waters are suitable for its practice; not all fish can be caught as easily as if you were using traditional gear (e.g., salmon, ocean fishing, bottom fishing); this is not an approach in which beginners will pick up and have immediate success; fly-fishing methods often conflict when used in close proximity to traditional methods of fishing; and fly-fishing gear is often two to three times more expensive than traditional gear, with a basic setup starting at $250 and higher.

Traditional Methods

Traditional methods of angling are what most people think of when they think of fishing. The simplest form is a baited hook, bobber, thin monofilament line, small lead weight, short rod and spinning reel. This is how most people learn to fish, and rightly so. Catching fish is as simple as casting your bait into a pool and waiting for the fish to strike. Beyond this simple approach lies a whole world of highly specialized techniques, including (but not limited to) drift fishing; side drifting; casting spinners, spoons and plugs; float fishing; back trolling; back bouncing; trolling; anchor fishing; plunking; mooching and jigging. As you can see, this is a highly diversified approach, and each of these is suitable for certain types of species.

Traditional gear also has its drawbacks, and many of these I associate with the use of bait: fewer and fewer waters are allowing bait fishing; bait needs to be purchased and used fresh; catch-and-release fishing is nearly impossible with bait because the fish take the hook so deep; bait can be messy and repugnant to some; and traditional gear riggings or setups can be complicated and gear-intensive.

Native Fish Species

RAINBOW TROUT
(Oncorhynchus mykiss)

Trout are the most popular, and some would say most sought-after, game fish in the world; they are stocked in more than 45 countries and on every continent except Antarctica. Not only are they good fighters, and challenging to fish for, but they taste great, especially cooked on an open campfire. The Oregon State record was caught in 1982 in the Rogue River; it weighed 28 pounds. The world record rainbow was caught in 1970 at Beel Island, Alaska weighing 42.2 pounds. A wide variety of trout can be caught in the same manner as the rainbow trout: Upper Klamath Basin Redband Trout *(Oncorhynchus mykiss newberrii)*, westslope cutthroat *(Oncorhynchus clarki lewisi)*, Lahontan cutthroat *(Oncorhynchus clarki henshawi)*, Alvord cutthroat *(Oncorhynchus clarki subsp)*, and redband trout *(Oncorhynchus mykiss gairdneri)*. Brown trout, brook trout, bull trout, sea-run cutthroat and lake trout (mackinaw) are discussed separately.

Rainbow trout, along with some of the above-mentioned varieties, are stocked by the millions in Oregon's cold lakes and streams—just in time for opening day. (The whole history and notion of the phrase "opening day," seemingly an American institution, is derived from the opening of trout season and no other species.) Rainbow trout, in their smaller stocked variety, provide fun and fair game for any youth with a bobber and worm. Larger wild rainbows found in rivers like the Deschutes, Metolius or Williamson are sophisticated creatures, befuddling and eluding the most advanced and experienced anglers. The trout's diversity of appeal, worthy of both beginner and experts alike, may be the primary reason this is such a popular fish.

Where and how you decide to fish for rainbow trout will largely determine your likelihood of success. Hatchery fish stocked in lakes and rivers are easier to catch than non-hatchery stocks. Obtain hatchery stocking schedules from the ODFW to find exactly where and how many fish will be supplied to a given lake or river. Wild fish must be found and located with analytical skills, an ability to read water, and an understanding of how trout live and feed in their environment.

Anglers need not limit their trout fishing to seasons. While many rivers and lakes have traditional seasons from April or May through October, many are open year-round and provide good fishing even in the dead of winter. For years, 80 percent of my trout fishing was between the months of October and March, leaving the summer months to other anglers. There are some drawbacks to winter

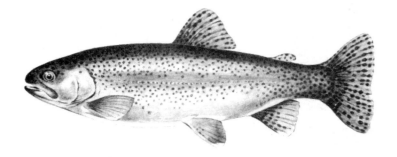

Rainbow Trout

© PAUL B. JOHNSON

trout fishing: the weather is often cold; it gets dark early; fly anglers will find limited insect hatches; and trout metabolism slows considerably (and therefore they feed less often) in water below 40°F, which is common in winter unless you're on a spring creek. Still, if you like fishing in the snow, on bright sunny winter days or rainy fall days, there are many surprises rarely witnessed by summer anglers.

Tackle, Tactics, and Tips

Whether fishing for trout in lakes or rivers, the equipment is the same. Spinning rods are often the lightest type of rod manufactured and come in lengths from 4.5 to 7.5 feet. G. Loomis makes several good models, including the all-SR782-2-GL2 rod. Spinning reels should be able to accommodate four- to six-pound test line, and several good choices can be had in the Abu Garcia Line of lightweight spinning reels, such as the 500 or 600 series. These rods will work for both spinners and bait.

The best fly rods are made of graphite and range from 6.5 feet to 9.5 feet. Trout rods need not hold any line weights larger than five or six pounds. The best all-around rod is a nine-foot five-weight, usually the first rod owned by beginning fly anglers. Manufacturers such as Echo, Temple Fork Outfitters, Thomas & Thomas, and Sage all make good entry-level as well as advanced rods. Fly reels should match the line weight of the rod. One- through four-weight rods in shorter sizes are adequate on small rivers. Shorter rods in six- to seven-foot lengths are better for smaller rivers where long casts are not a requirement. Longer rods in nine-foot lengths are good for lakes and bigger rivers such as the Deschutes, and they enable the caster to make longer casts, lob bigger nymphs and streamers and offer delicate dry fly presentations. Fly rods also come in different actions, or flexes: Beginners should start with soft or medium flexes; Advanced anglers have probably already gone through the process of selecting a fly rod for their style of fishing. Choosing a fly rod with a particular action is a matter of taste rather than expertise.

To avoid spooking trout, stay out of their line of sight. There are two ways to do this: 1). Approach the fish from behind, where they have a blind spot in their vision, or 2). Stay in a low crouch if you're to the side or in front of them. Standing tall by the bank is the surest way to spook trout. Both of these approaches correspond with what biologists understand about a trout's vision, namely that they can see approximately 160 degrees to the side of them and 30 degrees in from of them. A trout 10 feet deep in the water can see 20 feet of water surface above it.

Lakes

It is well-known that trout have a higher survival rate in lakes than they do in rivers. Oregon has an abundance of quality lake fisheries, most notably in the Cascade Mountains, which hold much bigger trout than local rivers. Trout act quite differently in lakes; they cruise, moving all the time to scout the shorelines and depths for food. In rivers, trout hold in pocket water and behind obstructions waiting for food to be delivered. The differences between lakes and rivers constitute a major difference in approach for anglers.

Options for fishing lakes include still fishing, trolling, and fly-fishing. Still fishing is perhaps the most popular and easiest method and doesn't require a boat like trolling does. The basic set-up is a hook, leader, bobber, fishing line, rod and reel. As fish seek comfort, cover and food, you will find them either higher or lower in the water column. Anglers can either drop down bait from above with a bobber or use a floating bait and anchor bait on the bottom. Bait such as night crawlers, cheese, a single salmon egg, small clump of PowerBait, or corn kernel can be suspended under a bobber to fish higher in the water column, four to six feet under the surface. To get near the bottom, remove the bobber, attach a small weight a foot or less from the hook and use a floating bait such as small marshmallows, Berkley's Power Nuggets, or clumps of cheese.

Spinners are a good option most of the year, either trolled behind a boat or cast and retrieved from a boat or shore. But because most spinners require a fast movement to keep the blades spinning, and therefore effective, they tend to work best in the summer and fall when fish are more active. Trout-sized Rooster Tails and Mepps Spinners in an assortment of colors such as white, yellow, red, black, and orange are all one needs.

Flies are a great option year-round and work best in shallower depths between 10 and 20 feet. If you plan to go beyond 20 feet with a fly outfit, you'll need special sinking lines. Casting and slow-stripping small leech patterns or nymphs is effective near the shore in spring and in deep water during summer. Perhaps one of the most famous lake flies is a size-eight black Woolly Bugger. These can be trolled, cast and stripped, or just allowed to sink and given an occasional twitch. Other colors that work well are white, maroon, red, and yellow. Effective basic nymphs include pheasant tails and hare's ears. Dry fly hatches are frequent on lakes with notable insects being *Callibaetis,* tricos, midges, chironomids, damsels, and dragonflies. Also present in lakes are water beetles, back swimmers, leeches, and small baitfish. It's a good idea for lake fly anglers to invest in a Type II clear intermediate sinking line, which will be useful whenever you're not fishing dry flies.

Fishing too deep or not deep enough is a common cause for not catching fish. Rather than changing your lures, fly or bait, try adjusting the depth at which you fish. This can be accomplished with the use of bobbers, strike indicators, and split shot. When using split shot, begin with the smallest shot you can find, using multiple weights on one line. This is a better way to fine-tune your depths than using one big weight.

Rivers

The very first thing one should do when walking up to a river is try and identify the four parts of a river: riffle, run, pool, and tail-out. Next, look for obvious obstructions in the form of rocks, undercut banks, downed trees, and overhanging brush, broken water and shadows or shade. Subtle and more difficult to detect are changes in the river's current and flow or depressions in the river bottom. The most important changes are back eddies where the river changes direction in pockets along the bank and current seams. Current seams can be found alongside any rock, downed tree, island or any other obstruction and are created by the meeting of two currents, one fast and one slow, the result of water being pushed or blocked by some obstruction. Locating depressions in the river bottom where trout hold is most difficult. One almost has to spend time not fishing and instead walking around in the river to detect these. It is time well spent if you can remember where you found depressions for the next time you're fishing.

Bait can be used with success in any part of the river: rolled along the bottom in a riffle, suspended or rolled on the bottom in a run and pool. Effective baits are the same you would use on a lake: night crawlers, salmon eggs, and PowerBait to name a few. Because spinners are often heavier than bait or flies, they require more water and are more effectively used in runs. Rooster Tails, Mepps Spinners and Rapalas are favorites of spin anglers. All these attractors can be cast into the deeper runs and pools and retrieved quickly before they hit bottom. Casting downstream or straight across is the best way to utilize the river hydraulics and keep the spinner off the bottom. Slower-moving rivers will require lighter spinners and quicker retrieves.

Fly-fishing is a matter of knowing what insects or other natural food forms live in the river and are available to fish. Flies for trout fall into three categories: dry flies, nymphs and streamers. Dry flies represent the adult form of a waterborne insect (mayflies, caddis, stoneflies, midges) or terrestrial insects (grasshoppers, ants, beetles, crickets) and are visible to the angler as they float on the surface of the

ENVIRONMENTAL FACTORS

It's important to understand that regardless how you decide to catch trout – bait, lure, or fly – trout don't change their behavior; bait and spin anglers catch trout in the exact same locations as fly anglers. Trout are found in colder rivers and lakes, and while they have a survival range which would indicate a greater tolerance for warm water (35-75°F), trout living at higher temperatures are less than desirable, becoming sluggish and lifeless. Optimum temperature ranges for fish feeding and movement are between 50 and 68°F. Even within this range, falling temperatures decrease feeding and rising temperatures increase feeding; a river or lake with water temperatures that have just fallen 5 or 6°F is likely to have fish that are off the feed. Temperatures above 68°F and below 50°F result in less feeding and movement, a kind of lethargy, from trout.

Because trout are always seeking comfort, food and cover, they move around a lot as the seasons change.

Other weather features can affect trout fishing such as whether the sky is overcast or sunny, low pressure systems or storms, lightening and thunder, rain and snow, warmer and cooler air conditions, and wind. Trout respond to these conditions in much the same way people do: Comfortable temperatures and less disturbing conditions make for better fishing. Wind, rain, snow, cold air, bright sun, and storms can all make fish wary and put them off the bite.

Temperature and weather are only two factors in determining when trout feed. The other major factor is insect and baitfish activity. Smaller fish below 12 inches feed almost exclusively on insects, plankton and other smaller food forms. Larger fish above 12 inches also feed on insects, but also take advantage of meatier offerings such as baitfish, snails, crawdads, leeches, salamanders, and mice. One rule of thumb is the bigger the lure the bigger the trout. Not always the case, but probably true 70 percent of the time.

---

water. Fish reveal their presence by coming to the surface to engulf these insects. The best stating point for fishing dry flies is attractor patterns. These are non-specific patterns that resemble a host of insects and therefore avoid complicated "matching the hatch" theories. Basic attractor dry fly patterns include the Adams, Royal Wolff, Humpy, and Stimulator. Any one of these dry flies can be used in various sizes with good effect on almost any river. Nymphs are fished under the water as representations of insect larva, pupa or other immature forms of the adult insects that live in the river prior to hatching. Since the angler cannot see nymphs, and strikes can be subtle and hard to detect, many anglers use a strike indicator. Strike indicators are floating attachments positioned on the leader and

are a good way to detect a strike. Small unnatural movement in the float that represents something other than an unencumbered drift will indicate strikes. Streamers are the third type of fly used and represent small baitfish and leeches. Streamers are used a lot like spinners, in that they are cast down and across in runs of deeper water. Popular streamers include Woolly Buggers, Muddlers, Zonkers, Zoo Cougars, Mickey Finns, Bucktail Caddis, and Egg Sucking Leeches.

Trout do 80–90 percent of their feeding below the surface. For fly anglers this makes nymphs and streamers an obvious first choice when exploring a new river and lake. In fact, if you're really uncertain about what approach to use, there are a few two-fly setups that help reduce your odds of getting skunked.

In the first set-up, tie on a larger dry fly such as a Stimulator or Humpy to use as a strike indicator. Attach to the bend of the dry fly hook a short piece of tippet, 8 to 12 inches, and tie on a smaller nymph. This gives trout two options and allows you to narrow down the odds of what works.

The second approach uses a streamer, such as an egg sucking leech or Muddler, with the same second piece of tippet, but shorter, six to eight inches, tied off the bend of the hook leading to a smaller nymph or egg pattern. Small egg patterns work especially well to catch larger trout in fall and spring. This system can also be used with two nymphs, two dry flies, and a nymph and soft hackle.

Recommended Waters

Rainbow trout: Chickahominy Reservoir, Crane Prairie Reservoir, Detroit Lake, Harriet Lake, Krumbo Reservoir, Metolius River, Prineville Reservoir, Rogue River, Timothy Lake, Wenaha River.

Upper Klamath Basin redband trout: Agency Lake, Davis Lake, Klamath River, Sprague River, Upper Klamath Lake, Williamson River, Wood River.

Redband trout: Ana River, Deep Creek, Crooked River, Deschutes River, Donner und Blitzen River, McKenzie River, North Fork Malheur River, Owyhee River.

Westslope cutthroat: Clatskanie River, Coast Fork Willamette River, Collawash River, North and East Forks of the Nehalem River, North Fork of the Middle Fork Willamette River, Oak Grove Fork of the Clackamas River, Upper Wilson River.

Lahontan cutthroat: Mann Lake, Willow Valley Reservoir.

Alvord cutthroat: Trout Creek.

COASTAL CUTTHROAT TROUT
(Oncorhynchus clarkii clarkii)

Also known as "sea-run," "Coastals" or "Harvest Trout," these fish have a long but spotty history on many of Oregon's coastal rivers and drainages. Long sought for their fighting spirit and unique pedigree as an ocean-run fish like steelhead, their numbers have been devastated, declining to remnant levels, as river habitats have been destroyed by timber harvesting, road building, and river use. Declining numbers combined with anglers' preferences for steelhead, have resulted in these fish falling out of favor with most anglers; that is, until lately. There has been a renewed interest in this forgotten fish, partly because of efforts on the part of conservation groups to restore sea-run habitats in many costal rivers. The ODFW has also made a concerted effort to improve sea-run populations. *Fly-Fishing Coastal Cutthroat Trout: Flies, Techniques, Conservation,* by Les Johnson, was published in 2004 and helps reacquaint anglers with the sea-run. (This is an updated version of *Sea-Run Cutthroat Trout,* last printed in 1971.) This is all good news for anglers who once again get to experience the pleasure of catching this feisty trout.

Sea-run cutthroat are hard to confuse with the rosy-colored rainbow trout. Coastals are often bright silver, sometimes showing shades of gold, and are deeply speckled with irregular dark spots. Sea-runs size between a pound and a pound and a half, 12–16 inches. Occasionally a fish of two pounds or more is caught, and 18-inch fish are common. The life cycle of the sea-run cutthroat spans about 10 years. At age two or three, a majority of sea-run cutthroat make a spring migration in May to saltwater. They feed in the bays, estuaries, and along coastlines, rarely venturing into the open ocean. After two to five months, they return to the river in the fall, typically October (hence the nickname "Harvest Trout"). The migration patterns are highly variable depending on the river. Some fish can return to freshwater rivers as early as July or as late as December or January.

Most anglers familiar with this fish can confirm their aggressive nature compared to rainbow and even brown trout. Sea-runs like to attack a fast moving fly or lure with shock-

© DUANE RAVER

Coastal Cutthrout Trout

ing quickness. Steelhead anglers frequently catch sea-runs with bright steelhead streamers. Tradition tells us that sea-runs like to hide in slack water around woody debris. This is true, but I catch at least as many fish in faster currents as long as I'm casting around and under brush. In my opinion, brush and obstructions are the key to locating sea-runs.

Tackle, Tactics, and Tips

No special equipment is needed; lightweight trout tackle and four- to six-pound test line is sufficient. Lures and flies should be brightly colored and impart a lot of flash or action. Faster retrieves seem to generate more strikes than slow ones. Because sea-runs like to hide, focus particularly around wood debris such as overhanging trees, downed logs, and brushy banks. Cast under these obstacles if possible in order to get the trout's attention. Casting a lure or fly a foot or two from structures can make a huge difference.

Recommended Waters

Clackamas, Kilchis, Nehalem, Nestucca, Rogue, Sandy, Santiam, and Trask Rivers, Siltcoos Lake.

BULL TROUT
(Salvelinus confluentus)

There are only three places in Oregon where bull trout may be legally retained: Lake Billy Chinook, Lake Simtustus, and the Deschutes River upstream from Lake Billy Chinook to Steelhead Falls. All other rivers and lakes either prohibit fishing or require catch-and-release fishing. One of the best catch-and-release fisheries in Oregon for bull trout over 10 pounds is the Metolius River.

Bull trout are a member of the char family and are native to Oregon and the Pacific Northwest. They require cold, clear water (59–64°F) and as such are an indicator species for how well a watershed is doing. The fact that they are on the endangered list for so many waters is some indication of how troubled many of our rivers are. Bull trout spawn in cold, clear tributaries of main lakes and rivers in September and October.

Bull trout are predacious, feeding on terrestrial and aquatic insects but also on sculpin, whitefish, small kokanee and trout, and other baitfish. Bull trout also take advantage of spawning fish and feed readily on the eggs of trout, kokanee the whitefish. Most bull trout average quite small, 8–12 inches. There are only a few places where they grow to enormous size. The Oregon state record catch was made in 1989 on Lake Billy Chinook and weighed 23.2 pounds.

Bull trout and brook trout can look remarkably similar: dark spots on a grey or dark olive background. Brook trout have three characteristics bull trout don't: dark markings on the dorsal fin, red on the paired fins and marbled,

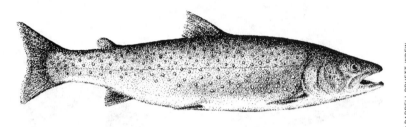

Bull Trout

worm-like markings on the back. Proper identification can make the difference between a legal and illegal catch.

Tackle, Tactics, and Tips

In rivers, bull trout are fished for with the same methods as rainbow trout and can be caught on all your favorite trout lures, bait and flies. Bull trout are particularly fond of baitfish patterns and so streamers such as bunny leeches, Woolly Buggers and spinners such as Rooster Tails work great.

In lakes, the most effective way to fish for bull trout is by trolling large lures like Rapalas, Quickfish, and flatfish, or by using any wobbling lure. The idea is to imitate a crippled baitfish, the primary food source for bull trout. Fly anglers should use streamers such as Clouser Minnows, weighted Zonkers, and weighted Woolly Buggers and rabbit leeches.

Recommended Waters

Legal harvest: Deschutes River upstream from Lake Billy Chinook to Steelhead Falls, Lake Billy Chinook, Lake Simtustus.

Catch-and-release: Beulah Reservoir, Imnaha River, Little Deschutes River, McKenzie River, Metolius River, Odell Lake, Wallowa River, Wenaha River.

STEELHEAD
(Oncorhynchus mykiss)

Steelhead, like salmon, are anadromous, meaning they are born in freshwater streams, migrate to the ocean for their adult phase and return to their native rivers to spawn. Steelhead will spend one to three years of their life in the ocean feeding on a rich diet of marine life. In that timespan, steelhead can grow from a smelt to an eight-pound fish or bigger. Unlike Pacific salmon, steelhead do not always die after spawning. Steelhead are known to be multiple spawners (iteroparous), making two and sometimes three trips out to the ocean and back. These multiple retuning fish are commonly called two- and three-salt fish. These are the big fish and can reach well over 18 pounds. The Oregon state record was caught in 1970 on the Columbia River weighing 35.8 pounds.

Steelhead and rainbow trout are the exact same species, differentiated only by their lifecycles. It still puzzles scientists why some trout become steelhead and some remain resident trout. Some suspect it is access to the ocean, but that doesn't account for why some fish never migrate and some do. To further muddy the waters, the offspring from one steelhead may include a mix of both resident rainbow trout and steelhead.

Juvenile steelhead live in rivers for their first few seasons, and anglers frequently catch them when fishing for trout. On such rivers as the Rogue and Umpqua, young steelhead are considered to be trout, while trout over 20 inches are labeled steelhead. The Rogue has one of the few juvenile steelhead sport-fisheries in the state. Called half-pounders, these are steelhead that have been to the ocean but return after their first year at sea. These fish are generally 14–18 inches and are attractive for their aggressiveness when taking a lure.

Steelhead will forever remain one of the most challenging and sought-after fish in the state. Hooking and landing a steelhead is incomparable with any other fish: They are all muscle, toned in the cold fast rivers in which they swim, and they're confident, tempered by their journey from ocean to river; They fight with power and determination, leaping into the air, and making hard fast runs that can strip an angler's line to the knot that secures it on the spool. Those who harvest steelhead find their meat delicious, and some prefer it to salmon. There are two runs of steelhead in Oregon: winter and summer. Some, but not all, rivers have both, and it all depends on stocking practices and river conditions. Summer steelhead are generally hatchery-raised fish that are sexually immature and return to rivers between the months of May and October. Winter steelhead are most commonly wild, sexually mature, and return to their native rivers between November and April. Summer fish spawn in the spring and winter fish spawn immediately after reaching their spawning grounds.

In recent years, hatcheries have developed a few more options for anglers desiring hatchery fish. A third stock of fish is becoming popular: the hatchery broodstock. These are hatchery fish bred to coincide with the winter run of fish. In effect, this gives anglers the opportunity to catch keeper hatchery fish during the winter runs. Rivers on which this occurs are Hood, Clackamas, Wilson, Nestucca and Siletz to name a few. Another recent hatchery practice to increase anglers' enjoyment is that of "recycling fish." This practice allows hatcheries to gather up a percentage of returning fish and release them back into the river in order to give anglers a second chance. Rivers on which this occurs in Oregon are the North Fork of the Santiam, Rogue, and Clackamas among others.

Tackle, Tactics, and Tips

The average steelhead weighs between six and 15 pounds. The most basic tackle set-ups allow for these weight differences. Without getting too specialized, most anglers choose graphite drift rods and spinning rods capable of handling six- to eight-weight lines. Steelhead rods, as opposed to salmon rods, tend to be stiffer through the midsection to allow good casting and a sensitive "touch" or soft action tip. The reason for the soft tip is to allow the angler to feel what is happening with the lure, bait or fly as it's moving through the water. Similar to trout fishing, steelhead fishing requires a degree of finesse when it comes to controlling your lure, bait or fly in the water. Reels should match the line weight and type of rod you're using. Spinning rods typically use spinning reels and drift rods use levelwinds. Beginning anglers should consider a spinning

© PAUL B. JOHNSON

Steelhead

rod for their first set-up. Levelwinds and drift rods are great tools, but somewhat specialized and can be difficult to operate until you have experience or instruction.

Fly anglers use rods of similar line weight to spin and drift anglers, six to eight weight, with matching reels. Disk drag reels can be an advantage when playing steelhead. Floating fly lines are a mainstay of summer steelhead fishing. Winter fishing is more technical and can require a variety of sink-tips and full sinking lines to get deeper in the water.

Most anglers agree, sharp hooks catch more fish, and nothing dulls a hook like getting caught on a snag, bouncing off rocks, or getting caught in debris. This problem can be solved by carrying a fine-toothed file in your vest or tackle box and periodically checking your hook for sharpness.

Locating Steelhead

It is generally conceded by most steelhead anglers that if you can get a fly, lure, or bait to a steelhead it will bite. The difficulty with this approach is, of course, locating the fish. Successful steelheading is dependant on one's ability to locate fish, or put another way, to read water. If you read *The Anatomy of Rivers and Lakes* in the Fishing Tips section then you have a head start. If you can learn to identify the various parts of a river (riffle, run, pool, tail-out) then you're halfway to locating steelhead. Like trout, steelhead require cover and comfort, but not food (at least that's the theory which is counter-pointed by the fact that they take flies, lures, and bait). What this means is steelhead are not like trout in that they rarely seek feeding lanes. Steelhead are on the move, and they want comfort, so they choose water that provides the greatest rest and cover. Good places to look for steelhead are around boulder clusters, ledges, depressions or pockets in the river bottom covered by four to six feet of water. All these areas break up the force of the current and provide cover and safety. A surprising number of steelhead can be found around boulders in tail-outs. The majority of steelhead are picked up along seams where fast and slow water meet, behind boulders in the middle of fast runs, and anywhere the water tends to back up against a tail-out or jutting piece of land. As long as there is current, and it's not too fast, or obstacles are present to break up the river's momentum, there is a good chance of finding a steelhead.

Since steelhead are constantly on the move, you should be too when fishing. There is no hard and fast rule other than to cover water thoroughly but quickly, and change runs or pools often; anglers who stay in one spot for hours miss opportunities elsewhere. It only takes a few well-positioned casts before you can determine the fish must be elsewhere.

Drift Fishing

Drift fishing, when done right, is a very precise way to deliver bait or other attractors such as yarn, corkies, and jigs directly to steelhead in any kind of water. It is a versatile approach that can be practiced either from the bank or from a boat (technically called side drifting). The basic set-up consists of a hook, four- or five-foot leader connected to a barrel swivel, and a small pencil lead or slinky weight attached to the swivel. The rig just mentioned is cast upstream and allowed to bounce along the bottom at the speed of the current (hence, drift fishing). Contact with the bottom is important and requires the angler's full attention not to get hung up by repeatedly lifting the rod tip and, if necessary, reeling in line prior to the weight getting stalled. Being able to detect where the bait is in the drift is facilitated by the sensitive rod tip discussed earlier. Tippet lengths and weights may need to be adjusted depending on the shallowness and nature of the river. Popular baits for this method include small clumps of salmon roe, sand shrimp, night crawlers, and artificial set-ups with corkies and yarn. Some anglers combine this technique with spinners, spoons, plugs, and jigs.

Float Fishing

Float fishing, another popular method of catching steelhead, is a variation on drift fishing; it utilizes a float to suspend the bait at various depths in the water column. This is a top-down approach, whereas drift fishing is a bottom-up approach. Float fishing requires a little more fine-tuning in order to keep your bait suspended at the right depth for each hole or run. This is a very effective method with the same baits listed above for drift fishing, but I think the real advantage with this method is in using jigs, those feathery lead-headed lures which steelhead can never resist. Spoons and lures are also used with this method.

BACK-TROLLING

Back-trolling, or pulling plugs, is an old technique developed by drift-boaters that has fallen out of favor with some anglers in light of more exciting drift- and float-fishing techniques, but it's an effective method nonetheless. Plugs (Hotshots, Wiggle Warts, Fatfish, and Tadpollys) work by diving to the bottom when counter pressure is applied on the lure. From a boat, this means anglers let out the lures 20–50 feet in front of the boat while the rower pulls back to create drag. The plug dives to the bottom and wiggles and wobbles, seducing the steelhead (and salmon) into striking. Plugs are difficult to use from the bank without the aid of a side-planer to keep the plug in the current. The other traditional fishing method is good ol' spinners and spoons. These are cast from the bank or boat and worked methodically through potential steelhead lies.

FLY-FISHING

Fly-fishing is also an effective method for catching steelhead, even if it's somewhat difficult and limited. Fly-fishing is not the most effective delivery system for getting a tempting lure to a fish. Success with fly gear requires more advanced skills than most anglers possess when starting out. Winter steelheading is especially difficult and not for the faint of heart when it comes to casting large flies with heavy sinking lines. To add to the difficulties, fly anglers frequently have to find their own water because their methods are simply

not compatible when used in the same pools and runs with traditional gear anglers; back casts, line mending, and floating line all create problems when mixed with the cast and drift techniques of drift anglers.

That said, here are a few tips for fly-fishing for steelhead. The trend on most rivers right now is nymphing. Most nymph rigs involve a two-fly setup under a large poly-foam or cork indicator. The lead fly is usually a weighted nymph such as a Kauffman Stonefly, or big Copper John, followed by a smaller dropper fly such as a prince nymph (some overzealous anglers use three flies, but you can imagine the potential for disaster that holds). Keep the flies separated on a eight- to 14-inch piece of tippet. From a boat, nymph fishing is not much different than drift fishing and is a matter of keeping a consistent dead drift off the side of the boat while moving with the current. Bank anglers can approach this kind of fishing by casting upstream, then using mends and an appropriate amount of slack line to keep the fly line from pulling the fly downstream.

A more traditional method of fly-fishing for steelhead employs the use of streamers, floating and sinking lines, and a fair amount of technical expertise to get a good drift (see *Suggested Reading* list). This method involves casting your streamer down and across the current, then allowing the fly to swing through the bottom of the run. Anglers tend to start at the top of a run and work their way downriver in two- or three-step increments until they reach the pool or tail-out. Traditional flies for this method include Green-Butt Skunks, Purple Perils, Skykomish Sunrises, Coal Cars, Spawning Purples, and various kinds of spey flies. Less traditional streamer patterns include starlight leeches, egg-sucking leeches, string leeches, and any other un-godly creation dreamed up at the "midnight-vise," provided it contains fluorescent feathers, long strips of rabbit fur, bead heads, cone heads, and lead-eyes.

Dry fly-fishing for steelhead is an innovative approach that works better for summer steelhead because the fish are more active and willing to move for the right offering. Surface strikes on a dry fly are explosive and powerful. The technique here involves skating a large buoyant dry fly such as a Bumble Bee, Wally Waker, or Bomber across the top of the water. The resulting look is the fly creating a wake, disturbing the water surface in such a way that it agitates a fish into striking. Fishing for summer steelhead during an October caddis hatch is a good time to employ a skated dry fly to imitate the clumsy surface skating action of these large caddis as they try to take flight.

Recommended Waters

Chetco, Clackamas, Columbia, Deschutes, Grand Ronde, Hood, Illinois, John Day, Nehalem, Nestucca, North Umpqua, Rogue, Sandy, Santiam, Siletz, South Umpqua, Trask, and Wilson Rivers.

CHINOOK SALMON
(Oncorhynchus tshawytscha)

Also known as the King Salmon, Tyee Salmon, Blackmouths, Springers (spring chinook), Upriver Brights (fall chinook), and June Hogs (summer chinook), chinook are the largest salmon species in Oregon and consequently the most popular with anglers. Chinook are caught for both sport and eating, but primarily the latter. Chinook can be caught in the open ocean, bays, tidewaters, and in freshwater rivers. The life cycle of a salmon is anadromous, meaning they are born in fresh water, spend a portion of their lives at sea and return to their native river to spawn. Most chinook rear in their natal river for one to two years, then spend two to five years in the ocean. Once returning salmon hit fresh water, they begin to die, and do die once spawning is completed.

Anglers want to find the freshest fish they can, and this means fishing in the lower ends of rivers and in bays. That said, a lot of fresh chinook are caught in upper portions of rivers such as the Rogue and Umpqua and they remain almost as fresh and bright as when they entered the river. The key point is that the longer the fish is in the river the less chance it will be a good eating fish, and less than desirable to catch as the fish are literally rotting to death.

Average chinook weigh between 10 and 15 pounds, but fish between 45 and 65 pounds are not uncommon. The Oregon state record is a longstanding one, caught in 1910 on the Umpqua River and weighing 83 pounds. There are two seasons salmon enter freshwater rivers to spawn: spring and fall. Spring chinook enter the rivers from April to July, and fall chinook arrive in September through December. There are some subtle distinctions on certain rivers, and sometimes there can be what's called a summer and winter run, but these are anomalies. Rivers such as the Nestucca, Nehalem, Wilson, Rogue, and Chetco have long tidal reaches, and fish may arrive

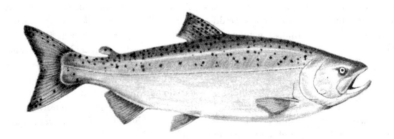

© PAUL B. JOHNSON

Chinook Salmon

in these areas a full month prior to ascending into freshwater. The first fall rains that raise the river's water level prompt the movement into fresh water. Fall chinook and coho salmon can usually be found in the same run. Fall chinook are preceded by summer steelhead and succeeded by winter steelhead, and overlap is quite frequent, making it possible for anglers to catch two or three different species at one time. Rivers like the Rogue, Umpqua and Wilson are famous for their overlapping runs of fish.

Some rivers such as the Umatilla have special regulations for jack salmon. Jack salmon are not a species of salmon, but a sexually immature salmon of any species and are distinguished from the adults by their size. Coho jacks are between 15 and 20 inches; any other salmon between 15 and 24 inches is considered a jack salmon. On most rivers in Oregon, except the Pistol River, one is not required to obtain a salmon/steelhead tag in order to catch and retain jack salmon.

Tackle, Tactics, and Tips

Although chinook are caught in both ocean and freshwater, tackle remains similar, but saltwater rods and reels need to be made of corrosion-resistant metals. Salmon rods come in many categories depending on the type of fishing you're doing. There are rods for float fishing, drift fishing, trolling, spinner fishing, plunking, mooching, jigging and back bouncing. A lot of these rods will double for several techniques. In general, rods used from a boat or shore that require leverage to lift heavy weights will be shorter and stiffer than rods used for casting spinners and floats from the boat or bank. Casting rods need to be stiff enough to power a 35-pound fish, but supple enough for casting. For plunking and trolling, a good general rod is a 7.5–9-foot, stiff, heavy-duty graphite rod with a sensitive tip. The sensitive tip allows anglers to feel subtle takes and to have some control over the position of their bait and casting. Anglers fishing rivers with floats and spinner techniques may

want something with slightly less backbone than an ocean rod for casting purposes. Anglers jigging for salmon prefer a heavy-duty rod of fiberglass construction with a stiff tip to allow good hook sets. Reels are usually levelwinds, constructed with good drag systems and enough capacity to handle 200–250 feet of 15–25-pound test line. Monofilament line is preferred for depths above 100 feet, but below 100 feet anglers like to switch to a low-stretch ultra-braid line for better hook sets.

There are many techniques used for catching salmon, depending where you choose to fish. The primary methods are trolling with plugs, spoons and spinners; mooching with herring or salmon eggs; and anchor fishing and bobber fishing with bait such as herring or eggs and jigs.

TROLLING

Both trolling and mooching occur in the bays and in tidewater. The most effective way to troll is to use a three-way swivel: attach one end of the swivel to your line, another to a leader bearing a one- to three-ounce weight and another leader with the attached plug, spinner or spoon. Troll slowly enough to keep your weight close to the bottom to deliver the bait, but not hitting the bottom.

MOOCHING

Mooching, which is a lot like jigging, is practiced in bays and tidewater where currents allow for a straight down presentation in easy currents. This method allows anglers to suspend a live or dead herring directly under the boat in the zone of salmon. Banana weights are popular for this technique, and are tied in the line six to 12 inches above the bait. Mooching can be done from either an anchored boat in still water or from a drifting boat, often called wind drifting. Mooching is a slow process, but its proponents swear by it.

ANCHOR FISHING

Anchor fishing uses a similar set-up to trolling, except the boat is anchored and the bait or plug is allowed to work against the current. Enough weight should be used to keep the bait near, but not on, the bottom. Most anglers look for their line to have a 45–60 degree angle to the water's surface. Any less or more of an angle means the bait is too high in the water or the weight is hung-up on the bottom.

BOBBER FISHING

Bobber fishing is most productive in water with current, like rivers or the heads of tidewater. Bobbers suspend bait from the top down. The key with this approach is to know the depth of your water and keep the bait suspended near the bottom without actually snagging on the bottom. Bobber fishing is also popular while fishing off of jetties and from a boat in bays when the tide is moving in or out and there is enough current to promote a drift. The preferred bait for this kind of fishing is herring, but salmon eggs also work.

River techniques include back bouncing with bait, back trolling with plugs and spinner fishing. Back bouncing is a method of lifting and dropping your weight, bouncing it on the bottom, so that the bait or lure is worked downstream. This technique is similar to anchor fishing, but with line releases to move the bait. Back trolling works with a plug or plug/bait combination downstream to a waiting fish. The boat must be held in the current to allow for the plug to dive with the resistance of the water. The boat then can be edged downriver, while maintaining tension on the diving plug. This method is a favorite of drift-boaters. Plugs for salmon include large flatfish, Kwickfish, and salmon-sized hotshots. Fluorescent colors such as orange, green and red work best. Casting spinners and spoons is always an effective technique. Spoons and spinners should be weighted to reach adequate depths and worked systematically across the river and through a run or pool. Coverage is the most important factor here, and the best way to do that is to cast, take a step downriver and repeat. Spinners include the Luhr-Jensen Clearwater Flash, Alsea Specials, Krystal Flash Salmon Spinners.

Recommended Waters

Alsea River, Chetco River, Clackamas River, Columbia River, Nehalem River and Bay, Nestucca River, Pistol River, Rogue River, Sandy River, Siuslaw River and Bay, Tillamook Bay, Umpqua River, Willamette River, Wilson River, Winchester Bay. Good winter runs on the Coquille, Elk, and Sixes Rivers.

COHO (SILVER) SALMON
(Oncorhynchus kisutch)

Also known as silvers, coho are an elusive salmon, and often protected in Oregon to help boost a population that started declining in the early 1970s. Anglers seek coho for both their sport and eating qualities. The distinguishing characteristic of coho versus chinook, other than size, is that coho can often be caught close to the surface, requiring little to no weight, and they often put on a surface show when hooked. Because of their surface feeding habits, fly anglers have a better than usual opportunity to catch coho. While there is a strong run of hatchery fish on some waters, a majority of the population is wild and off-limits to harvest. Open-ocean fishing along Oregon's shores is mostly off-limits to anglers, but occasionally there are brief openings each year. All rivers are closed to coho fishing unless exceptions are made in the Oregon Fishing Regulations. All coho spawn in fall, September through November, often coinciding with the fall chinook run. There are three coast lakes that are also good producers of coho salmon: Siltcoos, Tahkenitch, and Tenmile. In fact, the Oregon state record was caught out of Siltcoos Lake in 1966 weighing 25 pounds, 5.25 ounces. Average coho weigh 8–12 pounds and measure about two feet long.

Chinook and coho can be difficult to tell apart. The most reliable way to tell the difference, as recommended by the ODFW, is to look inside the mouth at the gum line in the lower jaw. On a chinook this area is black; on

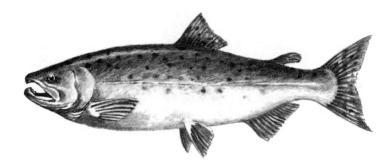

© BOB RACE

Coho (Silver) Salmon

a coho it's white. Other differences: there are smooth tail fin rays on a chinook, while the coho's are ribbed; the entire tail is spotted on a chinook, while only the upper tail lobe is spotted on a coho.

Tackle, Tactics, and Tips

Rods and reel will depend on the type of fishing you're doing. Because coho are smaller fish than chinooks, anglers can use lighter weight tackle like that associated with steelhead fishing. Bait and casting rods are generally made of graphite, with a stiff middle section and supple tip. Spinning and levelwind reels can be rigged with eight to 15-pound test monofilament line. Trolling and jigging rods can be slightly heaver and have stiffer tips. Seven- and eight-weight fly rods with matching reels and line are adequate.

All kinds of methods take coho, and the decision depends on where you're fishing. Trolling is the most popular method in saltwater bays and river mouths. Anglers troll spinners or herring and enough weight to fish between 20 and 50 feet of water. Sometimes no weight is required when coho are feeding on or near the surface. You can also troll "coho flies" in combination with a flasher. Popular colors for coho are fluorescent colors in orange, red, yellow, and pink. Mooching with herring is productive in deeper brackish water, at depths of 40 to 50 feet. Other methods include float fish, and simply casting spinners or flies over productive lies.

In rivers, coho are taken on spinners, spoons and diving plugs, but generally it's not necessary to go deep. Think of coho as holding in the same areas as steelhead, in shallower areas along ledges, current seams, runs, and around boulders.

Recommended Waters

Alsea River, Columbia River, Coos Bay, Coquille River, Nehalem River, Rogue River, Salmon River, Siltcoos Lake, Siuslaw River, Tahkenitch Lake, Tenmile Lake, Umpqua River, Wilson River, Young's River.

CHUM SALMON
(Oncorhynchus keta)

In many ways, Oregon is lucky to have a chum salmon run (also called Dog Salmon, Keta, and Calicos), the second-largest salmon next to the chinook. That is because Oregon, or Tillamook Bay to be exact, sits at the southernmost limit of the chum salmon's range, which is predominantly to the north in Washington, Canada and Alaska. This is a highly prized eating fish in those northern states, but here in Oregon the chum salmon has fallen on rough times. Declining populations have forced the ODFW to allow fishing on only two Oregon rivers, the Kilchis and Miami, and both have limited seasons and catch-and-release restrictions. These restrictions have been in place for a

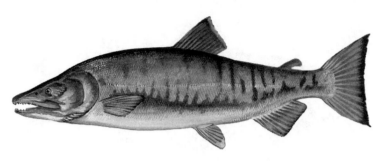

© DUANE RAVER

Chum Salmon

while, and there are signs that populations are rebuilding. Perhaps, if runs continue to improve, Oregon anglers will once again be able to enjoy the chum as more than a sport fish.

Chum salmon enter Oregon rivers in the fall, beginning in September and November, and average between 10 and 15 pounds. The Oregon state record was caught in 1990 on the Kilchis River weighing 23 pounds.

Tackle, Tactics, and Tips

Tackle for chum salmon should include heavy-weight graphite rods, spin or levelwind (bait casting) reels, and 20-pound test line. Fly anglers can use stiff seven- to nine-weight rods and matching reels and fly line.

All chum salmon are caught in rivers in Oregon. Chum are particularly aggressive and territorial, and they are a favorite among anglers because they take lures so readily. Traditional gear techniques for catching chum include drift fishing and casting spinners, spoons and plugs. The most popular color is green or chartreuse; other choices include fluorescent colors such as pink, purple and red. Chum are very popular with fly anglers who have no trouble getting these fish to take a fly. Large rabbit streamers in the above-mentioned colors work best.

Recommended Waters

Kilchis and Miami Rivers.

KOKANEE
(Oncorhynchus Nerka)

Kokanee, also known as silver trout, bluebacks, sockeye, silversides and redfish, are landlocked sockeye salmon, resident in many lakes in Oregon. The anadromous version of this fish populated Oregon waters in the past, most notably in the Grande Ronde and Deschutes watersheds, but are currently extinct. All existing kokanee populations inhabit lakes and are self populating, spawning in local tributaries. The Metolius is one such river that gets a sizable run from Lake Billy chinook.

Kokanee are known as great fighters and for their excellent-tasting meat. Kokanee average from eight to 20 inches with average catches below 14 inches. The larger the lake, and hence the lower the population density, the larger the average fish. Lake Billy Chinook, a sizable reservoir, is known for growing kokanee up to four pounds. The Oregon state record was caught at Wallowa Lake in 2001, weighing 6.12 pounds.

The primary food source for kokanee is plankton, but they are also known to feed on insects and larva. Kokanee like cold water—50°F and colder. Lakes that warm past this temperature drive these fish to the bottom, requiring anglers to fish at very deep levels, 100 feet or more. For this reason, kokanee flourish in lakes with depths exceeding 100 to 200 feet. Many anglers use fish finders to locate fish when they are at their deepest levels.

IMPROVING YOUR ODDS

Electronics have become a part of many anglers' fishing arsenals. The two most helpful items are **fish finders** and **GPS systems.** Fish finders help anglers determine depths, identify underwater structure and locate fish through sonar technology. GPS systems incorporate the use of hydrographic maps, which map the bottom of a lake and river, and can direct you to underwater features that are potential fishing areas. GPS systems also help you pinpoint and remember your position on the water. These two items—combined with a thermometer that can be lowered into the water to find the right temperatures where fish feed and rest—are just a few ways anglers try to improve their odds of catching fish.

Tackle, Tactics, and Tips

Trolling, jigging, and still-fishing are all productive methods for catching kokanee. Fishing at deeper depths is better suited to any length medium-action rods. Reels should be rigged with six- to eight-pound test line. Trolling is accomplished with the use of a string of trolling blades and a bright lures. Small spoons, spinners, or plugs painted in red, silver, or orange tipped with a small piece of bait such as a night crawlers work best. Trolling in a straight line is not nearly as effective as trolling in an s-curve pattern, which allows the lure to drop and vibrate in the turns. Troll very slowly for best results. Jigging is equally effective with mini-jigs and Buzz Bombs painted with fluorescent colors mentioned above. Bait such as white corn, maggots or small pieces of worm are added to the jigs. Still fishing is accomplished with weight and small spinners or bait.

Recommended Waters

Crescent Lake, Cultus Lake, East Lake, Green Peter Reservoir, Lake Billy Chinook, Metolius River, Odell Lake, Paulina Lake, Wallowa Lake, Wickiup Reservoir.

SACRAMENTO PERCH
(Archoplites interruptus)

The Sacramento perch (not really a perch) is the only native Western member of the sun-fish family. The only place to catch this fish in Oregon is on the Lost River east of Klamath Falls. The Lost River is, of course, where the state record fish came from in 1998, weighing 11.2 ounces. Sacramento perch provide good sport for such a small fish. They feed on insects, small crustaceans, and small minnows, and similar to other perch species, occupy weedy shorelines and are tolerant of warm waters.

Tackle, Tactics, and Tips

Use small marabou jigs, spinners and other lures in the weed beds or alongside the tulles wherever deeper water is present. Mid-spring and summer will prove to be the most productive times of year. Most baits work, including grubs and night crawlers. Also try any variety of small spinners or streamer flies that imitate baitfish.

Recommended Waters

Lost River.

STURGEON: WHITE AND GREEN

White sturgeon *(Acipenser transmontanus)* are also known as Pacific sturgeon, Oregon sturgeon, Columbia sturgeon, and Sacramento sturgeon. They are the largest freshwater fish in North America and can tip the scales at over 1,500 pounds and reach lengths of 20 feet. They

© BOB RACE

White Sturgeon

are found most abundantly in the Columbia River and along both the northern and southern coast in bays. Green sturgeon *(Acipenser medirostris)* are smaller and more rare, only existing in a few locations like the Columbia. The maximum size of green sturgeon is seven feet and up to 350 pounds. The appearance of both is similar, but they are a different color, as their names would suggest. Anglers catch surgeon for both sport, due to their enormous size, and eating. The same techniques for white sturgeon can be applied for green sturgeon.

A sturgeon's appearance is a little unsettling at first; it resembles some sort of prehistoric creature. A sturgeon's skeleton is made up of cartilage and, rather than scales, they have rows of bony plates for protection. There is no Oregon state record for sturgeon because the maximum size limit that may be removed from the water is 60 inches. Many sturgeon in the Columbia River are more than 100 years old.

Sturgeon are bottom dwellers and are most commonly found in freshwater, but they often migrate to saltwater bays and estuaries. They spawn in freshwater during the months of May and June and prefer cobbled bottoms for spawning areas. Females are known to produce 100,000 to several million eggs at one time. Primary food sources include other fish, shellfish, crayfish, clams and shrimp.

Tackle, Tactics, and Tips

Boat anglers can use shorter rods because casting is not imperative. Seven- to nine-foot rods are adequate. Fishing from the shore requires longer rods for casting leverage, and 11-foot rods are not uncommon. Levelwind reels should be rigged with at least 200 yards of 40–80-pound test monofilament or ultrabraid line.

Sturgeon fishing means fishing with bait. Because sturgeon are bottom feeders, rooting around in the mud, sand, and rocks for a meal, anglers must get their bait on the bottom. The most popular baits are whole smelt and shad. Some anglers will use pieces of salmon or clam meat as well. The most challenging aspects of sturgeon fishing are detecting the bite, knowing when to set the hook, and keeping bait on the bottom in deep, fast water. Weights can be huge, 16–24 ounces, but it all depends on the current and depth of the water. This also crates a lot of additional resistance when playing sturgeon, but that's the price one pays for getting to these fish. Once the bait is firmly anchored on the bottom, it is imperative that it be left alone and not moved. To accomplish this boats have to be anchored and secured so the current doesn't sweep the boat from side to side. It's important to check once in a while to make sure the bait is firmly anchored. If it keeps breaking loose, the weight may not be heavy enough. Because sturgeon do not have teeth they mouth the bait, sucking it in slowly, piece by piece. It is for this reason that anglers often have to abstain from setting the hook immediately. When it looks as if a sturgeon is beginning to take bait anglers need to wait for a solid take, and this can sometimes take a few agonizing seconds. When the bait is property engulfed, then anglers needs to give a hard hook-set.

Bait riggings are a matter of preference, but a majority of anglers attach a section of Dacron leader to the main line with a swivel. Then, a series of half-hitches are placed around the bait so that the smelt or shad is hanging upside down with the hook hanging out of the mouth of the bait. A sliding sinker is attached to the main line so it can work its way up and down the line.

Recommended Waters

Coos Bay, Columbia River between Bonneville Dam and the Columbia River estuary (smaller populations of fish can be found above Bonneville below The Dalles Dam and to a lesser degree further up in the river), Tillamook Bay, Winchester Bay, Yaquina Bay.

Non-Native Fish Species

BROWN TROUT
(Salmo trutta)

Also known as a German Brown and Loch-leven trout, the brown trout is a non-native species that thrives in many of Oregon's lakes and rivers. They provide great sport, are especially challenging to catch, and make good eating. Brown trout have distinctive brownish-yellow coloring with dark brown, black, and red spots. When compared to other types of trout, brown trout are noted for having a few distinguishing characteristics. First, while their preferred habitat is cold, clear rivers, they can tolerate higher water temperatures than most trout: up to 75°F. This makes them a good fishing opportunity even in summer, when some streams and lakes become low and warm. Second, brown trout on average grow to impressive size wherever they are. Even on small rivers like the North Fork of the Sprague, they can reach five pounds or more. Some Oregon lakes produce average-sized fish at five to six pounds. Fish of 10 pounds or more are common. The state record brown trout was caught in 2002 at Paulina Lake, weighing 28.5 pounds. Lastly, brown trout are wary. They prefer to eat at night and hide in the darkest cover they can find during the day. As a result these are not easy fish to catch, especially when undercut banks and logjams are present.

Brown trout are predacious, and their primary diet is baitfish minnows, but they also feed on insects (as many fly anglers can attest), leeches, and the occasional frog, mouse, and even small bird.

Tackle, Tactics, and Tips
Because of the size and strength of browns, consider using a slightly heavier rod with a faster action (stiff). Lightweight rods that fit this category will be fine. Spinning reels ought to have six- to eight-pound test line. Fly anglers can use faster five- to six-weight rods and matching fly line. On rivers, browns can be caught with bait, spinners and flies. Bait such as night crawlers, leeches and salmon eggs work great. Lures should be representative of small rainbow trout, brook trout or whitefish. Dry flies work when a hatch is present; otherwise, use basic nymphs such as hares ears and pheasant tails and streamers. Browns are especially known for having a preference for larger streamers such as a #4 or #6 Zoo Cougar, Zonker, Wooly Bugger, or rabbit leech. Regardless of the lure or bait you use, fish around and underneath obstructions. The closer you can cast or drift your lure near or under an obstruction, the better you chances. Lake anglers troll, still fish or cast lures and flies to the banks. Smaller browns can be caught on spoons, spinners and diving plugs. The larger trophy browns usually require heaver tackle and a lot more weight or downriggers to reach 100-foot depths. Trolling for bigger browns requires the use of larger lures such as Rapalas and Kwickfish, along with heavier 10–20-pound test line rigged on levelwind reels and medium-weight rods.

Recommended Waters
Agency Lake, Deschutes River, East Lake, Lake of the Woods, Miller Lake, North Fork Sprague River, Owyhee River, Paulina Lake, Sprague River, Suttle Lake, Wickiup Reservoir, Wood River.

BROOK TROUT
(Salvelinus fontinalis)

Also known as Speckled Trout, Aurora Trout, Brookie, Square-Tail, Speckled Char, Sea Trout, Common Brook Trout, Mud Trout, and Breac, average catches of brook trout range 10–12 inches and what they lack in size they more than make up for in fight. Larger lakes and rivers can produce brookies up to five pounds. The Oregon state record was caught in the Upper

Deschutes River, below Little Lava Lake, in 1980 and weighed 9 pounds, 6 ounces.

Brook trout are most commonly associated with small mountain lakes and the headwaters of small mountain streams. Most populations in Oregon are self-populating, using small tributaries or headwaters. Brook trout are voracious eaters, especially in high mountain lakes, and will eat anything that will fit in its mouth: aquatic insect larvae, terrestrial insects, and even smaller fish. Dry fly anglers do quite well fishing for brookies, as do streamer, spin and bait anglers. Brook trout are extremely popular with all anglers, especially youth.

Tackle, Tactics, and Tips
Both tactics and tackle are the same as for rainbow trout. If there is a difference it is the brook trout's propensity to chase an erratically jigged lure. Look for places around undercut banks in rivers and shelves in lakes to jig a small lure or fly. Float fishing is effective with single salmon eggs or power bait. Spin anglers can use a small Mepps, Rooster Tail or Blue Fox. As stated above, brook trout love to feed on the surface of rivers and lakes for hatching insects. Small attractor patterns such as an Adams will work in most cases. Nymphs, streamers and small wet flies also work but should be kept small, sizes 12 and under.

Recommended Waters
Allen Creek Reservoir, Crane Prairie Reservoir, Crooked River, Deschutes River (headwaters to Wickiup Reservoir), Devils Lake, Eagle Cap Wilderness Lakes, East Lake, Elk Lake, Hosmer Lake, Lava Lake, Little Cultus Lake, Little Lava Lake, Sparks Lake, Three Creek Lake, Todd Lake, Wickiup Reservoir, Waldo Lake.

LAKE TROUT
(Salvelinus namaycush)

Lake trout, or Mackinaw, are a non-native species to Oregon and a member of the char family rather than the trout family. Other chars in Oregon include brook and bull trout. Mackinaw are the largest of its species and are good for both sport and eating. Fish are regularly caught weighing 20 pounds or more. The Oregon state record was caught in 1984 in Odell Lake, weighing 40.8 pounds. Hailing from regions of Canada and the Great Lakes, lake trout like their water deep and cold (50–57°F; 53°F being optimum). This is also the water temperature at which most baitfish are found, the only food sources for Mackinaw. Mackinaw feed on minnows as well as trout, whitefish and kokanee. Early season (April/May) anglers can locate fish in 10 feet of water or less, just after ice-out, and along the edges of melting ice. Fall is a good time to fish a lake's rocky shoals or ledges when the females are getting ready to spawn and the males are building the nests. Spring is a good time to fish medium depths of 35–65 feet. Summer is when the water gets the warmest and fish are pushed deeper than 65 feet in order to find water at 53°F or less. The key to finding mackinaw is finding the right water temperature, which often means finding the right depth. Depth finders and fish finders work to help spot fish, and anglers can use portable water temperature devices that are lowered into the water to find optimum temperature ranges.

Tackle, Tactics, and Tips
There are two schools of thought when it comes to tackle: medium-sized tackle and heavy lines (20-pound test) or light tackle, softer rods and smaller test lines (six-pound test). Tackle is mostly a matter of preference, but both can be considered good options. Lighter tackle enables one to use less weight to get to the bottom and provide a more sensitive touch to detect strikes. The drawback to lighter tackle is the time it takes to land a fish. Heavier tackle lands fish quicker, but is also more difficult to manage at 60 feet or more. Popular spinner, plugs and spoons include Little Cleos, Sutton Silver Spoon, Rapalas, jigs, Williams Spoons, Lehr Jensen Crippled

Herring, Swedish Pimples, and Flutter Spoons. Some anglers also use No. 11 Mepps or Blue Foxes. Use a three-way swivel and attach the one- to three-ounce weight three feet below the swivel. Use about three feet of leader to attach the spinner or plug to the side swivel. Trollers begin by finding the bottom and then begin a slow troll, slow enough so you don't lose contact with the bottom.

Another, more difficult method for catching lake trout is with jigs. Jigging is accomplished with jigging spoons, swimming rap jigs, whitefish spoons, bass jigs and some kokanee jigs. These are fished vertically under the boat at depths where trout are known to be present. Depth finders are an invaluable tool with this approach. Tipping jigs with baitfish in often not necessary.

Recommended Waters
Crescent, Cultus, and Odell Lakes.

ATLANTIC SALMON
(Salmo salar)

These fish are known by a few names including quaniche, kennebec, and Sebago salmon. This is a true salmon and very sporting game fish from the East Coast. They were originally introduced into Oregon in 1951 from Quebec, Canada. These fish were planted in numerous lakes but most failed, except Hosmer and East Lake in Central Oregon. Because these fish do not naturally reproduce they have to be restocked every year. Today's stock of fish comes from a landlocked stock in Maine.

Atlantic salmon are noted as a great fighting fish, and they taste good on the table. The average catches range from 16 to 18 inches and can weigh two to four pounds. Larger fish up to seven pounds have been caught. Atlantic salmon feed a lot like trout in that they live off of insects, mainly the larvae (nymphs) of aquatic insects such as black flies, stoneflies, caddis flies, and chironomids. Good catches can be made on terrestrial insects such as crickets, grasshoppers, ants and beetles.

Tackle, Tactics, and Tips
No special equipment is needed to catch Atlantic salmon. Average trout gear, both lightweight spin gear and five-weight fly rods, is perfect. The two lakes in Oregon where anglers can find Atlantic salmon are generally fished by fly and spin anglers (Hosmer is fly-fishing only). Feeding fish can be taken on dries and non-feeding fish can be taken on your favorite trout lure or streamers. It's best to think of these fish as being similar to rainbow trout. Fish shorelines, rocky areas and places of overhanging brush and shade. A lot of Atlantic salmon are picked up by anglers jigging for kokanee.

Recommended Waters
East and Hosmer Lakes.

LARGEMOUTH BASS
(Micropterus salmoides)

Scrappy is about the best word that comes to mind when someone mentions largemouth bass. These are the most popular game fish in America and a bit overcrowded in Oregon by the presence of salmon and steelhead, but still the state's top warm-water fish. Anglers love the hard, explosive strikes, especially on top water lures; easy fishing, because they will take almost any presentation; and good eating. Largemouth bass should not be confused with the smaller variety of smallmouth bass which are a coldwater-loving fish.

Average catches of largemouth bass are between 14 and 16 inches. Maximum weights are around 10 pounds, and five- and eight-pound bass are quite common on many of Oregon's waters. The Oregon state record was caught in 2002 at Ballenger Pond weighing 12 pounds, 1.6 ounces. The unofficial world-record largemouth bass, as of the writing of this book, was caught in 2006 in Carlsbad, California and weighed 25.1 pounds. This new record topples the long-held record from 1932, when George Washington Perry caught a bass weighing 22 pounds.

© PAUL B. JOHNSON

Largemouth Bass

Largemouth bass are found in both lakes and rivers and are most active in water temperatures between 75 and 80°F. Spawning occurs in May to July or when waters reach 60°F. They are seldom found in water deeper than 20 feet and most often cruise the shallows around shorelines and among obstructions such as weedbed, vegetation, logs, pylons, and boat docks. Any obstruction that provides a degree of cover is attractive to a largemouth bass. Largemouth bass are known for being voracious and predatory eaters, feeding on minnows, larger carp, sunfish, tadpoles, frogs, leeches, crustaceans, mice, small birds and even their own young.

Tackle, Tactics, and Tips

Getting started in bass fishing is easy. All one needs to start is a light- to medium-action spinning rod, a spinning reel loaded with four- to six-pound test line, and a selection of bass lures mentioned below. Fly anglers can use the same medium-action rods (five- and six-weight), lines and reels to match, and a selection of streamers or surface poppers.

Largemouth bass can be caught on just about anything that moves in the water and looks or smells attractive. Popular baits include minnows, worms, and live bait. Bait is usually the best option in the spring. During the summer anglers switch to poppers and other surface plugs, and flies, to get the most excit-

ing action. Surface strikes from a large bass are what this fishing is all about. Underwater lures such as Rapalas, crankbaits and plastic worms are also productive and useful year-round. Using barbless hooks will help prevent snags when fishing around aquatic vegetation. Beyond this basic description, there are hundreds of options for catching bass, and just as many theories; but the fact remains that bass require little effort other than the ability to cast.

Recommended Waters

Columbia River, Cottage Grove Reservoir, Crane Prairie Reservoir, Davis Lake, Dorena Reservoir, Haystack Reservoir, Howard Prairie Reservoir, Hyatt Reservoir, Lake Billy Chinook, McKay Reservoir, Multnomah Channel, Ochoco Reservoir, Prineville Reservoir, Siltcoos Lake, Tahkenitch Lake, Tenmile Lakes, Wickiup Reservoir, Willamette River.

SMALLMOUTH BASS
(Micropterus dolimieu)

Also known as the brown bass, brownies, bronzebacks, smalls and smallies, these bass are becoming increasingly important as a game fish in Oregon, especially among river anglers. Found in both rivers and lakes, these are a coolwater-loving fish that prefer rivers more than the largemouth bass do. This bass is non-native but has been introduced with great success; Oregon is fortunate to have several world-class smallmouth bass fisheries on the John Day and Umpqua Rivers. Small-mouths provide exciting sport and make good eating.

Smallmouth bass love structure and slow water; logjams, rocky shorelines or points of land, overhanging brush and submerged vegetation provide optimal cover. Unlike their largemouth cousins, smallmouth can also be caught in open water, especially where breaks in the river or lake bottom occur, and in faster currents. Some bass angers speculate that smallmouth school up with like-sized fish. In other words, catching a 12-inch fish in one area will most likely result in similar-sized fish unless you move to a new area. Smallies are most readily found in lower, warmer sections of rivers such as the John Day and Umpqua. Unlike many species of fish, smallmouths are most active and easily caught during sunny bright afternoons in summer.

Average catches of smallmouth range 10–14 inches, but fish of six pounds or more are common. The record catch for the state of Oregon occurred in 2000 on Henry Hagg Lake weighing 8 pounds, 1.76 ounces. Anglers wishing to catch bigger fish improve their odds by fishing during spawning times in May and June when water temperatures hit 60–70°F.

Tackle, Tactics, and Tips

All one needs for catching smallies is light fly and spinning tackle. Trout gear works great: seven- to nine-foot rods rigged with four- to six-pound test line. Productive flies include rubber legged nymphs and streamers such as Clouser Minnows, Muddlers, Woolly Buggers, and crayfish patterns. Small surface deer hair poppers provide exciting surface action. Spin anglers can use small crank baits such as the Rebel Wee-R, rattling crankbaits and Rapalas.

Jigs of smaller variety are also effective. Rabbit hair jigs are very popular and preferred over plastic or rubber skirted jigs. When working

a jig, use your whole arm to work an up and down movement. Medium speeds are best, not moving the jig more than a few inches and no more than a foot at a time. Slower or faster retrieves may be needed depending on water conditions.

All of these lures are productive in muted colors such as olive, black, brown, burnt orange, and yellow. It's important to note that a majority of strikes occur as soon and the lure hits the water. Move away from areas that don't produce such quick strikes until you hit on water that does.

Recommended Waters

Columbia River, Henry Hagg Lake, John Day River, Lake Billy Chinook, Owyhee River, Siltcoos Lake, South Umpqua River, Tahkenitch Lake, Tenmile Lake, Umpqua River, Willamette River.

STRIPED BASS
(Roccus saxatilis)

Striped bass, also known as Stripers, Rockfish, Rock, and Linesides, have a place of prominence with many anglers in Oregon's history of angling. Introduced to the west coast in the late 19th century, its reputation as a worthy game fish grew among anglers. Oregon was renowned in the early and mid-20th century as producing good size and quality stripers, and much of the activity was centered near the mouth of the Umpqua River. Today, stripers are but a remnant population, and the future is not bright. Still, anglers can still find a few fish in the once productive areas of the Lower Umpqua River, Coos Bay, and Coquille River.

Stripers can get big. The Oregon state record was caught in 1973 in the Umpqua River and weighed 68 pounds. Average fish get well over 30 inches, the legal size limit for keepers. Stripers are also predatory in their feeding behavior and are often labeled as an ambush species. That is, they wait behind obstructions such as rocks, ledges, and logjams, then pounce on un-

© PAUL B. JOHNSON

Striped Bass

suspecting prey. Stripers also prefer the steady current of rivers, which provides not only a good supply of food, also but a steady flow of cold water (55–65°F) necessary for spawning purposes. Stripers spend quite a bit of time in the sea feeding on squid, crab, eels, and other fish. They enter the rivers to follow food or spawn. Look for stripers to be in tidewater from March to May. After May they begin a slow movement upriver, pausing in lower portions of bays to feed until spawning time in September and October. Fall is a great time to target stripers in the rivers and is especially popular with fly anglers who can use surface patterns to entice explosive, heart-stopping strikes.

Tackle, Tactics, and Tips

Tackle should be medium-weight graphite rods with either spinning reels or levelwinds (bait casting reels) rigged with 20-pound test line. Most stripers are targeted in the rivers, estuaries, and tidewater. Trolling plugs such as Quickfish baited with herring is standard practice. Some anglers simply troll frozen baits such as herring, anchovies, and smelt. Summer is a good time for fly anglers to fish for stripers with larger streamers and saltwater patterns such as Clouser Minnows, crab patterns and Crazy Charlies.

Recommended Waters

Coos Bay, Coquille River (between the bay and Myrtle Point), Lower Rogue River (be-tween Winchester Bay and the Smith River tributary), Lower Umpqua River.

WHITE HYBRID BASS

This species is a hybrid cross between the striped bass and the white bass. Hybrid bass are sterile and must be re-stocked every so often. The Ana Reservoir is the only location for these fish in Oregon and therefore is the home to the Oregon state record, caught in 2002, weighing 18.8 pounds. The Ana has been stocked with hybrid bass since 1982. Fish average between four to 10 pounds. They are hard fighters and make excellent eating.

Hybrid bass are both solitary and travel in packs. They are predacious and will eat almost anything alive, as long as it fits in their mouth. The easiest and main food source is other fish such as chub minnows and trout. Hybrid bass will also eat leeches, frogs, and insect larva. Winter and spring find this bass hunkered down on the bottom of the reservoir. Come summer, as the surface temperature rises, they move up into the top water.

Tackle, Tactics, and Tips

No special equipment is needed other than slightly heavier trout gear to land these bigger fish. Fly gear, spinning outfits and drift or trolling rods and reels all work in medium to fast actions. Still-fishing with bait, jigging, and trolling with baitfish lures and flies all work. Favorite baits for still fishing or plunking are frozen anchovies, chicken and beef liver, shrimp, and live and dead minnows. Lures such as small Quickfish plugs, Rapalas, and rainbow spinners can be trolled to imitate wounded or live baitfish, trout, or chub minnows. Fly anglers have better opportunities later in the year to find fish cruising the bank looking for leeches, swimming insects or small baitfish. Flies such as Woolly Buggers in white and Zonkers in natural colors are effective.

Recommended Waters
Ana Reservoir.

SUNFISH FAMILY

In addition to the bluegill, perch and crappie, all species of the sunfish family (Pumpkinseed, Green Sunfish, Redear Sunfish, and Warmouth) are non-native to Oregon and are commonly referred to as "panfish." These are warmwater-loving fish and can be found in almost any pond or slow-moving warm river in Oregon; they are therefore easy to catch and prove good eating. The lifecycles of all these fish are identical, as are the fishing methods. Most of these fish average between seven and eight inches, with larger fish reaching 12 inches and weights up to two pounds. Record catches in Oregon include green sunfish (11 ounces, Umpqua River, 1991); pumpkinseed sunfish (7.68 ounces, Lake Oswego, 1996); redear sunfish (1 pound 15.5 ounces, Reynolds Pond, 1992), Warmouth (1 pound 14.2 ounces, Columbia Slough, 1975).

Primary food sources for sunfish include insects, fresh-water shrimp, crustaceans, small shellfish, and baitfish. Fish can be found wherever they can find food, and that means generally around structure and along the shorelines.

Tackle, Tactics, and Tips
Basic light trout tackle is the only requirement for catching sunfish—the lighter the best for quality action. Use rods and reels suitable for four- or six-pound test line; the same goes for fly rods. Bait anglers need not use any hooks bigger than 10s or 14s, depending on the size of your bait. Either float your bait under a bobber or float, or anchor it on the bottom. When fishing the bottom, allow for about eight to 12 inches of leader between the weight and your bait. Successful baits include night crawlers, grubs, live nymphs, and pieces of crawdad tail. Spinner and light jigs (micro jigs, sizes 1/32 to 1/100 ounces) are also effective but should be keep small, one inch at the most. Flies are effective, but it's not so much the fly one uses as the action that attracts the fish. Don't use anything too big. Stick with small nymphs such as Hares Ears and Pheasant Tails, Adams dry flies and Woolly Bugger streamers.

Recommended Waters
Blue Lake, Columbia Slough, Cottage Grove Reservoir, Henry Hagg Lake, Middle Willamette, Pudding River, St. Louis Ponds, Tualatin River, Willow Creek Reservoir.

BLUEGILL
(Lepomis macrochirus)

Bluegill is a popular sportfish found in many warmwater lakes and rivers in Oregon, and it provides good eating. Technically they are a part of the sunfish family and commonly lumped into the group of fish known as panfish. Bluegill, also known as "gills" or "gillies" by aficionados, can grow to good size. The world record bluegill weighed 4 pounds, 12 ounces. The Oregon state record was caught in 1981 on a farm pond weighing 2 pounds, 5.5 ounces. Preferred water temperature is 60–85°F, and muddy or stained water is best. Bluegill are voracious eaters, as well as spawners, and feed heavily on baitfish, worms, crustaceans, and insects such as mayflies and caddis. As with most species, overpopulated waters will keep the average sizes small. Bluegill are a schooling fish, congregating in groups of 30 or more, so where you find one you will find many. Early

© BOB RACE

Bluegill

season finds most bluegills in one to 10 feet of water. Larger bluegill will hang out in deeper water of 35 feet or more. Most bluegill average six to eight ounces (seven to nine inches long)—maybe a little bigger during spawning periods in May when water temperatures hit the mid-60s. Most bluegill angling doesn't heat up until the water does, late spring and summer.

Tackle, Tactics, and Tips

Light tackle spinning and fly rods are all that is needed. Bait anglers use pieces of night crawlers, mealworms, grubs and nymphs. Use small hooks (#10) and a bobber to suspend the bait. Fishing around structure or aquatic vegetation is always the best way to start. Lures, flies and bait can be cast horizontally or straight under the boat. A lot of bluegill, especially the bigger ones, can be caught in deep water in the summer. Spin anglers use small spinners and bass poppers. Fly anglers have long known about a bluegill's propensity to feed on hatching insects; hence, dry flies can be quite effective. No need to match the hatch; an Elk Hair Caddis or small Adams will do the trick. Also try small nymphs and small baitfish streamers such as Zonkers and Woolly Buggers.

Recommended Waters

Cooper Creek Lake, Cottage Grove Reservoir, Dorena Lake, Fern Ridge Reservoir, Middle Willamette River, Moon Reservoir, Pudding River, Scappoose Bay, Smith and Bybee Lakes, Sturgeon Lake.

CRAPPIE

Crappie are a part of the sunfish family and commonly lumped into the category of panfish. Other common names for crappie include Papermouths and Specks due to the marbled effect on their scales. Crappie are easy to catch, provide good sport and are good easting.

There are two varieties, Black *(Pomoxis negromaculatus)* and White *(Pomoxis annularis)*, and both can inhabit the same water, although white crappie are more tolerant of silted or turbid waters. The black crappie is the most popular variety in the crappie family, and they prefer clear water with aquatic vegetation such as moss beds and tulles. Black crappie run a little bigger than the white crappie and can be finicky feeders. They commonly reach 1.5 pounds and average 8–12 inches. The Oregon state record black crappie was caught in 1995, in a Corvallis pond, weighing 4 pounds, 6.1 ounces. The record white crappie was caught in 1967, at Gerber Reservoir, weighing 4 pounds, 12 ounces.

Crappie are also a schooling fish and congregate in numbers in one to five feet of water around cover such as dock pilings, stumps, brush, weed beds and tulles. Spawning times are April and May. During summer you will find crappie schooling in deeper water. The primary food source is baitfish minnows, but they also feed on insects, tadpoles, crayfish and just about anything that is not too big to fit in their mouth.

Tackle, Tactics, and Tips

Light tackle spinning rods will provide the most action. A green, white, red, or yellow one-eighth ounce jig is the most common lure and can be fished directly under the boat or suspended with a bobber. Prepare to change lure colors often and move locations frequently to stay on top of the pods. Baits such as night crawlers, grubs, and crawdad meat can also be used.

Recommended Waters

Cold Springs Reservoir, Haystack Reservoir, Lake of the Woods, Ochoco Reservoir, Prineville Reservoir.

YELLOW PERCH
(Perca flavescens)

Yellow perch, with their seven distinct vertical bars, average only seven to nine inches. The Oregon state record perch was caught in 1971 at a pond in Brownsmead and weighed 2.2 pounds. Perch are not noted for their sport as much as for eating. When perch are located in a school many anglers experience a phenom-

enon of a feeding frenzy, and catching 15–20 perch in a matter of a half hour is no problem. Spawning occurs when water temperatures get above 45°F in April or May.

Yellow perch are primarily bottom feeders and take bait or lures with a subtle bite. They are found in water between five and 30 feet deep; they rest on the bottom at night and feed most heavily during the morning and evenings in shallow water. Perch love vegetation for the food it produces. Foods sources include minnows, insect larvae, plankton, and worms. Perch move about in schools, often numbering in the hundreds. If one spot is unproductive after a few tries, it is best to move to other spots until a school is located.

Tackle, Tactics, and Tips

There is no special tackle needed for perch fishing. Lightweight spinning trout gear or fly rods are sufficient. Strikes can be subtle and are better detected by a slightly stiffer-tipped rod. Use four- to eight-pound test line on a matching reel.

Fishing methods for catching perch include trolling, bobber fishing and jigging. Jigging occurs with leadheads or mini-jigs in sizes one 1/64- and 1/32-ounce sizes. Most anglers use skirted jigs. A "skirt" is a material that covers the hook and can be made of feathers, plastic, or animal hair. Slightly heavier leadheads, up to 1/8 ounce, are used when trolling or drift fishing. Also, slip-sinker lures, small spinner rigs, and floating jig-heads (either with a slip-

© BOB RACE

Yellow Perch

sinker rig or with a fixed sinker) all work and are popular methods.

Recommended Waters

Columbia River, Gerber Reservoir, Henry Hagg Lake, McKay Reservoir, Middle Willamette River, Multnomah Channel, Yamhill River.

CHANNEL CATFISH
(Ictalurus punctatus)

This is not the catfish that inhabits the local pond, unless the angler in your family is bringing home a 20-pound fish. "Channel cats" as they are commonly called, or "whiskerkitties," "spotted cat," "blue channel cat," "river catfish," or "fiddler" are the largest of the catfish family, and the most commonly eaten; in fact, they make up the majority of supermarket sales of fish. They are known to grow up to four feet long and weigh 50 pounds, but more common is a 20-pound fish at three feet long. Still a big catch! The Oregon state record was caught in 1980 on McKay Reservoir and weighed 36.8 pounds. The world record channel catfish weighed 58 pounds, and was caught in the Santee-Cooper Reservoir, South Carolina, in 1964.

Channel catfish love to hide in dark waters and seek out structure such as log jams, beaver dams, ledges and undercut banks. Other good places to find channel catfish are around rocky points, the rip-rap of dams, and even along smooth retaining walls. In early spring, catfish are attracted to the crawfish that are abundant around rocks that time of year. During spawning times in late spring and early summer, catfish spawn in rock crevices. Fishing begins as early as May and goes through October.

Catfish also prefer cooler waters than their smaller warmwater cousins, the brown bullhead catfish. In rivers, find areas of slow to moderate current, preferably with a sand or rock bottom rather than mud. The diet is varied and includes insects, small crustaceans, shellfish, leeches, worms, frogs, small birds and mammals. During summer, catfish also feed on moss and algae that can be found around rocks and retaining walls. Regulations often allow night fishing when channel catfish are present, so anglers can take advantage of their nighttime feeding habits.

Tackle, Tactics, and Tips

Fishing rods should be stout enough to land a 15-pound fish, but sensitive enough to detect a strike and maneuver the bait. Channel catfish are tough fighters, and most anglers would recommend erring on the side of heavier tackle. A medium-heavy seven- to nine-footer is adequate, with a good quality bait-casting reel or spinning reel spooled with at least 20-pound test line. Reels should have a good drag and large line capacity.

Hooks need to be large (#1/0 to #5/0), not

© PAUL B. JOHNSON

Channel Catfish

GOT STINK? NOT LIKE THIS!

Of all the stink-bait recipes for catfish I was privy to learn about, this one stands out as the king:

Find a locker plant that will let you have a set of beef lungs with the windpipe still connected. Hang the lungs up by windpipe, then pour fresh blood into the windpipe. When the lung is full, hang in a cooler until blood coagulates (leave in the cooler for 24 hours). After 24 hours, take the lung out of the cooler and slice it into cubes. (Because of its consistency, the lung absorbs the blood.) When you put the slices on the hook, the bait will stay on the hook, but the blood will still bleed out, re-liquefying in the water.

only to accommodate large bait but also get a good hook-set. A sliding or slip sinker rig is perhaps the most popular setup, but you can also use bobber drift fish techniques that float the bait a foot or so off the bottom. A good sliding or slip sinker rig is as follows: start with a 12–18-inch leader and attach the hook on one end; set it aside. Thread a barrel sinker or sinker-slide (a tubular device with a snap on it found in most tackle shops) through the end of the fishing line attached to the reel and followed by a small plastic bead. Tie on a barrel swivel to the end of your mainline (the bead should be between the swivel and weight). Pick up your leader with the hook tied on and attach it to the other end of the barrel swivel. When fishing this rig, your bait will be anchored, but suspended off the bottom. Depending on current you can pull up on the weight and let out line in order to walk the bait further downstream to cover more water.

Channel catfish are rarely caught on artificial lures and baits. Preferred baits are large shiners, anchovy, live and dead minnows, frogs, crayfish, leeches, night crawlers or cut baits of carp, bluegill, and shad. Those with the stomach for it can also use blood stinkbaits such as chicken gizzards and livers, beef liver, soured clams, raw spoiled shrimp, and aged or moldy cheese; or, a mix and blending of any of the above items.

Recommended Waters

Hells Canyon Dam, Brownlee Reservoir, Devil's Lake, Hells Canyon Reservoir, St. Louis Ponds.

BROWN BULLHEAD CATFISH
(Ictalurus nebulosus)

The brown bullhead catfish (a.k.a. Creek Cat, Mud Cat, Horned Pout, Red Cat, Minister, and Speckled Cat) is about as ubiquitous in Oregon's warm waters as algae growth. This is a highly adaptable fish, able to survive in waters over 82°F, they are easy to catch and can provide good sport when nothing else is biting. Also a night feeder like channel catfish, they feed mostly on dead matter (carrion), baitfish, crustaceans, shellfish, insects, worms and leeches. Average fish weigh one pound or less, 8–14 inches, but can reach three pounds. The Oregon state record was caught in 2001 on Henry Hagg Lake and weighed 3 pounds, 7 ounces.

Brown bullheads like shallow, weedy, muddy areas of lakes or large, slow-moving streams. This fish is a survivor, and the only survivor in many waterways that have been polluted by industrial toxins, agricultural run-off, and sewage overflows. Like many other catfish, brown bullheads feed on the bottom of lakes, ponds, and slow-moving rivers. Dark areas around submerged brush and snags, ledges, tree stumps, and undercut banks are all favorite hangouts.

Tackle, Tactics, and Tips

No special gear is required. If you own light tackle trout gear in the form of six- to seven-foot rods and spinning reels loaded with four-

BLACKENED CATFISH

4 catfish fillets

olive oil

$1/3$ lb. bacon

2 teaspoons each of the following: garlic powder, thyme, white pepper, black pepper, cayenne pepper, lemon pepper, cumin or chili powder, rosemary, crushed fennel seed

1 teaspoon allspice

1 teaspoon oregano

$1/2$ teaspoon salt

Fry the bacon, then discard the bacon and the retain grease. Combine all dry ingredients. Rub the fillets with olive oil, then coat each liberally with spices. Drop the fillets in hot bacon grease and cook until you can easily put a fork through them.

---

to six-pound test line, you're set for fun. Fish in water three to 10-feet deep. Focus on areas around obstructions, shorelines, and docks. Fishing is best starting at dusk or into the night up until midnight. Keep your bait on the bottom or slightly above. The best way to do this is either with a sliding sinkers system (see channel cat description above) or by suspending your bait with a bobber or float.

Recommended Waters

Antelope Reservoir, Cold Springs Reservoir, Columbia River (Lake Wallowa), Cooper Creek Lake, Cottage Grove Reservoir, Detroit Lake, Fern Ridge Reservoir, Henry Hagg Lake, Middle Willamette, Prineville Reservoir, Tualatin River, Warner Valley Lakes, Willow Creek Reservoir.

WALLEYE
(Stizostedion vitreum)

Also known affectionately as "Ol' Marble Eyes" and "Bug Eyes," walleye are a popular non-native game fish that have adapted very well to the Columbia River. The Columbia is also the only place to fish walleye in the state of Oregon. Walleye are highly sought after, and they are remarkable fighters as well as good eating.

Walleye are a cool-water fish that prefer slow to medium moving waters, preferably

stained. Walleye can reach 30 inches in length and weigh up to 15 pounds or more. The Oregon state record was caught in 1990 on the Columbia River weighing 19 pounds, 15.3 ounces. In the '90s, Oregon was a national destination for anglers to come and catch big walleye up to 19 pounds. Of late, the percentage of big walleye has declined and so has the river traffic, but there are still plenty of big fish to be had, with five- to eight-pound fish being the norm.

Walleye prefer water from 38–60°F. Spring is the most popular time to fish for walleye, during the spawning season when fish can be taken in 10 feet or less of water. Spawning starts on the Columbia when water temperatures reach 38–44°F in mid-April or early May. Anglers search for walleye in shallow areas such as river mouths and shoals that contain gravel, rock or sandy bottoms. Spring anglers also target the females that can be considerably bigger than the males. Other areas to locate walleye are just about anywhere small baitfish can be found such as on the edges of channels, gravel ledges, submerged humps, weedlines, and boulder areas. A lot of anglers will use top-water spinners and crankbaits during this time of year.

The rest of the year walleye are following the baitfish and can be found in shallow areas during morning and evening and deeper areas during the day. Fishing in 20–30 feet of water is standard. Bright, hot summer days may be the most difficult time to catch walleye without knowing where the submerged hums, rock gardens, shelves, and gravel ledges are located. Depth finders can be useful in identifying these areas.

Tackle, Tactics, and Tips

If walleye anglers are anything, they are unique in their style and preference for catching these fish. Walleye equipment varies from region to region, but in Oregon anglers tend to use medium-weight rods of slightly stiffer action. Spinning or levelwind reels are rigged with 10–20-pound test line. This basic setup is useful for both trolling and jigging. Ultralight tackle with four- to eight-pound test line is popular with some anglers, but should be considered for more specialized approaches and advanced techniques.

There are a lot of options for catching walleye, and many of them are utilized at different times of year and in varied water conditions. Blade baits, weighted minnow-shaped silver lures, are the hot ticket in spring when water levels are stable. Blade baits are fished vertically with a jigging action; the blade is raised sharply and then released to let it flutter back down. Spinners are trolled down river in slower currents, and crankbaits are trolled up river against the current. Other trolling methods include floating Rapalas, Northland Gumdrops, Husky Jerk's, Reef Runners, Walleye Flashers, Wally Divers and Shad Raps and Shad Rap RS's. Jigs are also popular. When fishing under the boat, anglers don't use a jig any heavier than it takes to stay near the bottom. The use of 1/4-ounce to 5/8-ounce leadheads is common, but heavier or lighter jigs may be necessary depending on water speed. Popular jigs include Northland Fire-balls, Northland Whistlers and various marabou and plastic skirted varieties. Popular colors include chartreuse, green, yellow pink and white. Anglers will often tip these jigs with bait such as minnows, leeches and night crawlers.

Recommended Waters

Columbia River below the dams at McNary, John Day, The Dalles, Bonneville and in the Multnomah Channel.

AMERICAN SHAD
(Alosa sapidissima)

Shad are an anadromous fish that were introduced to Oregon waters in the late 19th century, imported from the east coast. This is the largest member of the herring family and average 17–19 inches (3–4 pounds) with females running a couple inches bigger. The Oregon state record was caught in 2004 in the Willamette River weighing 6.6 pounds. Shad runs are impressive if for no other reason than their numbers. The peak run in 1990 on the Columbia River was over three million fish.

The uses of shad are mixed among angler options. Although the Latin name applied to this fish means "most delicious," not all anglers agree. Some love the taste of the fatty white meat, some find them too full of bones to be edible. A lot of anglers catch shad to use as bait to catch sturgeon. As a sport fish they are good fighters and quite popular with fly anglers on some rivers. Shad move into rivers to spawn from April to June.

Tackle, Tactics, and Tips

The equipment for catching shad is simple: Use lightweight spinning or casting rods, and spinning reels or levelwinds with six-pound test line. Fly anglers can use five- to six-weigh fly rods with matching reels and line and eight-pound test tippet.

Because shad have such delicate mouths, hooks should be small, #1 and #2. The simplest shad lure is a hook with three colored beads slid down on top of the hook. You can also use shad darts, small crappie jigs, lightweight wobbling spoons, and spinners. Spoons and spinners should be less than two inches long. Shad flies can usually be bought under that name and are simple creations on a size

#4 to #6 hooks made of materials in white, red or yellow.

If you are fishing from a boat you can use a simple plunking technique by sending out your lure with enough weight to anchor it on the bottom and wait for a strike. From the bank, cast upstream and let the current take your fly or lure to the bottom. Shad generally hold in faster currents in depths between four and 10 feet. If you're in a boat, find the edge of channels and then move to the shores and look for shelves at the required depth. From the bank, find areas of the river where the current pushes against the shore such as river bends or breaks in the water.

Recommended Waters

Columbia River (below Bonneville Dam), Coos River, Coquille River, Millicoma River, Sandy River, Siuslaw River, Smith River, Umpqua River, Willamette River.

Marine Species (non-salmonid)

BOTTOM FISH

Often overshadowed by more glamorous species such as salmon, halibut and snapper, bottom fish are abundant along Oregon's beaches, rocky headlands, jetties and bays. Caught for both sport and eating qualities, some anglers prefer the meat of these fish to salmon. All these species are best caught from shore, and in some cases a boat can be counterproductive. The one central attribute most of these fish share is that they all live and feed near structure such as rocks, cliffs, kelp beds, docks and pylons. Most fish are easily caught by baiting a hook or casting a jig or spinner and letting it work among the rocks. Those who have never fished for bottom fish owe it to themselves to check out these often-neglected species.

Surf Perch

Surf perch are abundant on the Oregon coast and can be found in surf zones off sandy beaches, in bays, and around rocks such as jetties. The most common perch in Oregon are the redtail surf perch (*Amphistichus rhodoterus*), pile perch (*Rhacochilus vacca*), and striped perch (*Embiotoca lateralis*). There are a few lesser varieties that may show up in anglers' catches: Silver, Walleye, and Shiner perch. Perch maintain a steady diet of crustaceans, but they also eat small crabs, shrimp, mussels, and marine worms. Spring and early summer (April to June) is the best time to catch perch, prior to spawning. Perch, especially redtail, school up in the spring around inland tidal areas prior to spawning, and this is when anglers catch the most fish. Pile perch and striped perch are readily available thought the year around docks, pilings, and rocky areas.

The three main species of perch are easy to tell apart. Redtail perch are silver with olive green molting, dark bars on the side, and a pink to deep purple tail. They can reach about 16 inches and weight of 1.5 pounds, but three-pound fish are common. Pile perch are distinguished by a black spot on the cheek and a deeply forked tail. Piles are the largest surf fish and can reach 17 inches; 10–14-inch fish are more common. Striped perch have orange and blue horizontal stripes and can reach 15 inches, but 9–13-inch fish are more common.

TACKLE, TACTICS, AND TIPS

Fishing for any of these species requires bait such as mussels, clams, and shrimp. Fishing for surf perch requires heavy rods capable of casting two to four ounce weights, sometimes more. A 10–12-foot rod will give you the leverage to cast further out into the breakers. Surf perch anglers stand on the beach and cast directly into the surf, letting the bait anchor on the ocean floor. Sometimes rod holds are used. The best fishing occurs in the hour before and an hour after high tide.

Fishing for pile and striped sea perch requires only lightweight tackle, such as a trout outfit, and no more than four-pound test line. Both of these species are caught primarily in bays around rocks, dock pilings and kelp beds where food is the most abundant. The easiest technique is to fish from a dock or pier and let your bait drop straight down along pilings. Use a #4 or #6 bait hook and 8–10-pound test line. Weights do not need to be very heavy, and one or two large spit shot is sufficient.

RECOMMENDED WATERS

Chetco Bay, Columbia River Estuary, Garrison Lake, Nehalem Bay, New River, Sand Lake, Siletz Bay, Yaquina Bay.

Lingcod
(*Ophiodon elongates*)

Lingcod are prized among rock fish for both their immense size and quality eating; many anglers prefer the taste of lingcod to salmon. The feeding habits of lingcod probably account for their massive size, which can reach

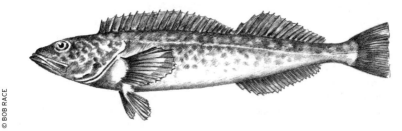

© BOB RACE

Lingcod

40 pounds or more. Enough 60-pound plus fish are caught each year to keep anglers guessing on the size limit of these fish. As young fish they feed mostly on crustaceans, but as adults they develop a taste for other fish and can be very predatory. In fact, lingcod will eat almost any reasonable baitfish offering that is placed in front of them.

When seeking lingcod, both boat and bank anglers are often met with challenging ocean conditions. The primary habitat is either deep ocean water (200–3,000 feet deep) or rocky areas and kelp beds close to shore around jetties and rocky headlands (75–125 feet deep). By far, the easiest way to catch lingcod is in shallower water near the shore, not only because they are more accessible but because they tend to concentrate their numbers in a few key areas, making themselves easier for anglers to find. To fish lingcod close to shore you need to start locating fish from December to March. This is the spawning season, and because the males of the species protect the nests until the eggs hatch, they are guaranteed to be in shallower water for several months. Females, which are often larger than the males, also maintain a position around the nest, and although they are not guarding it, they do hang around in shallow water for this period of time.

Fishing during certain tidal times can be a factor, especially if the tide is ripping at a few knots, which makes it difficult to hold over the fish in a boat or maintain a good presentation from the bank. Lingcod are known to bite best at low tide times. The best times to fish are when the tides allow an angler to make a good presentation (straight down from the boat or shore). High tide, slack tide, or times of moderate tides are the most opportune times to get the bait to the fish.

TACKLE, TACTICS, AND TIPS

Rods, reels and line are a matter of preference, but a good starter set would include a medium-weight casting rod and a levelwind reel with 20–40-pound test line. The heavier test line is to protection against the fish's sharp teeth, and some anglers use metal leaders. Make sure the rod you choose has a stiff midsection and supple tip; this will greatly aid in casting and controlling the lures or bait.

Lingcod are very aggressive and can be caught in a number of ways. Live bait is the preferred method, followed by dead bait and artificial jigs. Live bait includes the use of herring, anchovies, squid, mackerel and even small rockfish. Because of the sizes of live baits, large hooks in 5/0 to 6/0 are often necessary. Dead baits of these same species also work. Larger baits tend to catch bigger fish. Jigs are another method and can be very effective. Larger metal jigs pass for baitfish, as do skirted models in purple, blue, brown and black.

RECOMMENDED WATERS

Columbia River Estuary, Depoe Bay, Nestucca Bay, Rogue River Bay, Tillamook Bay, Yaquina Bay.

Kelp Greenling
(Hexagrammos decagrammus)

Kelp Greenling, also known as Greenling Sea Trout, Rock Trout, Spotted Rock Trout, Kelp Trout, and Kelp Cod, are abundant on the Oregon coast around jetties, kelp beds, rocky headlands and sometimes in bays. Indeed, as the various nicknames suggest, these fish are the rainbow trout of bottom fish: great sport, easy and fun to catch and also good eating. The greenling is also excellent bait for lingcod.

Greenling are generally found in water no deeper than 10 feet, but can go as deep as 60 feet. They feed on crustaceans, mussels, sea worms and small baitfish. Average sizes range from 0.5–1.5 pounds. Two-pound fish are not rare, and they have the potential to grow much bigger. Spawning occurs in October and November, but there is no better time to fish for greenling as they are ever present and available.

TACKLE, TACTICS, AND TIPS

There is no special gear necessary to catch greenling other than corrosion-resistant reels. Lightweight trout spinning gear in the form of seven- to eight-foot graphite rod and four- to six-pound test line is adequate.

Greenling can be taken on artificial lures and bait. Artificial lures include a half-ounce to 1.5-ounce metal jig or leadhead with a plastic skirt. These can be cast along the rocks and the edges of drop-offs and rock ledges where greenling like to hold. Bait is also effective, and the most popular choices are ghost shrimp, mussels, clams, and chunks of fish. The mouths of greenling are small, so the bait should also be keep small. Using #4 and #6 hooks will help. Fly anglers have also been known to catch greenling using saltwater flies such as crazy Charlies, and small Clouser Minnows.

RECOMMENDED WATERS

Columbia River Estuary, Coos Bay, Depoe Bay, Nehalem Bay, Nestucca Bay, Yaquina Bay.

Rockfish

There is a great variety of rockfish on the Oregon coast, but in general they all share a lot of the same characteristics; black rockfish are more readily available because they live at shallower depths, but all these species live at shallower depths at one time or another. All rockfish provide excellent sport and good eating. The most common rockfish on the Oregon coast include black rockfish *(Sebastes melanops)*, yelloweye rockfish *(Sebastes ruberrimus)*, canary rockfish *(Sebastes pinniger)*, copper rockfish *(Sebastes caurinus)*, and vermilion rockfish *(Sebastes miniatus)*. Black rockfish, also called sea bass, black snapper, and rock coos are the most common species and have a few attributes anglers like: they hold in shallow water near shore around rocks, jetties and kelp beds; and they take lures near the surface. They average about two pounds and are most commonly caught after their spawning cycle. Yelloweye rockfish can get large: 10–20 pounds and up to 36 inches. They are deep-water dwellers and can live between 150 and 300 feet. Canary rockfish are smaller than yelloweyes, growing to 30 inches at the largest, but are found in the same places. Copper rockfish are the smallest, but they are deep dwellers and can reach 23 inches. Vermilion are slightly bigger at 30 inches.

TACKLE, TACTICS, AND TIPS

The best places to begin looking for rockfish when they are shallow is near rocky shores around breakwaters, kelp beds and rocky headlands. Rockfish are not partial to any kind of bait and will take just about anything: mussels, clams, crabs, shrimp and squid strips, herring, and shiner perch. Lures include worm jigs, spoons, plugs, and large flies.

When rockfish are deep, you can find them around most rocky bottoms at depths of 250–750 feet. The usual rig is made up of three to six hooks above a sinker that is heavy enough to take the line to the bottom on a fairly straight course. Because of the depths fished, it takes a considerable amount of time to let down and haul up this rig; consequently the bait should be sufficiently tough to remain firmly on the hook while being nibbled and chewed upon by the quarry. Pieces of squid are ideal.

Recommended Waters

Chetco Bay, Columbia River Estuary, Coos Bay, Depoe Bay, Nehalem Bay, Netarts Bay, Tillamook Bay, Winchester Bay, Yaquina Bay.

Cabezon
(Scorpaenichthys marmoratus)

The largest member of the sculpin family, cabezon are not our friendly three-inch river sculpin. These ocean-tough fish with huge heads and pectoral fins can weigh 20 pounds and are fierce fighters. They are prized for their tasty white meat and produce thick fillets. The eggs of cabezon are extremely poisonous, and special care should be taken that they aren't touched when you're cleaning the fish for eating.

Cabezon are found most readily around hard, rocky, steep structure around reefs and headlands. Primary food sources are crabs and other crustaceans, but they also eat baitfish.

Tackle, Tactics, and Tips

The primary tackle is heavy jigging rods and larger levelwind reels capable of holding 200 feet or more of 10–15-pound test line. Most anglers use artificial lures, either metal jigs or leadheads skirted with plastic in orange, pink,

yellow, chartreuse, and brown. Because cabezon like to feed on baitfish, both live and dead bait also works. Try bait such as herring and sardines, and smaller rockfish. Lures that represent baitfish such as Crippled Herring, Point Wilson Darts, and Nordics also produce good catches. Whether you use jigs, bait, or lures, be sure to drift and bounce them among the rocks in the same darting fashion that you would imagine baitfish might make if they were trying to escape a predator. The more erratic the jigging motion, the more a cabezon may think he has found a crippled and vulnerable target.

Recommended Waters

Coos, Depoe, and Yaquina Bays.

Halibut
(Hippoglossus stenolepis)

"Fax me a halibut. Is that funny?" asks Jerry Seinfeld on an episode of the TV sitcom, *Seinfeld*. And, of course the answer from Elaine is, "No!" But if you were to try and fax a fish, there could be no better choice than the flat-profiled halibut. The story of halibut is a reverse saga of the ugly ducking story. Halibut start out looking like any other fish: normal, with an eye on each side of its head. Over time, the fish morphs into an ugly creature—modern art's version of a cubist fish—when both eyes and pectoral fins move to the same side

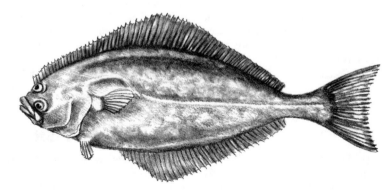

© BOB RACE

Pacific Halibut

and the body flattens. Looks, however, seem to make little difference to anglers, and the halibut is considered the heavyweight champion of Northwest ocean fish, a highly prized fishing and eating fish and can weigh anywhere between 200 and 400 pounds.

Halibut fishing along the Oregon coast has seen a steady resurgence in the last 20 years. The resulting increase in halibut has many anglers cheering, and catches of this difficult fish are far more frequent than they were in the years preceding 1976. Regulations for fishing halibut are strict and somewhat complex, and anglers need to pay attention to frequent and sudden changes. In Oregon, May is the most popular time of the year for targeting Pacific halibut. May 1 is the opening day for Pacific halibut in waters inside the 40-fathom line statewide and in all-depth waters north of Cape Falcon and south of Humbug Mountain. The spring all-depth Pacific halibut fishery between Cape Falcon and Humbug Mountain will be open May 11–13, 18–20 and 25–27; and June 1–3 and 8–10.

Halibut are bottom feeders and like to feed on and around underwater mountains and plateaus. Smooth bottoms of sand, gravel and cobble-sized boulders are their preferred habitat. Fishing these kinds of flats is much less frustrating, and far less tackle is lost than fishing for bottom fish around large jagged rocks. The state's most well-known halibut grounds are between the Whistler Buoy and Yaquina Head lighthouse on Yaquina Head off Agate Beach and near the edge of Hecceta Banks at two humps in the ocean floor: The Chicken Ranch and Halibut Hill. In these latter areas, halibut are fished for at 100 fathoms, 30–35 nautical miles out in the ocean. But perhaps more important when fishing for halibut is not deep water but finding flats and humps. Halibut may be taken in water as deep as 700 feet, or 15 feet, all depending on the terrain.

Tackle, Tactics, and Tips

It is safe to say that unless you're set up for deep-sea fishing, and if you are you know what you're doing, halibut fishing is best left to the pros, and there are numerous good charters on the Oregon coast. Charters will provide tackle, bait and lunches. Plus, you can avoid the hazardous problems associated with trying to boat a 200-pound fish. Proper techniques for boating one of these fish is an art unto itself, and the best know how to do it without putting either the boat or other anglers in peril.

Tackle for catching halibut varies depending on how deep one fishes. At levels above 150 feet, regular heavy salmon rigs will work because these fish are often between 40 and 80 pounds. Below these depths, anglers resort to very stiff rods with a roller tip and roller-stripping guide, braided Dacron fishing line, and reels that can hold 500 feet or more of line.

That said, halibut are well-known for taking both bait and jigs. The bait of choice is whole herring, the bigger the better. Other kinds of bait include whole squid, octopus pieces, live greenling and rock crab. Getting to the bottom involves a whole list of variables; common approaches include the use of wire spreaders, an L-shaped piece of heavy wire that prevents the bait from getting entangled in the fishing line. The use of weights will depend on the waters you're fishing and the ocean conditions. Weights as light as six ounces may work, but often heaver weights from 24 to 48 ounces are necessary in rough ocean conditions.

Jigging is another popular method for catching halibut. Many anglers use homemade or manufactured metal jigs, leadheads with plastic grubs bounced along the bottom. Spreaders mentioned above are also common with jig anglers, as are heavy weights.

Recommended Ocean Access Points

Coos Bay, Depoe Bay, Nestucca Bay, Tillamook Bay, Winchester Bay, Yaquina Bay.

LESSER GAME FISH

These are labeled "lesser" game fish because they are generally shunned by most anglers in pursuit of more noble species such as trout, steelhead and salmon. Not surprisingly, some of these fish come in and out of vogue. There has been a renewed interest in carp because of their size (5–20 pounds) and because they are known as good fighters. Whitefish, the bane of most trout anglers, can provide good sport when nothing else is biting.

Common Carp
(Cyprinus carpio)

The bottom-feeding, warmwater-loving carp is about as far removed from most angler's interests as one can get. Still, most anglers would be lying if they told you they have never considered what it would be like to hook one of these behemoths. The common knowledge at present is that they are great fighters and can be finicky eaters. Not surprising, but then again anglers will say anything to justify their efforts. One attribute of carp fishing which I find intriguing is the potential for sight-fishing. Regardless of the species, nothing compares to the anticipation that results from watching a fish swim toward your bait or lure, knowing that any second he'll take it. Believe it or not, sight fishing can be more difficult than blind fishing, and most anglers jerk the bait out of the fish's mouth before they ever have a chance to eat it.

TACKLE, TACTICS, AND TIPS

Use light to medium weight tackle. A large eight-pound fish can be quite a challenge on ultra-light trout gear. Carp are mostly vegetarians, eating decaying and live plant matter when it settles on the bottom. They prefer warm water, but can also be found in cold-water rivers. Carp have been known to eat such items as peas, yellow corn and dough balls. Special flies have been created which are nothing more than a representation of a brown dough ball. One suggested approach is to place the bait on the bottom and wait for a cruising fish. Just before the fish passes over the bait pop it off the bottom with a slight jerk, quick enough to disturb the surrounding sand or mud and draw the attention of the carp. Once you have their attention it's anybody's guess what may happen next.

RECOMMENDED WATERS

Columbia, Tualatin, and Willamette Rivers.

Mountain Whitefish
(Prosopium williamsoni)

The bane of most trout anglers, the native whitefish can be found in most rivers and lakes in Oregon and frequently live among trout populations. Their size averages between 13 and 15 inches, but can grow as big as two or three pounds. The Oregon state record catch was made in 1994 at Crane Prairie Reservoir weighing 4.14 pounds. Whitefish look like trout but are silver and have pointed mouths. Whitefish are most easily caught in winter when they school up in deep pools during their spawning cycles, but they are present all year. The Grande Ronde in northeastern Oregon has a little-known but excellent winter fishery for large whitefish.

TACKLE, TACTICS, AND TIPS

Standard trout tackle is the norm. Use six- to seven-foot spinning rods with four- to six-pound test line. Fly anglers can use standard nine-foot rods in five weight or less. Whitefish will take bait, lures and flies, but your offers should be small to match their small mouths. Anglers who fish small nymphs, size 14 and smaller, can have a difficult time keeping whitefish off the line in a heavily populated river. Whitefish will take a dry fly. You will know when whitefish are feeding on the surface because they make a popping sound or they strike very fast. Bait such as small grubs and pieces of worm work well.

RECOMMENDED WATERS

Crane Prairie and Wickiup Reservoirs, Crescent and Odell Lakes, Davis Lake, Deschutes River (mainstem from the headwaters to Lake Billy Chinook), Grande Ronde, Little Deschutes River, Little Lava Lake, Malheur River, Metolius River, Odell Creek, Paulina Lake, Suttle Lake, Odell Creek, Davis Lake, Metolius River system, Malheur River.

FISHING GEAR CHECKLIST

Fishing Apparel
- Fingerless gloves (winter)
- Long underwear (winter)
- Micro-fiber long-sleeve sun shirt
- Micro-fiber shorts and pants
- Rain shell or wading jacket
- Wading shoes or sandals
- Wading socks
- Wide-brimmed sun hat
- Windproof fleece jacket (winter)
- Wool hat (winter)
- Wool socks (winter)

Fishing Accessories
- Fishing vest or chest pack
- Float tube and kick fins
- Hip boots
- Inflatable life vest
- Landing net
- Lanyard
- Pontoon boat
- Tackle bag
- Waders (Gore-Tex or neoprene)
- Wading belt
- Wading boots (cleeted or felt)
- Wading cleets (if using felt soled boots)
- Wading gravel guards
- Wading staff

Tackle
- Extra lures, flies or bait
- Extra swivels and other connectors
- Floats
- Fly floatant
- Forceps
- Hooks
- Leaders
- Pliers
- Scissors or clippers
- Spare fishing line
- Spare fishing rod and reel
- Strike indicators
- Tippet
- Weights or split shot

Safety Equipment
In addition to the items below, always tell someone at home your travel plans, even if it's a day trip, and take a friend if possible.
- Cell phone
- Emergency food and water
- First-aid kit with booklet
- GPS
- List of emergency contacts (police, fire, rescue)
- Medications and medication card with contact information
- Red Cross first aid and CPR cards (highly recommended)
- Road and recreation maps
- Weather radio

Other Equipment
- Camera
- Binoculars
- Fishing license
- Insect repellent
- Multi-function knife
- Polarized sunglasses
- Sunscreen with SPF 30 or higher
- Trash bags

Traveling Kit
Travelers and backpackers require the basics that can be contained in a small space. Below is a list of the basic necessities.
- Compact fishing rod and reel (4, 5, or 6 piece rod)
- Guidebook or map of region
- Hat
- Fishing license
- Small box of lures, flies, tippet, leaders, weights, and floats
- Small first-aid kit

THE OREGON COAST

© CRAIG SCHUHMANN

BEST FISHING SPOTS

◖ Salmon
Columbia River Estuary, page 84
Tillamook Bay, page 96
Sixes River, page 126
Chetco River, page 134

◖ Smallmouth Bass
Lower Umpqua River, page 120

◖ Steelhead
Wilson River, page 97

◖ Hike-In Fisheries
Salmonberry River, page 94

◖ Places to Teach Kids to Fish
Columbia River Estuary, page 84

The Oregon Coast brings to mind different images

for many people: lighthouses, quaint coastal communities, windswept beaches, heavy rain gear, rugged coastlines, tidepools, and exotic wildlife. The angler, of course, thinks of fish – big anadromous fish.

The Oregon Coast is actually two distinct, but related, watersheds: the Northern Oregon Coastal Basin, from Astoria to Florence; and the Southern Oregon Coastal Basin, from Florence to Brookings. These two basins are made up of 20 subbasins, all of which drain directly into the ocean to form the Oregon Coastal Hydrologic Region. There are many differences in these two regions: "half-pounders" prevalent in the southwest zone are unheard of in the northwest zone; steelhead on average tend to be bigger in the north compared to their southern brethren; the northern coast receives a greater average rainfall; the southern coast has a higher concentration of lakes, warm-water fisheries, sand dunes, big rivers, and mountains.

Fortunately, your proximity to these basins is closer than you think. Resident anglers rarely need to travel more than a couple of hours to find good fishing on the coast. With 296 miles of coastline, from Astoria to the California boarder, any place along the I-5 corridor is within an hour's drive of 41 rivers, 12 bays, and 13 lakes. The section of coast you choose to fish is largely dependent on where you start. The northern coastal basin tends to be the province of the Willamette Valley and Portland anglers. Portlanders drive to Astoria or Tillamook and fish the Wilson, Trask, and Kilchis Rivers. Those in Salem need only drive west to Newport or Lincoln City to fish the Siletz or Alsea. Eugene, Roseburg, and Ashland anglers fish the southern half. From Eugene, it is a short drive to Florence for a chance at the Siuslaw. If starting in Roseburg, one can make a short hop to the Lower Umpqua, Coquille, or Coos Rivers. Medford and Ashland mark the gateways to the Rogue, Sixes, Elk, or Illinois Rivers. The greatest concentration of lakes on the coast is in Siltcoos and Coos County, beginning north of Florence at Lilly Lake and extending south towards Coos Bay at Tenmile Lake.

Salmon, more than any other species, symbolize the Northwest and

Oregon in particular. Fall and spring chinook, coho, and chum salmon all thrive on the Oregon Coast. They are a symbol for all that is wild in nature – from the dense Sitka spruce rainforests to the jagged coastline and frothing sea. This is their home and this is where anglers must go for the opportunity to tap into a fish as old as the continents themselves.

If salmon epitomize the Northwest, then steelhead – the game fish of game fish – epitomize its sport fish. Anglers have been known to chase these fish for years without a hookup, battling severe winter conditions suitable for the toughest Filson clothing and neoprene waders. Steelhead can be found in the same rivers as salmon, but unlike salmon, their migrations upriver are swift and determined, bypassing residence in tidewaters and estuaries for the swift currents of freshwater. Also unlike salmon, steelhead remain fresh and feisty hundreds of miles from the ocean and are the preferred game of fly anglers. The territory of steelhead is rugged, requiring anglers to have the skill to move through high gradient rivers in densely forested gorges. Drift boats are a mainstay on Oregon coastal rivers for anglers not wishing to scramble over moss-covered boulders or wade through swift river currents.

Not to be overlooked are the numerous other species found in rivers, lakes, bays, and estuaries on the Oregon Coast. Sea-run cutthroat, a once-thriving fishery, is slowly coming back from a decline in population. Important commercial fisheries in the port cities of Astoria, Newport, Charleston, Brookings, Port Orford, Garibaldi, Pacific City, Depoe Bay, Florence, Winchester Bay, Bandon, and Gold Beach all provide charters and guides that give anglers the opportunity to catch ocean salmon, albacore tuna, halibut, sturgeon, rockfish, and tuna.

As with many species, hatchery cutthroat, salmon, and steelhead are slowly being phased out in favor of their wild counterparts. As a consequence, many fisheries on the coast are becoming catch-and-release rivers and special regulations require anglers to be intimately acquainted with all regulations set by the Oregon Department of Fish and Wildlife (ODFW).

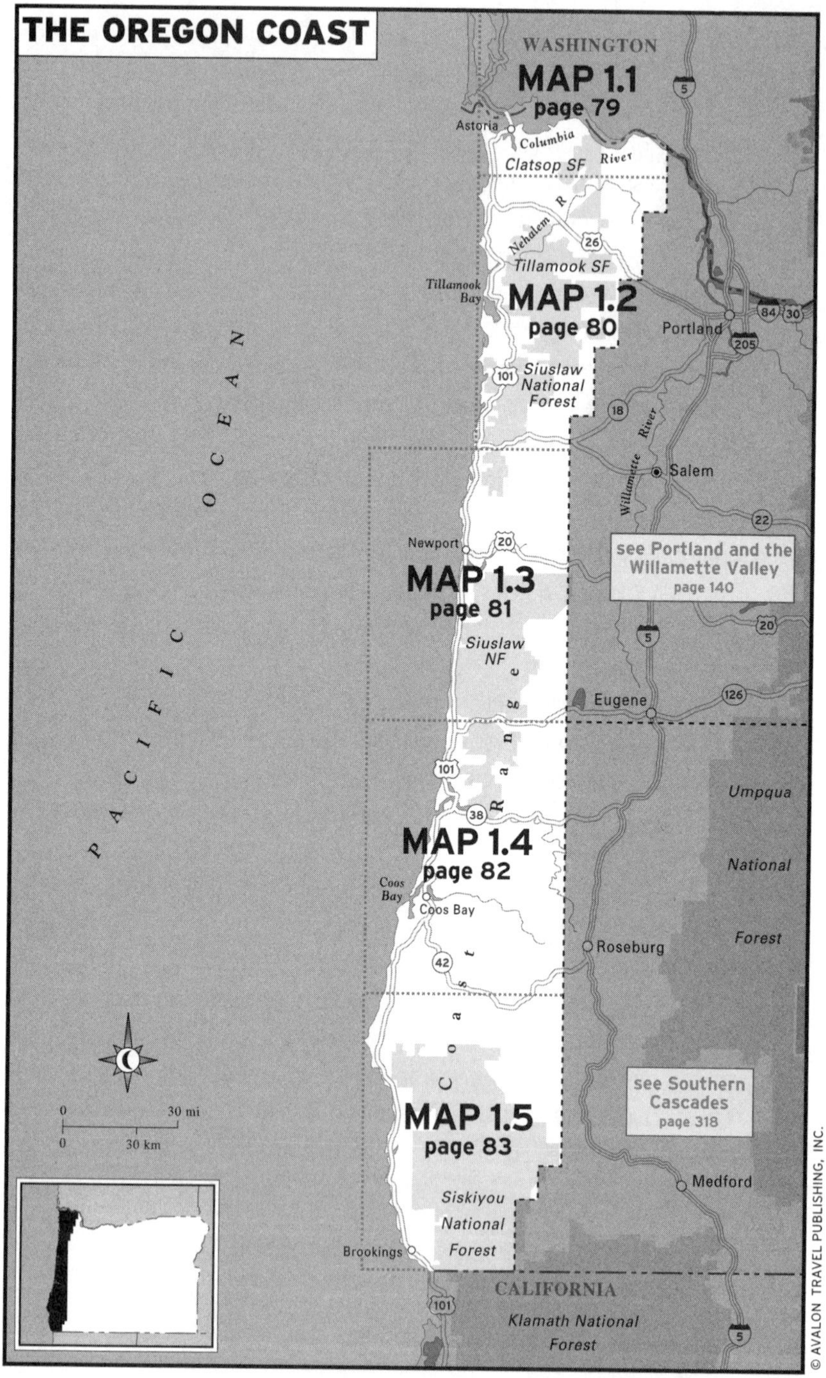

THE OREGON COAST

WASHINGTON

MAP 1.1
page 79

Astoria

Columbia River

Clatsop SF

Nehalem R.

26

Tillamook SF

Tillamook Bay

MAP 1.2
page 80

Portland

84/30

205

101

Siuslaw National Forest

18

Willamette River

Salem

22

see Portland and the Willamette Valley
page 140

Newport

20

MAP 1.3
page 81

Siuslaw NF

Coast Range

5

20

Eugene

126

101

38

MAP 1.4
page 82

Coos Bay

Coos Bay

42

Roseburg

Umpqua

National

Forest

Coast Range

MAP 1.5
page 83

see Southern Cascades
page 318

Medford

Siskiyou National Forest

Brookings

CALIFORNIA

101

Klamath National Forest

5

O C E A N

P A C I F I C

0   30 mi
0   30 km

Map 1.1

Sites 1-7
Pages 84-89

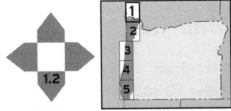

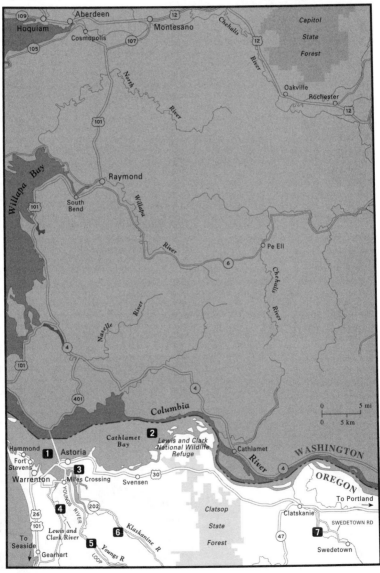

Map 1.2

Sites 8-28
Pages 90-105

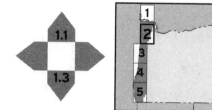

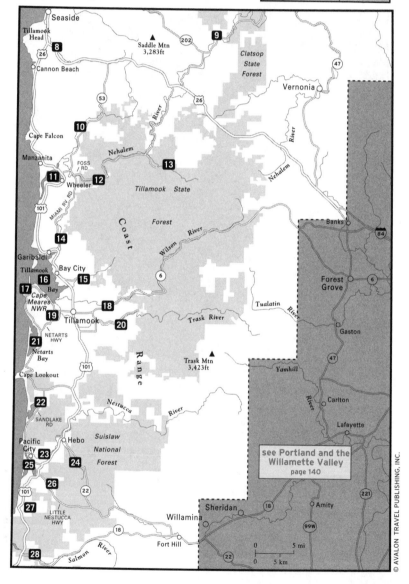

Map 1.3

Sites 29-43
Pages 106-115

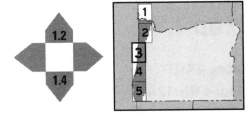

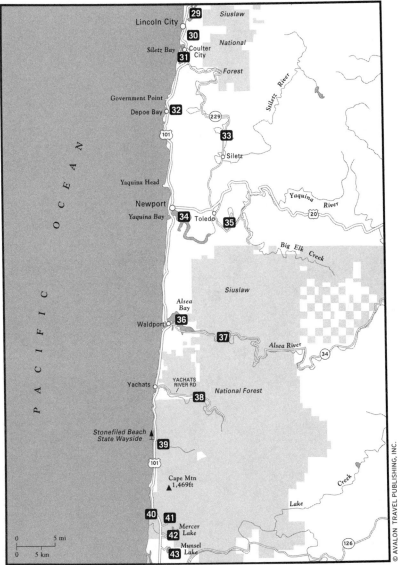

Map 1.4

Sites 44-57
Pages 116-124

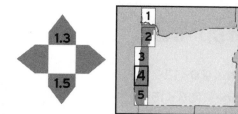

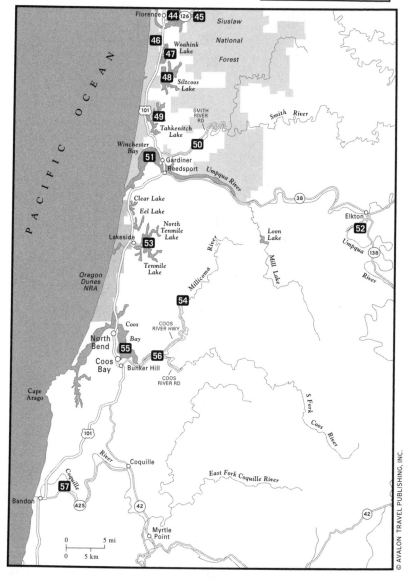

Map 1.5

Sites 58-71
Pages 125-135

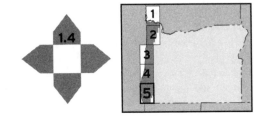

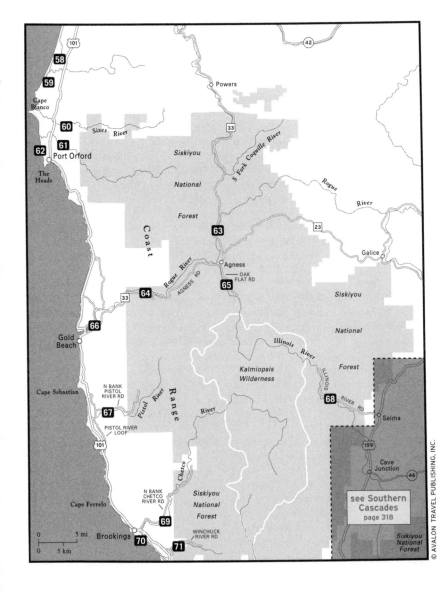

🚹 COLUMBIA RIVER ESTUARY

Buoy 10 to Astoria-Megler Bridge in Astoria

Map 1.1, page 79   **BEST ᶜ**

Crossing atop the Astoria–Megler Bridge from Washington to Oregon, one can't help but marvel at the sheer immensity of the Columbia River as 400,000 cubic feet per second of water butts up against the formidable force of the Pacific Ocean. Seemingly, there is no distinction between the ocean and freshwater as they mingle into a large watery estuary rich with aquatic life and fish. Life on the surface of the water is more visible in the form of small boats, commercial fishing vessels, sailboarders, cargo barges, sea birds, seals, sea lions, and marinas. This is an estuary teeming with life and human activity and one feels immediately charged upon arriving at the scene.

The Columbia is a river, but it is so much more. Historical, political, social, and environmental associations aside, this is the fifth-largest drainage basin in North America, making a journey of more than 1,200 miles and draining nearly 260,000 square miles of land from Oregon, Washington, Idaho, Montana, Wyoming, Nevada, Utah, and British Columbia.

All this water is accessible from a boat or various land points around the jetties, southern beaches, and the commercial logging and fishing communities of Astoria, Warrenton, and Hammond. The lowest reach of river is formally known as the Columbia River Estuary and it lies between the Pacific Ocean and the river mouth at Astoria–Megler Bridge. Buoy 10 forms the outermost edge of this estuary fishery, beyond which lies the Pacific Ocean. Beyond Buoy 10 is designated open-ocean fishing and is subject to fishing regulations imposed by the Western Pacific Fisheries Management Council. Check the fishing regulations before making a trip because angling rules are subject to last-minute changes with very little notice. Consult the latest printed regulations or local newspapers or call the ODFW for up-to-date information.

Of principal interest to the angler in this lower section are coho, fall and spring chinook, white and green sturgeon, bottom fish, and clams. Sturgeon is by far the greatest attraction with more than 80 percent of legal-size sturgeon in the Columbia Basin caught just off the shores of Astoria. The Columbia also has the greatest concentration of sturgeon in the world; their numbers are estimated at approximately one million between Bonneville Dam near Portland and the Pacific Ocean. Fishing is open year-round, but spring and summer tend to be the most productive and good catches coincide with the arrival of anchovies April–August. Numerous special regulations govern the legal catch and capture of sturgeon: legal size limits are 42–60 inches; catch limits are limited to one sturgeon per day, five per year; all hooks must be single-point and barbless. Sturgeon tags placed on sturgeon by the Oregon Department of Fish and Wildlife collect valuable biological information and should be returned to an ODFW office when a fish is kept. Anglers are asked to write down the tag information on nonkept fish and turn in the written information to the ODFW.

Anglers targeting sturgeon will want to concentrate on the areas between Desdemona Sands on the south side of Astoria–Megler Bridge and Gray's Bay Point to the north. Use fresh bait, no more than a day old, such as anchovies, herring, or smelt. The most popular fishing method is to use enough weight on your line to settle the bait on the river bottom and wait for the sturgeon to bite. Setting the hook after the first appearance of a bite is a sure way to lose the fish. Instead, wait for several pulls from the sturgeon while it engulfs the bait and then set the hook firmly.

Salmon fishing constitutes the other major fishery in the Columbia Estuary. Fall and spring chinook and coho are the primary species. Fall chinook usually enter the estuary and lower river in August. Spring chinook arrive in fishable numbers January–May. Angling regulations for these fish are subject to change so be sure to check with local authorities such as the ODFW for up-to-date information. Mostly this is a trolling fishery with bait such as herring or anchovies close to the surface of the water. The most popular areas for trolling are between Buoy 10 and Buoy 14 and the shipping channels near the bridge. These areas can get concentrated with anglers trolling the water, sometimes numbering in the hundreds. Boat access is good in Hammond, Warrenton, and Astoria.

Bank anglers can catch salmon as well as bottom fish, greenling, surf perch, rockfish, and lingcod on the incoming tide from the North and South jetties, the Clatsop Spit, and from public docks in surrounding towns. For those anglers interested in razor clams, the Clatsop beaches from the South Jetty to Seaside offer the best opportunities in the state. Try Clatsop Spit, Columbia Beach, and Sunset Beach for best results. Search for clams at low tides October–July.

One piece of advice: Hire a guide, learn the water from a professional, and severely cut down the learning curve required to catch fish in this difficult fishery. If you hire a guide, make plain your intentions to learn the water and find someone who will teach you. If your goal is a leisurely fishing trip to catch fish, then save yourself the frustration of doing it on your own and go with someone who knows the water. Not only is this a difficult fishery, but it can be very hazardous because of swells, incoming tides, and commercial river traffic headed to the various ports near Portland. Both guides and charters are abundant in the local towns of Astoria, Hammond, or Warrenton.

Species: Coho, fall and spring chinook, white and green sturgeon, bottom fish, steelhead, walleye, shad, bass.

Facilities: You will find plenty of good camping in Fort Stevens State Park, Kampers West Kampground in Warrenton, and farther south at Sunset Beach. The three primary boat ramps for access to the estuary are Jetty Sands at the South Jetty, Hammond Mooring Basin in Hammond, and Warrenton Marina in Warrenton. Fishing and camping supplies, food, lodging, RV camping, restrooms, restaurants can all be found in Astoria, Warrenton, Hammond, and Fort Stevens.

Directions: Astoria sits at the junction between Hwy. 30 out of Portland and North Coast Hwy. U.S. 101 from Seaside. The local communities of Warrenton, Hammond, and Fort Stevens all sit 2–3 miles west of Astoria on Hwy. 30 and U.S. 101.

Contact: ODFW, Astoria, 503/338-0106; Astoria District Department of Forestry, 503/325-5451; Hammond Marina, 503/861-0547; Warrenton Marina, 503/861-3822; Aldrich Point ramp, 503/325-9503; Yacht Club at Young's Bay, 503/325-7275; Tackle Time Charters and Bait and Tackle, 503/861-3693; Kampers West Kampground, 503/861-1814; Fort Stevens State Park, 503/861-1671; Sunset Lake Park, 503/325-9306; Charlton Charters, 503/861-2429; Chris Vertopoulos, 503/349-1377, www.northwestanglingexperience.com.

2 LOWER COLUMBIA RIVER
Astoria-Megler Bridge to Clatskanie
Map 1.1, page 79

This stretch of the Columbia is considered the river proper and begins from the Astoria–Megler Bridge and extends to St. Helens, or in this listing, Clatskanie. Markedly different from the Columbia Estuary, this water is more manageable in size, broken up by numerous islands and channels. A good river map will help you navigate the sloughs and channels of the river. Anglers in this stretch can catch sturgeon, spring and fall chinook, coho, steelhead, walleye, shad, bass, and panfish.

Fall and spring chinook, sturgeon, and coho are the primary species. Fall chinook usually enter the lower river in August. Spring chinook arrive in fishable numbers January–May. Angling regulations for these fish are subject to change so be sure to check with local authorities such as the ODFW for up-to-date information. Like the estuary, this is a trolling fishery with bait such as herring or anchovies close to the surface of the water. Clifton Channel and Blind Slough, both hot spots for salmon, are easily accessible at Aldrich Point boat ramp and are good starting points for spring chinook, coho, and perch. Wallace Island to Crims Island across from Clatskanie is also a good stretch for trolling for salmon.

Bank access is good from numerous beaches along Highway 30 at Aldrich Point launch, Bradley State Wayside, Westport boat ramp, and the adjoining Riverfront Road. Bait such as sand shrimp and cured roe are favorites for salmon and steelhead.

Both summer and winter steelhead can be caught from beaches and river mouths. Unlike salmon, which are content to mill around and feed in the estuary, steelhead are more determined to get into the rivers and currents. Thus a greater number of steelhead are caught above the Astoria–Megler Bridge than below. Summer steelhead are in the Columbia June–August before migrating into river mouths. Winter steelhead are in the river November–March. Access points and beaches mentioned above all provide good opportunities for bank angling. Fishing river mouths such as the Clatskanie and other smaller tributaries requires a boat.

Panfish, bass, and shad are all present anywhere in the river but especially around structure and away from the fast current of the main-stem river. Fish the shallower water from a boat or bank around structures such as pylons, boat ramps, weed beds, edges of channels, and sloughs. All the boat ramps and public areas provide an abundance of opportunities to catch these smaller game fish. Shad are in the river mid-May–June.

Sturgeon are plentiful in this area with the concentration of angling taking place on the Oregon side from Tongue Point upstream through the island channels and alongside the shipping channel. The best boat access for this area is at the John Day boat ramp east of Astoria. Fishing for sturgeon is open year-round, but spring and summer tend to be the most productive and good catches coincide with the arrival of anchovies April–August. Numerous special regulations govern the legal catch and capture of sturgeon: legal-size limits are 42–60 inches; catch limits are limited to one sturgeon per day, five per year; all hooks must be single-point and barbless. Sturgeon tags placed on sturgeon by the Oregon Department of Fish and Wildlife collect valuable biological information and should be returned to an ODFW office when a fish is kept. Anglers are asked to write down the tag information on nonkept fish and turn in the written information to the ODFW.

Species: Coho, fall and spring chinook, white and green sturgeon, bottom fish, steelhead, walleye, shad, bass, crappie, blugill.

Facilities: You will find camping nearby in Fort Stevens State Park, Kampers West Kampground in Warrenton, and farther south at Sunset Lake park. Several boat ramps along Hwy. 30 will get you to the water: Yacht Club at Young's Bay, East Mooring Basin in Astoria, John Day boat ramp, and Aldrich Point ramp east of Astoria, and Westport boat ramp in Westport. Fishing and camping supplies, food, lodging, RV camping, restrooms, and restaurants can all be found in Clatskanie, Astoria, Warrenton, Hammond, and Fort Stevens.

Directions: From Astoria drive east on Hwy. 30. Clatskanie is 30 miles from Astoria. The highway moves away from the river between the towns of Svensen and Clatskanie and it is necessary to take side roads to get to the river. A good local map will help you identify beaches, small marinas, and public access points in this area.

Contact: ODFW, Astoria, 503/338-0106; Astoria District Department of Forestry, 503/325-5451; Hammond Marina, 503/861-0547; Warrenton Marina, 503/861-3822; Aldrich Point ramp, 503/325-9503; Yacht Club at Young's Bay, 503/325-7275; Tackle Time Charters and Bait and Tackle, 503/861-3693; Kampers West Kampground, 503/861-1814; Fort Stevens State Park, 503/861-1671; Sunset

Lake Park, 503/325-9306; Charlton Charters, 503/861-2429; Chris Vertopoulos, 503/349-1377, www.northwestanglingexperience.com.

3 YOUNG'S BAY
in Astoria
Map 1.1, page 79

A limited sport fishery because of heavy commercial fishing and shallow depth, this freshwater bay near the mouth of the Columbia River in Astoria relies on hatchery runs of salmon, steelhead, and sea-run trout. Formed by the confluence of the Lewis and Clark, Young's, Klaskanine, and Wallooski Rivers, Young's Bay offers anglers good access to the several tidewater reaches into these rivers. The large commercial fishery in the bay can make sportfishing and boating tricky at best. One should be aware of commercial fishing times to avoid nets and fishing boats. It is advisable to check with marinas or sporting goods stores for up-to-date information before attempting either fishing or boating.

The most popular sportfishing is at the mouth of the bay during peak run times. As with most bays, this is a trolling fishery. Trolling herring or other bait, spinners, or a combination of the two is your best bet. Two boat ramps in Astoria offer access to the bay—the Young's Bay Yacht Club off Business Rt. 101 just before you cross the bay bridge and Tide Point ramp on Olney Avenue. Spring chinook come into the bay in early April and run through June. Fall chinook arrive July–October, followed by tule chinook and then coho. Tule chinook is a species native to the lower Columbia River. Winter steelhead arrive November–March, and sea-run cutthroat begin as early as July through the fall.

Species: Spring, and fall chinook, steelhead, and sea-run trout.

Facilities: Two primary boat ramps will grant you access to the bay: Young's Bay Yacht Club and Tide Point ramp. More boat ramps can be found in Warrenton. Camping is available at Kampers West Kampground and Fort Stevens

State Park. Food, supplies, RV camping, accommodations, and restaurants are all available in Astoria, Warrenton, and Hammond.

Directions: In Astoria, take business Rt. 101 west or south of Astoria to cross the bay at various points.

Contact: ODFW, Astoria, 503/338-0106; Astoria District Department of Forestry, 503/325-5451; Hammond Marina, 503/861-0547; Warrenton Marina, 503/861-3822; Aldrich Point ramp, 503/325-9503; Yacht Club at Young's Bay, 503/325-7275; Tackle Time Charters and Bait and Tackle, 503/861-3693; Kampers West Kampground, 503/861-1814; Fort Stevens State Park, 503/861-1671; Sunset Lake Park, 503/325-9306; Charlton Charters, 503/861-2429.

4 LEWIS AND CLARK RIVER
south of Astoria
Map 1.1, page 79

A tributary of Young's Bay on the lower Columbia, the Lewis and Clark River has runs of wild steelhead and a fair population of native cutthroat trout. As in most coastal rivers, the winter steelhead make their appearance December–March. Despite limited access there is some good water to be found along the Lewis and Clark Road. Look for turnoffs on the roadside and be aware of all No Trespassing signs. Farther up the river at the intersection of Lewis and Clark Road and Mainline Road there is a locked gate that leads down to the Warrenton Water Treatment Plant. Park near the locked gate and hike 0.75 mile to the river on the spur road to the left. All methods of fishing for steelhead and trout will take fish.

Species: Wild steelhead, native cutthroat.

Facilities: Camping is available at Kampers West Kampground and Fort Stevens State Park. For remote camping try Saddle Mountain State Park. Supplies, accommodations, and RV parks can be found in Astoria and Seaside.

Directions: From Astoria follow Business Rt. 101 south for 1.5 miles to Miles Crossing and continue south on the Lewis and Clark Rd. for 4.7 miles to the gate at Mainline Rd. Saddle Mountain State Park is off Saddle Mountain Rd.

Contact: ODFW, Astoria, 503/338-0106; Astoria District Department of Forestry, 503/325-5451; Tackle Time Charters and Bait and Tackle, 503/861-3693; Kampers West Kampground, 503/861-1814; Fort Stevens State park, 503/861-1671; Sunset Lake Park, 503/325-9306; Charlton Charters, 503/861-2429.

5 YOUNG'S RIVER
south of Astoria

Map 1.1, page 79

The Young's River is another tributary of Young's Bay south of Astoria. The Klaskanine, Young's River, and a few other tributaries come together to form the lower Young's River. The Young's River Falls nine miles upriver on Young's River Loop Road prevents any salmon or steelhead from getting into the upper river. Fishing is prohibited from the first highway bridge below Young's River Falls to the falls. Some fish are taken in the tidewater, which extends to a half mile below the falls. The Yacht Club Park and boat launch near Young's Bay will enable you to reach some of this water by boat. Small cutthroat can be caught in the river above the falls, accessible by logging roads above Young's River Loop Road. A good forest map will enable you to navigate the logging roads. Young's River Mainline Road will be your primary access into the upper reaches. Fish for trout with small spinners and flies. Search out pocket water and deeper holes for the best success.

Species: Salmon, steelhead, wild cutthroat.
Facilities: The boat ramp at the Yacht Club in Young's Bay will help you get access to the tidewater reach. Camping is available at Kampers West Kampground and Fort Stevens State Park. Supplies, accommodations, and RV parks can be found in Astoria and Seaside.
Directions: From Astoria drive south on busi-

ness loop 101 to Wireless Rd., which turns into Young's River Loop Rd. Young's River Loop Rd. turns into Young's River Mainline Rd. above Young's River Falls.

Contact: ODFW, Astoria, 503/338-0106; Astoria District Department of Forestry, 503/325-5451; Tackle Time Charters and Bait and Tackle, 503/861-3693; Yacht Club at Young's Bay, 503/325-7275; Kampers West Kampground, 503/861-1814; Fort Stevens State Park, 503/861-1671; Sunset Lake Park, 503/325-9306; Charlton Charters, 503/861-2429.

6 KLASKANINE RIVER
south of Astoria

Map 1.1, page 79

The Klaskanine is another tributary of Young's Bay and flows 20 miles out of the Clatsop State Forest. Coho, spring and fall chinook, winter steelhead, sea-run, and resident cutthroat are all present. The river breaks up into three forks quickly above tidewater, forcing the angler to choose which area to fish. The most productive areas of the river are the South and North forks. The North Fork along State Highway 202 is distinguished by good access on forest lands, hatchery runs of steelhead and salmon, a fish hatchery, and a healthy population of both resident and sea-run cutthroat and will be your best bet for productive fishing. The South Fork along Elk Mountain Mainline Road hosts wild runs of steelhead and sea-run trout, but access is sorely limited by private lands.

Winter steelhead arrive Thanksgiving–March. Fishing below the hatchery on the North Fork will give the best opportunity for catching steelhead. Spring chinook begin in early April till late May and fall chinook run July–December. Most fish are caught from the tidewater to just below the North Fork Klaskanine Fish Hatchery on State Highway 202. Sea-run trout arrive as early as July and are best fished during this time in the tidewater accessible from Klaskanine Park near Olney. The park can be reached either from Young's River Loop Road out of Astoria or from Olney off Highway 202 on Saddle Mountain Road. As autumn arrives, look to the upper reaches of the North Fork near the hatchery for sea-runs. Above the hatchery you will find good river access and bank fishing for a healthy population of resident cutthroat. Two good places to begin are at the North Fork Klaskanine Fish Hatchery and the primitive Klaskanine County Park at milepost 11 on Highway 202.

Species: Coho, spring and fall chinook, winter steelhead, sea-run and resident cutthroat.

Facilities: There is one boat ramp at Klaskanine Park. Camping is available at Kampers West Kampground and Fort Stevens State Park. Supplies, accommodations, and RV parks can be found in Olney, Astoria, and Seaside. The fish hatchery on the North Fork provides a good day-use area.

Directions: From Astoria drive south on Hwy. 202, which follows the North Fork before changing to the South Fork. The hatchery is 12 miles on Hwy. 202 from Astoria.

Contact: ODFW, Astoria, 503/338-0106; Astoria District Department of Forestry, 503/325-5451; Klaskanine Hatchery, 503/325-3653; Tackle Time Charters and Bait and Tackle, 503/861-3693; Yacht Club at Young's Bay, 503/325-7275; Kampers West Kampground, 503/861-1814; Fort Stevens State Park, 503/861-1671; Sunset Lake Park, 503/325-9306.

⑦ CLATSKANIE RIVER
west of Rainier
Map 1.1, page 79

This small stream enters the Columbia River just west of Rainier. Mostly fished by locals and those desiring wild winter steelhead, the Clatskanie also contains an abundant population of resident wild cutthroat in its scenic upper reaches and sea-run cutthroat in the lower river and tidewater. The most popular time of year to fish this river is during the winter steelhead run late January–March. Angler pressure is greatest during this time of year; otherwise the river is relatively unfished, providing opportunities for solitary fishing escapes. Sea-run cutthroat are available July–September in the lower sections and tidewater. The best access and opportunities for resident wild cutthroat are during the summer in the river's upper reaches from Miller Creek to Shaffer Road. Steelhead can be taken with drift rods baited with corkies or cured salmon roe. Spin anglers should use spinners in steelhead colors such as orange or silver. Fly-fishing can be productive for all species. To catch the resident cutthroats use simple nymphs and general attractor dry-fly patterns such as the Adams, Royal Wulff, or Humpy.

The lower river runs through mostly private lands and is difficult to get to without landowner permission. Knocking on a few doors in the lower section has been known to yield access from generous landowners. If you are granted access, be respectful and leave no trace by packing out all garbage. Reach the mouth and tidewater from a boat launch in Clatskanie.

Species: Winter steelhead, resident and sea-run cutthroat. All cutthroat trout and wild steelhead must be released unharmed.

Facilities: The Beaver Landing boat ramp in Clatskanie will enable anglers to get to the mouth and tidewater reaches. Supplies and accommodations can be had in Clatskanie or Rainier.

Directions: For boat ramp and lower river access, from Rainier drive west on Hwy. 30 14 miles to Clatskanie. Follow signs to Beaver boat ramp. For upper river access, from Rainier drive 4.5 miles west on Hwy. 30 to the intersection at Apiary Rd. and turn south. Drive 10 miles to Apiary. From Apiary follow the river on Apiary Rd. for approximately 10 miles and turn south on Shaffer Rd. Look for river access points along both Apiary and Shaffer Rds.

Contact: ODFW, Astoria, 503/338-0106; Reel Action Guide Service, 503/728-4154.

8 NECANICUM RIVER

in Seaside

Map 1.2, page 80

The Necanicum is a small but productive river, 22 miles long, that begins in the Coast Range by Saddle Mountain and drains into the sea at Seaside. This is often the first river on the north coast to clear after a rainstorm and is a good bet in fall when other rivers are high and muddy. It clears and drops so fast, that boaters should carry a bow saw or gas-powered saw—an uncommon piece of fishing equipment, but necessary for navigation after a storm.

The Necanicum is home to a good run of hatchery steelhead arriving November–Christmas, and a wild run of steelhead enter later in January and run through March. Wild coho are present in the fall, but are closed to fishing. Fall chinook enter the river in November and sea-run cutthroat arrive with the fall rains in October. According to some anglers, sea-runs are available in the tidal reaches during the summer. Resident trout can be caught anywhere above tidewater but especially in the upper reaches. Drift fishing, spinners, spoons, plugs, float fishing, and back-trolling are all productive fishing methods. Colder months and high waters might require weighted flies or sinking lines. Fly-fishing is very productive, especially for steelhead, trout, and sea-runs.

Most fish are caught below Highway 53 about 12 miles south of Seaside. Access is average with a mix of both private and forest lands. There are two primary drifts—Klootchie Creek to Johnson's Construction Company, and the latter on down to the Relief Pitcher Tavern in Seaside. Bank access is limited but there are a few choice spots for those interested. A short section of an old logging road from Klootchie Creek Park to the South Fork is good fly water. Parking at the South Fork will give you access to private timber lands, and there are several spots in Seaside such as the 12th Street bridge.

Species: Hatchery and wild steelhead, wild coho, fall chinook, sea-run and resident cutthroat.

Facilities: You will find boat ramps at Klootchie Creek Park, Johnson's Construction Company, and behind the Relief Pitcher Tavern. Camping is available at Circle Creek RV Park and Campground in Seaside and Ecola State Park a few miles south of Seaside. Fishing and camping supplies can be had in Seaside. Johnston Construction Company charges a $30 annual fee for use of the ramp.

Directions: From Seaside take U.S. 101 south to the Hwy. 26 turnoff and go east following the river. Klootchie Creek Park on Hwy. 26 is a good place to begin your explorations.

Contact: Seaside Chamber of Commerce, 800/444-6740; ODFW, Astoria, 503/338-0106; Klootchie Creek Park, 503/325-9306; Johnson's Construction Company, 503/738-7328; Trucke's One Stop 503/738-8863; Bud's Grocery, 503/738-6855; Chris Vertopoulos, 503/349-1377, www.northwestanglingexperience.com.

9 UPPER NEHALEM RIVER

near Elsie

Map 1.2, page 80

Densely forested and scenic, the Upper Nehalem River is populated with resident cutthroat, steelhead, and late-spawning salmon. Most anglers target the trout and occasionally steelhead. Fly anglers and those who use light spinning gear will find many appealing attributes in this area. It's smaller than the lower river, and expect to fish pools, pocket water, and short runs. Especially good fly water can be found on the river stretch between the towns of Vernonia and Elsie. Two public areas, Pope–Meeker Access and Big Eddy, are good starting places to begin fishing. A lot of the river is accessible from the road but be aware of No Trespassing signs because this area does contain quite a bit of private lands. A good Forest Service map will also help you discover public lands in these areas.

Species: Salmon, steelhead, resident cutthroat.

Facilities: Boat ramps and launches are available on the lower section of the river. Camping can be had at Big Eddy Campground. Supplies and accommodations can be found in Elsie, Jewell, Mist, and Vernonia.

Directions: From Elsie, drive two miles south on Hwy. 26 to Fishhawk Falls Rd. (Jewell Junction) and turn north. After two miles look for Pope–Meeker Access on your left at Pope's Corner. Continue to follow the river along Fishhawk Falls Hwy., eight miles to the junction at Hwy. 202 (Nehalem Hwy.). Several good river access points lie on this stretch of road; avoid all No Trespassing signs. Turn east on Hwy. 202 and follow the river toward Vernonia, 33 miles ahead, looking for riverside pullouts for fishing access. Highway 202 will eventually run back into Hwy. 26. Look for the big Eddy Campground on your right four miles north of Vernonia. To reach the headwaters, turn west at the Vernonia–Nehalem Rd. junction just south of Vernonia.

Contact: Wheeler Marina, 800/345-3029; Lyster's Bait and Tackle, 503/322-3342; Tillamook District Office, 503/842-2548; ODFW, Tillamook, 503/842-2741; Nehalem Chamber of Commerce, 877/368-5100; Chris Vertopoulos, 503/349-1377, www.northwest anglingexperience.com.

10 NORTH FORK NEHALEM RIVER

east of Nehalem

Map 1.2, page 80

Cousin to the Nehalem, the North Fork is far enough out of the way to get less pressure from the metro crowds and therefore it's easier to find solitude on the water. The river is characterized by a diverse ring of waters and habitats. The upper section is a fast, high-gradient river, reminiscent of coastal streams, whose source is the coastal rainforest and it is the best place to catch resident cutthroat, sea-run cutthroat, and the occasional stray steelhead from the hatchery. Anglers can reach this water from roadside turnouts, the fish hatchery, or a gated road closed off to vehicle traffic. The middle section of the river forms at the hatchery and extends to the take-out at Erickson's. This is mostly technical white water for experienced boaters only and consists mostly of pocket water fishing.

The lower section from Erickson's to the take-out at the mouth is a slow-moving stretch through farmlands and possesses deep holes and long channels. Most of the steelhead and salmon fishing is done at the hatchery with fewer fish caught in the lower stretches. Fall chinook appear in the river August–November. You can catch fin-clipped coho beginning early November. Hatchery steelhead enter the river beginning Thanksgiving, with a wild run following in February and March. Sea-run cutthroat are available in the tidewater beginning in July and in the upper river in fall with the onset of rains. Resident cutthroat are available most of the year above tidewater and into the upper reaches of the river.

There are two primary boating drifts. The first float is from the hatchery downstream to Erickson's. The second drift is from Erickson's to Aldervale ramp at the mouth of the North Fork. This lower stretch is perfect for novice boaters with little risk of danger.

Species: Fall chinook, fin-clipped coho, winter hatchery and wild steelhead, resident and sea-run cutthroat.

Facilities: Nehalem Hatchery, the Aldervale boat ramp, and one privately-owned ramp in between are good access points. The Erickson ramp was sold 2006. Supplies and accommodations can be found in Nehalem or Wheeler on Nehalem Bay.

Directions: From Nehalem, follow Hwy. 53, the Necanicum Hwy., for eight miles to the North Fork Nehalem Hatchery at milepost 8. Highway 53 follows the river from the hatchery to U.S. 101, where the river feeds into Nehalem Bay. Look for the Aldervale boat ramp between the hatchery and U.S. 101.

Contact: For the boat ramp at Erickson's or

shuttle service, contact Jim Erickson, 503/368-5365; Wheeler Marina, 800/345-3029; Lyster's Bait and Tackle, 503/322-3342; Tillamook District Office, 503/842-2548; ODFW, Tillamook, 503/842-2741; Nehalem Chamber of Commerce, 877/368-5100; Chris Vertopoulos, 503/349-1377, www.northwestanglingexperience.com.

11 NEHALEM BAY
south of Nehalem

Map 1.2, page 80

One of the great assets of the Oregon coast is its bays and jetties and all the opportunities they provide for a wonderful ocean experience without the risk of being drowned by a swell. Nehalem Bay is Oregon's fourth-largest on the coast but its feel is a tucked-away intimacy. The tidewater extends to Eck Creek on the Nehalem River via a long channel. Spring and early summer make this a good place for bottom and surf fish from various points along the highway. Perch, rockfish, and greenling can all be caught here. There is good access to the bay from beaches and rocky outcroppings along U.S. 101 and the South Jetty. The salmon enter the bay with the arrival of the fall rains and can be caught in the tidewater until November. Coho also show up in fall but only fin-clipped fish may be kept. Be sure to read all regulations regarding game fishing in the bay. Some anglers fish for sturgeon during the salmon season when the fishing is slow or on an outgoing tide. Trolling, spinners, bobbers, and most kinds of bait fishing are all productive methods of fishing.

Boating is very common on the bay and many anglers leave its confines to travel up the tidal waters trolling for salmon. Be aware that tide changes can be quick, unsettling, and dangerous for the inexperienced. Before boating in the bay make sure you get a tidal schedule and plan to be off the water or in a safe position for the changes. Both an outgoing and incoming tide transform the bay into a swift river.

The marinas in Nehalem Bay are exceptional for the resources they provide to anglers and their families. Boat rentals are abundant and, if you are feeling daring, you can rent a small outboard and troll the bay or fish its rocky areas for bottom fish. If getting to a secluded beach for a little surf perch fishing is more your style, ask one of the marinas to shuttle you out to North Jetty in the Nehalem Bay State Park for an afternoon.

Species: Perch, rockfish, greenling, fall chinook, coho, sturgeon.

Facilities: In addition to the fishing, Manzanita, Wheeler, and Rockaway Beach provide quaint and often rustic accommodations, quality restaurants, quirky shops, and perhaps the occasional old bookstore. One can spend an entire day on the docks chatting with the locals and throwing crab nets. Most places will even cook the crabs you catch and put them on ice for the drive back to the hotel, camp, or home. Boat ramps, food, lodging, and camping can also be found in Nehalem and Brighton. RV camping can be found at Paradise Cove RV Park or The Jetty Fishery.

Directions: From Nehalem drive south on U.S. 101 for two miles to Wheeler. The bay will be on your right.

Contact: Wheeler Marina, 800/345-3029; Lyster's Bait and Tackle, 503/322-3342; Tillamook District Office, 503/842-2548; ODFW, Tillamook, 503/842-2741; Nehalem Chamber of Commerce, 877/368-5100; Chris Vertopoulos, 503/349-1377, www.northwestanglingexperience.com; Paradise Cove RV Park, 800/345-3029; The Jetty Fishery, 503/368-5746; State Parks Reservations, 800/452-5687.

12 LOWER NEHALEM RIVER
east of Nehalem

Map 1.2, page 80

The third-largest river on Oregon's north coast draining more than 800 square miles of forested lands, the Nehalem travels more than 100 miles to the Nehalem Bay by Wheeler. Comprising many diverse settings, the Nehalem runs through dense rainforests of spruce trees and clear-cut hillsides in its upper reaches and rich agricultural lands in its lower sections. This is a popular river with salmon, trout, and steelhead anglers because of its close proximity to the Portland metropolitan area via Hwy. 26. It is best known for its large winter steelhead, but it is also home to some of the largest chinook in Oregon, some weighing as much as 70 pounds, and a healthy population of sea-run and resident trout. A major attraction of the Nehalem River area is its very close proximity to several other major fisheries, including the Salmonberry and Necanicum, making it possible to fish several major rivers in one day or weekend. The adventurous angler armed with a good forest map and a four-wheel drive vehicle can find some outstanding opportunities on the many small tributaries that feed this immense drainage system.

The Nehalem can be divided into two sections: the lower river from Nehalem Bay to the crossing at Hwy. 26 by Elsie and the upper section from Elsie to the headwaters through the towns of Jewell, Mist, and Vernonia. Although steelhead and salmon are known to travel as far as 100 miles in this river, most of the fishing takes place in the lower 15 miles of water, from the mouth of the Salmonberry River to Nehalem Bay, leaving the upper river to trout anglers. The lower 15 miles of river is best reached by drift boats in the main river and motorboats in the tidewater, with only occasional bank access. Productive fishing methods include trolling with spinners, bait, and plugs, drift fishing with roe and corkies, spin fishing, and fly-fishing.

Fishing on the Nehalem begins in the tidewater from the bay upriver to Roy Creek County Park. Salmon is the main species, except during the fall when sea-run cutthroat are present. Summer chinook are in the river in June and July and an early run of fall chinook come in with the fall rains. Wild coho are present but all wild fish must be returned unharmed. Many anglers troll with herring in the lower tidewater from the bay to Nehalem, switching to spinners and drift rigs up to the reach of tidewater at Roy Creek County Park. To catch sea-run cutthroat you can employ either brightly colored spinners or flies with a fast retrieve through slack water and around structures such as logs.

Winter steelhead occupy the lower river above tidewater December–March, with March being the best month. This lower section of river above tidewater is best reached by drift boat because of private lands that border most of the river. The highest put-in is at Beaver Slide just below Lost Creek. From Beaver Slide you can float to three take-outs: a private fee boat ramp at Mohler Sand and Gravel (two miles), Roy Creek County Park (six miles), or Aldervale at the confluence of the North Fork of the Nehalem (12 miles). The float from Beaver Slide to Roy Creek is the most popular. If you want less crowded waters try the float from Roy Creek County Park to Aldervale. Numerous boat ramps dot the tidewater section and bay, but if you don't have a motor, expect to do quite a bit of rowing.

Bank angling on the lower river is limited but good access can be found at Roy Creek Park and at Falls County Park. Guide Chris Vertopoulos recommends both Nehalem Falls and the area above Beaver Slide as the best places for bank anglers. Above the falls you will find better access at Spruce Run County Park and the Salmonberry River. Some of the best fly-fishing water is at the mouth of the Salmonberry River upstream about five miles to Spruce Run Campground. This water is not boatable. Much of the river is bordered by private lands and a good forestry map can allow good access while preventing trespassing. Wading in this river requires caution as it can be very slippery.

Species: Summer chinook, fall chinook, winter steelhead, wild coho, resident and sea-run cutthroat.

Facilities: Boat ramps for powerboats and drift boats, both within the reach of tidewater, can be had at the Hwy. 101 ramp, Aldervale, and at Roy Creek County Park. There are two drift-boat launches in the lower river at Mohler Sand and Gravel and Beaver Slide. Camping is available at Roy Creek County Park, Nehalem Falls Park, and upriver at Spruce Run Campground. Supplies and accommodations can be found in Nehalem or Wheeler on Nehalem Bay.

Directions: From Nehalem drive south on U.S. 101 to Hwy. 53. Turn east on Hwy. 53 and turn south on Foss Rd. Foss Rd. eventually turns into Lower Nehalem Rd. and ends 28 miles later at Hwy. 26. Boat ramps are in the first 15 miles of Lower Nehalem Rd. You will cross the Salmonberry River approximately 17 miles upriver.

Contact: Wheeler Marina, 800/345-3029; Lyster's Bait and Tackle, 503/322-3342; Tillamook District Office, 503/842-2548; ODFW, Tillamook, 503/842-2741; Nehalem Chamber of Commerce, 877/368-5100; Chris Vertopoulos, 503/349-1377, www.northwest-anglingexperience.com

13 SALMONBERRY RIVER
east of Nehalem

Map 1.2, page 80   **BEST (**

If there were one place in Oregon to build a cabin and live off the land, the Salmonberry River in the Tillamook National Forest would certainly top the list for its sheer beauty and seemingly wild environs. This is a small river with a very short run of only 18 miles, but it's a classic steelhead stream in every sense. It's a pristine rainforest setting with emerald water, and even the most determined angler may find it hard not to be distracted from fishing by the wonderful displays of nature found shadowing the river. Make no mistake, the high gradient flow and rugged terrain surrounding this river make this a challenging fishery. There are no roads here. The only access is limited to a hike-in trail from the mouth along an active railway. Recent efforts by conservation groups have made this a hiker-friendly trail, but exercise caution, especially when crossing long train trestles.

The Salmonberry River is said to have the healthiest intact run of native winter steelhead on the coast. The river itself is composed of swift runs, boulder pocket water, and gravelly bottoms. Any angler with a sense of adventure will find elegant runs, glides, and pools perfect for using traditional greased-line fly-fishing techniques. The river is subject to closures and off-limit fishing seasons so read the fishing regulations before making the trip. Steelhead enter the river as early as December, but the peak runs are in February and March. All steelhead are wild and must be released unharmed. Salmon fishing is prohibited. A solid run of sea-run cutthroat make an appearance in July and are best fished for in the lower two miles of river. All basic fishing techniques work here, from drift fishing to flies.

Species: Winter wild steelhead, sea-run and resident cutthroat.

Facilities: Parking and hike-in walking trail are at the Salmonberry River Trailhead. Camping can be had at Nehalem Falls, Spruce Run County Park, or Roy Creek along Foss Rd. and Lower Nehalem Rd. Supplies and accommodations are available in Nehalem and Wheeler.

Directions: From Nehalem drive south on U.S. 101 to Hwy. 53. Turn east on Hwy. 53 and turn south on Foss Rd. and travel 17 miles to the Salmonberry River Trailhead.

Contact: Wheeler Marina, 800/345-3029; Lyster's Bait and Tackle, 503/322-3342; Tillamook District Office, 503/842-2548; ODFW, Tillamook, 503/842-2741; Nehalem Chamber of Commerce, 877/368-5100; Chris Vertopoulos, 503/349-1377, www.northwes-tanglingexperience.com.

14 MIAMI RIVER
north of Tillamook

Map 1.2, page 80

The Miami is the northernmost tributary of Tillamook Bay and enters the bay just east of Garibaldi. At just under 14 miles long, the Miami is a small river with large runs of fish.

Wild winter steelhead, fall chinook, chum salmon, and resident and sea-run cutthroat all live in its waters. Bank access and public easements are on the most productive areas of the river, but the lower 6–7 miles is limited because of private property. At times, landowners have opened their property to fishing for a fee. Check with the local tackle shops or the Oregon Department of Fish and Wildlife to learn about the latest access points.

Steelhead are in the river December–March. Fall chinook and coho are present during the fall but not available to anglers. Next to steelhead and sea-run cutthroat, chum salmon provide the only other attraction and must be released unharmed. Although on the decline in recent years, the Miami is the only river, along with the Kilchis, to have chum salmon runs of fishable size. Chum come more readily to a fly than most salmon do, making this a popular fly-fishing river mid-September–mid-November. For chum salmon use brightly colored flies or other artificial bait in shades of green. Best bank access is in the Tillamook State Forest five miles above U.S. 101.

Species: Wild winter steelhead, fall chinook, chum salmon, resident and sea-run cutthroat.

Facilities: Camping is available at Barview Jetty County Park three miles north of Garibaldi. Fishing and camping supplies are available in Garibaldi, Bay City, and Tillamook.

Directions: From Tillamook drive north on U.S. 101 and take the Miami River Rd. junction just before entering Garibaldi. Miami Creek Rd., six miles north from Garibaldi, will take you east to the headwaters. Look for bank access along Miami River Rd. and again on Miami Creek Rd.

Contact: ODFW, Tillamook, 503/842-2741; Tillamook District Department of Forestry, 503/842-2545; Tillamook Chamber of Commerce, 503/842-7225; The Guide Shop, 503/842-3474; Garibaldi Bait and Store, 503/322-0282; Wilson River RV Park, 503/842-2750; Tillamook Sporting Goods, 503/842-4334; Dan Christopher, 503/491-9793, www.dan@qualityfishingadventures.com; Chris Vertopoulos, 503/349-1377, www.northwestanglingexperience.com.

15 KILCHIS RIVER
north of Tillamook
Map 1.2, page 80

The Kilchis flows 25 miles out of the rainforested Coast Range until it empties into Tillamook Bay north of Tillamook. This is a small river, but it hosts some of the larger runs of steelhead, salmon, and cutthroats on the coast. One of the fastest rivers to clear after a storm, the Kilchis needs only a day or two until it is fishable. When all the coastal rivers are blown out by storms, head to the Kilchis for some great fishing.

The river hosts wild winter steelhead November–March with the strongest runs in December and January. A few hatchery steelhead will come into the river beginning in fall because of a limited stocking program. Fall chinook, coho, chum salmon, and sea-run cutthroat all arrive at the same time in October, just before the fall rains. Cutthroats can also be caught in spring when water levels rise and are best fished for in the tidal waters.

The river is composed of at least two distinct sections with most of the fishing occurring in the lower reaches. The upper river around Kilchis County Park and extending into the Tillamook Forest is all bank access and is often disappointingly low, especially in summer. The lower river, on the other hand, has better habitat and holds a good population of resident trout and sea-run fish. This section is bordered by private land with some fee access points, such as Curl Bride Road, provided by generous landowners. Boating access can be had at Kilchis County Park, Cape Meers Landing (Logger Bridge), and the Highway 101 ramp. This six-mile section of river is the most productive for salmon and steelhead angling. Cape Meers Landing is about three miles up Kilchis Road and another 2.5 miles will get you to the county boat ramp at the county park. Both drifts are about three miles. The take-out is at Parks Landing 200 yards above U.S. 101 on Alderbrook Road.

Most standard fishing techniques work on this river. Boaters primarily back-bounce bait and work plugs through the deeper runs. Fly-fishing, drift fishing, and spinners all work from the bank or boat. Chum salmon seem particularly interested in fluorescent shades of green, pink, red, or purple, with green the preferred color.

Species: Hatchery and wild winter steelhead, fall chinook, coho, chum salmon, and sea-run cutthroat.

Facilities: Boat ramps at Kilchis County Park, Logger Bridge, and the Hwy. 101/Kilchis River Rd. ramp will get you access to the river. There's camping at Kilchis County Park. Fishing and camping supplies, accommodations, and restaurants can be found in Tillamook.

Directions: From Tillamook drive north on U.S. 101 a few miles to Kilchis River Rd. Follow this road for four miles to Kilchis County Park. To get to Logger Bridge, take the Kilchis Forest Rd. turnoff from Kilchis River Rd. The boat ramp will be on your right just after the junction. Kilchis Forest Rd. will take you into the Kilchis headwaters.

Contact: ODFW, Tillamook, 503/842-2741; Tillamook District Department of Forestry, 503/842-2545; Tillamook Chamber of Commerce, 503/842-7225; Cape Lookout State Park, 503/842-4981; The Guide Shop, 503/842-3474; Wilson River RV Park, 503/842-2750; Tillamook Sporting Goods, 503/842-4334; Dan Christopher, 503/491-9793, www.dan@qualityfishingadventures.com; Chris Vertopoulos, 503/349-1377, www.northwestanglingexperience.com.

16 TILLAMOOK BAY
west of Tillamook

Map 1.2, page 80	BEST (

Tillamook Bay is the crown jewel of this wonderful basin that boasts no fewer than five major salmon, steelhead, and trout rivers. The Tillamook Basin is rich farmland and there is an abundance of private lands, particularly around the lowlands of the basin where all these rivers empty into the bay. For this reason, the bay is going to be your best bet for access to river mouths and tidewater reaches and to the outer waters around the Pacific Ocean.

Tillamook Bay is an immense body of water—the second-largest in Oregon next to Coos Bay—and fishing the bay or breaching the Tillamook Bar is no small undertaking. Hazards such as tides, sandbars, discarded piling fields, and other boating obstacles make this a dangerous place if you don't know your way around. Consider hiring a guide or charter service for your first few outings. Offshore fishing over the Tillamook Bar is easily accessible from Garibaldi as are numerous charter services. Salmon and halibut are among the most sought-after species as are perch and rockfish. Most anglers fish the bay from a boat for ocean-fresh salmon, some as big as 70 pounds. Salmon are caught April–June and again September–November. Sturgeon move into the bay in winter and spring.

Boat anglers troll for salmon and the occasional steelhead. Numerous fishing holes populate the bay, including the popular Ghost Hole by Hobsonville Point near Garibaldi. Bank anglers will find a lot of access along U.S. 101 on the north shore and along Bayocean Road on the south shore. The highway stretch from Bay City to Barview is most popular for lingcod, rockfish, and perch. Concentrate your efforts around the rocky shores or the jetty. The mouth of the Miami is a popular bank fishery for fall chinook and chum salmon. Further bank access can be found at the western end of Bayocean Road, where you will find a locked gate closed to vehicle traffic. Follow this road by foot or bike to the South Jetty.

Species: Spring and fall chinook, ocean and chum salmon, sturgeon, halibut, rockfish, lingcod, perch, and steelhead.

Facilities: Boats can be launched directly into the bay from public ramps in Garibaldi and Bay City. Parks Landing on the Kilchis River and Carnahan Park ramp and Hoquarten Slough on the Trask are good all good launches to troll into the bay. Another option is Memaloose Point at the Oyster House Hole on Bay Ocean Drive. Camping is available at Cape Lookout State Park on Tillamook Head and Barview County Park a few miles north of Garibaldi. Fishing and camping supplies, accommodations, and restaurants can be had in Tillamook and Garibaldi.

Directions: To reach the southern end of the bay from Tillamook, head west on 3rd St., then right on Bayocean Rd. heading toward Cape Meers. To reach the eastern shore of the bay, drive north on U.S. 101 out of Tillamook. The road skirts the bay past Garibaldi to the Barview County Park.

Contact: ODFW, Tillamook, 503/842-2741; Tillamook District Department of Forestry, 503/842-2545; Tillamook Chamber of Commerce, 503/842-7225; Cape Lookout State Park, 503/842-4981; The Guide Shop, 503/842-3474; Tillamook Sporting Goods, 503/842-4334; Lyster's Bait and Tackle, 603/322-3342; Old Mill Marina Resort, 503/322-0324; Garibaldi Marina, 800/383-3828; Wilson River RV Park, 503/842-2750; Garibaldi Charters, 800/900-4665; Dan Christopher, 503/491-9793, www.dan@qualityfishingadventures.com; Chris Vertopoulos 503/349-1377, www.northwestanglingexperience.com.

17 CAPE MEARES LAKE
west of Tillamook

Map 1.2, page 80

Just down the road from Cape Lookout State Park, Cape Meares Lake is the largest lake in Tillamook County. The lake covers 90 acres and averages a depth of only 10 feet. Open year-round, it's best fished in the spring and fall when the aquatic vegetation is not so dense because of summer heat. Best access is along the road or out on the dike on the east shore. Boating is allowed but is better suited to ca-

noes and light watercraft. Winds and severe weather from its proximity to the ocean can pose a problem for boaters. The lake holds stocked trout, largemouth bass, brown bullhead catfish, and bluegill; occasionally the ODFW plants hatchery steelhead. Targeting bass and bluegill around structure and the lake edge can be productive. In summer, search out the deepest waters for trout. Small feathered spinners, bass poppers, streamer flies, and bait such as worms and sand shrimp all work in this lake.

Species: Hatchery trout, largemouth bass, brown bullhead catfish, and bluegill, hatchery steelhead.

Facilities: There is a free public boat ramp at the large gravel parking lot on Bayocean Rd. Camping is available at Cape Lookout State Park. Quick access to ocean beaches on scenic Tillamook Head can make for a nice diversion. Supplies, restaurants, and accommodations can be found in Tillamook.

Directions: From Tillamook head west on 3rd St., then right on Bayocean Rd. Follow Bayocean Rd. approximately nine miles until you see the lake on your right. Park near the lake at the large gravel area. Cape Lookout State Park is 10 miles south on Bayocean Rd.

Contact: ODFW in Tillamook, 503/842-2741; Tillamook District Department of Forestry, 503/842-2545; Tillamook Chamber of Commerce, 503/842-7225; Cape Lookout State Park, 503/842-4981; The Guide Shop, 503/842-3474; Wilson River RV Park, 503/842-2750; Tillamook Sporting Goods, 503/842-4334.

18 WILSON RIVER
east of Tillamook

Map 1.2, page 80   **BEST**

The Wilson River is a popular fishery because of its close proximity to Portland; you can drive only 70 miles and wet a line on one of Oregon's most productive and scenic steelhead streams. The Wilson is popular for other good reasons. An easily accessible boater's river, the bank access is good except in the lowermost regions. Spring chinook arrive in the river April–July with the peak run in late June. Fall chinook begin their run in September and last until December, with peak runs in November.

The Wilson draws most of its crowds for summer and winter hatchery and wild steelhead. Especially popular with fly anglers, the river with its long runs is conducive to popular methods of greased line and spey methods of fishing. Hatchery winter steelhead are in the river system November–March with peak runs in December. Wild winter steelhead appear in January and fish well until March. Summer steelhead enter the river in May and last through August. The Wilson as well as the Trask is known for holding fishable numbers of steelhead throughout the year.

Trout anglers can expect a lot of opportunities to catch resident and sea-run cutthroat. The aggressive sea-run cutthroats return from the ocean in full regalia July–August. Start in the tidewater at the beginning of the month and look to the upper river later in the season. Anglers are often surprised to find these fish as far as 20 miles from the ocean. A small resident trout population is available all year and provides terrific summer fishing in a rainforest setting.

Boat access is excellent with many good drifts, some technical, some easy. Boat anglers should look for river levels 4.5–6 feet. The lowest drift is from tidewater to Sollie Smith Bridge off Wilson River Loop Road and is good for drift and powerboats. Take the time to understand the tides and gravel bars if you go. Bank access is poor in this area.

Higher up in the river there are several good floats. The Mill's Bridge (The Guide Shop) to Sollie Smith Bridge is the most popular and easiest float on the river. If you don't feel like making the entire six-mile float there is a take-out at Donaldson Bar off Donaldson Road. Most of the fish are found in this stretch because hatchery plantings occur here and the fish don't go any higher in the river. Good

bank access is along most of Highway 6, especially at the Guard Rail Hole, one mile below Mills Bridge around milepost 5. Siskyville to Mills Bridge, Vanderzanden to Siskyville, and the extreme upper river are all technical water with steep boat slides and large boulders and should be attempted only by experienced boaters. Some good water exists in these areas and there is good bank access, often involving hikes into steep canyons off Highway 6.

Species: Summer and winter hatchery and wild steelhead, fall chinook, spring chinook, resident and sea-run cutthroat.

Facilities: Boats can be launched at Sollie Bridge Rd., Donaldson Bar, Mills Bridge, Siskyville Boat Slide, and Vanderzanden Boat Slide. Camping is available along Hwy. 6 at Keening Campground and Wilson River Campground. Fishing and camping supplies, shuttle service, and accommodations are available in Tillamook and at The Guide Shop.

Directions: From Tillamook drive south on U.S. 101 to the Wilson River Hwy. (Hwy. 6). After a few miles you will begin to see the river to the north. Look for The Guide Shop and Mills Bridge soon after. Highway 6 continues to follow the river for 39 miles.

Contact: ODFW, Tillamook, 503/842-2741; Tillamook District Department of Forestry, 503/842-2545; Tillamook Chamber of Commerce, 503/842-7225; Cape Lookout State Park, 503/842-4981; The Guide Shop, 503/842-3474; Wilson River RV Park, 503/842-2750; Tillamook Sporting Goods, 503/842-4334; Dan Christopher, 503/491-9793, www.dan@qualityfishingadventures. com; Chris Vertopoulos 503/349-1377, www. northwestanglingexperience.com.

🔢 TILLAMOOK RIVER
south of Tillamook

Map 1.2, page 80

The Tillamook River is one of five rivers that drains into Tillamook Bay. It forms in the mountains between U.S. 101 and the Pacific Ocean and flows south to the bay near the mouth of the Trask River. Most of the river, short of its formation in the mountains, flows through farmlands and is virtually inaccessible. Given its proximity to numerous other great salmon and steelhead rivers, the Tillamook would not be on my top 10 list for rivers to fish. Primarily a boating and tidewater fishery for salmon, winter steelhead, and sea-run cutthroat, most catches occur below the confluence of the Tillamook River and Trask River. The only reasonable fishing access occurs at the mouth of the river on a few public lands or by boat from the several boat launches.

Fall chinook come into tidewater in late September and October. Not all the salmon caught here are destined for the Tillamook River. Many salmon hold over in its tidewater before moving into other tributaries such as the Trask or Wilson River. Winter wild steelhead are caught December–January. Coho are in the river October–November, but the river is closed to coho angling. Sea-run cutthroat are plentiful July–September. Sturgeon are available in tidewater but in limited numbers.

Species: Fall chinook, sturgeon, winter steelhead, and sea-run cutthroat.

Facilities: Boaters have several options, beginning at the Carnahan Park ramp on the Trask River and Memaloose Point ramp below the mouth of the Tillamook River. Both boat put-ins require you to troll up into the mouth of the river. Another boat ramp can be found where Netarts Hwy. crosses the river at the Burton Frasier ramp. A good city map will help to navigate the streets of Tillamook. Anglers can fish the bank at Tillamook Tidewater, a public-access park with a disabled-friendly pier and boardwalk. More bank access is available along Fraser Rd. between Burton Frasier Bridge ramp and Tillamook tidewater. You can find supplies and accommodations in Tillamook. Cape Lookout State Park provides the most convenient camping. A visit to the Tillamook Cheese Factory is a nice and tasty diversion.

Directions: From Tillamook, drive west on the Netarts Hwy. headed toward Cape Lookout State Park. The highway crosses the river at the Burton Frasier ramp. Turn north on Bayocean Rd. to get to Memaloose Point boat ramp (Oyster House Hole).

Contact: ODFW, Tillamook, 503/842-2741; Tillamook District Department of Forestry, 503/842-2545; Tillamook Chamber of Commerce, 503/842-7225; Cape Lookout State Park, 503/842-4981; The Guide Shop, 503/842-3474; Wilson River RV Park, 503/842-2750; Tillamook Sporting Goods, 503/842-4334. Dan Christopher, 503/491-9793, www.dan@qualityfishingadventures. com; Chris Vertopoulos 503/349-1377, www. northwestanglingexperience.com.

20 TRASK RIVER
east of Tillamook

Map 1.2, page 80

The Trask is an especially scenic river flowing more than 50 miles until it empties into Tillamook Bay just south of town. Access is limited in the lower reaches below Loren's Drift but is excellent in the upper river where it enters forestlands. With an average rainfall of more than 200 inches per year, the forests are lush, and you might be inclined to enjoy the scenery as well as the great fishing. The fish range quite far in this fertile system with steelhead and cutthroats available in the underfished upper reaches of the North and South forks.

The river is divided into a few sections that will dictate your approach to this fishery. The lower river is a boater's river with little to no bank access except at the Loren's Drift boat ramp. Good water is available here both upriver and down. In most years you will need waders to move up and down the river to avoid walking on private lands. Fish the runs and tail-outs with flies such as black or purple Egg Sucking Leeches or conventional gear such as spinners and bobbers with cured roe. Lower water conditions will require smaller lures so as not to spook fish.

Above Loren's is the fish hatchery and

the most accessible water on the river all the way into the Tillamook State Forest. From the hatchery, move up- or downstream and tackle some great water for all species of fish. A hiking trail provides good access upriver. Downriver is a scramble over rocks and ledges and wading should be done with caution. This river is prone to high-water stages and can get deep, swift, and treacherous where it was safe to walk; avoid wading too far into the river during high-water months. It is illegal to fish within the hatchery boundaries, marked by yellow posts, during certain times of year. Both Loren's Drift and the hatchery are accessible via Chance Road on the south side of the river.

On the north side of the river along Trask River Road, access begins at Cedar Creek and continues among intermittent private properties to the Trask Park. Several popular fishing spots exist along this stretch as indicated by pullouts on the side of the road. A deep, steep canyon between Cedar Creek and the Dam Hole is composed of boulders and fast chutes. This section is fishable but not without some risk. Inspect this area carefully before taking the plunge. Just above the chutes across from Blue Ridge Creek, you will find the Dam Hole, recognized as a large pool below a narrow chute that prevents the fish from moving upriver until more water arrives. During high-water days, expect to see many local anglers here. Higher up into the river, Trask Park sits on the confluence of the South Fork and North Fork of the Trask and is your best access point for unlimited explorations and small-stream fishing. Once you feel the excitement of hooking a steelhead in these narrow waters you may never go back to the larger rivers. You can follow each fork by good roads and reach most of the water.

Winter steelhead are in the river December–April with peak runs in February and March. All steelhead are wild except for a few strays that come out of the Wilson River system. Average runs of summer steelhead may be caught May–October. As a general rule you can find steelhead year-round on the Trask. Fall chinook arrive in September and are available till November with peak months in October and November. Look for spring chinook April–June and later coho September–November. Only fin-clipped coho may be kept. Resident and sea-run cutthroat inhabit the river most of the year, with peak runs of sea-runs occurring in early summer and fall. During spawning season, you will get a front-row seat to the spawning ritual of salmon as they pass through riffles into large pools and migrate up streams no wider or deeper than a bathtub.

There are several good drifts for boaters, some of which are nontechnical, but the usual cautions will ensure a safe outing. The tidewater put-in is at the bridge by U.S. 101 with a take-out at 5th Street west of Tillamook. Higher upriver off Chance Road, you can put in at Loren's Drift and float to the U.S. 101 take-out. Cedar Creek to Loren's takes one past the fish hatchery water, but it is a more technical drift with rapids and boulders. The unofficial put-in at Cedar Creek is identifiable from a long boat slide down a rock hillside. Stone's Camp to Lower Peninsula or Last Chance is the uppermost drift and should be taken with caution. The water here is composed of swift runs and boulder-lined rapids. The water between Last Chance and Cedar Creek is unnavigable.

Species: Wild winter steelhead, fall chinook, spring chinook, coho, resident and sea-run cutthroat.

Facilities: Boat ramps are available at the U.S. 101 launch off Long Prairie Rd., Loren's Drift on Chance Rd., and Last Chance, Upper Peninsula, and Stone's Camp along Trask River Rd. Camping is available at Trask Park. Fishing and camping supplies, shuttle service, and accommodations are available in Tillamook.

Directions: From Tillamook drive east on Hwy. 6 to Trask River Rd. Trask River Rd. follows the north side of the river past the boat ramps and Trask Park. To get to the Trask fish hatchery, drive south on Trask River Rd., which turns into Long Prairie Rd., and turn east on Chance Rd. Follow this road to the end, where there is an anglers' parking lot above the hatchery. Watch for signs to Loren's Drift along Chance Rd.

Contact: ODFW, Tillamook, 503/842-2741; Tillamook District Department of Forestry, 503/842-2545; Tillamook Chamber of Commerce, 503/842-7225; Cape Lookout State Park, 503/842-4981; The Guide Shop, 503/842-3474; Wilson River RV Park, 503/842-2750; Tillamook Sporting Goods, 503/842-4334; Dan Christopher, 503/491-9793, www.dan@qualityfishingadventures.com; Chris Vertopoulos, 503/349-1377, www.northwestanglingexperience.com.

21 NETARTS BAY
southwest of Tillamook

Map 1.2, page 80

This bay provides little to no ocean access because the bar is shallow and generally covered by breakers. Of all the small tributaries that run into the bay, none hold fish; much of the bay is shallow with extensive mud flats exposed at low tide. Netarts Bay holds almost no interest to the angler except for some limited rockfish and perch in April and May. A small run of coho and chum salmon are known to inhabit the bay in fall, but angling is off-limits.

So why would you want to go to this little coastal community nestled in the Tillamook National Forest? Netarts is one of the five major bays on the Oregon Coast for crabbing and offers no fewer than five varieties of clams. The bay is very popular with sea kayakers and offers good crabbing even when other bays are blown out by heavy rains. Kids will love digging in the sand for clams or hauling in baskets of crab from the bay floor. September–November is the best time to try your hand at Dungeness and Redrock crab. Since there are no piers in the bay, you will need a boat to get to the best water. Check with the local moorage operators for rentals and infor-

mation about where to go for crabbing and clamming. Cockle, butter, gaper, little neck, and a few razor clams are available. Try the big flat off the spit at Cape Lookout State Park and the little flat on the north bay shore near the mouth. Both areas are easily accessible and provide an abundance of clams.

Species: Coho and chum salmon, rockfish, and perch.

Facilities: Netarts Bay RV Park and Marina offers boat ramps and rental boats and supplies for crabbing and clamming. Camping is close by at Cape Lookout State Park. Numerous scenic activities such as Cape Meares Lighthouse and Cape Meares State Park are also worth a side trip.

Directions: Netarts Bay is four miles southwest of Tillamook Bay near the small community of Oceanside, south of Cape Meares Lake. From U.S. 101 in Tillamook drive west on 3rd St. (Netarts Hwy.). Follow Netarts Hwy. for approximately 6.5 miles to Netarts.

Contact: ODFW, Tillamook, 503/842-2741; Tillamook District Department of Forestry, 503/842-2545; Tillamook Chamber of Commerce, 503/842-7225; Cape Lookout State Park, 503/842-4981; Cape Meares State Park, 800/551-6949; Netarts Bay RV Park and Marina, 503/842-7774; Tillamook Sporting Goods, 503/842-4334.

22 SAND LAKE
south of Tillamook

Map 1.2, page 80

Sand Lake is considered a tidal basin, formed at the mouth of Sand Creek. The bay hosts a few runs of anadromous fish, including fall and spring chinook, sea-run cutthroat and steelhead. Some surf perch can be caught on either side of the ocean inlet. Crabbing can be productive around the inlet and in the lake. Most of the fishing is accessible by boat and concentrated around the east side of the island. Fall chinook are available in November. Spring chinook can be caught April–May. A solid run of sea-run cutthroat are available July–August, but are catch-and-release only. Some steelhead are caught, but very few between February and March.

Bank anglers have access to the areas around the island, casting out into the bay with bait, spinners, or bobbers. Boaters have good access at the Whalen Island County Park, where the bridge crosses over to an island.

Species: Fall and spring chinook, sea-run cutthroat, steelhead, surf perch.

Facilities: Camping on the lake is available at West Winds, East Dunes, Sand Beach, and Whalen Island County Park. Fishing and camping supplies can be had in Pacific City and Hebo. Boat ramps exist at most of the campgrounds. Anglers and their families can find numerous recreational opportunities, including dune buggy–riding, boating, and bird-watching.

Directions: From Tillamook drive south on U.S. 101 and go west on Sand Lake Drive just north of Hemlock.

Contact: Siuslaw National Forest, 541/750-7000; Hebo Ranger District, 503/392-3161; Tillamook Chamber of Commerce, 503/842-7225; ODFW, Tillamook, 503/842-2741; Nestucca Valley Sporting Goods, 503/392-4269; Sand Lake Camping Reservation, 877/444-6777.

23 NESTUCCA RIVER
south of Tillamook

Map 1.2, page 80

Spanning close to 60 miles, the Nestucca originates in the densely forested Siuslaw National Forest and empties into the Nestucca Bay. This is a prize Oregon fishery mostly because of progressive fisheries management that has helped restore and build tremendous runs of steelhead, salmon, and sea-run and resident cutthroat trout. Current estimates by the Oregon Department of Fish and Wildlife claim that there are as many as 10,000 returning steelhead every year. The once-flailing cutthroat populations are showing up in record numbers, making this one of the best places on the Oregon coast to experience this aggressive fish. Most anglers fish from Blain downstream.

Boaters find the best fishing success pulling plugs, back-bouncing bait, drift fishing, and lures. Bank anglers find success drift fishing or float fishing with bait, corkies and yarn, and casting lures. Boating access is year-round, even in low-water months. This is good because steelhead are present most of the year. Winter steelhead season runs April–November with peak times December–January and again February–March. Summer steelhead make their strongest appearance April–October with peak runs in May and June and again in October. Spring chinook arrive May–July with a winter run appearing September–December. Sea-run cutthroat are present year-round but have peak seasons in April and May and again in August and October. Sea-runs are best fished with flies and bait. Flies should be brightly colored streamers.

Species: Fall and spring chinook, winter and summer steelhead, coho salmon, sea-run and resident cutthroats.

Facilities: The Nestucca is very boater-friendly with six drifts between the Fourth Bridge ramp and Woods ramp. Boats can be launched at First Bridge ramp, Bixby, Farmer Creek Wayside, Three Rivers, and Cloverdale. Several good campgrounds such as Rocky Bend, Alder Bend, Elk Bend, and Fan Creek line the remote upper stretches of the river. Shuttle service, supplies, and accommodations can be found in Beaver, Hebo, and Pacific City.

Directions: From Tillamook drive south on U.S. 101 for approximately 18 miles to Beaver. To get to the upper river and the First Bridge and Fourth Bridge boat ramps, drive east on Blaine Rd. out of Beaver. To get to the lower river, Hebo. and the remaining boat ramps, drive south out of Beaver on U.S. 101. Bixby, Farmer Creek Wayside, Three Rivers, and Cloverdale Boat ramps are all accessible off U.S. 101. Pacific City is approximately eight miles from Hebo.

Contact: Siuslaw National Forest, 541/750-

7000; Hebo Ranger District, 503/392-3161; Tillamook Chamber of Commerce, 503/842-7225; ODFW, Tillamook, 503/842-2741; Nestucca Valley Sporting Goods, 503/392-4269; Chris Vertopoulos, 503/349-1377, www.northwestanglingexperience.com.

24 THREE RIVERS

south of Hebo

Map 1.2, page 80

Three Rivers is a small but productive 14-mile tributary of the Nestucca River. It enters the Big Nestucca about a half mile north of Hebo near the junction of Highway 22 and U.S. 101. The river is managed primarily as a salmon and steelhead brood-stock stream and therefore is subject to more regulations than many other coastal streams. The Cedar Creek Hatchery is 1.5 miles upstream from Hebo. The river is closed from the hatchery weir to the mouth June 1–October 31. There is no boating on the river.

Seasonal fishing for resident cutthroat May–June and October is the best opportunity for fly anglers and those using light spinning gear; otherwise this is a popular traditional bait and spinner river. During the winter run of steelhead one can expect to encounter crowds concentrated at the mouth by the Three Rivers boat ramp. Popular public areas to fish are the mouth at Three Rivers boat ramp, the fish hatchery, and the upper reaches in the Siuslaw National Forest. Expect to encounter a lot of private property in the first few miles of river upstream from the mouth. Obey all No Trespassing signs or ask landowners for permission to cross private property.

Salmon and winter steelhead make their run as early as October. Fish for fall chinook November–March. Summer steelhead, which run during the closure of the lower river, are largely inaccessible because the hatchery weir blocks their movement into the upper river. Sea-run cutthroat are available in the fall but be prepared to compete with salmon and steelhead anglers. Some spring chinook enter the river May–June. Coho are present during the fall chinook run but angling for coho is illegal. The upper river is excellent habitat for trout, composed of gravelly river bottoms, boulders, and cut banks. Good access to this part of the river can be obtained along Highway 22. Anglers proficient at using fly and light spinning gear will have the best luck.

Species: Fall and spring chinook, summer and winter steelhead, resident and sea-run cutthroat.

Facilities: Three Rivers public boat launch is a gravel ramp with restrooms and parking. To get to the ramp, drive south of Hebo on U.S. 101 approximately two miles and look for the boat-ramp access road. Camping is available at Castle Rock Campground. Supplies and accommodations are available at Hebo and the nearby towns of Cloverdale and Pacific City south on U.S. 101.

Directions: From Hebo travel south on Hwy. 22 (Three Rivers Hwy.). Highway 22 will follow the river past the Cedar Creek Fish Hatchery and into the upper reaches. Look for roadside turnoffs indicating river access. Castle Rock Campground is five miles south of Hebo on Hwy. 22.

Contact: ODFW, Tillamook, 503/842-2741; Cedar Creek Hatchery, 503/392-3485; Chris Vertopoulos, 503/349-1377, www.northwestanglingexperience.com.

25 NESTUCCA BAY

south of Tillamook

Map 1.2, page 80

Formed by the Big Nestucca to the north and the Little Nestucca to the south, this productive fishery lies just 20 miles south of Tillamook. Some bank access is available but this is primarily a boat fishery and caution should be used the closer one gets to the tidal waters at the mouth. Some species of fish such as spring chinook and steelhead move through the bay very fast and are more readily caught in the upper tidal sections or in the rivers. An interesting angling opportunity exists north of Pacific City at Cape Kiwanda. A small dory fleet launches from the beach through the breakers and will take anglers 6–7 miles into open ocean for salmon, lingcod, and halibut. A trip to Cape Kiwanda is worth the trip if for no other reason than to watch the dories crash through the breakers.

Most anglers fishing the bay target the fall chinook available August–June. For best results try the upper tidewater, at the Airport Hole across from the airport at Pacific City, and Mid-Bay just north of the Fisher Landing boat ramp. Lower bay anglers have good luck at Cannery Hill at the mouth of the Little Nestucca and up into the Little Nestucca Channel. The mouth of the bay is productive for salmon as well as perch and greenling, but extreme caution should be used when approaching the bar. Spring chinook enter the bay May–June. Try the upper tidewater in fall for sea-run cutthroat.

Bank anglers have several good options in both the north and south bay. The mouth is accessible via a hiking trail through Bob Straub State Park. The Little Nestucca boat ramp is also good for anglers using bobbers and bait. Farther north try the areas around the boat ramp at Fisher Landing and Pacific City boat ramp. There is a nice county park with good bank access to the upper tidewater just south of Woods.

Species: Fall and spring chinook, lingcod, halibut, perch, greenling, steelhead, and sea-run cutthroat.

Facilities: Boaters have several options for access to the bay. At the northern end there are three boat ramps: Nestucca ramp off Brooten Rd., Pacific City ramp on the west shore, and Fisher Landing, also off Brooten Rd. To the south you can drop a boat in at the Little Nestucca ramp on U.S. 101 off Meda Loop Rd. Camping is available at Cape Kiwanda RV Park and Market Place and Webb County Park, both in Pacific City. Beach access, supplies, and accommodations are available in Pacific City and Dolph.

Directions: From Tillamook drive south on

U.S. 101 27 miles and follow the signs to Pacific City.

Contact: ODFW, Tillamook, 503/842-2741; Siuslaw National Forest, 541/750-7000; Hebo Ranger District, 503/392-3161; Cape Kiwanda RV Park and Market Place, 503/965-6230; Nestucca Valley Sporting Goods, 503/392-4269; Pacific City Inn, 503/956-6464.

26 LITTLE NESTUCCA RIVER
east of Pacific City

Map 1.2, page 80

This small but accessible river is well known for its scenic beauty, run of wild winter steelhead, and cutthroat trout. It originates in the forests above Dolph, east of Pacific City, and flows into the southern end of Nestucca Bay. The Little Nestucca Highway out of Dolph follows the river closely through scenic forestlands and affords anglers excellent access. Much of this river's popularity is due to the unlimited bank access along most of this highway. River management has phased out the hatchery run of steelhead in recent years, reducing the numbers of available fish. Because all wild fish must be released unharmed, this fishery is a catch-and-release river. Fall chinook arrive with the rains in October, but current regulations prohibit angling. Peak runs of winter steelhead occur in December and January but are available through March. Good numbers of wild resident and sea-run cutthroat can make for fun light-tackle fishing on a hot summer day. The bridge at U.S. 101 is a popular access for bank and boat anglers.

Species: Wild winter steelhead, wild resident and sea-run cutthroat, fall chinook.

Facilities: There is a boat launch where U.S. 101 crosses the Little Nestucca River. Convenient camping is available in Pacific City at Cape Kiwanda RV Park. Remote camping is available on the main stem of the Nestucca River. Supplies and accommodations are available in nearby Dolph and Pacific City.

Directions: From Pacific City drive south on Brooten Rd. to U.S. 101. Turn south on U.S.

101 and drive one mile to Little Nestucca Hwy. Turn east and follow the river for nine miles to Dolph. Look for river access points along this road. To reach the boat ramp at the highway crossing, stay on U.S. 101 0.5 mile past the Little Nestucca Hwy. Look for the ramp on the southeast side of the bridge.

Contact: ODFW, Tillamook, 503/842-2741; Siuslaw National Forest, 541/750-7000; Hebo Ranger District, 503/392-3161; Cape Kiwanda RV Park and Market Place, 503/965-6230; Nestucca Valley Sporting Goods, 503/392-4269; Chris Vertopoulos, 503/349-1377, www.northwestanglingexperience.com.

27 NESKOWIN CREEK
south of Nestucca Bay
Map 1.2, page 80

Just north of Cascade Head Scenic Area sits the hamlet of Neskowin. Originally named by settlers as Slab Creek because of the amount of slab wood that drifted onto the beach from an early shipwreck, it hosts a small wild winter steelhead river known today as Neskowin Creek. Then-Postmaster General Sarah Page overheard a local Indian call the river Neskowin, meaning "Plenty of Fish." Promptly after her encounter with the Indian, the postmaster requested the name of the town and river be called by the Indian name, and so it came to be. Today, Neskowin is a quiet community that honors its namesake. As for the river, it still has plenty of fish, but to protect it, strict regulations have been in effect for some time. In fact, the river is open only during November for the winter steelhead run. If you do plan to fish this river, be forewarned; access is very limited because of private lands. The only access points are at the mouth down the beach from the Neskowin Beach State Wayside and upriver via Slab Creek Road. If you fish this creek, be sure to check regulations for current closings and restrictions.

Species: Winter steelhead.

Facilities: There is no boating on this creek. A Forest Service campground lies five miles

south of Neskowin. Supplies can be bought in Neskowin.

Directions: From Nestucca Bay drive south four miles on U.S. 101. The highway follows the river for about a mile. Slab Creek Rd. just south of Neskowin follows the river just short of its headwaters.

Contact: Neskowin Creek RV Campground, 503/392-3082; Nestucca Country Sporting Goods, 503/965-6410; Eagle Charter, 503/965-2202; Camper Cove RV Park, 503/398-5334; Neskowin Beach State Recreation Site, 800/551-6949.

28 SALMON RIVER
north of Lincoln City
Map 1.2, page 80

One of two Salmon Rivers in Oregon, this short coastal stream of 24 miles intersects with the ocean just north of Lincoln City. The fish hatchery above Otis releases thousands of fall chinook and coho into the river each year, making this a popular fishery during the winter. With shallow riffles created by long gravel bars, this river is known for the best fishing after a few days of hard rain, when the flow allows fish to migrate upriver. Get to the river early after a good rain; this is one of the faster rivers on the north coast to clear after a storm.

The Salmon offers strong runs of winter steelhead, fall chinook, coho, and resident and sea-run cutthroat. Fishing access is limited with most occurring at the hatchery above Otis, along Highway 18 and at the access point by U.S. 101 downriver. Sea-run cutthroat enter the river in late July. Chinook arrive in fishable numbers in August, followed by coho. Peak fishing times for both species are in September and October. Steelhead are available December–March and are primarily of wild stock.

Bank anglers may want to bypass the lower river and head upriver on the North Bank Road to the bridge at Rose Lodge or the state lands in the Van Duzer Corridor. Here you will find small water with the potential for catching cutthroat in the summer and wild steelhead in the winter.

Species: Winter steelhead, fall chinook, coho, resident and sea-run cutthroat.

Facilities: Boats can be launched at the ramp at Three Rocks Rd. below the U.S. 101 Hwy. Bridge and motored upriver to a few popular fishing holes. Boaters usually stay within a mile stretch of the ramp. Buy supplies at tackle shops at the lower river and at several gas stations that line Hwy. 18. There are two RV and tent riverside camping areas: Lincoln City Resort on Hwy. 18, and higher upriver at Salmon River Evergreen Park near Rose Creek Lodge. Supplies are available in Otis.

Directions: From Lincoln City drive eight miles north on U.S. 101 to Otis. A 0.5 mile past the Otis turnoff on U.S. 101 lies the boat ramp. The North Bank Rd. from Otis will take you upriver to public access points. State Hwy. 18 out of Otis will take you higher up into the river and more fishing access.

Contact: Lincoln City Chamber of Commerce, 541/994-3070; Siletz Bay Lodge, 541/996-6111; Coyote Rock Resort and RV Park, 541/996-6824; Lincoln City Resort, 541/994-3646; Salmon River Evergreen Park, 541/994-3116; Bi-Mart, 541/994-3194; K&L Bait and Tackle, 541/994-9798.

29 DEVIL'S LAKE
south of Lincoln City
Map 1.3, page 81

Anglers beware when fishing this lore-filled lake, which, according to Indian legend, is occupied by a giant fish or marine monster and, "on occasion," dines on hapless anglers. Such legends make one stop and think what truth must lurk behind the myth. As it happens, no anglers in recent years have been reported eaten or otherwise lost on the lake, but no one's actually sure what "occasionally" means. It's not a huge attraction for most anglers, but it's a nice place to spend a few days relaxing in the campground and occasionally wetting

a line for whatever lurks in its depths. The lake is not small, covering about 700 acres. Its proximity to Lincoln City makes this a popular place for day-trippers and easygoing anglers. Consider this a great place for families with kids wanting easy fishing for legal-size trout and several warm-water species. Trout holdovers from previous years can reach 18–20 inches, possibly making them the best sport fish in the lake. Warm-water species include largemouth bass, black crappie, yellow perch, and channel catfish.

Species: Hatchery trout, largemouth bass, black crappie, yellow perch, and channel catfish.

Facilities: Devil's Lake State Park has a campground and a free boat launch. Several free boat ramps dot the lake. Camping and supplies are available at the lake and in nearby Lincoln City.

Directions: From Lincoln City drive north on U.S. 101 approximately two miles to Devil's Lake State Park.

Contact: Lincoln City Chamber of Commerce, 541/994-3070; Siletz Bay Lodge, 541/996-6111; Coyote Rock Resort and RV Park, 541/996-6824; Bi-Mart, 541/994-3194; K&L Bait and Tackle, 541/994-9798.

30 DRIFT CREEK
south of Lincoln City
Map 1.3, page 81

One of the great assets of the Oregon Coast is remote rivers in rainforest settings that beckon anglers wishing for solitude. Drift Creek is one such river and offers the adventurous angler the opportunity to catch big fish in a remote setting. The Drift Creek watershed contains one of the largest remaining stands of old-growth forest in the Coast Range. Here giant Douglas fir and western hemlock have been growing for hundreds of years, reaching heights of 200 feet or more, especially in the northern part of the area. Drift Creek enters the Siletz Bay at Cutler City after an 18-mile run out of the coastal range. Managed for a wild fish population, stocking was discontinued several years ago, making this a catch-and-release stream for all wild fish. The occasional hatchery fish can still be caught, but not for long.

Wild winter steelhead arrive January–March. Fall chinook make a strong showing in October and November. Wild cutthroat can be caught in most of the river with the best fishing in summer. Drift Creek is a bank fishery. Reach the lower river along Drift Creek Road and the upper river along logging roads and Drift Creek Trail. Most of the access in the first eight miles of road requires hiking into the river. Two camps give good access to the river. Drift Creek Camp offers good hike-in access both up- and downstream. Shooner Creek is the second camp and offers equally good access. A good Forest Service map will help you navigate the area.

Species: Wild winter steelhead, fall chinook, wild cutthroat.

Facilities: Two campsites are available on the river at Drift Creek Camp, and at Schooner Creek. Additional camping is available nearby at Devil's Lake State Park, 15 miles north on U.S. 101, and at Beverly Beach State Park, 15 miles south on U.S. 101. Supplies and accommodations are available in Cutler City and Lincoln City.

Directions: From Lincoln City drive south on U.S. 101 three miles to Cutler City. There you will find Drift Creek Rd. leading upriver for about 10 miles.

Contact: Lincoln City Chamber of Commerce, 541/994-3070; K&L Bait and Tackle, 541/994-9798; Siletz Moorage, 541/996-3671; Siletz Bay Lodge, 541/996-6111; Coyote Rock RV Park, 541/996-6824; Devil's Lake State Park, 541/994-2002; Beverly Beach State Park, 541/265-9278.

31 SILETZ BAY

south of Lincoln City

Map 1.3, page 81

Visitors to Lincoln City might enjoy a short trip south to this bay for a chance to catch fall chinook, perch, clams, and crab and to breathe some ocean air. U.S. 101 follows Siletz Bay for about five miles from Taft to the Kernville Bridge at the mouth of the Siletz River. If chinook salmon is your game, then you will want to be in the bay early August–September. Two areas are particularly good—the area around the bridge at Kernville and the banks between Taft and the jaws of the bay. Because much of the bay has been silted in, the best fishing happens at the extreme ends. Feathered spinners, Kwikfish lures, and bait such as sand shrimp are all popular fishing methods.

In spring and early summer the Siletz Bay attracts mainly perch anglers. Perch as big as three pounds are known to inhabit the areas around Kernville Bridge and the mouth of the Siletz River. Surf casters have excellent chances to catch redtail perch from the local beaches in Taft during low tides. When fishing the beaches look for areas where the beach drops off suddenly into deep water. Perch are best caught with sand shrimp, clam pieces, and kelp worms.

As if the dockside attractions, salmon fishing, and perch fishing were not enough, you can also catch crab from the local public docks and marinas around the bay and search for soft shell clams in the tidal flats between Cutler City and Kernville during low tides. Crabbing is best September–October and you can rent crab bait and traps from any number of marinas on the bay.

Species: Fall chinook, perch, surf perch.

Facilities: For boaters, Siletz Moorage, a fee ramp at the mouth of Siletz River, will be your best starting point. Other ramps and boat rentals are available along U.S. 101 as it parallels the bay. Boat moorages, boat rentals, fishing supplies, accommodations, and RV parks are available in Taft and Cutler City. The nearest camping is at Devil's Lake State Park, a 15-minute drive north on U.S. 101, or Beverly Beach State Park, south on U.S. 101.

Directions: From Lincoln City drive south on U.S. 101 2.5 miles to Taft. Both Cutler City and Kernville lie to the south on U.S. 101 another couple of miles.

Contact: Lincoln City Chamber of Commerce, 541/994-3070; K&L Bait and Tackle, 541/994-9798; Siletz Moorage, 541/996-3671; Siletz Bay Lodge, 541/996-6111; Coyote Rock RV Park, 541/996-6824; Devil's Lake State Park, 541/994-2002; Beverly Beach State Park, 541/265-9278.

32 DEPOE BAY
south of Lincoln City
Map 1.3, page 81

Considered the safest harbor on the west coast, Depoe Bay sits halfway between the coastal cities of Lincoln City and Newport. The most popular attractions for anybody visiting the bay exist right along U.S. 101, where you can park and watch the waves as they sweep into the shores seemingly right under your feet, or marvel as boats navigate the narrowest channel on the west coast on their way into the ocean. Depoe Bay has many attractions other than fishing, but the principal interest to anglers is the access it provides to open-ocean fishing. Charter companies and commercial fishing outfits abound in this small community. It has been estimated that 40,000–50,000 trips are made from Depoe Bay each year, and their catch rates per angler are the highest on the coast. One can easily book a charter trip on short notice June–October for any length of time, from a two-hour tour to a full-day excursion. Ocean anglers pursue many species, including salmon, halibut, lingcod, black sea bass, cabezon, kelp greenling, sea trout, rockfish, and striped perch. Catches are not guaranteed when hiring a charter, but all the companies have a very good reputation for high catch rates. Dress warmly and bring rain gear for all charter trips.

The shore angler has good access to both the bay and surrounding coastal areas. Nearby Pirate Cove, Whale Cove, Boiler Bay, and Cape Foulweather provide an excellent shoreline reef fishery. Consult with local tackle shops for the approaches to these areas.

Species: Salmon, halibut, lingcod, black sea bass, cabezon, kelp greenling, sea trout, rockfish, and striped perch.

Facilities: The south side of the bay has a good public boat ramp for those wishing to try the bay on their own. The nearest camping is in Devil's Lake State Park (13 miles north of Depoe Bay on U.S. 101) or Beverly Beach State Park (7 miles south on U.S. 101). Supplies, charter services, and accommodations are available in Depot Bay.

Directions: From Lincoln City drive south on U.S. 101 for 12 miles.

Contact: Lincoln City Chamber of Commerce, 541/994-3070; Devil's Lake State Park, 541/994-2002; Beverly Beach State Park, 541/265-9278; K&L Bait and Tackle, 541/994-9798; Tradewinds Charters, 800/445-8730; Black Rocket Charters, 503/366-0212.

33 SILETZ RIVER
south of Lincoln City
Map 1.3, page 81

The Siletz has one of the longest estuaries on the north coast, stretching 17 miles from bay to reach of tide. The entire river is approximately 80 miles long, stretching from the coastal rainforests in the Siuslaw National Forest to Siletz Bay. Unlike in most coastal rivers, the majority of the boating and fishing takes place in the upper reaches of the river, between Moonshine Park at milepost 53 and Morgan Park at milepost 25. There are four ramps between these two points, giving you the option of long or short drifts. The Siletz also features a section of fly-only water on the North Fork at the confluence with the South Fork and the Stott Mountain Bridge. The Siletz has the wild and scenic beauty one comes to expect of coastal streams but without the all-too-common ocean weather because of its inland location. Because the river muddies fast during a storm or runoff, this is one river where it pays to check flows before your outing. Look for river levels 4–6 feet for optimal conditions. One thing you can expect on this river is a lot of anglers. With 80 percent of the returning fish of hatchery stock, this is a meat fishery.

The Siletz has the only run of wild summer steelhead on the north coast. The predominant species are winter and summer steelhead, fall chinook, coho, and sea-run cutthroat. Hatchery steelhead are released between Moonshine Park and the Steel Bridge at milepost 57, an area that receives a lot of pressure for obvious reasons. Winter steelhead are in the river November–March with peak runs in February and March. Summer steelhead enter the river in May with peaks in June and early July, with a second opportunity at the summer run August–October. Some steelhead are always present in the river. Sea-run cutthroat move into tidewater in March and fish well into fall. Fall chinook and coho enter the bay July–August and are targeted in the lower 10 miles of tidewater from Kernville to Echo Creek.

Good bank access is available along most of the river: Moonshine Park and the gorge area above, Ojalla Bridge, and the North Fork fly-only water. The area above Moonshine is privately owned and subject to closure, so check the sign before proceeding. It is always a good idea to call the Georgia-Pacific land-use line. Both the North and South forks are notorious for car break-ins so don't leave any valuables for would-be thieves. This is a boater's river whether you use a drift boat or outboard. All boating is accessible from a single highway that traverses the entire river's length. No fewer than five public and private boat ramps are in the tidewater section between the bay and the reach of tide.

Species: Hatchery winter and summer steelhead, fall chinook, coho, sea-run cutthroat.

Facilities: Boat ramps from the bay to reach of tide are Siletz Moorage, Coyote Rock, Chinook Bend, Sportsman's Landing, and Storm Landing. The upper river includes six boat ramps, all of which are moderate to easy floats: Morgan Park, Ojalla Park, Mill Park, Hee Hee Illahee, Sam Creek, and Moonshine Park. The launch at Ojalla Park is a long slide and not

recommended as a take-out. It is advisable to scout all boat ramps before dedicating yourself to the drift. Nothing could be worse than arriving at the take-out and discovering it's not possible to reach. Camping is available on the Siletz at A. W. Jack Morgan Memorial Park, Devil's Lake State Park, and Beverly Beach State Park. Supplies and accommodations are available in Lincoln City, Culter City, Kernville, and Siletz.

Directions: From Lincoln City drive south on U.S. 101 to Kernville past Culter City. Highway 229 follows the north bank of the river into its uppermost reaches. Immonen Rd. follows the south bank.

Contact: Lincoln City Chamber of Commerce, 541/994-3070; Siletz Moorage, 541/996-3671; Siletz Bay Lodge, 541/996-6111; Coyote Rock RV Park, 541/996-6824; Devil's Lake State Park, 541/994-2002; Beverly Beach State Park, 541/265-9278; Bi-Mart, 541/994-3194; K&L Bait and Tackle, 541/994-9798.

34 YAQUINA BAY

in Newport

Map 1.3, page 81

Yaquina Bay is fed by the Yaquina River to the south. It's one of the more productive bays on the coast, and anglers catch everything from crab and bottom fish to salmon and sturgeon. Visitors can book ocean charters on short notice for any length of trip. Access to the open ocean is well provided for by a long jetty, which is known to be relatively safe for all craft. Ocean anglers can catch halibut, rockfish, lingcod, salmon, and the occasional tuna when the waters are warm enough to bring them closer to shore. Be sure to consult with local professionals or the Coast Guard before venturing into the ocean. Crabbing can be excellent year-round from the jetties to the public docks at South Beach. Crab nets and bait can be rented from several tackle shops in South Beach. The best salmon fishing in the bay is September–early November. The sturgeon fishery begins in January and goes through May in the best years. Bank anglers can fish from either of the two jetties for cabezon, striped perch, rockfish, and greenling. Perch fishing can be had at the Gas Plant dock and surrounding areas on the north shore.

Species: Winter steelhead, spring and fall chinook, coho, ocean salmon, halibut, bottom fish, lingcod, sturgeon, sea-run cutthroat, rockfish, tuna, cabezon, striped perch, and greenling.

Facilities: Boats can be launched for a fee at Newport Marina ($6) and Sawyer's Landing ($10–22 for a hoist, depending on boat size). Camping can be had at South Beach State Park or on the Yaquina River at Elk City Park. Supplies, accommodations, and RV parks are available in Newport and Toledo. Yaquina Bay sits in the coastal community of Newport, arguably one of the more cultured towns on the Oregon coast. In addition to great fishing, Newport offers numerous attractions such as the Newport Aquarium, the Newport Maria boardwalk, Moe's Restraints, the Sylvia Beach and Nybeach Hotels, and the performing arts center. Nybeach, a small community within a community, contains a small cluster of artists' galleries, coffee shops, antiquarian book stores, and good beach access.

Directions: Newport Marina is located just east of the south end of the Hwy. 101 bridge in Newport; Sawyer's Landing is on the north side of the bay; from the north end of the 101 bridge, follow Yaquina Bay Rd. east for four miles.

Contact: Newport Chamber of Commerce, 541/265-8801; Newport Marina, 541/867-3321; Sawyer's Landing, 541/265-3907; Harbor Village RV Park, 541/265-5088; Bittler Brothers, 541/265-7192; England Marine, 541/265-9275.

35 YAQUINA RIVER
east of Newport

Map 1.3, page 81

This is a medium-size river that enters Yaquina Bay south of Newport. The majority of fishing takes place in the bay and tidewater for chinook, but a limited number of anglers target steelhead and salmon up to the deadline at Eddyville.

Several good tributaries are accessible on the upper river around Elk City. Big Elk and Little Elk Creeks receive sustainable numbers of returning steelhead, chinook, and sea-run trout in the fall. The area is also known for its population of resident catch-and-release trout. Anglers wishing for some solitude and scenic wilderness might enjoy one of these tributaries; both are lined with good roads that provide plenty of access. Big Elk Creek, accessible from Elk City, has returning steelhead in December and January, fall chinook in October. A good place to begin fishing for trout is at the confluence of Big Elk Creek and the Yaquina River. Little Elk Creek is accessible from Eddyville, a few miles upriver from Elk City. The creek is closed to all angling except trout, but it provides ample access and sport for those so inclined.

Yaquina River chinook and coho move into the river from the bay in October and November. Winter steelhead can be caught in the river and tributaries December–March. Hatchery steelhead arrive in December and January followed by the wild fish in February and March. Target sea-run cutthroat from spring until fall. Bank access along most of the river is adequate. Look for turnoffs with paths leading to the river. Boat ramps may provide the best access, particularly at Elk City dock and ramp at the confluence of the Yaquina and Big Elk Creek. Anglers wishing to boat the river have a couple of options on the river at Cannon Park or Elk City dock and ramp. Drifts are easy and can be accomplished even by novice boaters. The lower river, closer to the bay, is accessible at Sawyers Moorage, River Bend Moorage, and Toledo boat ramp. These lower ramps will enable you to fish the tidal waters.

Species: Winter steelhead, spring and fall chinook, coho, sea-run cutthroat.

Facilities: Boats can be launched at Cannon Park, Elk City dock and ramp, Sawyer's Landing, River Bend Moorage, and Toledo boat ramp. Camping can be had at South Beach State Park or on the river at Elk City Park. Supplies, accommodations, and RV parks are available in Newport and Toledo.

Directions: From Newport, follow Hwy. 20 east for six miles to Toledo. Once in Toledo, you have two options. To access the lower river, turn south on Main St. and follow it to Butler Bridge. Cross that bridge and turn east on Hwy. 539 (Elk City Rd.), following the south bank of the river for 14 miles and passing through Elk City and Pioneer before intersecting Hwy. 20 again. To head straight for the upper river, stay on Hwy. 20 in Toledo and follow it eight miles east to Chitwood, where it rejoins the river. From Chitwood, Hwy. 20 follows the river for fives miles to Eddyville; from there you can follow Hwy. 180 further upstream.

Contact: Newport Chamber of Commerce, 541/265-8801; Sawyer's Landing, 541/265-3907; Harbor Village RV Park, 541/265-5508; Bittler Brothers, 541/265-7192; England Marine, 541/265-9275; Toledo Chamber of Commerce, 541/336-3183.

36 ALSEA BAY
south of Newport

Map 1.3, page 81

Alsea Bay sits near Waldport and is fed by the popular Alsea River system. Given its calm waters and great access via moorages and boat ramps, it's no wonder this is such a popular bay, particularly with novice salmon anglers and their families. There are seven ramps total and, with the exception of the Port of Alsea, all require a fee for access. Because of still waters, a boat with a motor is a must for all but the most determined. As for fishing, very few anglers find it necessary to travel very far beyond the launches for good catches. In fact, a majority of the fish are caught just off the docks, well within the reach of facilities.

The salmon season runs mid-August–October. The best fishing is in the lower main channel and at the mouth of the Alsea River.

The public docks in Waldport will be your best starting point for midchannel and King Silver boat ramp will get you to the mouth. Spring chinook and coho are present at certain times of the year but angling is prohibited. Perch anglers will have the best opportunities from the Highway 101 bridge to the public docks in Waldport and at Old Bridge Flats across the bay on the north shore. Steelhead are caught only rarely in the bay. A better bet is sea-run cutthroat. Try brightly colored streamers and lures fished in slack water and around structures. Bank anglers can find good access at the lower south-side bay flats for salmon and perch and at the secondary channel by Yaquina John Point and the public docks. Alsea Bay also offers opportunities for good crabbing and clamming. Check with local tackle shops for the best locations.

Species: Winter and summer steelhead, spring and fall chinook, coho, sea-run cutthroat, perch.

Facilities: Boats can be launched in the bay at the Port of Alsea or McKinley's Marina. Farther up into the reach of tide along Hwy. 34, boats can be launched for a fee at King Silver, Drift Creek Landing, Fishin Hole Trailer Park, Oakland's Marina, Happy Landing, Taylor's Landing, and Kozy Kove. Taylor's Landing provides camping. Further camping can be found upriver at Blackberry Park and Riveredge Group. Supplies, accommodations, and RV parks can be found in Waldport.

Directions: From Newport drive south on U.S. 101 15 miles to Waldport.

Contact: Waldport Chamber of Commerce, 541/563-2133; Waldport Ranger District, 541/563-3211; Jess's Bait and Tackle, 541/563-7060; Waldport True Value, 541/563-3199; Oakland Fish Camp, 541/563-5865.

37 ALSEA RIVER
east of Waldport

Map 1.3, page 81

The Alsea has a very loyal following of anglers—and for good reasons. Originating in the Coast Range west of Corvallis, the river attracts many midvalley anglers because of its close proximity and excellent fly angling in even the highest sections of the river on the South and North forks. After a 55-mile run, the Alsea enters the Alsea Bay near Waldport. The Alsea used to be a legendary producer of sea-run cutthroat but their numbers have declined in recent years. Still, there are plenty of resident trout and an improving population of sea-runs since it has become a catch-and-release stream. Bait is not recommended for these fish. Resort to small lures and flies and release all fish without harm.

August–October finds most anglers in the tidewaters between Tidewater and Alsea Bay fishing for an early season of fall chinook. Trolling spinners and bait are traditional methods but drift and float fishing are also effective methods. This river is best fished from a boat and there are no fewer than nine boat ramps in this lower stretch, all of which provide excellent access. Once the fall rains arrive, anglers move into the river and fish from Alsea to Tidewater. Because this is an early run, fresh salmon can still be had even late in the season. Again, there are an astonishing number of boat ramps in the upper river, 12 to be exact, beginning with the highest at Mill Creek Park. Float this river with caution. Some runs can be difficult for novice boaters.

Winter steelhead are plentiful throughout the river system. They enter the river as early as November and finish in March. November–January the run is primarily hatchery stock. The wild fish show a little later in February and March. Drift fishing with bait or corkies is without a doubt the best technique, but traditional spinners, plugs, and jigs will also do the trick, especially in low-water conditions. The fly-only section on the North Fork is very popular, providing a lot of the classic drifts necessary for greased-line methods.

Sea-run cutthroat move into the river in July and are best targeted in the tidal reaches until fall, when they move into the upper river with the arrival of rains. Once in the upper river

the fish can be caught all the way up to Alsea. Pay special attention to the tributary mouths at Five Rivers and Fall Creek. Sea-runs are an aggressive fish and react best to brightly colored streamer flies and lures.

Because of the numerous boat ramps, bank angling is good along most of Highway 34 from Waldport at the mouth to the South Fork. The best access is in the upper river away from private property and above Tidewater. Two fish hatcheries on the North Fork and Fall Creek each have excellent access. The forks are accessible by Forest Service roads, which will require a map for the best navigation.

Species: Winter and summer steelhead, spring and fall chinook, coho, sea-run cutthroat.

Facilities: River boat launches from lowest in the river to highest include: King Silver, Fishin Hole Trailer Park, Oaklands Marina, Happy Landing, Taylor's Landing, Kozy Kove, Barclay's Slide Creek, Hellion Rapids, Quarry Hole, Mike Bower Wayside, Drift Creek Landing, Blackberry Park, Hellion Rapids, Blackberry Park, Launching Forest Camp, County Launch, Stony Point, Missouri Bend Recreation Site, Forest Camp, Salmonberry Boat Landing, Campbell Park, Mill Creek Park. A good number of campgrounds dot the river from Taylor's Landing to Cedar Creek, including Blackberry Campground and Riveredge Group. Supplies, accommodations, and RV parks are in Waldport.

Directions: From Waldport drive east on Hwy. 34, which follows the river up to the South Fork and into Corvallis.

Contact: Waldport Chamber of Commerce, 541/563-2133; Waldport Ranger District, 541/563-3211; Jess's Bait and Tackle, 541/563-7060; Waldport True Value, 541/563-3199; Oakland Fish Camp, 541/563-5865; River Run Oregon Guide Service, 541/752-8350.

38 YACHATS RIVER

south of Yachats

Map 1.3, page 81

Yachats is a small river that runs 15 miles from its source in the Siuslaw National Forest to the ocean south of Yachats. Given its proximity to the Alsea and other northern waters, this isn't the first choice for fishing in the area, but on the plus side, fishing pressure is low and if you can navigate the public lands, you might be surprised by the availability of fish in this secluded setting. The Yachats's main attractions are winter steelhead and resident and sea-run cutthroat. You can reach the river at several points, beginning at its mouth from the Yachats Ocean Road State Wayside, and farther up at the Yachats State Park, Yachats Boat Landing, the bridge crossing at U.S. 101, and upriver along Yachats River Road. Steelhead enter the river November–March. Sea-run cutthroat are available in fall. Resident cutthroat can be found in the entire river system.

Species: Chinook, winter steelhead, sea-run and resident cutthroat.

Facilities: Campgrounds can be found at state parks along north U.S. 101 at Beachside State Recreation Site and Tillicum Beach and south on U.S. 101 at Cape Perpetua, Rock Creek, and Lanham. Supplies and beach access can be found in Yachats. Yachats is a pleasant place to visit with several bookstores, artists' galleries, coffee shops, and a fly-fishing shop.

Directions: From Yachats drive south about one mile on U.S. 101 to Yachats River Rd. Follow the river looking for access points. Higher up the road a series of logging roads offer access to the headwaters.

Contact: Yachats Area Chamber of Commerce and City of Yachats Visitors Center, 800/929-0477; The Dublin House Fly-Fishing Shop, 541/547-3703.

39 TENMILE CREEK
south of Yachats

Map 1.3, page 81

Nestled comfortably between two pristine wilderness areas, Cummins Creek and Rock Creek, and surrounded by numerous scenic coastal landmarks, this short and scenic 11-mile wild steelhead river is known and fished by only a handful of anglers. Lack of access

due to private lands and seasonal closures will be your greatest obstacles when considering this river. These two factors limit this river as a great small-stream fishery, not the abundance of wild winter steelhead. In fact, considering the restoration work being done by conservation groups such as the Audubon Society, this stream should enjoy an increasing stability in its anadromous fish populations. Be thankful, as fish management practices that prove successful on one stream strengthen the populations of wild fish elsewhere.

If you do find yourself in the vicinity of this stream November 1–March 31, the official fishing season, by all means stop and fish the upper reaches accessible from Tenmile Creek Road (Forest Rd. 56). A good place to begin your explorations would be at the Tenmile Creek campground. If you wish to travel into the headwaters you will need a good Forest Service map to help you navigate the logging roads. Because this river is so small, 15–30 feet wide, employ small-stream tactics and gear. Short spinning rods and fly rods will work best and help you cast around brushy banks. Be prepared to lose a few lures around the boulders and river debris, so pack some extra gear. Focus on pools, pocket water behind boulders, and deep runs with spinners, bobbers, or flies. Check with tackle shops in Yachats and Waldport or the local ODFW field office to get up-to-date information.

Species: Wild winter steelhead.

Facilities: Camping and fishing supplies are available in the nearby towns of Waldport and Yachats. Numerous campgrounds lie north and south of the river mouth, but the best camping can be had on Tenmile Creek at Tenmile Creek Campground and a few miles south on U.S. 101 at Rock Creek Campground. If hike-in camping is your passion, you might want to spend a day in one of the two wilderness areas, Cummins Creek and Rock Creek, for which all camping is free.

Directions: From Yachats drive south on U.S. 101 four miles to Hwy. 56 and turn east. This road follows the river, eventually turning into

Indian Creek Rd. and departs from the river. Fish along Hwy. 56, watching for No Trespassing signs in the first few miles. Best access points are going to be along the highway above Tenmile Creek Campground, which is 5.5 miles up Hwy. 56.

Contact: ODFW, Newport Field Office, 541/867-4741; Waldport Chamber of Commerce, 541/563-2133; Waldport Ranger District, 541/563-3211; Jess's Bait and Tackle, 541/563-7060; Waldport True Value, 541/563-3199; Tenmile Creek Campground, 541/563-3211; Tillicum Beach Campground, 800/280-2267; Rock Creek Campground, 541/563-3124.

40 LILY LAKE
north of Florence
Map 1.3, page 81

Imagine a lone float tuber sitting on a lake surrounded by reeds and sand dunes casting to the rhythms of the ocean and you have a pretty good idea of what Lily Lake is like. Lily Lake provides an opportunity for the solitude-seeker to fish a remote location for wild native cutthroat averaging 14 inches. The reason for Lily Lake's remoteness is the lack of roads leading to the shoreline. It's a walk-in fishery, and you must traverse a quarter-mile trail accessible from Baker Beach Road. The trail winds through a swamp for a part of the way so it is advisable to wear boots, waders, or other waterproof footgear.

Float tubes are easily carried to the lake and provide your best option for access because dense reeds make bank fishing very difficult at best. The only thing you're going to walk away with from this lake is good memories and a suntan because Lily is catch-and-release fishing only, restricted to artificial flies and lures. Fly anglers should look for fish feeding on hatching insects or just below the surface on small baitfish. Small leech patterns such as Woolly Buggers or damsel flies stripped in to the boat may work well. Spin anglers should cast and retrieve small feathered spinners or Rapalas in colors such as red, olive, or white.

Species: Wild cutthroat trout.

Facilities: There are no facilities on-site other than parking, but accommodations, food, and supplies are available in Florence. Camping is available a few miles south on U.S. 101 at the state campgrounds of Alder Dune or Sutton.

Directions: From Florence, drive 10 miles north on U.S. 101 to Baker Beach Rd. and turn west. Less than a 0.25-mile drive will put you at the marked trailhead leading to Lily Lake.

Contact: Waldport Chamber of Commerce, 541/563-2133; Waldport Ranger District, 541/563-3211; Jess's Bait and Tackle, 541/563-7060; Waldport True Value, 541/563-3199; Alder Dune Campground, 541/563-4473; Sutton Campground, 541/271-3611.

41 SUTTON LAKE
north of Florence
Map 1.3, page 81

Sitting six miles north of Florence on the east side of U.S. 101, Sutton Lake is approximately 100 acres composed of two bodies of water separated by a small channel. Sutton Lake Road, accessible from the north or south end of the lake, will take you around the east side to a campground and boat launch. This is another coastal lake that is lightly fished and therefore offers good opportunities for solitude and quiet. The lakeshore can be difficult to reach except at public areas. Dense brush forms a barrier abound the lakeshore and an abundance of lily pads and aquatic weeds make casting next to impossible. This provides good habitat for fish, but not anglers. Two places with access to the bank are areas along U.S. 101 or around the private docks near the channel. For better chances, launch a boat or float tube at the Sutton Lake ramp. Be aware that wind can be a problem because of this lake's proximity to the ocean; boaters should take caution. Trolling, spinning, bobber, or float fishing work for all species. Trout can be found in the deeper water and along the shore in the evenings. Bass and panfish can be found in the weed beds that surround the lake's edge.

Species: Wild cutthroat, stocked legal rainbows, yellow perch, and largemouth bass.

Facilities: Boat ramps, camping, and restrooms are all available at the lake. Alder Dune and Sutton campgrounds are at the north and south ends of the lake. Accommodations, food, and supplies are available in Florence.

Directions: From Florence drive six miles north on Hwy. 101. Drive east on Sutton Lake Rd.

Contact: Mapleton Ranger District, 541/902-8526.

42 MERCER LAKE
north of Florence
Map 1.3, page 81

Are you a bass angler? Mercer may be just the place for you. The lake is noted for its large, skittish largemouth bass that are, by all reports, difficult to catch. Perhaps perch are your fish? If so, there is a very healthy population of yellow perch, some averaging 14 inches. Whatever your fancy, you are likely to find it here, including trout and bluegill. Some large hatchery trout known as holdovers live in the deeper sections of the lake.

At 340 surface acres, Mercer is a fair-sized lake five miles north of Florence and adjacent east of Sutton Lake. The south shore is accessible by Mercer Lake Road. North Mercer Lake Road is a dead-end and provides no lake access. Some private lands border the lake. A lake resort supplies fishing gear and camping supplies as well as boat rentals. The only public dock is 2.5 miles around the north shore. Bank access is difficult because of brush and aquatic weeds. You would do well to consider this a boat fishery and save yourself the frustration of finding a suitable weed-free shoreline. Fish the weedy shoreline around logs and brush for bass and panfish. Fish the deeper sections and stream inlets and outlets for trout.

Species: Stocked trout, largemouth bass, yellow perch, bluegill.

Facilities: Boat ramps, rentals, and supplies are available at the lake. There is no camping on the lake. Siuslaw National Forest operates two campgrounds near the lake: Sutton and Alder Dune.

Directions: Take U.S. 101 five miles north of Florence to Mercer Lake Rd. Follow paved Mercer Lake Rd. 2.5 miles from Hwy. 101 to the public asphalt ramp. To reach Sutton Campground, drive four miles north of Florence on Hwy. 101 and turn left (west) on Campground-Vista Rd., which leads one mile to the campground. Alder Dune is located on Hwy. 101 0.5-mile north of that turnoff.

Contact: Florence Chamber of Commerce, 541/997-3128; Port of Siuslaw, 541/997-3040; The Sportsman Tackle Shop, 541/997-3336; Mapleton Ranger District, 541/902-8526; Siuslaw National Forest, 541/563-3124.

43 MUNSEL LAKE
north of Florence
Map 1.3, page 81

Munsel Lake sits 2.5 miles north of Florence east of Hwy. 101 on Munsel Lake Road. Comprising 93 surface acres, this is a very deep, clear lake and thanks to stocking techniques, holds many trophy specimens of trout and bass. Both trout and bass have been caught in the 5–7-pound range. This is primarily a boat fishery with very little bank access because of either private lands or brush-lined banks. You can launch a craft at the county boat ramp on the southern end. The topography tends to be steep shorelines with a lot of logs extending into the lake. Spring and fall tend to be the best times to fish. Focus on shallow coves or the creek inlet on the north shore. All methods of fishing work, including trolling, streamers, bass bugs, and bait.

Species: Hatchery trout, hatchery trophy trout, bass, perch.

Facilities: Restrooms, parking, and a boat ramp are all available at the lake. Nearest camping is at Sutton Lake. Accommodations, food, and supplies are available in Florence.

Directions: From Florence, drive 2.5 miles north on U.S. 101, then turn right (east) on Munsel Lake Rd. for one mile to the lake.

Contact: Florence Chamber of Commerce, 541/997-3128; Port of Siuslaw, 541/997-3040; The Sportsman Tackle Shop, 541/997-3336; Mapleton Ranger District, 541/902-8526.

4.4 NORTH FORK SIUSLAW RIVER

east of Florence

Map 1.4, page 82

The North Fork is a small bank fishery that empties into the Siuslaw east of Florence. Expect a small river with a width of only 30–50 feet in most places. This is not the best holding water; gravelly bottoms and limited cover make this place less than inviting for fish to take up residence. The North Fork is a marginal fishery and chances are this river is productive only a few days a year. A newcomer to this stream should not be expected to catch fish without a lot of research, perseverance, and hard work.

Primary species are winter steelhead February–March, sea-runs in the fall, and resident trout year-round. Access is good for most of its length with turnouts along the highway and a boat launch at Bender Landing. A good starting place is on the water above Minerva and 13 miles upriver at the Forest Service campground. Don't get discouraged if, when you arrive at the river, all you see is a shallow narrow waterway with very little holding water or fish cover. Your task is to pack your rod and begin hiking into those hidden places that only a few other anglers know about. This will be as much of an exploring adventure as a fishing trip. If by chance you can manage to find and hook fish on this river, then there is nothing stopping you from becoming a super angler who can catch fish anywhere. You stand to learn more by being successful on a river such as the North Fork with its tough conditions than on any other river.

Species: Sea-run and resident cutthroat, winter steelhead.

Facilities: Boats can be launched at Bender Landing, Houghton Landing, and the campground at Wilhelm Creek. Camping is available two miles north of Houghton Landing. Supplies and accommodations are available in Florence.

Directions: From Florence drive east a couple of miles on Hwy. 126 to North Fork Rd. Follow North Fork Rd. along the river. Houghton Landing is 9.6 miles upriver from Florence.

Contact: Florence Chamber of Commerce, 541/997-3128; Port of Siuslaw, 541/997-3040; The Sportsman Tackle Shop, 541/997-3336; Mapleton Ranger District, 541/902-8526.

4.5 SIUSLAW RIVER

east of Florence

Map 1.4, page 82

The Siuslaw is a long river at more than 100 miles and comprises numerous coastal drainages on its run west of Eugene to the bay in Florence. The major tributary and the place where a majority of the hatchery steelhead are released is Lake Creek near Swisshome. A few miles below Swisshome one encounters the reach of tide near Mapleton, below which most of the fishing occurs for chinook, steelhead, and shad. Surprisingly, given its many access points, and unique run of shad, this is not a heavily fished river. A few fly anglers take advantage of the good population of native and sea-run cutthroat, but even that is a small percentage compared to other coastal rivers.

The tidewater stretch from the bay to Mapleton is by far the most popular reach, as evidenced by numerous boat ramps. Above the tidewater, boating is restricted to drift boats but with equally good access. Some caution should be exercised when using a boat in this upper section because the river can be swift and technical.

Anglers wishing an abundance of bank access and a chance to catch winter steelhead, cutthroats, and shad should focus on the river between Mapleton and Lake Creek, accessible by

Hwy. 36. Steelhead begin their run in January and remain in the river until March. Fall chinook, caught primarily in the tidewater, can be found September–November. Sea-runs enter in fall, August and September, and can be found throughout the river. An on-again, off-again shad run appears May–June between Mapleton and Brickerville, sometimes moving as high as Swisshome. The lower river is primarily a boating affair, and anglers in this section are after chinook and shad and employ a variety of traditional bait and trolling techniques.

Species: Winter steelhead, chinook, sea-run and resident cutthroat, shad.

Facilities: One can find accommodations and complete fishing facilities in Florence, including paved public boat ramps, bait and outfitter shops, charter fishing, river shuttles, and boat rentals. Boats can be launched at Florence public ramp in Florence, Cushman RV Park and Marina, Siuslaw Marina, Midway Dock, Tiernan boat ramp, C and D dock, Mapleton Landing, Farnham Landing, Richardson Pole Slide, and Whittaker Creek. There are a campground, tackle shop, and wheelchair-accessible dock in Mapleton. East of Mapleton one can camp at Knowles Creek and Whittaker Creek.

Directions: From Florence drive east on Hwy. 126 to Mapleton. Highway 126 turns into Hwy. 36 at Mapleton. You can continue on Hwy. 36, following the river to Swisshome, and drive east on Stagecoach Rd. back to Hwy. 126 and the river. From Mapleton you can stay on Hwy. 126, bypassing a section of river. Drive south on Siuslaw River Rd. to get to the headwaters.

Contact: Florence Chamber of Commerce, 541/997-3128; Port of Siuslaw, 541/997-3040; The Sportsman Tackle Shop, 541/997-3336; Mapleton Ranger District, 541/902-8526.

46 CLEAWOX LAKE
south of Florence
Map 1.4, page 82

Cleawox Lake is the kind of place that family vacations are made of. In addition to the variety of easy fishing for a handful of different species, it's in the wonderful setting of Honeyman State Park on the border of Oregon Dunes National Recreation Area. Cleawox Lake is a popular fishery with campers and those wishing to catch stocked rainbow and warm-water species. At 82 surface acres, this is not a small lake but its size offers plenty of opportunities to discover private fishing holes. Motorboats are prohibited, but a nonmotor craft is all you need. Anglers can fish for many species in the lake, but focus on the trophy-size rainbow trout and largemouth bass. Other species include crappie, yellow perch, brown bullhead, and bluegill. It's a perfect place for families wishing to introduce their children to the joys of fishing.

Species: Trophy rainbow trout, largemouth bass, crappie, yellow perch, brown bullhead, and bluegill.

Facilities: Facilities include boat ramp, boat rentals, convenience store, and full-service campground. Supplies are available in Florence and North Beach.

Directions: Cleawox Lake is located three miles south of Florence on U.S. 101.

Contact: Florence Chamber of Commerce, 541/997-3128; The Sportsman Tackle Shop, 541/997-3336; Honeyman State Park, 800/551-6949; Oregon Dunes National Recreation Area, 541/271-3611

47 WOAHINK LAKE
south of Florence
Map 1.4, page 82

Woahink Lake on the eastern boundary of Honeyman State Park in one of the deepest lakes in Oregon and covers 350 surface acres. Better known by water-sport enthusiasts than by anglers, Woahink is a good place for family outings with lots of activities to distract young anglers when the fishing is slow. It is not, however, well suited to the serious angler. Much better opportunities are in the surrounding vicinity at Siltcoos Lake and the Siuslaw River.

Species: Hatchery rainbows, wild cutthroat, big yellow perch, largemouth bass.

Facilities: There are two boat ramps at the north end of the lake and camping in Honeyman State Park. Camping, boat ramps, supplies, and a day-use area are all available at the lake.

Directions: From Florence, head three miles south on U.S. 101.

Contact: Florence Chamber of Commerce, 541/997-3128; The Sportsman Tackle Shop, 541/997-3336; Honeyman State Park, 800/551-6949.

48 SILTCOOS LAKE

south of Florence

Map 1.4, page 82

Considered one of the top fisheries in the Northwest, this 3,000-acre lake is home to numerous warm-water species and anadromous fish. Trophy species of rainbow trout, wild cutthroat, sea-run cutthroat, steelhead, brown bullhead, yellow perch, crappie, bass, and bluegill can all be caught. Five-pound bass are common and rainbows have been known to reach 6–7 pounds. The setting is hard to beat with dense forests growing to the water's edge, but be prepared to deal with powerboats and wate-r sport enthusiasts. This is another great family vacation spot, but unlike the smaller lakes in the vicinity, this is an angler's lake.

An interesting feature of this lake is its outlet, the Siltcoos River, a two-mile-long river that runs through an old-growth spruce forest and empties into the ocean. Fall and spring provide opportunities for catching steelhead and sea-run cutthroat. Canoes, pontoon boats, and drift boats all work and can be taken out at the estuary near Wax Myrtle Campground. Bank-fishing access is good for the entire river's length and along several campgrounds near the river's mouth. Because of the size of Siltcoos Lake, anglers with boats will do the best. Consult with local shops for the best fishing times and areas. Fish concentrate in many of the lake's arms, which are fed by various tributaries, and around

islands. Good places for trophy and stocked rainbows are the Kiechle Arm and the mouth of Maple Creek Arm. Bass anglers do best in the Booth Arm, Fiddle Creek Arm, and Maple Creek Arm. Goat Island has good opportunities for catching warm-water species such as perch, brown bullhead, and crappie.

Species: Stocked rainbow trout, wild cutthroat, sea-run cutthroat, steelhead, brown bullhead, yellow perch, crappie, bass, bluegill.

Facilities: A boat ramp, camping, RV sites, accommodations, rentals, and supplies are available in nearby Westlake.

Directions: From Florence, travel south on U.S. 101 for six miles to the town of Westlake. Tyee Campground is located on Pacific Ave.; the parking area for the hiking trails is one mile south on U.S. 101, on the east side of the highway.

Contact: Florence Chamber of Commerce, 541/997-3128; The Sportsman Tackle Shop, 541/997-3336; Fish Mill Lodge and RV Park, 541/997-2511; Nightingale's Fishing Camp RV site, 541/997-2892; Honeyman State Park, 800/551-6949; Siltcoos Lake Resort, 541/997-3741; Lake's Edge RV Park and Marina, 541/997-6056; Westlake Resort, 541/997-3722.

49 TAHKENITCH LAKE

north of Reedsport

Map 1.4, page 82

Tahkenitch Lake spans 1,500 acres and borders 10,000 acres of undeveloped forestland, making the scenic value among the best on the coast. The lake has a good population of largemouth bass, some of which can reach 10 or more pounds. Good bass-fishing habitat can be found along the banks or in the Fivemile Arm on the east side. Rainbows are stocked annually and there is a small population of wild cutthroats. A very strong run of coho enter the lake in November, but angling is prohibited. The best fishing opportunities are for crappie, bluegill, and yellow perch. Don't expect too many bank angling opportunities.

Brushy banks and steep shorelines will require a boat. Fly anglers have a unique opportunity to fish a hatch of *Hexagenia,* a large yellow mayfly with an evening emergence. Focus your efforts on muddy banks along shores and islands. Don't be discouraged if one night you witness a large hatch and on the next no hatch. This bug is very sensitive to air temperature and emerges only during the hottest parts of the year. Most patterns are fished on a size 6 hook. Nymphs can be fished off the banks with a quick retrieve before the hatch.

Species: Coho, sea-run cutthroat, steelhead, largemouth bass, yellow perch, crappie, bluegill, rainbows.

Facilities: There are paved boat ramps and wheelchair-accessible piers at Tahkenitch boat ramp and Tahkenitch Landing. Camping is available at Tahkenitch Landing and Tahkenitch Campground. Local marinas offer boat rentals. Accommodations and supplies are available at the lake.

Directions: From Reedsport drive north eight miles on U.S. 101.

Contact: Tahkenitch Fishing Village, 541/271-5222; Reedsport/Winchester Bay Chamber of Commerce, 800/247-2155.

50 SMITH RIVER
north of Reedsport

Map 1.4, page 82

A major tributary of one of the great rivers on the coast, the Umpqua, the Smith enters Winchester Bay at Gardiner after a 75-mile run out of the coastal mountains. Smith River Road follows the river for approximately 30 miles before turning into logging roads. Not to be confused with the Smith River on the northern California border, Oregon's Smith River is equally productive and offers two unique fisheries for shad and striped bass. In addition, one can find wild runs of fall chinook, and steelhead.

Current regulations seeking to preserve spawning habitats and wild fish populations have placed a lot of restriction on anglers, making this essentially a catch-and-release sport fishery. An angler will find very few hatchery fish in these waters and coho are protected from angling. Striped bass must be released and trout angling has been prohibited for years. Be sure to check your regulations thoroughly before heading to the Smith. Fishing deadlines exist all over the river and species once fishable can quickly become off-limits. One positive consequence of catch-and-release fishing is it automatically reduces the number of anglers to those who are willing to release everything they catch. This reduced pressure means less crowded waters and more opportunities for solitude.

Early in the fall season the tidewater reach from the bay to Spencer Creek is the place to be for chinook and striped bass. Striped bass can also be caught in the spring, followed by a decent run of shad in May and June. A good starting place to target shad is around the Nole Ranch boat ramp. Boaters in the upper river may want to consider the drift from Dailey Pole Slide to the take-out at Dailey Ranch. The highest put-in is at Smith River Falls, a less popular float but just as productive. Numerous other boat ramps and campgrounds provide good bank access, as do turnouts along the highway.

Species: Fall chinook, steelhead, trout, striped bass, shad.

Facilities: Boat ramps are numerous along Hwy. 48. Camping can be had at several campgrounds on the river, including Fawn Creek, Smith River Falls, Vincent Creek, and Twin Sisters. Gardiner and Reedsport are well stocked with accommodations, supplies, and tackle shops.

Directions: From Reedsport drive a short distance on U.S. 101 to Gardiner and intersect Hwy. 48.

Contact: Reedsport/Winchester Bay Chamber of Commerce, 800/247-2155; Fisherman's Trailer Court and RV Park, 541/271-3536; Reedsport Outdoor Store, 541/271-2311; Englund Marine Supply, 541/888-6623; Osprey Fly Shop, 541/271-4463.

51 WINCHESTER BAY
southwest of Reedsport

Map 1.4, page 82

Winchester Bay was a once-booming commercial fishing community that has since seen its heyday because of the decline of coho fishing. Still, there exists a thriving charter business willing to take anglers out onto the ocean for a full day of salmon, halibut, and bottom fishing. The primary draws for most anglers wishing to fish Winchester Bay are its populations of sturgeon, salmon, stripers, rockfish, clams, and crabs. Both boat and bank access are plentiful, but boaters have the advantage because of the bay's size. Bank anglers may want to start at the South Jetty fishing for salmon, perch, and rockfish. Boaters can launch at the public docks in the lower bay and higher up in Reedsport. Consult with local marinas and tackle shops for the most productive waters.

Species: Winter and summer steelhead, fall and spring chinook, coho, sea-run cutthroat, smallmouth bass, striped bass, sturgeon, ocean salmon, halibut, stripers, rockfish, perch.

Facilities: There is a full-service marina with paved boat ramp, charter fishing, and boat moorage. The marina also provides boating and fishing supplies. Campgrounds are at Windy Cove in Winchester, Lake Marie, William Tugman State Park, and Ell Creek.

Directions: From Reedsport drive south on U.S. 101 about four miles to Winchester Bay.

Contact: Reedsport/Winchester Bay Chamber of Commerce, 800/247-2155; Fisherman's Trailer Court and RV Park, 541/271-3536; Reedsport Outdoor Store, 541/271-2311; Englund Marine Supply, 541/888-6623; Osprey Fly Shop, 541/271-4463; William Tugman State Park, 541/888-3778.

52 LOWER UMPQUA RIVER
east of Reedsport

Map 1.4, page 82   BEST (

Next to the Rogue and Deschutes Rivers, the Umpqua is one of Oregon's most famous and challenging rivers for steelhead and salmon.

The Umpqua is a long river, running 200 miles from its source in the Cascade Range east of I-5 to the ocean at Winchester Bay. The upper river North and South forks are legendary for their classic fly-fishing water and large steelhead. The lower river (also called the main stem) runs west of I-5 from River Forks, 10 miles west of Roseburg, to Winchester Bay.

Much of this river is accessible by jet sled or outboard motor, which makes sense considering this is a low-gradient river, dropping only 400 feet on its 100-mile journey from Roseburg to the ocean. If you decide to make your float in a drift boat, bring a motor to take you through the slack-water sections. Principal starting sections are above and below Elkton. Boaters should know there are some serious rapids in these sections.

The smallmouth fishery on the lower Umpqua is legendary among enthusiasts and guides. The low-gradient nature of this river provides excellent holding water and water temperatures for bass. The best fishing times are late May–October. Target the slack water, pools, or the edges of slow current with flies, poppers, top-water crankbaits, and spinners. Good places to start are from Elkton to Scott Creek boat ramp and Umpqua to Yellow Creek boat ramp. Look for bank-fishing opportunities at the boat ramps and between Scottsburg and Umpqua Wayside.

Salmon move into the river mid-March–July for spring chinook and August–September for fall chinook. A majority of these fish are targeted from the estuary to Reedsport and in the tidal waters around Scottsburg Park up to Elkton. The most common fishing technique is from anchored boats using spinners or bait.

Summer and winter steelhead are probably the river's second-biggest attraction. The fish here are bright chrome and can run as big as 20 pounds. Summer steelhead are in the river May–August with peak catches in June and July. Boaters should try Yellow Creek, Umpqua, or The Forks for the best chances of catching these great hatchery fish. Look for bank access at boat ramps and along the road from Tyee to Kellogg. Winter steelhead begin to show November–March, with peak runs in February and March. If you're after big, wild fish then this is your time to shine. Focus on the areas between Scottsburg and Elkton and at Sawyer Rapids near the RV park. Mehl Canyon Road out of Elkton offers good bank access. Drift boaters have several options, starting with the most popular drift between Elkton RV Camp to Sawyer Rapids. Other drifts can be had from Yellow Creek to Hutchison Wayside, Umpqua to James Woods boat ramp, and The Forks to Umpqua.

Shad make up the final fishery in the lower river. Any of the steelhead drifts are productive shad water May–June. These fish require small lures on light tackle. Try shad darts, spinners, jigs, or flies for best results.

Species: Winter and summer steelhead, fall and spring chinook, coho, sea-run cutthroat, smallmouth bass, shad.

Facilities: There are numerous private RV parks along Hwy. 38, and the Tyee County Park Campground across from Yellow Creek is good tent camping. Boat ramps line the river as do facilities for supplies and accommodations. Boat launches are at Umpqua State Wayside Park, Scottsburg Park, Scott Creek, Sawyer's Rapids, Yellow Creek, Osprey ramp, James Woods, Umpqua Landing, Cleveland Rapids, and River Forks Park. Boat shuttles can be had at any of the tackle shops in the nearby towns of Reedsport, Scottsburg, Elkton, Kellogg, or Roseburg.

Directions: From Reedsport drive east 36 miles on Hwy. 38 to Elkton. Highway 138 out of Elkton will lead you to the forks.

Contact: Reedsport/Winchester Bay Chamber of Commerce, 800/247-2155; Fisherman's Trailer Court and RV Park, 541/271-3536; Reedsport Outdoor Store, 541/271-2311; Englund Marine Supply, 541/888-6623; Osprey Fly Shop, 541/271-4463; Brent Lamm, 541/440-0558, www.umpquafishingguide.com.

53 TENMILE LAKES
south of Reedsport
Map 1.4, page 82

Bass, bass, and more bass—that's what you'll find at North and South Tenmile Lakes. The lake hosts several summer bass tournaments each year when anglers can catch 20–50 largemouth bass per day. When one understands the nature of this lake it's not hard to see why so many bass live here. In its 2,723 acres of surface area, its average depth is no more than 15 feet with very few deep holes. The best fishing occurs in summer when the water heats up to 70°F. Shallow shorelines, willows, docks, and other structures provide adequate protection and great holding water. Try the Colman and Temple arms in the South Lake and Lindross and Black's Arm in the North Lake. Of special interest to fly anglers and known to be of interest to bass are the evening emergences of a large yellow mayfly called *Hexagenia*. Most dry-fly patterns are tied on a size 6 hook and fished at dusk. Nymph patterns can be fished with a fast twitch around muddy banks before the hatch. *Hexagenia* are sensitive to air temperature and tend to emerge on hot days.

Tenmile Creek provides a novel fishery for salmon, steelhead, sea-run cutthroat, and chinook. It used to be home to hybrid bass, however these are no longer stocked and are all but nonexistant. Target chinook September–November. Steelhead can be caught December–March. Spring runs of the same species give anglers another chance. Anglers should start fishing for crappie and bluegill in early–late spring when the water temperature changes. Both hatchery and wild trout are available with the former being stocked 2–4 times a year.

Note: The lake hosts a large population of water-sport enthusiasts, usually not a good sign for angling; however, this lake is so big it might not matter. Numerous arms and coves will provide the isolation needed for concentrated fishing.

Species: Bluegill, largemouth bass, hybrid

bass, bullhead catfish, coho, steelhead, rainbow trout, and cutthroat, chinook, salmon, crappie.

Facilities: The county park provides picnic areas, a wheelchair-accessible pier, and paved boat ramp. Reach the North Lake through the lake channel or from the private boat ramp. There are no public campgrounds on the lake. Another public fishing dock is at South Lake access. The nearest camping is at Spinreel Campground on Tenmile Creek. Lakeside has facilities, supplies, and rentals.

Directions: From Reedsport drive south on U.S. 101 for 12 miles (U.S. 101 runs through Lakeside).

Contact: Osprey Point RV Resort, 541/759-2801; Tenmile Park and boat ramp, 541/759-3176; Lakeside Hardware and Tackle, 541/759-3448.

54 MILLICOMA RIVER

east of Coos Bay

Map 1.4, page 82

The main stem of the Millicoma is a short, eight-mile river beginning at the West and East forks near Allegany and emptying into the Coos River just above the reach of tide. The main stem is a boating river with almost no bank access. Anglers can launch a boat at Rooke and Higgins County Park and make a short five-mile float to the take-out at Dora's Place near the confluence with the Coos River. Anglers catch shad May–June with the best success occurring on the hottest days. Trolling for fall chinook is best September–November. Steelhead are present December–March but you'll have better success on the forks above Allegany. The only other fish is sea-run cutthroat and their numbers are strong August–October.

If it's steelhead or trout you're interested in then head to the scenic West and East forks above Allegany. Both rivers have good access in their upper reaches by way of logging roads and unimproved highways, but you will encounter a lot of private property in the lower reaches. On the East Fork, Glen Creek is a good place to begin looking for fishable water. Look for trout and steelhead in the pools and deeper runs and pay close attention to holding spots such as rocks that create pocket water. The West Fork is the preferred river for most anglers, with most of the fishing taking place in the Elliot State Forest and near the fish hatchery. There is a boat ramp at the county bridge 5.5 miles upriver and it can provide access to a lot of great water during high-water years. Boating is not recommended in low-water years nor is this a river for novices. Several rapids and tight chutes could be challenging to even the most experienced boater. While fishing the West Fork, the volunteer-run hatchery is worth a visit.

Species: Winter steelhead, spring and fall chinook, trout, shad.

Facilities: Boat ramps are available on the main-stem river at Rooke and Higgins County Park, Dora's Place, and at the county bridge 5.5 miles upriver on the West Fork. Camping on the West Fork is at the fish hatchery. Showers, barbecues, and restrooms are all available at the hatchery. Next door to the hatchery is an old Girl Scout Retreat Center open for camping. Supplies and accommodations are available in Coos Bay.

Directions: From Coos Bay, reach the river from either the north or south along U.S. 101. To the north take U.S. 101 six miles to East Bank Rd., turn east and drive south six miles to the Coos River Hwy. Coos River Hwy. follows the river for five miles before branching off to follow the Millicoma River on the way to Rook and Higgins Park, five miles upriver. Look for Dora's Place boat ramp and the confluence of the Coos River and Millicoma. Follow the Coos River Hwy. to Allegany, where the river splits into its two forks. For the southern route, drive south on U.S. 101 one mile to Bunker Hill and take the Coos River Rd. exit. Coos River Rd. follows the Coos River for approximately six miles before crossing the river and merging with Coos River Hwy.

Contact: Coos Bay Chamber of Commerce, 800/824-8486; Surplus Center, 541/267-6711; Bob's Sportfishing, 541/888-4041; Allegany Country Market, 541/267-2281; Ed O'Brian (hatchery), 541/267-2557; Sandbar Mobile and RV Park, 541/888-3179; Rooke and Higgins County Park, 541/396-3121; Myrtle Tree Park, 541/396-3121, ext. 354; Sunset Bay State Park, 800/452-5687; Brent Lamm, 541/440-0558, www.umpquafishingguide.com.

55 COOS BAY
southwest of Coos Bay
Map 1.4, page 82

Coos Bay, one of the largest bays on the southern coast, extends from the mouth at Charleston and sweeps around Coos Bay to the Coos River. Among the many inlets and tributaries anglers catch numerous species of fish, including winter steelhead, spring chinook, fall chinook, ocean salmon, coho, striped bass, shad, and trout. Charleston is home to a large commercial and charter fishery with an abundance of docks and marinas. The Charleston Boat Basin is a good starting place to launch a boat and begin asking questions at local tackle shops and marinas. Those wishing to fish the ocean can do so from Charleston either by charter or from personal watercraft, but consult with local marinas for advice about where to find your desired species of fish.

Chinook and coho are caught in the ocean May–September. Halibut, rockfish, cabezon, and greenling are also available. Jetties provide excellent fishing for a variety of rockfish, coho, and perch. Herring, Dungeness crab, and rock crab can be caught from docks in Charleston. The best clam flats are on the north spit and South Slough Flat. Winter steelhead run throughout the bay December–March followed by spring chinook April–June. Fall chinook arrive August–November with the strongest showing in October. Striped bass and shad can be caught May–June.

Species: Winter steelhead, spring and fall chinook, ocean salmon, coho, striped bass, shad, cutthroat trout, bottom fish, halibut, sturgeon, rockfish, cabezon, greenling, perch, herring.

Facilities: Charleston has a full-service marina with paved boat ramp, bait and outfitter shops, and charter fishing. Camping is available to the south along the coast at Sunset Bay, Shore Access State Park, and Cape Argo State Park. Accommodations and supplies can be had in the surrounding cities of Coos Bay, Barview, and Charleston.

Directions: From U.S. 101 in Coos Bay turn west on the Empire Coos Bay Hwy. to the Cape Arago Hwy., which will lead you to Charleston and the southern campgrounds.

Contact: Coos Bay Chamber of Commerce, 800/824-8486; Surplus Center, 541/267-6711; Bob's Sportfishing, 541/888-4041; Sandbar Mobile and RV Park, 541/888-3179; Betty Kay Charters, 541/888-9021; Sunset Bay State Park, 800/452-5687; Charleston Marina RV Park, 541/888-9512.

56 COOS RIVER
east of Coos Bay
Map 1.4, page 82

Just east of Coos Bay you will encounter a series of tributaries, all of which feed the Coos River and Coos Bay. The Coos River makes a short four-mile run through farmlands between Coos Bay and the reach of tide at the confluence of the Millicoma and the South Fork Coos Rivers. It's wide, deep, and slow; most anglers will classify this as trolling water and they wouldn't be wrong. Despite its short distance, it attracts many anglers and guides for fall chinook, steelhead, a declining striped bass population, sea-run cutthroat, and shad.

Coos River Road follows the south shore and Coos River Highway follows the north bank. Bank access is poor so be prepared to launch a boat at either Dora's Place just below the confluence of the Millicoma and Coos Rivers, Rooke–Higgins County Park on the Millicoma, or Myrtle Tree Park on the South

Fork Coos River. Floats are easy from the two rivers' put-ins. Winter steelhead can be caught December–March followed by spring chinook April–June. Fall chinook make their appearance August–November with the strongest showing in October. Coho show in November, but all coho angling here is illegal. Striped bass and shad show in May and June. Sea-run cutthroat can be fished in fall before their move into the upper river. When fishing for salmon in the Coos River, the best success is found by trolling spinners, bait, or a combination of the two. For steelhead try drift fishing with bobbers or casting spinners and spoons. Shad are partial to small spinners and shad flies.

Species: Fall chinook, steelhead, striped bass, sea-run cutthroat, shad.

Facilities: Camping can be found at Rooke and Higgins County Park on the Millicoma River and Myrtle Tree Park on the South Fork Coos River. More camping is available south of Coos Bay around Charleston at Sunset Bay State Park. Supplies and accommodations are plentiful in Coos Bay.

Directions: From Coos Bay you can reach the river from either the north or south along U.S. 101. To the north take U.S. 101 six miles to East Bank Rd., turn east and drive south six miles to the Coos River Hwy. Coos River Hwy. follows the river for five miles before branching off to follow the Millicoma River on the way to Rook and Higgins Park, five miles upriver. Look for Dora's Place boat ramp and the confluence of the Coos River and Millicoma. For the southern route, drive south on U.S. 101 one mile to Bunker Hill and take the Coos River Rd. exit. Coos River Rd. follows the Coos River for approximately six miles before following the South Fork Coos River on the way to Myrtle Tree Park.

Contact: Coos Bay Chamber of Commerce, 800/824-8486; Surplus Center, 541/267-6711; Bob's Sportfishing, 541/888-4041; Sandbar Mobile and RV Park, 541/888-3179; Rooke and Higgins County Park, 541/396-3121; Myrtle Tree Park, 541/396-3121, ext. 354; Sunset Bay State Park, 800/452-5687; Brent Lamm, 541/440-0558, www.umpquafishing-guide.com.

57 COQUILLE RIVER
east of Bandon

Map 1.4, page 82

The Coquille River is composed of a bay, main-stem river, and several forks stretching high into the Siskiyou National Forest. The bay has good bank access on the North and South jetties and at the public docks in Bandon for salmon, perch, bottom fish, and crab. Soft shell clams can be had in the flats next to the Bandon Treatment Plant. The Bandon Boat Basin and Bullard's State Park provide good boat access to the bay and open ocean.

The main river and the South Fork are home to wild and hatchery steelhead December–March with strongest showings in February and March, especially on the South Fork. Drift fishing, spinners, and fly-fishing are the most popular methods of catching steelhead. Concentrate on the longer runs and fish thoroughly behind rocks and in deeper pools. Salmon comprise the most popular fishing on the river—fall chinook arrive September–December with October and November the strongest months. Spring chinook make a small showing in May and June. Trolling the bay and tidewater with spinners, herring, and spinner/bait combinations are most effective. Sea-run cutthroats arrive in both the spring and fall with strongest showing in September and October. Try trolling small plugs in the tidewater or use flies and spinners against the bank and in slack waters. All the forks have strong populations of trout, especially the South Fork. Numerous boating ramps exist along the main river and into the forks. Rocky Point, Riverton, Sturdivant Park, Coquille, Argo, and Bryant ramp provide good drifts through the lower river. On the South Fork you can launch a boat at Beaver Creek or Baker Creek.

Species: Winter steelhead, fall and spring chinook, coho, bullheads, largemouth bass, striped bass, sea-run cutthroat, perch, bottom fish.

Facilities: The Port of Bandon provides a free boat launch for access to the bay. Other boat ramps within the reach of tide include Bullards Beach State Park, Rocky Point, and Riverton. To launch a drift boat on the main stem of the river try Sturdivant Park, Coquille, Argo, and Bryant boat ramp. Powers Rd. on the South Fork will take you to Beaver Creek and Baker Creek boat ramps. Camping can be had at Bullards State Park in Bandon, and on the South Fork at Powers County Park and Orchard Park. Fishing and camping supplies, shuttles, and accommodations are available in Bandon, Coquille, Myrtle Point, and Powers.

Directions: From Bandon drive east on Coquille–Bandon Hwy. (County Hwy. 42S) 17 miles to Coquille. Stay on Hwy. 42 south, passing through Myrtle Point, to get to the Middle Fork. Three miles past Myrtle you can take Powers Hwy. to the South Fork.

Contact: Bandon Chamber of Commerce, 541/347-9616; Coquille Chamber of Commerce, 541/396-4314; Bullard's State Park, 541/347-2290; Port-O-Call, 541/347-2875; Brent Lamm, 541/440-0558, www.umpquafishingguide.com.

58 NEW RIVER
north of Port Orford
Map 1.5, page 83

An area formally known as Storm Ranch, the New River is a unique freshwater channel that flows out of Flores Lake and runs north along a sand dune that separates it from the Pacific Ocean. It got its name from a rancher who, after a storm in 1890, saw the new body of water and said, "It's a new river." Today the New River is 120 years old and hosts good runs of wild chinook, steelhead, and sea-run and resident cutthroat. This is a river in flux, changing its mouth and length according to variables of weather and high water.

Look for chinook September–October.

Winter steelhead begin to show in December and are available till March. Sea-run cutthroat are available July–fall. All methods of fishing will take fish, but drift fishing with bobbers and sand shrimp or roe seems to be the most popular. For trout try flies or spinners. Most of the fish in this system are wild and so expect a catch-and-release fishery.

Bank access is excellent from either the outlet at Flores Lake or on the BLM property. From Flores Lake you can cross a footbridge to walk north along the river and look for rising fish. The bank is marshy with high brush, so use caution when scouting for fish. The BLM property provides unlimited access along the river's entire shore. There is one major float from the outlet at Flores Lake to the BLM take-out. Some boaters will launch at the BLM boat ramp and row or motor up- and down-river trolling for fish. Winds from the ocean can sometimes be brutal along the channel. The beaches by the mouth can provide excellent surf perch fishing.

Species: Wild chinook, wild winter steelhead, resident and sea-run cutthroat, surf perch.

Facilities: Boat ramps are at the outlet at Flores Lake and within the BLM property. The BLM property provides day-use facilities, hiking, and bird-watching. Buy supplies in Denmark.

Directions: From Port Orford, head north on U.S. 101 for approximately 12 miles. Turn west on Croft Lake Lane. To get to the mouth at Flores Lake follow the signs from Denmark off U.S. 101. Flores Lake is three miles to the west.

Contact: BLM, Coos Bay, 541/756-0100, www.or.blm.gov/coosbay/newriver.

59 FLORES LAKE
north of Port Orford
Map 1.5, page 83

Flores is a large, deep 250-acre freshwater lake isolated from the ocean by a sand-dune barrier. Its outlet at the southern end forms the New River and provides a nice deep channel for trout anglers. Trout and largemouth bass are this lake's main attractions. Some anglers in the know can catch winter steelhead, fall salmon, and sea-run cutthroat working their way into the tributaries. The lake is stocked every year with legal-size rainbows; some holdovers can get quite large. Largemouth bass, some as big as 6–7 pounds, are scattered throughout. Rainbows should be fished for in the deep parts of the lake and around the edges in the evening. Try trolling with small bait patterns or spinners. Bass are best fished for around obstructions and weedy shorelines. Best access is from a boat, although bank anglers can find a few good access points to some deeper holes. For the anadromous runs, fish during fall when the fish are moving into the lake from the New River. Because of the perpetual winds, Flores is popular with kite surfers, sailboarders, and the occasional Jet Skier.

Species: Rainbow trout, sea-run cutthroat, largemouth bass, steelhead, chinook.

Facilities: There is a boat launch at the north end of the lake. The nearest camping and day-use areas are on the lake at Boice County Park. Supplies and accommodations can be had in Port Orford or Bandon.

Directions: From Port Orford drive north on U.S. 101 about 12 miles. From U.S. 101, follow the sign to Flores Lake from Denmark to the south or Langlois to the north.

Contact: Port Orford Chamber of Commerce, 541/332-8055; Sixes Store and Tackle, 541/332-6666.

60 SIXES RIVER
north of Port Orford
Map 1.5, page 83   BEST (

The Sixes is a short small river, flowing about 40 miles from its source in the Siskiyou National Forest. Fishing is restricted to the lower 15 miles, but there are a lot of fish to be had in a short distance. The Sixes is a good winter steelhead and fall chinook fishery with limited access, especially in its lower reaches. This river can be populated with guides during the peak

runs in November and December, especially when other coastal rivers are high and muddy. Watch the boats and where they fish; chances are everyone will fish through the same spots. If possible, fish the opposite bank. Chances are that after the second or third boat, the fish are feeling pushed around and may seek refuge in nontraditional places.

The river mouth must breach the sandbar during the fall rains before any fish move into the river and this can make for a unique fishery during early fall when the fish are waiting to go into the river. Winter steelhead are present December–March. Fall chinook can be caught October–December. All methods of fishing are productive, including bobbers, bait, spinners, and plugs. Good populations of both sea-run and resident cutthroat are available at certain times of the year. Look for sea-runs in the tidal water and lower river in fall. Resident trout are available year-round in the upper reaches where the water turns into a series of pools, riffles, and pocket water.

Bank access is a problem, especially on the lower river. Tidewater bank access begins at the mouth in Cape Blanco State Park. Farther upriver you find access points and a few boat ramps along Cape Blanco Highway below U.S. 101 and at the Sixes store by the interstate crossing. The upper river access points are not well marked except at a couple of boat launches. Look for turnouts that have paths leading to the river and avoid any area with No Trespassing signs. Boaters have a few options for some easy floats through productive water. The highest put-in is at Edson Creek County Park, with take-outs at Mid-Drift or the Sixes River Store on U.S. 101. Each drift is about three miles. A longer drift can be had from the store to Cape Blanco State Park.

Species: Winter steelhead, fall chinook, coho, resident and sea-run cutthroat.

Facilities: Boats can be launched from behind the store where U.S. 101 crosses the river, upriver at Mid-Drift, and at Edson Creek County Park. A nice primitive campground is available approximately 15 miles east on

Sixes River Rd. day-use area. Buy supplies in Port Orford.

Directions: Five miles north of Port Orford, turn right at Sixes River. Travel approximately 11 miles on Sixes River Rd. From Bandon drive 25 miles south. To reach the river below U.S. 101, drive west on the Cape Blanco Hwy. south of the river crossing or north of the crossing take Airport Rd. to the west.

Contact: Port Orford Chamber of Commerce, 541/332-8055; Sixes Store and Café, 541/332-6666; Cape Blanco State Park, 541/332-6774; Brent Lamm, 541/440-0558, www.umpqua fishingguide.com.

61 ELK RIVER
north of Port Orford

Map 1.5, page 83

The Elk River runs 30 miles from its source in the Siskiyou National Forest at Salmon Mountain and Grassy Knob Wilderness before emptying into the ocean. The Elk and the Sixes are in close proximity to each other and share similar qualities: size, fish runs, size of fish, popularity, ability to clear quickly after a storm, limited access because of private lands, good fisheries at the mouth, and main drifts that are best reached by drift boat. The upper reaches are exceptionally small streams but easily accessible on forest lands. This is another popular guide river in the fall when other South Coast rivers are blown out.

The Elk is known for its wild winter steelhead and fall chinook runs. Most of the year, the Elk is blocked from entering the ocean by a sandbar, which accounts for its fall and winter runs of fish. The fall fish enter the river when the bar is breached by high waters. The mouth provides a unique and productive fishery before the breach when the fish are offshore waiting to move upriver. Winter steelhead begin their arrival in December and can be caught through March. Fall chinook can be caught as early as October when the river mouth is breached into December. In addition to salmon and steelhead the Elk gets

a good run of sea-run cutthroat that can be caught throughout the river but especially in the tidewaters starting in fall. The upper river has a decent population of resident cutthroat that can be fished for year-round. Use small spinners and flies to catch these fish.

There is some bank access on the lower river at the five-mile marker on Elk River Road and again near the seven-mile marker. The best access, however, can be found at the fish hatchery, eight miles upriver from U.S. 101. Here you will find lots of deep runs that are perfect for swinging a fly or drifting floats with egg patterns. Some anglers choose to stay at the Elk River Campground, a privately held campground that grants access to the river for campers only. There are two other access points on the lower river at the U.S. 101 crossing and at the mouth from Cape Blanco State Park. Once in the park walk about a mile south to the river.

Boat access is good, particularly on the productive lower stretches. The uppermost drift is a nine-mile stretch from the hatchery to the take-out at Ironhead. Another option is to use the ramp at the campground, six miles from the hatchery, for a small fee ($6).

Species: Winter steelhead, fall chinook, coho, sea-run cutthroat.

Facilities: Boat ramps are available at the fish hatchery, Ironhead boat ramp, Elk River Campground, and in Cape Blanco State Park. Camping can be had at the privately owned Elk River Campground, or at two primitive campgrounds approximately 15 miles up Elk River Rd. Buy supplies in Port Orford.

Directions: From Port Orford drive three miles north to Elk River Rd., which turns into Forest Rd. 5201. To reach the mouth at Cape Blanco State Park, cross the river on the interstate to McKenzie Rd. and drive west to the park.

Contact: Elk River Hatchery, 541/332-7025; Port Orford Chamber of Commerce, 541/332-8055; Sixes Store and Café, 541/332-6666; Elk River RV Park, 541/332-2255; Brent Lamm, 541/440-0558, www.umpquafishing guide.com.

62 GARRISON LAKE

west of Port Orford

Map 1.5, page 83

Scenic and close to camping, Garrison Lake is a 134-acre lake up to 30 feet deep, offering stocked rainbow, wild cutthroat, bass, and yellow perch. At one time there was a good population of bass, but due to overfishing and reduced stocking, they are of no consequence to the angler. Evidence of an ocean breach in 1999 may have had some effect on fish populations. Garrison is best fished from a boat and there are two good ramps at the south and north ends. Weeds can be a problem especially in the summer. A boat will help you gain access to the deeper water and fish the edges of the weed beds. Spin fishing, flies, and your bait of choice all work in the lake.

Species: Hatchery rainbows, wild cutthroat, bass, and yellow perch.

Facilities: The north and south ends of the lake have boat ramps. The nearest camping is at nearby Battle Rock State Park. There is good beach access and possible surf perch fishing to the north and south of the lake at Paradise Point State Wayside and Port Orford State Wayside. A day-use area provides good picnicking. Supplies and accommodations are available in Port Orford.

Directions: In Port Orford follow the signs west to the state waysides and Garrison Lake.

Contact: Port Orford Chamber of Commerce, 541/332-8055.

63 LOWER ROGUE: GRAVE CREEK TO AGNESS

west of Grants Pass

Map 1.5, page 83

With all due respect to such great Oregon rivers as the Umpqua and Deschutes, the Rogue is the most fabled and lore-filled river in Oregon. The Rogue is quite large, covering a distance of 155 miles and originating far east of the coastal range in the Cascades. The author Zane Grey fished on and wrote about the Rogue in the 1920s and '30s. Today, the Rogue attracts anglers from all over the world to fish its famous steelhead and salmon runs.

Grave Creek to Foster Bar is a 35-mile stretch of roadless Wild and Scenic Wilderness accessible only by foot or boat. This section of river is bracketed by Grave Creek Landing upstream and Illahe downstream. Jet boats are allowed into the wilderness as far as Blossom Bar, about 15 miles above Foster Bar; otherwise your options are a drift boat or internal frame raft. The wilderness section should be considered by only the most advanced boaters. White water, canyons, and large boulders make this some of the most treacherous water in Oregon. Several well-written boating guides cover this section of water in a river-mile-by-river-mile description.

This area has much to offer anglers, especially if they have more than a weekend to explore some truly wild country. Most float trips through this water are 3–5 days long. Fishing is excellent because of limited pressure and well worth the effort for backpackers, hikers, and rafters. Steelhead show in the summer August–October and in winter November–March. Chinook salmon are available in fall August–December and in the spring May–August. Coho enter the river August–October. A certain percentage of Rogue half-pounders, more abundant in the lower river below Foster Bar, winter over in the Wild and Scenic section by September–October.

Bank anglers can begin fishing this section of river from either end of the Rogue River Trail, which begins at Graves Creek and ends at Illahe. Along this 35-mile stretch of trail lies some marvelous fishing opportunities for both fly anglers and those who use traditional gear such as spinner and bait. The Rogue is considered a riffle fishery, that is, fish tend to hold either below or above a river drop, waiting to move upriver or resting after passing through the white water. Focus your angling skills on these two primary areas. Other areas where fish may hold are around boulders and tail-outs of long runs. Employ brightly colored flies and spinners or bait such as cured roe.

Below the Wild and Scenic section sits Illahe and the beginning of a very accessible stretch of river to Agness. Bank access is good at Foster Bar and the Illahe Campground. The tiny community of Agness is a good place to get supplies and hire a guide. The most popular drift is from Foster Bar below Illahe to the take-out at the gravel Lucas Bar below Agness. This area is home to spring and fall chinook, summer and winter steelhead, and a unique fishery of half-pounders.

Half-pounders deserve special mention because this stretch of river is famous for them. Classified not as a steelhead but as a trout, half-pounders are an immature summer steelhead that return to the river after less than a year in the ocean. Once in the river, half-pounders behave more like trout, making them the perfect prey of fly anglers with everything from a dry fly to a streamer. Anglers can fish for half-pounders without possessing a steelhead tag. Much smaller than the adults, averaging 12–16 inches, these fish are every bit as aggressive if not more so when coming to a fly. A unique feature of these fish is their feeding habits and their tendency to rise to a swinging wet fly or dry fly. Many unique fly patterns such as the Rogue River Special, Juicy Bug, and Golden Demon tied on double hooks have been developed or used with outstanding success on this river and have subsequently influenced the way steelhead anglers worldwide approach this difficult species. The flies tend to be smaller than most steelhead anglers are used to. Half-pounders enter the river in October and winter over in the waters between the mouth of the Illinois River and Foster Bar.

Species: Spring and fall chinook, coho, steelhead, Rogue half-pounders, trout.

Facilities: Boat access to the Wild and Scenic Rogue River begins at Grave Creek Landing with the take-out at Foster Bar. Special permits are required to float this section; they are obtainable on a lottery system from the U.S. Forest Service. Numerous backcountry lodges such as Marial, Paradise Bar, Half Moon Bar, Clay Hill, and Black Bar Lodge provide accommodations and meals to hikers and boaters. It is common for to book 3–5-day float trips that take you from lodge to lodge. Those wishing for hike-in camping can find primitive campsites along the Rogue River Trail between Foster Bar and Grave Creek. Camping is available at Indian Mary Park and Illahe Campground. RV parks, shuttles, accommodations, and supplies are available in Grants Pass, Marial, and Galice.

Directions: From Grants Pass take I-5 three miles to the Merlin exit. Drive west on the Merlin–Galice Hwy. road west approximately 25 miles to Grave Creek Landing. To reach Illahe, drive west from Graves Creek 45 miles on the circuitous Bear Creek Rd.

Contact: U.S. Forest Service Rand Information Center in Merlin, 541/479-3735; Indian Mary Park, 541/474-5285; McKenzie River Outfitters, 541/773-5145; Agness RV Park, 541/247-2813; Cougar Lane Lodge and Store, 541/247-7233; Old Agness Store 541/247-9181; Native Run Fly Shop, 541/660-0540; Chris Young Guide Service and Accommodations, 541/247-8115, www.fishtherogue.com; Marial Lodge, 541/474-2057; Paradise Lodge, 800/525-2161; Half Moon Bar Lodge, 888/291-8268; Clay Hill Lodge, 503/859-3772; Black Bar Lodge, 541/479-6507.

64 LOWER ROGUE: AGNESS TO GOLD BEACH

east of Gold Beach

Map 1.5, page 83

Below the confluence with the Illinois River the Rogue travels 27 miles to the Pacific Ocean, all of which is easily accessible from a boat or along the bank via Highway 595 (Jerry's Flat Rd.) on the south side and Highway 540 (North Bank Rd.) on the north side of the river. This stretch is accessible from I-5 near Grants Pass or, better yet, from Gold Beach on the coast. Steelhead show in the summer August–October and in winter November–March. Chinook salmon are available in fall August–December and in the spring May–August. Coho enter the river August–October. Rogue half-pounders enter the river between late summer and fall (see *Lower Rogue: Grave Creek to Agness,* for a description of half-pounders).

The reach of tide extends from the bay at the U.S. 101 bridge crossing four miles upriver to the Ferry Hole on the north side of the river. Bank fishing and boating, either powerboats or drift boats, is good in this stretch from either the north or south side of the river. Most anglers here are trolling or drifting for salmon and occasionally steelhead. Steelhead, however, are more easily caught above the reach of tide. A popular float for drift boats in this stretch begins at Huntley Park, two miles above tidewater. Other areas to fish are Indian Creek Park, Champion Mill, and Clay Banks.

Above the tidal reach you have access to the river from either the north or south sides. The drive from Gold Beach along Highway 595 (Jerry's Flat Rd.) is a scenic, windy road that parallels the south side of the river for most of its length and offers good opportunities for both bank fishing and boating. The first five miles of river above the reach of tide offers good bank fishing and unimproved boat ramps from numerous gravel bars such as The Willows, Coyote Riffle, Huntley Bar and Park, Orchard Bar, Lobster Creek boat ramp, and Quosatana Campground. Drift boats can float all this water with relative ease. Some caution should be used when driving onto the gravel bars in a non–four-wheel-drive vehicle; soft sand and large rocks could pose a problem for conventional cars. Spinner, flies, and drift fishing with bait are all productive techniques.

Highway 540 (North Bank Rd.) from Gold Beach is also a great drive on the north side of the river that dead-ends at the Lower Rogue River Trail. A good place to start fishing or put in a drift boat is at the Kimball Riffle seven miles upstream from U.S. 101. Other good access exists at Jim Davis Riffle near Lobster Creek.

The final section of river begins about a quarter mile below the confluence of the Illinois River below Agness. The Hotel Riffle and the boat ramp at Hog Eddy both offer good bank access and exceptional fly water for steelhead. The boat launch at Cougar Lane Store or Lucas Gravel Bar at the confluence with the Illinois River will give you access to a long stretch of river (approximately 12 miles) to the take-out at Quosatana Campground.

Species: Spring and fall chinook, coho, steelhead, Rogue half-pounders, trout.

Facilities: Boat ramps can be found along Jerry's Flat Rd. (Hwy. 595) at Huntley Park, Lobster Creek, Quosatana Campground, Lucas Gravel Bar, Cougar Lane Store, and Foster Bar. From the North Bank Rd. (Hwy. 540) a boat can be launched at Ferry Hole and Kimball Riffle. Camping is available at Indian Creek, Huntley Park, Lobster Creek, Quosatana Campground, Foster Bar, and on the Illinois at Oak Flat. Primitive hike-in campsites are available along the Rogue River Trail between Foster Bar and Grave Creek and along the Lower River Trail from Agness to North Bank Rd. RV parks, shuttles, accommodations, and supplies are available in Gold Beach and Agness.

Directions: From Gold Beach turn east from the south side of the U.S. 101 bridge in Gold Beach and drive east on Jerry's Flat Rd., which turns into Agness Rd. and follows the river up to Illahe. The north bank is accessible by turning east from the north side of the U.S. 101 bridge in Gold Beach. Follow this road 10 miles until it dead-ends at the Rogue River Trail.

Contact: Gold Beach Ranger District, 541/247-3600; Gold Beach Chamber of Commerce, 800/525-2334; Jot's Resort, 800/367-5687; Rogue Outdoor Store, 541/247-7142; Agness RV Park, 541/247-2813; Cougar Lane Lodge and Store, 541/247-7233; Old Agness Store, 541/247-9181; Native Run Fly Shop, 541/660-0540; Chris Young Guide Service and Accommodations, 541/247-8115, www.fishtherogue.com.

65 LOWER ILLINOIS RIVER
south of Agness

Map 1.5, page 83

The Lower Illinois River flows from Oak Flat at the northern end of the Kalmiopsis Wilderness Boundary to the confluence with the Rogue River near Agness. This short eight-mile stretch of river offers excellent opportunities to catch both Rogue half-pounders and native winter steelhead of 20 pounds or more. Both bank and boating access is excellent from Oak Flat. To boat this section, launch from one of the gravel bars at Oak Flat and take out at Cougar Lane near the confluence with the Rogue River. Bank anglers have the option of fishing a large area around Oak Flat or hiking the trail into the Kalmiopsis Wilderness at the southern end of the campground. Other bank access exists along Oak Flat Road on the way to the campground, but private property and No Trespassing signs will limit use. There is enough access at Oak Flat to warrant bypassing this area and avoid the risk of trespassing.

Note that the water here is big, wide, deep, swift, and very fishy—one can only imagine the fight that would ensue if hooking a native 20-pound steelhead. Anglers will be immediately drawn to the large runs, gravel bars, and boulders that sit 90 feet or more out in the river, but use extreme caution before wading. Wading more than 10 feet from the bank will put you waist-deep in a fast current over slippery rocks—enough to get away from brushy banks, but at the risk of going for a swim. Wading isn't necessary for bank anglers but be prepared to battle some high brush in certain sections; wading staffs and cleated boots are advisable. Both traditional gear anglers and fly anglers should be prepared to make long casts to reach holding water. Fly anglers might consider using spey rods for the best coverage. If you're not familiar with Rogue half-pounders you may scoff at the small ticks hitting your lure as it swings through the water, but those are actually 12–18 inch steelhead and if you set the hook you'll find out what all the fuss

is about. Fishing for half-pounders is best late August–late September. The winter steelhead arrive December–April.

Species: Trout, winter steelhead, Rogue half-pounders, fall chinook.

Facilities: Gravel bars at Oak Flat will enable you to launch a boat. The take-out is on Cougar Ln. at the confluence with the Rogue River. Get permission to use the Cougar Ln. boat ramp from the Cougar Lane Store. There are free primitive campsites at Oak Flat and Indian Creek Campgrounds. RV and tent camping, fishing supplies, and accommodations are at the Cougar Lane Store in Agness, and farther west at Gold Beach.

Directions: From Agness take Hwy. 33 west to Oak Flat Rd. (Rte. 450) and turn south. Oak Flat Rd. dead-ends at Indian Creek Campground and the Kalmiopsis Wilderness boundary. The best river access is around the campground and upriver on foot.

Contact: Illinois Valley Ranger District, 541/592-4000; Illinois Valley Visitor Center, 541/592-4076; Cougar Lane Lodge and Store, 541/247-7233; Old Agness Store, 541/247-9181; Native Run Fly Shop, 541/660-0540.

66 ROGUE RIVER BAY
in Gold Beach

Map 1.5, page 83

The Rogue Bay estuary comprises the area between the bay and Clay Banks at river mile 5 just below Jim Hunt Creek. The coastal mountains of the Siskiyou National Forest provide a spectacular backdrop to this excellent salmon fishery. Spring chinook begin their run late March–May. Fall chinook show July–September. Coho make their appearance August–October. Some steelhead may be caught, but because of the speed with which they move through they are rarely targeted until they pass the reach of tide at Clay Banks. This is primarily a trolling fishery, and anglers fish for salmon with plugs, spinners, and bait such as herring and anchovies. Fishing is concentrated from the North Jetty to the reach of tide at Clay Banks. Perch and lingcod are also caught from the North Jetty. Dungeness crab anglers use crab pots around Doyle Point on the North Jetty side.

Species: Spring and fall chinook, coho, steelhead, bottom fish, perch, lingcod.

Facilities: Boat launches are available at Jot's Resort and the Port Commission ramp at the South Jetty. Camping is available at Indian Creek Campground, Huntley Park, Lobster Creek, and Quosatana Campground. Additional camping, fishing supplies, RV parks, and accommodations can be had in Gold Beach.

Directions: The bay sits at the northern end of Gold Beach to the west of U.S. 101. To get to the South Jetty take the South Jetty exit off U.S. 101. To get to the North Jetty, cross the bridge over the bay and take your first left on Old Coast Drive.

Contact: Gold Beach Ranger District, 541/247-3600; Gold Beach Chamber of Commerce, 800/525-2334; Jot's Resort, 800/367-5687; Five Star Charters, 888/301-6480; Rogue Outdoor Store, 541/247-7142; Chris Young Guide Service and Accommodations, 541/247-8115, www.fishtherogue.com.

67 PISTOL RIVER

south of Gold Beach

Map 1.5, page 83

The Pistol is a small but rugged river originating at the confluence of a series of small tributaries just 20 miles up in the Siskiyou National Forest. The Pistol has had much of its fish habitat destroyed from years of logging, which stripped the river of its spawning beds and holding water. Some rehabilitation work has helped restore the river's ecosystem, but much remains to be done. Meanwhile, the river has seen improvements in its runs of winter steelhead, fall chinook, and sea-run cutthroat. A small but steady population of resident cutthroat can provide a fun afternoon of trout fishing.

River access is extremely limited by private lands bordering most of the river. Anglers will find the best opportunities at the Pistol River State Park along U.S. 101 and upriver via the North Bank Pistol River Road. A day-use area five miles upriver provides some access as so various roadside turnouts along the first eight miles of Pistol River Road. Use caution when getting to the river along the road—No Trespassing signs are frequent but by no means a reliable indicator of all private property. The day-use area is actually private land that a landowner allows people to use and is identified by a small turnoff leading to the river. After eight miles the road dissipates into a network of logging roads bordered by private lands. Some landowners in both the upper and lower sections of the river allow access. The Pistol General Store can provide the names and phone number of those owners willing to grant angler access. Should you venture into the upper reaches it is advisable to obtain a Siskiyou National Forest map to negotiate the many forks, road changes, and public lands.

Most of the fishable water in the upper reaches of the river is boulder runs in deep canyons. Access to these areas can be strenuous at best. Expect to fish pocket water behind boulders and deep pools created by narrow chutes. Spinners, flies, and drift gear are your best approach. Lower reaches of the river consist of gentle currents flowing through farmland and provide the best opportunity to catch fresh steelhead and active sea-run cutthroat with flies or bait and spinners. Steelhead enter the river December–March. Sea-run cutthroat are available in the river when the river mouth is breached by fall rains in September and October. A small run of stray half-pounders migrates over from the Rogue in September and October.

Species: Winter steelhead, fall chinook, sea-run cutthroat, half-pounders.

Facilities: There is a day-use area at milepost 5. Supplies are available at the Pistol General Store and in Gold Beach.

Directions: From Gold Beach take U.S. 101 south 15 miles. Look for the Pistol River Rd.

turnoff after crossing the river. You can also reach the river via Pistol River Loop Rd. just north of where U.S. 101 crosses the river.

Contact: Jot's Resort, 800/367-5687; Gold Beach Ranger District, 541/247-3600; Gold Beach Chamber of Commerce, 800/525-2334; Pistol River General Store, 541/247-2735; Pistol River Fire Station, 541/247-6765.

68 UPPER ILLINOIS RIVER

north of Cave Junction

Map 1.5, page 83

The Illinois River forms in California and flows north through Cave Junction, Oregon, until entering the Rogue River just below Agness. The 25-mile path through the northern section of the Kalmiopsis Wilderness is designated Wild and Scenic River and is accessible only by foot or boat. Boating, however, is limited to experts only—this water is some of the most challenging in the country and should not be taken lightly. The wilderness section divides the river into upper and lower reaches. Deciding which section to fish before a trip can save a lot of driving because the two sections can be breached only by a full day's drive.

Anglers attempting to fish this beautiful and scenic tributary of the Rogue River have their work cut out for them, but the effort can result in a 20-pound steelhead. Other than the upper reaches east of Cave Junction where there is a good population of trout, the fishing below Cave Junction is limited to winter steelhead up to 20 pounds and Rogue half-pounders. Fishing for half-pounders is best late August–late September. The winter steelhead arrive December–April. For successful fishing, learn these waters firsthand, understanding the demanding schedules these fish must keep to get through miles of treacherous white water and troubled-water conditions. Otherwise a fishing guide would be a good investment. The entire river is limited to catch-and-release fishing and only artificial flies and lures may be used.

Above the Kalmiopsis Wilderness from Cave Junction to Briggs Creek Ranch, the river is accessible by road but borders a lot of private property until one enters the Siskiyou National Forest boundary near County Road 4103 For 15 miles the river runs through boulder sections, long tail-outs, and pools. Because this is a catch-and-release river, the Illinois attracts far more fly anglers than traditional gear anglers. Those interested in traditional wet–fly-fishing with spey flies or hair wing patterns such as a Green Butt Skunk are in luck. Long tail-outs with interspersed boulders make this classic steelhead fly-fishing water. Traditional gear anglers do as well using spinners, floats, and drift fishing. Boulder sections and pocket water are better suited for nymphing, drift fishing, and float fishing with yarn and artificial egg patterns. Wading can be treacherous so carry a staff and wear spiked or felt-soled boots. March is the best time to fish this section of the river for hefty steelhead.

Species: Trout, winter steelhead, half-pounders.

Facilities: There is camping at Briggs Creek on County Rd. 4103 and at Store Gulch and Sixmile on the Illinois River Rd. Camping and fishing supplies can be had in Cave Junction or Grants Pass. Steve Bonner of Native Run Fly Shop in Grants Pass is an excellent resource for fly-fishing information.

Directions: From Cave Junction drive north on Hwy. 199 nine miles to the Illinois River Rd. in Selma and turn west. Briggs Creek is 24 miles ahead. Follow the river, watching for occasional river access, until you get to the Siskiyou National Forest boundary at County Rd. 4103, at which point there is no more private property. Route 4103 will dead-end at Briggs Creek and the Kalmiopsis Wilderness Boundary.

Contact: Illinois Valley Ranger District, 541/592-4000; Illinois Valley Visitor Center, 541/592-4076; Native Run Fly Shop, 541/660-0540.

69 CHETCO RIVER

in Brookings

Map 1.5, page 83   **BEST (**

The Chetco is a splendid South Coast river that begins in the spectacular Kalmiopsis Wilderness and travels 50 miles west to Chetco Bay. The upper sections of the river provide the solitude and wilderness experience one comes to expect of most coastal streams. Bank fishing and boat access are excellent and easily reached from the main highway that follows the north side of the river. Salmon, winter steelhead, and native wild resident and sea-run cutthroat are all present at certain times of the year. The winter steelhead run ranks among the best in the state and is no secret among anglers. The Chetco is noted for having a very loyal following of anglers, many of whom fish only the Chetco.

Beginning in September, the salmon move into the tide reaches of the Chetco River and begin moving into freshwater with the arrival of fall rains. Good catches of salmon are available through December in the lower reaches of the river. Winter steelhead make their appearance starting in December and exist in catchable numbers throughout the river until March, January being the peak month. Fly anglers will find some of the best fishing for winter steelhead during low-water months in spring from Loeb State Park upriver. Gravelly river bottoms and long drifts are conducive to traditional greased-line techniques as well as nymphing and sinking lines. Other exceptional fly-fishing can be found at Nook Bar, Redwood Bar, and the South Fork of the Chetco. Fly anglers and light-gear spin anglers should not ignore the year-round cutthroat fishing on the main stem of the river and its tributaries.

Both the North Bank and South Bank roads offer access to the river, but only the North Bank Road follows the river into its upper reaches. The Oregon Department of Fish and Wildlife provides a number of good access points on both sides of the river. Two popular fishing spots on the South Bank Road are Tide Rock, two miles from the highway, and the Piling Hole, four miles from the highway. Both are excellent salmon and steelhead spots with the most popular methods of fishing being trolling with bait, drift fishing with bait and/or corkies and yarn, and fly-fishing. The North Bank Road provides excellent bank and boat access beginning at Morris Hole, just two miles upstream from the highway. Farther up you'll find Social Security boat ramp, the walk-in access at the mouth of the North Fork of the Chetco River, Myrtle Grove, Albert A. Loeb State Park, Ice Box Hole, Miller Bar, and Nook Bar. Access to the bars is generally good, but exercise caution when driving onto bars in non–four-wheel drives. Most standard fishing methods apply with drift fishing, spinners, and fly-fishing being the most productive methods. The Chetco is very drift boat–friendly with plenty of nontechnical drifts through gentle rapids.

Species: Salmon, winter steelhead, native wild resident and sea-run cutthroat.

Facilities: Camping is available at Harris Beach Campground two miles north of Brookings and on the Chetco at Alfred A. Loeb State Park and Redwood Campground. Loeb State Park offers many amenities such as rental cabins, electrical sites with water, restrooms, showers, and day-use and picnic areas. A large grove of mature myrtlewood trees attracts many visitors. Boat ramps exist at Morris Hole, Social Security boat ramp, Miller Bar, and Nook Bar. Supplies and accommodations can be had in Brookings.

Directions: From Brookings, go south on U.S. 101 to the North Bank Chetco River Rd. and turn east. To reach the South Bank Chetco River Rd. continue south over the highway bridge and turn east just after the bridge.

Contact: Siskiyou National Forest–Chetco, 541/412-6000; Alfred A. Loeb Campground, 800/452-5687; Brookings Chamber of Commerce, 800/535-9469; Loring's Lighthouse Sporting Goods, 541/469-2148; Gold River Guides, 541/412-0754.

70 CHETCO BAY
in Brookings

Map 1.5, page 83

This is billed as one of Oregon's top small-craft ports, and small crafts and even canoes find it easy to reach the ocean with the protection of Chetco Cove. Off-shore angling is very popular here for bottom fish, halibut, and salmon. The best place to begin exploring the bay and beaches is at the Chetco River South Jetty on Chetco Bay. Here you will find a public fishing pier and jetty, both wheelchair-accessible. The beach access in front of Driftwood RV Park and the Beachfront Inn provide excellent surf perch fishing April–June. One approach to getting local fishing information is to politely ask anglers on the jetty how they are doing or just observe their techniques while you enjoy the great ocean views. Most anglers are more than willing to answer a few questions to help a visitor to the area.

Chinook are in Chetco Cove beginning late July–August. Most anglers find success trolling with bait such as anchovies and baitfish and spinners for fall chinook. Chetco Bay provides ample opportunities for both boaters and jetty anglers, including bottom fishing for the popular black rockfish, fall chinook, perch, and crab. If you don't have a boat there are numerous guide services and charters to escort you for a fee. (It's advisable to call ahead for the most productive offshore fishing seasons.) Chinook begin to inhabit the bay and tidal reaches of the river beginning in late September and lasting until the fall rains, when they move into the Chetco River. Try fishing from the jetty or trolling the bay in late September for best results. Trolling, float fishing, and fly-fishing are all productive methods. The tide's reach ends at Joe Hill Creek on North Bank Chetco River Road.

Species: Fall chinook, black rockfish, perch, winter steelhead, halibut.

Facilities: A boat launch, public fishing pier, and jetty, all wheelchair-accessible, are available at the Port of Brookings by the South Jetty. Reservation camping is available two miles north of Brookings at Harris Beach Campground Parking. Restaurants, RV camping, bait and tackle shops, and fishing charter services are all available in Brookings or within the jetty community.

Directions: From Brookings head south on U.S. 101. After crossing the Chetco River follow exit signs to Lower Harbor Rd. The South Jetty is accessible from Boat Basin Rd. The Port of Brookings Harbor provides a boat ramp for bay and ocean anglers. The upper bay and tidal sections of the river are accessible from North Bank Chetco River Rd. and South Bank Chetco River Rd. on the north and south ends of the U.S. 101 bridge crossing Chetco Bay. Motorized boats are prohibited above tidewater.

Contact: Siskiyou National Forest–Chetco, 541/412-6000; ODFW, Gold Beach, 541/247-7605; Brookings Chamber of Commerce, 800/535-9469; Loring's Lighthouse Sporting Goods, 541/469-2148; Tradewinds Sportfishing, 541/469-0337; State Parks Reservations, 800/452-5687; Driftwood RV Park, 541/469-9089; Harris Beach Campground, 541/469-2021.

71 WINCHUCK RIVER
south of Brookings

Map 1.5, page 83

Just one mile north from California's border and seven miles south of Bandon, the Winchuck is Oregon's most southern river. At one time this river was popular for its run of winter fish, but it has since fallen out of favor with most anglers because of regulation changes that limit access.

Access is difficult in the first five miles because of private property. It becomes better as one enters the Siskiyou National Forest nine miles upriver. The best access points to the river are at two campgrounds, Winchuck and Ludlum House, and at the river mouth at Winchuck State Wayside Day-Use Park; Winchuck Campground is nine miles from U.S. 101 and Ludlum House Campground is 11 miles. Fishing above Wheeler Creek is prohibited. The entire river below the forest boundary borders private lands and is inaccessible without landowner permission. Recent regulation changes do not permit angling from a floating device.

The river hosts fall chinook salmon November–January, winter steelhead December–March, and sea-run and resident cutthroat year-round. You might be surprised when you arrive to find either high water during heavy rains in the winter spring and fall, or extremely low and clear conditions in the summer. This is a small river in a heavily wooded area, easily crossed in most places. Approach the river with stealth so as to not spook fish. Because this river clears so easily after a storm, clearwater conditions can make angling particularly difficult. Most typical fishing methods apply, from spinner and bait to flies. During low-water years you would be well advised to pack light fishing gear and concentrate on the native cutthroat population for the best action. Focus your fishing on the deeper pools and runs for best results. A productive trip to this river should be planned according to weather conditions and fish runs, all of which can be obtained by contacting one of the agencies or guides below.

Species: Fall chinook, winter steelhead, sea-run and resident cutthroat.

Facilities: Camping with facilities is available at Winchuck Campground and Ludlum House Campground. There is a day-use area with beach access at Winchuck State Wayside. Supplies, accommodations, and RV parks are available in Brookings.

Directions: From Bandon drive seven miles south on U.S. 101. The day-use area is on the west side of U.S. 101. To reach the upper river turn east onto Winchuck River Rd., 0.5 mile north of the day-use area on U.S. 101. Winchuck River Rd. eventually turns into Forest Rd. 1108. Both campgrounds are accessible from the Forest Service roads.

Contact: Siskiyou National Forest–Chetco, 541/412-6000; ODFW, Gold Beach, 541/247-7605; Brookings Chamber of Commerce, 800/535-9469; Loring's Lighthouse Tackle, 541/469-2148.

PORTLAND AND THE WILLAMETTE VALLEY

© BOB HEIMS/US ARMY CORPS OF ENGINEERS

BEST FISHING SPOTS

◖ Salmon
Lower Willamette River: Oregon City to
Columbia River, **page 150**

◖ Smallmouth Bass
Henry Hagg Lake, **page 150**

◖ Places to Teach Kids to Fish
Blue Lake, **page 149**

◖ Most Accessible for Disabled Anglers
Henry Hagg Lake, **page 150**

Portland and the Willamette Valley stretches from

north to south, between the Coast Range on the west and the Cascades to
the east. The valley is home to Oregon's largest metropolitan areas – Portland, Salem, Albany, Corvallis, and Eugene. Rich agricultural lands and flat
river bottomlands surround each of these cities and extend into the foothills
of the mountains. The countryside south of Portland is home to an abundance of small, proud farming communities, all wonderful places to visit
not only for good fishing, but for local summer fairs, bed-and-breakfasts,
antique stores, vineyards and wineries, fruit and nut orchards, vegetable
farms, dairies, flower and plant nurseries, and historical sites.

   The centerpiece of the region is the Willamette River, a 185-mile tributary of the Columbia River and the central drainage for all rivers and
creeks in the Willamette Valley. The valley breaks down into three primary
areas. The lower Willamette Valley ("lower" referring to its proximity to
the mouth of the Willamette) lies within a 15-mile radius around Portland
and includes the Columbia River and cities south of Portland. The middle
Willamette Valley stretches from Salem to Corvallis and Albany. The upper
Willamette Valley extends from Albany south to areas above Eugene and
Springfield and to the border of the Umpqua National Forest. Each of these
areas is unique, but they are all linked by the Willamette River.

   Salmon and steelhead are ubiquitous, inhabiting the whole valley as they migrate their way into rivers and streams to spawn. Because of either number or regulations, these fish get harder to catch the farther "up," or south, one goes in the Willamette Valley. Some catches are made on the upper Willamette above Willamette Falls in Oregon City, but for the most part salmon and steelhead fishing is best, odd though it may seem, around Portland.

Trout fishing anywhere in the Willamette Valley is limited to the upper-most areas of most rivers, higher-elevation lakes, and wherever stocking takes place. The Eugene/Springfield area is a haven for big trout on the Willamette and McKenzie Rivers and constitutes the primary sport fishery. The upper reaches of the Tualatin, Pudding, Molalla, Butte Creek, and Yamhill are also productive for trout, both wild and stocked.

Warm-water fishing is far more prevalent in the Willamette Valley and makes up three-quarters of the spots in this region. Several good fisheries lie between St. Helens and Troutdale, but the best warm-water fishing, bar none, is on Sauvie Island and on the Columbia and Willamette Rivers. Anglers can explore miles of river from shore or a boat, tapping into good catches of walleye, large and smallmouth bass, fat crappie, plump bluegill, big catfish, and even larger sucker fish. South of Portland, anglers can catch bass and panfish on the Willamette River above the falls in Oregon City, and on the lower reaches of the Tualatin, Molalla, and Pudding Rivers.

PORTLAND AND THE WILLAMETTE VALLEY

Longview

WASHINGTON

Woodland

St Helens

Vancouver

Columbia River Gorge National Scenic Area

Gifford Pinchot National Forest

MAP 2.1 page 141

Portland

Tigard

see The Columbia River Gorge and Mount Hood page 180

Mt Hood National Forest

Wilsonville

Trask Mtn 3,423ft

Elsie

Clatsop State Forest

Tillamook State Forest

Siuslaw National Forest

Grand Ronde

Sheridan

Willamette

River

Coast Range

see The Oregon Coast page 78

Salem

Gates

Clackamas River

Cascade Range

Detroit Lake

Eddyville

Corvalis

Albany

MAP 2.2 page 142

Green Peter Reservoir

Sweet Home

see Southern Cascades page 318

Vida

Willamette River

Fern Ridge Reservoir

Eugene

Vendetta

0   10 mi

0   10 km

© AVALON TRAVEL PUBLISHING, INC.

Map 2.1

**Sites 1-17
Pages 143-161**

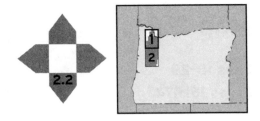

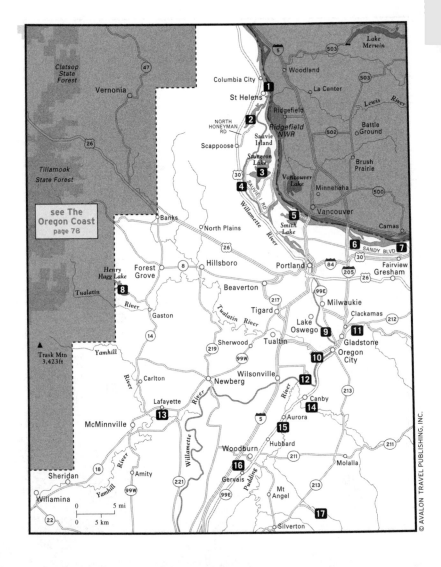

Map 2.2

Sites 18-29
Pages 161-174

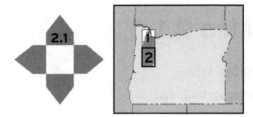

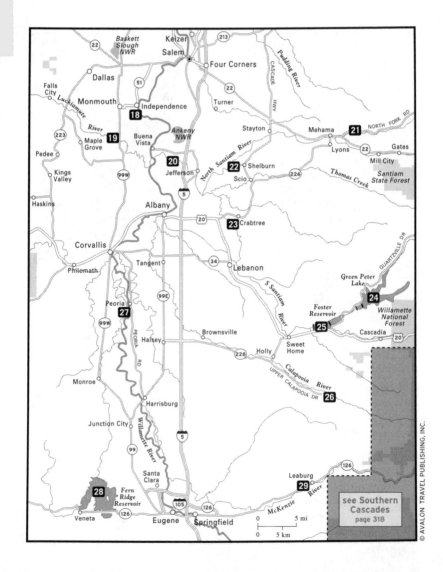

1 COLUMBIA RIVER

Rainier to Troutdale

Map 2.1, page 141

The Willamette Valley section of the Columbia River forms the Portland/Vancouver Basin. This is perhaps one of the most popular, productive, and accessible reaches of the Columbia as the narrow, womblike confines of the Columbia Gorge give way to the sprawling, fertile farmlands of the Willamette Valley. The river widens and becomes less discernable among the islands, channels, and sloughs, then flows between Portland and Vancouver, generating a tremendous amount of commercial use and shipping traffic. Just below Portland, the Columbia and Willamette combine forces at Kelley Point Park. The whole basin from Troutdale to Rainier is a watery mess of marshes, lakes, and smaller tributaries.

Sturgeon, salmon, steelhead, shad, bass, and panfish make up the major catches in this section of the Columbia River. Regulations change frequently on these waters, so check the ODFW publications and website for updates. Summer and winter steelhead are present June–August and November–March, respectively. The best catches are made between Government Island and the mouth of the Sandy River near Troutdale, and from the beaches and tributary inlets around Sauvie Island and Rainier. Fall chinook are present August–September and are caught primarily around river mouths such as the Sandy and Willamette, islands such as Government Island, and in channels such as those found in front of the decommissioned Trojan nuclear power plant. Sturgeon are present all year, but the best catches are made February–May around St. Helens, Trojan, and the Sandy River mouth. Shad are a popular sport fish and a source of bait for sturgeon anglers. Shad arrive from the ocean in May and last through early July; they can be caught in the faster currents and shallower waters on the sides or tips of islands. Bass and panfish are abundant in sloughs and slack water anywhere near the riverbank. Good catches are made downstream from the boat launch at Chinook Landing.

Both boat and bank anglers have good opportunities for all species. There are 17 public or private boat ramps and marinas between the towns of Troutdale and Rainier. With the exception of boat ramps on the Multnomah Channel and Willamette River, all boat launches on the Columbia put you in productive water. Multnomah Channel and Willamette River ramps will require anywhere from 1–3-mile cruise to reach the Columbia. Perhaps the two most popular boat launches are those at Chinook Landing, near Troutdale, and Scappoose Bay. These two launches, approximately 40 miles apart, cover the upper and lower/middle sections of this stretch respectively. Scipios Globe Landing and Rainier Marina give good access to the lowest section, 15 miles west from the nearest upriver put-in and Scappoose Bay.

The best bank access on the river is from the roadside beaches at Sauvie Island (Reeder, Willow Bar, Walton, North Unit) near the towns of St. Helens (Shell Island wig jetties, Columbia City), Prescott (Prescott and Laurel Beach), and Rainier (Rainier Beach and Dibble Beach). The areas around Sauvie Island tend to be best for sturgeon bank anglers, while the areas around St. Helens to Rainier are better for steelhead and salmon. Almost all bank fishing is done in the plunking style with bait and heavy lead weights.

Species: Spring and fall chinook, bluegill, crappie, sunfish, yellow perch, brown bullhead catfish, steelhead, shad, sturgeon, bass.

Facilities: Camping is available at Scappoose Bay RV Park and on Sauvie Island at Reeder Beach Resort RV Park. There is also camping at Jantzen Beach RV Park, on Hayden Island in North Portland. It has 169 sites for RVs, none for tents, and offers all imaginable services. Supplies and accommodations are available throughout the Portland metropolitan area.

There's a boat ramp for the lower section in Rainier; the public marina there charges $2 per day for launch and parking; pump-out facilities are also available. St. Helens also has a public marina with a ramp onto the Columbia; the ramp is open 7 A.M.–5 P.M. year-round and charges $3 per launch, plus $3 per day for overnight parking. Warren has a boat ramp at the Scappoose Bay Marina (see *Scappoose Bay* listing in this chapter).

The middle section of river can be accessed at M. James Gleason Ramp (open sunrise to sunset, $4 per car). The upper section is best reached from Chinook Landing Marine Park (open sunrise to sunset, $5 per car).

Access to Multnomah Channel can be had from ramps at Fred's Marina, Cassidy/Marina Way Moorage, Brown's Landing, Gilbert River Ramp, Larson's Moorage, and the Sauvie Island Boat Ramp, which is operated by Metro Regional Parks and Recreation Department. Fred's, Cassidy, and Larson's are along Hwy. 30 near the Sauvie Island turnoff.

Brown's Landing, Gilbert River, and Sauvie Island boat ramps are all on Sauvie Island, and parking permits (daily $3.50, annual $11) are required to park in any of the wildlife areas. Purchase permits at the Cracker Barrel Store (15005 N.W. Sauvie Island Rd.) just after you cross the bridge onto the island, through the Oregon Department of Fish and Wildlife, or at the Reeder Beach RV Country Store.

Directions: To reach Reeder Beach Resort RV Park from Portland, drive 10 miles west on Hwy. 30 and turn right onto Sauvie Island Rd. Cross the bridge onto the island, then drive 2.1 miles and turn right onto N.W. Reeder Rd. The entrance to the park is 5.5 miles ahead on the right. To get to Jantzen Beach RV Park, drive four miles north from Portland on I-5 and take Exit 308 (Jantzen Beach), which will put you on Hayden Island Drive. Go west on Hayden Island Dr. for 0.5 mile to the park.

For the boat ramps: St. Helens Marina is at 134 N. River St. in St. Helens. From Portland, drive 27 miles west on Hwy. 30 and turn right (north) on Columbia Blvd. in St. Helens. Drive 1.2 miles on Columbia Blvd. and turn left (west) on N. 1st St. Go 0.1 mile

and turn right (north) on Wyeth St. Wyeth becomes River St., and you'll reach the park in 0.1 mile.

Rainier Public Marina is at the foot of E. 3rd St. in Rainier. From Portland, drive 45 miles west on Hwy. 30 to Rainier, then turn right (north) on E. 3rd St. The boat ramp is 500 feet ahead at the end of the road.

M. James Gleason Boat Ramp, operated by Metro Regional Government, is at N.E. 43rd Ave. and Marine Drive in Portland. To reach it from downtown Portland, take I-5 north for 3.7 miles to Exit 307 (Marine Dr.). Travel east on Marine Dr. for 2.9 miles to the park on the left.

Chinook Landing Marine Park, also operated by Metro, is adjacent to Blue Lake Park in Fairview. From Portland, drive east on I-84 for 13 miles and take Exit 14 (Fairview). Go 0.3 mile north on 207th Ave. to Sandy Blvd. Turn right (east) onto Sandy and travel east for 0.7 mile to 223rd, then turn left (north). Proceed one mile north to the park.

Contact: Portland Oregon Visitors Association, 503/275-9750; Rainier Chamber of Commerce, 503/556-7212; St. Helens/Scappoose Chamber of Commerce, 503/397-0685; Oregon Parks and Recreation Department, 800/551-6949; ODFW, Corvallis, 541/757-4186; Metro Regional Parks and Greenspaces Department 503/797-1850; Reeder Beach Resort RV Park, 503/621-3098; Jantzen Beach RV Park 503/289-7626; St. Helens Marina, 503/397-4162; Scappoose Bay Marina 503/541-3939; Fred's Marina, 503/286-5537; Cassidy/Marina Way Moorage, 503/286-2157; Brown's Landing, 503/289-7879; Gilbert River boat ramp, 503/397-2353; Larson's Moorage, 503/286-1233.

◪ SCAPPOOSE BAY
south of St. Helens

Map 2.1, page 141

Five miles south of St. Helens, Scappoose Bay forms a small backwater tributary of the Multnomah Channel, which runs into the

Columbia River. The upper bay extends south about five miles in a series of pools connected by narrow waterways. Most of this upper area is shallow, with marginal fish populations, but it attracts some anglers who use canoes and kayaks to navigate the inlets and waterways. Most anglers focus on the much more productive lower bay. The environment is river bottomlands, appreciated for its wildlife, tall stands of cottonwoods, oaks, and the forested backdrop of the Tualatin Mountains.

Many anglers use the bay as a jumping-off point for access to the Columbia River, a short five-mile trip from Scappoose Marina (the only access point to the bay). The only bank fishing is around the marina on hiking trails both up- and downstream a few hundred yards, making this a better boat fishery. Except during high water, anglers with larger boats are restricted to waters downstream from the Scappoose Marina boat launch.

Primary catches include warm-water species of bass, perch, crappie, bluegill, and carp; the mouth of the bay is a popular sturgeon fishery. Log rafts, pylons, boat docks, downed trees, and riverbank brush attract good numbers of fish. From the marina, move north down the west bank for the best water. A few smaller bay arms can be found on the west bank closer to the Columbia. Fish these smaller backwaters and the entire bay with jigs, bass bugs, and bait such as worms or eggs. Catfish and carp are thick on the bay bottom and easily caught with a worm or small piece of cheese. (Fly angling is not commonly practiced, but that doesn't mean it won't work.) Carp are not commonly thought of as a sport fish but are fast becoming popular with many fly anglers because of their size, strength, and finicky eating habits.

Several creeks flow into Scappoose Bay and can be fished at the mouths by boat: McNulty Creek enters the north end; Honeyman and Scappoose enter from the south. These creeks contain bass, perch, and crappie and some trout at the mouths in the upper reaches, but they are virtually unavailable elsewhere

without permission from landowners to cross private lands.

Species: Largemouth bass, crappie, bluegill, perch, brown bullhead catfish, carp, sturgeon.

Facilities: Full-service Scappoose RV Park, operated by Columbia County, has tent sites and full hookup sites with picnic tables and fire grills. River access is at the Scappoose Bay Marina, in Warren. The marina (open 24 hours) has a three-lane boat ramp, large parking lot, boat and trailer storage for rent, a fishing dock and walking bridge, restrooms, large picnic areas, a small grocery store, gazebo, and nature trails. The fee is $3 per day, which includes the launch. Accommodations and supplies are available in St. Helens and Scappoose.

Directions: From St. Helens, drive eight miles south on Hwy. 30 to Scappoose. For the Scappoose RV Park, turn left (northeast) on N.E. Westlane Rd. and drive 0.5 mile to N. Honeyman Rd. Turn left (north) on N. Honeyman Rd. and go 0.1 mile to the park. For the marina, turn right (east) onto Bennett Rd., three miles north of Scappoose. Take an immediate left (north) onto Old Portland Rd., and continue 0.4 mile to the marina.

Contact: St. Helens/Scappoose Chamber of Commerce, 503/397-0685; ODFW, Corvallis, 541/757-4186; Scappoose RV Park, 503/543-3225; Scappoose Bay Marina, 503/397-2888.

❸ STURGEON LAKE
on Sauvie Island
Map 2.1, page 141

Sauvie Island, 10 miles north of Portland, is both an active farming community and a popular recreation area composed of river-bottom vegetation such as tall grasses, cottonwood trees, large oak trees, and blackberries. The forested backdrop of the Tualatin Mountains looms on the western skyline. Its canoe and kayak trails, hiking trails, Columbia River beaches, country roads, and fresh produce farms are popular features, but the central feature is Sturgeon Lake, a 3,500-acre warmwater fishery providing fair to good fishing for largemouth bass, crappie, bluegill, perch, and brown bullhead catfish.

Sturgeon Lake is accessible from surrounding roads, boat ramps on the lake or in the Multnomah Channel, or by hiking trails across Game Management lands. Fishing season on Sauvie Island is April 16–September 30, and a special Sauvie Island Wildlife Area parking permit is required for all recreational parking. Boating on the lake is suitable for small motorboats, jet sleds, canoes, and kayaks.

Sturgeon Lake boat ramp on Oak Island is perhaps the most convenient access to the lake. Once launched, cruise the shorelines looking for bass with surface poppers, fish jigs around debris for crappie and perch, or fish the bottom with bait for brown bullhead. There are so many little pockets, channels, arms, and sloughs that boating the lake can feel like working through a maze. Near the north end of the lake, either the Gilbert River or Pete's Slough will lead you to the Multnomah Channel (three miles) or McNary Lake (two miles), respectively. Gilbert River is also the access point for reaching the Multnomah Channel and the Columbia River, and it has a small population of walleye. To start at the bottom end, launch your boat at the Gilbert Lake ramp, where the Gilbert River and Multnomah Channel meet, and follow the Gilbert River south to Sturgeon Lake or north to the Multnomah Channel.

Bank access is best from surrounding roads: Reeder Road, which leads to the northern end of the lake; Oak Island Road, which leads to the boat launch and more access; or along the west bank off Steelman Road. Cast spinners, bait, or bass poppers just about anywhere, but especially around structure.

Species: Largemouth bass, crappie, perch, brown bullhead catfish, bluegill, walleye.

Facilities: Reeder Beach Resort RV Park has the closest camping. Boat ramps are at Gilbert River (operated by Columbia County Parks) and Sturgeon Lake (operated by ODFW), both of which are on Sauvie Island. Parking permits are required to park in any of the wildlife areas on Sauvie Island; daily permits are $3.50 and annual permits are $11. Buy permits at the Cracker Barrel Store (15005 N.W. Sauvie Island Rd.), just after you cross the bridge onto the island; through the Oregon Department of Fish and Wildlife; or at the Reeder Beach RV Country Store. Supplies are available at the Sauvie Island General Store and in Scappoose.

Directions: To reach Sauvie Island and Reeder Beach Resort RV Park from Portland, drive 9.3 miles west on Hwy. 30 and turn right onto Sauvie Island Rd. Cross the bridge onto the island, then drive 2.1 miles and turn right onto N.W. Reeder Rd. The entrance to the park is 5.5 miles ahead on the right. To reach Gilbert River boat ramp, continue on Reeder Rd. for six miles past the RV park (making a total of 11.5 miles), then turn left (south) onto Gilbert River Boat Ramp Rd. Follow this road approximately one mile to the ramp. To reach Sturgeon Lake boat ramp, drive a total of 1.3 miles on Reeder Rd., then turn left onto Oak Island Rd. Travel 2.7 miles on this road, and just after crossing a dike, turn right. The ramp is 0.2 mile ahead down this road.

Contact: Portland Oregon Visitors Association, 503/275-9750; Metro Regional Parks and Greenspaces Department, 503/797-1850; ODFW, Corvallis, 541/757-4186; Sauvie Island Wildlife Area, 503/621-3488; Columbia County Parks, 503/397-2353; Reeder Beach Resort RV Park, 503/621-3098.

◪ MULTNOMAH CHANNEL
on Sauvie Island

Map 2.1, page 141

The Multnomah Channel, a popular and productive fishery, divides Sauvie Island from Oregon's mainland. The Multnomah Channel starts near the mouth of the Willamette River and runs 25 miles from the tip of Sauvie Island to St. Helens. Most of this area is river bottomlands and rich agricultural fields; cottonwoods, oaks, and blackberries line the banks. The scenic Tualatin Mountains form a nice backdrop to the west.

Fishing season on Sauvie Island is April 16–September 30 and a special Sauvie Island Wildlife Area parking permit is required for all recreational parking. It's popularly fished for spring chinook, and other catches such as shad, walleye, sturgeon, bass, and panfish are also possible. Spring chinook begin to show as early as January and can be caught until May. Shad make up the second-biggest catches in the channel, occurring May–July. Early spring is the best time to catch larger walleye as they wake from winter and prepare to spawn. Summer is best for spot catches of bass, perch, brown bullhead catfish, and crappie.

Boaters can access the channel from six boat ramps or marinas along the channel, either on the Sauvie Island side or from Highway 30; motor downriver from Cathedral Park on the Willamette or from Scappoose Bay near St. Helens for additional access. But Sauvie Island provides perhaps the best access—a majority of the chinook and shad are caught near Coon Island, about two miles south of the Gilbert River ramp, or 10 miles north of the Sauvie Island ramp. Two methods are used here: trolling and anchor fishing in what are commonly known as hog lines. (Hog lines are easily discernable wherever a line of boats are anchored adjacent to each other spanning the river.) Most fall and spring chinook are caught with either of these methods using herring or other bait, large plugs, wobblers, and spinners. Trollers move slowly, keeping the bait on the bottom or in water of 20 feet or less. Other good places to catch salmon are at the mouth of the channel near St. Helens or up top at the starting point with the Willamette River.

The channel is on public lands so accessibility is generous except in a few places where posted. Highway 30, which parallels the Channel, or Sauvie Island along Sauvie Island Road provides access, most of which is from roadside turnouts and involves scrambles down to the river. Boat ramps offer reliable bank access; the most popular is Gilbert River ramp at the northern end of the channel.

Species: Spring chinook, shad, sturgeon, walleye, bass, perch, brown bullhead catfish, crappie.

Facilities: The closest camping is at Reeder Beach Resort RV Park. Access to Multnomah Channel can be had from ramps at Fred's Marina ($5, open 24 hours), Cassidy/Marina Way Moorage ($3.50), Brown's Landing, Gilbert River ramp, Larson's Moorage, and the Sauvie Island boat ramp, which is operated by Metro Regional Parks and Recreation Department.

Brown's Landing, Gilbert River, and Sauvie Island boat ramps are all on Sauvie Island, and parking permits are required to park in any of the wildlife areas on Sauvie Island. Daily permits are $3.50 and annual permits are $11. Buy permits at the Cracker Barrel Store (15005 N.W. Sauvie Island Rd.), just after you cross the bridge onto the island; through the Oregon Department of Fish and Wildlife; or at the Reeder Beach RV Country Store. Supplies are available in Portland, St. Helens, and Scappoose.

Directions: To reach Sauvie Island and Reeder Beach Resort RV Park from Portland, drive 9.3 miles west on Hwy. 30 and turn right onto Sauvie Island Rd. Cross the bridge onto the island, then drive 2.1 miles and turn right onto N.W. Reeder Rd. The entrance to the park is 5.5 miles ahead on the right.

For the mainland boat ramps: From Portland, drive west on Hwy. 30; Fred's Marina, Cassidy Marina, and Larson's Moorage are along this road. For Fred's, drive 7.7 miles on Hwy. 30 and turn right (north) onto N.W. Marina Way; the marina is 0.3 mile along this road. Cassidy is 0.1 mile past Fred's on N.W. Marina Way. For Larson's, drive 9.1 miles on Hwy. 30 and turn right (northeast) onto N.W. Larson Rd., which is the entrance to the moorage.

For the Sauvie Island boat ramps: From Portland, drive 9.3 miles west on Hwy. 30 and turn right onto Sauvie Island Rd. Cross the bridge onto the island, then drive three miles to the ramp on the left. For Brown's Landing, from the Sauvie Island Bridge, drive 7.3 miles on Sauvie Island Rd. to the marina. To reach Gilbert River boat ramp, after crossing the bridge onto Sauvie Island, drive 2.1 miles on N.W. Sauvie Island Rd., then turn right onto N.W. Reeder Rd. Continue on Reeder Rd. for 11.5 miles, then turn left (south) onto Gilbert River Boat Ramp Rd. Follow this road approximately one mile to the ramp.

Contact: Portland Oregon Visitors Association, 503/275-9750; Metro Regional Parks and Greenspaces Department, 503/797-1850; ODFW, Corvallis, 541/757-4186; Sauvie Island Wildlife Area, 503/621-3488; Columbia County Parks, 503/397-2353; Reeder Beach Resort RV Park, 503/621-3098; Fred's Marina, 503/286-5537; Cassidy/Marina Way Moorage, 503/286-2157; Brown's Landing, 503/543-6526; Larson's Moorage, 503/286-1233.

5 SMITH AND BYBEE LAKES
Lower Columbia River north of Portland
Map 2.1, page 141

These two adjacent lakes include smaller lakes and the Columbia Slough; both offer fair fishing for warm-water species. Bybee (200 acres) is the larger and better of the two; Smith tends to be shallow and less productive. The lakes are situated in bottomlands of scrub brush, blackberries, cottonwoods, and oak trees in the vicinity of the main north/south flyway. This area is especially popular with canoeists, kayakers, bird-watchers, and hikers.

Spring, when water levels are higher, provides the best fishing; midsummer is not as productive, and anglers would do better at Sauvie Island's Sturgeon Lake. Ample amounts of underwater structure, grasses, logs, and overhanging brush provide habitat for all species of warm-water fish. All fishing methods work in either lake: Jigs tipped with bait are popular for catching crappies and perch; bait such as worms or eggs settled on the bottom will take catfish; lures such as

Rapalas or surface poppers are productive for largemouth bass.

Bank access is good from hiking trails that surround both lakes. Boating is limited to canoes or kayaks and provides access to either lake through connecting channels or the Columbia Slough via a couple of portages.

Species: Crappie, brown bullhead catfish, bluegill, perch, largemouth bass.

Facilities: The closest camping is at Jantzen Beach RV Park on Hayden Island in North Portland. It has 169 sites for RVs (none for tents) and offers full services. There is a free boat ramp near a parking lot on N. Marine Dr., which is also the hiking trailhead. Buy supplies in Jantzen Beach.

Directions: To reach Jantzen Beach RV Park, drive four miles north from Portland on I-5 and take Exit 308 (Jantzen Beach), which puts you on Hayden Island Drive. Go west on Hayden Island Drive for 0.5 mile to the park. To reach the parking lot and boat ramp, take I-5 to Exit 307 (westbound N. Marine Dr.). The exit road continues for about one mile before making a right turn onto N. Marine Drive. Drive two miles on N. Marine Dr.; look for a brown and white "Smith and Bybee Lakes Wildlife Area" sign. Turn left into the driveway and proceed about 0.1 mile to the parking lot on the left. The boat ramp is 0.2 mile past the parking lot.

Contact: Portland Oregon Visitors Association, 503/275-9750; Metro Regional Parks and Greenspaces Department, 503/797-1850; ODFW, Corvallis, 541/757-4186; Jantzen Beach RV Park, 503/289-7626.

6 COLUMBIA SLOUGH
north of Portland
Map 2.1, page 141

The Columbia Slough originates at Fairview Lake, five miles west of Troutdale, and parallels the Columbia River for 18 miles to Kelley Point Park, where it meets the Willamette River. This is a slow-moving body of water, stagnant in places, with densely lined banks of brush, blackberries, and cottonwood trees. Part of the largest urban wetland in the United States (Smith and Bybee Lakes Wildlife Area), this is a nice wilderness escape for Portlanders. Unfortunately, this is also one of the most polluted waterways in the country and is recommended for exploration only; the deterrents of pollutants far outweigh the desire to fish.

The fishery contains mostly warm-water species and the occasional steelhead or salmon. Regulations do not allow for salmon and steelhead fishing, but warm-water fishing is fair to good for bass, large carp, crappie, perch, and brown bullheads. Access is good along most of its length, and waters higher up near the Parkrose neighborhood may be less polluted. Boating is possible in kayaks and canoes only, and there are several portage points between Fairview Lake and Kelley Point Park. Bank fishing is also possible from boat-launch sites and road crossings. Bait, lures, and flies all work and should be fished principally around obstructions and streamside vegetation.

Species: Largemouth bass, large carp, crappie, perch, and brown bullheads.

Facilities: Camping is available at Jantzen Beach RV Park, on Hayden Island in North Portland. It has 169 sites for RVs (none for tents) and offers full services. The city of Fairview's Lakeshore Park, at Fairview Lake and the eastern end of the slough, has a free canoe dock and a nearby free launch site on the slough. Buy supplies in Portland.

Directions: From Portland, drive four miles north on I-5 and take Exit 308 (Jantzen Beach), onto Hayden Island Drive. Go west on Hayden Island Drive for 0.5 mile to Jantzen Beach RV Park.

Contact: Portland Oregon Visitors Association, 503/275-9750; Metro Regional Parks and Greenspaces Department 503/797-1850; ODFW Corvallis, 541/757-4186; Portland Parks and Recreation, 503/823-7529; City of Fairview, 503/665-7929; Columbia Slough Watershed Council, 503/281-1132, www.columbiaslough.org; Jantzen Beach RV Park, 503/289-7626.

7 BLUE LAKE
in Fairview near Portland

Map 2.1, page 141   **BEST (**

One of the nice things about Portland is that it provides close escape from city life. Blue Lake, less than 15 miles from downtown Portland, is one such place. Its scenic forests offer a busy, family-friendly environment to catch stocked trout and resident populations of bluegill, perch, crappie, and catfish. Young anglers will have a field day catching easy, legal-size trout with everything from bait to spinners and flies.

Because the rest of the shore is private property, anglers are restricted to bank fishing from the public access area. A boat is also a good way to discover less-fished areas and deeper water holding bigger fish. To beat the crowds, bring your own boat, float tube, or canoe or rent one from the general store. Think of Blue Lake as a nice place to go when you have only an afternoon and can't get away to the mountains or other favorite fishing spots.

Species: Stocked legal-size trout, and native bass, bluegill, perch, crappie, sunfish.

Facilities: Blue Lake Regional Park, operated by Metro Regional Government (8 A.M.–sunset year-round, $4 per car) has public (and wheelchair-accessible) fishing docks, a swimming beach and play area, boat and canoe rentals (May 1–Sept. 30), walkways, and bike paths. Buy supplies in Troutdale.

Directions: From Portland, take I-84 east to Exit 14 (Fairview) and turn north (left) onto N.E. 207th Ave. Drive 0.3 mile and turn east (right) onto N.E. Sandy Blvd. Follow Sandy for 0.7 mile, then turn north (left) onto N.E. 223rd Ave. Travel north on this road for 0.8 mile to the park entrance on the left.

Contact: Portland Oregon Visitors Association, 503/275-9750; Metro Regional Parks and Greenspaces Department, 503/797-1850; ODFW, Corvallis, 541/757-4186.

8 HENRY HAGG LAKE
southwest of Forest Grove

Map 2.1, page 141   BEST (

Henry Hagg Lake is far enough outside the city to be in the countryside, but close enough that you can have an excellent day of fishing and be home in time for supper. The lake is secluded among the forested foothills of the Cascade Range, but don't expect a lot of solitude; Henry Hagg is very popular among metropolitan anglers, especially during the best fishing times—spring and fall. The primary catches are rainbow trout but warm-water fish have flourished, providing good sport for bass, crappie, perch, and bluegill.

The lake consists of 1,100 acres, 12 miles of shoreline, and numerous arms all fed by smaller tributaries. In fact, there are approximately a dozen tributaries, all of which carry cold water year-round and attract many resident anglers. Its deepest point is near the dam (110 feet) extending north to the center of the lake; average depths are 51 feet and 25 feet around the shoreline. The lake is open to all methods of fishing March 5–November 20. Boats are allowed, but there is a 10 mph speed limit. One bass per day may be kept in addition to the regular limit of five trout per day.

Because of the lake's depth and configuration, boat anglers have an easier time catching fish than bank anglers do. Two boat ramps service the lake on the west and east shores. Good bank fishing can be had from the boat ramps, the dam, and from two wheelchair-accessible piers at Elk Point Picnic Area and at the west shore ramp.

Hagg Lake attracts many bass anglers who fish the shallower waters in spring with lures, worms, poppers, and jigs around the mouths of tributaries such as Tanner and Sain Creek (near the north end and western side of the lake, respectively). Hagg Lake produced two state record catches of smallmouth bass; the most recent record of 8 lbs. 1.76 ounces was caught in 2000. Largemouth bass are also present, albeit in smaller numbers, but can reach 4–7 pounds. Trout continue to be a big attraction with more than 70,000 legal-size fish stocked every year; holdovers from previous years can reach 4–7 pounds. All sizes of trout can be caught on any kind of bait, spinner, and fly. During spring and fall, look for smaller trout along the shorelines and bigger trout in the deeper areas near the center. Perch, bluegill, and catfish are all present and can be found with jigs and bait around docks, shallow coves, and structure.

Species: Trout, perch, brown bullhead catfish, bluegill, smallmouth bass, largemouth bass, crappie.

Facilities: Washington County operates boat ramps and fishing piers at the lake (sunrise–sunset year-round, $5 per vehicle, $6 with boat), as well as picnic areas and recreation areas. There's no camping, but supplies and accommodations are available in Forest Grove and Hillsboro.

Directions: From Forest Grove, go south on Hwy. 47 for 5.9 miles, then turn west (right) onto Scoggins Valley Rd., at a sign for Hagg Lake. Drive 3.7 miles on this road to the park entrance. A park map will guide you to the boat ramps.

Contact: ODFW, Corvallis, 541/757-4186; BLM, Salem, 503/375-5643; Washington County Facilities and Parks Services Division, 503/846-8715; Convention and Visitors Bureau of Washington County, 503/644-5555.

9 LOWER WILLAMETTE RIVER: OREGON CITY TO COLUMBIA RIVER
north of Oregon City

Map 2.1, page 141   BEST (

The Lower Willamette contains 25 miles of river popular for its runs of salmon and steelhead. It's surrounded by bottomlands and metropolitan areas, a majority of which are blocked from view by stands of cottonwood, oaks, and Douglas fir that line the banks. The river between Oregon City and downtown Portland has some very scenic stretches with minor waterfalls, sandy beaches, interesting rock formations, and cliffs.

The Willamette is big, not quite as big as the Columbia, but more manageable because it's narrower. Primary catches here are spring and fall chinook and coho, followed by sturgeon, steelhead, shad, and smallmouth bass, and panfish. Most of the fishing between the mouth and Oregon City is contained in a few productive areas where fish seem to hold in the greatest numbers: between the Fremont Bridge in Portland and the Multnomah Channel; between Lake Oswego and Ross Island; and below Willamette Falls in Oregon City and West Linn. Good boat ramps offer access to all of these areas (the river is most suitable to powerboats) and there's also good bank fishing. Because this is an immense and complex fishery, consider hiring a guide for the first few times on the river. Guides will help improve your catch and are a valuable source of information to help you become a self-sufficient angler.

Salmon: Fall chinook are in the river September–October, and spring chinook February–early July, with peak runs in April and early May. Boat anglers should begin fishing for salmon in the lower river: the mouth near the Multnomah Channel; near St. Johns at Cathedral Park; in Portland under the Fremont Bridge. As the run progresses upriver, concentrate in the areas around Ross Island and Willamette Falls. The most popular methods for catching salmon are anchor fishing and trolling plugs, spinners, and bait such as herring. Coho salmon are present August–October with good showings in September. More elusive than chinook, coho are considered a prize catch, and most anglers go after them by trolling plugs and spinners.

Steelhead: The second-most popular species are more frequently caught in small tributaries such as the Clackamas River. Summer steelhead are present March–September, with peak catches April–May; winter steelhead arrive January–March and November–December. Boat anglers catch steelhead with many of the same methods used to catch salmon, and often in the same holes, but with slightly smaller plugs and spinners. The most popular places to catch steelhead are at the mouth of the Clackamas River at Clackamette Park and near Willamette Falls.

Bank anglers fishing for salmon and steelhead need not go any farther than Clackamette Park or a mile downstream at Meldrum Bar. Other popular spots include St. Johns' Cathedral Park, near the mouth, and Mary S. Young Park in West Linn. Use bait such as sand shrimp, prawns, or salmon roe; other methods include spinners and plugs such as Kwikfish, spoons, and plugs. Plunking is popular for most species.

Sturgeon: Though in the river all year, the best catches occur March–July in the deepest holes on the river. Depth finders will help find these deep holes, but good places to start are: in the shipping channels between the Fremont and St. Johns bridges, especially around Swan Island; Willamette Falls in Oregon City; and a few areas around Sellwood on the downriver side of the bridges. Bank anglers are successful at Mary S. Young Park, in West Linn, and at Meldrum Park.

Smallmouth bass and panfish: Most active June–August, these can be caught in slack water. Likely places for bass are around the rocky islands between Oregon City and Lake Oswego. Shad migrate into the Willamette May–June and are mostly caught near Willamette Falls.

Species: Spring and fall chinook, coho, shad, summer and winter steelhead, sturgeon, bass, crappie, bluegill, yellow perch, brown bullhead catfish.

Facilities: Camping is available at three RV parks: Reeder Beach Resort RV Park, on Sauvie Island, has 65 sites (no tents); Jantzen Beach RV Park, on Hayden Island in north Portland, has 169 sites for RVs (no tents) and full services; and, most convenient, the RV Park of Portland, along the river on Nyberg Rd. in Tualatin, has 112 mostly full-hookup sites (no tents). Supplies and accommodations are available in Oregon City, Gladstone, Milwaukie, and Portland.

There are 10 boat ramps between Willamette Falls and the mouth. On the east side of the river you can launch a boat at any of these locations, which are listed south to north. None of these east-side ramps charges a fee:

- **Sportcraft Marina:** A full-service marina and watercraft store with a free paved ramp.
- **Clackamette Park:** A large, paved ramp and an RV park with free day use.
- **Meldrum Landing:** In Gladstone's Meldrum Bar Park is a paved, two-lane ramp. There are restrooms and a picnic area.
- **The Oak Grove Boat Ramp:** A concrete ramp, paved parking, and portable restrooms are available in River Villa Park.
- **Swan Island Boat Ramp:** A paved ramp, a dock, and plenty of parking are on Swan Island Lagoon in the heavily industrial Port of Portland area.
- **Cathedral Park:** A paved ramp, dock, wheelchair access, and restrooms are directly under the St. Johns Bridge.

The following locations, also listed south to north, are on the west side of the river. They are all free, except Fred's.

- **Bernert's Landing:** West Linn's Willamette Park has a paved boat ramp as well as playing fields, picnic areas, and restrooms.
- **Cedar Oak Boat Ramp:** This paved ramp is part of West Linn's Cedar Island City Park, which has restrooms and picnic areas.
- **Staff Jennings Marina Boating Center:** Practically under the west end of the Sellwood Bridge in southwest Portland, this has a paved ramp and a full range of boats and boating supplies.
- **Fred's Marina:** A paved ramp is available 24 hours a day (but charges a $5 fee) north of Portland at the entrance to Multnomah Channel.

Directions: For the east-side ramps around the Clackamas River, take Exit 9 (McLoughlin Blvd.) off I-205 in Oregon City. Sportcraft is under the expressway, Clackamette is half a mile north on McLoughlin, and Meldrum Landing is two miles north of there (go west on Meldrum Bar Park Rd.). Keep going north on McLoughlin (which is also Hwy. 99E) for two miles to Oak Grove Ramp (west on Courtney Ave.). The Milwaukie Ramp is another two miles north on McLoughlin.

For the east-side ramp at Swan Island: Travel west on I-205 for nine miles, then go north on I-5 for 14 miles to Exit 302 (Swan Island). From that exit, follow Going St. north and Basin Ave. west to the ramp—a total of about 1.3 miles. Cathedral Park is in St. Johns; from the same Exit 302 on I-5 north, take Hwy. 30 towards St. Helens for five miles, then cross the St. Johns Bridge. After that, make quick rights onto Syracuse, Burlington, Salem and Crawford Sts. to get under the bridge.

For the west-side ramps in West Linn: Access Willamette Park via Exit 6 off I-205, which is three miles west of Oregon City. Turn right onto 10th St. After 0.1 mile, turn left onto Willamette Falls Dr., follow that road 0.3 mile, then turn right onto 6th St. Go 0.1 mile, turn left onto 5th Ave., then take an immediate right onto 4th St., which becomes Volpp St. The ramp will be on your left. To reach the Cedar Oak Ramp, take Exit 8 (West Linn) from I-205, then travel north on Hwy. 43 for four miles.

To reach Staff Jennings Marina from Oregon City, travel one mile west on I-205 and take Exit 8 for Hwy. 43 (Macadam Ave.). Follow Macadam for nine miles to the marina on your right, just north of the Sellwood Bridge. And for Fred's on the Multnomah Channel, take Exit 302 off I-5 north and follow Hwy. 30 for 7.7 miles, then turn right (north) onto NW Marina Way; the marina is 0.3 miles along this road.

Contact: Portland Oregon Visitors Association, 503/275-9750; Oregon City Parks Department, 503/657-8299; Portland Parks and Recreation, 503/823-7529; City of Gladstone, 503/656-5225; City of Milwaukie, 503/786-7555; West Linn Parks and Recreation, 503/557-4700; Metro Regional Parks and Greenspaces Department, 503/797-1850; Clackamas County Parks Department,

503/353-4414; ODFW, Corvallis, 541/757-4186; Fred's Marina, 503/286-5537; Sportcraft Marina, 503/656-6484; Fisherman's Marine and Outdoor, 503/557-3313; Guide Service Northwest, 503/297-5159; Martin's Big Fish Adventures, 503/680-9787; A&B Pro Guides and Charters, 503/720-9033.

🔟 TUALATIN RIVER

in the Willamette River watershed

Map 2.1, page 141

The long and winding Tualatin runs 75 miles from its headwaters above Gaston to its confluence with the Willamette in Oregon City. Below Gaston the river enters farmlands on the outer edge of Forest Grove and Hillsboro before descending into Tualatin and West Linn. While the river holds wonderful potential, family-friendly parks, and easy fishing, there is very little to recommend to the serious angler. The headwaters west are bordered by private property; access is better in the lower river, but the fishing is marginal. In addition, the Tualatin has been a dumping ground for many agricultural and commercial uses for many years, which has hurt the fishing and riparian areas. Restoration efforts are in process, but improvement has been slow as far as fisheries are concerned.

Fishing is permitted for all species with bait May 28–October 1 from the mouth to the Highway 210 bridge at Scholls. All trout must be released. The most exciting water is near the mouth, which has a series of rough rapids and good holing water in long runs. (It also has hatchery steelhead and salmon in November and December, but steelhead and salmon fishing is off limits.) Access is limited to a few areas, and only experienced boaters should consider the rapids. There are no official boat ramps, but there are approximately 12 unofficial ramps at parks and road crossings. You may float through the wildlife refuge and fish from a boat, but the land within the refuge is off-limits. Good places for both bank and boat anglers are Tualatin County Park, Cook Park, and Brown's Ferry Park. For salmon and steelhead, start lower in the river near West Linn at the mouth or a little higher up in the river. Warm-water species can be caught at any of the access locations.

Species: Trout, bass, bluegill, perch, sunfish, brown bullhead catfish.

Facilities: RV Park of Portland on Nyberg Rd. in Tualatin provides camping. It has 112 mostly full-hookup sites. River access is available at Sholls Bridge on Hwy. 210, Schamburg Bridge on Tualatin–Sherwood Rd., and 99 West Bridge in Tualatin. Parks with access are Rood Bridge Park in Hillsboro (ramp), Cook Park on Durham Rd. in Tigard (small ramp), Tualatin Community Park (improved ramp), Browns Ferry Park (dock only) on Nyberg Rd., Shipley Bridge on Stafford Rd., and Fields Bridge and Willamette Park in West Linn. Willamette Park has a paved boat ramp onto the Willamette. All of these areas are free, and each park has picnic areas and restrooms. Brown's Ferry Park rents canoes and kayaks June–September. Supplies are available in Tigard, Tualatin, Forest Grove, and Hillsboro.

Directions: Take I-5 south to Exit 289 (Tualatin). Turn right (west) onto S.W. Nyburg Rd. and then, after 0.1 mile, stay straight to go onto S.W. Tualatin–Sherwood Rd. After 0.4 mile, turn right (north) onto S.W. Boones Ferry Rd., which enters the Tualatin Community Park in 0.3 mile. To reach Cook Park, take I-5 south and follow Exit 291 (Carman Drive). Turn right (southwest) onto S.W. Upper Boones Ferry Rd. and follow it 0.5 mile to S.W. Durham Rd. Turn right (northwest) on Durham Rd. and follow it 0.9 mile to S.W. 92nd Ave. Turn left (south) on 92nd and follow it 0.5 mile to where it dead-ends into the park.

Contact: Portland Oregon Visitors Association, 503/275-9750; Convention and Visitors Bureau of Washington County, 503/644-5555; City of Hillsboro, 503/681-6120; City of Tualatin, 503/692-2000; West Linn Parks and Recreation Department, 503/557-4700; City of Tigard, 503/639-4171; ODFW, Corvallis,

541/757-4186; Friends of the Refuge (FOR), 503/972-7714; Tualatin River National Wildlife Refuge, 503/590-5811; Tualatin Riverkeepers, 503/620-7507; RV Park of Portland, 503/692-0225; River City Fly Shop, 503/579-5176, www.rivercityfly.com; G.I. Joe's, Lake Oswego, 503/635-1064.

11 LOWER CLACKAMAS RIVER: ESTACADA TO OREGON CITY

southeast of Oregon City

Map 2.1, page 141

The Clackamas River is a popular and important spawning tributary of the Willamette River that runs 80 miles from the Mount Hood National Forest in the Cascade Range to its confluence with the Willamette near Oregon City. Along this 26-mile stretch are rapids, deep pools, long gravel bottom runs, and underwater shelves. The lowest sections are a mix of metropolitan areas, river-bottom stands of cottonwood trees and thick blackberry bushes that give way upstream to Douglas fir forests near Estacada. Primary catches in the lower river include hatchery and wild species of winter and summer steelhead, spring chinook, and coho, many of which can be found in the river most of the year.

Spring chinook peak in their migration April–May, but fish can be present late January–first part of October. Fall chinook have a much shorter window, mid-August–September, with peak catches in mid-September. Coho salmon migrate upriver August–March, and peak runs can occur anytime during these months. Winter steelhead arrive in two waves, an early hatchery run and a late wild run. Early-run winter fish begin to enter the Clackamas in November, and most of them spawn in tributaries below River Mill Dam in January and February. The late run of wild steelhead, larger in size, begins to enter the river in January, with peak runs in March. By April and May a majority of the winter fish have moved over North Fork Dam. A few

summer steelhead enter the river as early as February, but good numbers are not observed until mid-April. They spawn in January and February the following year. Trout anglers have good opportunities to catch the elusive sea-run cutthroat trout, which enter the river from the ocean in September and October. Sea-run trout can be found in the main river, but they fairly quickly make their way into the larger tributaries such as Eagle Creek below River Mill Dam.

All methods of fishing are allowed, including bait. The river is open to hatchery chinook and steelhead fishing all year. Hatchery coho can be caught August 1–October 31. There are no boating restrictions, and the river will accommodate drift boats, jet sleds, rafts, and smaller craft capable of navigating white water. Bank angling is limited to parks and a few roadside pullouts; otherwise this is primarily a boat fishery. Three of the most popular places to fish from the bank are just upstream from the mouth at Clackamette Park, High Rocks, and Riverside Park. All three areas are productive for salmon and steelhead, especially the deep holes around High Rocks, but situated as they are within metropolitan areas, one may expect to compete with many anglers. If it is quieter fishing you are looking for, skip this lower water and head for equally good water upriver at McIver and Barton parks on the way to Estacada and at the ODFW property from Carver Bridge to the mouth of Clear Creek. The effort required to get to these spots is minor (just a little driving) and will take you away from 70 percent of the anglers who fish this river.

Boating is one way to avoid other anglers, but unfortunately not other boats, and with five boat ramps there are plenty on this river. Again, the most popular drifts are those in the lower river from the Carver to Clackamette Park (eight miles). You will also encounter a majority of the bank anglers on this stretch, requiring some consideration not to disturb another angler's water. If you want to avoid most boat traffic, float the upper stretches near River Mill Dam. McIver to Barton (eight miles) or Barton to Carver (5.5 miles) are both easy, pleasant drifts with lots of steelhead and salmon water. The first rapid downriver from the put-in at McIver can be dangerous, requiring scouting during high water. McIver to Carver (13.5 miles) is also a good drift, especially when the steelhead and salmon fishing is spotty and you need to cover lots of water to find the fish.

Fishing from a boat or bank is productive with all kinds of gear, including lures, bait, and flies. Lures such as spoons and plugs are standard methods and produce a majority of the catches. Bait is effective under floats or when side-drifted from a boat or drift-fished from shore. The most popular baits are cured salmon roe, sand shrimp, and worms. Corkies and yarn are good substitutes for bait. Fly anglers frequently take fish by swinging flies on floating or sinking lines with streamers such as Green Butt Skunks and Egg Sucking Leeches. Nymphs are productive in shallow riffles, pocket water, and faster runs. Sea-run cutthroat are frequently caught by steelhead anglers and take readily to brightly colored, fast-swinging flies and lures.

Species: Hatchery summer steelhead, hatchery and wild winter steelhead, spring chinook, coho, sea-run cutthroat trout.

Facilities: Boats can be launched from Clackamette Park, Riverside Park, Carver, Barton Park, and Milo McIver State Park. Clackamette Park, at the mouth in Oregon City, also includes an RV park, though day use is free. Milo McIver State Park (day use $3), just west of Estacada, offers a boat ramp, RV and tent campsites, and all other services.

Barton Park and Carver boat ramp are both run by Clackamas County. Each charges a $3-per-vehicle day-use fee on weekends Memorial Day–Labor Day. Barton Park also has camping available. Supplies can be had in Estacada, Clackamas and Oregon City.

Directions: From Portland travel south on Hwy. 99E (S.E. McLoughlin Blvd.) for 13 miles to the bridge over the river in Oregon

City. Immediately south of the bridge, turn right (west) into Clackamette Park.

All the following places are along the river southeast of Portland, in or near Clackamas. Directions start from the intersection of I-205 and Hwys. 242/212 in Clackamas. To reach that intersection from Portland, travel east of Portland on I-84 for 4.9 miles, then follow I-205 south for 12.5 miles and take Exit 12A (Estacada). For Riverside Park and the High Rocks Area, follow Hwy. 224/212 east for 0.5 mile, then turn right (southwest) onto S.E. Evelyn St. After 0.6 mile, Evelyn becomes S.E. Mangan Dr., and after 0.2 mile on Mangan, turn right on S.E. Water Ave. The park is 0.2 mile ahead. For Barton Park, follow Hwy. 224/212 for 3.3 miles to where Hwys. 224 and 212 split. Stay on Hwy. 224 and follow it for another 6.4 miles to S.E. Bakers Ferry Rd. Turn right here, and the park entrance is in 0.2 mile. For Carver boat ramp, follow Hwy. 224/212 for 3.3 miles to where Hwys. 224 and 212 split. Stay on Hwy. 224 and follow it for another 1.1 miles to Springwater Rd. in Carver. Turn right here, and you'll drive over the bridge in 0.1 mile; the ramp is at the far end. For Milo McIver State Park, follow Hwy. 224/212 for 3.3 miles to where Hwys. 224 and 212 split. Stay on Hwy. 224 and follow it for another 1.1 miles to Springwater Rd. in Carver. Turn right here, and you'll reach the park in 9.5 miles.

Contact: Portland Oregon Visitors Association, 503/275-9750; Oregon City Parks Department, 503/657-8299; Clackamas County Parks Department, 503/353-4414; Oregon Parks and Recreation Department, 800/551-6949; ODFW, Clackamas, 503/657-2000.

12 MIDDLE WILLAMETTE: NEWBERG TO WILLAMETTE FALLS

in West Linn above Willamette Falls

Map 2.1, page 141

This section of the Willamette covers 22 miles from Rogers Landing in Newberg to Willamette Park. The river here is scenic, lined with tall stands of cottonwoods and the occasional backdrop of forested hills. One will get a sense of seclusion, particularly in the narrows above Willamette Park. Along this stretch are two state parks and four boat ramps. Anglers can move past the falls via the Willamette Locks, which can be found on the north river bank below Willamette Park. Allow approximately 45 minutes to make the transition.

If catching steelhead and salmon is your goal, then this water will be of limited interest. Some salmon and steelhead can be caught around the mouth of tributaries such as the Molalla and Tualatin Rivers, but for the most part this area is too slow and wide to produce any likely holding spots for these species. Some sturgeon hold in the deeper holes around Champoeg State Park. On the other hand, if bass and panfish are what you are after, then you're in luck, because both can be found in abundance.

Most anglers who launch powerboats do so to move up and down the river, pulling out at the same place they launched. Canoes and kayaks can move up and down the river with little difficulty or can float down to the next take-out. Boat anglers concentrate on four areas: the river in front of the mouth of the Tualatin River at Bernert Landing, Rock Island one river mile up from Bernert Landing, the mouth of the Molalla River, and the deep water holes in front of Champoeg State Park. For bass and panfish, work the shorelines and river mouths with bait, lures, jigs, and bass plugs. Trolling any of this tackle is a trouble-free and productive method, and you're never quite sure what you're going to catch. If you're canoeing or kayaking, simply trail a spinner off the back of the boat and stay close to shore. A good indication that you are moving too far from shore is when you stop hitting fish. Look for tributary inlets or sloughs for more opportunities.

Bank anglers can reach the river from any of the state parks, most of which have docks and/or good shore access. The only real bank access for salmon or steelhead is at Bernert

Landing at Willamette Park or at the mouth of the Molalla River via a short hike upriver from Molalla State Park. Champoeg State Park, Hebb Park, and Wilsonville Memorial Park provide more opportunities for bass and panfish from the docks or shoreline. The primary fishing methods from the bank include casting lures and bait.

Species: Salmon, steelhead, large and small-mouth bass, perch, crappie, bluegill, brown bullhead catfish, channel catfish, sturgeon.

Facilities: Four free boat ramps serve this stretch of river. Bernert Landing boat ramp, at the northern end, is in West Linn's full-service Willamette Park. The next ramp south is Clackamas County's Hebb Park, just downstream from the historic Canby Ferry on the west bank; Hebb has a paved ramp, picnic areas, and restrooms. Molalla River State Park (year-round, no fee) offers a boat ramp, picnic areas, and restrooms—but no camping. Boones Ferry public ramp in Wilsonville is part of Boones Ferry Marina, which also has moorage and a fuel dock. Camping is available at Champoeg State Park (year-round, day-use $3 per vehicle). There's a boat dock in summer and miles of hiking trails along the river. Supplies are available in West Linn and Wilsonville.

Directions: For Willamette Park take Exit 6 off I-205 in West Linn. Turn right onto 10th St. After 0.1 mile, turn left onto Willamette Falls Dr., following that road 0.3 mile. Turn right onto 6th St. and continue 0.1 mile. Turn left onto 5th Ave., then take an immediate right onto 4th St., which becomes Volpp St. The ramp will be on your left. To reach Hebb Park from West Linn, go eight miles west on I-205 to I-5 south, then follow I-5 to Exit 286. From here, go east on Advance Rd. for 2.6 miles, then turn right (south) on Mountain Rd. Follow Mountain Rd. 0.5 mile to Hoffman Rd., then go left (east) on Hoffman for 1.8 miles to the park. Boones Ferry Marina is in Wilsonville (Exit 283 off I-5). Travel south on Boones Ferry Rd. for 0.3 mile to the bottom of the hill at the river. To reach Molalla

River State Park, start in Canby and travel north on N. Holly St. for 2.2 miles to the park entrance.

Contact: Champoeg State Park, 503/678-1251; Boones Ferry Marina, 503/678-1295; Oregon Parks and Recreation Department, 800/551-6949; West Linn Parks and Recreation, 503/557-4700; Clackamas County Parks Department, 503/353-4414; ODFW, Corvallis, 541/757-4186.

13 YAMHILL RIVER
southwest of Portland in the
Yamhill watershed

Map 2.1, page 141

The Yamhill River runs 60 miles, beginning with two forks, North and South, that originate in the Coast Range and join forces in McMinnville. From McMinnville the river flows to its confluence with the Willamette River north of Dayton. Much of the upper river lies in scenic forest, fed by smaller creeks, which eventually give way to farmlands, bigger creeks, and quaint Willamette Valley communities the closer you get to McMinnville. Trout are available in both the North and South forks, and bass and panfish such as perch and bluegill can be caught in the lower river below McMinnville. Steelhead and salmon are present throughout during the winter and fishing has been allowed in previous years, but it is now closed. Use of all types of bait and lures is allowed during the regular fishing season March 1–October 31. Trout fishing is catch-and-release only.

Canoes and kayaks can be used to float most of the river and its forks. Larger boats such as drift boats can be used on either fork from unofficial roadside put-ins during high-water years. Popular drifts on the South Fork are from Fort Hill to Willamina and on the North Fork from Pike to Westside Road. Small motorboats have access to the lower Yamhill River from the river mouth on the Willamette up to Lafayette Locks Park just above Dayton. The Dayton boat ramp offers access to this part of the river. Lafayette Locks Park provides the best bank access on the lower river, and many anglers jig for warm-water species in the tanks of the old locks.

Both the North and South forks have good access along Highways 47 and 18, respectively. Look for roadside turnouts and avoid areas marked with private-property signs. Expect smaller water comprising pools, pocket water, and some runs. Flies such as attractor dry flies and nymphs will work well. Most small lures such as Rooster Tails will also take fish. Use bait such as worms and eggs. West of Pike on the North Fork and north of Willamina on the South Fork you'll find unlimited bank access into the headwaters. All of this area is dotted by other small fishable streams, many of which contain Yamhill County parks, such as Willamina Creek (Blackwell Park north of Willamina), Mill Creek (Stuart Grenfell Park west of Sheridan), Deer Creek (Deer Creek Park northeast of Sheridan), and Salt Creek on the South Fork and Turner Creek (Menefee Park west of Yamhill), Haskins Creek, Baker Creek (Metsker, Huber, Juliette, Powerhouse and Ed Grenfell parks, all west of McMinnville), and Panther Creek on the North Fork.

Species: Trout, bass, perch, bluegill, steelhead, and salmon.

Facilities: This area is also dotted with numerous wineries, filbert orchards, and old immigrant towns such as Yamhill, Amity, Carlton, Dundee, and Lafayette. These are great places to pick up big sandwiches and milkshakes, visit historical landmarks, and buy fresh fruit in the U-pick orchards. Camping is available at Sleepy Hollow RV Park in Lafayette. It has both tent and full hookup sites, as well as showers, cable TV, and Internet access. Supplies are available in McMinnville.

Directions: For Dayton and Lafayette Locks Park on the main-stem Yamhill: From Portland travel south on Hwy. 99W for 14.8 miles, then turn left (southwest) onto Hwy. 18. After 1.3 miles, turn left (south) onto Hwy. 221, which reaches Dayton in 0.5 mile. For the Dayton boat ramp, turn left (northeast) onto

Ferry St. and follow it 0.3 mile to Water St. Turn right (southeast) onto Water St. and follow until it ends 0.1 mile later. To reach Lafayette Locks Park, stay on Hwy. 99W when it intersects Hwy. 18. Follow 99W for 2.2 more miles, then turn left (south) onto Locks Rd., which dead-ends into the park in 0.6 mile. To reach Sleepy Hollow RV Park, stay on 99W until it enters Lafayette one mile west of the turnoff to the park.

North Fork: From Forest Grove, travel south on Hwy. 47 for 6.9 miles to Patton. Turn right (west) onto Old Hwy. 47, and after 0.4 mile turn left (south) onto S.W. Patton Valley Rd. Follow this for 2.9 miles, then make a slight left onto N.W. Mount Richmond Rd. After 5.4 miles on this road, turn right (west) on Hacker Rd., which will take you into Pike. The Westside Rd. take-out is southwest of Yamhill; from there, travel west on Moores Valley Rd. for 1.8 miles, then turn left (south) on Westside Rd., which crosses the North Fork in 0.1 mile.

South Fork: From Salem, follow Hwy. 22 west for 22 miles. To reach Willamina, continue on Hwy. 22 for 3.8 miles past Fort Hill (a total of 25.8 miles from Salem), then turn right (north) on Hwy. 18 and follow it 1.8 miles to Willamina.

Contact: Oregon State Parks, 800/452-5687; ODFW, Corvallis, 541/757-4186; Yamhill County Parks, 503/434-7463, www.co.yamhill.or.us; Yamhill Valley Visitors Association, 503/883-7770; Sleepy Hollow RV Park, 503/864-3740.

14 MOLALLA RIVER
near Portland in the Willamette watershed
Map 2.1, page 141

Originating in the Cascade Mountains above Molalla, the Molalla River runs 45 miles through fertile farmlands to meet with the Willamette near Canby. This river used to have a reputation for producing large hatchery and wild winter steelhead and was often favored by fly anglers during the 1970s and '80s because of its small size and classic fly-

fishing–style runs. Nested among river-bottom stands of cottonwoods and farmlands, it has always provided a nice secluded getaway 20 miles from Portland. The river still produces big steelhead, but their numbers have been reduced since hatchery plantings were discontinued in 1998. But don't let the lack of hatchery fish detour you from this wonderful river. The river today is only lightly fished by a few local anglers who still consider this one of the best winter steelhead streams in Oregon.

Trout and some bass are present throughout the river. Bass are predominantly found in the lower river at the mouth, and trout inhabit the upper river above Molalla. Fish the lower river from the vicinity of Canby (Knights Bridge) to the mouth for a late run of wild winter steelhead February–April, though fish can arrive as early as December. A small run of spring chinook are present May–July and occupy the same stretch of water in the deeper holes; they are usually caught by back-trolling or plunking with bait or larger plugs. All methods of fishing are permitted, including bait. Fishing season for steelhead and chinook is open all year.

The river is suitable for jet sleds during high-water times and is accessible from the Willamette River upstream one-half mile from Molalla River State Park, but most anglers either use drift boats or fish from the bank. During midsummer and late fall the river is too low to run in anything but a kayak or canoe. Plugs, spinners, drift fishing with bait or corkies, and flies all work. There are four popular boat ramps offering differing length drifts of 2–12 miles or longer. These drifts include Meadowbrook Bridge near Molalla to Wagonwheel near Union Mills (four miles), Wagonwheel to Knights Bridge west of Canby (12 miles), and Knights Bridge to Molalla River State Park, north of Canby on the Willamette River (four miles). Boaters should expect a few larger rapids that can sometimes prove hazardous because of large boulders in the river.

Bank anglers can avoid the problems of trespassing on private property by fishing from any of the boat-launch sites or from other road crossings and parks. The river crossing on the Canby/Marquam Highway, 1.5 miles south of Canby, is a great access point with several miles of accessible river. Knight's Bridge is also a good access point with several large pools interspaced with productive runs. Anglers can walk to the river on hiking trails from Molalla River State Park to reach the mouth and some of the best water on the river. Above Molalla on Dickey Prairie Road, the upper river rolls through timber harvest lands and is accessible from logging roads. The upper river is very scenic with forested foothills and rock canyons. Natural campsites can be found along the river once you hit the forested lands on Dickey Prairie Road. Hiking along any part of the river will reveal good holding water for trout and the occasional steelhead.

Species: Wild winter steelhead, spring chinook, trout, and bass.

Facilities: Molalla River State Park (year-round, no fee) offers a boat ramp, picnic areas, and restrooms—but no camping. The nearest camping is at Feyrer Memorial Park, operated by Clackamas County; it offers 20 sites. Supplies are available in Canby and Molalla.

Directions: To reach Feyrer Park, start in Woodburn and travel east on Hwy. 211 for 12.7 miles. At the east end of town, turn right (south) on Feyrer Park Rd. and follow it three miles to the park. To reach Molalla River State Park, start in Canby and travel north on N. Holly St. for 2.2 miles to the park entrance.

Contact: Molalla Chamber of Commerce, 503/829-6941; ODFW, Corvallis, 541/757-4186; Clackamas County Parks Department, 503/353-4414; Oregon Parks and Recreation Department, 800/551-6949.

15 PUDDING RIVER
southwest of Canby

Map 2.1, page 141

The Pudding River is a slow-moving, winding tributary of the Molalla River originating in the foothills of the Cascade Range near Silver Falls State Park east of Salem. Fishing is only fair for trout and warm-water fish such as bass, but the river has high exploratory value for anglers wishing for something a little different close to Portland. The Pudding River is fed in the upper reaches by many smaller tributaries (Butte, Abiqua, and Silver creeks), all of which have historically provided important spawning grounds for hatchery and native salmon and steelhead. The Pudding and Molalla Rivers meet approximately one-half mile up from the mouth of the Molalla near Molalla River State Park. As the name may suggest, this river runs off-color year-round because of its muddy bottom. From its origin, the river runs north in a twisting fashion through farmlands and river bottomlands. The river below Woodburn has especially dense, almost impenetrable, banks of blackberries, cottonwood trees, and tall grasses.

Primary catches here are trout in the upper reaches and tributaries near Silverton, Mount Angel, and Woodburn and bass and panfish in the lower river below Aurora. Steelhead and spring chinook salmon are present in very small numbers, but they are mostly passing through the river to get to the colder, cobbled Butte, Abiqua, and Silver creeks. Winter steelhead are in the river mid-February–May; spring chinook in April and May. Both these species, once stocked in the upper creeks, have not been stocked since 1988, and what remains is a remnant population of both wild and stocked fish. The river is restricted to artificial flies and lures only, and all trout are catch-and-release.

There is no official public access, leaving anglers to fish either around road crossings or launch a boat at Molalla State Park on the Willamette and motor upriver from the mouth. Small boats may be launched at most road crossings. The lower river is crossed on Highway 99E in Aurora and on Arndt Road, west of Canby. Here anglers can get into the river and walk up- or downstream or launch a small canoe or kayak. The river is also crossed near

Woodburn, most notably on Highway 211 east of town. Other road crossings are near Silverton on Hazel Green Road, and east of Salem on Highway 213 (Silverton Rd.), Sunnyview Road, and State St.

Unless you're after trout, the best way to experience this river is upstream from the mouth in a motorized boat or jet sled. Here you can cruise the winding channel, encased in dense streamside vegetation, and look for likely spots to begin fishing. There are numerous hidden back eddies (ponds) and sloughs, many created by beaver dams, which hold good populations of fish. It is also possible to fish both the Molalla and Pudding in one day. Your chances of seeing another person on the lower river is unlikely.

Species: Trout, bass, perch, bluegill, sunfish, brown bullhead catfish, small populations of winter steelhead and spring chinook.

Facilities: Molalla River State Park (year-round, no fee) offers a boat ramp, picnic areas, and restrooms—but no camping. The nearest camping is at Feyrer Memorial Park, operated by Clackamas County; it offers 20 sites. Supplies can be had in Aurora and Woodburn.

Directions: From Canby, take Hwy. 99E south 3.7 miles to reach Aurora and the river crossing there; the bridge is just before you enter the town. For the Arndt Rd. crossing, go west on Knights Bridge Rd. from Canby. Cross the Molalla River in 0.5 mile and keep going. In 0.6 mile the road will turn left (south); 0.3 mile later it will dead-end into Arndt Rd. Turn right (west) and cross the Pudding in 0.2 mile. For the crossing near Woodburn, travel 11 miles south of Canby on Hwy. 99E, then turn left (east) onto Hwy. 211, which crosses the Pudding in 0.8 mile. To reach Feyrer Park, start in Woodburn and travel east on Hwy. 211 for 12.7 miles. At the east end of town, turn right (south) on Feyrer Park Rd. and follow it three miles to the park. To reach Molalla River State Park, start in Canby and travel north on N. Holly St. for 2.2 miles to the park entrance.

Contact: Molalla Chamber of Commerce, 503/829-6941; ODFW, Corvallis, 541/757-4186; Clackamas County Parks Department, 503/353-4414; Oregon Parks and Recreation Department, 800/551-6949.

16 ST. LOUIS PONDS
west of Gervais
Map 2.1, page 141

St. Louis Ponds is a compound of seven constructed ponds near Gervais, south of Woodburn. It is managed by the ODFW as a day-use area for warm-water fishing and dog training, and it provides fair to good fishing in a pleasant setting of mowed fields, grasslands, and tall stands of cottonwood and oak trees. From the main parking lot, anglers can walk down pleasant, shaded hiking trails to any one of the seven ponds. Principal catches include stocked legal-size trout, largemouth bass, channel catfish, bluegill, crappie and sunfish. The ponds are open all year from dawn to dusk. Boats (and swimming) are not allowed on any of the ponds. Most of the ponds develop aquatic weed problems in the summer, making fishing difficult. The weed problem is being addressed by the ODFW, but until it finds a solution it might be best to avoid this area in the summer; spring and fall produce the best fishing, anyway.

All methods of fishing can be used, including bait, and no special equipment is needed. Bait such as worms, eggs, and PowerBait all work. Any assortment of small lures such as Rooster Tails, Woolly Buggers, and surface poppers are good for catching bass. Consider this fishery a good place to bring children who are just learning to fish. More serious anglers may find sport in the largemouth bass and crappie populations.

Species: Stocked legal-size trout, largemouth bass, channel catfish, bluegill, crappie and sunfish.

Facilities: The park at St. Louis Fish Ponds (Mar. 1–Oct. 15) is open for day-use only and provides picnic tables, comfort stations, accessible restrooms, concrete pathways to fishing sites, and picnic tables. Supplies and accommodations are available in Gervais and Woodburn.

Directions: From Gervais, travel northwest on St. Louis Rd. for two miles and turn south into the park.

Contact: St. Louis Fish Ponds, 503/588-5304; ODFW, Corvallis, 541/757-4186.

17 BUTTE CREEK
northeast of Silverton
Map 2.1, page 141

This attractive, fast-flowing mountain stream in the middle of the Willamette Valley, along with the Upper Molalla, Silver Creek, and Abiqua Creek, have become favorite places of solitude to go exploring for smaller wild cutthroat trout. Butte Creek originates in the Santiam State Forest east of Salem. While the upper river is accessible from logging roads, there is not much reason to fish anywhere but the public access area in Scotts Mills. Here you will have access to miles of river once you're in the water. The river is composed of pools, riffles, small waterfalls, and pocket water. The trout are not large (7–11 inches), but they are wild and abundant. Fishing for trout is catch-and-release only with artificial lures and flies. Angling for steelhead and salmon is not permitted, but they are present in late February through May.

Because of low summer flows, the best times to fish Butte Creek and surrounding creeks is in late spring, after the winter runoff, and again in fall. When you approach any of these creeks, think "pocket water." Fish flies such as nymphs or attractor dry flies and spinners such as Rooster Tails in the pools and deeper runs. The fish here are not picky and will take almost anything remotely attractive. Use light tackle gear such as 3- and 4-weight rods for the best action.

Species: Wild cutthroat trout and steelhead.

Facilities: Scotts Mills Park (year-round, no fee) is a day-use area providing parking, picnic tables, fire pits, playground equipment, and restrooms. There is no camping in the area. Supplies and accommodations can be had in Silverton and Mount Angel. There is also small general store and restaurant in Scotts Mill. Attractions in the area include fresh produce and fresh-cut flowers available from makeshift roadside stops. Walden West Hosta is an internationally renowned nursery in Scotts Mill that propagates rare hostas, and should not be missed; Mount Angel is famous for its Oktoberfest celebration and historic buildings; Mount Angel Abbey offers a retreat house, good walking trails, an interesting library and art gallery, bookstore, and very hospitable staff.

Directions: From Silverton, travel northeast on Hwy. 213 for 4.8 miles. Turn right (east) onto Silverton–Scotts Mills Rd. and follow it 2.3 miles, at which point it becomes 3rd St. in Scotts Mills. Turn right (south) on Crooked Finger Rd. at the eastern edge of town, just before 3rd St. crosses the creek. The park is 0.1 mile south on Crooked Finger Rd.

Contact: Mount Angel Chamber of Commerce, 503/845-9440; Silverton Area Chamber of Commerce, 503/873-5615; Marion County Parks Department, 503/588-5304; ODFW, Corvallis, 541/757-4186; Mount Angel Abbey, 503/845-3025; Walden West Hosta, 503/873-6875.

18 MIDDLE WILLAMETTE: ALBANY TO NEWBERG
from Albany to Newburg
Map 2.2, page 142

Angling is fair to good for warm-water species such as bass and panfish and marginal for steelhead and salmon in this 72-mile section of the Willamette. Although salmon and steelhead are present, this is mostly pass-through water for them, and finding good holding locations is difficult at best. Trout, ubiquitous around Eugene, are less likely to be caught in the main river, but they can occasionally be found around river mouths or in deeper holes.

Unlike the river below Newberg, which is slow-moving because of being backed up by Willamette Falls, this water runs faster and is more characteristic of a free-flowing river, with pools bracketed by riffles, gravel bars, and shallows. Average depth is considerably lower, 12–15 feet. Boaters are more inclined to drift from one point to the next. Powerboat pilots have to be careful to avoid dangerous, shallow areas. The scenery doesn't change much from that of the lower river, except there are fewer hills, but the river is still lined with dense stands of cottonwood trees and thick undergrowth of blackberries and other scrub brush. There are two operating ferries on this stretch: at Wheatland and Buena Vista.

Boaters have their choice of 11 boat ramps between Rogers Landing in Newberg and Hyak Park in Albany. Since bass and panfish are prevalent through the entire river, there is no one good place to fish. The best bets are always around river mouths, and there are four main ones in this stretch: Yamhill, Santiam, Luckiamute, and Calapooia. Side channels and sloughs, such as Lambert near Wheatland Ferry, are always a good bet, and they are prevalent over this entire stretch. Islands such as Windsor, upstream from Willamette Ferry, are good places to find concentrations of warm-water fish and the occasional steelhead or salmon. Wherever you launch a boat, you will find an abundance of good water for fishing.

Species: Trout, steelhead, salmon, largemouth and smallmouth bass, crappie, perch, bluegill, brown bullhead catfish, channel catfish.

Facilities: Listed from north (Newberg) to south (Albany), here are the boat ramps for this section:

Rogers Landing in Newberg, operated by Yamhill County Parks, is a concrete ramp with a large parking area that charges $3 per vehicle. San Salvador Park, about 10 miles southwest of Newberg, has a paved ramp and restrooms for no fee. Supplies are available in Albany and Newberg.

The ramps at Wheatland Ferry and Willamette Mission State Park are across the river from each other. The Wheatland Ferry ramp is concrete and is on the west bank. Willamette Mission State Park, on the east bank, also has eight miles of trails along the river, and it is home to the nation's largest black cottonwood tree, which is more than 250 years old. There's a $3-per-vehicle day-use fee.

Wallace Marine Park in West Salem has two ramps. The northern, older ramp is gravel and best suited for canoes and kayaks. The southern ramp is the primary one. About 10 miles southwest of Albany, Riverview Park in Independence has a concrete ramp and restrooms. The ramp at the Buena Vista Ferry, halfway between Salem and Albany, is concrete and has restrooms onsite.

There is plenty of access to the river in, or just west of, Albany. Bowman Park at the east end of town has a paved ramp, barbecue grills, restrooms and hiking trails. Takena Landing Park has a boat ramp and docks, barbecue grills, restrooms, and trails. Across the river from Takena are Bryant Park and Montieth River Park. Neither has a boat ramp, but both offer bank access to both the Calpaooia and Willamette Rivers. Hyak Park, just west of town on the north bank, has a boat ramp and moorage, family picnic tables, and accessible restrooms.

Directions: To reach Rogers Landing in Newberg, take Hwy. 99W south onto River St.; the park is at the intersection of River and 14th Sts. For San Salvador Park, start in Newberg and travel south on Hwy. 219 for 7.7 miles to St. Paul. Turn right (west) on Blanchet Ave. and follow it for 3.3 miles to the park. To reach Wallace Marine Park from Albany, travel 20 miles north on I-5 to Exit 253 (Oregon Hwy. 22). Turn left (west) on Hwy. 22 and follow it four miles to where it crosses the river in downtown Salem. Just after the bridge, turn right (north) onto Oregon Hwy. 221 and follow it 0.4 mile north to Glen Creek Rd.; turn right (east) and go 0.3 mile to the park. To reach Riverview Park from Albany, travel west on U.S. 20 for four miles, then go right (north) on Independence Hwy., which leads 17 miles to Independence. The park is on your right as you enter the town.

To reach Wheatland Ferry and Willamette Mission State Park, from Newberg take Hwy. 99W south for 6.5 miles, then take Hwy. 18 southeast for 1.3 miles to Hwy. 221. Follow 221 for 9.6 miles to Wheatland Rd., which leads one mile east to the ferry (daily 5:30 A.M.–9:45 P.M., $1–4, depending on vehicle size) and the west-bank ramp. The east end of the ferry is in the state park.

Farther south, reach the Buena Vista Ferry by taking Hwy. 51 (Corvallis Rd.) south from Independence for two miles, then following Davidson Rd. east 1.4 miles to Buena Vista Rd., which leads to the ferry (7 A.M.–5 P.M. Wed.–Fri., 9 A.M.–7 P.M. Sat.–Sun., $1–5) in three miles.

Contact: Newberg Chamber of Commerce, 503/538-2014; Salem Chamber of Commerce, 503/581-1466; Albany Chamber of Commerce, 541/926-1517; Monmouth and Independence Chamber of Commerce, 503/838-4268; Yamhill County Parks, 503/434-7463; Salem Parks and Recreation, 503/588-6336; ODFW, Corvallis, 541/757-4186; Steelheaders West Tackle shop, 541/744-2248; The Caddis Fly Angling Shop, 541/342-7005, www.thecaddisfly.com

19 LUCKIAMUTE RIVER
north of Corvallis
Map 2.2, page 142

The Luckiamute River (pronounced "lucky-mute") is a tributary to the Willamette River originating in the coastal mountains of the Siuslaw National Forest northwest of Corvallis. It offers fair to good fishing for wild trout and smallmouth bass. After a 30-mile run, the river enters the west side of the Willamette a quarter mile downstream (and across from) from the Santiam River. The Luckiamute gathers numerous other small tributaries in its headwaters, flows west through the towns of Pedee and Maple Grove, and picks up the Little Luckiamute in the vicinity of Mitchell. Most of the upper river flows through scenic forests. Below Mitchell to the Willamette, the river flows through farmlands and tall cottonwood stands of the Willamette Valley.

Both steelhead and salmon are present during spawning periods but are off-limits to anglers. The primary fishing here is for trout in the upper waters and smallmouth bass in the lower reaches. The lower river, composed mostly of slow-moving water, is accessible from either Luckiamute Landing State Park off Buena Vista Road or from Sarah Helmick State Park east of Mitchell. At Luckiamute Landing, good access can be had along the river through the brush once you leave the trails or from a canoe or kayak. The upper river has unlimited bank access in the forest above Hoskins on Luckiamute Road. The river here is too small to boat, and anglers can expect faster flows with pools and riffles.

All fishing for trout is catch-and-release with artificial lures and flies only. Nymphs and attractor dry flies will take trout in the upper waters; bass poppers, jigs, and artificial worms will take bass and small panfish in the lower river.

Species: Trout, smallmouth bass, bluegill.

Facilities: Sarah Helmick State Park (year-round, no fee) has a picnic area, electricity, water, and restrooms. Luckiamute Landing, on the Willamette south of Buena Vista, has primitive camping for boaters only, a vault toilet, and hiking trails. It is managed by Willamette Mission State Park.

Directions: To reach Sarah Helmick State Park, start in Corvallis and drive north on Hwy. 99W for 15.7 miles. Turn left (west) on Old Fort Rd., then left again into the park after 0.2 mile. To reach Luckiamute Landing, start in Buena Vista and travel south on Buena Vista Rd. for two miles. Just after you cross a concrete bridge, look to the left for a gravel road and a mailbox with the number 8989. Follow this driveway, which is shared with a private residence, for 0.7 mile, and when it splits, stay left for the trailhead parking; the residence is to the right. It's a mile walk from the trailhead to the river. To reach the upper river, start in Corvallis and drive north on Hwy. 99W for 12.9 miles to Airlie Rd. Follow this road for 7.9 miles to Maple Grove, which is on the Luckiamute. From here, travel west on Maple Grove Rd. for 3.6 miles to Hwy. 223, then follow 223 west for 0.5 mile to Pedee, also on the river. Follow Hwy. 223 for an additional 5.2 miles to Kings Valley, and for the last two miles you'll be driving along the river; 2.3 miles south of Kings Valley, Hwy. 223 intersects Hoskins Rd. Turn right (west) here, reach Hoskins in 1.7 miles, and from there take Luckiamute Rd. into the headwaters.

Contact: Oregon Parks and Recreation Department, 800/551-6949; Willamette Mission State Park, 503/393-1172; Siuslaw National Forest 541/750-7000; ODFW, Corvallis, 541/757-4186.

20 SANTIAM RIVER
north of Albany
Map 2.2, page 142

The main stem of the Santiam is a short, 12-mile river that forms from the convergences of the North and South forks approximately five miles upriver from I-5, north of Albany, and empties into the Willamette River. This productive stretch of river is home to seasonal runs of steelhead and salmon as well as resident smallmouth bass. The river here flows through farmlands and is bordered by mostly private property.

Hatchery summer steelhead arrive in mid-April and can be caught through July. A small run of wild winter steelhead is present March–May. Chinook enter the river in May and can be caught through October. Only hatchery fish may be retained, and all wild fish must be released unharmed. Steelhead fishing is open all year, and hatchery chinook may be caught January 1–August 15 and again November 1–December 31. All angling methods are permissible, including bait.

Boats are the best and most popular way to get to the river because of limited bank access. Boat access to the main river can be had from boat ramps on the North Fork and from two ramps on the main stem at Jefferson Junction boat ramp at I-5 and Jefferson Site boat ramp, four miles upstream. Jet sleds are popular here, and a lot of anglers launch from the Buena Vista boat launch downstream on the Willamette River, then motor up into the Santiam. Buena Vista is the next take-out for drift boats launching at the Jefferson Site ramp.

Most steelhead are caught from a boat by back-trolling plugs and spoons or side-drifting and float fishing with bait such as sand shrimp and salmon roe and jigs. Salmon may be caught with the same methods in the deeper holes, but include back-bouncing large plugs rigged with herring. Bank anglers are restricted to two areas, the Jefferson Junction boat ramp and Jefferson Site boat ramp. Drift fishing is popular for steelhead, and plunking catches most of the salmon. Smallmouth bass are found principally in the river confluences with the North and South forks. Look for bass around the shoreline with underwater structure, back eddies, or slack water, and against rocks. Bass crankbaits, plastic worms, and jigs all work as effective bass lures.

Species: Spring chinook, hatchery summer and wild winter steelhead, smallmouth bass.

Facilities: The closest camping is on the North and South forks of the Santiam. A concrete boat ramp (no fee) at the Santiam Rest Area near milepost 241 on I-5 is managed by the Oregon Department of Transportation. Low-water conditions in summer may make the water inaccessible from this ramp. Call ODOT to check on this ramp. There's also an improved ramp near Jefferson. Supplies and accommodations are available in Salem and Albany.

Directions: To reach the improved Jefferson ramp, take I-5 north from Albany, and after four miles take Exit 238 (Jefferson), then take Jefferson Hwy. east for three miles. The ramp is under the bridge you cross to enter the town.

To reach the Jefferson Junction ramp, stay on I-5 for three more miles, then take Exit 241 (Rest Area). The ramp is just west of the interstate.

Contact: ODFW, Salem, 503/378-6295; Oregon Department of Transportation, 541/967-2111; City of Jefferson, 541/327-7268; Creekside Fly-Fishing Guides and Outfitters, 877/273-3574

21 LITTLE NORTH SANTIAM
in Willamette National Forest

Map 2.2, page 142

The Little North Santiam is the main tributary of the North Santiam and originates from the confluence of Opal and Battle Ax creeks in the Opal Creek Wilderness. It flows approximately 25 miles to the North Santiam near Mehama, where Highway 22 crosses the river. This is a stunningly beautiful river composed of pools, runs and pocket water, rock gorges, the occasional waterfall, and surroundings of lush forests and foothills of pine and cedar trees. Because of its proximity to the productive North Santiam, most anglers overlook this stream, making it relatively underfished.

A few wild winter steelhead enter the stream and are available February–May. Both wild rainbow and cutthroat trout are available throughout the river but become more abundant the higher in the river you go. Steelhead fishing is open all year, and trout fishing is open during the regular fishing season. Hatchery steelhead may be retained, but all wild fish, including trout, must be released unharmed. Use of bait is allowed.

This is a bank fishery, and access is unlimited from good Forest Service roads that follow the river from the mouth near Mehama, to the dead-end road 20 miles east on Forest Road 2209. From the dead-end, a good hiking trail will lead you the extra five miles upriver into Opal Creek Wilderness and the confluence of Opal and Battle Ax creeks. In fact, this is one of the loveliest hikes you can go on in Oregon. Opal Creek Wilderness is the largest,

low-elevation, uncut watershed in the state and is revered for its massive trees, peaceful creek, and easy hiking. Just more than three miles in, you'll reach Jawbone Flats at the confluence of Battle Ax and Opal creeks, also the home of the Opal Creek Ancient Forest Center, a nonprofit group that hosts educational programs about old-growth forests.

Five miles below where the Forest Service road dead-ends, the Shady Cove campground provides easy river access and hiking trails. Fish for steelhead in the lower 2.5 miles, where the river is bigger and composed of faster, deeper runs and good pocket water. Steelhead are also caught up higher around Elkhorn Valley Park, eight miles from the mouth. Trout become more abundant the higher you go in the river. If you do decide to hike upriver into the wilderness, both Opal and Battle Ax creeks have fair fishing for small wild trout.

Anglers fishing for steelhead can use flies, lures, and bait. No special techniques are needed other than ensuring your tackle gets down to the fish. Swing weighted streamers such as Egg Sucking Leeches, or use a sink tip line with hairwing flies such as Green Butt Skunks, Purple Perils, Silver Hiltons, or Spawning Purples. Gear anglers can use spoons or spinners in gold or silver, and drift gear can be quite productive with corkies and yarn or bait such as worms, eggs, or sand shrimp.

For trout, fish nymphs, dry flies, or streamers. Nymphs would constitute the majority of fishing, but summer hatches of caddis and other insects can warrant the use of attractor dry flies such as an Adams, Royal Wolff, or Humpy. You can fish streamers such as Woolly Buggers in the longer runs by casting across and down.

Species: Wild winter and hatchery steelhead, wild and cutthroat trout.

Facilities: Shady Cove Campground, operated by the National Forest Service, has 13 sites, some of which will handle a vehicle with a trailer. There's no drinking water. Elkhorn Valley Recreation Area, operated by the BLM, has 24 sites for tents or RVs up to 18 feet, as well as drinking water. Parking at National Forest trailheads requires a Northwest Forest Pass ($5 per day; $30 annually), which is available from most sporting goods or outdoors shops or from Nature of the Northwest in Portland. Supplies are available in Stayton and Mehama.

Directions: From Salem, travel east on Hwy. 22 to milepost 23 and a flashing light at the Swiss Village Restaurant. Turn left (north) here on North Fork Rd., which is marked "Little North Santiam Recreation Area." To reach Elkhorn Recreation Area, travel about 15 miles to Forest Rd. 201 (Elkhorn Drive), turn right, and travel 0.5 mile. To reach Shady Cove Campground, continue on North Fork Rd. for about four miles to Forest Rd. 2207, turn right, and travel about 2.5 miles to the campground.

Contact: BLM Salem, 503/375-5646; ODFW, Salem, 503/378-6295; Willamette National Forest Detroit District, 503/854-3366; Nature of the Northwest, 503/872-2750, www.naturenw.org; Opal Creek Ancient Forest Center, 503/892-2782; Creekside Fly-Fishing Guides and Outfitters, 877/273-3574.

22 NORTH SANTIAM

near Salem in Willamette National Forest

Map 2.2, page 142

The North Fork of the Santiam is a very productive fishery for hatchery summer steelhead, winter wild steelhead, spring chinook, and trout. The river runs 60 miles from Big Cliff Dam below Detroit Reservoir to the confluence with the main-stem Santiam near Jefferson. This is a large river with big runs, deep holes, and dangerous rapids. The river is beautiful and its surroundings are spectacular: densely forested banks, steep cliffs descending to the river, and lush forest undergrowth. Fishing pressure is greater than normal but limited to locals in the Salem/Albany/Corvallis areas.

The river hosts salmon, steelhead, and trout, and all methods of fishing are permitted, including bait. Steelhead fishing for hatchery fish is open year-round, but the greatest concentration of summer runs occur May–October, with peak runs in June and July. The winter run of steelhead is entirely wild, entering the river in December, and are available in fishable numbers February–May. Steelhead are found throughout the river in good numbers from Big Cliff Dam, a barrier to the migration of all fish upriver. All wild fish must be released unharmed.

Spring chinook enter the river mid-May–July, with peak catches in June. Wild winter steelhead and chinook fishing is January 1–August 15 and November 1–December 31. Although spring chinook fishing is good throughout the river, many anglers concentrate on the lower sections of the river in the main-stem Santiam River, or on the North Santiam between Stayton and Mill City.

Trout fishing is good throughout the river and gets better the closer you get to Big Cliff Dam. All trout are wild and catch-and-release fishing is required for all trout. Nymphs, dry flies, and streamers are all effective. The Santiam gets good hatches of caddis and assorted mayflies during summer.

Fly-fishing is very popular on the North Santiam and has been the home river to several notable anglers and fly-tiers, including Dave McNeese, John Shewey, and Rich Youngers. Tactics for summer steelhead include floating lines, 7–8-weight rods, and streamer patterns such as Green Butt Skunks, Silver Hiltons, Purple Perils, and Spawning Purples. The Purple Matuka was specifically developed for this river and remains a very popular producer. Greased-line techniques are standard practice with this type of gear. More recent and experimental patterns can be bought from Rich Younger's shop, Creekside Fly-Fishing in Salem.

Traditional gear anglers fishing for steelhead have great success on the North Santiam with drift rigs, plugs, and spinners. Popular baits are night crawlers, salmon eggs, sand shrimp, and crayfish. Corkies and yarn work well when the water is low and clear in the summer. Spoons and lures should be used in brighter colors of orange, purple, pearl, and green. Salmon are caught with plugs such as Hot Shots and Wiggle Worts and salmon eggs.

Both bank and boating access is excellent from numerous parks that dot the river along the 60-mile stretch between Big Cliff Dam and the mouth. Additional parks and boat ramps are available on the main-stem Santiam and farther downstream on the Willamette at Buena Vista Ferry. The Santiam is a difficult river to float because there are numerous Class II, III, and IV rapids in most stretches. Get a good river guidebook before attempting any of this water. Boats suitable for this water are drift boats and rafts equipped to handle white water.

Drifts can be of any desired length. Starting at Packsaddle Park, five miles downriver from Big Cliff Dam, some of the more popular drifts are: Packsaddle Park to Mill City (6.5 miles), Mill City to Mehama (8.5 miles), Mehama to Stayton (10.5 miles), and Stayton to Jefferson (19 miles). There are other take-outs between each of these drifts that can either shorten or lengthen your drift. There is a mandatory portage above Stayton Bridge, and a boat slide has been constructed to enable anglers to rope their boats around the danger. Boaters need to check regulations for special angling restrictions around Mill City.

Bank anglers have virtually a lifetime of choices to reach this river. There are good access points at all 10 boat ramps, and the five miles of river below Big Cliff Dam is all open access. Popular starting points are John Neal County Park at the mouth of the Little North Santiam and the BLM property at Fisherman's Bend below Mill City.

Species: Summer and winter steelhead, spring chinook and trout.

Facilities: Camping is available at two campgrounds on the river. Fisherman's Bend, operated by the BLM, offers 18 tent sites, 21 hookup sites, and trail access to a mile of river,

as well as a day-use area and boat ramp. John Neal Memorial Park, operated by Linn County, has 40 sites for tents or self-contained RVs (no reservations) and also a day-use area with a boat ramp. There are eight other public ramps along the North Santiam, all of them free and open year-round. Packsaddle Park (Marion County) also has picnic tables, fire pits, and restrooms. North Santiam State Park also has restrooms, hiking trails, and restrooms. Buell Miller, Mehama Bridge, and Stayton Bridge (all run by Linn County) offer pit toilets and no other amenities; Kimmel Park (Mill City) has a pole-slide put-in for rafts; and Green's Bridge has restrooms, parking, and a gravel ramp. Marion County's Minto Park, a take-out spot only for rafts, also has picnic tables, fire pits, and restrooms. Supplies are available in Albany and Stayton.

Directions: To reach all of these campgrounds and boat ramps, start by driving east on Hwy. 22 from Salem. Then follow each of these directions:

For Stayton Bridge, follow Hwy. 22 for 13.6 miles to Stayton, then turn south on Stayton–Scio Rd. On the south edge of town, just before crossing the river, turn left (east) onto Access Rd., which leads 0.2 mile down to the ramp.

For Buell Miller boat ramp, stay on Stayton–Scio Rd. and follow it for 6.2 miles to Shelburn, then turn north on Hess Rd.; the ramp is two miles ahead, at the end of Hess Rd.

For Green's Bridge, stay on Stayton–Scio for six miles past Shelburn to the crossing of the North Fork.

For Mehama Bridge, take Hwy. 22 for a total of 23 miles from Salem, and when you arrive in Mehama, turn south on Hwy. 226 (Albany–Lyons Hwy.). This road crosses the river on the south side of town, and the ramp is under the south end of the bridge.

For John Neal County Park, after crossing the river in Mehama, continue south on Hwy. 226 for 1.4 miles to the park entrance, which is also 13th St.

For North Santiam State Park, travel on Hwy. 22 for 2.1 miles past Mehama (25.1 miles from Salem) and turn right (south) onto Dewitt Ln., following a sign for the park, which is 0.8 mile ahead at the end of the road.

For Fisherman's Bend campground and boat ramp, take Hwy. 22 a total of 32 miles east of Salem. The entrance is on the right.

For Minto Park, stay on Hwy. 22 for 2.5 miles past Fisherman's Bend; the entrance to the park is on the right. Packsaddle Park is one mile past that.

Contact: ODFW, Salem, 503/378-6295; BLM, Salem, 503/375-5646; Linn County Parks Department, 541/967-3917; Creekside Fly-Fishing Guides and Outfitters, 877/273-3574, www.creeksideflyfishing.com.

23 SOUTH SANTIAM
southeast of Albany in Willamette National Forest

Map 2.2, page 142

The productive South Fork of the Santiam makes an 80-mile run from its source in the Willamette National Forest to its confluence with the North Santiam five miles above I-5 near Albany. The river is compounded near Sweet Home at Foster Reservoir before continuing to the confluence with the North Santiam. Above the reservoir the river runs through densely forested lands, scenic and breathtaking in places, and borders the Menagerie Wilderness for a stretch. The river below the dam enters Lower Pleasant Valley and a mix of farmlands and forests to the mouth. Steelhead and salmon are blocked from entering the upper river by Foster Dam. Though there may be some trout in the lower river, most trout fishing takes place above Foster Dam.

The lower river is open for hatchery steelhead from the mouth to Foster Dam, year-round. Spring chinook fishing is open in the same stretch January 1–August 15 and again November 1–December 31. All fish-

ing methods are allowed, including bait. Wild trout, steelhead, and salmon must be released unharmed. Winter steelhead arrive in December with peak runs January–March; summer steelhead arrive May–October with peak catches June–August. Spring chinook arrive May–August and peak in June.

Anglers use jet sleds, drift boats, and rafts on the river. The concentration of boat ramps and fishing for salmon and steelhead are between Foster Dam and Lebanon. A majority of the bank angling takes place in the first three miles of river below Foster Dam, particularly at Andrew Wiley Park, where anglers can take advantage of the fish's inability to migrate over the dam. This area is very popular and crowded with both bank and boat anglers. If crowds are not your thing, you can fish from the bank or a boat below Sweet Home at Waterloo Park or Gills Landing with equally good success.

Popular floats on this river are Andrew Wiley Park at Foster Dam to Northside Park in Sweet Home (three miles), Sweet Home to Waterloo Park (11 miles), Waterloo to Lebanon at Gills Landing (five miles), Lebanon to Crabtree (11 miles), and Crabtree to Jefferson (10 miles). The take-out at Crabtree requires a special permit from the Linn County Road Department. Class I and II rapids dominate the river, and there are two mandatory portages at Waterloo Falls, downstream from Waterloo Park, and Lebanon Dam, below Gill's Landing.

Fishing techniques vary from flies to traditional methods of lures and bait. Fly anglers should not attempt to fish among gear anglers below the dam. Instead, they can move downriver to the parks below Sweet Home. Summer steelhead fishing includes floating lines and classic steelhead streamer patterns such as Green Butt Skunks and Purple Perils. Winter steelhead fishing can use the same flies in combination with a sink tip or full sinking line. Traditional gear anglers catch steelhead on brightly colored jigs or bait such as sand shrimp, night crawlers, and salmon roe on drift rigs or under floats. Salmon are primarily caught using spoons and plugs from a boat or bait such as salmon roe from the bank.

The upper river, above Foster Reservoir, runs primarily through forested public lands, and great access can be had from numerous parks and campgrounds along Highway 20. No specific place is better here because trout are equally distributed throughout the river. Scenic starting points can be found at Cascadia State Park, eight miles east of the lake on Highway 20, and Trout Creek Campground, 16 miles east on Highway 20 from the lake.

Species: Hatchery summer steelhead, wild winter steelhead, spring chinook, and trout.

Facilities: Linn County's Waterloo Park, in Waterloo, has a 120-site campground with full hookups and showers and also a year-round day-use area with two boat ramps. Gill's Landing, part of River Park in Lebanon, has a boat ramp and 21 RV sites, each with electricity and Internet. Above the dam, there are 25 primitive campsites at Cascadia State Park, as well as good bank access. Willamette National Forest has three campgrounds even farther upstream: Trout Creek, Yukwah, and Fernview. Other camping is available at Foster Reservoir. Andrew Wiley Park, operated by the Corps of Engineers (who built Foster Dam just above it) offers a free, year-round boat ramp plus restrooms and picnic tables. There's also a free boat ramp at Northside Park in Sweet Home. Supplies are available in Jefferson and Lebanon.

Directions: From Albany, take I-5 north for four miles. Take Exit 238 (Jefferson), then take Jefferson Hwy. east for three miles. The Jefferson ramp is under the bridge you cross to enter the town. To reach the take-out at Crabtree from Albany, travel east on I-5 for 14 miles to the town of Lebanon, then travel north on Hwy. 20 for 6.9 miles, then turn right (east) on Hwy. 226. You'll cross the river in 1.1 miles. Gill's Landing is in Lebanon; travel east on Grant St. to the edge of town.

To reach Waterloo Park, start in Lebanon and drive south on Hwy. 20 for 5.2 miles and turn left (east) on Waterloo Rd. This road leads 0.8 mile to the park, turning into Gross St. along the way.

Northside Park is in Sweet Home. From Hwy. 20, travel north on 12th St. for 0.2 mile, then turn left (west) onto Poplar St. and, one block later, right (north) on 11th St., which leads north into the park. The boat ramp at Andrew Wiley Park is at the eastern end of Sweet Home. From Hwy. 20 eastbound, turn left (north) onto 53rd Ave. and follow it for 0.2 mile into the park.

Cascadia State Park and the campgrounds in Willamette National Forest are above Foster Dam on the South Santiam. To reach Cascadia, start in Sweet Home and take Hwy. 20 east for 14.4 miles to the park entrance. Trout Creek, Yukwah, and Fernview campgrounds are scattered along the same road 8–11 miles east of Cascadia.

Contact: Sweet Home Chamber of Commerce, 541/367-6186; Linn County Parks and Recreation, 541/967-3917; ODFW, Salem, 503/378-6295; Linn County Rd. Department, 541/967-3919; Army Corps of Engineers Foster Dam office, 541/367-5124; Lebanon Parks Department, 541/258-4917; Oregon Parks and Recreation Department, 800/551-6949; Willamette National Forest Sweet Home District 541/367-5168; Creekside Fly-Fishing Guides and Outfitters, 877/273-3574, www.creeksideflyfishing.com.

24 GREEN PETER LAKE
east of Sweet Home
Map 2.2, page 142

Green Peter is a massive reservoir (3,700 acres) in the Santiam watershed about four miles northeast of Foster Reservoir. It is fed by numerous small tributaries, most of which make up the lake's many arms, and two major ones, the Middle Fork of the Santiam and Quartzville Creek. Fishing is good for kokanee, trout, and largemouth bass, with kokanee making up the majority of the catches. Anglers will no doubt find this a scenic reservoir surrounded by the forested foothills of the Willamette National Forest. Boaters will particularly enjoy exploring the abundance of coves and tributary arms.

Two boat ramps service the lake on the north shore, and bank anglers will find a network of logging and Forest Service roads around most of the lake, all navigable with a good Willamette National Forest Service map. The easiest places to begin are the boat launches at Thistle Creek Park and Whitcomb Creek Park, or along Quartzville Drive on the north shore. All these places provide good bank access for trout, bluegill, and early season kokanee.

Kokanee, the lake's main attraction, are caught in shallow waters (20–30 feet deep) around the lakeshore in spring and deeper waters (80–100 feet) during summer. The limit on kokanee is a generous 25 fish per day with no size limit. Balance jigs, Nordic Jigs, or Buzz Bombs in different colors (red, green, pink, pearl) all work. Some anglers attach a small piece of white corn on the jig hook. Fish early in the morning, before the wind kicks up and moves the boat around, taking your lure out of the holes.

Trout can be caught with trolled lures or streamers such as Woolly Buggers or Zonkers. In spring, concentrate your fishing around the tributary mouths and in the shallows around the shorelines and structure. In summer, fish the deep, cooler water toward the center of the lake. Fish for bass in the same locations, but use surface poppers, crankbaits, and Rapalas.

Species: Trout, kokanee, largemouth bass, bluegill.

Facilities: Whitcomb Creek Park (mid-Apr.–mid-Oct.), operated by Linn County, has 38 campsites with drinking water but no RV hookups. There are also a boat ramp, restrooms, and picnic and swimming areas. Thistle Creek boat ramp, which extends to the winter lake levels, has vault toilets and is open all year for no charge. Supplies are available in Sweet Home.

Directions: From Sweet Home, drive 5.8 miles east on Hwy. 20, then turn left (north) on Quartzville Rd. Continue on this road for 7.9 miles to reach Thistle Creek boat ramp and for 11.4 miles to reach Whitcomb Creek Park.

Contact: Sweet Home Chamber of Commerce, 541/367-6186; Linn County Parks and Recreation, 541/967-3917; ODFW, Salem, 503/378-6295; Willamette National Forest Sweet Home District, 541/367-5168; Creekside Fly-Fishing Guides and Outfitters, 877/273-3574, www.creeksideflyfishing.com.

25 FOSTER RESERVOIR

east of Sweet Home

Map 2.2, page 142

Foster is a 1,200-acre reservoir on the South and Middle forks of the Santiam River near Sweet Home. It offers fair to good catches of stocked rainbow trout, largemouth and smallmouth bass, and bluegill. The lake is surrounded by the Cascade foothills of the Willamette National Forest, providing a pleasant backdrop for anglers.

The reservoir is open to all methods of fishing, including bait, and there are no limits on size or numbers of bass that can be retained; all wild fish, including trout, must be released unharmed. Both the Middle and South Fork arms are open to fishing only during the regular trout season of April 23–October 31.

The most popular places for most boaters and bank anglers are just behind the dam, along the north shore on North River Drive, and in the South and Middle Fork arms. Both arms are accessible by boat for a short way into backed-up water or from Highway 20 and Quartzville Drive. Three boat ramps (Gedney Creek on the north shore, Calkins Park on the south shore, and Sunnyside Park on the Middle Fork Arm) offer access to their respective parts of the lake.

Either the north shore or the Middle Fork Arm is the best place to begin both boat and bank fishing, and either will get you away from the congestion around the dam. There is plenty of good habitat here in the form of sunken logs, tree stumps, and vegetation to find all species of fish. Trout fishing is especially popular in both the arms. Popular methods for trout include bait such as worms or eggs and trolling spinners and flies. Bass are frequently taken on surface poppers and jigs fished around obstructions. Troll lures near and around changes in the lake bottom.

Species: Stocked trout, bass, bluegill.

Facilities: Gedney Creek boat ramp, operated by Linn County, has parking and restrooms, and is open year-round for no charge. Sunnyside County Park's campground has 130 hookup sites and 35 for tents. The day-use area is open all year and includes a boat ramp, moorage, and picnic shelter. Calkins Park has an unimproved ramp and restrooms. Supplies are available in Sweet Home.

Directions: From Sweet Home, follow Hwy. 20 east to the reservoir's south shore. Calkins Park is two miles past the dam. To reach Sunnyside County Park, drive a total of 5.8 miles from Sweet Home and reach Quartzville Rd. Turn left (north) here, and in 1.3 miles you'll enter the park. To reach Gendey Creek boat ramp on the north shore, go 3.6 miles east on Hwy. 20 from Sweet Home, then turn left (north) on Foster Dam Drive. Follow this for 0.8 mile, crossing the dam, then turn right (east) on North River Dr., which in 0.4 mile will take you to the ramp.

Contact: Sweet Home Chamber of Commerce, 541/367-6186; Linn County Parks and Recreation, 541/967-3917; ODFW, Salem, 503/378-6295; Army Corps of Engineers Foster Dam office, 541/367-5124; Willamette National Forest Sweet Home District, 541/367-5168; Creekside Fly-Fishing Guides and Outfitters, 877/273-3574, www.creeksideflyfishing.com.

26 CALAPOOIA RIVER
south of Albany

Map 2.2, page 142

The Calapooia River originates in the Willamette National Forest on the west flanks of Tidbits Mountain, running 85 miles to its confluence with the Willamette River in Albany. The lower river flows through private property and farmlands of the Willamette Valley. Fishing is restricted to artificial flies and lures only, and all wild fish must be released unharmed. Access can be had at the mouth of the Willamette River, the Corvallis/Albany KOA on Highway 34, and by road crossings in Crawfordsville, Brownsville, and Albany. This water is slow-moving and suitable for canoes and kayaks in the spring when water levels are higher. Good fishing can be had from the mouth via Takena Landing. The upper river is in a forested mountain region accessible by good roads into the headwaters and offers fair to good fishing for wild trout. The area above Calapooia is on Forest Service property, and the river is followed by good roads for 21 miles to the headwaters. When navigating the upper roads, have a good Willamette National Forest Service map.

Species: Wild trout, largemouth and smallmouth bass, perch, bluegill.

Facilities: The Albany/Corvallis KOA has camping, cabins, a snack bar, firewood, and bicycle rentals. Takena Landing Park, on the north shore of the Willamette River in Albany opposite the mouth of the Calapooia, has a boat ramp and docks, barbecue grills, restrooms, and trails. On the south side, bracketing the Calapooia, are Bryant Park (west) and Montieth River Park (east). Neither has a boat ramp, but both offer bank access to both the Calpaooia and Willamette Rivers. Albany's Bowman Park, on the Willamette River, also has a boat ramp. Supplies are available in Albany.

Directions: In Albany at Hwys. 20 and 99E, drive north on Hwy. 20 for 0.1 mile and turn left (west) on 8th St. Follow 8th seven blocks (0.3 miles) to Vine St., turn right (north) on Vine, follow it 0.3 mile and turn left on 3rd St., which turns into Bryant Way and leads into the park. To reach Montieth Park, go north on Hwy. 20 for 0.6 mile, then turn left (west) onto Water Ave., which leads 0.2 mile to the park. For the KOA, drive 5.1 miles from Albany south on Hwy. 99E, then turn right (west) on Hwy. 34. Follow Hwy. 34 for 2.2 miles and turn left (south) onto Oakville Rd., which leads to the KOA in 0.1 mile.

For the upper river, from Albany go east on Hwy. 20 for two miles and then take I-5 south for 16.5 miles. Take Exit 216 (Brownsville) and, from there, follow Hwy. 228 for 3.8 miles east to Brownsville. This town is on the Calapooia, and for the next 10.9 miles, to Holley, Hwy. 228 follows the river southeast. At Holley, Linn County operates McClun Wayside, which offers access where County Rd. 759 crosses the Calapooia (this is also the site where trout stocking takes place). From here, Calapooia Rd. turns southeast, leaving Hwy. 228, and following the river upstream into the headwaters.

Contact: Albany Parks and Recreation, 541/917-7777; Albany/Corvallis KOA, 541/967-8521; Linn County Parks and Recreation, 541/967-3917; Willamette National Forest Sweet Home District, 541/367-5168; ODFW, Corvallis, 541/757-4186; BLM Salem, 503/375-5646.

27 MIDDLE WILLAMETTE: SPRINGFIELD TO ALBANY

from Island Park in Springfield to Hyak Park in Albany

Map 2.2, page 142

This description covers 65 miles of the Willamette River. Three significant changes occur in this upper river. First, it gets broken up into channels, developing more islands, riffles, deceptively fast currents, and several challenging rapids around Eugene. As on most of the river in this stretch, boating is limited to rafts, drift boats, and jet sleds. Second, trout begin to inhabit the river from Peoria, south of Corvallis, and increase in numbers higher up in the river, especially around Santa Clara and Eugene. Steelhead also become more of an option at river mouths such as the McKenzie below Eugene and the Coast Fork and South

Fork above Eugene. Below Corvallis the river is once again slow, and fishing is limited to warm-water species such as bass and panfish, with few opportunities for steelhead or salmon. Third, this section of the Willamette is far more rural than you find from Albany to Portland, with fewer towns and services. Boat ramps are spread out over longer distances, which is a consideration for anglers using rafts and drift boats. Regardless of which section you decide to fish, the Willamette remains a beautiful river, isolated from developed areas with tall stands of cottonwood trees and dense bank brush. Mountain backdrops begin to appear as you get closer to Eugene.

Two good places for warm-water anglers to begin are Willamette Park and Crystal Lake boat ramps in Corvallis and Michaels Landing eight miles downriver. Canoes, kayaks, and drift boats can float from Willamette Park to Michaels Landing and find good numbers of bass and panfish in channels, sloughs, and around abundant river debris. The float from Michaels Landing to Hyak Landing is approximately 11 miles. Jet sleds can be used in this part of the river, but prop boats should be very wary of shallows, deadheads, and other dangers. Anglers can float down from Peoria Park to Corvallis (10 miles) for fair warm-water fishing and some trout. McCartney Park to Peoria Park is the longest float in this section (15 miles) and offers better trout fishing than warm-water fishing. Anglers attempting to boat any part of this river are well advised to obtain a river guidebook such as that published by the Oregon State Parks Department. Bank access is good at all the boat launches listed here, as well as at other parks in the vicinity.

Trout anglers need only go to Eugene for the best opportunities to catch fish up to 20 inches. This area is particularly popular for fly anglers who find good hatches of stone flies, mayflies, and caddis throughout the year. The early spring blue-wing olives and March browns are two highlights. Caddis come off in April and last all summer. Four boat ramps in this section give good access to underfished water. Popular drifts start at Island Park above the I-5 Bridge in Eugene but also pose some of the most formidable rapids on the river. Less experienced boaters should begin lower in the river at Alton Baker Landing and float down to Whitely Landing (approximately six miles) or Hileman Landing (approximately eight miles). Another popular option is to start on the McKenzie River at Armitage Park and float five miles downriver to Hileman Landing. The mouth of the McKenzie provides the best opportunity to catch summer steelhead May–October.

Bank anglers can fish from any of the landings or from Skinner Butte and Maurie Jacobs parks in Eugene. A novel bank fishery, and one that has garnered a lot of attention in previous years, is the water by the Valley River Center shopping mall in Eugene. Here, anglers park in the mall parking lot and walk down to the river to good riffles.

Species: Trout, steelhead, salmon, large and smallmouth bass, crappie, perch, bluegill, brown bullhead catfish, channel catfish.

Facilities: There are 10 boat ramps on this stretch of river. Corvallis ramp in that town is paved but has no other amenities. Peoria Park, about eight miles south of Corvallis, has a concrete ramp and restrooms, and boaters may spend one night in the campground. McCartney Park (about 10 driving miles south of Peoria), is sometimes under water in winter, has a concrete ramp and, in spring and summer, portable restrooms and picnic tables. Call Linn County Parks to check on the status of this ramp.

Harrisburg Park in Harrisburg has a paved ramp and restrooms. Christensens Landing (paved, no other facilities) and Marshall Island Landing (paved with restrooms) are very near each other a few miles southeast of Junction City. Hileman Landing (gravel) and Whitely Landing (asphalt), a little farther south, on the northern outskirts of Springfield, have no other amenities.

Island Park (6 A.M. to 10 P.M. year-round), on the McKenzie River in Springfield, is managed by that town's Willamalene Parks District. It has a concrete ramp, restrooms, shelters, electric outlets, and hiking trails.

Alton Baker Park in Eugene is a large, developed park near the University of Oregon. The boat ramp there is unimproved, and parking is limited.

Other areas that offer bank access include Skinner Butte and Maurice Jacobs parks in Eugene, and Truax Island and Riverside Landing just south of Albany. Supplies are available in Springfield.

Directions: Peoria Park is in the small community of Peoria. To get there from Corvallis, start east on Hwy. 34 and, 1.2 miles out of town, turn right (south) on Peoria Rd., which leads nine miles to Peoria. To reach McCartney Park, start in Harrisburg and head north on Peoria Rd. for three miles, then west on McCartney Rd. two miles to the ramp.

For Christensens Landing, go south of Harrisburg about six miles on Coburg Rd., then turn right (west) on Crossroad Ln., which becomes gravel in its two-mile run to the river. For Marshall Island Landing, start in Junction City and travel east, then south, on River Rd. for a total of four miles to Hayes Ln., which heads east two miles to the ramp.

To reach Hileman Landing and Whitely Landing, start in Santa Clara. Go north on River Rd. for just under a mile, then turn east on Wilkes Drive, which leads one mile east to Whitely Landing. For Hileman Landing, continue north on River Rd. for another mile, then turn east on Beacon Drive for a mile and north on Hileman Rd. into the park.

Contact: Convention and Visitors Association of Lane County, 541/484-5307; Albany Chamber of Commerce, 541/926-1517; Springfield Area Chamber of Commerce, 541/746-1651; Linn County Parks Department, 541/967-3917; Willamalene Park District of Springfield, 541/736-4104; ODFW, Corvallis, 541/757-4186; Steelheaders West Tackle shop, 541/744-2248; The Caddis Fly Angling Shop, 541/342-7005, www.thecaddisfly.com

28 FERN RIDGE RESERVOIR
west of Eugene

Map 2.2, page 142

Fern Ridge is a popular, 9,360-acre recreation reservoir nine miles west of Eugene. It offers fair fishing for stocked trout, bass, and other warm-water species. This is a scenic lake near the forested foothills of the Siuslaw National Forest, but don't expect a lot of solitude and quiet. The overall depth of the reservoir is a shallow 11 feet (33 feet at its deepest point). Most of the recreational boating is limited to the areas around the dam, leaving a majority of arms and coves available for anglers. This is good, because a majority of the fish are here, with the exception of the area around the dam.

The lake is open year-round and is a popular early spring, fall, and winter fishery, when the summer skiers have left. The half dozen arms that make up the lake are all fed by smaller, cold-water tributaries and provide a good haven for all species of fish year-round. Bait, flies, and lures are all allowed and work equally well.

Bank angling opportunities are good; the best places to start are around the dam, below the dam in Kirk Pond, and in the vicinity of the four boat ramps scattered around the lake. Bait such as worms and PowerBait fished under a bobber is the number one approach when working along the bank. Spinners and flies also work when trolled at various depths and speeds.

Boaters have the option of launching from four sites, two at the north end and two at the south. The whole lake is accessible for trolling. The best water lies in the lake arms and at the end of each arm, where a tributary is generally found. The coves also provide good largemouth bass habitat around fallen trees and other underwater obstructions. The deeper waters around the dam are good for trolling for all species, but this area can be crowded in summer.

Species: Trout, largemouth bass, crappie, bluegill, brown bullhead catfish.

Facilities: Lane County operates three parks at the reservoir. Amenities at Orchard Point Park

(8 A.M.–dusk; $3 per vehicle 9 A.M.–7 P.M. May 1–Sept. 30, no fee rest of the year) include a marina with boat ramp, food, sundries, boat fuel, picnic areas, and rentable sailboats and Jet Skis. Perkins Peninsula Park (9 A.M.–7 P.M. May 1–Sept. 30, $3 per vehicle) has a boat ramp with parking, hiking trails, and picnic areas. Richardson Park (mid-Apr.–mid-Oct.) has campsites as well as a large marina and boat ramp. Day-use fee (May 1–Sept. 30) is $3 per vehicle. Fern Ridge Shores RV Park (year-round) also has a boat ramp ($5), though the water typically doesn't reach it until mid-April. Supplies are available in Veneta.

Directions: Fern Ridge Reservoir is approximately eight miles west of Eugene on Hwy. 126. Driving west on that highway, you will first come to Perkins Peninsula Park on the right. To reach Fern Ridge Shores RV Park, take Hwy. 126 approximately one mile west of Perkins Park, then turn right (north) on Ellmaker Rd. After 1.1 miles on Ellmaker, turn right (east) on Jeans Rd., which will lead you 1.3 miles into the park. Richardson Park and Orchard Point Park are on the lake's northern shore. For these, start in Eugene and travel north on Hwy. 99W for 6.1 miles, then turn left (west) on Clear Lake Rd. Orchard Point is 5.5 miles ahead on this road. To reach Richardson Park, go another 2.2 miles on Clear Lake Rd., then turn left (south) on Richardson Park Rd., which enters the park in 0.3 mile.

Contact: Convention and Visitors Association of Lane County, 541/484-5307; ODFW, Corvallis, 541/757-4186; Fern Ridge Wildlife Area, 541/935-2591; Lane County Parks, 541/682-2000; Orchard Point Concessions, 541/461-7886; Richardson Park Marina, 541/935-2005; Fern Ridge Shores RV Park, 541/935-2335.

29 McKENZIE RIVER
east of Springfield

Map 2.2, page 142

The magnificent McKenzie originates at Clear Lake in the Willamette National Forest and flows 89 miles, skirting Springfield before entering the upper Willamette River. The river above Springfield flows through picturesque forests and gorges, while the lower river flows mostly through farmlands. This is one of the best trout fisheries in the state, and it's good to better for steelhead, depending on the size of the runs from the Willamette. There is also a marginal but improving spring chinook run.

Trout are plentiful in the entire river, including both cutthroat and native "McKenzie River" redsides. Hatchery fish are available above Leaburg Dam and wild fish below. Expect average catches of 12–14 inches, with some bigger fish nearing 20 inches. Summer steelhead can be fished for year-round and arrive in the river in May and June; they are caught below Leaburg Dam. The most popular area for steelhead is the five miles of river from Leaburg Dam downstream to Leaburg. Current fishing regulations for salmon are in flux and often limit fishing to certain parts of the river, so check with ODFW for the latest regulations. The entire river is restricted to artificial flies and lures, except for the area between Hayden Bridge on Marcola Road and Forest Glen boat ramp, which is open to bait fishing April 23–December 31. Trout and steelhead seasonal regulations are imposed on other parts of the river, so consult the ODFW regulation guide. All wild fish must be returned to the river unharmed.

The McKenzie is a great trout stream for fly anglers, with multiple hatches of mayflies, stone flies, and caddis most of the year. These hatches provide good opportunities to match the hatch or simply use attractor patterns such as an Adams, Royal Wulffs, or small yellow Humpies. Winter hatches include blue-wing olives, winter stone flies, and midges. March–May sees the emergence of March brown mayflies, perhaps the most popular and productive hatch of the year. In April, March browns are joined by golden stones, pale morning duns, yellow "sally" stone flies, and caddis for the remainder of the year till

August. From August the blue-wing olives return, and caddis will continue to hatch until October. General nymphs such as Hare's Ears and Pheasant Tails are good between hatches, but get them on the bottom of the river with weight. Streamers and Soft Hackles are great any time of day.

Traditional gear anglers fishing for trout and steelhead use spinners, spoons, plugs, and drift-fishing techniques with corkies and yarn or jigs. Color can be important during different times of the year; orange, red, purple, silver, and gold are favorite shades.

Upper River (Leaburg Dam to Headwaters): While there are many campground and boat ramps in the upper reaches (Forest Glen to Clear Lake) it's not very productive fishing. Most anglers start fishing below Blue River, where the South Fork and main river meet. All this water is productive for trout. From here anglers can float drifts of any length, 1–20 miles, starting from 10 launch points. Or they can bank fish from any launch or along the roadside on Highway 126. Good places to start bank fishing are at Howard J. Morton or Dorris county parks. Most of this water is composed of Class I and II rapids, the most dangerous being near Rennie Landing. There is a mandatory portage around Leaburg Dam south of Leaburg. The most popular and productive drifts begin from Forest Glen boat launch near Blue River. Anglers can float downstream to Finns Landing (3.5 miles), Shepards Landing (four miles), McMullens Landing (five miles), Rennie Landing (10 miles), Dorris Park and nearby Helfrich Landing (14 miles), and Eweb Slip at Leasburg Dam (19 miles).

Lower River (Leaburg to the Mouth): Ten boat ramps dot the lower river, and bank access is only fair because of private property, making boating a better option. Still, there are good access points at each of the boat ramps, especially Armitage Park on I-5, Rodakowski, and Hayden Bridge—all in Springfield. For bank fishing for steelhead below the dam, start at either the Greenwood Drive ramp or from road access along Highway 126 between Greenwood and the dam. Armitage State Park is the lowest take-out on the river, the next lowest being five miles downriver on the Willamette River at Heileman Landing. Popular drifts in this section include Leaburg Dam to Hendricks Bridge Wayside (15 miles), Hendricks Bridge Wayside to Hayden Bridge (15 miles), and Hayden Bridge to Armitage (eight miles). There are numerous take-outs between these points to either shorten or lengthen your float.

Species: Native and hatchery cutthroat and redside trout, summer steelhead, spring chinook salmon.

Facilities: There are numerous camping options in the area. Willamette National Forest operates three campgrounds (May–Sept.) in the area east of Blue River: Delta, Mona, and Lookout. It also operates a string of sites along the upper McKenzie, the nearest of which are McKenzie Bridge and Paradise; both have boat launches onto the McKenzie. Patio RV Park is in the McKenzie Bridge area. Supplies are available in Springfield.

Directions: Springfield is across the Willamette River from Eugene. Follow the specific directions below to reach these free boat ramps, which fall under various administrations.

Armitage Park (Lane County) has a concrete ramp, picnic tables, and restrooms. From Eugene, travel north on Coburg Rd. for 4.4 miles to the Armitage Park, on the north edge of town. Rodakowski (BLM) has a concrete ramp and restrooms. In Springfield, travel east on Hayden Bridge Rd., turn north on Harvest Ln. and follow it 0.7 mile to the BLM ramp at Rodakowski. Hayden Bridge Ramp

(Lane County) has a pole-slide ramp and parking. For the Hayden Bridge Ramp, travel east on Hwy. 126 to Marcola Rd., starting north and then turning east, to cross the river in 1.4 miles.

The rest of the sites mentioned lie along Hwy. 126, the McKenzie River Hwy., east of Springfield. Hendricks Bridge (Oregon State Parks) has a concrete ramp and restrooms (six miles); Leaburg Landing (Lane County), in Leaburg, has only a gravel ramp (14 miles); Greenwood ramp in Greenwood (ODFW) has an asphalt ramp (17 miles); Eweb Slip at Leaburg Dam (City of Eugene) has a pole-slide ramp (19 miles); Helfrich Landing (ODFW) has a gravel ramp (26 miles); Dorris Park (Lane County) has an asphalt ramp, picnic tables, drinking water, and restrooms (27 miles); Rennie Landing (ODFW) has just a gravel ramp (32 miles); McMullen's Landing and Shepards Landing (ODFW) both have only a pole-slide (37 miles); Finn Rock Landing (Lane County) has a gravel ramp (39 miles); Forest Glen Landing (Lane County) has a gravel ramp and restrooms (43 miles).

Contact: Convention and Visitors Association of Lane County, 541/484-5307; Oregon Parks and Recreation Department, 800/551-6949; Willamette National Forest McKenzie River Ranger District, 541/822-3381; ODFW, Salem, 503/378-6295; BLM, Salem, 503/375-5646; Steelheaders West Tackle shop, 541/744-2248; Patio RV Park, 541/822-3596; Belknap Hot Springs, 541/822-3512, www.belknaphotsprings.com; The Caddis Fly Angling Shop, 541/342-7005, www.the caddisfly.com.

THE COLUMBIA RIVER GORGE AND MOUNT HOOD

© BOB SCHUHMANN

BEST FISHING SPOTS

❰ **Rainbow Trout**
Lower Deschutes River: Pelton Dam to
Trout Creek, **page 227**

❰ **Steelhead**
Lower Deschutes River: Mack's Canyon to Maupin,
page 213

❰ **Family Fishing**
Lost Lake, **page 198**

❰ **Places to Teach Kids to Fish**
North Fork Reservoir, **page 190**

❰ **Most Accessible for Disabled Anglers**
Lower Deschutes River: Mack's Canyon to Maupin,
page 213
Timothy Lake, **page 216**

Less than 20 miles east of I-5 between Portland

and Salem, the Cascade Mountains begin their ascent from rolling foothills
to the alpine highlands of Mount Hood and Mount Jefferson. Flowing west
through these hills are three drainages: the Clackamas, North Santiam, and
the great Columbia River Gorge. Most Oregonians and much of the nation
are familiar with the Columbia River Gorge (commonly referred to as "the
Gorge"). How could they not be? It is often the first place locals drag visitors to admire waterfalls and misty mountain scenery, catch glimpses of
spawning salmon in the streams, or go hiking on rainforest trails. In many
respects the Columbia Gorge typifies everything Americans have come to
associate with the Northwest, and although it may be a cliché to take every
out-of-state relative to Multnomah Falls, locals secretly love it.

The north-south Cascade wall divides the high desert of Oregon's
eastern two-thirds from its temperate-rainforest western side. There
are fish on both sides of this great dividing line, and how far you travel
depends entirely on which species, experience, or setting you're looking
for. The rivers, lakes, and reservoirs of this region are contained in seven
wilderness areas, three national forests, and seven designated Wild and
Scenic Rivers – all part of larger Columbia River Basin. There are very
few warm-water fisheries here, and most of the best trout fishing is in
lakes and reservoirs. Steelhead and salmon are present in a half dozen
rivers. Kokanee, landlocked sockeye, and large bull trout are present in
a surprising number of fisheries on the east side. And, unlike a majority
of regions in Oregon, most of this land is publicly accessible.

The ponderosa forests, sagebrush, and rattlesnakes of the Cascades'
east side seem a different world from the lush west side. The reservoirs,
lakes, and rivers are big with a more rugged feel than their western coun-

terparts, and they hold the region's only warm-water fisheries. Most prominent here is the popular Lower Deschutes River, perhaps Oregon's most sought-after destination fishery for steelhead and trout. The Metolius is a beautiful spring creek holding big rainbows and bull trout that will test even the most advanced angler. Boating and reservoir enthusiasts will relish the open waters of Lake Billy Chinook for its prized catches of kokanee. Pine Hollow Reservoir will excite enthusiasts wanting bass, bluegill, and brown bullhead catfish.

Those living in and around Portland will enjoy fishing the west side of the Cascades. As a former Portlander, I know what it's like to be surrounded by rivers too high or low to fish, while dreading yet another 2.5-hour drive over to the east side. With a few exceptions, fishing the west side means steelhead and salmon in the rivers and trout in the lakes. Anglers should understand that, for the most part, catching good numbers of larger trout in rivers means heading east of the Cascades to fish the Deschutes, Metolius, or Hood Rivers. Instead, take advantage of the lakes on Mount Hood. Some of the best trout fishing in Oregon is available in the region's lakes; Timothy, Harriet, Lost, Detroit and Olallie are great producers of big trout and are favored by all types of anglers. Very few places in Oregon have such a concentration of great lakes in close proximity to each other. Explore the upper Clackamas and Sandy Rivers as well, particularly the Upper Clackamas, which receives very little pressure for steelhead. You may want to make the Deschutes or Metolius your home river, but nothing says home like a 20-minute drive after work to the solitude of a float tube on a mountain lake.

The diversity and beauty of this region, and some of the great destination fisheries it holds, are among the reasons Oregon is not just a great place to fish, but also a great place to live.

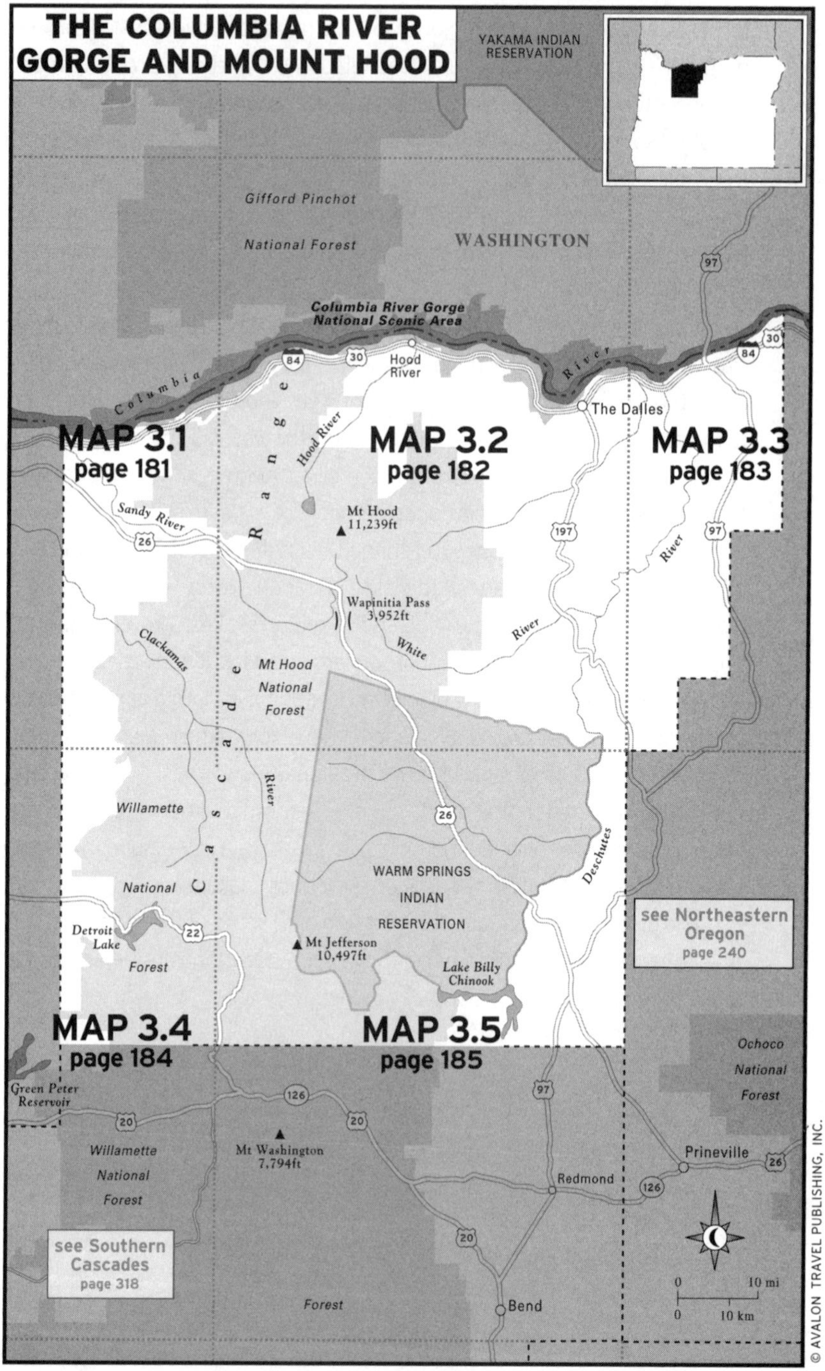

THE COLUMBIA RIVER GORGE AND MOUNT HOOD

YAKAMA INDIAN RESERVATION

Gifford Pinchot

National Forest

WASHINGTON

Columbia River Gorge
National Scenic Area

Hood River

The Dalles

Columbia

Range

Hood River

MAP 3.1
page 181

MAP 3.2
page 182

MAP 3.3
page 183

Sandy River

Mt Hood
11,239ft

Wapinitia Pass
3,952ft

White

River

Clackamas

Cascade

Mt Hood
National
Forest

River

Willamette

National

WARM SPRINGS

INDIAN

RESERVATION

Deschutes

see Northeastern
Oregon
page 240

Detroit
Lake

Forest

Mt Jefferson
10,497ft

Lake Billy
Chinook

MAP 3.4
page 184

MAP 3.5
page 185

Green Peter
Reservoir

Ochoco

National

Forest

Willamette

National

Forest

Mt Washington
7,794ft

Redmond

Prineville

see Southern
Cascades
page 318

Forest

Bend

0   10 mi

0   10 km

© AVALON TRAVEL PUBLISHING, INC.

Map 3.1

Sites 1-6
Pages 186-191

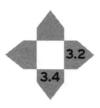

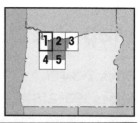

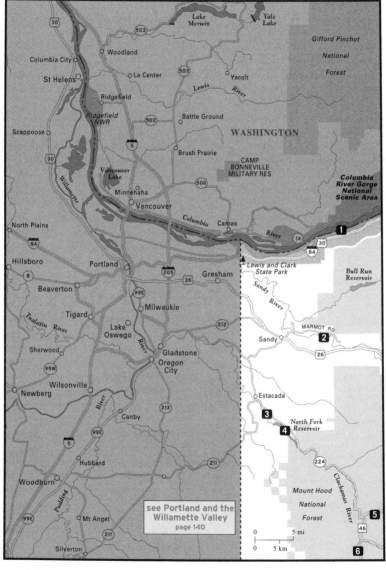

Map 3.2

Sites 7-34
Pages 193-218

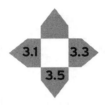

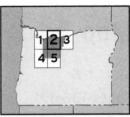

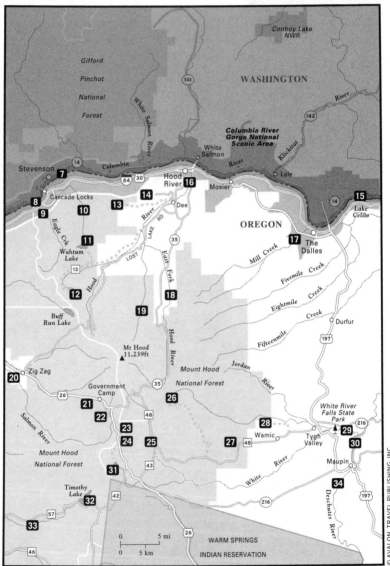

Map 3.3

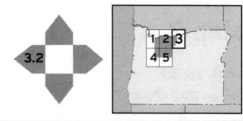

Site 35
Page 219

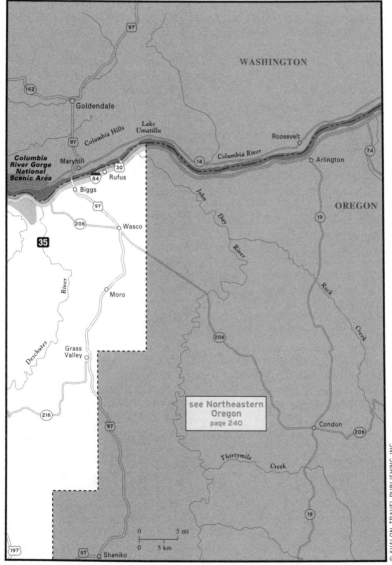

Map 3.4

Sites 36-39
Pages 222-224

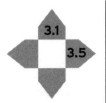

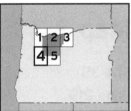

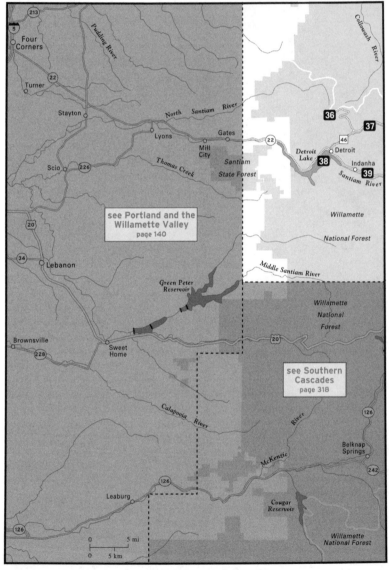

Map 3.5

Sites 40-47
Pages 225-233

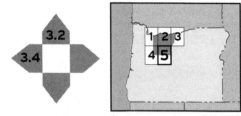

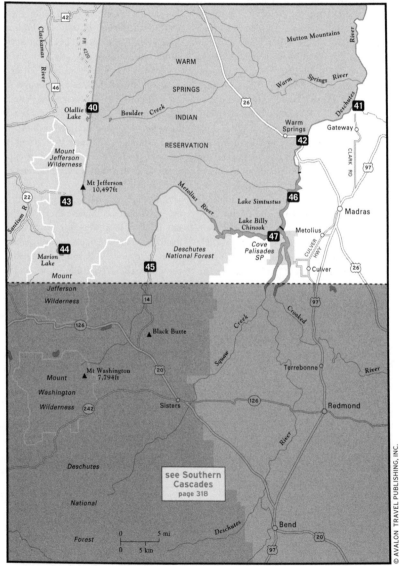

❶ COLUMBIA RIVER: BONNEVILLE DAM TO TROUTDALE

east of Portland

Map 3.1, page 181

This 23-mile stretch of river, from the outflow of Bonneville Dam to the mouth of the Sandy River at the eastern edge of Troutdale, is the most scenic section of the Columbia Gorge National Scenic Area, with its high mountain walls, waterfalls, hiking trails, state parks, and areas of interest such as Crown Point and Bonneville Dam Visitor Center and Fish Hatchery. Well-known tributaries such as Tanner Creek and the Sandy River can be fished for steelhead and/or salmon and trout. Numerous smaller tributaries supply a steady flow of cold water running off the mountains into the Columbia, attracting anglers and fish alike. The Columbia is famous for its runs of salmon, steelhead, and shad, and it is home to resident populations of sturgeon, nonnative walleye, smallmouth bass, and the intrusive northern pike minnow. Access is easy from numerous points on I-84, which parallels the river and offers boat ramps, state parks, beaches, and river inlets. Bank access is more limited than boating but still good. Boating is the preferred, and often necessary, means to fish the river.

Boating any part of the Columbia is dangerous and should not be taken lightly. Nautical maps are necessary to navigate the islands, shallow shelves, and other obstacles. Winds from the Pacific Coast can beat this water to a froth, and waves have been known to swamp all kinds of boats. The Gorge receives the worst weather within a 50-mile radius of Portland, and winter storms can make driving and boating fatal propositions. This is also a major shipping channel, and boaters should be current on their ability to read buoy markers.

The most popular fisheries here are fall chinook, steelhead, and sturgeon, followed by coho and jack salmon, shad, and walleye. Northern pike minnow is not popular as a game fish, but a $6 reward is given for every fish that is caught and delivered to fish stations around the area. Fall chinook arrive in the last part of August and can be caught into October, but September tends to be the best month. Current fishing seasons for chinook and coho are August 1–December 31. Spring chinook fishing has a very limited fishing season and it is in constant flux. Historically, they could be caught only below the I-5 bridge near Vancouver, Washington. They are present near Bonneville Dam April–early May, but fishing may or may not be available (check current regulations). Jack salmon, two-year-old chinook in the 21–24-inch range, have their season June 16–July 31. Steelhead season is open for winter and summer steelhead January 1–March 31 and June 16–December 31. Summer steelhead tends to be more popular than winter steelhead because of severe winter weather conditions.

Sturgeon is available year-round, as are walleye (also known as "Marble Eyes"). Walleye, a nonnative eastern game fish, has adapted remarkably to the Columbia and average catches can be 5–15 pounds. Barring any major spring runoffs, peak walleye fishing times tend to be February–April when the fish are getting ready to spawn, but good fishing can be had until late fall. Shad are available early May–July, but fishing is closed April 1–May 15. Smallmouth bass are present throughout the river system but can't be caught until early summer or when the waters begin to warm after spring runoff, usually in early July.

Fishing regulations can be complicated and ever-changing, so consult the latest sportfishing regulations published by the ODFW and check local newspapers or the ODFW website for updates (ignorance of the rules is not an excuse, and anglers are required to know all updates before fishing).

Islands, river inlets, and channels make the most popular fishing spots in the river. A host of islands from Troutdale to Bonneville Dam provide excellent habitat in the form of gravel bars, channels, shallow flats, and both slow- and fast-moving water. Reed Island is the southernmost island in this stretch, followed by Sand, Skamania, Pierce, Ives, Hamilton, and Bradford just below Bonneville Dam. Salmon, steelhead, and walleye are all fished for around the islands and river inlets. Islands that garner the most attention are Hamilton and Ives, both near the dam. In fact, a majority of the fishing in this stretch takes place in the first 12 miles below Bonneville. Anglers troll with plugs and spinners and jig with bait or leadheads or both. Bait fishing or plunking is especially popular for bank anglers for all species at the base of Bonneville Dam or a little lower around the mouths of Moffett, McCord, and Tanner creeks and the Sandy River. Sturgeon is fished from the bank around Bonneville Dam and at Tanner Creek. Boat anglers have the best luck from Dobson Park and in the channels around Bradford Island.

Smallmouth bass are scattered throughout the river and can be found in areas of slower water around Beacon Rock and in slack-water coves up and down the river. Spinners, bass spinnerbaits, and Rapalas all work for bass. Shad fishing is popular from the bank at Bonneville Dam and from a boat below the dam at Bradford Island and Tanner Creek. Anglers use shad darts and small spinners fished near the bottom.

Species: Salmon, steelhead, sturgeon, shad, walleye, smallmouth bass, northern pike minnow, trout, fall and spring chinook, coho, jack salmon.

Facilities: Camping is available at Rolling Hills and Portland Fairview RV parks in Troutdale and Ainsworth State Park. Viento and Memaloose campgrounds are available upriver on I-84 past the Bonneville Dam. Viento State Park is a full-service campground with tent and RV sites, restrooms, showers, and electricity. Memaloose State Park is bigger with full RV facilities and tent sites and accepts reservations. Boat ramps are available at Sundial Marina boat ramp near the mouth of the Sandy River and east on I-84 at Rooster Rock State Park, Dalton Point, and below the Bonneville Dam at Coverts Landing (The Fishery). Supplies and accommodations can be had in Troutdale and Cascade Locks and in the Greater Portland Metropolitan Area.

Directions: From downtown Portland, drive approximately 15 miles east on I-84, exiting the highway at Exit 18 east of Troutdale across the Sandy River Bridge to Lewis and Clark State Park. From Lewis and Clark State Park, east I-84 follows the Columbia River 28 miles to Bonneville Dam. Rooster Rock (Exit 25), Dalton Point (Exit 29), Coverts Landing (Exit 35), and Bonneville Dam (Exit 40) can all be reached from I-84 east of Lewis and Clark State Park.

To reach Sundial Marina from Lewis and Clark State Park, drive west on I-84 one mile to the next off-ramp (Exit 17). At the bottom of the ramp turn north on N.W. Graham. Follow Graham Rd. north and then west for 1.5 miles to N.W. Sundial Rd. Turn north on Sundial Rd. and drive 0.6 mile to the dead-end at Sundial Marina and Beach.

Contact: West Columbia Gorge Chamber of Commerce, 503/669-7473; Columbia River Gorge National Scenic Area, 541/308-1700; Oregon Parks and Recreation Department, 800/551-6949; ODFW, Clackamas, 503/657-2000; Rolling Hills RV Park, 503/666-7282; Portland Fairview RV Park, 503/661-1047; Viento State Park, 541/374-8811; Stewart's Fishing Shop in Troutdale, 503/666-2471; Don Schneider's Reel Adventures, 877/544-7335; Hook Up Guide Service, 503/666-5370; NorthwestGuides.com, 877/734-7466.

❷ SANDY RIVER
east of Portland

Map 3.1, page 181

The Sandy River offers great year-round fishing near Portland; no more than a 50-mile drive is required to reach its farthest point. To be in the Mount Hood National Forest, surrounded by swift cold rivers, dense rain-soaked forests, and thriving populations of salmon and steelhead in 50 miles or less is a privilege not too often advertised by solitude-loving Oregonians. The Sandy is no secret, though, and it is well known to most steelhead and salmon anglers as a quality year-round local fishery.

The Sandy River is fed by glaciers on the western slopes of Mount Hood. Many sizable tributaries such as Bull Run, Little Sandy, Salmon, and Zigzag Rivers add to its run, creating a large river in its lower stretches. The Sandy is 50 miles long from its headwaters to the confluence with the Columbia River near Troutdale, but only the lower half below Marmot Dam is available for steelhead and salmon fishing. The river is characterized by classic boulder-strewn runs, deep holes, and plenty of pocket water in the riffles. Much of the river is shallow, making wading a pleasure, but all serious wading should be accompanied by a wading staff and cleated wading boots.

Both summer and winter steelhead can get up to 15 pounds. Salmon provide the other great fishery with both spring and fall chinook and coho. For successful fishing on the Sandy, time the runs. If it rains, get on the river shortly thereafter as the river begins to clear, especially in winter; if there's no rain for a while, stay home and await the next storm. The river is open to salmon and steelhead fishing from Marmot Dam near Sandy to the mouth. Spring chinook enter the river in April and can be caught through June. Fall chinook arrive in August, but the best fishing is in October. All chinook can be caught during the regular fishing season, February 1–October 31. Coho are present and can be caught during the appointed fishing season August 1–October 31. Steelhead are in the river year-round, and fishing is open the entire year for hatchery fish.

Bank fishing is abundant and the most popular way to fish the river. Several parts of the river, particularly above Oxbow Park, are remote and accessible only by descending deep forested canyons or hiking through old-growth forests; anglers who love to hike to secluded holes will be in heaven. As high

as Marmot Dam are good roads that follow the river to the mouth. At some points the road veers away from the river, requiring a healthy hike to find water; start at one of the parks: Lewis and Clark, Dabney, Oxbow, and Dodge. More adventurous anglers can explore the upper reaches at Revenue Bridge and Marmot Dam and from access points along PGE and Marmot roads. Much of this upper water runs through canyons, and walking can be strenuous as there are no established trails.

Boating is popular in river boats with some tougher rapids up high. Boaters interested in floating the river have several options. Angling from a floating device is allowed from the only power-line crossing downstream from Oxbow Park to the mouth. All floats above Oxbow require the angler to fish from the shore and break down equipment before drifting to the next spot. There are a couple of good drifts from Oxbow to the mouth, suitable for drift boats and rafts: Oxbow County Park to Dabney State Park and Dabney to Lewis and Clark State Park. Both of these stretches are relatively easy, but there are some Class I rapids requiring negotiation around rocks and structure. High water or low water can make these runs more technical.

Species: Winter and summer steelhead, spring and fall chinook, coho.

Facilities: Lewis and Clark State Recreation Site (year-round, no fee) has a boat ramp, picnicking, and restrooms. Dabney State Park (year-round, $3), approximately three miles upstream from Lewis and Clark, is a popular day-use area with no camping but plenty of picnicking, recreation, restrooms, and a boat ramp. Oxbow Regional Park ($3 day-use), five miles farther up the Sandy, has 67 campsites plus picnic tables, drinking water, restrooms, and a boat ramp. Many more accommodations and lodging options are available in Portland, Troutdale, and Sandy.

Directions: From Portland, travel east on I-84 for 15 miles and take Exit 18. At the end of the ramp, turn south (left) and drive 100 yards to the parking lot of Lewis and Clark State Park.

To reach Dabney State Park, go to the same exit, but at the end of the ramp turn south (left) onto the Historic Columbia River Hwy. and drive three miles to the park. To reach Oxbow Regional Park, take I-84 east 14 miles to Exit 17. Turn south on 257th and drive three miles to Division St.; turn east (left) and go seven miles to the park. The upper river near Dodge Park, Marmot Rd., and PGE Rd. is most easily reached from Sandy. Drive east on Hwy. 26 to the east end of Sandy, then turn north on Teneyck Rd. Drive north on Teneyck Rd. for two miles to Marmot Rd. Turn east on Marmot Rd. Marmot Rd. follows the river and intersects PGE Rd. in about two miles. Turn south on PGE Rd. and drive approximately four miles to reach the base of Marmot Dam. To reach Dodge Park, travel north on Teneyck Rd., passing Marmot Rd., for approximately six miles to Dodge Park.

Contact: Portland Oregon Visitors Association, 503/275-9750; West Columbia Gorge Chamber of Commerce, 503/669-7473; Oregon Parks and Recreation Department, 800/551-6949; ODFW, Clackamas, 503/657-2000; BLM, Salem, 503/375-5646; The Fly-Fishing Shop in Welches, 800/266-3971; Stewart's Fishing Shop in Troutdale, 503/666-2471; Marty Sheppard, 503/622-1870, littlecreekjd@earthlink.net.

❸ CLACKAMAS RIVER
Estacada to headwaters
Map 3.1, page 181

The Clackamas River originates in the Olallie Lake area and flows 49 miles through the Mount Hood National Forest to North Fork Reservoir, southeast of Estacada. Feeding this river are numerous sizable tributaries, such as the North Fork, South Fork, Oak Grove Fork, Hot Springs Fork, and Collawash River; they all come together to create a rugged river. This area is also popular among whitewater enthusiasts who play in the big rapids. Thick forests of Douglas fir, old-growth forests, deep gorges, and tall Cascade foothills define the area. Hik-

ing trails to and along the river lead through ferns, mosses, and wild huckleberry bushes.

Anglers can catch trout, winter and summer steelhead, coho, and spring chinook salmon. Summer steelhead are present starting in mid-June or as early as March. Winter steelhead arrive in the upper river in April and May and can be present all year. Coho salmon in the upper river are mostly a late-returning run of wild fish and enter this section starting in December, but are available through May. The spring chinook fishery has been on the rise since 1980, and good numbers of fish are available in April and May. Trout are present all year.

Ninety percent of the fishing in the upper river takes place from the bank because of ease of access and dangerous boating conditions. (This water can be quite treacherous and should be left to advanced boaters.) Good roads (Highway 224 and Forest Rd. 46) and river hiking trails follow the river for its entire length and offer unlimited access. Start bank angling above North Fork Reservoir near Memaloose Campground; from here you can walk upriver on trails or drive on Highway 224 to 13 other campgrounds on the way to the headwaters. Access points include the Big Eddy Day Use Area, Carter Bridge, Armstrong, Roaring River, and Three Lynx. River Ford Campground at the confluence of the Collawash and Clackamas Rivers is a popular access point and provides both good steelhead and trout water. Look for roadside turnouts near Ripplebrook Guard Station and hike through the forest to the west for secluded access to great fishing water.

Angling is limited to artificial flies and lures only. Fly anglers are partial to swinging streamers, such as hair wing patterns and spey flies, or skated dry flies on floating line for both summer and winter steelhead. Winter fly-fishing may require the use of sinking or sink tip lines to get deeper in the runs. Try fishing with steelhead nymphs such as size 6 Copper Johns and stone flies in deeper runs and pocket water. Drift anglers are partial to corkies and yarn or floats and jigs. Use jigs and yarn in orange, salmon, and various shades of pink for best results. Spin anglers can use spoons and spinners in large sizes such as a No. 4 Blue Fox. Again, use colors in pink and orange but include some spoons in silver or gold. Trout fishing is best with flies such as attractor dry flies and nymphs. Spinner anglers can use Rooster Tails and Mepps Spinners to the delight of trout all day.

Species: Summer and winter steelhead, spring chinook, coho, trout.

Facilities: Camping is available at 13 or campgrounds along Hwy. 224 and Forest Rd. 46 between North Fork Reservoir and the headwaters. All campgrounds include running water, garbage facilities, restrooms, RV and tent sites, and river access trails. There are no official boat ramps, but anglers can launch rafts wherever they find suitable places along roadsides. Big Eddy Day Use Area is a popular launching point for rafts and kayaks. There are several hot springs in the area at Austin and Bagby. Supplies and accommodations can be had in Estacada.

Directions: From Estacada drive southeast on Hwy. 224, which follows the river for 41 miles to Forest Rd. 46. Turn east on Forest Rd. 46, which tracks the river 20 miles into the headwaters. Use a good Forest Service map to help you navigate the upper reaches toward Olallie Lake.

Contact: Estacada Chamber of Commerce, 503/630-3483; Mount Hood National Forest Clackamas River District, 503/630-6861; Clackamas County Parks Department, 503/353-4414; ODFW, Clackamas, 503/657-2000; Promontory Park Store and Marina, 503/630-5152; Fisherman's Marine and Outdoor, 503/557-3313; Estacada Tackle, 503/630-7424.

4 NORTH FORK RESERVOIR

south of Estacada on the Clackamas River

Map 3.1, page 181   BEST (

Of little interest to serious anglers, North Fork Reservoir is perfect for families, especially those with young children being introduced to fishing. The environment is very scenic, surrounded by the cooling shade of fir forests. It is a short drive from Portland (35 miles) and makes a nice day or overnight camping trip from the city. North Fork Reservoir is small (350 acres), narrow, and runs four miles along the adjoining highway, which is blocked from view by the forest. Most of the fish caught here are stocked rainbow trout, 10–14 inches. Some wild fish exist, but only fin-clipped trout may be retained. Fishing opens a little later than normal, May 28, and closes October 31.

Anglers can use a boat or fish from the bank. Boats are launched from Promontory Park Store and Marina or at the North Shore boat ramp near the dam. Small rowboats, rafts, or propelled boats with an electric or gas motor is all that is required. The most successful angling takes place from the marina up to the lake inlet where the trout are stocked. Bank angling can be had from all points around the reservoir, which is on Forest Service property, but some places are hard to get to because of the dense forests. The best places to start are out in front of the resort on the docks, the North Shore boat ramp near the dam, or near the inlet. Bait and trolling are the primary means of catching fish. Fish both the shallower water near the inlet and the deeper water out in the middle and downstream near the dam. Fly anglers can troll Woolly Buggers and leech patterns. Spin anglers can troll Rooster Tails and Mepps Spinners in various colors. Fish bait such as worms, PowerBait, or cheese under a bobber.

Species: Rainbow Trout, wild species of cutthroat, brown trout, brook trout, and bull trout.

Facilities: Promontory Park Campground at the reservoir is operated by Portland General Electric, which built the dam that created this reservoir. It offers 50 campsites, showers, restrooms, boat ramps and dock, a grocery store, and boat rentals. The north-shore boat ramps are just off Hwy. 224 near the dam. Supplies and accommodations can be had in Estacada.

The local resort sells groceries, fishing tackle, and has boat rentals.

Directions: From Estacada, travel seven miles east on Hwy. 224 to the resort entrance on the west side of the road.

Contact: Portland General Electric Parks Department, 503/464-8515; ODFW, Clackamas, 503/657-2000; Mount Hood National Forest Clackamas River District, 503/630-6861; Promontory Park Store and Marina, 503/630-5152; Fisherman's Marine and Outdoor, 503/557-3313; Estacada Tackle, 503/630-7424.

5 HARRIET LAKE
near Estacada in the Clackamas River watershed

Map 3.1, page 181

On the Oak Grove Fork of the Clackamas River, seven miles below Timothy Lake, Harriet is a modest-size lake (23 acres) secluded in a richly forested environment in the Clackamas watershed. Just 60 miles from Portland, Harriet makes for a good day or overnight excursion for both serious anglers and families wishing to catch larger rainbow, brook, and brown trout.

Harriet's popularity stems in part from its generous stocking program, which introduces 16,000 legal rainbows (8–10 inches) every year April–September, and 800 trophy fish of 16 inches or larger in August. Naturally reproducing browns, cutthroat, and brook trout are also present. Harriet is one of the few lakes west of the Cascades to produce lunker brown trout of four pounds or more. The lake is open all year, but snows or bitter cold and rainy weather can restrict or deter access November–late March. Fishing is restricted to artificial flies and lures only.

Harriet is fished well both from a boat and the bank. The eastern end of the reservoir near the inlet is where you want to be in the early spring and fall, when the brown and brook trout are moving up the Oak Fork Tributary to spawn. From a boat you can move out to the south shore, where the river generates a good current well into the lake. Cast flies or spinners into this moving water for good chances at catching larger rainbows and browns. Several deeper holes also exist in this part of the lake. Position your boat above these deep holes and let your flies and lures swing through the bottom on slow-moving currents. There are lots of snags in the water, so expect to lose a few rigs and bring plenty of backups. Both the inlet and outlet of the lake offer good bank-access water, particularly the inlet. Here you will often see small mayflies hatching in summer and fall—and lots of rising fish. Other areas of the reservoir provide only fair fishing compared to the eastern end.

Species: Stocked trophy and legal-size rainbow trout; brown, brook and cutthroat trout.

Facilities: The campground at Harriet Lake, operated by the dam's builder, Portland General Electric, has 13 sites with picnic tables and fire grills. It also has drinking water, pit toilets, and a free fishing pier and boat ramp.

Directions: From Estacada, drive 27 miles southeast on Hwy. 224 to the ranger station at Ripplebrook. Here, the road becomes Forest Rd. 46. Stay straight ahead when Rd. 46 turns right (south) just past the station; this will put you headed east on Forest Rd. 57. Follow Rd. 57 for 7.5 miles, then turn left (west) on Forest Rd. 4630. This road leads one mile to Lake Harriet.

Contact: Mount Hood National Forest Clackamas District, 503/630-6861; Portland General Electric Parks Department, 503/464-8515; ODFW, Clackamas, 503/657-2000; Fisherman's Marine and Outdoor, 503/557-3313; Estacada Tackle, 503/630-7424.

6 COLLAWASH RIVER/ HOT SPRINGS FORK
south of Estacada in the Clackamas River watershed

Map 3.1, page 181

There are very few good trout streams near Portland, requiring most anglers to drive to central Oregon or learn to still-water fish the lakes of Mount Hood. The Collawash and its tributary, Hot Springs Fork, are both surprisingly good trout streams in scenic forests on the upper Clackamas River. These rivers offer the chance at some bigger trout within a shorter drive.

The Collawash River runs approximately 13 miles from its headwaters on the northern side of Collawash Mountain, near the Breitenbush River drainage, to the confluence with the Clackamas River at River Ford Campground. Along the way it picks up the Hot Springs Fork, two miles above River Ford, where Forest Roads 63 and 70 come together. The Hot Springs Fork runs approximately 10 miles from its source in the Opal Creek Wilderness. Both rivers are restricted to artificial lures and flies only, and the season opens May 28. Steelhead and salmon may be present, but restrictions do not allow anglers to catch them. Neither river is suitable for boating, but bank access is unlimited along both.

The main catches on both rivers are rainbow trout averaging 10–14 inches, with some bigger fish exceeding 16 inches. Small brook trout are available in the upper reaches of both rivers, and so are bull trout. Angling for bull trout is prohibited, and all fish must be released unharmed. Both rivers are comparable in size, flow, and type of water. Expect riffles, plunge pools, and pocket water. River banks can be brushy, requiring anglers to get into the water to reach good holding water; waders or hip boots may prove to be an asset. Use shorter rods in seven-foot lengths to help you make short casts into tight pockets. Fly anglers can use any type of high-floating attractor fly such as a Humpy or Royal Wulff, or they can drift small nymphs under an indicator. Spin anglers can use small Rooster Tails or spoons in the same manner, paying special attention to deep holes around rock cliffs.

Start fishing the Collawash along the roadside between River Ford Campground and the junction of Forest Roads 70 and 63. Raab Campground on this stretch offers good bank access. Above this point, a very windy Highway 63 will take you farther upstream to marginal fishing in very small waters. For the most part anglers can avoid the headwaters for better fishing down below. The Hot Springs Fork is best fished from Kingfisher Campground on Forest Road 70 and along the road to the Bagby Hot Springs Trailhead. From Bagby Hot Springs the river is accessible by good hiking trails. Anglers can avoid most of the upper river in exchange for adequate fishing around Kingfisher Campground. The trail to Bagby Hot Springs gives good river access, but it can be quite crowded and rowdy with partying bathers. If you do decide to go to Bagby, do so during the work week and avoid evenings.

Note: Bagby Hot Springs, once a pleasant place to bathe in hot mineral-rich waters, has since become a magnet for the party crowd. Behavior inappropriate for children is common and safety has become an issue. Don't leave valuables in the car and avoid the squatter camps along the river, which should be considered dangerous areas. Report threatening behavior to Forest Service officials at Ripplebrook Ranger Station.

Species: Rainbow and brook trout.

Facilities: Raab Campground is on the main-stem Collawash, and Kingfisher is on the Hot Springs Fork. Each has tent sites, fire pits with grills, and pit toilets. Kingfisher has drinking water; Raab does not have drinking water. Buy supplies in Estacada.

Directions: From Estacada, drive 27 miles southeast on Hwy. 224 to the ranger station at Ripplebrook. Here, the road becomes Forest Rd. 46. Follow Rd. 46 to the south for three miles to Forest Rd. 63; this intersection is at the confluence of the Collawash and Clackamas Rivers. Take Rd. 63 to the right (south); Raab Campground is 1.5 miles ahead on the right. To reach Kingfisher, go 1.5 miles past Raab and turn right (southwest) onto Forest Rd. 70; this intersection is where the Hot Springs Fork joins the main-stem Collawash. Take Rd. 70 one mile to the campground on the left. Rd. 70 follows the Hot Springs Fork four more miles to the trailhead for Bagby Hot Springs.

Contact: Mount Hood National Forest Clackamas District, 503/630-6861; ODFW, Clackamas, 503/657-2000; Fisherman's Marine and Outdoor, 503/557-3313; Estacada Tackle, 503/630-7424.

7 COLUMBIA RIVER: BONNEVILLE DAM TO THE DALLES DAM
behind Bonneville Dam

Map 3.2, page 182

The Columbia River behind Bonneville Dam, known as the Bonneville Pool, is the last in a series of reservoirs on the Columbia River before the river runs unencumbered to the Pacific Ocean. Anglers visiting this part of the Columbia River are treated to a variety of landscapes, from the lush western edge of the Columbia Gorge to the arid eastern end—a transition that defines western and eastern Oregon. The drive from Bonneville Dam to Hood River is bordered by the steep mountainous slopes of Columbia Gorge National Scenic Area: Oregon on the south bank and Washington on the north. East of Hood River, the eastern Cascade slopes and foothills give way to the arid but rich farmlands of the Columbia Plateau. Driving still farther east to The Dalles reinforces the sense that you are in the desert, and the river stands out as a refreshing contrast among the often-brown hills and ridge rock.

Anglers in this region are met with an array of fish species, including salmon, sturgeon, steelhead, walleye, smallmouth bass, and shad. Sturgeon and the nonnative walleye make up a majority of the catches here. Smallmouth bass fishing is becoming increasingly popular, and good runs of steelhead and fall chinook salmon are also present. Good but tough access can be had by bank anglers; boaters have the distinct advantage here. Several good tributaries (Eagle, Herman, and Lindsey creeks and

Hood River) flow into this section of river, offering good mouth and river fishing.

Salmon: Current regulations allow salmon fishing for chinook and coho August 1–December 31, with September being the best time of the year. Coho are restricted to harvest of adipose fin-marked fish between Bonneville Dam and the Hood River Bridge. Jack salmon, two-year-old chinook in the 21–24-inch range, may also be caught June 16–July 31. These restrictions and seasons are bound to change from year to year, so be sure to check with local regulations before making your trip. Anglers fish for salmon with plugs, Flatfish, or bait such as herring around river inlets, islands, and flats. Most fish can be taken in 10–15 feet of water. Good places to begin fishing are around the mouth of Hood River near Hood River and at Herman and Lindsey creeks near Bonneville Dam. Also, the area below the Hood River Bridge in Hood River and below the Dalles Dam is all productive water.

Steelhead: Present in the river June–November. The fishing season extends January 1–March 31 and June 16–December 31. Most of the steelhead in the river are on the move to their home waters on the Deschutes, John Day, Grand Ronde, and Snake Rivers. It is well known among anglers that steelhead will pause at river mouths where the water runs cooler than in the Columbia. Some fish are known to move into their nonnative rivers before continuing their upstream journey. By and large, steelhead are caught with plugs and spinners trolled at river mouths or bait cast into currents. A boat is handy in these situations, as river access for bank anglers is limited. Boaters can also find steelhead hanging out in shallower water alongside deeper channels and in gravel areas around islands. Good places to begin fishing are around the mouth of Hood River and at Herman and Lindsey creeks.

Walleye: A burgeoning fishery with the potential for trophy fish up to 15 pounds or more, this is a main attraction here and up higher in the river in Lake Celilo, Lake Umatilla, and

Lake Wallula. February–April tends to be the best time for a chance at trophy fish, but fishing is good all year. Popular fishing methods include vertical jigging with roundhead jigs tipped with night crawlers and plastics, and by blade-baiting below the dams. Worm harnesses are trolled downstream, and crankbaits and stickbaits are trolled upstream. There are two good places to begin: below the bridge at The Dalles, and in the Rowena area west of The Dalles. Anglers fishing for walleye should look for transition points in the river bottom and wherever baitfish such as shad, steelhead, and salmon smolts are available. Some anglers use depth finders to find these areas.

Sturgeon, bass, and shad: Popular places to fish for sturgeon are below the interstate bridge in The Dalles and around Stevenson, Washington. Shad are fished for below the interstate bridge in The Dalles during May and June. Bass are abundant and can be found throughout the river in areas of slack water, coves, and inlets and anywhere structure is present.

Bank access is readily available from boat ramps and parks such as Mayer, Memaloose, and Koberg Beach. Additional access can be had along I-84 at pullouts, but this practice is not recommended. Technically, cars may not be parked on the highway except for emergencies, but this doesn't seem to stop a lot of anglers from doing so; theft and break-ins may also be a problem on the highways.

Species: Spring and fall chinook, coho, and jack salmon; steelhead, walleye, sturgeon, smallmouth bass, shad.

Facilities: Camping is available at Viento and Memaloose state parks. Viento is a full-service campground, with tent and RV sites, restrooms, showers, and electricity. Memaloose State Park is bigger and accepts reservations. The nearest boat ramp to Bonneville Dam is at Port of Cascade Locks. More boat ramps are available farther east at Hood River Marina, Mayer State Park, and Port of The Dalles. Accommodations and supplies can be had in Cascade Locks, Hood River, and The Dalles.

Directions: From Bonneville Dam, I-84 follows the river east for 48 miles to The Dalles. Boat ramps are available at Port of Cascade Locks (Exit 44), Hood River Marina (Exit 63), Mayer State Park (Exit 76), and Port of The Dalles (Exit 87). To reach Viento State Park from Cascade Locks, take I-84 east for 10.5 miles to Exit 56/Viento State Park. At the end of the ramp, turn north onto Viento Rd.; this will lead you 0.2 mile into the park. Memaloose State Park is accessible only to westbound traffic on I-84, so from Cascade Locks you'll have to go east to Exit 76 (Rowena). Then head back to the west for three miles to the Memaloose exit. Stay straight on the access road for 0.5 mile to reach the campground.

Contact: Hood River County Chamber of Commerce, 541/386-2000; West Columbia Gorge Chamber of Commerce, 503/669-7473; Hood River County Parks Department, 541/387-6889; Columbia River Gorge National Scenic Area, 541/308-1700; Oregon Parks and Recreation Department, 800/551-6949; ODFW, The Dalles, 541/296-4628; BLM, Salem, 503/375-5646; Viento State Park, 541/374-8811; Columbia Basin Guide Service, 541/276-0371; Young's Fishing Service, 800/270-7962; Stewart's Fishing Shop in Troutdale, 503/666-2471.

8 LOWER EAGLE CREEK
near Troutdale in Columbia River Gorge
Map 3.2, page 182

Eagle Creek, a small tributary of the Columbia River, originates from two forks: one in the Mark O. Hatfield Wilderness and one at Wahtum Lake. The river runs into the Columbia River just above Bonneville Dam and is crossed by I-84. This area offers all the scenic splendor that one expects in the Gorge: deep forest, hiking trails, waterfalls, lush plant life, cool clear waters, and excellent opportunities to view salmon and steelhead as they make their upstream migration.

The lower river has a reputation as a fine

steelhead and salmon river, but it's devoid of trout. The primary salmon and steelhead water in the lower river is from the mouth to the railroad bridge. This area is regulated consistently with the Columbia River from Bonneville Dam upstream to the Oregon–Washington border. Some fishing is also available upstream to the fish hatchery deadline when water levels are good enough to let fish pass upriver. Separate regulations are imposed on this water: steelhead can be caught January 1–March 31, May 28–August 15, and December 1–31; salmon fishing is open May 28 August 15. There's only about 0.3 mile of water between the mouth and the hatchery. The greatest concentration of anglers is at the mouth and a little way upstream to the highway bridge. Most of this water stays deep and cool for salmon and steelhead to refresh themselves. Steelhead and salmon are in the river August–November.

The lower river attracts anglers using traditional tackle, such as spinners, plugs, drift gear, and bait. During exceptionally good runs anglers can line the banks shoulder to shoulder. Fly anglers would be well advised to fish higher up in the river or move to Herman Creek, as their tactics can be incompatible with these traditional methods of fishing.

Species: Salmon, steelhead.

Facilities: Parking at the trailhead requires a Northwest Forest Pass ($5 per day; $30 annually), available from most sporting goods or outdoors shops or from Nature of the Northwest in Portland. Eagle Creek Campground, operated by the Forest Service, has 20 sites, each with a picnic table and a fire pit with a grill. There is also a bathhouse and drinking water. No reservations are accepted, except for groups. Additional lodging, as well as supplies and restaurants, are available in Portland, Troutdale, and Cascade Locks.

Directions: From Troutdale, drive 25 miles east on I-84 and take Exit 41. After crossing the creek at the end of the ramp, turn south (right). In 50 yards, the campground road leads left; stay right for a series of parking lots for the Eagle Creek Trail, spread along a 0.5 mile of the creek. Trail 435 (Eagle Creek Trail) follows the river for 7.5 miles, to a point just above 7.5 Mile Camp, a series of backpack sites stretched along the creek. From its intersection with trail 433 (Eagle-Tanner Trail), Eagle Creek Trail climbs another seven miles to Wahtum Lake. Eagle-Tanner Trail follows Eagle Creek for 0.8 mile, crosses it, follows the west bank for 0.4 mile, then climbs away from it.

Contact: West Columbia Gorge Chamber of Commerce, 503/669-7473; ODFW, Clackamas, 503/657-2000; Columbia River Gorge National Scenic Area, 541/308-1700; Gorge Fly Shop, 541/386-6977; BLM, Salem, 503/375-5646; Nature of the Northwest, 503/872-2750, www.naturenw.org; The Fly-Fishing Shop in Welches, 800/266-3971; Stewart's Fishing Shop in Troutdale, 503/666-2471.

9 UPPER EAGLE CREEK

near Troutdale in Columbia River Gorge

Map 3.2, page 182

The upper river of Eagle Creek is a fine trout fishery for rainbows, cutthroat, and brook trout, and it attracts numerous anglers who enjoy hiking through the forest in search of quality water. The river can be fished for trout from hiking trails that start at the fish hatchery and follow the river its entire length. A slightly later trout season applies here, May 28–October 31. Light tackle combined with flies, lures, or bait is all that is required to have a successful time. Fish the pocket water in the runs and deeper pools below the water falls. Trout are small, 10–12 inches, but fun on light tackle.

Species: Rrainbow, cutthroat, and brook trout.

Facilities: Parking at the trailhead requires a Northwest Forest Pass ($5 per day; $30 annually), which is available from most sporting goods or outdoors shops or from Nature of the Northwest in Portland. Eagle Creek

Campground, operated by the Forest Service, has 20 sites, each with a picnic table and a fire pit with a grill. There is also a bathhouse and drinking water. No reservations are accepted, except for groups. Additional lodging, as well as supplies and restaurants, are available in Portland, Troutdale, and Cascade Locks.

Directions: From Troutdale, drive 25 miles east on I-84 and take Exit 41. After crossing the creek at the end of the ramp, turn south (right). In 50 yards, you will see the campground road leading left, and 50 yards past that you will come to the trailhead parking area.

Contact: West Columbia Gorge Chamber of Commerce, 503/669-7473; ODFW, Clackamas. 503/657-2000; Columbia River Gorge National Scenic Area, 541/308-1700; Gorge Fly Shop, 541/386-6977; BLM, Salem, 503/375-5646; Nature of the Northwest, 503/872-2750, www.naturenw.org; The Fly-Fishing Shop in Welches, 800/266-3971; Stewart's Fishing Shop in Troutdale, 503/666-2471.

🔟 HERMAN CREEK

near Cascade Locks in Columbia River Gorge

Map 3.2, page 182

Herman Creek is a good salmon and steelhead fishery in its lower section and a fine trout fishery, with some bigger fish, in its upper waters. There is no shortage of scenic splendors as this river reflects the lush forested areas of the Columbia Gorge. Hikers and anglers alike can take pleasure and experience a measure of solitude among the cool, moist ferns, mosses, and tall Douglas firs.

The lower river from the mouth to the railroad bridge is under regulations consistent with the Columbia River from Bonneville Dam upstream to the Oregon–Washington border. A small run of steelhead enters the river June–October. Salmon are in the river August–November. One reason for the river's unpopularity is the imposition of special regulations from the mouth to the fish hatchery,

which closes this part of the river during prime fish runs, August 16 –November 30. For this reason, fishing in this part of the river is less congested because anglers are forced to try to hit early or late arrivals of spawning fish. This can be unpredictable at best, especially since hatchery returns on Herman Creek are not as big as on Eagle Creek. Nonetheless, when fishing is permitted, anglers have more opportunity to stretch out and enjoy relative peace on even the most productive water. Flies, lures, and bait are all allowed and equally productive. The most popular methods are float and drift fishing, followed by fly-fishing. Fly anglers have better opportunities here than on Eagle Creek to fish closer to the mouth of the river and not conflict with traditional angling methods.

The upper river extends from the railroad bridge to the headwaters. Chinook, coho, and steelhead fishing is open under special regulations January 1–March 31, May 28–August 15, and December 1–31. Do not plan to hit too many anadromous fish in this reach, but trout fishing is good and some bigger trout of 16 inches or more live in the deeper pools. All of the river in this section must be reached by hiking trails into the headwaters. Carry light tackle rod and reels, and fish with flies, lures, or bait. Some weight may be needed in the form of split shot to get down in the deeper holes.

Species: Fall chinook, coho, summer steelhead, steelhead, trout.

Facilities: Camping is available at Herman Creek Horse Camp near Herman Creek's confluence with the Columbia. There are seven sites, drinking water, and a restroom. Supplies and accommodations can be had in Cascade Locks.

Directions: From Cascade Locks, drive two miles to the east end of town on Wa Na Pa St. (Hwy. 30), pass under I-84, and turn left onto Forest Lane. To reach Herman Creek Horse Camp, follow Forest Ln. for two miles to the signed road on the right, leading 0.1 mile to the campground. Next to the campground is a parking area for Herman Creek Trail (No. 406); parking here requires a Northwest Forest Pass ($5 per day; $30 annually), which is available from most sporting goods or outdoors shops or from Nature of the Northwest in Portland.

Contact: West Columbia Gorge Chamber of Commerce, 503/669-7473; ODFW, Clackamas. 503/657-2000; Columbia River Gorge National Scenic Area, 541/308-1700; Gorge Fly Shop, 541/386-6977; Nature of the Northwest, 503/872-2750, www.naturenw.org; The Fly-Fishing Shop in Welches, 800/266-3971; Stewart's Fishing Shop in Troutdale, 503/666-2471.

11 WAHTUM LAKE
near Dee in Mount Hood National Forest
Map 3.2, page 182

Wahtum is a large hike-in lake (62 acres) situated in the Mark O. Hatfield Wilderness on the northwestern slopes of the Mount Hood National Forest and is one of the sources of the popular Eagle Creek in the Columbia Gorge. This area receives an above-average amount of rainfall, creating a lush forest floor of ferns and mosses beneath towering Douglas firs that extends right up to the lake. Some folks not used to this kind of forest may find the environment somewhat claustrophobic—lacking sun and warmth because of the dense forest canopy—but these are the qualities that make Oregon forests unique and inviting. Be sure to come equipped with rain gear and warm clothes.

Unlike some of the smaller lakes in the region (North and Black lakes) Wahtum is deep at 30 feet or more, but it holds the same crystal-clear water. Numerous shoals can be found between the deep and shallow areas along the bank and are great places to begin trolling flies or lures from a float tube or raft for larger trout. All methods of fishing are allowed, and standard regulations and fishing seasons apply with no special restrictions. The lake is always accessible by opening day on May 28.

Fishing on Wahtum is fair to good for brook trout 8–10 inches long. Some bigger fish are present (16 inches) and can be caught with a little extra effort in the deeper water. Fly anglers should be conscious of any insect activity that may bring fish to the surface. A small dry fly such as an Adams, Griffiths Gnat, or Elk Hair Caddis will work best in the summer. Streamers and small nymphs such as Pheasant Tails, trolled or stripped back to the angler, are good when no fish are rising. Consider using a full sinking line in intermediate weight to get your wet flies deeper. Spinners such as Rooster Tails or bait such as worms and PowerBait work well cast from the bank or raft and trolled in the deeper waters.

Species: Brook trout.

Facilities: The Wahtum Lake campground has five sites, a pit toilet, and no other facilities. For all supplies and other accommodations, look in Hood River. Parking at the trailhead on Rd. 1310 requires a Northwest Forest Pass ($5 per day; $30 annually), which is available from most sporting goods or outdoors shops or from Nature of the Northwest in Portland.

Directions: From Dee, take Hwy. 35 south, across the bridge over the Hood River and immediately bear west (right) on Lost Lake Rd. In another five miles, bear west (right) on Forest Rd. 13, following a sign for Wahtum Lake. Take Rd. 13 for five miles and bear west (right) on Rd. 1310 (Scout Lake Rd.). Continue on Rd. 1310 for six miles to a pullout on the right. If the paved road turns to gravel, you've gone too far. The campground is on the road; Wahtum Lake is in the basin directly below the pullout—at the bottom of 254 stairs.

Contact: Hood River County Chamber of Commerce, 541/386-2000; ODFW, Clackamas, 503/657-2000 or 541/308-1700; Mount Hood National Forest, Hood River District, 541/352-6002; Gorge Fly Shop, 541/386-6977; Nature of the Northwest, 503/872-2750, www.naturenw.org; The Fly-Fishing Shop in Welches, 800/266-3971; Stewart's Fishing Shop in Troutdale, 503/666-2471.

12 LOST LAKE
east of Portland in Mount Hood
National Forest

Map 3.2, page 182   **BEST (**

Lost Lake—possibly the most photographed lake in Oregon next to Crater Lake—is a spectacle not to be missed. The lake provides stunning views of Mount Hood framed by high rolling foothills and gorgeous lush forests. Heavy snowfalls can inhibit access until April or May, making it prudent for early-season travelers to check with the Forest Service for road conditions. Lost Lake's cold, clear waters cover 231 acres and average 75 feet deep. Caution should be used around shorelines, which can drop off quickly to 25 feet or more. The center of the lake is the deepest point at 175 feet. Three miles of shoreline are accessible by good hiking trails. Powerboats are not allowed, but small electric motors can be used and provide a good option for trolling. The lake hosts a healthy variety of wild and stocked trout and a small population of kokanee. Rainbow, brown, and brook trout are all present. Rainbow trout average 10–16 inches, and brown trout can reach 18 inches or more. Brook trout are scarce and average 8–12 inches. A remnant self-sustaining kokanee population is available from previous stocking efforts, but anglers may find their populations too low for satisfactory fishing. Bank fishing is good around the lake perimeter with starting points at the campground and resort. Better fishing can be had from a boat, pontoon boat, or float tube.

Flies, bait, and lures are all allowed and perform equally well when trolled from a boat or float tube along the shoals between the shallow and deeper water. Flasher and bait combinations work especially well for kokanee. Bait fishing is good from the bank or boat; use eggs and worms and PowerBait in fluorescent colors such as green, pink, and orange. Lures such as Rooster Tails and Hot Shots can be trolled slowly at deeper depths for a good chance to pick up bigger trout.

Fly-fishing is limited to either surface activity when mayflies are emerging or streamers stripped or trolled on full sinking fly line. The best dry–fly-fishing occurs mid-July–August when the *Hexagenia limbata* mayflies are hatching. *Hexagenia,* often called the "big yellow may," are a unique and unpredictable hatch occurring on only a handful of lakes and rivers in Oregon (Lost Lake, Williamson River) and bring the biggest fish to the surface. They emerge dusk–dark, and they come off best when hot days are followed by warm evenings. There is no mistaking the size 6 adults as they sit scattered on the surface like small sailboats waiting for their wings to dry before taking flight. Trout, the smart devils, capitalize on this insect's need for an extended drying period and feed voraciously on the surface. Before the full-blown emergence, anglers can strip Hex nymphs to imitate the struggling insect as it swims to the surface. The nymphs are fast swimmers with an undulating motion, so retrieve your nymph quickly to attract the fish's attention. Muddy shoals in 15–20-foot-deep water are ideal, as are areas near the bank. Spin anglers can participate in this action by using a bobber to cast a dry fly or nymph. Rooster Tails in yellow will work quite well as a nymph imitation.

Species: Rainbow, brown, and brook trout, kokanee.

Facilities: Families will enjoy this area for its nice campgrounds, full-service resort, and hiking trails into old-growth forests. Camping is available at the Lost Lake Resort at the north end of the lake or at Lost Lake Campground on the eastern shore. Basic facilities provide water, restrooms, picnic tables, and nice tent sites overlooking the lake. The resort offers boat rentals and a general store. Supplies and accommodations are available in Hood River.

Directions: From Hood River, follow Dee Hwy. south for 8.5 miles and turn right onto Forest Rd. 13 (Lost Lake Rd.). The resort is 14 miles ahead, at the end of the road.

Contact: Hood River County Chamber of Commerce, 541/386-2000; Hood River County Parks Department, 541/387-6889; ODFW, The Dalles, 541/296-4628; Lost

Lake Campground, 503/666-0700; Gorge Fly Shop, 541/386-6977, www.gorgeflyshop.com; The Fly-Fishing Shop in Welches, 800/266-3971; Stewart's Fishing Shop in Troutdale, 503/666-2471.

⓭ NORTH LAKE AREA
near Dee in Mount Hood National Forest

Map 3.2, page 182

North Lake is one of a handful of small brook trout lakes interconnected by hiking trails and marginal logging roads in the vicinity of Mount Defiance near the Columbia Gorge in the Mount Hood National Forest. Other lakes include Rainy, Black, Bear, and Warren. All these lakes provide fair to good fishing in a secluded forest setting of dense Douglas fir and surrounding foothills—perfect for summer hike-in fishing and camping. These lakes are small (10 acres or less) and shallow (eight feet or less), and sit 3,000–4,000 feet in elevation. Snow can hinder access November–late April. Flies, lures, and bait are all allowed, and standard lake regulations apply with no special conditions.

Don't expect to catch large trophy brook trout at any of these lakes; however, smaller nine-inch fish with the occasional 16-inch fish are caught. Shorelines are often littered with dead snags, providing good fish habitat and the occasional natural fishing platform. Cold, clear waters provide an abundance of insect populations, making these lakes especially attractive to fly anglers using nymphs, dry flies, and small leech patterns. Spin anglers can use small Rooster Tails and bait such as worms or PowerBait. The fish are not picky here, and almost anything thrown into the water will work. Lake shorelines are accessible by trails or off-trail bushwhacking, but float tubes could prove to be a real asset, especially to fly anglers who will be hindered on their back-cast by brush and trees when casting from shore.

Species: Brook trout.

Facilities: There are backpacker campsites at each lake with no facilities; parking at all these

trailheads requires a Northwest Forest Pass ($5 per day; $30 annually), which is available from most sporting goods or outdoors shops and from Nature of the Northwest in Portland. Additional accommodations and supplies can be had in Hood River.

Directions: From Dee, take Punch Bowl Rd. north for one mile to where it crosses the Hood River at Punch Bowl Falls. Continue on this road, which after the falls turns into gravel Forest Rd. 2820 (Dead Point Rd.). Follow this road for 10 miles to the parking area for the Wyeth and Mount Defiance trails, and then follow these directions. For North Lake, take Trail No. 411 (Wyeth Trail) down to the lake. For Bear Lake, take Trail No. 413 (Mount Defiance Trail) 0.5 mile to Trail No. 413-A (Bear Lake Trail). Follow this trail 0.7 mile to the lake. For Warren Lake, take Trail No. 413 (Mount Defiance Trail) 1.7 miles (including a climb of 1,000 feet to summit the mountain) to Trail No. 417 (Warren Lake Trail). Follow Trail No. 417 0.5 mile to the lake.

The following trailheads are past the Wyeth/Defiance Trailhead on Rd. 2820. For Rainy Lake, drive one mile past the Wyeth/Defiance Trailhead to a parking area on the right. The lake is 0.1 mile down Trail No. 409 from here. For Black Lake, drive 0.7 mile past the Rainy Lake turnout at the lake.

Contact: Hood River County Chamber of Commerce, 541/386-2000; Mount Hood National Forest Hood River District, 541/352-6002; ODFW, Clackamas, 503/657-2000; BLM, Salem, 503/375-5646; Nature of the Northwest, 503/872-2750, www.naturenw.org; Gorge Fly Shop, 541/386-6977; The Fly-Fishing Shop in Welches, 800/266-3971; Stewart's Fishing Shop in Troutdale, 503/666-2471.

⓮ KINGSLEY RESERVOIR
southwest of Hood River

Map 3.2, page 182

If solitude and peace are what you require in a fishing experience, then Kingsley Reservoir (also known as Green Point Reservoir) might not be your best option, at least in midsummer. Scenically situated at 3,200 feet in elevation, Kingsley Reservoir covers a large area (60 acres) in the Mount Hood National Forest among pine forests and meadows, and it abounds in nonangling activities such as motorbiking and mountain biking, and it hosts numerous sponsored events throughout the season. Don't be surprised if you arrive to find the campground full, parking lots congested with cars, and people swimming in your favorite fishing spot.

The fishing here isn't highly rated; the only catch is stocked trout ranging 10–12 inches. However, young anglers can catch fish here all day with bait and bobber combinations or spinners. Spinners, flies, and bait are all permitted and work equally well; fish are not fussy and will take just about anything offered. Baits such as worms and PowerBait are sure to please any fish in the vicinity. For more of a challenge, you can use spinners such as Rooster Tails or Bangtails, or flies such as streamers and nymphs. Any of these combinations can be trolled in the deeper waters to good effect.

To avoid congestion when the lake is busy, launch a boat from the campground and travel to remote parts of the lake, or hike across the dam to the west shore. Bank fishing from both the dam face and west shore is excellent and provides a measure of solitude from crowds and motorcycles. Alternatively, limit your fishing to early spring, after the roads are clear in May, or late fall. The reservoir is open all year, as long as access is not blocked by snow. Boats are allowed with gas motors, but there is a 10 mph speed limit, so there is no water-skiing.

Species: Stocked rainbow trout.

Facilities: There is a 20-site campground, operated by Hood River County, with a pit toilet and boat ramp but neither showers nor drinking water.

Directions: From Hood River, follow Dee Hwy. south for 8.5 miles, then turn right (west) onto Lost Lake Rd., which crosses the East Fork Hood River in 0.2 mile and intersects Punchbowl Rd. Turn right (north) onto Punchbowl Rd. and follow it 1.5 miles to Kingsley Rd. Turn right (north) here and follow it 6.5 miles to the campground at the reservoir.

Contact: Hood River County Chamber of Commerce, 541/386-2000; Hood River County Parks Department, 541/387-6889; ODFW, The Dalles, 541/296-4628; Gorge Fly Shop, 541/386-6977, www.gorgeflyshop.com.

15 COLUMBIA RIVER: DALLES DAM TO JOHN DAY DAM

east of The Dalles

Map 3.2, page 182

This 22-mile reservoir is in the Columbia Plateau, an arid region of Oregon characterized by wheat farmlands, barren mountainsides, and rimrocks. Winds blow consistently here, as evidenced by the proliferation of kite surfers and sailboarders, and the sun beats heavy in the summer. Spring is a particularly nice time to be here, when the hills are still green and the sun is not quite as intense. Still, come prepared for anything, especially if you plan to boat the river. One of Oregon's most famous fisheries, the Deschutes River, flows into this part of the river just above The Dalles.

Lake Celilo gets its name from the former Celilo Falls, a traditional Native American fishing site that has since been covered up by the placement of The Dalles Dam. Celilo Park, east of The Dalles, offers an interpretive site that recounts the falls' history and is a worthy stop for interested anglers. Considered one of the more productive pools on the Columbia River, Lake Celilo offers better than average fishing for salmon, sturgeon, steelhead, walleye, and smallmouth bass. Most catches are made from boats, as there is very little productive bank access, except in a few select places such as French Giles Park, John Day Dam, and the Rufus gravel pit complex for walleye, sturgeon, and smallmouth bass. Bank anglers wishing to catch salmon and steelhead are better off going to the river below the John Day Dam or the Deschutes River.

The mouth of the Deschutes, 12 miles east of The Dalles, is by far the most popular area for boaters to catch salmon and steelhead, and it is the best place to start. Both species find this water suitable for resting before carrying on to their home waters. On any given day during the fish run, 50–100 boats can be seen trolling plugs, spinners, and bait in these productive waters.

Salmon, when available, are present during August and December. Complicated restrictions are often in place, depending on size of run and tribal negotiations and change with dizzying frequency. Steelhead are present July–September. All wild steelhead must be released unharmed. Trolling plugs is the most standard fishing practice, but bait such as salmon roe also works. Sturgeon fishing is a major attraction on this stretch of river. The best starting point is below The Dalles Dam at Giles French Park. Walleye fishing garners an equal amount of prestige in this water. As in other areas of the Columbia, the best fishing occurs February–April when walleye are getting ready to spawn. Catches are still good throughout the summer and into fall. Again, this is primarily a boat fishery, with a majority of the catches being made around the mouth of the Deschutes and near Rufus up to the John Day Dam. Smallmouth bass are present throughout spring–fall; look for them in slack water, coves, inlets, and around structure.

Species: Salmon, steelhead, sturgeon, smallmouth bass, walleye.

Facilities: Primitive and hookup campsites are available at the Deschutes River State Recreation Area, which has picnic tables, fire grills, drinking water, and restrooms—but no showers. Tent and RV campsites can be had in The Dalles at View Point and Lone Pine RV parks. Boat ramps are available at Celilo Park, east of The Dalles, Heritage Landing at the mouth of the Deschutes, and Giles French

Park below the John Day Dam. Supplies and accommodations can be had in The Dalles and at Biggs Junction.

Directions: From The Dalles, travel east on I-84 for 12 miles to Exit 97. At the end of the ramp, turn right and drive 50 feet to the Biggs–Rufus Hwy. Turn left here and drive one mile, cross the river, and turn right to the Deschutes River State Recreation Area entrance. East I-84 follows the Columbia River from The Dalles to John Day Dam. Celilo Park boat ramp and Heritage Landing (Exit 97) and Giles French Park (Exit 109) are all accessible from I-84 east of The Dalles.

Contact: The Dalles Chamber of Commerce, 541/296-2231; West Columbia Gorge Chamber of Commerce, 503/669-7473; Columbia River Gorge National Scenic Area, 541/308-1700; Oregon Parks and Recreation Department, 800/551-6949; ODFW, The Dalles, 541/296-4628; BLM, Salem, 503/375-5646; View Point Trailer Court, 541/296-5797; Lone Pine RV Park, 541/506-3755; Columbia Basin Guide Service, 541/276-0371; Young's Fishing Service, 800/270-7962.

16 HOOD RIVER
southwest of Hood River

Map 3.2, page 182

Hood River is an enigma among Oregon rivers. Most anglers know it exists, since it's only 50 miles east of Portland, but one would be hard-pressed to find an angler outside of Hood River or The Dalles who ever fishes it. It's quietly known as a locals' river, and it is rarely talked about in fishing circles outside of its tight community of anglers. There must be something good here, and there is, thanks to progressive hatchery programs that have turned this sleepy little river into a contender when it comes to returns of both winter and summer steelhead.

Hood River originates from the eastern flanks of Mount Hood and is fed by glaciers and numerous tributaries such as the Middle Fork, East Fork, and West Fork. Hood is also considered a freestone river, meaning the river bottom is composed of gravel and boulders, creating long runs and deep pools. Its waters are often milky from sediment from the glaciers. The upper river is draped in beautiful forests while the lower river flows through fertile farmlands and apple orchards near Hood River. Fishing for steelhead and salmon is open to all methods of fishing but restricted to the river's lower 4.5 miles below Powerdale Dam. There is a fine catch-and-release fishery for trout (rainbows and brown) both above and below the dam. Above the dam the river is restricted to artificial flies and lures only. The West Fork and its tributaries are closed to fishing, as are the Clear Branch (middle fork) and Pinnacle Creek.

Steelhead fishing is the primary draw for most anglers, followed by salmon and then trout. The winter run of steelhead is composed of both hatchery and wild fish returning late January–May, with peak runs in April. Approximately 50,000 winter steelhead are planted every year, and annual returns are in the vicinity of 1,500–3,000 fish. Both hatchery and wild fish return to the river at the same time, unlike most rivers, where the returns are staggered with wild fish following hatchery returns. The main reason for this is that the hatchery fish are grown entirely from wild brood stock, which makes their instincts similar to those of their wild cousins. Summer steelhead are in the river year-round, and peak catches can occur early spring–late fall. Winter steelhead can reach 20 pounds, and summer fish average 10 pounds. When returning hatchery fish are in excess of production needs, a certain number of fish may be returned to the mouth to provide for additional angler opportunities. This is a fish-management practice that is becoming more common on many rivers, such as the Rogue.

Fishing for steelhead is successful with bait, flies, and lures. Drift anglers fish with bait such as roe or shrimp and nonbait tackles such as colored corkies and yarn. Spinners and spoons are effective in various colors such as orange and chartreuse. Flies, both nymphs and streamers, work equally well. Egg Sucking Leeches or Sting Leeches are particularly effective when swinging downstream through deeper holes. Salmon fishing is marginal, and regulations change from year to year. The river is now closed to chinook but open to coho fishing all year. Their appearance in the river can happen anytime the last two weeks of September–November. When coho do bite, which is not often, they are usually taken on spoons, spinners, or bait such as salmon roe. Trout are restricted to catch-and-release fishing through the entire river. The season starts a little later here and runs May 28–October 31. Bait is allowed below the dam, but the upper river is restricted to artificial flies and lures only. Successful anglers take trout on everything from bait to spinners and flies. Work the pocket water, deeper holes, and around brush for best results.

Species: Summer and winter steelhead, coho, chinook, rainbow and brown trout.

Facilities: Access points for the lower river can be had at two places: below the Powerdale Dam and upriver from the I-84 crossing at the Dam Powerhouse. A good hiking trail follows the lower river for four miles between the dam and river mouth. Boating is not practiced except near the boat ramp at the mouth where anglers run out to the Columbia.

Directions: For the lower section between Powerdale Dam and the mouth, start at the intersection of Hwys. 30 and 35 at the east end of Hood River. Drive south 0.6 mile on Hwy. 35 and turn west (right) on Power Canal Rd., which leads 0.5 mile down to a parking lot at the dam. A trail from there extends four miles along the river to the mouth. To drive to the mouth, take Hwy. 30 north from the interchange with Hwy. 35, going toward the Hood River Bridge over the Columbia. Just before the toll booth turn west (left) on E. Marina Way and follow it one mile to a series of parking lots at the mouth. To reach the upper river, start at the Hood River airport and go south on Tucker Rd., which becomes

Hwy. 281 (Mount Hood Hwy.) one mile south of the airport. This highway follows the river for five miles to where the East and West forks come together.

Contact: Hood River County Chamber of Commerce, 541/386-2000; Tucker Park, 541/386-4477; ODFW, The Dalles, 541/296-4628 or 541/308-1700; Gorge Fly Shop, 541/386-6977, www.gorgeflyshop.com.

17 MILL CREEK

southwest of The Dalles in Mount Hood
National Forest

Map 3.2, page 182

Mill Creek is a fair, small trout stream that originates in The Dalles municipal watershed and flows into the Columbia River at the western edge of The Dalles. Anglers will encounter a combination of lush scenic forests and the remnants of a once-thriving timber operation (hence the name Mill). The creek is restricted to catch-and-release fishing for trout during the season, May 28–October 31; bait fishing is not allowed.

It's too small for boats, so all fishing on Mill Creek is from the bank and is accessible from roads. The river can be fished from numerous road crossings in The Dalles (Hwy. 30, Mosier–The Dalles Hwy., and West 1st St.) and in the upper river from Mill Creek Road. Much of the land surrounding the river in The Dalles is private, so stay in the river once you get in it from a bridge crossing. The upper eight miles of river is all forestlands, and access is unlimited. There are no hiking trails to speak of, so be prepared for some bushwhacking.

Small tumbling streams such as Mill Creek rarely hold trout over 12 inches, but catching these fish on light tackle can be fun, especially for younger anglers. Use short 3–4-weight spin and fly rods and your favorite small lure in gold or silver. Fly anglers can use small nymphs under an indicator or attractor dry flies with great success.

Species: Rainbow trout.

Facilities: There are no campgrounds along this stream; all the accommodations an angler would need are available in The Dalles. Supplies can be had in The Dalles.

Directions: Three roads cross the river near its mouth in The Dalles: Hwy. 30, Mosier–The Dalles Hwy., and W. 1st St. From the intersection of Hwy. 30 and Webber St., go southeast on Hwy. 30 for 0.4 mile to reach the Hwy. 30 bridge. To reach the Mosier–The Dalles Hwy. bridge, go northeast on Webber St. for 0.2 mile, then turn southeast on Mosier–The Dalles Hwy. for 0.5 mile. To reach the W. 1st St. bridge, travel northeast on Webber St. 0.3 mile and turn southeast on W. 1st St., then go southeast on that street 0.6 mile to the bridge. To reach the upper sections of the river, from Hwy. 30 just east of the bridge over Mill Creek, travel south on Mount Hood St. for one mile, then veer west (right) onto Mill Creek Rd., which follows the creek for eight miles to the confluence of the North and South forks.

Contact: The Dalles Chamber of Commerce, 541/296-2231; Columbia River Gorge National Scenic Area, 541/308-1700; ODFW, The Dalles, 541/296-4628; Gorge Fly Shop, 541/386-6977, www.gorgeflyshop.com.

18 EAST FORK HOOD RIVER

south of Hood River

Map 3.2, page 182

The East Fork (the only fork in the Hood River system open to fishing) is a modest rainbow trout stream that joins the main river near Dee. The upper river flows through scenic forested lands composed of waterfalls and meadows in the Mount Hood National Forest before draining into the agricultural communities of the Hood River Valley. Angling for steelhead and salmon is not permitted, though they are present. All trout fishing is restricted to catch-and-release fishing with flies and artificial lures. The season starts a little later here and runs May 28–October 31.

The best fishing and access occurs a couple

of miles north of Dee on Highway 35 at Tollbridge County Park. From here the river is
followed by the highway, but anglers will want
to get on the hiking trails to reach the river;
bank access from Forest Service hiking trails
is unlimited once you are beyond the forest
boundary at Tollbridge. Expect a small, non-
boating river composed of runs, deep holes,
and pocket water. Trout are present throughout the system, but they get smaller the higher
you go. Larger fish seem to hang out in the
lowest sections, where they have more room to
move around. Small tackle in the form of ultralight spinning rods and 3–4-weight fly rods
is all that is necessary. Use small spinners such
as Rooster Tails to fish behind boulders and at
the base of waterfalls in the deeper pools. Fly
anglers can use small nymphs under an indicator to fish the pocket water or try attractor
dry flies in smaller sizes such as an Adams,
Elk Hair Caddis, or Stimulator.

Species: Rainbow trout.

Facilities: There are four campgrounds along
this river: Toll Bridge County Park is at the
point where Hwy. 35 first joins the river,
Routson County Park is just upstream from
there, and two Forest Service campgrounds—
Sherwood and Nottingham—are along the
river farther upstream. All four have boat
access. Toll Bridge has 87 sites for tents and
RVs, as well as a group picnic shelter and a
playground. Routson has 20 sites, drinking
water, and flush toilets. Sherwood has 14 tent
sites and a pit toilet. Nottingham has 23 tent
sites and pit toilets. Supplies can be had in
Hood River.

Directions: From Hood River, travel south
on Hwy. 35 for 17 miles to Toll Bridge Park,
which is on the East Fork at the point where
it intersects Hwy. 35. The highway follows
the East Fork for the next 18 miles to its
headwaters. Along the way, Routson Park is
six miles south of Toll Bridge; Sherwood and
Nottingham are 11 and 12 miles farther south,
respectively.

Contact: Hood River County Chamber of Commerce, 541/386-2000; Hood River County Parks

Department, 541/387-6889; Toll Bridge Park,
541/352-5522; Mount Hood National Forest
Hood River District, 541/352-6002; ODFW,
The Dalles, 541/296-4628; Gorge Fly Shop,
541/386-6977, www.gorgeflyshop.com.

19 LAURANCE LAKE
near Parkdale in Mount Hood National Forest
Map 3.2, page 182

Situated at an elevation of 2,980 feet near the
base of Mount Hood, 127-acre Laurance Lake
is a large and scenic irrigation reservoir whose
outflow forms the Middle Fork of Hood River.
The area is surrounded by tall hills, healthy
stands of Douglas fir trees, and rocky hillsides.
Much of the surrounding forest comes down
to the lake, but because of its size and patchy
hillsides, there is a feeling of space.

The lake's average depth is 15 feet; it's 105
feet at its deepest point near the dam. Some
summer irrigation drawdowns occur, but they're
not significant enough to discourage angling.
Fishing is open April 23–October 31 and is
restricted to flies and artificial lures only to protect the bull trout population. Only hatchery
fin-clipped trout and bass may be retained. All
wild fish must be released unharmed. During
heavy snow years, the lake may not be accessible
until end of May. Laurance Lake's banks are
often shallow and lined with willows and aquatic grasses providing good insect populations
and habitat for resident trout and bass. Boats
with electric motors are useful for trolling (gas
engines are prohibited). Most anglers choose
float tubes, pontoon boats, or bank fishing.
Bank fishing is good along the south shore near
the campground, east of the dam and around
the bridge crossing Pinnacle Creek.

Anglers can expect to catch 9–12-inch
rainbows, cutthroat, and bull trout. A small
population of smallmouth bass also inhabits
the lake. Good insect hatches of *Callibaetis*
and *Hexagenia* are present in the summer starting in mid-July. *Hexagenia,* often called the
"big yellow may," are a unique and unpredictable size 6 mayfly occurring on only a hand-

ful of lakes and rivers in Oregon (Lost Lake, Williamson River) and bring the biggest fish to the surface. They emerge dusk–dark, and they come off best when hot days are followed by warm evenings. Other flies such as small nymphs and streamers also work well during no-hatch times. Try trolling or stripping leeches on clear intermediate sinking line.

Spin anglers can use any assortment of lures such as Rooster Tails to imitate small baitfish or rainbow smolts. When casting lures, allow enough time to sink before retrieving. Flies and lures may be trolled with success in the deeper parts of the lake for a chance at bigger fish. Bass are caught with either flies or bass lures. Top-water poppers work well in the spring for fly anglers and spinnerbaits are good for casting rods. Evening, morning, and early-season fishing is best around the bank and near tributaries such as Pinnacle Creek and Clear Fork. During summer when the surface water warms, try trolling in the deeper water with spinnerbaits, plugs, or streamers.

Species: Rainbow, cutthroat, and bull trout, smallmouth bass.

Facilities: Kinnickinnick Campground, operated by the Forest Service, has 20 sites with picnic tables, fire pits, grills, and vault toilets—but no drinking water.

Directions: From Parkdale, go south on Clear Creek Rd. for three miles to Forest Rd. 2840 (Laurance Lake Rd.). Turn right and drive four miles to the campground on the right.

Contact: Hood River County Chamber of Commerce, 541/386-2000; Mount Hood National Forest Hood River District, 541/352-6002; ODFW, The Dalles, 541/296-4628; Gorge Fly Shop, 541/386-6977, www.gorge-flyshop.com.

20 SALMON RIVER
south of Zig Zag in Mount Hood
National Forest

Map 3.2, page 182

The Salmon River is a tributary of the Sandy River and joins its parent river near Brightwood

on Highway 26. It originates on the slopes of Mount Hood and flows 31 miles through the Mount Hood National Forest and the mountain community of Welches. Back before regulations were imposed and stocking was ceased, the Salmon River was a favorite river for Portland anglers wishing to catch winter and summer steelhead, chinook, and coho salmon in an intimate forest setting. This was made more attractive by the creation of a fly-only section of water in the upper river. The river is as beautiful today as it was back then, minus the ability to catch anadromous runs of fish. Still, the Salmon River is a good wild cutthroat river and offers opportunities to hike into pristine forest settings in the Mount Hood National Forest.

The upper river in the Mount Hood National Forest is composed of a series of waterfalls, shallow runs, deep pools, white water, and large logjams. The lower river has less of a gradient but still holds good water in the form of deep pools. Do not expect any big fish (10–14 inches), but what you do catch are wild and native. All fishing on the Salmon is restricted to artificial lures and flies only. This is not a boatable river, but bank access is unlimited in the forest stretch above Welches. From Welches to Wildwood Recreation Area and near Brightwood, the river flows through some private property, limiting access. Good bank access can be had in the lower river at Wildwood Recreation Area and in the upper river from Trail No. 742.

Trail No. 742 is one of the most scenic trails in the Mount Hood National Forest. The trail follows the river, and anglers can jump into any stretch they think holds fish. The river is composed of nice runs, pocket water, and deep pools. Flies and lures both work. Cast attractor dry flies such as Royal Wulffs and Humpies in the faster water and behind rocks. Nymphs and streamers all work in the deeper pools. Spinners such as Rooster Tails and bangbaits are productive just about anywhere.

Species: Wild cutthroat trout.

Facilities: Access to the lower river is available at the BLM's Wildwood Recreation Area in Welches; $3 per vehicle parking fee. Camping is available at the Forest Service's Green Canyon Campground, on the river south of Zig Zag; 15 tent sites, no drinking water. Camping is also available near the upper river at Trillium Lake. Supplies can be had in Welches or Zig Zag. Trail No. 742 has picnic spots with tables and numerous good primitive campsites.

Directions: From Zig Zag, follow Hwy. 26 west for two miles and turn south into the Wildwood Recreation Area. For access to the rest of the lower river, follow Salmon River Rd. south from Zig Zag. The first trailhead for Trail No. 742-A is 2.7 miles up. The bridge over the river, with parking for Trail No. 742 leading upstream, is 4.9 miles up. To reach the upper river and the east end of Trail No. 742, from Zig Zag follow Hwy. 26 for 13 miles to the Trillium Lake turnoff (Forest Service Rd. 2656). Follow Rd. 2656 south for 1.8 miles, then turn left (southwest) just past Trillium Lake Campground, staying on Rd. 2656. Stay on this road for 1.9 more miles, then turn right on Forest Service Rd. 2656–309. The trailhead is two miles ahead on the right.

Contact: Mount Hood Visitor Information Center, 503/622-4822; Mount Hood National Forest Zig Zag District, 503/622-3191; BLM, Salem, 503/375-5646; ODFW, Clackamas, 503/657-2000; The Fly-Fishing Shop in Welches, 800/266-3971.

21 MIRROR LAKE
west of Government Camp
Map 3.2, page 182

Eight-acre Mirror Lake attracts many visitors, mostly hikers and trail runners, for its scenic views of Mount Hood, strenuous uphill hike, and alpine beauty. It is close to Government Camp and is conveniently situated on Highway 26, 50 miles from Portland.

With so much good trout fishing in the Mount Hood National Forest, there's little to recommend Mirror Lake to anyone who values good fishing above hiking. The hike into Mirror Lake can be strenuous and crowded; the fish are exceedingly small (6–8-inches); and

hikers can make the environment can feel like a county park. Still, where there are fish you will undoubtedly find anglers, and Mirror Lake gets its share. To avoid crowds, fish this lake after Labor Day weekend and into fall before the snows can block access. Fall is a good time to find bigger fish who have avoided the summer angling pressure. Younger anglers will have fun with the smaller, easy-to-catch fish.

Mirror Lake is open all year; however, winter snows can block access November–April. Angling is restricted to artificial flies and lures only. Attractor dry flies such as an Adams or Griffith Gnat will match any hatch on the lake. Streamers such as Woolly Buggers and leech patterns work well, as do nymphs. Rooster Tails and bangbaits will work all year with great success.

Species: Stocked rainbow trout.

Facilities: There are backpacker campsites at the lake with no facilities. Lodging and supplies can be had in Government Camp. The closest camping is at Trillium Lake.

Directions: From Government Camp, drive one mile west on Hwy. 26 and park along the left (south) side of the road, just before Hwy. 26 turns to the north. Parking at the trailhead requires a Northwest Forest Pass ($5 per day; $30 annually), which is available from most sporting goods or outdoors shops or from Nature of the Northwest in Portland. From this trailhead, Trail No. 664 leads 1.5 miles to the lake, climbing 700 feet in the process.

Contact: Mount Hood National Forest Zig Zag District, 503/622-3191; Mount Hood Visitor Information Center, 503/622-4822; ODFW, Clackamas, 503/657-2000; Nature of the Northwest, 503/872-2750, www.naturenw.org; The Fly-Fishing Shop in Welches, 800/266-3971.

22 TRILLIUM LAKE
east of Government Camp
Map 3.2, page 182

Trillium is a popular, 57-acre lake on the south side of Mount Hood in the Mount Hood National Forest. This scenic lake offers stunning views of Mount Hood, dense fir forests, nice campgrounds, and good fishing that create a family-friendly atmosphere. Trillium is especially popular with fly anglers for its shallow depths—no more than eight feet on average and 16 feet at its deepest point near the dam—and prolific hatches of mayflies such as *Callibaetis,* caddis, and chironomids.

Beginning each May, Trillium is stocked with 3,000 legal-size rainbows, and more than 8,000 are added through the year. In addition to the legal-size fish, about 800 trophy fish of 16 inches or larger are stocked in August. Fishing is open all year, but the lake is available only after the snowpack melts sometime in the first part of May. Fishing is good all through the summer, but serious anglers will want to take advantage of the lake's ice-out period or fall, when fish are foraging and extra feisty.

Fish can be caught either from the bank or from a boat. Boats can be launched from a good ramp in the campground, but gas motors are prohibited. Float tubes and canoes may prove to be the better option because of the lake's shallow depth and manageable size. Fly anglers will especially appreciate a float tube or pontoon boat to make back casts away from the dense foliage and trees that line the banks. Bank angling is easy from hiking trails that surround the lake or from the fishing dock near the campground.

During hatch times fly anglers can match the hatch or simply put on a small Adams or other mayfly patterns with high success. Trolling or stripping nymphs and leech patterns will prove effective when concentrated around the banks and in the deeper water. Spinners such as Rooster Tails work great, as do baits such as worms, PowerBait, and small eggs.

Species: Stocked rainbow and trophy trout.

Facilities: Sailboarding is popular on the lake, as are canoeing and still-water kayaking. Trillium Lake Campground, operated by the Forest Service, has 57 tent sites, drinking water, hiking trails, fishing dock, and boat ramp for $16 per night. Supplies can be had in Government Camp.

Directions: From Government Camp, drive two miles east on Hwy. 26 and turn right onto Trillium Lake Rd. It is a short three-mile drive to the bottom of the hill on Trillium Lake Rd. Continue straight on Trillium Lake Rd. 0.5 mile to reach the Trillium Lake Campground. Supplies, gas, and other accommodations can be had in Government Camp.

Contact: Mount Hood Visitor Information Center, 503/622-4822; Mount Hood National Forest Zig Zag District, 503/622-3191; ODFW, Clackamas, 503/657-2000; Nature of the Northwest, 503/872-2750, www.naturenw.org; The Fly-Fishing Shop in Welches, 800/266-3971.

23 TWIN LAKES
southeast of Government Camp

Map 3.2, page 182

These two popular hike-in lakes on the south slope of Mount Hood offer fair to good fishing for stocked brook trout. Anglers will enjoy the short 1–1.5-mile hike through scenic pine forests. Lower Twin Lake (12 acres) and Upper Twin (10 acres) are both small enough that bank fishing is easy. Both lakes are approximately 50 feet deep or more at their deepest points. It would be fairly easy to walk to the lakes with a float tube or pontoon boat, but this probably is not necessary given the lakes' small size. Both lakes fish equally well, with fish averaging 9–12 inches. Some holdover fish from previous years are present and make up the larger fish in the lake at 14 inches or more. Both lakes are open all year, and there is no limit to the number of brook trout that may be harvested. Access is limited in the winter because of high average snowfalls and doesn't become available to foot traffic until late April. Flies, lures, and bait are all allowed and work equally well in the deep water and against the shorelines. Some small hatches of mayflies occur in the midsummer and fall.

Species: Brook trout.

Facilities: There's a backpacker camp at lower Twin Lake and a Forest Service campground near the trailhead at nearby Frog Lake. Supplies can be had in Government Camp.

Directions: From Government Camp, travel east on Hwy. 26 for 8.5 miles and look for the parking lot near the Pacific Crest Trail on the left. Parking at the trailhead requires a Northwest Forest Pass ($5 per day; $30 annually), which is available from most sporting goods or outdoors shops or from Nature of the Northwest in Portland.

Contact: Mount Hood Visitor Information Center, 503/622-4822; Mount Hood National Forest Hood River District, 541/352-6002; ODFW, Clackamas, 503/657-2000; Nature of the Northwest, 503/872-2750, www.naturenw.org; The Fly-Fishing Shop in Welches, 800/266-3971.

24 FROG LAKE
east of Government Camp
Map 3.2, page 182

Eleven-acre Frog Lake offers stunning views of Mount Hood and is set among dense fir forests covering both the lakeshore and surrounding foothills. Good campgrounds and hiker-friendly trails make this a good overnight family outing close to Portland. Frog Lake's popularity may rest in the fact that it is stocked with more than 6,000 legal-size rainbow trout in mid-May. These fish average 8–10 inches, but holdovers from previous years can reach 15 inches or more. All methods of fishing are permitted, including bait. The lake is open all year, but snow will inhibit access December–late April.

Frog Lake is quite shallow, with an average depth of 3–6 feet. Nonmotorized boats may be launched from the campground to troll the deeper waters near the center. Float tubes and pontoon boats work equally well and will help provide a good back cast for fly anglers. Bank angling is good from all points around the lake on hiking trails. A good place to begin bank fishing is within the campground. Ef-

fective fly-fishing techniques include stripping nymphs and small streamers such as leeches and Woolly Buggers. Small attractor dry flies such as an Adams will take fish feeding on the surface during summer and fall. Spinners such as Rooster Tails and small Rapalas will imitate the baitfish populations greedily consumed by the trout. All baits work, such as worms and eggs floated under a bobber.

Species: Stocked rainbow trout.

Facilities: The Forest Service campground at Frog Lake has 33 sites, pit toilets, boat-launching facilities, and drinking water. Supplies can be had in Government Camp.

Directions: From Government Camp, travel east on Hwy. 26 for nine miles and turn left (southeast) on Forest Service Rd. 2610; the campground is 0.5 mile down this road.

Contact: Mount Hood Visitor Information Center, 503/622-4822; Mount Hood National Forest Hood River District, 541/352-6002; ODFW, Clackamas, 503/657-2000; The Fly-Fishing Shop in Welches, 800/266-3971.

25 UPPER WHITE RIVER
east of Government Camp
Map 3.2, page 182

The upper White River may be familiar to anglers who have driven over Barlow Pass on Highway 35 to Hood River. Even though it runs off-color most of the time because of glacier sediment, the White River holds a fair amount of fish for anglers willing to drive off the beaten path to discover its secrets. The upper river—from a point above a series of waterfalls near Tygh Valley to the southeastern slopes of Mount Hood—flows through a nice alpine valley and is scenically forested beginning at White River Campground.

The upper river is a rough-and-tumble stream for most of its run, originating from the White River Glacier near the Timberline Ski Area. The most productive water is below the Highway 35 river crossing at several campgrounds 10 miles south on Highway 48. The fish are not big (9–12 inches), but neither is the river. Small gear such as ultralight spin rods and 4-weight fly rods are perfect. Nymphs, attractor dry flies, Woolly Buggers, and an assortment of spinners in smaller sizes are all you will need. The lower you go in the river, the bigger the fish get. Expect fish up to 16 inches or more in the area around Graveyard Butte and above the falls in Tygh Valley.

This is not a boating river, and bank access is limited to areas around bridges and campgrounds; nonetheless, access is good, especially in the upper reaches in the Mount Hood National Forest. Best places to start are at Barlow Crossing, White River, and Keeps Mill campgrounds in the upper river off Highway 35, and southwest of Tygh Valley at a few roadside crossings. The entire river is restricted to artificial lures and flies only.

Species: Wild rainbow trout.

Facilities: Primitive camping can be had along Barlow Rd. (Forest Service Rd. 3530) on the river at Barlow Crossing, White River, and Keeps Mill. Camping near Tygh Valley is limited to the Deschutes River campgrounds at Oak Springs or Buckhollow (10 miles east) or near Pine Hollow and Rock Springs Reservoir (10 miles west). Buy supplies in Government Camp or Tygh Valley.

Directions: From Government Camp, drive two miles east on Hwy. 26, then turn north on Hwy. 35 toward Hood River. Follow Hwy. 35 for five miles to Forest Rd. 48, which is to the south just after Hwy. 35 crosses the White River. Paved Rd. 48 roughly follows the north bank of the White River for the next 14 miles. Eight miles below Hwy. 35, you'll reach Forest Rd. 43, which branches right (west) and crosses the river to Barlow Crossing Campground. From Barlow Crossing you can drive up and down the river 20 miles on Forest Rd. 3530. Four miles below Rd. 43, Rd. 48 reaches gravel Rd. 4885, which drops three miles right (south) to the river and Keeps Mill Campground. Two miles past its intersection with Rd. 4885, Rd. 48 reaches Forest Creek Campground, at which point this road leaves White River.

To reach the area near Tygh Valley from Barlow Crossing, drive south on Forest Rd. 43 approximately 10 miles to the junction with Hwy. 26. Drive south on Hwy. 26 for four miles to Hwy. 216 and turn east. Follow Hwy. 216 east for approximately 10 miles, passing Bear Springs Ranger Station and Pine Grove. Two miles east of Pine Grove, turn north on Victor Rd. toward Wamic. Drive north and then east on Victor Rd. 2.5 miles to Smock Rd. Turn north on Smock Rd., which crosses the river near Graveyard Butte in one mile. Staying east on Victor Rd. for 15 miles will put you one mile east of Tygh Valley. Stay east on Victor Rd. for two more miles of river access above the falls.

Contact: Hood River County Chamber of Commerce, 541/386-2000; ODFW, The Dalles, 541/296-4628; Mount Hood Visitor Information Center, 503/622-4822; Bear Springs and Barlow Ranger District, 541/467-2291; Pine Hollow Lakeside Resort and RV Park, 541/544-2271; Gorge Fly Shop, 541/386-6977.

26 BADGER LAKE
south of Hood River
Map 3.2, page 182

There are too many easily accessible lakes on Mount Hood to recommend Badger except to the most experienced four-wheel drivers and those tolerant of partying youth. Roads to the lake are deeply rutted, and rock slides frequently block parts of the road; be prepared with a good spare tire and plenty of supplies. Young people looking for a place to party have adopted Badger during the summer and can make overnight camping less than peaceful. Still, Badger Lake does provide good fishing for stocked rainbow trout of 10–14 inches in a scenic, secluded setting.

Badger Lake is relatively underfished, allowing some fish to reach 17 inches or more. The lake covers 30 acres and is 45 feet deep in the center. Fly anglers will be pleased with good insect hatches of mayflies. Unconfirmed reports suggest there may even be the presence of a small *Hexagenia* hatch (big yellow may). If *Hexagenia* are present they will most likely come off in late July. Boating is allowed, but pulling a boat over the extremely rough road is inadvisable. Anglers would be better off using float tubes and pontoon boats. Good hiking trails surround the lake. Access to the lake is usually blocked by snow until the first part of July.

All methods of fishing are permissible, including bait. Use bait such as worms, Power-Bait, and eggs floated under a bobber. Spinner anglers can cast or troll Rooster Tails in any color, but orange will best imitate the abundant crayfish population. Fly anglers should watch for insect hatches with big fish rising to the surface to feed. A small Adams or Griffith Gnat should work in most cases. If not, try terrestrial patterns such as ant, beetle, or grasshopper worked tight against the bank. Troll streamers such as Woolly Buggers and small leeches out in the middle for a chance at bigger fish. Crayfish patterns can be fished on the bottom among rocks.

Species: Stocked rainbow trout.

Facilities: The campground at the lake has four primitive tent-only sites. Parking here requires a Northwest Forest Pass ($5 per day; $30 annually), which is available from most sporting goods or outdoors shops or from Nature of the Northwest in Portland.

Directions: Driving to this lake is not recommended for vehicles without high clearance. From Hood River, take Hwy. 35 south for 37 miles to Forest Rd. 48, just past Bennett Pass. Turn left (east) onto Rd. 48, and follow it 16 miles to Forest Rd. 4860. Turn left (north) onto Rd. 4860 and drive eight miles to Forest Rd. 140. Bear right (east) and go four miles to the lake.

Contact: Mount Hood National Forest Hood River District, 541/352-6002; ODFW, The Dalles, 541/296-4628; Nature of the Northwest, 503/872-2750, www.naturenw.org.

27 ROCK CREEK RESERVOIR
west of Tygh Valley

Map 3.2, page 182

Rock Creek Reservoir holds the same diversity of fish species as Pine Hollow Reservoir, but in a more quiet and remote setting. A mix of ponderosa pine and oak forests surrounds the lake, and willows line the banks. Rocky shore outcroppings and underwater weed beds provide good habitat for bass, bluegill, and trout. What you will not find here is a resort and water-skiing during the summer. Rock Creek is better suited to anglers who like remote settings without the busyness of summer disturbing their fishing.

Rock Creek Reservoir is 100 acres and averages a shallow 10 feet for most of the lake. The deepest area (32 feet) is near the dam and receives a majority of the fishing pressure from trollers. Both bank and boat access are good. Most bank angling takes place on the north shore, around the dam and to the east. Gas motors are not allowed on the lake, and most anglers use cartop rowboats, canoes, pontoons, and float tubes. All these self-powered boats will give you good access to the deeper parts of the lake and shorelines.

Large numbers of legal-size trout are stocked every year, including a few trophy fish of 16 inches or bigger. Average catches are 12–14 inches, but 16–18-inch fish are not uncommon. Other species of fish include largemouth bass, bluegill, and brown bullhead catfish. All methods of fishing are permitted, including bait. The best fishing methods in order of success are trolling, spinner fishing, bait fishing, and fly-fishing. Trollers use Rapalas, Flatfish, and Rooster Tails. Spin anglers can use plugs, spoons, and spinners. Bait such as worms, eggs, and PowerBait work well when fished under a bobber. Fly anglers should be conscious of any surface insects hatching, or should fish streamers and nymphs trolled or stripped back. The lake is open year-round.

Species: Stocked legal and trophy trout, largemouth bass, bluegill, brown bullhead catfish.

Facilities: A campground and boat ramp are on the south shore, with 33 campsites available, and additional campsites are scattered elsewhere along the reservoir's shore. RVs are welcome, but there are no hookups. Drinking water, restrooms, picnic tables, and fire pits are all available.

Directions: From Tygh Valley turn west at a flashing yellow light in the middle of town. Drive west through town on Wamic Market Rd., reaching Wamic in approximately five miles. From Wamic, continue west on Wamic Market Rd. for another five miles until reaching the lake and campground.

Contact: Hood River County Chamber of Commerce, 541/386-2000; ODFW, The Dalles, 541/296-4628 or 541/308-1700; Pine Hollow Lakeside Resort and RV Park, 541/544-2271; Gorge Fly Shop, 541/386-6977, www.gorgeflyshop.com.

28 PINE HOLLOW RESERVOIR

south of The Dalles in Tygh Valley

Map 3.2, page 182

Pine Hollow Reservoir is a scenic, 240-acre reservoir situated in a semiarid climate. Willows, pine, and oak trees lining the reservoir banks make this an especially beautiful environment in the fall. Fishing is open all year, and all methods of fishing are permitted, including bait. Boating is permitted, but a 10 mph speed limit has been set for certain times of the year. Faster limits—fast enough for water-skiing and Jet Skis—are permitted on the west end of the lake July 1 Labor Day weekend.

More fish are caught by trolling spinners, spoons, and flashers from a boat, but bank fishing is also productive. Good places to begin bank fishing are at the south and east public boat ramps, near the dam, and along the dikes on the northeast shore. Rooster Tails, Mepps Spinners, and bait such as worms or eggs floated under a bobber work almost anytime of year. The entire shoreline is accessible

to the public 10 feet above the high-water line, with the exception of the southeast corner in front of Camp Morrow. In low-water years this means you can walk almost anywhere around the lake to bank fish. The deepest area of the lake is between the dam and the east public boat ramp.

A good number of legal-size rainbow trout (8–10 inches) are stocked every year, plus a few trophy-size fish over 16 inches. Holdovers from previous years get big by the second or third year and can reach 30 inches or more. Admittedly, these larger fish are rare, but a fair number of trout can be caught in the 16–24-inch range. Included among these prized trout are a fair number of largemouth bass that can reach five pounds or more. Also present in the lake are bluegill and brown bullhead catfish, both of which make good sport in the summer.

An overall shallow depth of 15 feet also makes this a popular place for fly anglers fishing from pontoon boats or float tubes. Sporadic hatches of mayflies occur along the banks during the summer. Streamers and nymphs can be trolled or stripped through the water to catch bigger fish.

Species: Stocked legal and trophy trout, largemouth bass, bluegill, brown bullhead catfish.

Facilities: The only camping is at Pine Hollow Lakeside Resort and RV Park, which provides a full-service campground with a store, full RV hookups, showers, laundry facilities, playground, tent sites, fishing and swimming docks, boat rentals, and day-use area. There are two boat ramps, one at the resort and one at the south end of the lake. The nearby Wasco County Fair offers cotton candy, Tilt-A-Whirls, and rodeos August 17–20.

Directions: From The Dalles, take I-84 east to Exit 87, Hwy. 197. Drive south on Hwy. 197 for 31 miles to Tygh Valley. Turn right into Tygh Valley at a flashing yellow light. Take Wamic Market Rd. (between the storage building and the tavern). Go four miles and then turn right at Ross Rd. Go 3.5 miles and turn left at Pine Hollow Lakeside Resort and RV Park.

Contact: Hood River County Chamber of Commerce, 541/386-2000; ODFW, The Dalles, 541/296-4628 or 541/308-1700; Pine Hollow Lakeside Resort and RV Park, 541/544-2271; Gorge Fly Shop, 541/386-6977, www.gorgeflyshop.com.

29 LOWER WHITE RIVER

south of Tygh Valley

Map 3.2, page 182

Lower White River extends 2.5 miles upstream from the Deschutes River to a series of waterfalls. Scenic and desolate, this canyon stretch produces some big trout, 20 inches plus, and good runs of summer steelhead. This is not a boating river, and the best access to this river is from the hiking trail at White River Falls State Park, which will lead you from the mouth to the falls.

Anglers visiting this river can expect sizable rapids interspersed with deep pools and pocket water. Perhaps the only deterrent that keeps most anglers from visiting this river—other than they don't know it exists—is the difficult hiking and unpredictable water conditions. Expect quite a bit of walking up and down steep hills to negotiate around canyon walls. Slow to clear during spring runoff and exceptional warm summers on Mount Hood, this river can stay high and muddy for weeks. The best times to fish are in spring, before the runoff, before the summer glacier melt, and again in fall when cold weather returns to the mountain.

The lower river is open to fishing the entire year for trout and steelhead and is regulated under the Deschutes River regulations. Fishing is restricted to artificial lures and flies only. Steelhead anglers will want to fish this river August–September and sometimes into October. For steelhead, fish either flies or lures. Fly anglers can use standard 7- and 8-weight rods and floating lines with hair-wing streamer patterns (Green Butt Skunks and Purple Perils). This is also good nymphing

water, and some steelhead will take a skated dry fly. Spin anglers can use Blue Fox Spinners, spoons in fluorescent colors, and drift rigs with corkies and fluorescent yarn. Trout are present all year. Watch for salmon fly hatches followed by golden stones and an assortment of smaller mayflies in June. Mid- to late summer produces good hatches of caddis. Five- and 6-weight rods will handle any trout and the occasional steelhead.

Species: Wild redband trout and summer steelhead.

Facilities: White River Falls State Park is day-use only but does offer river access and a trail leading 2.5 miles along the river, down to the Deschutes. Camping is available at several BLM sites on the east bank of the Deschutes, including White River, Oak Springs, and Blue Hole. Comfortable camping and great amenities can also be had west of Tygh Valley at Pine Hollow Reservoir. Supplies and other accommodations can be had in Tygh Valley or Maupin.

Directions: From Tygh Valley, reach White River Falls State Park by driving four miles north, then east on Hwy. 216 (Tygh Valley Rd.) to the park on the right. To reach the BLM campgrounds on the Deschutes, continue another four miles east on Hwy. 216 to the Shears Bridge over the Deschutes. One mile past this bridge, turn right (south) on Deschutes River Access Rd.; BLM campgrounds are three, four, and five miles along this road. You can also reach the river from Tygh Valley by driving southeast on Tygh Valley Rd. for one mile to where it crosses the river. From here, turn right (west) along Davison Grade Rd. or left (east) along Tygh Valley Rd. for access in both directions.

Contact: Hood River County Chamber of Commerce, 541/386-2000; ODFW, The Dalles, 541/296-4628; Mount Hood Visitor Information Center, 503/622-4822; Oregon Parks and Recreation Department, 800/551-6949; BLM, Prineville, 541/416-6700; Pine Hollow Lakeside Resort and RV Park, 541/544-2271; Gorge Fly Shop, 541/386-6977.

30 LOWER DESCHUTES RIVER: MACK'S CANYON TO MAUPIN

near Maupin

Map 3.2, page 182   **BEST (**

This 25-mile section of the Deschutes is popular for great roadside access and fine steelhead and trout water. The river here flows through a canyon, like the river below Mack's Canyon, and consists of the same series of slow, calm stretches with intermittent rapids. Shears Falls, 18 miles south of Mack's Canyon Campground, forms a natural barrier that migrating fish have to navigate before making their way into the section above Maupin. Boating in this section is recommended for advanced boaters only, and Shears Falls is a mandatory portage. In summer, the river from Maupin to Shears Falls is very popular among white-water rafters, and the endless parade of giggling and splashing boaters can be less than conducive to quality fishing.

The most popular methods for access to this part of the river are from drift boats or rafts; on foot from the bank; and using jet sleds. Angling from a floating device is off-limits for the entire river, requiring anglers to get out of the boat before fishing. The river between Shears Falls and Mack's Canyon is followed by a good but washboarded gravel road. Along this stretch, access to the east bank is unlimited, and anglers can stop anywhere they see a nice riffle or tail-out. Boats can be launched from three ramps between Mack's Canyon and Shears Falls. This section of river may be the easiest section to float, but it still requires competent rowing skills and the ability to read rapids and avoid obstructions. Jet sledding on the Deschutes has been a controversial issue, and restrictions have been imposed on their use. Contact the Parks and Recreation Department for the latest regulations.

Above Shears Falls to Maupin, a paved road follows the river for eight miles, granting unlimited access to the east bank. Boaters will find this stretch more challenging as there are a few Class III and IV rapids. Only one

boat launch offers access to this part of the river—at Maupin County Park. The mandatory take-out is just above the falls at Sandy Beach. You do not want to miss the Sandy Beach take-out, and it is highly recommend you scout the take-out before launching.

Steelhead and trout are present and can be fished for all year. Salmon are also present during spring and fall; however, they are c off limits to all fishing. Steelhead make their appearance between Mack's Canyon and Shears Falls in late July and can be available till November. Steelhead do not pass above the falls to reach the upper river until late August. Fishing regulations are the same for the entire river: artificial flies and lures only, with the exception of a three-mile stretch from Shears Falls downriver three miles to the upper railroad trestle, which is open to bait fishing.

Trout fishing is excellent over the entire stretch of river and attracts mostly fly anglers for the prolific hatches of mayflies, caddis, and stone flies. Stone flies move to this section of river from the area below Mack's Canyon late May–early June and provide some of the most exciting fishing of the year. Subsequent hatches include golden stones, blue-winged olives, pale morning and evening duns, and caddis. Caddis, in fact, make up the primary food source of trout midsummer–fall. Five- and 6-weight rods with floating line are all you need to fish nymphs, dry flies, and streamers. Nymphs and streamers are always good options during nonhatch times.

Steelhead are fished with both lures and flies. Fly anglers use stout 7- and 8-weight single hand or spey rods rigged with floating lines. Popular steelhead patterns include Green Butt Skunks, Red Butt Skunks, Purple Perils, Spawning Purples, Coal Cars, and Signal Lights. Cast your fly down and across in likely runs and wait for the steelhead to strike at the bottom of the swing. Other popular methods of steelhead fishing include skated dry flies and nymphs with an indicator. Spin anglers can use drift rigs with corkies and yarn or spoons such as Stee-Lees or Little Cleos.

Orange, purple, and green tend to be the best colors for spinners, yarn, and corkies.

Species: Wild redband trout, summer steelhead, chinook salmon.

Facilities: Boater passes are required all year for use on the Lower Deschutes River from Pelton Dam to the confluence with the Columbia River. Anyone using a watercraft or any other floating device for transport must have in his/her possession a boater pass. Passes are available from the boater pass website and from a number of vendors throughout Oregon, such as G.I. Joe's. Access may be restricted to a limited number of boaters on certain sections of the river during peak use periods, and there may be group size limitations. Cost varies depending on time of year and duration. Contact the Prineville BLM for up-to-date information on the boater pass program.

Beavertail and Mack's Canyon campgrounds, and the Maupin County Park, are the only areas with drinking water. All other campgrounds are primitive, providing restrooms and garbage service only. Free day-use areas are along the Deschutes River Access Rd. at Maupin County Park, Grey Eagle, Blue Hole, Lower Blue Hole, Surf City, and Sandy Beach. Fee campgrounds and restrooms are available between Maupin and Shears Falls on the Deschutes River Access Rd. at Oasis, Blue Hole, Oak Springs, and White River. Blue Hole provides a wheelchair-accessible fishing platform, restrooms, and picnic areas. Camping below Shears Falls is available along the Max Canyon Access Rd. at Mack's Canyon Campground, which provides outhouses, drinking water, and a boat launch. Other fee campgrounds can be had along Mack's Canyon Rd. at Rattlesnake Canyon, Beavertail, Jones Canyon, Twin Spring, and Pine Tree.

The only boat ramp between Maupin and Shears Falls is at Maupin County Park. The mandatory take-out for this stretch is eight miles downriver at Sandy Beach above Shears Falls. Longer floats can be had from numerous put-ins above Maupin. Below Shears Falls, anglers can launch a boat at Pine Tree, Twin

Springs, and Beavertail campgrounds. The lowest take-out before descending into Mack's Canyon and committing to a 30-mile stretch of river is at Mack's Canyon Campground. Supplies, accommodations, fly shops, and hardware stores can be had in Maupin. River shuttles can be had for a fee from the Oasis Resort.

Directions: From Maupin, drive south on Hwy. 197 for 0.5 mile, to where the highway bridge crosses the Deschutes. Cross the bridge, driving south on Hwy. 197, and make an immediate turn to the north on Bakeoven Rd. Follow Bakeoven Rd. 0.5 mile, passing Maupin City Park, to the Deschutes River Access Rd. Turn north on the Deschutes River Access Rd. and follow the river 6.5 miles to Shears Falls. From the beginning of the access road the following campsites, boat ramps, and day-use areas can be reached: Grey Eagle (1.5 miles), Blue Hole (three miles), Oak Springs (3.5 miles), White River (five miles), Sandy Beach (six miles), and Shears Falls (6.5 miles). To get from Shears Falls to Mack's Canyon Campground, at Shears Falls the Deschutes River Access Rd. dead-ends into Hwy. 216. Turn east on Hwy. 216 and drive one mile to Mack's Canyon Access Rd. Turn north on Mack's Canyon Access Rd., a graded gravel road. Mack's Canyon Access Rd. dead-ends 18 miles ahead at Mack's Canyon Campground. From the beginning of the access road, the following sites can be reached: Buckhollow (0.5 mile), Pine Tree (three miles), Twin Springs (four miles), Oakbrook (6.5 miles), Jones Canyon (eight miles), Gert Canyon (8.5 miles), Beavertail (9.5 miles), Rattlesnake (10.5 miles), and Mack's Canyon (18 miles).

Contact: Deschutes River Boater Pass Information, 866/588-7277, www.boaterpass.com; Maupin Chamber of Commerce, 541/395-2599; BLM, Prineville, 541/416-6700; ODFW, Bend, 541/388-6363; Oregon Parks and Recreation Department, 800/551-6949; National Forest Service, Bend, 541/383-4000; Barlow Ranger District, 541/467-5101; Maupin City Park, 541/395-2252; Deschutes RV Park, 541/395-2204; Deer Brook RV Park,

541/328-6225; Deschutes Motel, 541/395-2626; John Hazel and Company, Deschutes Angler, 541/395-2441, www.johnhazel.com; The Oasis Guide Service and Resort, 541/395-2611, www.deschutesriveroasis.com; Deschutes Canyon Fly Shop, 541/395-2565, www.flyfishingdeschutes.com; G.I. Joe's, Bend, 541/388-3770.

31 CLEAR LAKE
south of Government Camp

Map 3.2, page 182

Clear Lake (600 surface acres) is a large lake in the White River watershed on the south side of Mount Hood about nine miles from the Warm Springs Indian Reservation boundary. This is a very popular fishing lake, scenically situated in a forested valley of juniper and pine forests consistent with the drier climate of central Oregon. With its nice campground and proximity to Portland (80 miles), this is an ideal spot for families and younger anglers.

Much of Clear Lake's popularity is owed to generous stocking programs, which introduce more than 14,000 legal-size trout every May. It is also the recipient of a successful brood-stock program, meaning good numbers of fish 10 pounds or bigger can be caught. Stocked rainbows average to 12 inches, and brook trout can reach five pounds or more. All methods of fishing are permissible, including bait. Boats are allowed with gas motors, but a 10 mph speed limit has been set. The lake is open all year, but snowfalls may prohibit access November–late April. Summer irrigation drawdowns can affect the lake's size but not enough to deter anglers for most of the summer and fall.

Bank and boat angling are both popular and effective. During summer drawdowns anglers can walk out onto the dry shoals and cast into deeper waters. The best place for bank anglers to start is at the campground on the east shore and around the dam. Boaters have some advantage at Clear Lake with the ability to troll in the deeper waters near the

dam and out in the middle. The east shore from the dam to past the campground and into the northeast cove is popular with boaters who fish the rocky outcroppings around points of land. Additional coves are laid out in the west and northwest corners of the lake. The north end of the lake is reputed to have several natural cold-water springs, identified by green water, which can attract fish in the hotter months.

Fly anglers will appreciate Clear Lake as a producer of prolific hatches of assorted mayflies *(Callibaetis)*, chironomids, damsels, and other waterborne insects. There is an abundance of crayfish and baitfish, so patterns and imitations of these food forms work extremely well. Crayfish patterns should be fished close to the bottom where the naturals live among the rocks and natural springs. Streamers such as Woolly Buggers and small Mole Hair Leech patterns and nymphs can be strolled or stripped along the shorelines and in deeper water on full sinking lines. Spin and bait anglers can use Rapalas to imitate baitfish and orange spinners to imitate crayfish. General spinners such as Rooster Tails in an assortment of colors will also work well when trolled or cast to the bank and retrieved. Some anglers troll with flashing blades, making big S-turns in the water to imitate an escaping baitfish.

Species: Stocked legal and brood-stock rainbow trout, brook trout.

Facilities: Clear Lake Campground, operated by the Forest Service, has 28 sites with picnic tables, fire grills, drinking water, firewood, and pit toilets. A boat ramp is nearby. Supplies and accommodations can be had in Estacada or Government Camp.

Directions: From Government Camp, drive east on Hwy. 26 for 11 miles to Forest Rd. 2630. Turn south and drive one mile to the campground on the right.

Contact: Mount Hood Visitor Information Center, 503/622-4822; Mount Hood National Forest Hood River District, 541/352-6002; ODFW, Clackamas, 503/657-2000; The Fly-Fishing Shop in Welches, 800/266-3971.

32 TIMOTHY LAKE

on the Oak Grove Fork of the Clackamas River
in Mount Hood National Forest

Map 3.2, page 182   **BEST (**

Timothy Lake is a popular, richly diverse fishery close to Portland and surrounded by everything expected from the western side of the state: tall stands of Douglas firs, diverse undergrowth of ferns, mosses, and smaller deciduous tress, and a tremendous amount of shade and rain. Timothy Lake holds a surprisingly diverse fish population, with kokanee and four species of trout. In addition to brown, cutthroat, and brook trout, Timothy Lake is also the yearly recipient of 18,000 legal-size rainbows (10–14 inches), including a good brood-stock program supplying fish of 10 pounds or more. Stocking begins in May and runs through June. All fishing methods are legal, including bait. Fishing is good year-round but access may be limited by winter snowfalls November–late March.

The lake is fairly large (1,290 acres) and deep (80 feet near the south shore). Even average depths are surprisingly deep (45 feet) and begin almost abruptly at the shoreline around the entire lake. Boats, float tubes, and pontoon boats are the best options, although good catches are also made from the bank. Boats may be used with a gas motor, but there is a 10 mph speed limit. Good bank access can be had all around the 10 miles of shoreline from good hiking trails, but the best water is often right in front of each of the four campgrounds on the south shore. Here, the water is some of the deepest in the lake and holds all species of fish, especially during the heat of summer. Four boat ramps on the south shore provide plenty of access to the entire lake. Some of the deepest trolling water is in 80 feet of water off the south shore from the dam to the northeastern corner of the lake. The center of the lake is popular trolling water, but it's not as deep as that along the south shore.

Fly anglers will be pleased to know that Timothy Lake is well known for producing prolific hatches of mayflies *(Callibaetis, Hexagenia)*, chironomids, damsels, and other assorted aquatic insects. The best dry-fly-fishing occurs mid-July–August when the *Hexagenia limbata* mayflies are hatching. *Hexagenia,* often called the "big yellow may," are a unique and unpredictable hatch occurring on only a handful of lakes and rivers in Oregon (Lost Lake, Laurance Lake, and Williamson River) and bring the biggest fish to the surface. They emerge dusk–dark, and they come off best when hot days are followed by warm evenings. There is no mistaking the size 6 adults as they sit scattered on the surface like small sailboats, waiting for their wings to dry before taking flight. Terrestrial fishing is also good in the summer, and anglers can fish patterns to represent ants, grasshoppers, beetles, and termites. Timothy has an abundance of crayfish and baitfish, and patterns in both these food forms will take the largest fish in the lake.

Spin anglers can use a variety of techniques such as trolling with flashers and spinners, casting and retrieving spinners and small Rapalas from the shore, or using bait such as worms, grubs, and eggs under a bobber or float. Spin anglers can also participate in the *Hexagenia* hatch by casting flies with a casting bobber or fishing bright yellow Rooster Tails retrieved quickly from the banks and along muddy shoals.

Species: Stocked legal-size and broodstock rainbow trout, brown, brook and cutthroat trout, kokanee.

Facilities: There are five Forest Service campgrounds at the lake: Gone Creek, Oak Fork, Pine Point, Hoodview, and Meditation Point. All but Meditation Point have drinking water, boat launching, firewood, and picnic tables; Pine Point also has a wheelchair-accessible fishing dock. Meditation Point, accessible by foot or boat only, has four sites with picnic tables and fire grills, but no drinking water. Supplies and accommodations can be had in Government Camp.

Directions: From Government Camp, drive 17 miles east to Forest Rd. 42. Turn right (west) on Rd. 42 and drive eight miles to Forest Rd. 57. Turn right (west) on Rd. 57. Mileages from there are Gone Creek in one mile, Oak Fork in two miles, Hoodview in three miles, and Pine Point in four miles. To reach Meditation Point, take a boat to the north shore of the lake, or continue on Rd. 57 for 0.5 mile past Pine Point Campground, cross the dam, and park in a lot at the far side of the dam. A trail leads 1.1 mile from there to the campsite.

Contact: Mount Hood Visitor Information Center, 503/622-4822; Mount Hood National Forest Zig Zag District, 503/622-3191; ODFW, Clackamas, 503/657-2000; The Fly-Fishing Shop in Welches, 800/266-3971; Fisherman's Marine and Outdoor, 503/557-3313; Estacada Tackle, 503/630-7424.

33 OAK GROVE FORK OF THE CLACKAMAS RIVER

south of Estacada

Map 3.2, page 182

This small but respectable trout fishery originates in the Mount Hood National Forest seven miles above Timothy Lake and flows 25 miles west to its confluence with the Clackamas River near Ripplebrook Guard Station. It is captured on its journey by two lakes, Timothy and Harriet, both good producers of trophy trout. Situated in a dense forest of Douglas fir, this river is sure to please the intrepid angler who loves to scramble over fallen trees and large boulders to reach trout-rich pocket water.

Anglers can catch wild rainbows in the lower river below Lake Harriet and rainbows, browns, and brook trout between Lake Harriet and Timothy Lake. Fish on average are small, 10–12 inches, but some bigger fish can be caught in the deeper holes. The brown trout are present as spawners from Lake Harriet and are more readily available in fall and spring. The entire river is limited to artificial flies and lures only, and a two-fish harvest limit, minimum eightinches, has been imposed. Fly anglers will do well on nymphs and attractor

dry flies such as an Adams or Royal Wulff. Spin anglers can cast use small Rooster Tails and bangbaits of various colors into pocket water and deeper holes.

The Oak Grove Fork is too small for boats, but bank access is great from several roads that follow the river from Ripplebrook Guard Station to Timothy Lake and above. Anglers can start at one of two places for the best fishing. From the Ripplebrook Guard Station, anglers can follow the river's lower five miles on good roads (Forest Rd. 4630 or Highway 57) east to Lake Harriet and pull off to the side of the road at any point to venture to the water. The outflow and inflow into Harriet Lake can be especially good in spring and fall when trout are in their spawning cycles. The second option is to start above Lake Harriet, driving east on Highway 57, which follows the river to Timothy Lake. Here, anglers can also scramble down to the river from the roadsides or hike up from the inflow at Lake Harriet to the outflow from Timothy Lake. There is about a mile of river access above Timothy Lake on Highway 57 that is also open to angling; brook trout are the dominant species.

Species: Rainbow, brown, and brook trout.

Facilities: Nearby camping is at Timothy Lake and Lake Harriet and also at Forest Service campgrounds at Rainbow and Ripplebrook, both of which are in the area around Ripplebrook Ranger Station. Each of these has tent sites but no drinking water. Supplies and other accommodations can be had in Estacada.

Directions: From Estacada, drive 27 miles southeast on Hwy. 224 to the ranger station at Ripplebrook. Here, the road becomes Forest Rd. 46. For Rainbow Campground, drive 100 yards to the campground on the right. Ripplebrook Campground is another 100 yards ahead on the left. To reach the river, stay straight ahead when Rd. 46 turns south; this will put you headed east on Forest Rd. 57, which parallels the Oak Grove Fork on the south bank for five miles to Lake Harriet. You can also get to the north bank here by taking Forest Rd. 4630 from Ripplebrook

Ranger Station; this road rejoins Rd. 57 one mile east of Harriet Lake. Following Forest Rd. 57 east seven miles from Harriett Lake will take you along the river up to Timothy Lake. To reach the water above Timothy Lake continue on Forest Rd. 57 from the west end of Timothy Lake, skirting the south shore for one mile. The river will appear to the east side of the highway. Highway 57 dead-ends at Clackamas Lake.

Contact: Estacada Chamber of Commerce, 503/630-3483; Mount Hood National Forest Clackamas District, 503/630-6861; ODFW, Clackamas, 503/657-2000; Estacada Ranger Station, 503/630-8700; Clackamas County Parks Department, 503/353-4414; Fisherman's Marine and Outdoor, 503/557-3313; Estacada Tackle, 503/630-7424.

34 LOWER DESCHUTES RIVER: LOCKED GATE TO MAUPIN

near Maupin

Map 3.2, page 182

The "Locked Gate," as it has come to be known, sits at the end of a six-mile access road that follows the river upstream from Maupin. This water is significant for a few reasons: ease of access, good steelhead runs and trout water, and relatively easy floats with take-outs above the more difficult rapids. If you're looking for a good half-day float or just want to learn how to run a drift boat, this is a hard place to beat. Runs are short enough that you can float a section in the morning and again in the evening.

The river is composed of long flat runs below rapids, perfect for resting summer steelhead, and good soft water for trout. Summers are hot, and white-water rafters dominate the river from Harpham Flats (3.5 miles downriver from the Locked Gate) to the take-out in Maupin. Regulations allow anglers to fish for steelhead and trout year-round with artificial flies and lures. As with the rest of the Deschutes, there is no fishing from a float-

ing device. Three official boat ramps and one unofficial boat ramp near the Locked Gate enable anglers to make concentrated drifts of 1–6 miles.

Rafters and drift boaters have a few options. Rope your boat or raft down the hillside at the Locked Gate; a good winch, a rope, and a strong friend will make this task easier. This gives an extra mile of water above the nearest official boat ramp (Nina Creek Campground) and puts you 3.5 miles above Harpham Flats, where most white-water rafters launch their boats. It also puts you in great steelhead water from the get-go; row to the opposite side of the river and upstream as far as you can and begin fishing the run on the west bank. At least 2–3 good runs can be fished in this section before reaching Nina Creek Campground. The second option is to launch at Nina Creek Campground and take out at Harpham Flats, Wapinitia Campground, or Maupin County Park in Maupin. Above Wapinitia, you will encounter Class I and II rapids; below Wapinitia, the river turns angry with Class III and IV rapids (Wapinitia and Boxcar). For this reason, inexperienced boaters are strongly recommended to take out at Wapinitia. Jet sleds are allowed on the river but have proved to be a controversial issue, and restrictions have been imposed on their use.

Bank angling is unlimited along the access road or by walking upstream from the Locked Gate. If you do walk past the Locked Gate pay attention to No Trespassing signs before jumping in the water. The other option is to stay in the water and walk upstream to desired areas.

Steelhead are in this part of the river late August–November. Fly anglers use single-hand casting rods or spey rods in sizes 7- and 8-weight with floating lines. The most effective method is to swing hairwing steelhead flies such as Green Butt Skunks or Purple Perils in the long seams between the slow and fast water. Drift and spin anglers can use a variety of techniques, including corkies and yarn, larger Rooster Tails, and spoons in silver, orange, and gold. Plugs are always effective when combined with a planer to keep the plug out in the current. Trout are present year-round in good numbers. Expect average catches around 12–16 inches, with bigger fish reaching 20 inches. Stone-fly hatches begin in late May; this 2–3-inch-long insect can inhabit every bush along the bank and bring the biggest trout to the surface. Other good hatches of mayflies (blue-wing olives, pale morning and evening duns) follow the salmon flies. Caddis makes up the bulk of the trout's diet midsummer–fall. Nymphs and streamers work well during no-hatch times.

Species: Wild redband trout, hatchery and wild steelhead.

Facilities: Boater passes are required all year for use on the Lower Deschutes River from Pelton Dam to the confluence with the Columbia River. Anyone using a watercraft or any other floating device for transport must have in his/her possession a boater pass. Passes are available from the boater pass website and from a number of vendors throughout Oregon, such as G.I. Joe's. Access may be restricted to a limited number of boaters on certain sections of the river during peak use periods, including group size limitations. Cost varies depending on time of year and duration. Contact the Prineville BLM for up-to-date information on the boater pass program.

Fee campgrounds are available along the Upper River Access Rd. and include Wapinitia, Harpham Flat, Long Bend, Devil's Canyon, and Nena Creek. A free day-use area is available at Nina Creek. All campgrounds are primitive and supply restrooms and garbage cans only. Boat ramps are available along the Upper River Access Rd. at Wapinitia, Harpham Flat, Devil's Canyon, and Nina Creek. Supplies, accommodations, fly shops, and hardware stores can be had in Maupin. River shuttles can be had for a fee from the Oasis Resort.

Directions: From the Hwy. 197 bridge at the south end of Maupin, drive one mile south on Hwy. 197, passing the Oasis Resort, to the Upper River Access Rd. Upper River Access Rd. is easy to miss because it looks like a driveway. If you round a big bend and start heading east up a long grade, you have gone too far. The access road begins where the bend starts. Drive south on Upper River Access Rd. The road dead-ends after eight miles at the Locked Gate. From the beginning of the Upper River Access Rd. you can drive to Wapinitia (four miles), Harpham Flat (4.5 miles), Long Bend (5.5 miles), Devil (six miles), and Nina Creek (7.2 miles).

Contact: Deschutes River Boater Pass Information, 866/588-7277, www.boaterpass.com; Maupin Chamber of Commerce, 541/395-2599; BLM, Prineville, 541/416-6700; ODFW, Bend, 541/388-6363; Oregon Parks and Recreation Department, 800/551-6949; National Forest Service, Bend, 541/383-4000; Barlow Ranger District, 541/467-5101; Maupin City Park, 541/395-2252; Deschutes Motel, 541/395-2626; Deschutes RV Park, 541/395-2204; Deer Brook RV Park, 541/328-6225; John Hazel and Company, Deschutes Angler, 541/395-2441, www.johnhazel.com; The Oasis Guide Service and Resort, 541/395-2611, www.deschutesriveroasis.com; Deschutes Canyon Fly Shop, 541/395-2565, www.flyfishingdeschutes.com; G.I. Joe's, Bend, 541/388-3770.

35 LOWER DESCHUTES RIVER: MACK'S CANYON TO COLUMBIA RIVER

near The Dalles

Map 3.3, page 183

This 25-mile stretch of river is rugged with no access points other than at the terminus ends, running through steep canyons and under high rimocks, some of which extend 2,000 feet or more from the river. The country is arid and covered with junipers, grasses, and sagebrush. The river itself contains stretches of flat water between sometimes long rapids rated from Class I to Class VI. Only highly experienced boaters should attempt to run this section of river in a drift boat, raft, or jet sled. Jet sleds are a frequent sight on this water, shuttling anglers from hole to hole at the wee hours of the morning or waning hours of the day to get to favorite steelhead spots.

Floating the river in a drift boat or raft is perhaps the most popular method (canoes are not recommended). Anglers launch a boat at Mack's Canyon (57 road miles from The Dalles) and make a 2–3-day drift to Heritage Landing boat ramp at the mouth. Any shorter amount of time on this drift would not allow enough time to fish. A second way is to bike or hike on the walking trails on either side of the river, which extend the entire section of river from Mack's Canyon Campground to the river mouth. A third and less practical approach is to use a jet sled. A jet sled is a shallow-bottom aluminum boat that uses a concealed prop housed in a jet shoe, enabling low draft and the mobility to run heavy shallow water. Jet sledding on the Deschutes has been a controversial issue, and restrictions have been imposed on their use. Contact the Parks and Recreation Department for the latest regulations.

Anglers will be treated to year-round fishing for sizable native redband trout, a superb run of summer steelhead, and a growing population of spring and fall chinook salmon. Steelhead begin to appear in this section of river beginning in July but can be caught through November on good years; average sizes range 6–8 pounds. Larger fish are present, so do not be surprised if you happen to hook a 15–18-pound fish. Trout average 12–16 inches but can go as big as 20 inches or more. Fishing is restricted to artificial flies and lures only—no bait. Only hatchery steelhead can be retained (two per day), and trout are limited to two fish per day with a minimum length of 10 inches and a maximum of 13 inches. All wild fish must be released unharmed. Spring and fall chinook are present, but as of the printing of the 2006 regulations angling was closed for the entire river. Fishing is prohibited from a floating device in the entire river, so anglers are forced to anchor and step out of the boat before fishing.

The Deschutes is most famous for its fly-fishing and is a veritable bug factory most of the summer. For trout, use nymphs, dry flies, and streamers. Five and 6-weight rods loaded with floating line are perfect. The most significant insect hatches for trout on this part of the river begin in mid-May with the salmon fly hatch. This large-bodied insect (2–3 inches in length) makes for legendary trout fishing when hatches are thick, covering every bush along the river's edge. Stimulators and Macsalmons in orange are perfect patterns for matching the hatch. Successive hatches include golden stone flies, blue-wing olives, pale morning and evening duns, green drakes, and caddis. Caddis are probably the most significant hatch next to the salmon fly hatch and make up a majority of the fishes' diet by midsummer into fall. Patterns that represent the nymphs of any of these insects work well during nonhatch times. Favored nymphs tend to be black Kaufmann Stones and Pheasant Tails. More advanced fly anglers can use emergers and wet flies to great advantage.

Steelhead fishing does not rely on insects to bring fish to the surface. Use a floating fly line on a 7- or 8-weight rod and deliver your choice of one of hundreds of streamer or spey patterns downstream on a tight line swing. Standard steelhead patterns for the Deschutes are general hairwing flies, and their developers include a who's who of great Northwest anglers. Other approaches to catching steelhead on the Deschutes include the skated dry flies and nymphs. Fishing nymphs for steelhead often requires an indicator because of light takes. Spin anglers are not left out of the loop and find great success for both trout and steelhead. Steelhead take most readily to plugs (Wiggle Worts, Flatfish, or Hot Shots) and larger spoons such as a Stee-Lee or BC Steel. A planer will help you deliver a plug into good holes from the bank. Drift fishing is popular with corkies, Spin-N-Glows, Winged Cheaters, and yarn. Trout are taken on small spinners such as Rooster Tails and Rainbow Spinners.

Species: Wild redband trout, summer steelhead, chinook salmon.

Facilities: Boater passes are required all year for use on the Lower Deschutes River from Pelton Dam to the confluence with the Columbia River. Anyone using a watercraft or any other floating device for transport must have in his/her possession a boater pass. Passes are available from the boater pass website and from a number of vendors throughout Oregon, such as G.I. Joe's. Access may be restricted to a limited number of boaters on certain sections of the river during peak use periods; group size limitations apply. Cost varies depending on time of year and duration. Contact the Prineville BLM for up-to-date information on the boater pass program.

Deschutes River State Recreation Area has tent and hookup sites and a biker/hiker trail that parallels the river. Get to the hiking trail from the south end of the parking lot and anglers can walk upriver 23 miles into the Mack's Canyon Campground. Across the river is Heritage Landing, a free boat ramp. On this side, a hiker trail extends two miles upstream, and beyond that, anglers can walk (with caution) on the railroad grade. Camping is allowed anywhere you can pitch a tent on the hiking trails upstream from the Deschutes River State Recreation Area or Heritage Landing.

All official campgrounds on the Deschutes are fee camping and operated by the BLM. Beavertail, Mack's Canyon, and Maupin County Park are the only areas to supply drinking water. Primitive camping, outhouses, drinking water, and a boat launch is available at Mack's Canyon Campground. Other fee campgrounds can be had along Mack's Canyon Rd. at Rattlesnake Canyon, Beavertail, Jones, Twin Spring, and Pin Tree. If you want to start your drift above Mack's Canyon Campground, boat ramps are available at Pine Tree, Twin Springs, and Beavertail campgrounds. Supplies and accommodations can be had in The Dalles, Maupin, or Biggs Junction.

Directions: To reach the Deschutes River mouth, from The Dalles travel east on I-84 for 11 miles and take Exit 97. Travel east on Hwy. 206, driving 2.6 miles to reach Heritage Landing, and turn south onto Moody Rd., just before Hwy. 206 crosses the Deschutes. The Deschutes River State Recreation Area is across the bridge on Hwy. 206, 0.4 mile past Moody Rd. Turn right into the campground entrance. The hiking trail is in the parking lot at the south end of the campground. To reach Mack's Canyon Campground, from The Dalles drive east on I-84 for 1.5 miles to Exit 87. Turn south on Hwy. 197 and drive 31 miles to the Hwy. 216 junction (Shears Bridge Hwy.). Turn east on Hwy. 216 and drive eight miles to the Deschutes River bridge. Continue driving east on Hwy. 216, crossing the bridge, and drive for one mile to Mack's Canyon Rd., a gravel road. Drive north on Mack's Canyon Rd. 18 miles to where the road dead-ends at Mack's Canyon Campground. You will see a parking area and boat ramp as you enter the campground.

Contact: Deschutes River Boater Pass Information, 866/588-7277, www.boaterpass.com; The Dalles Chamber of Commerce, 541/296-2231; Maupin Chamber of Commerce, 541/395-2599; Columbia River Gorge National Scenic Area, 541/308-1700; Oregon Parks and Recreation Department, 800/551-6949; Deschutes River State Recreation Area, 541/739-2322; ODFW, The Dalles, 541/296-4628; ODFW, Bend, 541/388-6363; BLM, Prineville, 541/416-6700; National Forest Service, Bend, 541/383-4000; Barlow Ranger District, 541/467-5101; John Hazel and Company, Deschutes Angler, 541/395-2441, www.johnhazel.com; The Oasis Guide Service and Resort, 541/395-2611, www.deschutesriveroasis.com; Deschutes Canyon Fly Shop, 541/395-2565, www.flyfishingdeschutes.com; G.I. Joe's, Bend, 541/388-3770.

36 ELK LAKE
northeast of Detroit
Map 3.4, page 184

A small 60-acre lake situated in the mountains above Detroit Reservoir, Elk Lake is surrounded by nice forests and has a good campground. It's good for decent catches of stocked rainbows and kokanee and bank access is easy, but float tubes and small boats will make the job easier. Trout average 7–10 inches with some bigger fish present. Flies, lures, and bait all work and are permissible. The lake is open year-round, but snow will block passage until July. The road to the lake should be attempted only with four-wheel drives. The best times to fish Elk Lake are during July and again in fall.

Species: Stocked rainbow trout, kokanee.

Facilities: There is a large campground at the lake with no facilities other than restrooms and picnic tables. Hiking trails reach out from the lake and will take you to other area lakes, such as Twin Lakes, Pansy, and Welcome lakes.

Directions: From Detroit, drive northeast on Hwy. 46 (Breitenbush Rd.), which can be caught from the north end of town just before crossing the Detroit Lake Bridge. Drive northeast on Hwy. 46 for 4.5 miles to Forest Rd. 4697. Turn north on Rd. 4697 and drive 7.5 miles up a steep windy grade to reach the lake. You will pass Dunlop Lake to the east in approximately five miles. Once Elk Lake is in sight, follow Forest Rd. 4697 to the west end to reach the campground.

Contact: BLM, Salem, 503/375-5643; ODFW, Corvallis, 503/757-4186; Willamette National Forest, 503/854-3366; Detroit Ranger Station, 503/854-3366; Oregon State Parks and Recreation Department, 800/551-6949; Detroit Lake Marina, 503/854-3423; Detroit Lake State Park, 800/551-6949; Mongold Day Use Area, 800/551-6949; Detroit Lake RV Park, 503/364-7337; Hoover Campground, 503/854-3366; All Seasons Motel, 503/854-3421; Breitenbush Hot Springs, 503/854-3320; P&A Lake Detroit Market, 503/854-3433.

37 BREITENBUSH RIVER
east of Detroit
Map 3.4, page 184

Breitenbush River originates from two forks, North and South, and flows 15 miles west out of the Cascade Range to its confluence at the eastern end of Detroit Lake. It is crossed at the mouth by Highway 22 at the eastern edge of Detroit. The river runs through forests and canyons for most of its run, creating nice scenery and solitude. Anglers can expect a small river composed of pools, runs, and pocket water and fair to good fishing for slightly larger trout. Both stocked and wild trout are present and can be harvested for up to five fish per day. Trout average 12–16 inches, and a few catches up to 18 inches are possible. The main river below the forks offers better fishing for larger fish. The forks are also good, but more for exploratory reasons than quality fishing. Some brook trout are present in the upper headwaters.

The main river and forks are followed by Highway 46 and Forest Rd. 4685 from Detroit, making river access easy. Hiking through the forest from the highway leads to secluded spots rarely fished by any other anglers. The fish here are not picky. You can fish any of this water with your favorite nymphs, attractor dry flies, spinners, or bait. The river is open April 23–October 31 and has no restrictions on fishing methods, including bait.

Good bank access points can be had from four campgrounds that line the river from the reservoir to the headwaters. In good water years, boating is available in the Detroit Reservoir Breitenbush Arm upriver for approximately one mile. Beyond this point the river is accessible only on foot and by the roads.

Species: Stocked and wild rainbow trout, brook trout.

Facilities: Three primitive fee campgrounds can be had along the river at Humbug (year-round), and at Cleator Bend and Breitenbush (May–Sept.). Restrooms and picnic tables are provided. Supplies and accommodations can be had in Detroit. Anglers wishing to boat the lower river can do so from Lakeshore State Park or Detroit Lake Marina. Accommodations can be had at Breitenbush Hot Springs, but reservations should be made well in advance.

Directions: From Detroit drive northeast on Hwy. 46 (Breitenbush Rd.), which can be caught from the north end of town just before crossing the Detroit Lake Bridge. Drive northeast on Hwy. 46, which follows the river for six miles to just below the river forks. Along this road you will pass campgrounds Humbug (two miles), Cleator Bend (four miles), and Breitenbush (4.5 miles). To reach the North Fork, travel east on Hwy. 46 for one mile before passing the joining of the forks at the junction with Forest Rd. 4685. Another three miles of river are available on the south side of Hwy. 46 before it departs from the river to the north. To fish the South Fork, drive one mile east of Breitenbush Campground on Hwy. 46 and turn south on Forest Rd. 4685. This road follows the river south for approximately three miles before starting a steep ascent to Crown Lake.

Contact: BLM, Salem, 503/375-5643; ODFW, Corvallis, 503/757-4186; Willamette National Forest, 503/854-3366; Detroit Ranger Station, 503/854-3366; Oregon State Parks and Recreation Department, 800/551-6949; Detroit Lake Marina, 503/854-3423; Detroit Lake State Park, 800/551-6949; Mongold Day Use Area, 800/551-6949; Detroit Lake RV Park, 503/364-7337; Hoover Campground, 503/854-3366; All Seasons Motel, 503/854-3421; Breitenbush Hot Springs, 503/854-3320; P&A Lake Detroit Market, 503/854-3433.

38 DETROIT LAKE

east of Salem in Willamette National Forest

Map 3.4, page 184

Detroit Lake is a large, scenic reservoir popular for a variety of recreation, including Jet Skis, water-skiing, and pleasure boating. Consisting of 3,000 surface acres when full, it is subject

to extreme drawdowns, making boating access impossible in some years. There are 33 miles of shoreline, all densely forested with Douglas fir trees and surrounded by high rolling foothills.

Detroit Reservoir is stocked annually and throughout the year with more than 100,000 legal-size rainbow trout (8–10 inches). With the proliferation of resident trout, average catches range 12–16 inches, and bigger fish are available up to 20 inches or more. There are annual spring stockings of kokanee, chinook fingerlings, and a few adult chinook salmon 7–10 pounds. Fishing is open all year, but trout bigger than 24 inches must be released unharmed August 16–October 31. All methods of fishing can be used, including bait.

Good catches can be made from the bank, but you'll need a boat to catch the bigger fish. Spin fishing and bait fishing with worms and eggs are most popular from numerous roadside pullouts along the north shore, or at Lakeshore State Park and Mongold Day Use Area. Bank anglers wishing for a little more solitude can find good access on the south shore at Cove Springs and Southshore campgrounds. During low-water years, anglers can walk out on the uncovered shoals to fish deeper water. The most popular launch spot is at Lakeshore State Park; it gives instant access to Piety Island and the inlets of Breitenbush and the North Santiam Rivers, all good producers of trout. Mongold Day Use Area is a better launch point to fish the deep water of Blowout and Kinney arms, both good producers of trout, chinook, and kokanee. Kokanee and chinook salmon lie 80–100 feet deep during summer, and 20–50 feet deep during spring and fall. The main methods for catching salmon are trolling rigs such as plugs or flashers. Contact the Detroit Ranger Station and ask about water levels before launching.

Species: Trout, kokanee, landlocked chinook, brown bullhead catfish.

Facilities: A full-service campground with RV sites is available on the north shore at Lakeshore State Park. South shore campgrounds include

Southshore and Cove Creek. Boat ramps can be had at each of these campgrounds, as well as at Mongold Day Use Area ($3 day-use fee) and Detroit Marina. Supplies and other accommodations can be had in Detroit.

Directions: From Salem, take Hwy. 22 east and drive 43 miles, passing through Stayton and Lyons to Detroit Dam. From the dam, drive east on Hwy. 22 for five miles, following the north shore and passing Mongold Day Use Area (two miles) and Lakeshore State Park (3.5 miles) to reach Detroit. To reach the south shore from Detroit, drive southeast on Hwy. 22 for three miles to Hwy. 10 (Idanha Rd.). Turn south on Hwy. 10 and drive three miles to reach Cove Creek Campground or four miles to reach Southshore Campground.

Contact: BLM Salem, 503/375-5643; ODFW, Corvallis, 503/757-4186; Willamette National Forest, 503/854-3366; Detroit Ranger Station, 503/854-3366; Oregon State Parks and Recreation Department, 800/551-6949; Detroit Lake Marina, 503/854-3423; Detroit Lake State Park, 800/551-6949; Mongold Day Use Area, 800/551-6949; Detroit Lake RV Park, 503/364-7337; Hoover Campground, 503/854-3366; All Seasons Motel, 503/854-3421; Breitenbush Hot Springs, 503/854-3320; P&A Lake Detroit Market, 503/854-3433.

39 UPPER NORTH SANTIAM RIVER

near Detroit in Willamette National Forest

Map 3.4, page 184

The upper North Santiam is probably familiar to most anglers who have driven over to Bend from Salem. It's a classic-looking trout stream, with brush-lined banks, towering Douglas fir trees, long riffles, and deep pools. The upper river runs approximately 30 miles from its source in the Eight Lakes Basin in the Mount Jefferson Wilderness to Detroit Reservoir.

The upper North Santiam River has a mix of hatchery and wild trout, both of which can be harvested at five fish per day. Stock-ing programs are superb, with nearly 50,000 legal-size trout (8–10 inches) and 7,000 larger trout (more than 12 inches) introduced into the river April–August. Holdovers from previous years can reach 16 inches-plus. All methods of fishing are permitted, including bait. The river opens on April 23 and closes October 31.

This is not a boating river, but bank access is excellent for nearly 16 miles along Highway 22 from Hoover Campground at the east end of the reservoir past Detroit to the highway bridge crossing at Forest Rd. 2267. Above the bridge crossing, the headwaters are accessible to the east from Forest Service roads and hiking trails into the Mount Jefferson Wilderness. Good places to start are at any of the four campgrounds on Highway 22 and along Highway 22 at roadside turnouts. Marion Forks Campground, just above the fish hatchery halfway between the reservoir and the bridge crossing, is perhaps the best place to begin. The headwaters are less productive, holding smaller brook trout.

Anglers can expect shallow runs, deep holes, and plenty of pocket water behind rocks and logs. Light but stout tackle in the form of 5-weight rods is best and will allow you to make longer casts. Waders are recommended if you're going to get into the water. Fly anglers can use attractor dry-fly patterns such as Royal Wulffs and Humpies during the summer when hatches of insects are present. Nymphs and streamers also work when fishing in the deeper runs and pocket water. Spin anglers can use Rooster Tails and bangbaits in the same locations. Bait such as worms and eggs will be productive anywhere, but especially in the deeper pools.

Species: Rainbow and brook trout.

Facilities: Fee camping is available along Hwy. 22 above Detroit at Hoover, Whispering Falls, Riverside, and Marion Forks campgrounds. Camping in the headwaters is limited to backpacker sites from Trail No. 3427 in the Mount Jefferson Wilderness. Supplies and accommodations can be had in Detroit. Other accommodations can be had at Breitenbush Hot Springs, but reservations should be made well in advance of your expected trip.

Directions: From Detroit, drive southeast on Hwy. 22, which follows the river for 16 miles to Forest Rd. 2267; campgrounds and roadside pullouts are available along this highway from Detroit at Hoover (two miles), Whispering Falls (six miles), Riverside (six miles), and Marian Forks (seven miles). To reach the headwaters, drive east on Hwy. 22 16 miles to Forest Rd. 2267, signed for Big Meadows Horse Camp. Turn east on Rd. 2267 and drive three miles to the dead-end at the trailhead for Trail No. 3427. This trail will take you into the Mount Jefferson Wilderness and the headwaters of the Santiam River.

Contact: BLM, Salem, 503/375-5643; ODFW, Corvallis, 503/757-4186; Willamette National Forest, 503/854-3366; Detroit Ranger Station, 503/854-3366; Oregon State Parks and Recreation Department, 800/551-6949; North Santiam State Park, 800/551-6949; Hoover Campground, 503/854-3366; Breitenbush Hot Springs, 503/854-3320; All Seasons Motel, 503/854-3421; P&A Lake Detroit Market, 503/854-3433.

⑳ OLALLIE LAKE
east of Government Camp in Mount Jefferson Wilderness

Map 3.5, page 185

Olallie is a popular, 200-acre lake situated among ponderosa pine forests on the border of the Mount Hood and Willamette national forests. Good campgrounds and a full-service resort make this a great place for families to come and spend a weekend teaching their kids to fish. Serious anglers will appreciate the opportunities to catch larger brood-stock trout that are introduced into the lake every year by the ODFW. Olallie Lake is stocked annually April–July with 14,000 legal-size rainbow trout 8–10 inches and 500 trophy fish 16 inches or bigger. Combine these fish with winter holdovers, and in 2–3 years an-

glers have the opportunity to catch 30-inch trout. Some brook trout are present, but not in fishable numbers. Fishing is open all year, but snows can block access to the lake November–May. All methods of fishing are permitted, including bait.

The most successful fishing is done by trolling spinners or flashers from a boat or float tube; motors are of any kind are prohibited. The deepest water is at the lake's north end by the resort and at the south end near Peninsula Campground, and both areas provide good trolling water for bigger fish. The rest of the lake is fairly shallow, 10–20 feet, and provides good bank fishing and float-tube water from just about anywhere from a good hiking trail that goes three miles around the lake. Campgrounds are always a good place to start, and there are four scattered about the lake, plus one resort that rents boats. Bait such as worms or eggs work well when cast from the bank and fished under a bobber. Fly anglers can use nymphs and streamers such as Woolly Buggers trolled or stripped on clear sinking line. Keep an eye out for insect hatches along the banks during the morning and evenings and use a small Adams, Griffith Gnat, or other attractor pattern.

Species: Stocked legal and brood-stock trout, brook trout.

Facilities: Camping is available at four rustic campgrounds, two on the south shore (Tent Camp and Peninsula) and two on the north shore (Paul Dennis and Olallie Lake) which provide restrooms and picnic tables but no drinking water. Supplies can be had in Government Camp. Olallie Lake Resort has a small general store and rents cabins, yurts, and boats.

Directions: From Government Camp drive nine miles east on Hwy. 26 to Hwy. 42, which is two miles south of the Clear Lake turnoff. Turn east on Hwy. 42 and drive 26 miles to Forest Rd. 4220, signed for Olallie Lake. Turn south on Rd. 4220 and follow it another 25 miles to Olallie Lake. There is a fork at the lake entrance. Turning southwest will take you to the southern end of the lake and several campgrounds (Tent Camp and Peninsula) in 1.5 miles. Turning to the southeast will take you past the resort to two other campgrounds (Paul Dennis and Olallie Lake) in less than a mile.

Contact: BLM, Salem, 503/375-5643; ODFW, South Willamette, 503/757-4186; Willamette National Forest, 503/854-3366; Oregon State Parks and Recreation Department, 800/551-6949; Olallie Lake Resort, 541/504-1010.

41 LOWER DESCHUTES RIVER: TROUT CREEK TO LOCKED GATE

in Madras

Map 3.5, page 185

Great steelhead and trout fishing, scenic remote canyons, sandy beach campgrounds, and dangerous white water can all be found on this 30-mile section of river. Bank fishing is limited to a few choice spots, making this primarily a boating section. Trout Creek forms the uppermost part of this section. The next take-out is 30 miles downstream at the Locked Gate or near Maupin. Most floats through this section require 2–3 days and should be considered minor expeditions because of remoteness (there is no place to walk to for help). Whitehorse Rapids is the most formidable section, a three-mile Class IV rapid that eats boats for lunch. The entry into this rapid is the most dangerous on the river, a telling fact concealed in aptly named "Oh Shit! Rock!" Bank anglers are restricted to a few limited access points: Trout Creek Campground, South Junction, and on roads from the Locked Gate upstream. Fishing is good at Trout Creek, but private property prevents downstream access. South Junction provides some of the best bank access in this part of the river. There's a good campground, and 1.5 miles of river offer a generous amount of steelhead and trout water. From the Locked Gate, anglers can walk upstream on a good road, but private property dominates. Stay in the water, and you should be fine.

Steelhead and trout fishing is excellent through this entire section of river. Steelhead are in the river late August–November. Fishing techniques for fly anglers include heavy 7- and 8-weight rods rigged with floating line. Streamers such as Green Butt Skunks, Purple Perils, and Freight Trains are cast down and across current seams. Nymphs and skated dry flies also work. Spin anglers use spoons, spinners, and drift rig setups with corkies and yarn. Trout fishing highlights start with the salmon-fly hatch in late May or early June. Use Stimulators and Macsalmons to match the salmon-fly hatch. Other hatches of mayflies (blue-wing olives, pale morning and evening duns), golden stone flies, and caddis make up the rest of the summer hatches. Spin anglers can use Rooster Tails and Bangtails cast into riffles and pockets.

Note: The entire west bank is property of the Confederated Tribes of Warm Springs, and fishing is restricted from the bank out to the middle of the river. Steelhead fishing is open all year, but trout fishing is open only April 23–October 31. Both of these restrictions change to year-round fishing and unlimited bank access at the Warm Springs Reservation Boundary near the powerboat deadline (indicated by a white sign) 10 miles upriver from the Locked Gate (river mile 69). Angling from a floating device is never allowed on the Deschutes. The river is open to artificial flies and lures only.

Species: Wild redband trout, native and hatchery steelhead.

Facilities: Boater passes are required year-round on the Lower Deschutes River from Pelton Dam to the confluence with the Columbia River. Anyone using a watercraft or any other floating device for transport must carry a boater pass. Passes are available from the boater pass website and from a number of vendors throughout Oregon such as G.I. Joe's. Access may be restricted to a limited number of boaters on certain sections of the river during peak use periods, and group-size limitations may apply. Cost varies depending on time of year and duration. Contact the Prineville BLM for up-to-date information on the boater pass program.

Camping is available at Trout Creek; restrooms and garbage collection are available. Boaters have unlimited camping access on the east bank of the river below Trout Creek to the Warm Springs Reservation Boundary. Both the east and west banks are open for camping from the Warm Springs Reservation Boundary (at the powerboat deadline) to the Locked Gate and below to Maupin. The South Junction campground provides drive-in access to the river, restrooms, and garbage collection. Trout Creek has the only boat launch, which commits boaters to a 30-mile stretch of river to the take-out below the Locked Gate near Maupin. Supplies and accommodations can be had in Madras, Warm Springs, or Maupin. River shuttles can be had for a fee from the Oasis Resort.

Directions: From Madras, start at the north end of town at the junction of Hwys. 26 and 97. Turn northeast on Hwy. 97 and drive three miles to Clark Drive. Turn north on Clark Dr. and drive nine miles, passing through Gateway. Continue driving west on Clark Dr. through Gateway and turn right on the Trout Creek Access Rd. (following the signs to the Deschutes River and Trout Creek BLM) after passing the railroad tracks. This rough road will lead you to Trout Creek Campground in 4.5 miles.

For South Junction, from Madras drive northeast on Hwy. 97 for 30 miles to the Hwy. 197 junction. Turn north on Hwy. 197 and drive 0.25 mile to the signed South Junction Access Rd. Turn west on South Junction Access Rd. and drive 10 miles on a winding gravel road down a steep canyon to the bottom of the hill. Turn north at the fork in the road to reach the campground in 0.5 mile. Driving one mile down this road will take you to several remote campsites away from the main camping area. It's about a 0.25-mile hike to the river downhill and across the railroad tracks.

For Maupin and the Locked Gate, from Madras drive northeast on Hwy. 97 for 30 miles to Hwy. 197 and turn north on Hwy. 197. Follow 197 another 20 miles to Maupin. Just before you reach Maupin you will come down a steep grade and drive through a hairpin turn as the river comes into view; Upper River Access Rd. will be to the south (a hard left) at the bottom of the hill. Turn south on Upper River Access Rd. Upper River Access Rd. dead-ends eight miles later at the Locked Gate. Along this road you will pass numerous campgrounds and boat take-outs. From the beginning of the Upper River Access Rd. you will pass Wapinitia (four miles), Harpham Flat (4.5 miles), Long Bend (5.5 miles), Devil (six miles), Nina (7.2 miles), and finally reach the Locked Gate (eight miles).

Contact: Deschutes River Boater Pass Information, 866/588-7277, www.boaterpass.com; Maupin Chamber of Commerce, 541/395-2599; BLM, Prineville, 541/416-6700; ODFW, Bend, 541/388-6363; Oregon Parks and Recreation Department, 800/551-6949; National Forest Service, Bend, 541/383-4000; Barlow Ranger District, 541/467-5101; Confederated Tribes of Warm Springs, 541/553-1161; Department of Natural Resources, Warm Springs, 541/553-3548; Deschutes Motel, 541/395-2626; Deschutes RV Park, 541/395-2204; Deer Brook RV Park, 541/328-6225; John Hazel and Company, Deschutes Angler, 541/395-2441, www.johnhazel.com; The Oasis Guide Service and Resort, 541/395-2611, www.deschutesriveroasis.com; Deschutes Canyon Fly Shop, 541/395-2565, www.flyfishingdeschutes.com; G.I. Joe's, Bend, 541/388-3770.

42 LOWER DESCHUTES RIVER: PELTON DAM TO TROUT CREEK

near Warm Springs

Map 3.5, page 185   BEST (

This 13-mile stretch of river is some of the most popular and congested trout-fishing water on the Deschutes. All of this water is a nice, easy float with few hazards. Hikers have good bank access to great holding water for both trout and steelhead. The river here flows through agricultural lands and is bordered by Warm Springs Indian Reservation on the west bank. Both bank and boat anglers can expect good pocket water, islands, long steelhead drifts, and streamside vegetation providing good holding water for big trout. Steelhead fishing is open all year, but trout fishing is restricted to April 23–October 31. Fishing from a boat is prohibited, and tackle is restricted to artificial flies and lures only. Fishing here is restricted to the east bank out to the middle of the river, where tribal restrictions take effect. Anglers wishing to fish along Warm Springs Reservation property or the western side of the river's center can do so in a six-mile zone from Dry Creek to Trout Creek, but only after buying a tribal fishing permit. Tribal areas are marked with good signs.

Boaters have the advantage on this river, but bank anglers do equally well because of good access. The best bank access can be found at Mecca Flat and Trout Creek. A good 7.5-mile hiking trail connects these two points and is accessible from either end. There is no access below Trout Creek because of private property. Other access points can be found at Dry Creek on the reservation side (tribal permits required) and upstream from the boat launch at Warm Springs Access. Dry Creek is accessible via roads that take you through the scenic Warm Springs Reservation. Access to the water above Warm Springs Access is limited to one mile of river on the east bank before running into private property. This water is relatively underfished; most anglers are getting downstream from the boat ramp. Anglers can either hike upstream from the boat ramp or use several pullouts along Highway 97 south of the boat ramp.

Drift boats and rafts can be launched from the ramp at Warm Springs Access for a good one-day float to the take-out at Trout Creek. Caution: The access road into Trout Creek is notoriously rough and muddy with deep ruts; four-wheel drives are necessary. This stretch of river is especially popular for fishing around the islands that run down the center of the river. Boats can be anchored at the top or bottom of these islands while the angler casts a fly or lure from the bank out into the adjacent current. Pay particular attention to the ends of these islands, where several currents come together to create good holding water for trout and steelhead. When fishing the islands stay to the east side unless you have a tribal permit and are within the permitted zone as indicated by signs.

The highlight of the trout season occurs during the salmon-fly hatch in late May and early June. There are big, clumsy insects (2–3 inches long) that drop into the water from tree branches and streamside vegetation, and into the mouths of willing trout. Patterns such as Stimulators and Macsalmons are perfect for matching the hatch. The salmon-fly hatch is followed by other mayfly hatches (blue-winged olives, pale morning and evening duns) and caddis. Caddis is the primary food source for trout midsummer–fall. During non-hatch times anglers can use nymphs such as Kaufmann Stones, Hare's Ears, and Pheasant Tails fished under a strike indicator. Wet flies and streamers such as Soft Hackles, Woolly Buggers, and Zonkers work well when cast down and across. Most anglers find 5-weight rods and floating line to be adequate for most presentations.

Steelhead are in the river August–November, with September being the most productive month. Slightly bigger tackle is required in the form of single-hand or spey rods in 7- and 8-weights. Floating line is standard for all approaches, including streamers and nymphs. Streamers such as Green Butt Skunks, Purple Perils, and Coal Cars are popular patterns most of the year. Nymph fishing is becoming more popular for summer steelhead, as is skated dry flies. Spin and drift anglers can catch both species on a variety of spinners, spoons, and corky and yarn rigs. Larger spinners in purple, orange, gold, and silver are good for steelhead. For trout use smaller Rooster Tails and bangbaits cast into the seams and pocket water.

Species: Wild redband trout, wild and hatchery steelhead.

Facilities: You can buy tribal fishing permits on the reservation at the Department of Natural Resources or Warm Springs Market, and off the reservation at the Rainbow Market, at the crossing of the Deschutes and Hwy. 97 south of Warm Springs. You can also buy permits at G.I. Joe's stores around the state and in Bend.

Boater passes are required all year for use on the Lower Deschutes River from Pelton Dam to the confluence with the Columbia River. Anyone using a watercraft or any other floating device for transport must have in his/her possession a boater pass. Passes are available from the boater pass website and from a number of vendors throughout Oregon such as G.I. Joe's. Access may be restricted to a limited number of boaters on certain sections of the river during peak use periods, and group-size limitations may apply. Cost varies depending on time of year and duration. Contact the Prineville BLM for up-to-date information on the boater pass program.

Fee camping is available at Mecca Flat, Trout Creek, and Dry Creek. Camping at Dry Creek requires a tribal fishing permit. None of these campgrounds has facilities other than restrooms and garbage collection. There is a good 7.5-mile hiking trail between Mecca Flat and Trout Creek. The only boat ramp in this reach is available at Warm Springs Access at the Hwy. 26 river crossing south of Warm Springs on the west side of the highway. The take-out is 10 miles downriver at Trout Creek, beyond which the boater is committed to a 30-mile float to Maupin. Supplies and accommodations are available in Warm Springs or Madras. River shuttles can be had for a fee from the Oasis Resort.

Directions: From Warm Springs drive south on Hwy. 26 to the Deschutes River crossing.

Crossing this bridge takes you off the reservation. The boat launch access road is a few hundred yards to the west of the highway. Driving another couple of hundred yards down the access road will take you into a parking lot next to the boat ramp.

For Mecca Flat Campground, from the Warm Springs Access boat ramp drive straight across Hwy. 26 to an unnamed dirt road on the southeast side of the highway bridge. The access road lies between the Rainbow Market and a trailer park. Follow this road straight for two miles to the parking lot at Mecca Flat. The hiking trail and campground are to the north. From here, you can walk or use mountain bikes for access to the river for 7.5 miles to Trout Creek.

For Dry Creek Campground, from Warm Springs drive two miles north on Hwy. 26 from the Deschutes crossing to Agency–Simnasho Rd. (signed for Kah-Nee-Ta Resort). Drive three miles on Agency–Simnasho Rd. to an unnamed dirt road signed for Dry Creek. Turn east on this road and drive two miles to the campground and parking lot. Anglers may fish only in front of the campground and downstream six miles to the area opposite Trout Creek. The area is well marked with boundary signs; if in doubt, err on the side of not fishing.

For Trout Creek, from Warm Springs drive south on Hwy. 26 for 14 miles to the Hwy. 97 junction in Madras. Turn northeast on Hwy. 97 and drive three miles to Clark Drive. Turn north on Clark Dr. and drive nine miles, passing through Gateway. Continue driving west on Clark Dr. through Gateway and turn right on the Trout Creek Access Rd. (following the signs to the Deschutes River and Trout Creek BLM) after passing the railroad tracks. This rough road will lead you to Trout Creek Campground in 4.5 miles.

Contact: Deschutes River Boater Pass Information, 866/588-7277, www.boaterpass.com; Maupin Chamber of Commerce, 541/395-2599; BLM, Prineville, 541/416-6700; ODFW, Bend, 541/388-6363; Oregon Parks and Recreation Department, 800/551-6949; National Forest Service, Bend, 541/383-4000; Barlow Ranger District, 541/467-5101; Confederated Tribes of Warm Springs, 541/553-1161; Department of Natural Resources, Warm Springs, 541/553-3548; Warm Springs Market, 541/553-1597; Rainbow Market, 541/553-1176; Kah-Nee-Ta Vacation Resort, 800/831-0100; Maupin City Park, 541/395-2252; Deschutes Motel, 541/395-2626; John Hazel and Company, Deschutes Angler, 541/395-2441, www.johnhazel.com; The Oasis Guide Service and Resort, 541/395-2611, www.deschutesriveroasis.com; Deschutes Canyon Fly Shop, 541/395-2565, www.flyfishingdeschutes.com; G.I. Joe's, Bend, 541/388-3770.

43 PAMELIA LAKE

near Detroit in Mount Jefferson Wilderness

Map 3.5, page 185

Pamelia is a 50-acre hike-in lake surrounded by nice fir forests in an alpine setting. Splendid views of Mount Jefferson can be had from many points around the lake. Scenic beauty aside, Pamelia may hold little appeal to serious anglers. Both rainbows and brook trout are abundant, but small. Trout average 7–10 inches with very few bigger fish. Nevertheless, you will catch lots of fish, and there is no limit on brook trout. The lake is open all year, and all fishing methods are permitted, including bait. Bank access is good around the whole lake, and good catches can be made by casting spinners, eggs, worms, or small streamer flies. A float tube may help increase the action, giving anglers access to the deeper, middle section of the lake and brushy shorelines. Consider taking light tackle to increase the sportiness of these fish. Ultralight spinning rods and fly rods in 2- and 3-weights are ideal.

Species: Wild rainbow and brook trout.

Facilities: Natural campsites are available at the lake and the trailhead. Anglers are encouraged to practice no-trace camping when staying at the lake. Supplies and other accommodations are available in Detroit.

Directions: From Detroit drive 14 miles east on Hwy. 22, passing through Idanha, to Pamelia Rd. (Forest Rd. 2246). Turn east on Pamelia Rd. and drive approximately six miles to where the road dead-ends at the trailhead for Trail No. 3439. Hike east on this trail for two miles to reach the lake.

Contact: BLM, Salem, 503/375-5643; ODFW, South Willamette, 503/757-4186; Willamette National Forest, 541/225-6300; Detroit Ranger District, 503/854-3366; Oregon State Parks and Recreation Department, 800/551-6949; All Seasons Motel, 503/854-3421; Breitenbush Hot Springs, 503/854-3320; P&A Lake Detroit Market, 503/854-3433.

44 MARION LAKE

near Detroit in Mount Jefferson Wilderness

Map 3.5, page 185

Marion is a large, hike-in alpine lake surrounded by fir forests, large rock scree slides, and wonderful views of volcanic Three-Fingered Jack and Mount Jefferson. The lake is 261 surface acres, averages 64 feet deep, and is 180 feet at its deepest point near the northeast shore. There are 3.5 miles of shoreline, much of which is accessible by scrambling over rock slides and through brush. Float tubes can be a real asset here, the only issue being packing them to the lake. All methods of fishing are permitted, including bait. The lake is open all year, but snow will hinder access November–first part of July. This is a backpacker's lake, and although day trips are certainly possible, overnight trips provide a fuller experience—and the opportunity to fish other nearby lakes.

Wild rainbow, cutthroat, and brook trout are all present and can reach impressive sizes. Average catches range 12–15 inches, but fish up to five pounds are available. These fish are not picky, making most any approach productive. Many anglers use streamers such as Woolly Buggers or Zonkers to imitate leeches and small baitfish. These can be cast out from the bank and stripped back or trolled from a float tube. Spinners will do the same thing, and Rooster Tails and bangbaits in various colors will catch a lot of fish. Of course, bait always works, and night crawlers and eggs floated under a bobber have a chance of picking up some pretty big fish. Change fishing spots often on lakes like this; fish tend to favor certain parts of the lake at different times, sometimes deep, sometimes shallow. Once you find the fish, it should be no trouble catching your fair share.

Species: Wild rainbow, cutthroat, brook trout.

Facilities: Camping is limited to natural sites around the lake and at the trailhead parking lot. There are no facilities, and anglers are encouraged to practice no-trace camping. A good Forest Service map for the Mount Jefferson Wilderness can clue you into hiking trails that lead to other fishable lakes. Supplies and other accommodations can be had in Detroit.

Directions: From Detroit, drive east on Hwy. 22 for 16 miles to the Marion Forks Ranger Station. Turn southeast on Marion Forks Rd. (Forest Rd. 2255) and follow it six miles to where it dead-ends at Trail No. 3436. The lake is about two miles east on this trail.

Contact: BLM, Salem, 503/375-5643; ODFW, South Willamette, 503/757-4186; Willamette National Forest, 541/225-6300; Detroit Ranger District, 503/854-3366; Oregon State Parks and Recreation Department, 800/551-6949; All Seasons Motel, 503/854-3421; Breitenbush Hot Springs, 503/854-3320; P&A Lake Detroit Market, 503/854-3433.

45 LOWER METOLIUS RIVER
north of Sisters in Deschutes National Forest

Map 3.5, page 185

The lower Metolius River runs 16 miles from the Lower Bridge to Monty Campground at the head of the Metolius River Arm on Lake Billy Chinook. Ponderosa pine forests dominate this predominantly arid region, and the river is lined with thick stands of willows. The river here runs fast, deep, and narrow with dangerous rapids, logjams, and big boulders.

Anglers will do a lot of walking between areas of accessible holding water, mostly back eddies, separated as they are by dense brush or fast, wide runs too deep to wade. The only access is via good hiking trails and logging roads on the east bank between Lower Bridge Campground and Monty Campground on Lake Billy Chinook. Floating the river is possible, but only in white-water rafts or kayaks and by experienced boaters. A half mile of river is available on the west bank from Lower Bridge downriver to Candle Creek Campground and the boundary of the Warm Springs Indian Reservation, beyond which fishing is prohibited.

Beauty and big fish aside, there is very little that is friendly or welcoming about this stretch of river. Hot weather and dry, dusty conditions prevail; wading is treacherous if not potentially fatal; and thick brush frequently blocks access to the best water. Wading should be considered only by those with the proper gear (leak-proof waders, cleated boots, wading belt, and staff) and physical stamina; this is not a river you want to turn your back on. Catching fish on the lower river requires a high degree of patience, perseverance, expert ability, and moxie. The allure of this area is obviously big fish (bull trout and rainbows), most of which have never seen an angler, but unless it gets more developed in the future, consider this a frontier for serious anglers.

Bull trout average five pounds in this stretch, and finding a 10-pounder is not much of a problem. Between December and April the bull trout all but disappear into the tributaries to spawn. Average trout catches will be 14–16 inches but can reach five pounds or more. During fall the river gets a large run of kokanee, but these fish provide little sport, as they are often starting to die. Regulations restrict anglers to artificial flies and lures only. This is the only section of the Metolius open to lures. The river is open year-round and the roads are plowed to Lower Bridge, making it accessible most of the year.

Summer hatches can be excellent beginning in July with salmon flies, followed by golden stones, green drakes, numerous mayfly hatches, and caddis. (If you are at all familiar with green drakes but have never managed to find a good enough hatch, this is the place to start looking.) Grasshoppers and other terrestrial patterns, especially large flying ants, work well in summer. During the kokanee run in fall try drifting very small egg patterns for bull and rainbow trout. For those so inclined, big weighted streamers such as Egg Sucking Leeches, four-inch-long Bunny Streamers in white or black, Woolly Buggers, and Articulated and String Leeches work well. Indicator nymphing was invented for this type of river, but flies should be heavy and dead-drifted close to the bottom. Bait and spin anglers can use larger Rooster Tails, spoons, and plugs. Drift fishing may be productive in the fall with corkies and yarn for bull trout.

Get your flies and lures on the bottom of the river and don't waste your time on unproductive water. Begin using half again as much weight as you think you need; you can always scale down. The bottom of the river is where the fish hold. The cold, fast currents don't encourage much movement from the fish, and because of the food-rich waters they don't have to move much anyway. If you're not catching fish, you may not be getting deep enough. Productive water is going to be in the form of back eddies, along the banks under brush, and in current seams. Ignore fast-flowing, featureless sections and move right to river bends, downed logs, and swirling back eddies.

Species: Wild rainbow, brown, and bull trout, kokanee.

Facilities: Three fee campgrounds are available below the Hwy. 99 bridge: Lower Bridge, Candle Creek, and Monty on Lake Billy Chinook. Additional fee campgrounds are available above the Hwy. 99 bridge at Canyon Creek Campground, Allen Springs Campground, and Pioneer Ford Campground. Supplies and upscale accommodations can be had in Camp Sherman and in Sisters.

Directions: From Sisters drive nine miles northwest on Hwy. 20 (Santiam Hwy.) to Hwy. 14, signed for Camp Sherman and the Metolius River. Turn north on Hwy. 14 and drive 14 miles to Lower Bridge. Lower Bridge Campground will be to your right just before you cross the river. Keep driving north on Hwy. 14 across the river to reach Candle Creek in approximately 0.5 mile. To reach Monty Campground and the mouth of the Metolius River on Lake Billy Chinook from Sisters, drive northwest on Hwy. 20 for five miles to Indian Ford Rd. Turn north on Indian Ford Rd. and make an immediate turn to the south on Forest Rd. 11. Drive 19 miles north on Forest Rd. 11 to the junction with Forest Rd. 1170. Turn east on Rd. 1170 and drive 12 miles, passing Perry South campground to the dead-end road at Monty Campground. River access is upstream on the east bank.

Contact: Sisters Area Chamber of Commerce, 541/549-0251; ODFW, Bend, 541/388-6363; Sisters Ranger District, 541/549-7700, www.metoliusriver.com; House on the Metolius, 541/595-6620; Cold Springs Resort and RV Park, 541/595-6271; Lake Creek Lodge, 800/797-6331; Metolius River Lodges, 800/595-6290; Kokanee Café, 541/595-6420; Camp Sherman Store and Fly Shop, 541/595-6711, www.campshermanstore.com; The Fisher's Place in Sisters, 541/549-3474.

46 LAKE SIMTUSTUS
south of Warm Springs

Map 3.5, page 185

A popular recreational lake, Lake Simtustus occupies a narrow, seven-mile canyon between Round Butte Dam and Pelton Dam. The lake's coolness provides a refreshing contrast to this arid country marked by basalt rock and forests of juniper and pine trees. But most anglers don't come here for the stark beauty as much as for the resident populations of large kokanee, rainbow, brown, and bull trout, and a small population of smallmouth bass.

Lake Simtustus is open to all methods of fishing, including bait, April 23–October 31. This and Lake Billy Chinook are the only fisheries in Oregon that permit the retention of bull trout: one over 24 inches per day is included as part of the trout limit of five fish per day. Kokanee must also be included in the daily limit for trout. Because of the difficult, steep terrain around most of the lake there is practically no bank access except at a few boat ramps and campgrounds; 99 percent of the fishing on the lake is done from a boat.

The principal fishery here is in the upper four miles of water and higher up in an area known as "The Narrows." This is where a majority of the fish are concentrated in the deep, cool waters below the dam. Kokanee are the main catch and can run up to two pounds, although the average catch is between 15–22 inches. Kokanee are caught on jigs fished under the boat and trolling spinners. Rainbow and brown trout make up the next most popular species, with average catches 12–16 inches, but they grow much bigger. The only rainbow trout to be stocked in Lake Simtustus are steelhead smolts. Most anglers who catch the large fish are trolling flashers, large spinners, and Rapalas very deep near Round Butte Dam. Bull trout are occasionally caught and also run big, 10–15 pounds. Bull trout are not targeted but show up when trolling for rainbow trout. Smallmouth bass are present in small numbers but are overshadowed by the trout fishing.

Species: Kokanee, rainbow, brown, and bull trout, smallmouth bass.

Facilities: Camping and boat ramps are available at Pelton Park near the dam, privately owned Lake Simtustus RV Park and Campground, and on the reservation side at Indian Park. Pelton Park has 71 campsites, restrooms, showers, picnic area, boat launch, and a general store. Lake Simtustus RV Park and Campground is a full-service facility. Indian Park is primitive camping with no amenities. Supplies and other accommodations can be had in Madras, Redmond, and Bend.

In addition to an Oregon state fishing license, anglers are also required to buy a tribal angling permit before fishing. You can buy permits by contacting the Warm Springs Natural Resources Office, from several locations on the Warm Springs Indian Reservation, or from fishing shops in Sisters, Madras, and Bend, from Cove Palisades Marina on Lake Billy Chinook, and from G.I. Joe's stores around Oregon.

Directions: From Warm Springs drive three miles south on Hwy. 26 to the Pelton Dam turnoff at Elk Drive. Drive south on Elk Drive for four miles, passing the dam to your west, to reach Pelton Park. Lake Simtustus RV Park and Campground is two miles up the road from Pelton Park. To reach Indian Camp from Warm Springs, turn south on Jackson Trail Rd. 0.25 mile before crossing the Deschutes on Hwy. 26. This is a sometimes rough road, and it's dangerous when wet. Follow Jackson Trail Rd. approximately 14 miles to the dead-end at Indian Park.

Contact: Bend Chamber of Commerce, 800/905-2362; Madras Chamber of Commerce, 800/967-3564; ODFW, Bend, 541/388-6363; U.S. Forest Service, Sisters, 541/549-7700; U.S. Forest Service, Bend, 541/383-4000; BLM, Prineville, 541/416-6700; Confederated Tribes of Warm Springs, 541/553-1161; Department of Natural Resources, Warm Springs, 541/553-3548; Pelton Park Store and Marina, 541/475-0516; Pelton Park (reservations hotline), 503/464-8515; Lake Simtustus RV Park and Campground, 541/475-1085; Madras Marine, 541/475-2476; Culver Marine, 541/546-3354, Numb-butt Fly Shop and Outfitters, 888/248-8309; Patient Angler Fly Shop, 541/389-6208; Deschutes River Anglers, 541/617-1571. Guides: Check with one of the local fishing shops or call Rick Arnold, 541/317-4103, www.trophytroutguide.com.

47 LAKE BILLY CHINOOK
north of Bend
Map 3.5, page 185

Lake Billy Chinook is a large, 3,915-acre reservoir behind Round Butte Dam, extending up three canyons that form the mouths of the Crooked, Deschutes, and Metolius Rivers. The remote and desolate terrain evokes the stark desert beauty commonly associated with Central Oregon waters: canyon walls, topped by rimrocks, and large plateaus that can reach a few thousand feet above the water. Summers can be quite hot and desert winds can blow with fierce determination.

Lake Billy Chinook is open to fishing in the arms above Round Butte March 1–October 31. The balance of the reservoir, below Round Butte, is open all year. The predominant catches are wild kokanee and trophy bull trout, and to a lesser degree rainbow trout and smallmouth bass. (Lake Billy Chinook is one of only two places in Oregon where bull trout can be legally harvested.) All methods of fishing are permitted, including bait. One bull trout of 24 inches or more may be retained. The limit on kokanee is 25 per day; that's a big feast of fish. Special tribal angling permits are required to fish the Metolius Arm.

There is very little productive bank angling except for a few places around public boat ramps, campgrounds, and bridges along Jordan Road at the road crossings over the Crooked and Deschutes Rivers. Anglers should expect to use a boat for 99 percent of the fishing, and even these are limited to a few select places: at Cove Palisades Park on the Crooked River Arm and a few miles down the road at the Deschutes River Arm. From either spot it is an 8–10-mile troll out to the confluence of the two arms with the Metolius River Arm. Fortunately there is little need to go very far into the lake to make good catches. Serious anglers have their favorite spots on the reservoir, and many are willing to travel long distances to fish these areas. A popular fishing area for both kokanee and bull trout is at the confluence of the Deschutes and Crooked River arms at The Island.

Another popular boat-launch area is on the Metolius River Arm at Perry South. The drive to reach this area is a bit longer and the roads can be windy, but some anglers consider this the most productive fishery on the lake because it holds the coldest water, favored by bull trout and kokanee. All species of fish can be found anywhere in the reservoir, but the Metolius River Arm seems to hold the greatest concentration of fish. The entire north bank of the Metolius River Arm is owned by the Confederated Tribes of Warm Springs and is off-limits. A tribal fishing permit is required to fish this arm of the reservoir.

Because most angling is limited to boats, trolling is the most popular method of fishing. Good catches of bull trout are made by trolling Rapalas, plugs, or other large baitfish imitations. Kokanee are found 60–100 feet deep in water of 45°F. The primary method is to troll plugs, red Wedding Rings, or lures with white corn or worms. Troll in large S-curves rather than a straight line to cover more water. Brown and rainbow trout are caught primarily in the upper reaches of each of the arms. Here, fly anglers have a better chance in shallower waters and moving currents. Streamers work best, unless a hatch is discovered, and then small attractor patterns such as an Adams and Griffith Gnat are productive. Bass are caught primarily along the shorelines in each of the arms. Average catches of brown and rainbow trout range 12–16 inches, but fish up to 10 pounds are present. Bull trout run bigger at 5–20 pounds, but average catches range 16–24 inches. Kokanee run in typically smaller sizes, 12–16 inches. What kokanee lack in size they more than make up for in their fight and delicious meat. Bass on average run small, 10–16 inches.

Lake Billy Chinook's future is in for some exciting changes with attempts to restore anadromous fish runs back to the middle and upper Deschutes, Crooked River, and Metolius River. Historically, summer steelhead and spring chinook migrated up all these rivers to spawning beds. Reservoir renovations that will restore these runs were to be completed in 2008, and fish stocking programs (steelhead and salmon) were to get under way in 2007. Expected returns of adult fish were projected for 2010. This means there will be opportunities to catch ocean returning salmon and steelhead in the reservoir and the rivers—a dream come true for many anglers.

Species: Bass, kokanee, rainbow, brown, bull trout.

Facilities: A tribal fishing permit is required to fish the Metolius River Arm of the reservoir; purchase one at the Cove Palisades store or at sporting goods stores and fly shops in Sisters, Madras, and Bend. Within Cove Palisades State Park (day-use $3) there are two campgrounds with boat ramps: Crooked River Campground has 91 electrical sites with water, tent sites, and three deluxe cabins, and lesser cabins and yurts; Deschutes Campground has 82 full hookup sites, 92 tent sites with water nearby, and three group tent areas. Two privately owned marinas can be found at the east end of the lake at Cove Palisades State Park and at the west end at Three Rivers Marina. Both offer boat rentals, restaurants, camping and fishing supplies, and boat slips. Another primitive fee campground and boat ramp can be found at the west end of the Metolius River Arm at Perry West. Supplies and accommodations can be had in Bend, Madras, and Redmond.

Directions: From Bend, drive north on Hwy. 97, through Redmond, 29.2 miles to Culver Hwy. Turn northwest on Culver Hwy. and drive 2.3 miles to Iris Lane. Turn west on Iris Ln. and drive one mile to Feather Drive. Turn north on Feather Dr. and drive two miles to Fisch Lane. Turn west on this road, which turns into Frazier Dr. after one mile, and then another mile to Peck Rd. Turn west on Peck Rd. and follow it 0.5 mile to Cove Palisades Park. Once in the park, Peck Rd. turns into Jordan Rd. To get to the Crooked River Campground and Deschutes River Campground, follow Jordan Rd. south from the park entrance two miles and 3.5 miles respectively. For Three Rivers Marina on the Metolius River Arm, drive south on Jordan Rd. from the Deschutes River Campground for six miles to the Grandview Junction. Turn east on Forest Rd. 1172 and follow it approximately 16 miles to the marina. For Perry West Campground from the Grandview junction, turn west onto Graham Rd. and drive seven miles to where Graham Rd. turns into Hwy. 64 at Fly Lake. Drive north on Hwy. 64 approximately 11 miles to the dead-end at the campground.

Contact: Bend Chamber of Commerce, 800/905-2362; Madras Chamber of Commerce, 800/967-3564; ODFW, Bend, 541/388-6363; U.S. Forest Service, Sisters, 541/549-7700; U.S. Forest Service, Bend, 541/383-4000; BLM, Prineville, 541/416-6700; Confederated Tribes of Warm Springs, 541/553-1161; Department of Natural Resources, Warm Springs, 541/553-3548; Cove Palisades State Park, 800/551-6949; Cove Palisades State Park (campground, cabin, or boat slip reservations), 800/452-5687, Cove Palisades Marina, 541/546-3521; Lake Billy Chinook Houseboats (Three Rivers Marina), 541/546-2939, www.lakebillychinook.com; Madras Marine, 541/475-2476; Culver Marine, 541/546-3354; Numb-butt Fly Shop and Outfitters, 888/248-8309; Patient Angler Fly Shop, 541/389-6208; Deschutes River Anglers, 541/617-1571. Guides: Check with one of the local fishing shops or call Rick Arnold, 541/317-4103, www.trophytroutguide.com.

NORTHEASTERN OREGON

COURTESY OF DAVE POWELL, USDA FOREST SERVICE,
WWW.FORESTRYIMAGES.ORG

BEST FISHING SPOTS

❰ Smallmouth Bass
John Day River: Service Creek to
  Clarno Rapids, **page 287**
Brownlee Reservoir, **page 311**

❰ Steelhead
Lower Grande Ronde River, **page 269**

❰ Family Fishing
Wallowa Lake, **page 276**

❰ Hike-In Fisheries
South Fork Walla Walla River, **page 262**
Minam River, **page 273**
Eagle Cap Wilderness, **page 277**

Northeastern Oregon is an enigma to most

Oregon anglers: It poses problems of distance, accessibility, and knowledge. The region is diverse and downright rugged in places; travel here from anywhere other than the eastern border states is going to seem like visiting a faraway world. Seven mountain ranges divide the region and 10 wilderness areas, contained in four national forests, are scattered throughout. You'll encounter the arid and agricultural lands of the Columbia Plateau, the alpine peaks of the Blue Mountains, and the fertile but arid ranchlands of the Snake River Plain. The climate is drier and more extreme – expect hot summers and cold winters. Only the northern end of the Blue and Wallowa Mountains, receiving cool coastal air via the Columbia River Gorge, resemble the rain-soaked forests of the Oregon Coast or Mount Hood.

A trip from Portland or the Willamette Valley will range from 2.5 hours to a full day's drive. So why would any sane angler drive more than 200 miles inland – bypassing the Sandy, Clackamas, and Deschutes Rivers – to catch a steelhead or trout? The reasons include variety, solitude, and the mystery of the unknown. Northeastern Oregon offers some of the state's most remote and scenic steelhead and salmon fishing; world-class smallmouth bass fisheries; opportunities for multiday float, horse-packing, and fly-in wilderness trips; exotic warm-water fisheries for large catfish and sturgeon; hikes to remote alpine lakes and river headwaters for big trout and large winter whitefish; and a chance to exchange city life for a week with your favorite fishing hat, backpack, pack rod, and a small assortment of spinners and flies.

The Columbia River watershed breaks down into three smaller subregions: the Middle Columbia, the Middle Snake River, and the Lower Snake River. Within each are river basins such as Lower John Day, Willow, Upper and Lower Grand Ronde, Imnaha, Powder, and Umatilla. Most of the major rivers have their source in a handful of wilderness areas, and access is often limited to hiking trails, multiday float trips through rugged canyons, wilderness pack trips, and fly-in lodges. Any river that drains into the Columbia — and all of them in this region do so — has the potential to host anadromous fish populations, as more than a dozen streams do. The region's most famous steelhead and salmon river is the Snake, especially Hell's Canyon. The Grand Ronde River, the area's second-best-known river, has only one steelhead run: a summer run that does not arrive until the rivers begin to fill in late October. This may be the region's biggest secret: that summer-run fish are caught October–January, or even as late as May. By February, Portlanders have all but forgotten the local summer runs, as they chase fresh winter-run steelhead on their local streams. Meanwhile, northeast anglers are catching steelhead in the middle of winter.

Other than the Snake, Grand Ronde, and John Day, most rivers in the northeast are relatively unknown. The Umatilla, Walla Walla, Wenaha, Imnaha, Wallowa, Lostine, Minam, and Catherine Creek all host runs of summer steelhead and salmon, and the majority of these streams are set in pristine wilderness areas. The region is also home to a fair amount of warm-water fisheries. Several unique warm-water fisheries on the Snake River attract anglers wishing to catch perch and channel catfish. Smallmouth bass predominate in the lower sections of most rivers connected to the Columbia or Snake. The John Day and Snake River reservoirs are fast becoming destination fisheries for anyone looking for 100-fish days. And Northeastern Oregon is also a land of lakes — especially alpine lakes, the greatest concentration of which can be found in the Anthony Lakes Area and Eagle Cap Wilderness.

The Northeast region has the greatest concentration of Wild and Scenic Rivers — 15 rivers share this distinction. Despite the lack of fishing pressure, these rivers will remain protected and well-managed for future generations to discover and enjoy. Northeastern Oregon is a diverse and intriguing part of the state, waiting to be explored. A journey to this area requires a little extra planning to account for distances and other obstacles, but when the journey is the goal, you're sure to have the experience of a lifetime.

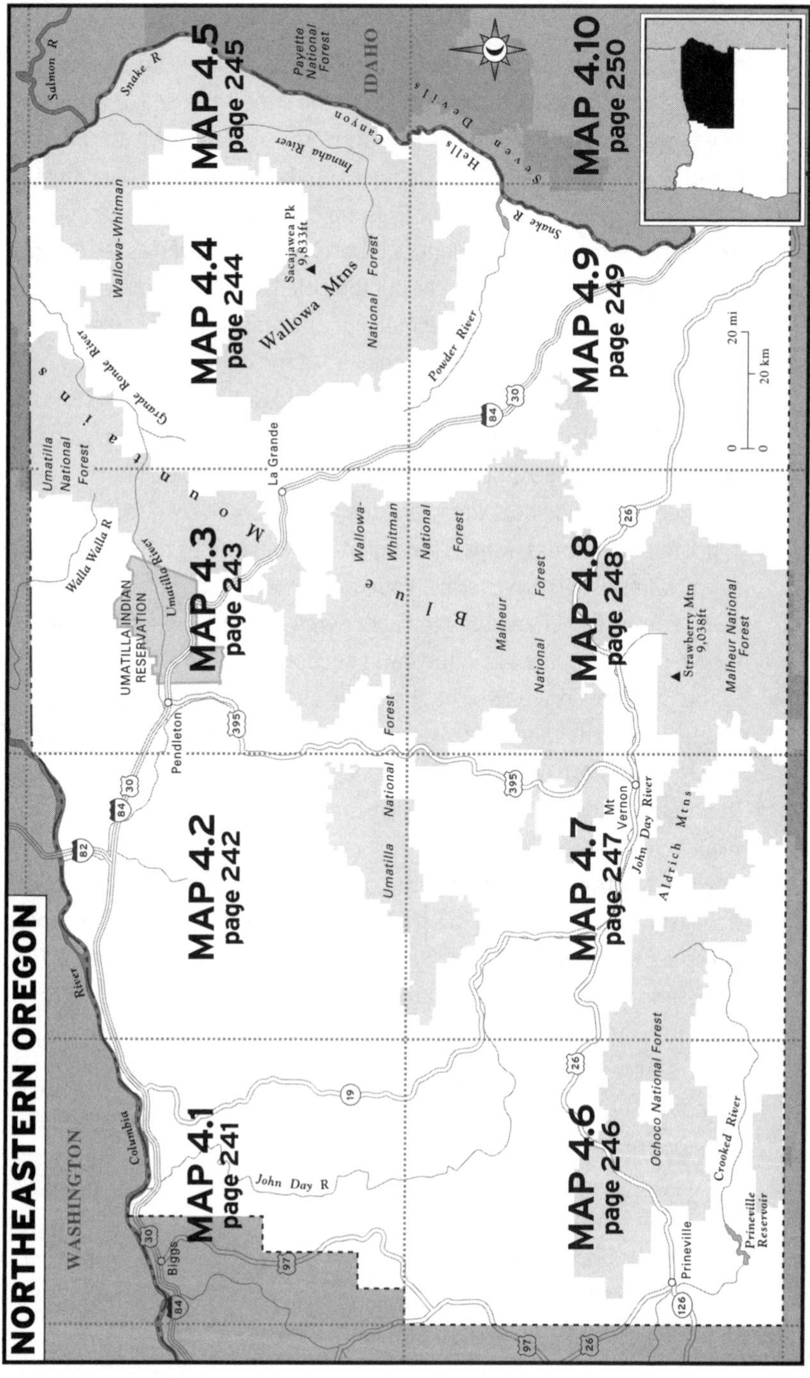

NORTHEASTERN OREGON

MAP 4.1
page 241

MAP 4.2
page 242

MAP 4.3
page 243

MAP 4.4
page 244

MAP 4.5
page 245

MAP 4.6
page 246

MAP 4.7
page 247

MAP 4.8
page 248

MAP 4.9
page 249

MAP 4.10
page 250

WASHINGTON

IDAHO

Columbia River

John Day R

Biggs

Pendleton

La Grande

Prineville

Mt Vernon

Prineville Reservoir

Crooked River

Ochoco National Forest

John Day River

Aldrich Mtns

Strawberry Mtn
9,038ft

Malheur National Forest

Malheur National Forest

Wallowa-Whitman National Forest

Umatilla National Forest

Umatilla National Forest

Umatilla Indian Reservation

Walla Walla R

Umatilla River

Grande Ronde River

Wallowa Mtns

Sacajawea Pk
9,833ft

Wallowa-Whitman National Forest

Imnaha River

Snake R

Salmon R

Payette National Forest

Hells Canyon

Seven Devils

Snake R

Powder River

Blue Mountains

Blue Mountains

20 mi

20 km

0

0

© AVALON TRAVEL PUBLISHING, INC.

Map 4.1

Sites 1-3
Pages 251-254

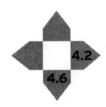

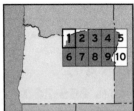

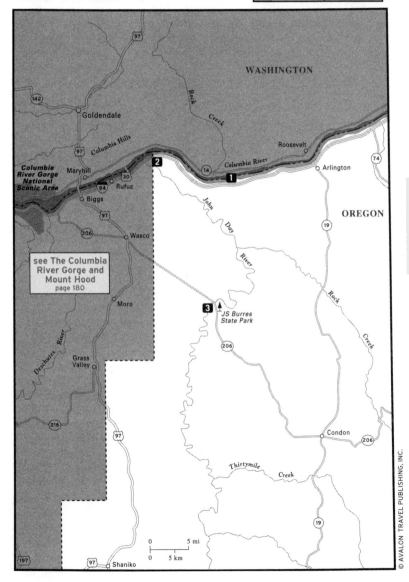

Map 4.2

Sites 4-8
Pages 256-260

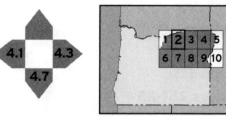

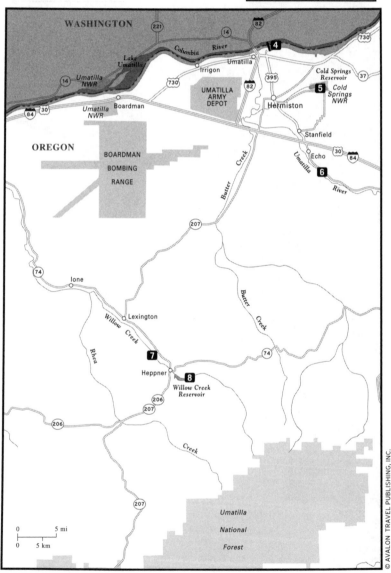

Map 4.3

Sites 9-16
Pages 261-266

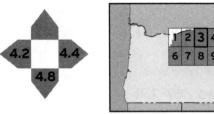

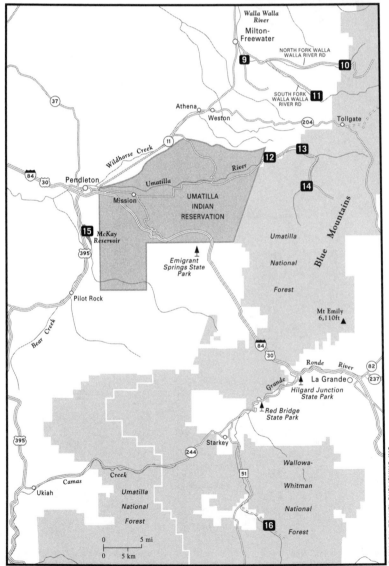

Map 4.4

Sites 17-28
Pages 267-281

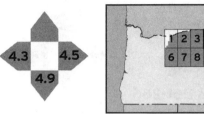

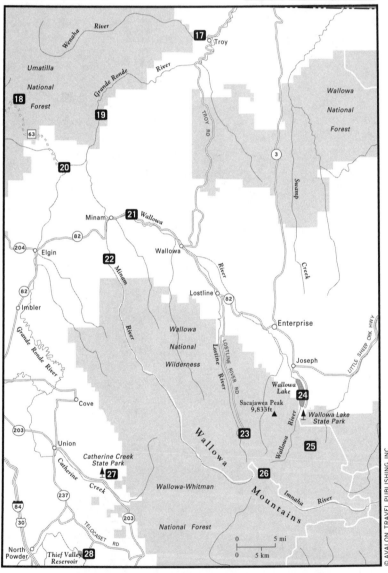

Map 4.5

Sites 29-31
Pages 282-286

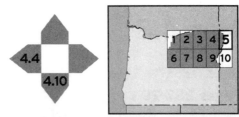

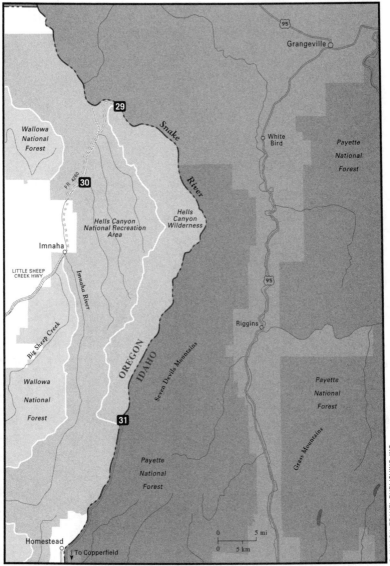

Chapter 4

Map 4.6

Sites 32-37
Pages 287-293

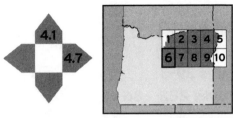

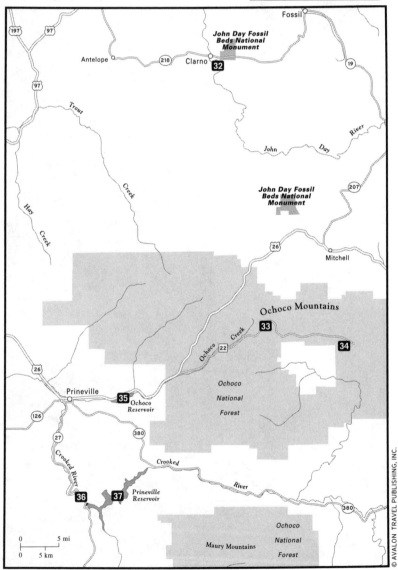

Map 4.7

Sites 38-42
Pages 295-300

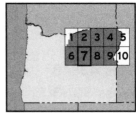

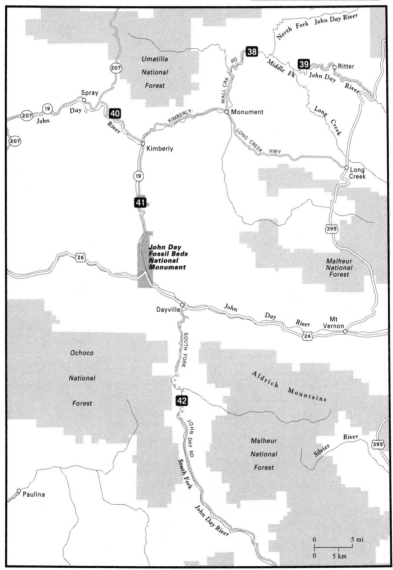

Map 4.8

Sites 43-48
Pages 301-305

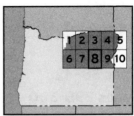

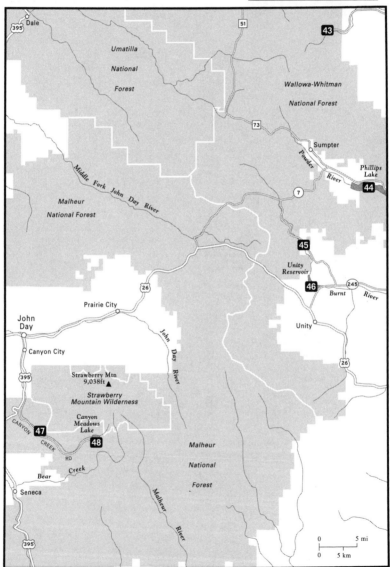

Map 4.9

Sites 49-53
Pages 306-309

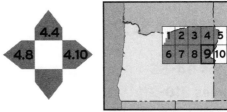

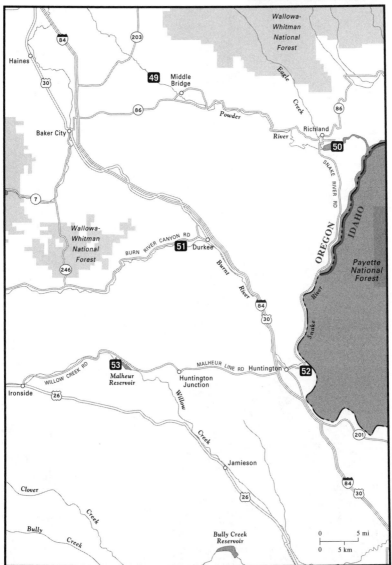

Map 4.10

Sites 54-55
Pages 310-311

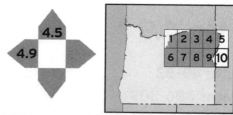

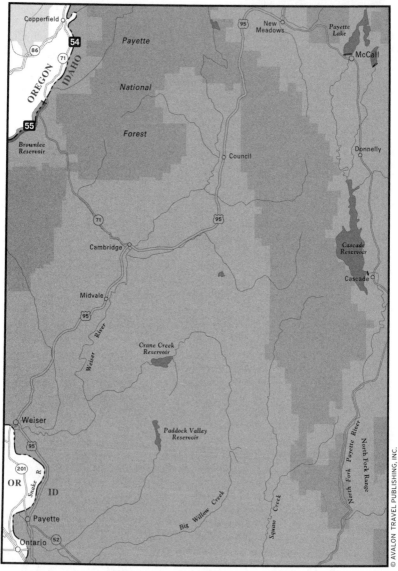

1 COLUMBIA RIVER: LAKE UMATILLA

east of Rufus

Map 4.1, page 241

Lake Umatilla is one of four major reservoirs on the Columbia River. Also known as the John Day Dam Pool, this stretch of the Columbia River runs 75 miles from the John Day Dam near The Dalles to the McNary Dam in Umatilla. For approximately 50 miles, I-84 parallels the entire reservoir until Boardman, where Highway 730 will take you the rest of the way upriver to Umatilla and McNary Dam. The drive from The Dalles to Umatilla is through the Columbia Plateau, an ecoregion characterized by sagebrush, grasslands, wheat fields, and high winds. If you are driving to this area from the lush and scenic Columbia Gorge, prepare yourself for a stark contrast in landscape.

Although there isn't much for the eye, this section of the Columbia River provides year-round hunting and fishing opportunities that rival anything in the state. Access and camping facilities are plentiful, as are towns providing fishing and camping supplies. Several significant tributaries such as the John Day, Willow Creek, and Umatilla Rivers flow into this section of the Columbia, providing great opportunities to catch summer runs of steelhead and salmon. The river itself hosts a healthy mix of both cold- and warm-water species, including trout, shad, smallmouth bass, channel catfish, largemouth bass, crappie, walleye, bluegill, sturgeon, and yellow perch. While there is some bank access along the river at parks and roadside pullouts, a majority of this water is best fished from a boat to reach the most productive water.

Walleye: Lake Umatilla has garnered a national reputation for its walleye fishery. The state record fish (19 pounds, 15.3 ounces) was taken from this section of the Columbia in 1990. All successful walleye fishing requires a boat to troll the appropriate depths and find structures such as gravel bottom, rock structures, submerged land masses, ledges, and sandy flats. Depth finders and topographical river maps can help to identify good holding water. Tackle should be kept close to underwater structures or the river bottom, 20–30 feet deep if necessary. Average catches are 4–9 pounds with larger fish reaching 16–18 pounds. Walleye feed almost exclusively on smaller fish such as minnows, smolts, shad, and small baitfish such as sculpin. For this reason, it may be helpful to determine where these smaller fish live in the river and use imitative patterns such as plugs or flashers. Bait such as large night crawlers also work. Timing and an understanding of spawning habits is critical to catching walleye. Walleye spawn in May, when the water begins to warm, and prespawning fish can be very aggressive. Serious anglers begin fishing in early April for the feistier fish. Postspawning walleye fishing is good until fall and early winter.

Smallmouth Bass: Enthusiasts of smallmouth bass will find much to like about Lake Umatilla. Bass average 3–4 pounds, with six-pound fish not uncommon. Fishing is good from spring, when the water begins to warm, until late fall. Most anglers concentrate on the upper reaches of the river between the towns of Irrigon and Umatilla, though other good areas include the boat launches in Blalock, Arlington, and Boardman. Both bank and boat anglers have equal opportunities for excellent sport. Bank anglers may want to start at Umatilla Park in Umatilla. Boaters can launch a craft at any number of ramps between Blalock and Umatilla, or at Le Page Park at the mouth of the John Day River. The John Day River Arm of Lake Umatilla is a popular smallmouth bass fishery.

Techniques for catching smallmouth bass include finding suitable habitat along shorelines and around structures. Look for weed beds, brush, rocks, logs, pylons, and other areas that may provide good cover for bass and baitfish. A general rule of thumb when catching smallmouth bass is to go deeper on sunny days and shallower on cloudy days. Plugs, crankbaits, minnow patterns, and plastic worms all work. Vary your retrieves and depth until you begin catching fish. Avoid sticking in one piece of water for too long. Work water thoroughly, but move often to increase your chances of stumbling upon a good cache of fish.

Salmon and Steelhead: The best opportunities to catch these two species are near McNary Dam and at the mouths of the John Day River near John Day Dam, Willow Creek, a few miles east of Arlington, and Umatilla River in Umatilla, since river mouths and tributaries concentrate the fish more than the wide-open Columbia. If you attempt to fish Lake Umatilla for steelhead, concentrate your efforts around obstructions or currents with gravel or rocky bottoms—any place a steelhead may stop for rest. Spoons, plugs, and bait fished close to the bottom are all good approaches. Your chances are highly dependent on run size, commercial fishing, and water temperatures. September–January are the best steelhead months, with fall chinook arriving in October. Steelhead fishing is open January 1–March 31 and June 16–December 31. Chinook season begins August 1 and closes on December 31.

Sturgeon: Sturgeon are present in Lake Umatilla, but their declining numbers lead most anglers to seek more productive water in the lower sections of the Columbia River around Bonneville Dam. If you do go for sturgeon, remember to use barbless hooks for quick release and check the ODFW website for changes in regulations. The most productive water is in channels or areas of depression in the river bottom, where food and dead matter collects. Shad is the most popular form of bait. Bait should be kept on the bottom, which can be challenging depending on river depths and current. Weights as small as five ounces or as large as 40 ounces may be required. Most anglers employ leaders of 8–15 inches. A slider sinker rig will help keep bait on the bottom.

Other warm-water species present in Lake Umatilla include shad, largemouth bass, yellow perch, crappie, carp, and catfish. Shad are in the river April–June. Perch and crappie can be caught around most docks or in shallower water along shorelines, and around islands where there is minimal current. Try both the John Day Arm and Umatilla Arm of Lake Umatilla for these warm-water species.

Species: Fall chinook, steelhead, shad, smallmouth bass, channel catfish, largemouth bass, crappie, walleye, bluegill, sturgeon, yellow perch, and carp.

Facilities: Camping is available at the Deschutes River State Recreation Area, Quesnel Park, Boardman Park, and Hat Rock State Park. RV owners will find full-service hookups as well as tent sites near the water at Arlington Marina and RV Park, Boardman RV Park, and Umatilla Marina and RV Park. Supplies and accommodations are available along I-84 in numerous small towns including Biggs, Arlington, Boardman, and Umatilla.

There are numerous boat ramps between the John Day Dam and McNary Dam:

- **Le Page Park:** At the mouth of the John Day River, two miles east of the John Day, this park has a fee ramp, restrooms, parking, and picnic facilities.
- **Blalock Canyon Ramp:** This free gravel ramp is launches into a backwater area connected to the main river.
- **Port of Arlington:** A free, concrete ramp with parking and restrooms in Arlington.
- **Quesnel Park:** A free, concrete ramp with parking and restrooms east of Heppner Junction.
- **Boardman Park:** A free, concrete ramp with parking and restrooms in Boardman.
- **Patterson Ferry:** Free use of a concrete ramp, including parking (but no restrooms), is available west of Umatilla.
- **Irrigon Marina Park:** This free concrete ramp in Irrigon also has parking and restrooms.
- **Umatilla Marina:** This is anther free ramp with parking and restrooms in Umatilla.

Directions: From Rufus, the site of the John Day Dam, drive east on I-84 following the river 50 miles to Boardman. Many of the boat ramps can be found along this stretch of road at Le Page State Park (4 miles), Port of Arlington (27 miles), Quesnel Park (41), Boardman Park (50 miles). The Deschutes River Recreation State Park is 11 miles west of Rufus on I-84. Numerous signs along the interstate help identify significant towns, parks, fishing access points, and camping areas. Five miles east of Boardman take Exit 168 off I-84 and drive north on Hwy. 730 toward the towns of Irrigon and Umatilla. Irrigon is eight miles from I-84, and river access can be had at Irrigon Marina and Park and Paterson Ferry. Umatilla is approximately 15 miles from the interstate turnoff and river access can be had at the Umatilla Marina just below McNary Dam.

For the boat ramps: To reach Irrigon Marina, drive seven miles northeast on Hwy. 730, which becomes Main St. in Irrigon. Drive east on Main St. for 0.1 mile and turn north on 8th St. Drive 0.3 mile to 7th St., turn west onto 7th St., and drive 0.1 mile to the marina. To reach Patterson's Ferry from I-84, drive northeast on Hwy. 730 for three miles to Patterson Ferry Rd. Turn north on Patterson Ferry Rd. and drive three miles to the dead end at Patterson Ferry boat ramp.

To reach the Umatilla Marina, follow Hwy. 730 northeast from I-84 15 miles into Umatilla where Hwy. 730 turns into 6th St. From 6th St. turn north onto Switzler Ave., which becomes 1st St. after 0.2 mile. Follow 1st St. 0.3 mile and turn west onto Quincy Ave. Drive 0.1 mile to the end at Umatilla Marina.

Contact: Heppner Chamber of Commerce, 541/676-5536; BLM, Prineville District, 541/416-6700; ODFW, Dalles, 541/296-4628; ODFW, Heppner, 541/676-5230; Deschutes River Recreation State Park, 541/739-2322; Irrigon Park and Marina, 541/922-4933; Willow Creek RV Park, 541/676-9618; Morrow County Parks, 541/989-9500; Pioneer RV Park, 888/408-6100; Hat Rock Campground, 541/567-0917; Umatilla Marina and RV Park, 541/922-3939; Balanced Catch, 541/564-0626; High Desert Marine, 541/567-8419;

River's Bend Outfitters, 541/296-5949, www.riversbendoutfitters.com; Young's Fishing Service, 800/270-7962, www.fishyfs.com; Columbia Basin Guide Service, 541/276-0371, www.columbiafishing.net/index.htm; Blue Mountain Anglers and Fly Shop, 541/966-8770, www.blumtn-anglers-flyshop.com/home.html.

2 COLUMBIA RIVER: JOHN DAY ARM
at Lake Umatilla east of The Dalles
Map 4.1, page 241

The John Day River is a major tributary of the Columbia River, flowing more than 275 miles from its source in the Blue Mountains of Wallowa–Whitman National Forest. The John Day Arm of the John Day River concerns the lower nine miles of the John Day River from the mouth, south to Tumwater Falls. The falls form an impassable barrier into the upper river. The river here shares many of the physical characteristics of most of the John Day Basin: towing cliffs, narrow canyons, and an arid desert landscape with precious little shade. This is strictly a boat fishery with no bank access except at the boat launch near I-84 at the confluence of the John Day and Columbia Rivers at Le Page Park. Fishing here can be excellent for summer steelhead, smallmouth bass, channel catfish, brown bullhead catfish, and crappie. Steelhead fishing is open from the mouth to Tumwater Falls January 1–March 31 and June 16–December 31; otherwise fishing is open year-round for all other species but closed to salmon fishing. Bass 12–16 inches must be released.

Most of the steelhead fishing is concentrated in the two miles of river below the falls where the fish stack up waiting to move upriver. Many John Day steelhead are caught by trolling such lures as Spin-N-Glows, small plugs, and rainbow blade spinners. In areas with current, anglers might try sand shrimp or worms under a float. Smallmouth bass can be caught along the cliff banks and around structure. Popular lures are flies such as poppers and small Rapalas. Crappie can also be found around the banks and shallower water, especially in spring during the spawning season; otherwise anglers will have to find schools of fish in the deeper water. Catfish are caught with bait around rocky areas and on mud flats.

Species: Summer steelhead, smallmouth bass, channel catfish, brown bullhead catfish, crappie. Closed to salmon.

Facilities: Fee camping and a day-use area are available at La Page Park at the confluence of the John Day and Columbia Rivers, offering tent and RV sites, picnic areas, showers, drinking water, and restrooms. There is a boat-in fee campground four miles upriver from the mouth at Phillippi Park that offers tent camping, running water, picnic tables, restrooms, and two boat ramps for tying up boats. Supplies and accommodations can be had in The Dalles.

Directions: To get to La Page Park from The Dalles, drive east on I-84 approximately 39 miles to Exit 114 and turn south from the off-ramp into the park. Parking is available in the day-use area and in the campground.

Contact: The Dalles Area Chamber of Commerce, 800/296-2231; BLM, Prineville District, 541/416-6700; ODFW, The Dalles, 541/296-4628; Dufur RV Park, 541/467-2449; Columbia Basin Guide Service, 541/276-0371; Deschutes River Recreation State Park, 541/739-2322; Inn at The Dalles, 800/982-3496.

3 JOHN DAY RIVER: CLARNO RAPIDS TO COTTONWOOD ACCESS

east of The Dalles

Map 4.1, page 241

Above Tumwater Falls near at the head of the John Day Arm of Lake Umatilla on the Columbia River, the John Day runs for 35 miles through private lands with virtually no public access except for those brave anglers who are willing to knock on doors and ask permission. Fishing access resumes at river mile 40 at Cottonwood Access on Highway 206. From here, the river is publicly accessible for 70 miles south to Clarno Rapids, but only from a boat. Anglers wishing to fish this stretch have to do so from a raft or drift boat launched below Clarno Rapids at the John Day River Scenic Wayside (Clarno Rapids should not be attempted), committing to a 3 –5 day drift to Cottonwood Access. This is the longest and most remote section of the John Day, but adventurous anglers are well rewarded with great fishing and wonderful scenic beauty. The land here is arid and stark, composed of narrow canyons and towering cliffs. Floats through this section should be considered minor wilderness expeditions with very few places to turn to for help should something life-threatening happen on the river.

Primarily, this is an early-season and winter fishery for steelhead and smallmouth bass. Steelhead make their appearance October–December and into spring. Smallmouth bass are available all summer, and catches can run up to 100 fish per day, but because of severe irrigation draws the river is not really floatable July–September. Anglers wanting to fish for smallmouth bass during this time should turn to the river near Service Creek to Clarno Rapids, above this section, where the water maintains a larger and more consistent flow. Fishing and water levels pick up again after September, just in time for summer steelheading.

Bass fishing is open all year and bag limits are set at five fish per day, with only one over 16 inches; all bass 12–16 inches must be released unharmed. The smallmouth bass fishery on the John Day has developed a reputation as one of the best in the country. It is estimated that there are more than 1,000 fish per mile of river, averaging 12–13 inches or about one pound. Larger fish up to 18 inches are common, with some exceeding six pounds. Methods for catching bass on the John Day differ according to the time of year. During the cooler spring months, anglers will be required to go deeper with diving crankbaits, bait, and weighted nymphs and streamers. Bait is often discouraged on the John Day because of the difficulty of releasing fish unharmed. This is also the best time of year to hit the biggest fish in the river, before spawning. As summer approaches and the waters warm, fishing becomes a simpleminded game and smaller bass will hit just about anything thrown on top of the water. Poppers are a particular favorite with fly and spin anglers. Don't be shy about using dry flies or drifting nymphs under an indicator.

Steelhead may be fished for the entire year. There is a two-fish limit per day of hatchery steelhead and 20 per year. All wild fish must be released unharmed. John Day steelhead tend to be on the small side, averaging 5–7 pounds. All methods of fishing are permitted for both bass and steelhead, including bait. Most traditional fishing techniques work in the river for catching steelhead. Side drifting, drift fishing, float fishing, flies, lures, and drift rigs are all productive. Look for runs where boulders and current meet and create pockets for resting steelhead. The John Day attracts many fly anglers who hope to catch a large steelhead swinging dry flies or streamers. Salmon are present during the spring but off-limits to angling.

Species: Smallmouth bass, summer steelhead.

Facilities: Fee camping is available near Clarno Rapids at Shelton State Wayside and at the take-out at J. S. Burres State Park on Hwy. 206. Fee camping is also available at the confluence of the John Day River and Columbia River at Le Page Park. Camping is available to boaters anywhere along the river, but the BLM requires no-trace camping in all boat-in campsites, including packing out garbage and solid human waste. Fires are not allowed during summer. BLM in Prineville can provide you all the updated regulations regarding boating, camping, and river use.

Boat ramps are available at the John Day Scenic River Wayside in Clarno and at J. S. Burres State Park. Supplies and accommodations can be had nearby at Biggs Junction on I-84 and The Dalles.

Directions: To reach Cottonwood Access and J. S. Burres State Park from The Dalles drive 20 miles east on I-84 to Biggs Junction (Exit 104). Turn south at the end of the off-ramp onto Hwy. 97. Drive southeast on Hwy. 97, passing through Biggs Junction, eight miles to the Hwy. 206 junction. Turn east on Hwy. 206, passing through Wasco, and follow the highway for another 16 miles to the river at J. S. Burres State Park at the Cottonwood Recreation Site.

To reach the put-in at John Day River Scenic Wayside follow the above directions to the Hwy. 206 junction, but rather than turning onto Hwy. 206, keep driving southeast on Hwy. 97. In three miles Hwy. 97 will make a southward turn. Follow Hwy. 97 south 48 miles, passing through Grass Valley and Kent to Shaniko. In Shaniko, Hwy. 97 bends to the west; turn south on Hwy. 218 and drive 18 miles to Antelope. Stay on Hwy. 218 through Antelope. Now you're headed east toward Clarno. It's approximately 16 miles between Antelope and Clarno. In Clarno, cross the river to reach the John Day River Scenic Wayside on the north side of the road.

Contact: Wheeler County Visitor Information, 541/763-2355; BLM, Prineville District, 541/416-6700; ODFW, John Day, 541/575-1167; River flow information: U.S. Department of Commerce, River Service Center, 503/261-9246, www.oregon.wr.usgs.gov; John Day Fossil Beds Information Line, 541/987-2333 or 541/987-2333; Shelton State Wayside, 503/575-2773; Shuttle information: Wheeler County Visitor Information, 541/763-2355; J&Z Shuttles, 541/468-2182 or 541/468-2447; Fishing Guides: Marty Sheppard, 503/622-1870, littlecreekjd@earthlink.net; Gorge Fly Shop, 541/386-6977, gorgeflyshop@gorge-flyshop.com.

◪ COLUMBIA RIVER: LAKE WALLULA

east of Umatilla

Map 4.2, page 242

Lake Wallula, also known as McNary Dam Pool, comprises 11,640 acres and is the fourth and last in a series of pools on the Columbia River before the river turns north into Washington. It is formed behind McNary Dam just east of Umatilla and is followed by Highway 730 for 15 miles to the Oregon/Washington border. There are two highlights in this stretch of water: the area directly behind the McNary Dam and Hat Rock State Park. Both places provide good boat launches and easy bank-fishing access.

Smallmouth bass are the highlight game fish here, followed by salmon, steelhead, walleye, and panfish. Smallmouth bass are most successfully taken along the banks, around islands, and in slack-water areas during the summer when the water gets above 65°F. Bass of six pounds or more are not uncommon. The best place to fish for bass is from the boat launch at Hat Rock State Park. Anglers should begin by fishing around the islands along weed beds and river debris with plugs, worms, and Rapalas. Bank anglers can catch smallmouth from either of the two boat ramps mentioned above.

Anglers can fish for fall chinook August 1–December 31, but September is the peak month. Summer steelhead can be caught January 1–March 31 and again June 16–December 31. The peak steelhead time is in November. Most of the chinook and steelhead catches occur right behind the dam at the buoy line, but their numbers are limited compared to the lower river around Bonneville Dam. Bank anglers have a less than average chance of catching salmon and steelhead from the bank, but it can be done from the two boat ramps.

Walleye, sturgeon, and channel catfish are present and can be found especially in the channels and deeper water, which often requires a boat. Warm-water fish such as crappie, bluegill, brown bullheads, and perch are abundant and can be fished for either from the boat or from the bank. All these panfish are found mostly in slack-water areas against the bank and around docks or river obstructions such as trees, logs, and rocky areas. Trout may be present but it is illegal to fish for them.

Species: Smallmouth bass, walleye, fall chinook, summer steelhead, sturgeon, channel catfish, white crappie, black crappie, bluegill, brown bullhead, yellow perch.

Facilities: There are two boat ramps, one at McNary Dam and the other at Hat Rock State Park. The McNary Dam ramp is a fee site and provides parking and restrooms. Hat Rock State Park provides a free boat launch with parking and restrooms. Fee camping is also available at Hat Rock State Park. A third, less used natural dirt boat ramp is available in the Cold Springs Recreation Area, two miles east of Hat Rock State Park. Supplies and accommodations can be had in Umatilla, Hermiston, and Boardman.

Directions: From Umatilla follow Hwy. 730 east 1.7 miles to McNary. Turn north on Devore Rd. and drive 0.7 mile to McNary Dam and the boat ramp. To reach Hat Rock State Park from Umatilla, drive east on Hwy. 730, 8.9 miles to Hat Rock State Park Rd. Turn north on Hat Rock State Park Rd. and drive 0.3 mile to the park entrance. To reach the Cold Springs Recreation Area, conntinue on Hwy. 730, two miles east of Hat Rock State Park. Turn north on the unnamed dirt road across from the Pendleton–Cold Springs Hwy. and drive 0.5 mile to the dead-end and the boat ramp.

Contact: Umatilla Chamber of Commerce, 541/922-4825; BLM, Vale District, 541/473-3144; ODFW, Heppner, 541/676-5230; Willow Creek RV Park, 541/676-9618; Morrow County Parks, 541/989-9500; Pioneer RV Park, 888/408-6100; Hat Rock Campground, 541/567-0917; Umatilla Marina and RV Park, 541/922-3939; Balanced Catch, 541/564-0626; High Desert Marine, 541/567-8419; River's Bend Outfitters, 541/296-5949, www.riversbendoutfitters.com; Young's Fishing Service, 800/270-7962, www.fishyfs.com; Columbia Basin Guide Service, 541/276-0371, www.columbiafishing.net/index.htm; Blue Mountain Anglers and Fly Shop, 541/966-8770, www.blumtn-anglers-flyshop.com/home.html.

5 COLD SPRINGS RESERVOIR
east of Hermiston in Cold Springs National Wildlife Refuge

Map 4.2, page 242

Cold Springs Reservoir, four miles east of Hermiston, is an integral part of Cold Springs National Wildlife Refuge, established in 1909 by Theodore Roosevelt. It is intended as a resting and feeding ground for migrating waterfowl and is home to an abundance of wildlife, including hawks, bald eagles, mule deer, pheasant, and quail, and it's popular with hunters, wildlife enthusiasts, and photographers. Characteristic of a low-elevation lake, the banks are dense with willow brush and overhanging cottonwood trees. Submerged logs and other debris make this perfect habitat for large, solitude-seeking warm-water species such as white and black crappie, brown bullheads, largemouth bass, carp, and perch. Bank fishing is limited to the areas around the inlet and dam face because of the dense shoreline around most of the lake, making a small boat or canoe with an electric motor the best means to get at the fish. Gas motors are prohibited. The reservoir is open to fishing March 1–September 30. October 1–February 28 or 29, fishing is permitted from the dam face and along the inlet channel.

At maximum capacity, the lake covers 1,500 acres with an average depth of 36 feet and a maximum depth of 70 feet. There are 10 miles of shoreline accessible via walking trails. Cold Springs Reservoir is susceptible to low-water years, sometimes reducing its size to a mere 500 acres. Check with the Hermiston Irrigation District for up-to-date water levels. The best fishing often occurs in spring and fall when water levels are higher and more stable.

Most anglers come to Cold Springs to fish for crappie, which are found throughout the lake and can average 14–16 inches. To begin, focus your attention around brush and submerged cover along the bank in the morning and evening using spinners or streamer flies in shallower water. During the heat of summer, fish bait or jigs in deeper holes. Erratic retrieves are the best attention-getters. Other species such as brown bullhead catfish are caught more often in the early and late hours of the day, in shallow water, and along the bank or at the inlet. Use bait such as worms or shrimp and settle the bait on or near the bottom. Bass can be caught around shore or underwater structure using weedless worms or baitfish patterns moved slowly along the bottom.

Species: White and black crappie, brown bullheads, largemouth bass, carp, perch.

Facilities: Cold Springs has two free primitive boat ramps at the south end of the lake and restrooms. Boats are allowed with electric motors only. There is no camping at Cold Springs Reservoir. The nearest camping is at several RV parks and Hat Rock Campground. Supplies and accommodations are available in Hermiston and Umatilla.

Directions: From Hwy. 395 in Hermiston drive east one mile to the Highland Hills Rd. turnoff. Turn east on Highland Hills Rd. and drive for three miles to East Loop Rd. Turn northeast on East Loop Rd. and drive five miles to the entrance of Cold Springs National Wildlife Refuge, which will be to north. Turn north into the refuge; parking and boat ramps can be had just after entering the refuge property.

Contact: Hermiston Chamber of Commerce, 541/567-6151; ODFW, Heppner, 541/676-5230; BLM, Vale District, 541/473-3144; Federal Refuge Regulations Information Line, 509/545-8588; Hermiston Irrigation District, 541/567-3024; Pioneer RV Park, 888/408-6100; Hat Rock Campground, 541/567-0917; Umatilla Marina and RV Park, 541/922-3939; Balanced Catch, 541/564-0626; High Desert Marine, 541/567-8419.

6 LOWER UMATILLA RIVER

southeast of Umatilla in the Umatilla
National Forest

Map 4.2, page 242

The Umatilla River is born on the western flanks of the Umatilla National Forest, gathering two river forks, before descending through the Umatilla Indian Reservation and the low farmlands and cities of Pendleton, Hermiston, and Umatilla. Anglers wishing to catch salmon, steelhead, and warm-water species are restricted to the lower river between the Highway 11 bridge in Pendleton to the mouth at the Columbia River. Trout anglers visiting this area should consider the upper river. Most anglers are drawn to the Umatilla River looking for an opportunity to catch seasonal steelhead, hatchery spring chinook, fall jack salmon, and hatchery coho adult salmon. Because of the need to reintroduce salmon to the river in 1981 after their extinction in the early 20th century, salmon fishing has only recently become permitted. Anglers should read the latest restrictions and seasonal openings from year to year, as they might change with river management policies.

Salmon and steelhead fishing is restricted to the lower river from the Highway 730 bridge near the mouth to the Umatilla Indian Reservation boundary upstream from the Highway 11 bridge at Pendleton. The river is open for hatchery summer and winter steelhead January 1–April 15 and September 1–December 31, though the best fishing is September–mid-April. Spring chinook enter the river March–mid-April, and angling is open from the Highway 730 bridge to Three Mile Dam April 16–May 21, with a limit of two per fish day and 10 spring chinook per year. Spring chinook angling is also open from Three Mile Dam to the Indian reservation April 16–June 30, limit two fish per day and 10 per year. Angling for fall chinook salmon is limited to jacks (fall chinook under 24 inches). Jacks enter the river with the adults in late August and September, with the best catches occurring in October. Coho salmon enter the river in September and are best caught in October. Coho and jack salmon fishing is open from the Highway 730 bridge to the reservation boundary September 1–November 30, limit of two fish.

Techniques for catching salmon and steelhead should take into consideration the shallow water levels. Spinners such as a Blue Fox, spoons, and drift gear are all productive. Bait can include worms, shrimp, or salmon eggs drifted under floats or weighted with pencil lead. Fly anglers can use weighted streamers such as Egg Sucking Leeches or a slow sink tip line during the winter when flows are higher. Summer fly angling can be accomplished with floating lines and weighted or unweighted streamers in smaller sizes. If you're unsure about what techniques to use, you can always try to find local information by talking with other anglers or asking questions at the local hardware store.

Access to this lower river is generally good but often restricted to public access points because of private lands. Some of the best bank access is at road crossings, parks, highway pullouts and within the city limits of Pendleton, Hermiston, and Umatilla. Good bank access points are also available at Echo State Park near Stanfield, Steelhead Park in Hermiston, and along Umatilla River Rd. near Three Mile Dam. Don't expect to be fishing alone in these waters as the local population is very enthusiastic about its fish.

Boating on the lower river is allowed and practiced by many anglers. Drift boat and rafts are your best option because of the shallowness of the water. Some caution is required because there are numerous diversion dams (Stanfield, Cold Springs, Westland, and Three Mile) that are impassable and possibly dangerous during low-water years. Scouting and checking water levels is always a good option before undertaking a drift. A good starting drift is a 7.5-mile float from the paved ramp adjacent to the ODFW office east of Pendleton to the ramp at Reith. Other unimproved ramps can be found at Yoakum, Barnhart, the Power

Plant Gravel Bar, and at the Babe Ruth ramp in Pendleton.

Warm-water fishing is open all year from the footbridge in Umatilla to the Highway 730 bridge. Upstream from the footbridge, warm-water fishing is closed April 16–May 24. Smallmouth bass, perch, and crappie are all available and best fished for during the warmer months.

Species: Steelhead, hatchery coho, spring and fall chinook, jack salmon, perch, crappie, smallmouth bass.

Facilities: Camping is available in Umatilla National Forest at Tollgate, Mount Chalet, and North Fork Umatilla Wilderness. There are several campgrounds, RV parks, supplies, and accommodations around the towns of Umatilla and Pendleton. All boat ramps are free and mostly unimproved. Two concrete ramps can be had in Pendleton, one at the Babe Ruth ramp across from the ballpark and another adjacent to the ODFW offices east of Pendleton. Unimproved boat ramps are available west of Pendleton along Rieth Rd. in Barnhart and Rieth and at the intersection of Yoakum Rd. and Rieth Rd.

Directions: The lower river is easily followed by roads from the Hwy. 730 bridge crossing, 1.5 miles west of Umatilla, north to Pendleton. From the Hwy. 730 bridge crossing drive less than a mile east along Hwy. 730 to River Rd. and turn south. River Rd. follows the river for six miles before becoming Umatilla–Stanfield Hwy. in Hermiston. From Hermiston, you can turn west on Bridge Rd. to a river crossing access point or continue driving south on Umatilla–Stanfield Hwy., crossing under I-84 and Echo. In Echo, the road name changes again to Old Pendleton River Rd. and later Reith Rd. 10 miles southeast of Echo. Drive southeast on Old Pendleton River Rd. for 10 miles (the river will be to your south) and follow Rieth Rd. another eight miles to Rieth. Several of the boat ramps mentioned above are along this road at the junction of Yoakum Rd. (11 miles from Echo), in Barnhart (15 miles from Echo), and Reith (18 miles from Echo).

To reach Pendleton from Rieth, keep driving east on Rieth Rd. for two miles, crossing under I-84 and merging onto Hwy. 11. Highway 11 will reach downtown Pendleton in approximately 2.5 miles and more river access in town.

Contact: Pendleton Chamber of Commerce, 800/547-8911; Umatilla National Forest in Pendleton, 541/278-3716; BLM, Vale District, 541/473-3144; ODFW, Heppner, 541/676-5230; Umatilla Indian Reservation, 541/276-4109; AC RV Park, 541/278-1731; Arrowhead RV Park, 541/276-8484; Pioneer RV Park, 888/408-6100; Hat Rock Campground, 541/567-0917; Umatilla Marina and RV Park, 541/922-3939; Balanced Catch, 541/564-0626; High Desert Marine, 541/567-8419; Blue Mountain Anglers and Fly Shop in Pendleton, 541/966-8770.

⑦ WILLOW CREEK

south of Heppner in the Umatilla
National Forest

Map 4.2, page 242

Willow Creek is an 80-mile tributary of the Columbia River originating in the Umatilla National Forest south of Heppner. Below Heppner the water is captured in Willow Creek Reservoir, forming a tail-water fishery from the Willow Creek Dam to the Columbia River. Not a destination fishery by any means, Willow Creek can be a nice afternoon diversion for anglers with children visiting Willow Creek Reservoir. The river is inaccessible above the reservoir because of private property. Below the dam, the creek is heavily stocked with legal trout in Heppner. Anglers wishing to fish the creek can begin by driving north along Willow Creek Road below the dam to Heppner, looking for inviting spots or roadside pullouts. County roads follow the river below Heppner, and a good city map may be able to help you navigate this area. Within Heppner there is good bank fishing access in designated places such as Hager Park.

Species: Trout.

Facilities: Camping is available at Willow Creek Reservoir. Accommodations and supplies are available in Heppner.

Directions: To get to Hagar Park from Heppner drive south on Hwy. 74 and turn east onto East May St. (drive 0.1 mile), south onto Court St. (drive 0.1 mile), and southeast on Cowins St. The Hagar Park entrance will be on the east side of Cowins St. in approximately 0.1 mile. Anglers can reach the area from Hager Park to Willow Creek Dam along Willow Creek Rd. To get to this area, follow the directions to Hager Park, but after driving 0.1 mile on Court St., turn southeast onto Hagar St., which turns into Willow Creek Rd. and continues to the dam. The river follows the east bank of the river for 0.2 mile before reaching the reservoir.

Contact: Heppner Chamber of Commerce, 541/676-5536; BLM, Vale District, 541/473-3144; ODFW, Heppner, 541/676-5230; Willow Creek RV Park, 541/676-9618; Morrow County Parks, 541/989-9500; Heppner Hardware, 541/676-9961.

8 WILLOW CREEK RESERVOIR

south of Heppner

Map 4.2, page 242

Willow Creek Reservoir is a 110-acre irrigation impoundment situated in a grassy, hilly plain one mile south of Heppner. Fed by two forks of Willow Creek, it is a nice year-round fishing retreat and offers easy fishing access for both the boat and bank angler. Concrete boat ramps, fishing docks, brush-free banks, and campgrounds make this an accessible multiday fishing spot and should be considered a good option for families whose goal is catching fish. Some of the banks are steep and covered in riprap rock, which may present a challenge to smaller children. There are no boating restrictions.

The primary fish species are rainbow trout, largemouth bass, black crappie, white crappie, smallmouth bass, bluegill, pumpkinseed, and brown bullhead. Annual stockings of legal-size rainbow trout in April and May are the main attraction for early-season anglers. Holdovers from previous years can get quite large, some exceeding 18 inches. A good place to start hunting for trout is in the deeper water on the south shore along Willow Creek Road. Walk or drive down Willow Creek Road from the boat ramp and parking area. Look for areas along the shore where riprap rock forms the bank. Gear anglers will want to try spoons, plugs, or Rooster Tails. Vary your retrieve until you find the right action to attract fish. Fly anglers can use weighted nymphs or streamers such as Woolly Buggers or Zonkers, varying the retrieve until you get a bite. Boat anglers will want to fish the same water, trolling along the shore or casting to the bank and retrieving back to the boat.

Later in the summer and fall, when the trout have moved to deeper, cooler water, anglers begin targeting the warm-water species. Perch are best fished for around the inlets with a jig and erratic retrieves. Bass hold on both the north and southwest shores around underwater obstructions and can be caught with plastic worms and crankbaits. Fish for catfish in the deeper waters with bait such as worms or shrimp, letting the bait settle on the bottom of the lake.

Species: Trout, largemouth and smallmouth bass, black crappie, white crappie, perch, bluegill, pumpkinseed, brown bullhead, rainbow trout.

Facilities: There is a free boat ramp, dock, parking area, and restrooms at the far eastern shore of the lake, which you reach as you drive into the reservoir area from Willow Creek Rd. Camping can be had at Willow Creek Campground on the western shore. Campground fees include tent sites as well as RV sites with water, electric, and sewer. The campground is run by the City of Heppner. Showers, restrooms, drinking water, and telephones are all available. Supplies and accommodations are available in Heppner.

Directions: From Heppner, travel south one mile on Cowins St. to the park entrance. To reach the reservoir from I-84, take Exit 147, which is nine miles east of Arlington. After exiting the highway turn south on Hwy. 74 (Heppner Hwy.) and drive 57 miles to Heppner. In Heppner, turn east onto East May St. (drive 0.1 mile), south onto Court St. (drive 0.1 mile), and southeast onto Hagar St. Hagar St. turns into Willow Creek Rd. and will lead to the reservoir in approximately 0.2 mile. The campground is also along Willow Creek Rd.

Contact: Heppner Chamber of Commerce, 541/676-5536; BLM, Vale District, 541/473-3144; ODFW, Heppner, 541/676-5230; Willow Creek Campground and RV Park, 541/676-9618, www.heppner.net/wcpd; Morrow County Parks, 541/989-9500; Willow Creek Water Levels, 541/865-3229.

❾ WALLA WALLA RIVER
in Milton–Freewater

Map 4.3, page 243

Situated near the Oregon border near Milton–Freewater, the Walla Walla River is a short tributary of the Columbia River hosting runs of steelhead and a healthy population of trout, especially in its upper reaches. The main stem of the river flows about 12 miles in Oregon before crossing the border into Washington. It originates from the North and South forks in the Blue Mountains, five miles east of Milton–Freewater.

The main attractions of this river are steelhead and trout. Steelhead fishing is open from the Oregon border to the confluence with the forks January 1–April 15 and throughout December. Fish harvest is limited to hatchery fish and is restricted to flies and artificial lures. Unfortunately, there is very little access to the river because of private property, and permission from landowners is required to cross nonpublic lands. Some public access and good steelhead water can be had at Marie Dorian County Park north of Milton–Freewater. If you're desperate to fish this river and can't seem to find any access in Oregon, you can always sneak over to Washington and fish Swegle Public Fishing Area and McDonald Bridge Public Fishing Area, but you didn't hear it here.

Species: Steelhead, trout.

Facilities: Harris Park provides nice camping and RV facilities on the South Fork, 13 miles from Milton–Freewater. Supplies, accommodations, and RV parks with camping can be had in Milton–Freewater, Pendleton or Walla Walla, Washington.

Directions: To reach Marie Dorian County Park from Milton–Freewater drive south on Hwy. 11 one mile to Walla Walla River Rd. and turn east. Follow Walla Walla River Rd. 1.5 miles to Couse Creek Rd. Turn south on Couse Creek Rd. to the river crossing and the entrance to Marie Dorian County Park. To get to the upper river, take Hwy. 11 south of Milton–Freewater a couple of miles to Walla Walla River Rd. In 5–6 miles you will come to the confluence of the river forks. To get to Harris Park Campground, drive east on Walla Walla River Rd. to the forks and take the South Fork River Rd. seven miles to the end.

Contact: Milton–Freewater Chamber of Commerce, 541/938-5563; Umatilla National Forest in Pendleton, 541/278-3716; BLM, Vale District, 541/473-3144; ODFW, Heppner, 541/676-5230; Blue Mountain Anglers and Fly Shop in Pendleton, 541/966-8770; Harris Park, 541/938-5330; Henry's Ace Hardware, 541/938-5398; Trails West RV Park, 509/301-0650.

❿ NORTH FORK WALLA WALLA RIVER
east of Milton–Freewater

Map 4.3, page 243

The Walla Walla River North Fork is one of two forks that converge five miles east of Milton–Freewater to form the Walla Walla River. The North Fork originates off the west-facing slopes of the Blue Mountains in the Umatilla National Forest and runs 20 miles to its confluence. Decent populations of rainbow trout 8–12 inches inhabit the river. Bull trout are also present in good numbers but angling is for them is prohibited. The first eight miles of river is followed closely by the North Fork Walla

Walla Road, but private property prevails until you reach forest lands at the road's dead-end. From the dead-end road a good hiking trail (No. 3222) will take you into the headwaters. Expect a small river with shallow runs and pools. Fish can be found in classic holding water around obstacles, behind rocks, and in faster water. Dry flies, nymphs, and small spinners all work. Because the North Fork suffers from irrigation draws and water levels can drop significantly, warming the water and reducing the fishing potential in summer, spring and fall are the best times to fish this river when water levels are more stable. The North Fork is restricted to catch-and-release fishing with flies and artificial lures.

Species: Rainbow trout.

Facilities: Camping is available at Harris County Park on the South Fork of the Walla Walla River. Supplies and accommodations can be had in Milton–Freewater and Pendleton.

Directions: From Milton–Freewater drive south on Hwy. 11 one mile to Walla Walla River Rd. Turn east on Walla Walla River Rd. and drive approximately five miles before it turns into the North Fork Walla Walla River Rd. (Forest Rd. 680). North Fork Walla Walla River Rd. follows the river for approximately seven miles before dead-ending at Trailhead No. 3222.

Contact: Milton–Freewater Chamber of Commerce, 541/938-5563; Umatilla National Forest in Pendleton, 541/278-3716; ODFW, Heppner, 541/676-5230; Blue Mountain Anglers and Fly Shop in Pendleton, 541/966-8770; Target Meadows Campground, 509/525-6290; Harris County Park, 800/452-5687.

11 SOUTH FORK WALLA WALLA RIVER

east of Milton-Freewater

Map 4.3, page 243   BEST (

The South Fork of the Walla Walla is one of two forks that come together five miles east of Milton–Freewater to form the Walla Walla River. The South Fork originates in the Blue Mountains of the Umatilla National Forest and runs 30 miles west from its headwaters to its confluence. The trout here are not large, 10–12 inches, but they are plentiful. The river environment is somewhat arid, characterized by steep, shaded canyons, pine forests, and plenty of bank vegetation. The water in the South Fork runs exceptionally cold year-round, making this a nice place to fish even when summer temperatures can reach 100°F.

Access to the river is excellent both from roads and by hiking trails. The first nine miles of river is followed by the South Fork River Road and good access is provided by roadside turnouts and a short hike through the forest. South Fork River Road dead-ends into Harris County Park, a nice campground on the river, and hiking trails pick up where the roads left off. Trail No. 3225 follows the river for approximately 12 more miles. It is the hike-in section from Harris Park that really reveals the river's pristine beauty and splendor and anglers can get as remote as they wish to catch good numbers of small trout. The hiking is comfortable on good trails, but it often skirts high above the river, requiring anglers to make a sometimes-steep decent to get to the fishable water. Be sure to bring along plenty of water and snacks and watch for rattlesnakes.

Fishing gear and tactics for the South Fork should be kept simple and small. Regulations restrict fishing to the use of artificial flies and lures only, no bait. Shorter lightweight rods are the best for casting into tight pockets and small holding water. A small selection of nymphs such as Pheasant Tails and attractor dry flies will keep you in fish all day. Spin anglers can use small Rooster Tails and other spinners with single barbless hooks for easy fish release. Bull trout are also present in the river, but off-limits to fishing. The river is open for fishing May 27–October 31.

Species: Rainbow trout, bull trout.

Facilities: Fee camping is available at Harris County Park. Amenities include tent sites, RV sites, drinking water, restrooms, and fire pits. Supplies and accommodations can be had in Milton–Freewater and Pendleton.

Directions: From Milton–Freewater drive south on Hwy. 11 one mile to the Walla Walla River Rd. Turn east on Walla Walla River Rd. and drive approximately five miles to the South Fork Walla Walla River Rd. (Forest Rd. 680). Turn southeast on South Fork Walla Walla River Rd. and drive approximately nine miles to the dead-end at Harris Park Campground. The trailhead and parking can both be found in the campground.

Contact: Milton–Freewater Chamber of Commerce, 541/938-5563; Umatilla National Forest in Pendleton, 541/278-3716; ODFW, Heppner, 541/676-5230; Blue Mountain Anglers and Fly Shop in Pendleton, 541/966-8770; Target Meadows Campground, 509/525-6290; Harris County Park, 800/452-5687.

12 UPPER UMATILLA RIVER

east of Pendleton in the Umatilla
National Forest

Map 4.3, page 243

The upper Umatilla River flows 30 miles west, mostly through the Umatilla Indian Reservation, from the western flanks of the Blue Mountains in the Umatilla National Forest to Pendleton. This small but scenic, forested river provides good fishing for smaller wild redband trout. Public access to the upper river above Pendleton begins only after driving 24 miles east on County Highway 900, through the Umatilla Indian Reservation to Ryan Creek (the eastern boundary of the reservation). From Ryan Creek, upriver to the confluence of the river forks at Umatilla Forks Campground, anglers have unlimited bank access to six miles of river, along County Highway 900. Fishing on the Indian reservation property is allowed with a special tribal permit.

From the confluence of the two river forks

at Umatilla Forks Campground to Ryan Creek, the river flows through scenic forest lands and consists of small runs and pocket water. Fishing is good for wild redband trout but restricted to catch-and-release fishing with artificial flies and lures. Bull trout are also present, but it is illegal to target them and if you do by chance hook one, it must be released unharmed. Fishing is open during the regular fishing season May 27–October 31. Good starting places to begin fishing are at the Bingham Springs area, four miles upriver from the confluence of Ryan Creek, and below the Umatilla Forks Campground. Both of these places provide good water to test your dry fly, nymph, or spinner fishing skills. Attractor dry-fly patterns such as Royal Wulffs and Humpies in smaller sizes will produce fish all day. Early in the morning you can search the deeper pools with small nymphs and streamer patters such as Woolly Buggers. Spinners such as Rooster Tails will also work well in the deeper holes and runs.

Species: Wild redband trout.

Facilities: You can buy a tribal permit from the Tribal Administration Office near Pendleton. Fee camping is available at the Umatilla Forks Campground. Camping is also available in Umatilla National Forest at Tollgate, Mount Chalet, and North Fork Umatilla Wilderness. There are several campgrounds, RV parks, supplies, and accommodations around the towns of Umatilla and Pendleton.

Directions: To reach the upper river from Pendleton, drive east out of Pendleton on Hwy. 11 (Oregon–Washington Hwy.) four miles to the Umatilla–Mission Hwy. Turn south on the Umatilla–Mission Hwy. and drive approximately two miles to Mission Rd. in Mission. Turn east on Mission Rd., which turns into Cayuse Rd. after two miles. Keep driving east on Cayuse (which turns into Bingham Rd. after passing through Thorn Hollow), and drive approximately 18 more miles, passing through the Umatilla Indian Reservation, to the confluence of Ryan Creek. Ryan Creek comes in on the south side of the highway across the river. At this point, Bingham Rd. turns into County Hwy. 900. Umatilla Forks Campground is approximately seven miles east of Ryan Creek on County Rd. 900.

Contact: Pendleton Chamber of Commerce, 800/547-8911; Umatilla National Forest in Pendleton, 541/278-3716; BLM, Vale District, 541/473-3144; ODFW, Heppner, 541/676-5230; Umatilla Indian Reservation, 541/276-4109; AC RV Park, 541/278-1731; Arrowhead RV Park, 541/276-8484; Pioneer RV Park, 888/408-6100; Hat Rock Campground, 541/567-0917; Umatilla Marina and RV Park, 541/922-3939; Balanced Catch, 541/564-0626; High Desert Marine, 541/567-8419; Blue Mountain Anglers and Fly Shop in Pendleton, 541/966-8770.

13 NORTH FORK UMATILLA RIVER

east of Pendleton

Map 4.3, page 243

The Umatilla Forks North Fork is one of two forks that come together 32 miles east of Pendleton to form the Umatilla River. The North Fork originates in the North Fork Umatilla Wilderness in the Blue Mountains and runs six miles west to its confluence, three miles east of Bingham Springs. This is a small hike-in river, flowing through deep canyons and surrounded by thick pine forests. Fishing is good for wild redband trout, 9–12 inches. Regulations restrict anglers to catch-and-release fishing with the use of artificial flies and lures only. Bull trout and chinook salmon are also present but fishing is prohibited for both species. The trailhead for fishing this river is easily accessible from the Umatilla Forks Campground, three miles east of Bingham Springs on River Road. The trailhead for North Fork Trail (No. 3080) follows the river for approximately five miles. Fishing the river along the trail can be strenuous because much of the trail follows the river at the top of a steep canyon, requiring anglers to scrabble down steep hillsides to reach the river.

Tackle and techniques for fishing the river should be kept small and simple; leave the steelhead gear in the car and break out the light tackle equipment. Ultralight spinning rods and short fly rods (seven feet) will allow you to cast easily into tight pockets behind rocks and upstream. Fly anglers can use a simple indicator nymph rig and cast upstream into riffles or around obstructions such as logs and rocks. Two fly approaches work great with this technique. Dry flies can produce a lot of excitement. Use high-floating attractor patterns such as Humpies, Royal Wulffs, hoppers, or other deer hair flies for good visibility to both angler and fish. Cast above you in the currents and to the side in pocket water. If fish are present it will take only a split second for them to strike. Spin anglers will want to use small Rooster Tails or similar spinners in various colors, striking the pockets where you think fish may be resting. Quick retrieves of the spinner will ensure fast action from the fish.

Species: Wild rainbow trout.

Facilities: Fee camping is available at the Umatilla Forks Campground three miles east of Bingham Springs. Wilderness camping is available along the river wherever a tent can be pitched; no-trace camping is encouraged. Supplies and accommodations can be had in Pendleton.

Directions: From Pendleton drive east on Mission Rd., which turns into Cayuse Rd. in about five miles. In another 10 miles Cayuse Rd. turns into Bingham Rd. (County Hwy. 900). Stay east on Bingham Rd. approximately 20 miles to the Umatilla Forks Campground. (The campground is on Bingham Rd., which is also known as County Hwy. 900.) Free parking is available in the campground at the trailhead.

Contact: Pendleton Chamber of Commerce, 800/547-8911; Umatilla National Forest in Pendleton, 541/278-3716; ODFW, Heppner, 541/676-5230; Blue Mountain Anglers and Fly Shop in Pendleton, 541/966-8770.

14 SOUTH FORK UMATILLA RIVER

east of Pendleton

Map 4.3, page 243

The South Fork of the Umatilla is one of two forks that come together 32 miles east of Pendleton to form the Umatilla River. The South Fork originates at the base of Black Mountain in the Umatilla National Forest and runs north approximately 12 miles to its confluence at Umatilla Forks Campground three miles east of Bingham Springs. The river is characterized by small riffles and runs flowing through steep canyons. Summer flows can get quite low, making this a better place to fish in spring and fall. The river holds good populations of small wild rainbow trout, 9–12 inches, and bull trout. Fishing for bull trout is prohibited. The South Fork is open for fishing May 27–October 31. All fishing is limited to catch-and-release fishing with artificial flies and lures.

The river is easily accessible from both roads and hiking trails. The lower four miles of river is followed south by Forest Road 32. Pullouts are available along the road. Trail No. 3076 also follows the entire length of the river and originates at the Umatilla Forks Campground. The South Fork has recently come under concentrated efforts to restore damage to riparian areas, such as erosion, that have been caused by overuse from both recreationalists and logging practices. Visiting anglers can do their part in the restoration efforts by avoiding freshly planted streamside vegetation and using fragile riverbanks with care. Tackle and techniques should be kept light and simple. Ultralight spinning rods and short fly rods (seven feet) will allow you to cast easily into tight pockets behind rocks and upstream. Fly anglers can use a simple indicator nymph rig and cast upstream into riffles or around obstructions such as logs and rocks. Two fly approaches work great with this technique. Dry flies can produce a lot of excitement. Use high-floating attractor patterns such as Humpies, Royal Wulffs, hoppers, or other deer hair flies for

good visibility to both angler and fish. Cast above you in the currents and to the side in pocket water. If fish are present it will take only a split second for them to strike. Spin anglers will want to resort to small Rooster Tails or similar spinners in various colors, striking the pockets where you think fish may be resting. Quick retrieves of the spinner will ensure fast action from the fish.

Species: Wild rainbow trout.

Facilities: Fee camping is available at the Umatilla Forks Campground three miles east of Bingham Springs on Bingham Hwy. Unimproved natural campsites are available along the river wherever a tent can be pitched; no-trace camping is encouraged. Supplies and accommodations can be had in Pendleton.

Directions: From Pendleton drive east on Mission Rd., which turns into Cayuse Rd. in about five miles. In another 10 miles Cayuse Rd. turns into Bingham Rd. (County Hwy. 900). Stay east on Bingham Rd. approximately 20 miles to the Umatilla Forks Campground and the confluence of the North and South forks of the Umatilla River. Forest Rd. 32 from the campground follows the South Fork River south four miles. At four miles anglers can park at the trailhead to Trail No. 3076 and hike along the river for the remaining eight miles.

Contact: Pendleton Chamber of Commerce, 800/547-8911; Umatilla National Forest in Pendleton, 541/278-3716; ODFW, Heppner, 541/676-5230; Blue Mountain Anglers and Fly Shop in Pendleton, 541/966-8770.

15 McKAY RESERVOIR

south of Pendleton in McKay Creek Wildlife Refuge

Map 4.3, page 243

Eight miles south of Pendleton, McKay Reservoir (Mc-EYE) is part of a larger refuge called McKay Creek Wildlife Refuge. The reservoir is only a part of the 1,837 acres of open water, marsh, and grasslands that are home to abundant wildlife, migrating waterfowl, and numerous species of warm-water fish such as black crappie, yellow perch, bluegill, brown bullhead, largemouth bass, and channel catfish. Fishing is permitted March 1–September 30. The daily limit is three bass, none of which can exceed 15 inches.

Situated in a sage and grassland valley at an elevation of 1,320 feet, the reservoir covers 1,300 acres but can be reduced to 80 acres during low-water years. If you're planning a midsummer trip you might want to check with the Hermiston Irrigation District for up-to-date water levels. The average depth is 50 feet, and the deepest point (115 feet) is near the north end of the lake, due east of the boat ramp. There are 10 miles of shoreline, all accessible to the angler during the normal fishing season. Two boat ramps offer access to the lake on the west shore at both the south and north ends. During low-water conditions, only the northern ramp near the dam will accommodate bigger boats. There are no restrictions on boat or motor usage, but it's always a good idea to check with the Oregon Department of Fish and Wildlife before dragging that big cruiser down the gravel roads.

Spring, when the water levels are higher and the temperature lower, is the best time of year to target fish. There is very little structure in the water to provide cover for fish. Focus your attention on the brush-lined shores when the water levels are high. Bass provide the greatest game here, with some largemouths tipping the scales at nine pounds. A depth finder will help you find larger fish, such as the channel catfish, in the deeper waters at the southern end of the lake. The state-record channel catfish was caught here in 1980, weighing 36 pounds, 8 ounces. Perch fishing is good with the average fish measuring eight inches. Brown bullheads run a little bigger at 15 inches.

Species: Black crappie, yellow perch, bluegill, brown bullhead, largemouth bass, channel catfish.

Facilities: No camping is allowed at the lake, but there are restrooms. Boat ramps are at the north and south ends of the lake. Camping

can be had at Emigrant Springs State Park, Oregon Trail RV Park, Arrowhead RV Park, Brook RV Park, and Hat Rock Campground on the Columbia River. Supplies are available in the nearby town of Pendleton.

Directions: From Pendleton take Hwy. 395 south, across I-84, then drive eight miles to the McKay Reservoir turnoff.

Contact: Pendleton Chamber of Commerce, 800/547-8911; Umatilla National Forest in Pendleton, 541/278-3716; BLM, Vale District, 541/473-3144; ODFW, Heppner, 541/676-5230; Hermiston Irrigation District, 541/567-3024; Blue Mountain Anglers and Fly Shop in Pendleton, 541/966-8770; Emigrant Springs State Park, 541/983-2277; Oregon Trail RV Park, 541/276-4957; Hat Rock Campground, 541/567-0917; Arrowhead RV Park, 541/276-8484; Brooke RV Park, 541/276-5353.

16 UPPER GRANDE RONDE RIVER

west of La Grande

Map 4.3, page 243

The Grande Ronde originates in the Anthony Lakes area of the Blue Mountains. From Grande Ronde Lake it makes a 200-mile journey, through a designated Wild and Scenic section, to the Snake River in Washington state. Steelhead, trout, bull trout, and mountain whitefish are all present. A majority of the river from La Grande to the headwaters is followed by good roads with better than average bank access. Highway 84 west out of La Grande follows the river to Hilgard, where it is picked up by Highway 244 south. Between Hilgard and the steelhead fishing deadline at Meadow Creek near Starkey, there is good access from a couple of state parks. From Starkey, the river is followed by good Forest Service roads all the way into the headwaters on the slopes of the Blue Mountains.

Boating is not feasible in this section, but bank fishing is good for native steelhead and wild trout. Steelhead make their appearance in the upper river beginning in January. The steelhead season is open January 1–April 15 and September 1–December 31. Wild trout are available all year. The best places to begin fishing for steelhead or trout are either along Highway 244 at Hilgard Junction State Park or along I-84 off Exit 256 (the first exit west of La Grande), and at Five Points Creek confluence near Hilgard. Along Highway 244, Red Bridge State Park offers good water and hike-in possibilities downstream through the adjacent Forest Service lands. Anglers can ask for permission to fish near the steelhead deadline from the proprietors at Camp Elkanah. Forest Roads 51 and 5125 will lead you into the headwaters in the Wallowa–Whitman Forest, and it provides additional access for trout fishing and camping.

Fishing methods on this stretch are similar to those used in the lower river: traditional gear and flies. This is not really plug water; instead, stick to steelhead and trout lures. Water conditions are at their peak when there is adequate flow and the water is not off-color. At these times use larger, brightly colored spinners for steelhead and concentrate on the longer, deeper runs. Drift anglers can use bait under a float or weighted techniques with Spin-N-Glows. Fly anglers should use nymphs under an indicator or try streamers on a floating or short sink tip line. Streamer fishing and skated dry flies should always involve a series of mends to counter the pull on the fly line by the current. This technique will slow down the swing of the fly, thus enabling the steelhead to take the fly without being spooked. The Grande Ronde is noted for steelhead that rise to a skated dry fly, so don't ignore this possibility.

Trout fishing is effective with the use of spinners in smaller sizes and bait, such as night crawlers or flies. Search for pocket water around obstructions with spinners or nymphs. Don't ignore slicks or seams where two currents come together; seams are great holding water for trout. Shaded areas around brushy banks are always promising areas for wily trout.

Species: Wild trout, mountain whitefish, steelhead.
Facilities: Camping is available at Hilgard Junction and Red Bridge State Park. Three campgrounds can be found in the Wallowa–Whitman Forest, two on Forest Rd. 51 and one on Rd. 5125. Supplies, RV parks, and accommodations can be had in La Grande.
Directions: From La Grande take I-84 west approximately five miles to the Hwy. 244 junction. Drive south on Hwy. 244 for eight miles, following the river, passing Hilgard and Red Bridge state parks. Another three miles will put you in Starkey. To reach the headwaters from Starkey, drive south on County Hwy. 51 13 miles, following the river to Forest Rd. 5125. Turn southeast on Forest Rd. 5125 and drive seven miles to the confluence of the forks. A Forest Service map for the Wallowa–Whitman National Forest showing the locations of roads and the river above the confluence will help you navigate the headwaters section.
Contact: Union County Chamber of Commerce in La Grande, 541/963-8588; Wallowa–Whitman National Forest, 541/523-6391; Wallowa Mountains Visitors Center, 541/426-5546; BLM, Vale District, 541/473-3144; ODFW, La Grande, 541/963-2138; Four Seasons Fly Shoppe, La Grande, 541/963-8420; Camp Elkanah, 541/963-5050.

17 WENAHA RIVER
west of Troy
Map 4.4, page 244

The Wenaha originates in the Blue Mountains of the Wenaha–Tucannon Wilderness in the Umatilla National Forest and runs 35 miles to its confluence with the Grande Ronde at Troy. The majority of the river flows through a heavily forested canyon, and runs, pools, and pocket water created by large boulders characterize the river. Because rocks can be slippery, use extra caution when navigating this area on foot and wading in the cool, swift waters. There are no roads with access to the river except in the lower few miles, making this a hike-in fishery. Highlights include beautiful scenery, large rainbows, hatchery and wild steelhead, and catch-and-release fishing for bull trout.

Hike into this river from Trail No. 3106 outside Troy. The trail follows the river for 30 miles to its headwaters. Trout fishing is best after the spring runoff until late fall. Trout season is open May 27–October 31. Trout average 10–15 inches with some larger fish present. The Wenaha is one of the few rivers in Oregon that permits catch-and-release fishing for bull trout. All trout can be targeted with either nymphs or dry flies such as Royal Wulffs and Humpies. During the heat of the summer water levels tend to drop, creating perfect conditions for terrestrial patterns such as grasshoppers, ants, and beetles. Bull trout seem to have an affinity for nymphs as well as streamers. Try casting a weighted Woolly Bugger into faster currents and around structures for best results. Because of the potential for slightly larger fish, a 5-weight rod will be your best choice.

Steelhead fishing is limited to the lower six miles of river between the mouth and Crooked Creek. Steelhead season is open January 1–April 15 and September 1–December 31. Steelhead can generally be found in the river late October–January or later. Fly-fishing is particularly popular with most anglers on the Wenaha, although spin angers also do well. Carry larger medium-action rods or 6–7-weight fly rods. Fly anglers tend to use traditional Northwest steelhead hairwing patterns such as Green Butt Skunks, Purple Perils, and Juicy Bugs. Don't ignore nymphs as an option in the pocket water and in deeper runs. Also, streamers such as Egg Sucking Leeches can produce good results. Spin anglers can use Rooster Tails in an assortment of colors; red, black, and purple are the most popular colors.

Species: Wild rainbow trout, wild and hatchery steelhead, bull trout.

Facilities: There are no developed campgrounds so anglers wishing to camp on the river will have to find suitable natural campsites. The nearest accommodations and supplies can be had in Troy.

Directions: From Troy drive south on Troy Rd. less than 0.5 mile to Wenaha Game Rd. and turn west. Follow Wenaha Game Rd. approximately two miles to the end. Parking is available here at the trailhead to Trail No. 3106. Anglers can follow this trail into the river's headwaters.

Contact: Union County Chamber of Commerce in La Grande, 541/963-8588; Wallowa County Chamber of Commerce (Troy, Joseph, Enterprise), 800/585-4121; Elgin Chamber of Commerce, 541/437-3100; Umatilla National Forest in Pendleton, 541/278-3716; ODFW, La Grande, 541/963-2138; Minam Motel, 877/888-8130; River View Cabin, 541/828-7070; Troy Wilderness Resort, 541/828-7741; Shiloh Oasis Resort, 541/828-7741; Grande Ronde Outfitters and Lodge, 541/828-7902, granderonde@tds.net; Little Creek Outfitters, 541/963-7878, www.littlecreekoutfitters.net.

18 JUBILEE RESERVOIR
east of Pendleton in the Umatilla National Forest

Map 4.4, page 244

Jubilee Reservoir is a scenic lake in the Umatilla National Forest well suited for camping and families. Serious anglers intending to catch trophy trout will be disappointed as much by the size of the fish as the crowds, but families should enjoy the ease of fishing and efficient camping facilities. Jubilee is open year-round, but snows will block access until the first week in July.

The lake sits at an elevation of 4,700 feet and is approximately 90 acres, forming the headwaters of Mottet Creek. There are 2.5 miles of shoreline with accessible hiking and biking trails. The average depth is 16 feet, and the deepest point (45 feet) is at the southern end of the lake near the boat ramp. Fishing is best after it has been stocked in spring and again in July. Because of the popularity of this lake and the annual kids' fishing event, the lake gets fished out quite fast. Bait, spinners, and flies all work, with no particular strategy being the best. Don't expect any lunker-size trout, but a simple bobber and worm or small spinner will catch pan-size fish all day and keep the kids engaged.

Species: Rainbow trout.

Facilities: There are 50 campsites, a day-use area ($3), four picnic sites, restrooms, drinking water, hiking trails, and a boat ramp. There is an annual kids fishing day. Camping facilities are fully accessible to wheelchairs. Buy supplies in the nearby town of Pendleton.

Directions: From Pendleton drive northeast on Hwy. 11 approximately 20 miles to the Hwy. 204 junction and turn east toward Tollgate. Continue on Hwy. 204 for 20 miles to Tollgate. Just east of Tollgate take Forest Rd. 64 north. Stay on Forest Rd. 64 for approximately 12 miles until you reach Forest Rd. 63. Turn south on Forest Rd. 63 and drive one mile to the entrance to Jubilee Lake Campground.

Contact: Pendleton Chamber of Commerce, 800/547-8911; Umatilla National Forest in Pendleton, 541/278-3716; BLM, Vale District, 541/473-3144; ODFW, Heppner, 541/676-5230; Blue Mountain Anglers and Fly Shop in Pendleton, 541/966-8770; Emigrant Springs State Park, 541/983-2277; Oregon Trail RV Park, 541/276-4957; Hat Rock Campground, 541/567-0917; Arrowhead RV Park, 541/276-8484; Brooke RV Park, 541/276-5353.

19 LOWER GRANDE RONDE RIVER

north of La Grande

Map 4.4, page 244   BEST (

The Grande Ronde is probably the most popular steelhead fishery in Northeastern Oregon, averaging more than 5,000 fish caught every year. The lowest and most productive part of the river runs from the Wallowa confluence near Minam to the Washington state line. This 43 miles of river includes 26.4 miles that

are designated Wild and Scenic, and 17.4 miles are designated recreational with excellent bank access. Steelhead are the primary species, but there are also good numbers of smallmouth bass, trout, and large mountain whitefish. Trout fishing is good throughout most of the river, with smaller fish 10–14 inches. Bass are generally caught around Troy in the slower water and pools. Winter holds surprises for the angler not shy about catching whitefish. Large whitefish, 20–24 inches, inhabit these waters and make for good sport with the locals. The steelhead season here is January 1–April 15 and September 1–December 31. Bait, flies, and lures are all allowed, and any wild fish must be released unharmed. Trout season is open May 27–October 31. Bull trout are present but may not be targeted and must be released unharmed.

All the steelhead caught in this river are considered summer-run fish, even though they don't enter the river until October. The movement of fish upstream coincides with fall rains needed to raise the water levels, enabling fish to pass rugged chutes and obstacles. In low-water years, such as in 2005, the fish did not begin to move into the river in fishable numbers until mid-November. When this happens the steelhead begin staging in the lower river and at the confluence with the Snake River. The Washington stretch gets a lot of attention during these times of year. In normal years the Grande Ronde fishes well from October until as late as March. Checking water levels through the USGS website will help anglers plan successful trips.

Both boating and bank angling are popular here. The river is suitable only for drift boat and rafts and caution should be used because there are numerous rapids and large boulders. The most popular floats begin in Minam on the Wallowa River or Palmer Junction on the Grande Ronde and require three days to reach the pullouts at Wildcat Creek, nine miles south, above Troy, or in Troy at two ramps, Troy Access No. 1 or Troy Access No. 2. This part of the river includes a designated

Wild and Scenic section from Rondowa at the confluence of the Grande Ronde and Wallowa Rivers to Wildcat Creek. There is no bank access from Palmer Junction to Wildcat Creek. Should you not want to attempt multiday trips on your own, several good outfitters provide first-class service.

Shorter one-day floats can be had from Wildcat Creek or nearby Mud Creek, nine miles downriver to the take-outs at Troy. There are two boat ramps near Troy; Troy Access No. 1 and Troy Access No. 2. The latter will add about two miles to your drift. Anglers who float the river below Troy do so only when water levels permit. The only reasonable pullouts below Troy are near the Highway 129 bridge in Washington state. This is a good 15-mile float, but you will need licenses for whichever state you decide to fish. Most anglers resort to bank angling below Troy, as access is good and trouble-free.

The best bank fishing access is from Wildcat Creek through Troy to the Washington border. Troy Road follows the river from Mud Creek Campground, two miles below Troy, turning into Grande Ronde Road, which continues to the Washington border. Bank access can be had anywhere along either of these two roads. The best approach when fishing from the bank here is to drive along the road until you spot an inviting piece of water. Find a roadside pullout and hike down to the river. Fishing methods for steelhead vary depending on what part of the river you fish. The Wild and Scenic section, a three-day float, tends to attract more fly anglers, while the area below Wildcat Creek attracts both traditional gear anglers and fly anglers. Productive fly-fishing techniques include both streamer and dry flies. In fact, many anglers come to the Grande Ronde specifically to catch steelhead on a skated dry fly. Streamers and greased-line methods are more traditional but equally effective on the bigger runs.

Species: Summer steelhead, trout, smallmouth bass, mountain whitefish.

Facilities: All boat ramps on the river are free.

Available boat ramps can be found at Minam State Recreation Area in Minam, Palmer Junction near Lookingglass, Wildcat Creek, Mud Creek nine miles south of Troy, and in Troy at Troy Access No. 1 and Troy Access No. 2. Camping supplies and accommodations can be had in Troy, Minam, Elgin, and La Grande.

Fee camping is available in Minam at the Minam State Recreation Area. Free camping is available on BLM lands around Wildcat Creek and Mud Creek, and at Griz Flats on the Wenaha River. Other accommodations can be had in Troy. Among these are an anglers' lodge run by Dave Flynn of Grande Ronde Steelhead and Outfitters.

The BLM has imposed special camping regulations on the Wild and Scenic section of river between Rondowa, at the confluence of the Grande Ronde and Wallowa Rivers, to the Wildcat Creek section. Camping is allowed anywhere you can pitch a tent, but no-trace camping is required, meaning all waste, including solid human waste, must be packed out. Human waste is generally managed with a five-gallon bucket filled with kitty litter or sand. Fires are discouraged except in cooking pans.

Directions: From La Grande, take Hwy. 82 north approximately 20 miles to Elgin. Continue north on Hwy. 82 for another 14 miles, crossing Minam Hill Summit (elevation 3,638 feet), to Minam. Troy is approximately 90 miles from Minam. To reach Troy, take Hwy. 82 east out of Minam and drive 30 miles to Hwy. 3 (Enterprise–Lewiston Hwy.). Turn north on Hwy. 3, drive 47 miles to Grande Ronde Rd., then turn west. Stay on Grande Ronde Rd. (sections unpaved) for 17 miles until you arrive at Troy.

To reach Lookingglass Creek from La Grande, drive northeast on Hwy. 82 from the intersection of Business Rte. 30 in downtown La Grande. In approximately two miles the highway will cross the river near Island City and in another mile you will pass through Island City. Continue driving northeast on

Hwy. 82 for approximately 20 miles to reach Elgin. From Elgin, you can get to Lookingglass Creek and the confluence of the Wallowa River by driving north on Hwy. 42 out of Elgin and following the road 15 miles to Merts Store on Moses Creek Lane. Turn east on Moses Creek Ln. and drive two miles to reach the river. Follow the river north on Moses Ln. to reach Lookingglass in approximately one mile.

Contact: Union County Chamber of Commerce in La Grande, 541/963-8588; Wallowa County Chamber of Commerce (Troy, Joseph, Enterprise), 800/585-4121; Umatilla National Forest in Pendleton, 541/278-3716; BLM, Vale District, 541/473-3144; ODFW, La Grande, 541/963-2138; ODFW, Enterprise, 541/426-3279; Four Seasons Fly Shoppe, La Grande, 541/963-8420, www.4seasons@eoni.com; Joseph Fly Shoppe, 541/432-4343, www.josephflyshoppe.com; Minam Motel, 877/888-8130; River View Cabin, 541/828-7070; Troy Wilderness Resort, 541/828-7741; Shilo Oasis Resort, 541/828-7741; Grande Ronde Outfitters and Lodge, 541/828-7902, granderonde@tds.net; Little Creek Outfitters, 541/963-7878, www.littlecreekoutfitters.net; Shuttle service and raft rentals: Minam Store, 541/437-1111.

20 MIDDLE GRANDE RONDE RIVER

La Grande to Wallowa River confluence

Map 4.4, page 244

The Grande Ronde River from La Grande to Palmer Junction, upstream from the confluence with the Wallowa River, is only marginally attractive to most anglers. From La Grande the river flows east through a valley of agricultural lands with numerous diversions and channels for irrigation. This section of river does hold steelhead in January and trout during the fishing season, but most of the water is bordered by private property and is inaccessible unless you ask permission from landowners. It is not until you get to Elgin,

where the river resumes its flow into a canyon, that the river again holds promise for steelhead and trout anglers. Most of the steelhead are caught between the towns of Elgin and Palmer Junction in early winter; trout fishing is best in the summer. From Palmer Junction upstream to Meadow Creek, the steelhead fishing deadline, the river is open January 1–April 15 and September 1–December 31. Bait, flies, and lures are all allowed, but any wild fish must be released unharmed.

During higher river flows boating is possible between Elgin and Palmer Junction at Lookingglass Creek, but some caution should be exercised. Anglers should scout all put-ins, take-outs, and water conditions before attempting this run. The next take-out below Palmer Junction is a three-day float to Wildcat Creek. There is a gravel bar launch on Clark Creek Road near Elgin Park. Bank fishing is limited to a few parks and river easements around bridges in La Grande, Island Park, and Elgin. Riverside Park in La Grande offers good river access, as does Elgin Park. Further access can be had along the road from Lookingglass Creek to the confluence with the Wallowa River.

Fishing tactics remain similar to those used on the lower river. Flies, spinners, and bait all work with equal success. Steelhead anglers using traditional gear can rely on large steelhead spinners, plugs, and drift rigs with Spin-N-Glows or bait. Float fishing may be possible, but it doesn't seem practiced much. Fly anglers can use streamers, nymphs, and skated dry flies. All anglers should concentrate on areas around boulders and in deeper runs, especially where drop-offs are present. Trout anglers will want to concentrate on the pocket water along shorelines, behind rocks, and in back eddies. High-floating attractor patterns such as Royal Wulffs and Humpies are sure to catch a slew of trout. If dry flies don't produce, switch to streamers such as Woolly Buggers or nymphs. Use an indicator with nymphs and ensure a good dead drift through pocket water.

Species: Trout, bull trout, steelhead.

Facilities: Primitive camping is available in Minam at the Minam State Recreation Area, on BLM lands around Wildcat Creek and Mud Creek, and at Griz Flats on the Wenaha River. An unimproved gravel bar launch is available in Elgin on Clark Creek Rd. and also at Palmer Junction at Lookingglass Creek. Camping supplies and accommodations and RV parks with tent sites can be had in Troy, Minam, Elgin, Island City, and La Grande.

Directions: To get to Riverside Park in La Grande, start at the intersection of business Rte. 30 and Hwy. 82 and go east on Hwy. 82 for 0.2 miles to N. Spruce St. Turn north on N. Spruce St. and drive one mile to reach the entrance of Riverside Park. Parking is available in the park. To reach Elgin from La Grande, take Hwy. 82 north approximately 20 miles. Continue north on Hwy. 82 for another 14 miles to reach Minam. To reach Lookingglass Creek from La Grande, drive northeast on Hwy. 82 from the intersection of business Rte. 30 in downtown La Grande. In approximately two miles the highway will cross the river near Island City and in another mile you will pass through Island City. Continue driving northeast on Hwy. 82 for approximately 20 miles to reach Elgin. From Elgin, you can get to Lookingglass Creek and the confluence of the Wallowa River by driving north on Hwy. 42 north out of Elgin and following the road 15 miles to Merts Store on Moses Creek Lane. Turn east on Moses Creek Ln. and drive two miles to reach the river. Follow the river north on Moses Ln. to reach Lookingglass in approximately one mile.

Contact: Union County Chamber of Commerce in La Grande, 541/963-8588; Wallowa County Chamber of Commerce (Troy, Joseph, Enterprise), 800/585-4121; Elgin Chamber of Commerce, 541/437-3100; Umatilla National Forest in Pendleton, 541/278-3716; BLM, Vale District, 541/473-3144; ODFW, La Grande, 541/963-2138; ODFW, Enterprise, 541/426-3279; Wallowa Mountains Visitors Center, 541/426-5546; Four Seasons Fly Shoppe, La Grande, 541/963-8420, www.4seasons@eoni.com; Joseph Fly Shoppe, 541/432-4343, www.josephflyshoppe.com; Minam Motel, 877/888-8130; River View Cabin, 541/828-7070; Troy Wilderness Resort, 541/828-7741; Grande Ronde Outfitters and Lodge, 541/828-7902, granderonde@tds.net; Little Creek Outfitters, 541/963-7878, www.littlecreekoutfitters.net; Shuttle service and raft rentals: Minam Store, 541/437-1111.

21 WALLOWA RIVER
north of La Grande

Map 4.4, page 244

The Wallowa River flows 80 miles out of Wallowa Lake to its confluence with the Grande Ronde River approximately six miles northwest of Minam at Rondowa (so called because it is the meeting of the Grande Ronde and Wallowa Rivers). It is noted for both its year-round trout fishing and summer steelhead that appear in the river February–April. A majority of the river from Wallowa Lake north (downriver) to Wallowa is bordered by private property and access is not available to anglers. Odd as it may seem for such a long river, most of the fishing occurs in the last 14 miles of river, from Wallowa to the confluence at the Grande Ronde River.

The best access for both boat and bank anglers is between the towns of Wallowa and Minam. The river here is followed closely by Highway 82 for all of its length, providing good roadside access at turnouts, parks, and state waysides. Six miles west of Wallowa, anglers can reach the river at Wallowa Lake State Wayside. Park at the wayside and walk up- or downriver on good trails. Another access point is at Rock Creek, approximately 12 miles east of Minam. This is a popular starting place for steelhead and trout anglers. There is no improved access to the river at Rock Creek and anglers will have to blaze their own trails. From Rock Creek downstream to the beginning of Big Canyon, two miles west of Minam, anglers can park at any roadside turnout and walk down to the river wherever promising water can be spotted. Another good access point is at Minam State Park, two miles below Minam, which offers improved facilities and trails along the river.

Boaters have two options for floating the river, suitable only for a drift boat or raft. The first float is five miles, from Big Canyon to Minam State Park. The boat launch at Big Canyon does not have a ramp; boats are simply launched from the roadside near the confluence of Deer Creek. The second option is to float from Minam State Park to Wildcat Creek on the Grande Ronde (a 2–3-day float). There used to be a take-out at Rondowa, a few miles below Minam, but the road washed out in past years and has not been repaired. Both floats involve a high degree of risk because of white water and large boulders and should be attempted only by experienced boaters familiar with the river.

Fly anglers fishing for trout in the lower river can step up to larger weighted flies and medium-weight trout tackle suitable for making longer casts. Rods in the 5–6-weight range will handle just about all this water. Larger rods (6 and 7) will be required to land and safely release larger steelhead. Spin and bait anglers can use light tackle for trout and larger medium-weight rods for steelhead.

A smaller hike-in section of river exists above the Wallowa Lake, coming into the lake at the south end near the Wallowa Lake State Park. The river here is small and runs cold and clear, providing good catch-and-release fishing for wild rainbow and brook trout with artificial lures and flies. Trails into this section of river are accessible from the Wallowa Lake State Park at the southern end of Wallowa Lake.

Species: Rainbow, bull, and brook trout, steelhead.

Facilities: Fee camping is available at Minam State Park and Wallowa Lake. Free camping is available along the Lostine River Rd. on the Lostine River. The only official boat ramp on the river is free and can be had at the river

crossing in Minam. Supplies and accommodations can be had in the towns of Minam, Wallowa, Enterprise, and Joseph.

Directions: To get to Minam from La Grande, drive northeast on Hwy. 82 approximately 34 miles. The entrance to Minam State Park is in Minam on the north side of Hwy. 82. To reach the river above Minam, drive east on Hwy. 82 out of Minam, passing through Wallowa, Lostine, and Enterprise, following the river for 32 miles to reach Joseph and Wallowa Lake. The boat ramp at the river crossing in Minam, and fishing access areas such as Big Canyon, Rock Creek, and Wallowa State Wayside are all along Hwy. 82 between Minam and Wallowa. The headwaters of the Wallowa above Lake Wallowa can be reached from Trails 1820 and 1804 at the South Park Picnic Area in Wallowa Lake State Park. To reach Wallowa Lake State Park from Joseph, drive one mile south on Hwy. 82 to reach the lake. Highway 82 follows the lake four miles to its southern end and Wallowa Lake State Park. Parking is available at the trailheads in the park's South Park Picnic Area.

Contact: Union County Chamber of Commerce in La Grande, 541/963-8588; Wallowa County Chamber of Commerce (Troy, Joseph, Enterprise), 800/585-4121; Wallowa–Whitman National Forest, 541/523-6391; Wallowa Mountains Visitors Center, 541/426-5546; BLM, Vale District, 541/473-3144; ODFW, La Grande, 541/963-2138; Joseph Fly Shoppe, 541/432-4343, www.josephflyshoppe.com; Minam Motel, 877/888-8130; Four Seasons Fly Shoppe, La Grande, 541/963-8420.

22 MINAM RIVER
north of La Grande in the Eagle Cap Wilderness

Map 4.4, page 244   BEST (

The Minam River flows almost entirely through the Eagle Cap Wilderness from its origin at Blue Lake. It joins its parent river, the Wallowa, 50 miles to the north in Minam. In 1988, a 39-mile section of river was designated

Wild and Scenic from its headwaters at the southern end of Minam Lake to the Eagle Cap Wilderness boundary, one-half mile downstream from Cougar Creek. Special fishing regulations restrict anglers to the use of flies and artificial lures only. Road access is available in the lower nine miles of river, but this is primarily a hike-in fishery with a unique fly-in opportunity to stay at a remote lodge. Some anglers choose to take horseback trips into this country. No matter how you get to the river, this is sure to be the experience of a lifetime.

The first 18 miles of river including the forks begins as a steep drainage that runs off the slopes of the highest mountains in the Eagle Cap Wilderness. Beginning in the vicinity of Minam Lodge, the river begins a gentle decent with wide runs and riffles flowing through a heavily forested valley. Below the lodge the river flows through deep basalt canyons and rimrocks that inspire a sense of awe. Wildlife is diverse and abundant in all these areas and is popular with big game hunters in the fall and winter. Cougar, wolverines, bighorn sheep, mule deer, elk, black bear, river otter, and bald eagle all live in the Minam River Valley.

It's easy to get sidetracked with the splendor and beauty of this place. There are several options for reaching the river: By car, anglers can get to the lower nine miles of river from Minam to Meads Flat. From Meads Flat to the headwaters, a good hiking trail (No. 1673) traverses the river for 40 miles, granting unlimited fishing access. Approximately 7.5 miles upstream of the trailhead sits the Minam River Lodge. You can also work your way from Blue Lake at the headwaters, downriver past the lodge to Minam Flats.

Trout fishing season on the Minam is open during the regular season May 27–October 31. Anglers can begin fishing as soon as the spring runoff stabilizes water conditions, sometime in late July, but many anglers prefer this river in the late summer, such as in August when insect hatches are more prolific and the fish are for-

aging for winter. The Minam does not receive any stocked fish, and its entire populations of rainbow trout, brown trout, brook trout, and bull trout are completely wild. Rainbow and brown trout average 8–15 inches, with some larger fish available. Brook trout and bull trout are 8–10 inches.

The Minam is a major spawning tributary for the Grande Ronde stock of chinook salmon, and those fish are present in the river July–mid-September. Salmon and steelhead angling are prohibited, and anglers should be careful not to disturb spawning reds while wading the river or fishing for trout. The Minam is well suited to fly-fishing, but spinner fishing is also effective. Light tackle gear is best, such as ultralight spin rods and 3- and 4-weight fly rods. The most productive fishing in early summer will occur on nymphs and streamers. Weight your flies so you're sure to be near the bottom. In late summer and fall, watch for prolific hatches of insects such as caddis and even terrestrials such as ants, beetles, or grasshoppers. If you're unsure about the best approach to use, you can always try what has come to be known as the "hopper/dropper method." This method involves a two-fly rig of a grasshopper or larger dry fly and a smaller nymph, such as a Hare's Ear or Copper John. Tie a piece of tippet about 8–12 inches off the bend of the larger fly, and attach the nymph. The larger fly is meant to act as a strike indicator for the nymph, with the advantage that the fish may take the dry fly.

Species: Trout, salmon, steelhead.

Facilities: Natural campsites are available anywhere in the Eagle Cap Wilderness. Approximately 7.5 miles upstream of the trailhead at Meads Flat is the Minam River Lodge, a full-service public lodge open to hikers for lodging and meals. Tent sites are available around the lodge. The lodge also runs an outfitting service, books float-fishing trips and backcountry wilderness excursions on horseback, and rents rafts for self-guided trips downriver to the towns of Minam or Troy on the Grande Ronde. Two landing strips can accommodate small planes for those wishing to fly in. Buy supplies in Minam before hiking into the wilderness. The Minam Lodge does not have supplies for purchase. Camping outside the wilderness can be had at the Minam State Recreation Area. More supplies and accommodations can be had in Wallowa and La Grande.

Directions: From La Grande take Hwy. 82 north approximately 20 miles to Elgin. Stay on Hwy. 82 north for another 14 miles, crossing Minam Hill Summit (elevation 3,638 feet), to Minam. The entrance to Minam State Park is in Minam on the north side of Hwy. 82. To reach the lower nine miles of river, drive south on Deer Creek Rd. off Hwy. 82, two miles east of Minam. In approximately two miles, turn west at the fork on a four-wheel drive road. Follow this road nine miles along the river to the parking lot at the trailhead.

Contact: Union County Chamber of Commerce in La Grande, 541/963-8588; Wallowa–Whitman National Forest, 541/523-6391; Wallowa Mountains Visitors Center, 541/426-5546; ODFW, Enterprise, 541/426-3279; Four Seasons Fly Shoppe, La Grande, 541/963-8420; Minam Motel, 877/888-8130; Minam River Lodge, 541/432-6545; Minam Lodge Outfitters, 541/562-8008.

23 LOSTINE RIVER
south of Lostine

Map 4.4, page 244

The Lostine is not a destination fishery, but because of its proximity to such rivers as the Minam, Wallowa, and Catherine Creek, not to mention several wilderness lakes and its scenic values, this river is a must-see for anyone who appreciates the challenge of catching an abundance of small, wild trout in a small stream. The Lostine is a small but scenic river that flows 31 miles from Eagle Cap Wilderness in the Wallowa–Whitman National Forest to its confluence with the Wallowa River west of Lostine. All fishing on this river is done from the bank; there are no boating opportunities.

Reached by a good road out of Lostine, all but the lowermost parts of the river are accessible to the angler. The headwaters form at Minam Lake, a few miles above the Eagle Cap Wilderness boundary, and flow for a few miles before picking up the East Fork near Two Pan Campground on Forest Road 8210. Two Pan Campground also provides a good jumping-off place to fish the forks or area lakes in the Eagle Cap Wilderness. Below the confluence, the river begins to channel into a small canyon until it emerges into the lower valley and makes its way through agricultural and private lands. The entire river is great fly-fishing water, especially the lowest section. Ask permission from local landowners to fish this area; they are known to be generous in honoring such requests.

The Lostine fishery comprises mostly small wild trout and native bull trout, and it acts as spawning habitat for salmon in the early winter and spring. Salmon fishing is illegal, and anglers have been asked to use special caution not to disturb the spawning reds when fishing for trout. Bull trout are present but off-limits to anglers. Any accidental catches of bull trout must be returned to the river unharmed. Lostine trout are not big, but they are wild and plentiful. The best fishing times are midsummer–fall, but the river is fishable once water levels subside after the spring runoff. The trout average 7–11 inches and display nice colors from the cold water. As with most streams flowing out of the wilderness, tackle is restricted to artificial lures and flies to protect the bull trout.

Fishing the Lostine is a straightforward affair: nymphs, dry flies, and small spinners on light tackle gear. Ultralight spinning rods and 3–4-weight fly rods are all that is required to have a successful day. Nymphs will work better in the early season; switch to dry flies during the summer and fall. Use medium- to small-size attractor patterns such as Humpies, Royal Wulffs, and terrestrial patterns to entice trout from around rocks, in pools, and along brushy banks. Spin anglers can do the same with a small Rooster Tail, varying your retrieve and depth until you hit on the right combination of factors.

The two river forks are hike-in fisheries with good access from the end of Forest Road 8210 at Two Pan Campground. Two hiking trails, Nos. 1670 and 1662, follow the main river and East Fork, respectively. The main fork is bigger, and anglers may find more success there. Access points along Rd. 8210 can be had at five other campgrounds and several other trailheads.

Species: Trout.

Facilities: There are six primitive campgrounds along Forest Rd. 8210 (Lostine River Rd.) with no facilities other than restrooms. Supplies and accommodations can be had in Lostine and Enterprise.

Directions: From Lostine drive south on Forest Rd. 8210 (Lostine River Rd.). Follow this road for 24 miles to a dead-end at Two Pan Campground. Trails 1670 and 1662 will take you along the upper Lostine and East Fork, respectively.

Contact: Union County Chamber of Commerce in La Grande, 541/963-8588; Wallowa County Chamber of Commerce (Troy, Joseph, Enterprise), 800/585-4121; Wallowa–Whitman National Forest, 541/523-6391; ODFW, Enterprise, 541/426-3279; Joseph Fly Shoppe, 541/432-4343, www.josephflyshoppe.com; Four Seasons Fly Shoppe, La Grande, 541/963-8420.

24 WALLOWA LAKE
south of Joseph

Map 4.4, page 244   **BEST (**

The quaint town of Joseph, gateway to the Hells Canyon Recreation Area and Eagle Cap Wilderness, hosts this 1,500-acre, glacier-formed lake one mile south of town. The lake offers a variety of activities and is family-friendly, so anglers and nonanglers alike will be able to find what interests them. Expect to see lots of recreational boaters. Nestled at 4,380 feet among the breathtaking Wallowa Mountains,

Wallowa Lake is home to record-breaking rainbow trout, kokanee, lake trout, and bull trout. (Fishing for bull trout is prohibited in the lake and in the inlet streams.) The lake is fed by two forks of the Wallowa River coming out of Eagle Cap Wilderness. All tributaries to the lake are closed September 1–October 31 to protect spawning kokanee. The Wallowa River outlet can provide some good year-round trout fishing. The average depth is 170 feet, and the deepest point (300 feet) is near the middle and southern end of the lake. There are 8.5 miles of shoreline, all accessible by the angler, but most use boats to reach the fish.

May, June, and July are the best times to target the abundant populations of kokanee (landlocked sockeye salmon) that can reach 20 inches. It is estimated that 30,000 kokanee are caught every year, with the state record of 6 pounds, 12 ounces caught in 2001. For best results fish the northwest end of the lake. Lake trout (mackinaw) are present, although no longer stocked. These fish can run big, but you have to go deep (200 feet and more) to get their attention. Spinners, bait, and jigs all work for the mackinaw and kokanee. Depth finders can be invaluable for finding fish that lie in deeper waters. Search for trout on the southern shoreline, close to shore, around structures or shoals both in and out of the water. Spinners such as Rooster Tails trolled or pulled back to the angler are productive. Bait such as worms is effective under a bobber. Fly anglers can begin using searching patterns such as Woolly Buggers and small nymphs, being conscious of any insect emergences that may occur in the warmer parts of the day.

Species: Rainbow and lake (mackinaw) trout.

Facilities: Popular as a jumping-off point for travelers headed into Hells Canyon, the lake is considered by many vacationers as a destination spot for boating and other activities such as hiking, horseback riding, and general tourism. Expect to see lots of water-sport enthusiasts such as pleasure boaters, water skiers, and Jet Skiers. For a fee, boat ramps, boat rentals, and camping can be had at Wallowa Lake State Park. Amenities at the park include water, showers, restrooms, cabins, and RV hookups. Accommodations and supplies can be had in Joseph or at other private resorts.

Directions: From Joseph drive one mile south on Hwy. 82 to reach the lake. Highway 82 follows the lake four miles to its southern end and Wallowa Lake State Park. Parking is available in the park at day-use parking sites.

Contact: Joseph Chamber of Commerce, 541/432-1015, www.josephoregon.com; Wallowa–Whitman National Forest, 541/523-6391; BLM, Vale District, 541/473-3144; Wallowa Mountains Visitors Center, 541/426-5546; Hells Canyon Chamber of Commerce, 541/742-4222, www.hellscanyonchamber.com; ODFW, La Grande, 541/963-2138; Joseph Fly Shoppe, 541/432-4343, www.josephflyshoppe.com; Eagle Cap Fishing Guides, 800/940-3688; Wallowa Lake State Park, 800/551-6949; Joseph Hardware, 541/432-2271; Eagle Cap Chalets, 541/432-4704; Five Peaks RV Park, 888/432-4605.

25 ANEROID LAKE
south of Joseph in the Eagle Cap Wilderness
Map 4.4, page 244

One of the most-visited lakes in the area, Aneroid is a 39-acre lake in the pristine Eagle Cap Wilderness. This hike-in–only lake sits at an elevation of 7,520 feet and offers the angler a chance to catch sizable brook and rainbow trout in relative solitude. It can be reached by following Trail No. 1804 from the southern end of Wallowa Lake State Park; Aneroid Lake is approximately six miles from the trailhead. It's a somewhat strenuous hike, with an elevation gain of 2,320 feet, much of it in the first two miles. Packing a float tube may be an option for those in excellent physical condition—and the drive to do so.

Fishing is good in the summer but better in the fall when fish are foraging for the winter. Good insect populations are active throughout warmer weather. Snow can block entrance to the

lake until July, so be sure to check with the local Forest Service office for up-to-date trail conditions. There are plenty of campsites around the lake. A Wallowa–Whitman Forest Service map showing the location of Eagle Cap Wilderness can help you identify other lakes in the area. Fishing in Eagle Cap is open year-round but spring comes late, mid-July, and winter comes early, early September. Generally, high lake trout are more opportunistic and not picky when it comes to feeding. Basic spinners such as Rooster Tails in smaller sizes will do the job. Fly anglers can employ small streamers and nymphs for best results, varying the retrieve until the right speed is producing strikes. Dry flies such as an Adams or emerger pattern are good searching patterns before, during, and after insect hatches.

Species: Rainbow and brook trout.

Facilities: Camping is permitted anywhere a tent can be pitched, but campers are asked to keep at least 200 yards back from the water and practice no-trace camping. All camping is primitive, limited to natural campsites. Supplies are available in Joseph.

Directions: From Joseph, drive south on Hwy. 82 (Joseph–Wallowa Lake Hwy.) five miles to entrance of Wallowa Lake State Park at the south end of Wallowa Lake. Cars may be parked at the trailhead, which is at the southern end of the park. Trail No. 1804 begins here. It is approximately six miles from the trailhead to Aneroid Lake.

Contact: Joseph Chamber of Commerce, 541/432-1015; Wallowa–Whitman National Forest, 541/523-6391; ODFW, La Grande, 541/963-2138; Wallowa Mountains Visitors Center, 541/426-5546; Joseph Fly Shoppe, 541/432-4343, www.josephflyshoppe.com; Wallowa Lake Lodge, 541/432-9821.

26 EAGLE CAP WILDERNESS
west of Enterprise in the Wallowa-Whitman National Forest
Map 4.4, page 244   **BEST (**

Noted for its pristine high-alpine lakes, meadows teeming with wildflowers, abundant wildlife, looming granite peaks, and glaciated valleys, Eagle Cap Wilderness remains much the same today as it did when local Native American tribes used this land to hunt big game and gather huckleberries. Anglers wishing for a truly remarkable backcountry experience cannot go wrong in choosing this as one of their choice summer fishing spots and family recreation areas. In the Wallowa Mountains of the Wallowa–Whitman National Forest, Eagle Cap Wilderness is Oregon's largest designated wilderness (361,446 acres) and is home to many peaks over 9,000 feet. It is also home to more than 75 lakes, several of which are sources for major rivers such as the Wallowa, Minam, Lostine, and Imnaha. Because no wheeled vehicles are allowed within wilderness boundaries, anglers must reach these waters either by foot or on horseback and they have approximately 534 miles of trails to choose from.

Most of the lakes are situated above 7,000 feet in elevation, with many above 8,000. Because of the extreme elevations, the fishing season starts late at all lakes in the Eagle Cap Wilderness. The first opportunity for access to the wilderness begins in late June with the arrival of the spring thaw. By early September winter will begin to arrive, making for a fairly short fishing season. Anglers should contact the local Forest Service office when planning an early-season trip to ensure that trails are passable and lakes are thawed. As with most alpine lakes, anglers should not expect large fish or a great variety of species. Deep, glacier-cold waters, a lack of food, and harsh winters allow only the toughest fish to survive. The dominant species are brook trout that get no bigger than 7–4 inches; however, most of the lakes have self-sustaining populations of fish, which reduces the need for stocking and keeps their numbers in good fishable quantity. Many lakes have above-average depths between 30–90 feet or more. Lake surface areas range from a half acre to 40 acres and up. Expect fast and steep elevation gains on most of the hikes from the trailheads into the wilderness. The farther

you get away from the main trails, the less likely you are to see other people.

Since it is not possible to list all the trailheads and corresponding lakes here, what follows is a short list of good places to start. Anglers can begin their trip preparations by buying three good maps from the Forest Service. These maps are: *The Forest Recreation Map for the Wallowa–Whitman National Forest, The Wilderness Map for Eagle Cap Wilderness,* and the *Wallowa Ranger District Map for Eagle Cap Wilderness.* Maps cost about $60 and are available by calling Nature of the Northwest, the Wallowa Mountains Visitors Center, or visiting the Wallowa–Whitman National Forest offices in Baker City.

Wallowa Lake Trailhead and the **Lakes Basin Management Area:** Two trails can be found here, East Fork Wallowa (No. 1804) and West Fork Wallowa (No. 1820). From the East Fork trail anglers can reach Aneroid Lake and Roger Lake, not to mention the East Fork of the Wallowa River. Both these lakes and the Wallowa River provide good summer fishing for brook trout. The West Fork Trail (No. 1820) allows anglers to fish the West Fork of the Wallowa River and also Frazier Lake and Little Frazier Lake. Spur trails to the west of West Fork Trail lead to more lakes such as Moccasin Lake, Glacier Lake, Prospect Lake, and the upper headwaters of the Lostine River.

Two Pan Trailhead: This area is densely populated with lakes and also provides access to the headwaters of the pristine Lostine River for good opportunies to catch wild rainbow trout. The East Fork Lostine River Trail (No. 1670) gives anglers access to Mirror, Minam, and Blue lakes. There are several trailheads to be found along Forest Road 8210 before you reach Two Pan Campground. These are Frances Lake Trail (No. 1663) and Maxwell Lake Trail (No. 1674), which is at the Shady Campground, one mile north of Two Pan Campground. Both these lakes are larger bodies of water that produce good summer fishing for brook trout. From the Maxwell Lake Trail you can reach other lakes including Steamboat Lake, Long Lake, and John Henry Lake.

West Eagle Trailhead: The West Eagle Trail (No. 1934) gives access to several good brook trout lakes including Echo, Traverse, Diamond, and Tombstone. This is also a good place to reach the Upper Minam River for a chance at wild rainbow trout. Close to West Eagle Trailhead is East Eagle Trailhead (Forest Rd. 7745) and Main Eagle Trailhead (Forest Rd. 7755), both off Forest Road 77 on the way to West Eagle Trailhead. Main and East Eagle Trailheads lead to lakes such as Lookingglass, Eagle, Crater, and Bear, as well as various forks on Eagle Creek.

Other equally productive areas to consider are the **Cornucopia Trailhead** northwest of Halfway and **Fish Lake Trailhead** 21 miles north of Halfway.

Several rivers have their origins in Eagle Cap Wilderness and offer good small-stream fishing for rainbows, brook, and cutthroat trout. The trout fishing season for rivers is May 27–October 31. All fishing on rivers in the wilderness is restricted to artificial flies and lures only. Lakes are open year-round, but only accessible in summer unless snowshoeing and ice fishing are your thing. Fishing tactics on wilderness lakes are open for bait, lure, and flies. In general, alpine fish are opportunistic and will take anything short of a rib-eye steak. The best gear is going to be light tackle, ultralight spinning rods, and 3–4-weight fly rods. Keep your lures small. Gold and silver flash will attract anything in the lake. Fly anglers can use nymphs, leeches, or dry flies. On deeper lakes, look for underwater shelves in 5–10 feet of water and areas with cover such as brushy banks, rocks, or downed logs. Inlets and outlets can be especially productive in the early and late months.

Species: Rainbow trout, brook trout, cutthroat trout.

Facilities: Parking at any wilderness trailhead requires a Northwest Forest Pass ($30 per year, or $5 per day). Likewise, all visitors to the Eagle Cap Wilderness must obtain a required Wilderness Visitor Permit before entering the area. Only one permit per group is necessary, and there is no fee for the permits. The self-issue registration/permit boxes are at each trailhead near the information board. Most trailheads have areas for overnight camping. Camping is available in the wilderness anywhere a natural campsite exists. The Forest Service requires no-trace camping in all wilderness areas. Supplies, accommodations, and Forest Service offices can be had in Joseph, Enterprise, and La Grande.

Directions: From Joseph, drive south on Hwy. 82 seven miles to the southern end of Wallowa Lake. The highway dead-ends at Wallowa Lake Campground. The parking and the Wallowa Lake trailhead are available at the southern end of the campground.

To reach Two Pan Trailhead from Lostine, drive south on Forest Rd. 8210 for 17 miles. The road dead-ends at Two Pan Campground. Parking is available at the trailhead.

To reach West Eagle Trailhead from La Grande, drive southeast on Hwy. 203 for 27 miles, passing through Union, to the turnoff for Forest Rd. 77. Turn east on Forest Rd. 77 and drive approximately 15.5 miles to West Eagle Meadows. The campground and trailhead are to the east side of the road. To reach Main Eagle from West Eagle, continue driving east on Forest Rd. 77 four miles to Forest Rd. 7755. Turn north on Forest Rd. 7755 and follow the road to the dead-end West Eagle Trailhead and campground. East Eagle is reached from West Eagle by driving east on Forest Rd. 77 for 10 miles to Forest Rd. 7745. Turn north on Forest Rd. 7745 and drive six miles to the dead-end road at the East Eagle campground and trailhead.

To reach Cornucopia Trailhead from Halfway, drive northwest on County Rd. 413 approximately 13 miles to reach the dead-end at the trailhead and campground. Parking is available at the trailhead.

To reach the Fish Lake Trailhead from Halfway, drive north on County Rd. 1005 and drive three miles, at which point the road turns into County Rd. 999. Drive approximately 0.5 mile on County Rd. 999 and turn northwest on Forest Rd. 66 (Fish Lake Rd.). Follow Forest Rd. 66 14 very windy miles to Fish Lake Campground on the south side of the road. The trailhead is approximately 0.5 mile past the campground entrance. Park at the trailhead. Continuing north on Forest Rd. 66 from Fish Lake Campground will take you to two other trailheads, Horse Lake and Twin Lakes, two and four miles respectively.

Contact: Union County Chamber of Commerce in La Grande, 541/963-8588; Wallowa County Chamber of Commerce (Troy, Joseph, Enterprise), 800/585-4121; Nature of the Northwest, www.naturenw.org, 503/872-2750; Wallowa–Whitman National Forest, 541/523-6391; Wallowa Mountains Visitors Center, 541/426-5546; ODFW, La Grande, 541/963-2138; Northwest Forest Service Pass Information Line, 800/270-7504; Joseph Fly Shoppe, 541/432-4343, www.josephflyshoppe.com; Four Seasons Fly Shoppe, La Grande, 541/963-8420; Eagle Cap Fishing Guides, 800/940-3688.

27 CATHERINE CREEK
east of Union in Eagle Cap Wilderness
Map 4.4, page 244

Catherine Creek headwaters are in Eagle Cap Wilderness, like the Lostine River, from which it runs 32 miles to its confluence with the Grande Ronde River near Cove. In addition to being a wonderful trout stream, Catherine Creek also boasts a respectable run of summer steelhead, which begin to appear February–April. This is a bank-fishing river only. Catherine Creek originates from two forks that flow out of the southwest corner of Eagle Cap Wilderness. Highway 203 follows the creek for most of its length to Union. The upper forks are easily accessible from Forest Service roads that spur off Highway 203 above Catherine Creek State Park and from trailheads that lead into the Eagle Cap Wilderness. Trails No. 7785 and No. 600 offer access to

the North Fork and South Fork, respectively. The North Fork is probably the more scenic of the two, but both hold an equal amount of wild rainbow trout up to 14 inches. The river is open for trout fishing May 27–October 31, and the best times of year to fish are after the spring runoff mid-July–fall. Intrepid anglers may also wish to take advantage of the upper river's proximity to wilderness lakes in the Eagle Cap Wilderness.

Bull trout and spawning salmon are present throughout the river; however, both are off-limits to anglers. Apparently there have been problems with salmon poaching, especially in the forks, necessitating frequent patrols to the upper waters by law enforcement for most of the summer and fall. Use caution not to disturb the salmon spawning grounds when chasing trout.

Steelhead fishing is open January 1–April 15 and September 1–December 31. Steelhead are available in the river late winter–early fall but may not be fished for above the second Highway 203 bridge near Catherine Creek State Park. Hatchery fish may be kept, but most of the fish are wild, making this effectively a catch-and-release fishery. Despite private lands in the lower steelhead water, there are several good access points that should provide ample opportunities to catch fish: Catherine Creek State Park near the headwaters and Union State Park in Union. Both provide good pools and runs for casting spinners, flies, or bait. Another popular fishing spot exists downstream from the sewage treatment plant between Union and Union Junction. Other areas lie along Highway 203 at bridge crossings and along the highway at visible pullouts. If you are unsure about access, consult a good local BLM or Forest Service map, or stop by the local ODFW office for more information.

Tactics for trout should involve light tackle rods and lures appropriate for small-stream fishing. Ultralight spinning rods and 3- and 4-weight fly rods are best. Nymphs and dry flies all work; neither approach is better than the other. Using two-fly setups such as a nymph dropped below a dry fly will cover your bases. Steelhead anglers should use heavier equipment suitable to bigger fish. Medium-action spinning rods and 6- or 7-weight fly rods will be appropriate. Streamer flies such as Egg Sucking Leeches and nymphs will take most steelhead. Spin anglers will want to use a larger spinner in various colors until they hit on the right combination.

Species: Rainbow trout, steelhead.

Facilities: Catherine Creek State Park provides a nice setting by the river for camping, but it has few services other than restrooms. Two other primitive campgrounds can be had on the North Fork at North Fork Catherine Creek Campground and Buck Creek Campground. Supplies and accommodations can be had in Union, La Grande, and North Powder.

Directions: To reach Catherine Creek State Park from Union, drive south on Hwy. 203 for eight miles to reach the entrance of Catherine Creek State Park on the south side of the road. To go higher up in the river, toward the river's headwaters, keep driving south on Hwy. 203 a couple of miles until you reach Forest Rd. 7785 (North Fork Catherine Creek Rd.). Drive east on Rd. 7785 a few miles to reach North Fork Catherine Creek Campground. Buck Creek Campground can be reached off Spur Rd. 7787 a mile before you reach North Fork Catherine Creek Campground.

Contact: Union County Chamber of Commerce in La Grande, 541/963-8588; Wallowa–Whitman National Forest, 541/523-6391; Wallowa Mountains Visitors Center, 541/426-5546; BLM, Vale District, 541/473-3144; ODFW, La Grande, 541/963-2138; Four Seasons Fly Shoppe, La Grande, 541/963-8420.

28 THIEF VALLEY RESERVOIR
east of North Powder on the North Powder River

Map 4.4, page 244

Like most northeastern Oregon reservoirs, Thief Valley Reservoir is surrounded by barren terrain with little or no shade and features high afternoon winds and large trout. On the North Powder River at an elevation of 3,100 feet, this irrigation reservoir grows good-size trout and several warm-water species. Although susceptible to drought, drying up completely in some years, Thief Valley is stocked regularly to ensure healthy fish populations.

The reservoir is approximately two miles long, a half mile wide, and consists of 200 acres of water when full. The average depth is 20 feet with a maximum depth of 40 feet at the southern end. There are 7.5 miles of shoreline, available to the angler year-round. There are no boating restrictions, but most people find small boats and float tubes to be adequate for reaching the fish. A favorite spot for locals practiced in the art of ice fishing, Thief Valley's major fishing seasons occur from ice-out in early April–late fall. On good, nondrought years expect 14–20-inch rainbow trout. Warm-water species such as crappie, brown bullhead, largemouth bass, and bluegill are all present, sometimes overwhelming the trout populations. The best trout fishing is early spring or late fall, leaving the hotter months for bass and warm-water anglers. Fly anglers should concentrate on attractor patterns such as leeches and small nymphs trolled back to the angler. Look for hatching insects during the most comfortable parts of the day—which here means early mornings and late afternoons and evenings—and start with small Adams. Spin anglers should concentrate on tackle typically used for trout, such as a small Mepps Spinner or Rooster Tail. Fish can be targeted in the shallower areas near the bank during morning and evening. Troll or fish the deeper water during the day or middle of the summer.

Species: Trout, crappie, brown bullhead, largemouth bass, bluegill.

Facilities: There are a free boat ramp, 10 primitive campsites, and a restroom on the eastern shore of the lake. There's no drinking water and very little shade, so come prepared with plenty of liquid. Supplies and accommodations can be had in either North Powder or La Grande.

Directions: From North Powder take Hwy. 237 east and drive five miles to Government Gulch Rd. Turn east on Government Gulch and drive two miles to Telocaset Rd. Turn southeast on Telocaset Rd. and drive four miles to Thief Valley Rd. Just before you reach Thief Valley Rd., the reservoir will be visible to the south. Turn southwest on Thief Valley Rd. to reach the reservoir in approximately three miles. Parking, camping, and a boat ramp are at the dead-end of Thief Valley Rd.

Contact: Union County Chamber of Commerce in La Grande, 541/963-8588; Wallowa–Whitman National Forest, 541/523-6391; Wallowa Mountains Visitors Center, 541/426-5546; BLM, Vale District, 541/473-3144; ODFW, La Grande, 541/963-2138; Four Seasons Fly Shoppe, La Grande, 541/963-8420.

29 HELLS CANYON ON THE SNAKE RIVER

east of Joseph

Map 4.5, page 245

If you're looking for the famous Hells Canyon on the Snake River, you have found it. This Wild and Scenic section of the Snake River runs from Hells Canyon Dam to the Washington–Oregon border—roughly 72 miles of river. All the land adjacent to the river on the Oregon side is public land and has been designated wilderness. The canyon itself is unsurpassed as a natural wonder in the United States: though it's only 10 miles wide, numerous ridges tower 5,000 feet above the river; He Devil Mountain soars 8,000 feet above the river, creating the deepest gorge in the United States. Wildlife is also abundant, and anglers have opportunities to see bighorn sheep, ospreys, eagles, chukar partridges, deer, turkeys, elk, bears, and otters. Unlike the days when this region was home to the Shoshone and Nez Perce tribes, the Hells Canyon of today is a commercially exploited recreation area that attracts visitors from all over the globe,

which can make the canyon less than peaceful, especially on weekends.

This is not an easy river to get to, often requiring travel on winding gravel roads. From Oregon there are two road access points: at Hells Canyon Dam and at Dug Bar, eight miles above the confluence of the Imnaha River. Otherwise, you have to travel over to Idaho, where the river is accessible from Pittsburg Landing, Wolff Creek, and Dry Creek. There are many hike-in opportunities to reach the river within the Hells Canyon Wilderness. One of the most popular hikes is the Battle Creek Trailhead off the Hells Canyon Rim Road; this trail reaches the river about four miles down from the dam. Another popular trail is the Dug Bar Trail at the end of Dug Bar Road. This trail follows the river to Saddle Creek. Other popular trails include Granite Creek, Buck Creek, Freezeout, and Indian Crossing. Anglers attempting to hike any of these trails, or to find other trails to the river, are advised to buy a copy of the Hells Canyon National Recreation Map from the Forest Service.

Boats can be launched at Hells Canyon Dam and Dug Bar in Oregon and at Pittsburgh Landing in Idaho. Boaters should beware that certain sections of this river from Pittsburgh Landing upriver to the dam include some treacherous Class III and IV rapids, and boating should be left to experts with experience in negotiating big white water. Several good river maps are available for do-it-yourselfers. Boating permits are required to float the upper section of river.

Anglers fishing from the bank or a boat can expect to catch smallmouth bass, channel catfish, trout, steelhead, and sturgeon. Bass are plentiful and can reach three pounds or more. The bag limits on bass are six per day, with no restriction on size. Smallmouth bass fishing is best beginning in April when the water has warmed to 65°F, until the cold weather arrives in September or October. Poppers, bass crankbaits, Rapalas, and plastic worms all work. Focus on areas around structures, in pools and against the bank.

Trout fishing is open year-round and the fish are abundant in the cool waters, averaging 8–20 inches. Any trout over 20 inches is considered a steelhead downstream from Hells Canyon Dam. Trout fishing is good all year, but better in the spring, beginning in April. During the heat of summer, trout fishing is best in the morning and evening. Watch particularly for caddis hatches during summer evenings and fish current seams around rocks and riffles. Look for smaller areas of moving current such as river mouths or tributaries for best success. Bait, flies, and spinners all work.

Summer steelhead begin to show in the river in October, with November–February the best time. The mouth of the Imnaha is particularly good for bank anglers. Most steelhead are caught by trolling plugs and casting bait and spinners. Single-point barbless hooks are required for all steelhead fishing tackle. Only hatchery fish may be kept; wild fish must be released unharmed and should not be taken from the water.

Sturgeon are available in Hells Canyon and can reach enormous sizes of nine feet or more. Sturgeon are protected on the entire Snake River, and all fish must be released unharmed without being removed from the water. Tackle is restricted to single-point barbless hooks.

Channel catfish are present and can be as big as 20 pounds. Anglers catch these primitive fish by settling large pieces of dead bait on the bottom of the river.

Spring chinook are present in the fall, and angling has been permitted in the past, but as of the 2006 fishing season all salmon fishing is closed and probably will remain so until there is an increase in numbers of returning fish. Anglers should check with ODFW annually for the most current regulations.

Species: Smallmouth bass, channel catfish, trout, steelhead, sturgeon.

Facilities: Fishing licenses from either Oregon or Idaho are valid on the Snake River when angling from a floating device or launching watercraft. You must buy the required state license when fishing tributaries or landforms within either state.

Boats can be launched for free at three places: Hells Canyon Dam, Dug Bar near the Oregon–Washington border, and at Pittsburgh Landing in Idaho. Camping is very limited unless you're boating or hiking the river. The only camping on the Oregon side accessible by car is at Dug Bar Campground, a Forest Service campground, which has a fee campsite. There are two boat-in campsites at Cache Creek, nine miles north (downriver) from the Hells Canyon Dam and at Kirkwood, approximately four miles upriver from Pittsburg Landing. Kirkwood and several other places on the river have preserved historical attractions such as Native American archaeological sites and homesteads from the frontier days.

Boaters can camp on the river, but it is highly regulated because of overuse and environmental damage. There is no camping at the Hells Canyon Dam put-in, and camping is restricted to one night at Granite and Saddle creeks, both boat-in campsites, eight and 12 miles north of the Hells Canyon Dam. Camping is also available anywhere natural campsites allow a tent to be pitched, and this includes camping for those who hike into the canyon. Boaters must carry out human waste, and float boaters must show proof of approved receptacles before launch. Campfires are prohibited year-round. Because of fluctuating flows, camp high above the river.

River permits are required for boaters floating from Hells Canyon Dam to Rush Creek from the Friday before Memorial Day–September 10. Application for permits runs Dec. 1–Jan. 31 (permit applications must be *received* by Jan. 31); the lottery is in early February. You are most likely to draw a permit for May or Sept.; the worst odds are for July and Aug., because these are the most popular times for boating the river. Launch dates must be confirmed by Mar. 15. Boaters can call the Forest Service Office beginning Mar. 16 to try to claim unconfirmed dates that may better suit their preferences for being on the river. The group limit is 30. Advance permits are not required for trips starting at Pittsburg Landing (mile 32).

Aside from the many angling opportunities, recreationalists can also choose from a variety of activities—white-water rafting, jet-boat rides, air tours, and wilderness pack trips.

Directions: From Joseph, drive east on Hwy. 350 (Little Sheep Creek Hwy.) for 30 miles to where the road dead-ends in Imnaha. Once in Imnaha, turn north on gravel County Rd. 735 (Lower Imnaha Rd.). County Rd. 735 turns into Forest Rd. 4260 approximately six miles north of Imnaha and Dug Bar Rd. near the Snake River. Parking is available at the Dug Bar Campground or anyplace along the river.

Contact: Wallowa County Chamber of Commerce (Troy, Joseph, Enterprise), 800/585-4121; Joseph Chamber of Commerce, 541/432-1015; Hells Canyon National Recreation Area, managed by the Wallowa–Whitman National Forest, 541/523-6391; BLM, Vale District, 541/473-3144; Whitman Unit Pine Ranger District, 541/742-7511; ODFW, Enterprise, 541/426-3279; Idaho Power recording that gives the release from Hells Canyon Dam, 800/521-9102; Wallowa Mountains Visitors Center, 541/426-5546; Hells Canyon Chamber of Commerce, 541/742-4222, www.hellscanyonchamber.com; Joseph Fly Shoppe, 541/432-4343, www.josephflyshoppe.com; Eagle Cap Fishing Guides and Natural History Guided Tours, 541/432-9685; Hells Canyon Adventures II, 541/785-3352; Diamond W Outfitters, 541/577-3157; Scotty's Hells Canyon Outdoor Supply, 800/785-3358; Hells Canyon Shuttle Service, 800/785-3358, float@hellscanyonshuttle.com; Rapid River Outfitters, 208/628-3862.

30 IMNAHA RIVER
north of Joseph in the Eagle Cap Wilderness

Map 4.5, page 245

One of the pleasures in writing a book of this nature is discovering new and exciting places to fish. The Imnaha is one such discovery. In a very remote northeast corner of the state, this is not a river that is well known except by a handful of anglers. What anglers don't know about this river is sure to pique their interest in this remote country.

The Imnaha originates on the eastern side of Eagle Cap Wilderness in the Wallowa Mountains; the North and South forks join forces about seven miles above Indian Crossing Campground. From its source the river flows 77 miles to its confluence with the Snake River near Eureka Bar. The entire river, including the South Fork, was designated a Wild and Scenic River in 1988 and it flows through two special management areas: Eagle Cap Wilderness and Hells Canyon National Recreation Area (HCNRA). The river is deeply gorged for most of its run, making access to this remote but beautiful river sometimes difficult and strenuous. There is no boating on the river, so all anglers must either fish from the bank or wade. The entire river is open for trout fishing May 27–October 31. The Imnaha is one of the few rivers in Oregon that allows catch-and-release fishing for bull trout. All methods of fishing are permitted, including bait.

The upper river extends west from the border of Eagle Cap Wilderness at Indian Crossing Campground and includes the North and South forks. This section of river is accessible on foot only via Trail No. 1816, which starts at Indian Crossing Campground. From Indian Crossing Campground, the hike is approximately seven miles, following the main river to the confluence of the forks. The main river provides the best fishing in bigger water, but both forks contain good quantities of wild rainbow trout and bull trout. Expect a high-gradient river characterized by lots of pools and pocket water. Anglers should consider carrying lightweight tackle suitable for short casts up into pools and behind structures. Wading boots are a plus if you plan to get into the water. Both nymphs and dry flies will work, as will small spinners. Because some of the flows are faster, some weight may be needed to get down quickly in the deeper pockets. This water is best fished after spring runoff, with the best fishing July–September.

The middle section of the Imnaha extends 40 miles east (then north), from Indian Crossing Campground, passing through the area of Pallette Ranch, to Imnaha (midpoint between the mouth and the headwaters). The river in this section produces good numbers of wild rainbow trout, bull trout, and whitefish. River access is a mix of both public and private property. From Indian Crossing Campground 16 miles downriver to Pallette Ranch, the river flows exclusively through public lands and is accessible from Imnaha River Road (Forest Rd. 3960). Six Forest Service campgrounds can also be found in the first 11 miles of road east of Indian Crossing Campground. The 24 miles of river below Pallette Ranch to Imnaha flows exclusively through private property and is inaccessible to anglers, except for those willing to ask landowners for permission. Private property is well defined by the presence of No Trespassing signs. Again, the best fishing times are during summer and fall, when the river has stabilized from the spring runoff.

The lower river extends 22 miles north from Imnaha to the mouth on the Snake River. This section of river produces good catches of rainbow trout, bull trout, summer-run steelhead, and a few smallmouth bass near the mouth. The steelhead fishing deadline is in a section at Big Sheep Creek, which enters the Imnaha at Imnaha. The river here flows through a mix of public and private property, but mostly the latter. Anglers who pay attention to No Trespassing signs can find limited public access along this road, particularly downstream from Horse Creek, which is 10 miles north of Imnaha. The best public access is near the mouth of the river on Trail No. 1713, which starts at Cow Creek Bridge, four miles south of the river mouth. The hiking trail follows the river four miles north along the west bank to Eureka Bar on the Snake River. Lots of good water can be found along this trail for both trout and steelhead and the occasional

smallmouth bass. Steelhead fishing from the mouth to Big Sheep Creek is open January 1–April 15 and September 1–December 31. Steelhead begin to show in the river with the arrival of the fall rains in October. November and December are the best fishing months. Anglers can catch steelhead with traditional tackle such as spinners and bait or with fly-fishing gear.

Since 2001, anglers have been allowed to fish for hatchery chinook salmon. This broodstock strain can reach 12–30 pounds. Chinook return to the river between June and the first week in July; only fin-clipped fish may be kept. Salmon can be caught in the entire river, but the best fishing is in the first 30 miles of river from the mouth. Because the salmon season is only open pending good returns of fish, check the latest ODFW regulations before venturing out.

Species: Wild rainbow and bull trout, hatchery and wild steelhead, hatchery spring chinook, smallmouth bass, whitefish.

Facilities: There are six primitive, fee Forest Service campgrounds near the upper river at Blackhorse, Ollokot, Coverdale, Hidden, Evergreen, and Indian Crossing. Fee camping is also available near the Imnaha River mouth at Dug Bar Campground. Supplies, accommodations, and information can be had in Joseph.

Directions: From Joseph, drive east on Hwy. 350 (Little Sheep Creek Hwy.) for 30 miles to where the road dead-ends in Imnaha. Once in Imnaha you can follow a good gravel road north, headed downstream on County Rd. 735 (Lower Imnaha Rd.) or south headed upstream on County Hwy. 727 (Upper Imnaha Rd.). County Rd. 735 turns into Forest Rd. 4260 approximately six miles north of Imnaha and to Dug Bar Rd. near the Snake River.

From Joseph, reach Dug Bar Landing by driving east on Imnaha Hwy. for eight miles, then turning north on Hwy. 350 (Little Sheep Creek Hwy.) for 22 miles to Imnaha. Once in Imnaha, follow Lower Imnaha Rd. for six miles downstream (north) until it intersects

Dug Bar Rd., which leads 24 winding miles to the campground. Parking is available at the Dug Bar Campground or anyplace along the river.

To reach the upper river from Joseph, drive east on Hwy. 350 (Little Sheep Creek Hwy.) approximately eight miles and turn south on Hwy. 39 (Wallowa Mountain Loop). You will reach Blackhorse Campground on the Imnaha River in approximately 38 miles on the east side of the road. One mile south of Blackhorse, at Ollokot Campground, turn west on Forest Rd. 3960 and drive approximately 10 miles, passing Coverdale, Hidden, and Evergreen campgrounds, to the dead-end at Indian Crossing Campground. The trailhead for Trail No. 1816 starts at Indian Crossing Campground and will lead you into the headwaters and the forks.

Contact: Wallowa County Chamber of Commerce (Troy, Joseph, Enterprise), 800/585-4121; Joseph Chamber of Commerce, 541/432-1015; Hells Canyon National Recreation Area managed by the Wallowa–Whitman National Forest, 541/523-6391; BLM, Vale District, 541/473-3144; Whitman Unit Pine Ranger District, 541/742-7511; ODFW, Enterprise, 541/426-3279; Wallowa Mountains Visitors Center, 541/426-5546; Hells Canyon Chamber of Commerce, 541/742-4222, www.hellscanyonchamber.com; Joseph Fly Shoppe, 541/432-4343, www.josephfly-shoppe.com.

31 HELLS CANYON RESERVOIR

northeast of Baker City

Map 4.5, page 245

Hells Canyon Reservoir is the lowest reservoir on the Snake River, extending 21 miles from Oxbow Dam at Copperfield north to Hells Canyon Dam. Below Hells Canyon Dam the river flows free through the designated Wild and Scenic stretch to the Columbia River.

Hells Canyon Reservoir is a placid and scenic part of the Snake River on the southern boundary of the Hells Canyon Wilderness. Geographically, this area is composed of the same rugged landscape as Hells Canyon below Hells Canyon Dam, but most of the great features are now under the reservoir's waters. What remains is just the tip of the iceberg, so to speak, of what must have been an expansive area with towering canyon walls and rugged steep terrain. The Oregon side is a mix of private property and wilderness in the lower section around Hells Canyon Dam. As a fishery, this area is less than remarkable, mostly limited to warm-water species such as crappie, bass, sturgeon, and channel catfish.

Bank fishing and boating are both popular from several parks and access points. The only bank fishing on the Oregon side is in Copperfield at Copperfield Park and along eight miles of river north of Copperfield (downriver) on graveled Forest Road 1039. Access points along this Forest Service road can be had from roadside turnouts or from two campgrounds, Westfall and Ashby Creek. An additional access point is from Cooper Creek Trailhead (No. 1890) at the dead-end of Forest Road 1039. Here, the trail will take anglers an additional seven miles downriver before ending in trailless wilderness. Hells Canyon Campground in Idaho, reached from the river crossing in Copperfield, provides further bank access, but anglers wanting to fish from the Idaho bank will need to buy an Idaho license.

Boating is the most effective method to fish Hells Canyon Reservoir because it allows anglers to ply the deeper waters for channel catfish and sturgeon. There are two boat ramps that offer access to this part of the reservoir: The first is one mile downstream from Copperfield on the Oregon side at Tunnel ramp; the second is at Hells Canyon Creek, 11 miles below Oxbow Dam on the Idaho side. This is placid water with few boating hazards other than shallow shelves. Water levels tend to fluctuate throughout the year, sometimes reaching very low levels.

The most targeted fish species in Hells Canyon reservoir are smallmouth bass, followed by crappie, sturgeon, and channel catfish. Fishing for most of these species is only marginal, and much better catches can be had in either Oxbow or Brownlee reservoirs. Compared to those in the Oxbow and Hells Canyon stretches, the channel catfish are small, 14–20 inches. Channel cats are primarily caught with bait rigs that place the bait on the bottom of the reservoir near muddy bottoms. Bass, crappie, and bluegill can all be caught around shorelines, structures, and in deeper water. Bass anglers can use surface poppers, Rapalas, or plastic worms cast at shorelines and around structures in the river. Crappie can hover at depths of 25 feet or more and prefer the motion of small jigs and bait such as worms. The bridge at Copperfield is a popular place to fish for crappie. Sturgeon are present in small numbers because they don't reproduce in the Snake River reservoirs. Any sturgeon caught must be released unharmed. Trout are best fished for around creek and river inlets and against shorelines around structure.

Species: Smallmouth bass, channel catfish, crappie, bluegill, trout, sturgeon.

Facilities: Fishing licenses from either state are valid on the Snake River when angling from a floating device or launching watercraft. You must buy the required state license when fishing tributaries or landforms within either state.

Fee camping is available on the river in Copperfield at Copperfield Park and north of Copperfield on Forest Rd. 1039 at Westfall and Ashby Creek campgrounds. Free primitive camping is available along Trail No. 1890, at the end of Forest Rd. 1039. Hells Canyon Campground in Idaho offers fee camping. There is a free boat ramp one mile downstream from Copperfield on the Oregon side at Tunnel ramp and also at Hells Canyon Creek, 11 miles below Oxbow Dam on the Idaho side. Supplies and accommodations can be had in Baker City and along Hwy. 86 at Richland, Halfway, and Copperfield.

Directions: From Baker City, drive east on Hwy. 86 for 75 miles to Copperfield, where you will find a majority of the facilities mentioned above. To get to Hells Canyon Dam and Hells Canyon Campground, follow Hwy. 86 0.5 mile east out of Copperfield to the river crossing. Turn north, crossing the river to the Idaho side. From the river crossing it is approximately 10 miles to north to Hells Canyon Campground, 11 miles to Hells Canyon Creek boat launch, and another 30 miles to Hells Canyon Dam.

Contact: Wallowa County Chamber of Commerce (Troy, Joseph, Enterprise), 800/585-4121; Joseph Chamber of Commerce, 541/432-1015; Hells Canyon National Recreation Area managed by the Wallowa–Whitman National Forest, 541/523-6391; BLM, Vale District, 541/473-3144; Whitman Unit Pine Ranger District, 541/742-7511; ODFW, Enterprise, 541/426-3279; Wallowa Mountains Visitors Center, 541/426-5546; Hells Canyon Chamber of Commerce, 541/742-4222, www.hellscanyonchamber.com; Hells Canyon Park and Copperfield Park Information, 541/785-3323; Idaho Power's Recreation Information Line, 800/422-3143; Stuzman Hells Canyon Guide Service, 541/742-4828; Rapid River Outfitters, 208/628-3862; Brownlee Reservoir Charters, 208/257-3703; Joseph Fly Shoppe, 541/432-4343, www.josephflyshoppe.com; Scotty's Hells Canyon Outdoor Supply, 800/785-3358; Hells Canyon Shuttle Service, 800/785-3358, float@hells-canyonshuttle.com.

32 JOHN DAY RIVER: SERVICE CREEK TO CLARNO RAPIDS

east of The Dalles

Map 4.6, page 246   BEST (

The John Day River between Service Creek and Clarno Rapids consists of 47 miles of river with great fishing opportunities for smallmouth bass and summer steelhead. This is the most popular section of river for both anglers and white-water enthusiasts. The river here is designated Wild and Scenic and flows through some exquisite country characterized by steep canyon walls, painted hills, abundant wildlife, and deceptively gentle flows. Most of the river is carried down a shallow gradient but several Class II–IV rapids are present, and anglers should carry a river guidebook to make navigation easier. Bank access to this part of the river is limited to access points at boat ramps such as Service Creek, Twickenham, Priest Rapids, and at the John Day Scenic River Wayside. The most effective and fun way to fish here is by drift boat, raft, or canoe. Anglers can construct trips of any length between 1–5 days. Service Creek (river mile 157) to Clarno Rapids (river mile 110) is the longest float at 47 miles. Two shorter sections in this stretch include Service Creek to Twickenham (12 miles), and Twickenham to Clarno (35 miles). A primitive boat ramp can be found six miles west of Twickenham at Priest Hole.

All methods of fishing are permitted, including bait. Steelhead fishing is open year-round, but steelhead are present late October–February or March. There is a two-fish limit per day of hatchery steelhead and 20 per year. All wild fish must be released unharmed. John Day steelhead tend to be on the small side, averaging 5–7 pounds. Most traditional fishing techniques work in the river for catching steelhead. Side drifting, drift fishing, float fishing, flies, lures, and drift rigs are all productive. Look for runs where boulders and current meet and create pockets for resting steelhead. The John Day attracts many fly anglers who hope to catch a large steelhead swinging dry flies or streamers.

Bass are present and open to fishing year-round, but they don't become active until the warmer weather beginning in April, with some of the most active fishing late April–September. The smallmouth bass fishery on the John Day has developed a reputation as one of the best in the country. It is estimated that there are more than 1,000 fish per mile of river, averaging 12–13 inches or about one pound.

Larger fish up to 18 inches are common, with some exceeding six pounds. Bag limits for bass are set at five fish per day, with only one over 16 inches. All bass 12–16 inches must be released unharmed. Methods for catching bass on the John Day differ according to the time of year. During the cooler spring months, anglers will be required to go deeper with diving crankbaits, bait, and weighted nymphs and streamers. Bait is often discouraged on the John Day because of the difficulty of releasing fish unharmed. This is also the best time of year to hit the biggest fish in the river, before spawning. As summer approaches and the waters warm, fishing becomes a simpleminded game and smaller bass will hit just about anything thrown on top of the water. Poppers are a particular favorite with fly and spin anglers. Don't be shy about using dry flies or drifting nymphs under an indicator.

Note: Although salmon are present in the river, salmon fishing is prohibited in the John Day River System.

Species: Smallmouth bass and steelhead.

Facilities: Several archaeological and pale-ontological sites such as the John Day Fossil Beds and Picture Gorge make nice diversions for families. Free riverside camping is available along the river at natural campsites from Service Creek to Clarno Rapids. Because the river bank is composed of a mix of both public and private lands, boaters need to carry either a Prineville District BLM map showing the section of river between Service Creek and Clarno Rapids or use a river guidebook to identify publicly accessible lands. The BLM requires no-trace camping at all boat-in campsites, including packing out garbage and solid human waste. Fires are not allowed during summer. BLM in Prineville can provide you all the updated regulations regarding boating, camping, and river use.

Fee car camping is available at Service Creek. There is no camping available at Clarno Rapids, Twickenham, or Priest Rapids; Service Creek is the closest camping to all these places. Boat ramps are available at

Service Creek, Twickenham, Priest Rapids, and John Day Scenic River Wayside at Clarno Rapids. Supplies and other accommodations can be had in The Dalles, Biggs Junction, Condon and Fossil.

Directions: To get to Service Creek from The Dalles drive 20 miles east on I-84 to Biggs Junction (Exit 104). From the base of the I-84 off-ramp turn south onto Hwy. 97. Drive southeast on Hwy. 97 eight miles to the Hwy. 206 junction. Turn east onto Hwy. 206, passing through Wasco and crossing the John Day River near Cottonwood, and follow the highway for another 50 miles to Condon. From Condon, turn south on Hwy. 19, headed toward Fossil and Service Creek. Highway 19 reaches Service Creek in approximately 42 miles. Parking and restrooms are available at Service Creek.

To reach Clarno and the boat ramp at the John Day Scenic River Wayside from Service Creek, drive north on Hwy. 19 out of Service Creek 22 miles to Fossil. At Fossil, turn south on Hwy. 218 and drive 40 miles to the wayside on the north side of the road before crossing the river. Twickenham boat ramp can be reached from Service Creek by driving south on Hwy. 207 15 miles to Girds Creek Rd. Turn north on Girds Creek Rd. and drive seven miles to reach the river crossing. Twickenham is on the south side of the river. Parking is available at the boat ramp. The boat ramp at Priest Hole River Access can be found by driving west on Girds Creek Rd. from Twickenham six miles. Priest Hole Access is on the south side of the river with parking available at the ramp.

Contact: Wheeler County Chamber of Commerce, 541/763-2698; Wheeler County Visitor Information, 541/763-2355; BLM, Prineville District, 541/416-6700; ODFW, John Day, 541/575-1167; River flow information: U.S. Department of Commerce, River Service Center, 503/261-9246, www.oregon.wr.usgs.gov; John Day Fossil Beds Information Line, 541/987-2333 or 541/987-2333; Shuttle information: Wheeler County Visitor Information, 541/763-2355; J&Z Shuttles, 541/468-2182 or 541/468-2447; Fishing Guides: Marty Sheppard, 503/622-1870, littlecreekjd@earthlink.net; Gorge Fly Shop, 541/386-6977, gorgeflyshop@gorgeflyshop.com.

33 WALTON LAKE
east of Prineville
Map 4.6, page 246

Walton Lake is extremely accessible for anglers of all abilities, providing ample opportunities to catch stocked trout 8–10 inches and larger trout near 18 inches. The ponderosa pine forest surrounding the lake provides pleasant scenery and the campgrounds are well shaded from the hot Central Oregon summer sunshine. At 25 acres, with an average depth of 12 feet and 25 feet at its deepest point, Walton Lake is manageable for both the boat and bank angler. Boats rarely need to be more than a float tube or canoe; motors are prohibited. A good hiking trail of 0.8 mile surrounds the entire lake, making bank fishing a matter of relative ease. The lake water remains cool and clear for the entire year as a result of natural underwater springs, providing ideal conditions for a well-developed fishery. Walton is a year-round lake, but fall and winter can be cold in this high desert area.

Flies, spinners, and bait are all allowed and produce equally well. Bait such as worms or cheese combinations will ensure quality catches, as will flies such as small leeches. Keep on eye out for insect hatches and the opportunity to fish with dry flies in the morning and evening. Because of the clear water conditions, employ spinners such as Rooster Tails in smaller sizes and muted colors so as not to spook trout.

Species: Rainbow trout.

Facilities: Camping and a day-use area are all available at the lake. Water, restrooms, picnic tables, tent sites, and limited RV camping are available. A boat ramp, disabled fishing access, and swimming area are all available close to the campground.

Directions: From Prineville drive east on Hwy. 26 for 14 miles. Turn south on Hwy. 23, which turns into Forest Rd. 22 (Ochoco Ranger Station Rd.) and drive 14 miles, following signs to the lake.

Contact: Prineville–Crook County Chamber of Commerce, 541/447-6304; Ochoco National Forest, 541/416-6500; BLM, Prineville District, 541/416-6700; ODFW, Prineville, 541/447-5111; Crook County Parks and Recreation, 541/447-1209; Walton Lake State Park, 541/447-9645; R&R Grocery and Sporting Goods, 541/447-7231; Numb-butt Fly Shop and Outfitters, 888/248-8309; Patient Angler Fly Shop, 541/389-6208; Deschutes River Anglers, 541/617-1571; Cent Wise Sporting Goods, 541/548-4422.

34 ALLEN CREEK RESERVOIR

east of Prineville

Map 4.6, page 246

Allen Creek Reservoir is a 200-acre irrigation impoundment with a strong rainbow trout population, sitting at an elevation of 4,716 feet. Tucked away in the Ochoco Mountains in a region called Big Summit Prairie, this is a scenic area and partly due to its remoteness, likely devoid of people most of the year. This hike-in fishery requires a walk of 1.5 miles to reach the lake. Navigating the Forest Service roads into the lake will be challenging. Have a good Forest Service map for the Ochoco National Forest showing the location of this lake and a four-wheel-drive vehicle to negotiate the spur roads and difficult terrain. The reservoir is open all year to anglers, but the roads are not passable until the spring thaw in late June.

Fishing the lake is relatively easy, with good bank access provided by hiking trails encircling the lake. Float tubes or pontoon boats are helpful for trolling and reaching deeper areas of the lake but are not necessary. Trout are the only species available, and their numbers are strong. Average catches are 14–16 inches, with a plentiful supply of fish over 20 inches.

All methods of fishing are permissible, including bait, artificial lures, and flies. Bait anglers should suspend their bait just off the bottom of the lake. Worms and PowerBait all work. Flies such as small leech patterns and Woolly Buggers in burgundy, red, or black should entice a fish or two. Keep an eye peeled for insect hatches and the opportunity to throw out a dry fly or emerger pattern. Small nymphs such as chironomids suspended under a strike indicator and stripped very slowly will surely appeal to larger trout. Rooster Tails and Mepps Spinners should be kept small. Vary the color of your spinners and the speed at which you retrieve them until you hit on the right combination.

Species: Rainbow trout.

Facilities: Allen Creek Horse Camp on Forest Rd. 22 provides the nearest car camping. Restrooms and tables are available, but you must bring your own water. Primitive campsites are available on the lake. Be sure to use no-trace camping techniques by packing out what you pack in. The nearest supplies are in Prineville or at one of the resort stores near Ochoco Reservoir.

Directions: From Prineville drive east on Hwy. 26 for 14 miles. Turn south on Hwy. 23, which turns into Forest Rd. 22 (Ochoco Ranger Station Rd.) and drive 14 miles, following the signs to Walton Lake. From Walton Lake follow Hwy. 22 east approximately nine miles to Allen Creek Horse Camp. Follow the trail from the horse camp about 1.5 miles to reach the lake.

Contact: Prineville–Crook County Chamber of Commerce, 541/447-6304; Ochoco National Forest, 541/416-6500; BLM, Prineville District, 541/416-6700; ODFW, Prineville, 541/447-5111; Crook County Parks and Recreation, 541/447-1209; R&R Grocery and Sporting Goods, 541/447-7231; Numb-butt Fly Shop and Outfitters, 888/248-8309; Patient Angler Fly Shop, 541/389-6208; Deschutes River Anglers, 541/617-1571; Cent Wise Sporting Goods, 541/548-4422.

35 OCHOCO RESERVOIR
east of Prineville
Map 4.6, page 246

Ochoco Reservoir, six miles east of Prineville, is a scenic and popular recreation spot for boaters, anglers, and campers, and it's another good site for families. As at other reservoirs, Ochoco's waters are heavily relied on by farmers for irrigation, resulting in dramatic water-level fluctuations during the summer. For this reason, it is best fished in the winter, spring, and fall to coincide with higher water levels and cooler temperatures. The reservoir comprises 950 acres, with an average depth of 30 feet and a maximum depth of 100 feet near the dam. There are 9.5 miles of shoreline accessible by Highway 26 on the north shore and by unimproved roads on the south shore. The reservoir is open for fishing year-round, and the primary species are trout and illegally introduced black crappie. All methods of fishing are permitted.

Anglers hoping to catch trout are in luck, because Ochoco can grow them big. Average trout run 12–14 inches with 16-inch fish common. A few lunkers of six pounds or more are caught every season. Common tackle includes flies, spinners, and bait. Trolling is by far the most popular method of taking trout. Rooster Tails, Mepps Spinners, flashers, and weighted flies such as Woolly Buggers or baitfish patterns are all good choices. Fly anglers may also want to employ full sinking intermediate or type II lines to get closer to the bottom. The north and south shores above the dam, and the north shore in front of the state park and RV park, are all popular places to troll spinners and flies. Bank anglers can walk down from Highway 26 to fish from shore or cast a line from one of the camping areas. The inlets of Ochoco Creek and Mill Creek at the far eastern end of the lake also provide good opportunities for bank anglers. Lures such as Rooster Tails and flies will work, but bait such as worms, cheese, or PowerBait is far more effective fished from the bank.

When the summer heat sets in, anglers will be forced to ply the deeper waters for their prey and this requires the use of a boat. Trout, especially, will seek deeper and cooler waters, requiring anglers to go deep with their tackle. Use brightly colored lures and fish them close to the bottom. Depth finders may be helpful for finding concentrations of fish.

Black crappies are abundant, but their future is uncertain. The cooler waters of Ochoco are not ideal habitat for creating a long-term fishery of healthy fish. Still, anglers wishing to catch these fish have their opportunity now, and they can be good sport. Crappies hang out in schools, primarily around underwater structure such as logs. Red, white, and yellow rubber-skirted jigs are the best tackle. Crappies are enticed by erratic movement; move your jig with start-and-stop motions, letting it sink for a second before beginning another retrieve. Fly anglers can use a similar approach with weighted lures such as Woolly Buggers or small Zonkers.

Species: Rainbow trout, black crappie.

Facilities: Ochoco Lake State Park provides a campground with drinking water, showers, restrooms, boat ramp, and hiking trails. Other camping can be had at Crystal Corral RV Park and Lake Shore RV Park. Crystal Corral provides both a store and café. Lake Shore has a general store, marina, boat ramp, and boat rentals. Buy supplies in Prineville or one of the general stores at the RV parks. Accommodations are available in Prineville.

Directions: From Prineville drive east on Hwy. 26 for six miles to the park entrance on the south side of the road. Both the campground and lake are right next to the highway.

Contact: Prineville–Crook County Chamber of Commerce, 541/447-6304; Ochoco National Forest, 541/416-6500; BLM, Prineville District, 541/416-6700; ODFW, Prineville, 541/447-5111; Crook County Parks and Recreation, 541/447-1209; Lakeshore RV Park and Store, 541/447-6059; Crystal Corral RV Park, 541/447-5932; Ochoco Lake State Park, 503/447-4363; Ochoco Lake Campground, 541/447-1209; Ochoco Divide Campground,

541/447-9645; R&R Grocery and Sporting Goods, 541/447-7231; Numb-butt Fly Shop and Outfitters, 888/248-8309; Patient Angler Fly Shop, 541/389-6208; Deschutes River Anglers, 541/617-1571; Cent Wise Sporting Goods, 541/548-4422.

36 CROOKED RIVER
in Prineville
Map 4.6, page 246

The Crooked River is probably responsible for more Oregonians getting started in fly-fishing than any other river in Oregon, except maybe the Deschutes. Slow, gentle currents, easy access, feisty rainbows, abundant and diverse insect hatches—the Crooked River is an every person's river. It has an estimated fish population of 2,000–8,000 redband trout per river mile; anglers can stake out a piece of water, and within 100 yards above and below their chosen water, can catch fish all day long. Although this is every person's river, it's not a river for everybody. The fish are small, 12 inches on average with some larger fish occasionally caught; the water remains turbid all year thanks to the sentiment-laden bottom of Bowman Dam; and the crowds can be overwhelming during the best fishing times. But, as with all great trout streams, one has to deal with pros and cons, and the pros certainly outweigh some of the cons.

This section of the Crooked River covers the 17 miles from Bowman Dam at the north end of Prineville Reservoir to the city of Prineville. The Crooked River is a tail-water fishery, meaning it receives its water from dam releases. Most tail-water fisheries are noted for having consistent flows, steady supplies of cold water, and abundant insect populations—and the Crooked River is no exception. The Crooked River is open year-round, with some of the best fishing in winter, early spring, and fall. However, be warned that spring run-off or heavy winters can cause high, raging waters and fishing should be avoided at these times. Summer heat also slows fishing because

of warm-water conditions. It is best to call one of the local fly shops in Bend or Sisters to get a fishing report before making your trip.

The river is open to artificial flies and lures year-round and to bait fishing May 28–October 31. The river is closed to all fishing 150 feet below Bowman Dam. A standard limit of two trout per day, with an eight-inch minimum length and only one trout over 20 inches, may be kept. This is a bank-only fishery with no boating options. Highway 27 from Prineville follows the river for its entire length and offers unlimited access. The most popular water is contained in the first eight miles of river below the dam, where fish populations are said to be the strongest. This is also where anglers will find the bulk of campgrounds, set fairly close together.

The river produces daylong hatches of blue-winged olives, chironomids, and caddis in the early season, switching to morning and evening hatches of caddis during the summer. During the days when no hatches are present, nymphs such as Pheasant Tails, Hare's Ears, and scuds can provide good action. If you do decide to nymph or even dry–fly-fish in the summer, be prepared to deal with a lot of aquatic weeds, requiring a regular cleaning of your flies. Streamers and Soft Hackles are also an option. Woolly Buggers, small leeches, and Soft Hackles all work well when cast downstream and swept along the current. Keeping your tackle light will ensure a good fight while not overtiring a fish; 3- ,4-, and 5-weight fly rods rigged with floating lines will handle any fish you catch. Spin and bait anglers don't need to get fancy to have fun. Most anglers do well on spinners such as Rooster Tails and small Mepps Spinners cast on ultralight spin rods and 4–6-pound test line. Bait such as worms, PowerBait, or small freshwater shrimp all work.

Species: Redband trout.
Facilities: Eight fee campgrounds are available on the river, all primitive but including toilets and garbage cans. Beginning at the dam these are: Big Bend, Poison Butte, Devil's Postpile,

Cobble Rock, Chimney Rock, Lower Palisades, Lone Pine, and Greenwood. Supplies, accommodations, and ice-cream cones can be had in Prineville. Fishing shops can be had in Sisters, Redmond, and Bend.

Directions: Highway 27 out of downtown Prineville follows the river for 17 miles to the base of Bowman Dam at Prineville Reservoir. All the listed campgrounds can be found along this road in the last 12 miles of river below the dam.

Contact: Prineville–Crook County Chamber of Commerce, 541/447-6304; Ochoco National Forest, 541/416-6500; BLM, Prineville District, 541/416-6700; ODFW, Prineville, 541/447-5111; Crook County Parks and Recreation, 541/447-1209; Prineville Reservoir State Park, 541/447-4363; Prineville Reservoir Resort, 541/447-7468; R&R Grocery and Sporting Goods, 541/447-7231; Sun Rocks RV Park and Campground, 541/447-6540; Numb-butt Fly Shop and Outfitters, 888/248-8309, www.numb-butt.com; The Riffle Fly Shop, 800/411-3330, www.theriffleflyshop.com.

37 PRINEVILLE RESERVOIR
south of Prineville
Map 4.6, page 246

Prineville Reservoir, 17 miles south of Prineville and within an hour's drive of Redmond and Bend, is a destination fishery and popular recreation site. Prineville is a large, high-desert lake with 41 miles of shoreline, covering five square miles during high water and three square miles during low-water years. At an elevation of 3,235 feet, lighter snow packs allow this fishery to be used year-round, including a devoted group of ice anglers. The average depth is 51 feet, and the maximum depth is 130 feet near the dam. It is fed by the Crooked River, which also offers an excellent tail-water trout fishery below Bowman Dam. Stocking programs for trout are superb. Every May, 170,000 fingerling rainbow trout are planted by the ODFW. The average sizes for legal-size fish have increased by 20 percent so

anglers now have a better chance of catching trout up to 16 inches, with some bigger trout present. Precipitous drops in water levels during droughts and heavy irrigation make for a less-than-stable environment to raise truly large fish. Prineville Reservoir is also well known for its warm-water fisheries, including largemouth and smallmouth bass, black crappie, and brown bullhead catfish.

All methods of fishing are permitted at Prineville Reservoir. Bag limits for large and smallmouth bass are restricted to fish larger than 12 inches; otherwise, there are no special restrictions on fishing on the reservoir. The best trout fishing occurs in winter and spring when trout are prone to live in shallower waters and along shorelines. Warm-water conditions push fish into the deeper, cooler waters, making them tougher to catch. Early-season trout fishing begins in spring and is productive around most docks, shorelines, islands, points, and cliffs that reach into the water. Shore anglers will find plenty of good access around campgrounds, the resort, and for three miles along Juniper Canyon Road northeast of the resort. Big Island, Little Island, and the resort are all popular starting points for trout anglers with a boat. Both Big Island and Little Island sit in the middle of the reservoir directly across from Prineville State Park, to the north and west, respectively. Bait anglers are partial to cheese combinations, night crawlers, and eggs. Trolling is very productive on most of the lake. Try flashers, worms, spinners, or flies such as Woolly Buggers or scud imitations.

Prineville's warm-water fishery is well known by anglers, especially for catches of large and smallmouth bass. Largemouth bass can reach eight pounds, but the 4–6-pound range is more common. In spring, beginning about mid-April, these bass are spawning in the upper end of the reservoir, and anglers should begin fishing above the Jasper Point boat ramp. Focus your attention on the shallower, brushy water in the coves. Once the summer heat begins to set in starting around mid-July, bass can be found throughout the lake, in all the usual places: around obstructions such as stumps or brush and along shorelines. If smallmouth bass are your desired species then search the cooler waters in the main body of the lake. Concentrate on rocky points, rocky shorelines, and gravel bars. Productive tackle choices for both species include spinners, spinnerbaits, plugs, flies, and worms. Experiment with lure color, retrieve techniques, and depth to find the most productive combination.

Other warm-water species include brown bullhead catfish and black crappie, and both can be found in abundance. Crappie average 6–7 inches and can be found in shallower areas near the upper end of the reservoir and at the resort docks. Jigs and bait such as worms are both productive. Bullhead catfish are more solitary than most species and tend to hug the muddy sections of the reservoir's bottom. Begin at one of two places—near the dam or in the upper part of the reservoir—and move on to Roberts Bay and Bear Creek Bay. Worms are the bait of choice for most catfish anglers.

Species: Rainbow trout, largemouth and smallmouth bass, black crappie, brown bullhead catfish.

Facilities: With great amenities such as five campgrounds and a resort (also with camping), numerous boat ramps, hiking and biking trails, and boat rentals, Prineville Reservoir is especially attractive to families. Boaters will find many hidden beaches secluded in the reservoir's coves, good for camping, sunbathing, barbecues, fishing, and unfettered fun. The most popular and developed campgrounds on the reservoir are at Prineville State Park and Prineville Reservoir Resort. Other established but more primitive campgrounds can be had at Chimney Rock, Jasper Point Campground, Powder House Cove, and Roberts Bay East, all of which charge a nightly fee for camping. All but Chimney Rock have boat ramps and all boat ramps are free with the exception of Prineville Reservoir Resort. Prineville Resort

and Prineville Reservoir State Park have RV hookups and showers; campsites should be booked in advance to ensure a spot. Boat rentals and a store can be had at Prineville Resort. Roberts Bay East is the most primitive campground, lacking water and restrooms. Hiking trails are abundant from all the campgrounds. Supplies and accommodations can be had in Prineville, Bend, and Redmond.

Directions: There is no single road that will get you to the reservoir and around the lake. Several roads from Prineville will get you to various sections, so it's a good idea to have your plans worked out ahead of time.

To get to the east end of the reservoir and Bowman Dam: Approaching the city of Prineville from the west on Hwy. 26, drive east on Hwy. 26 approximately one mile toward the center of Prineville to the Hwy. 27 (Crooked River Hwy.) turnoff. Turn south on Hwy. 27, following the river to your west, and drive for 19 miles, crossing the dam and the eastern end of the reservoir. A paved road will take you south across the dam and in one mile you will reach Powder House Cove. To reach Juniper Bay and Roberts Creek from the dam, keep driving south on Hwy. 27, which becomes a good unpaved road just past Powder Cove. Drive south on Hwy. 27 for 10 miles to Salt Creek Rd. junction. Turn northeast on Salt Creek Rd., still driving on good unpaved roads, and continue 10 miles to Roberts Bay Area and then another two miles to the dead-end of Salt Creek Rd. at Juniper Point Area.

To get to Prineville Reservoir Resort and the state park: From Prineville, follow Hwy. 308 south and take the Juniper Canyon Rd. turnoff. Drive south 14 miles to the state park and 16 miles to the resort. A few primitive, rough roads from the state park will take you higher into the northern section of the reservoir, but these are recommended only for four-wheel-drive vehicles.

Contact: Prineville–Crook County Chamber of Commerce, 541/447-6304; Ochoco National Forest, 541/416-6500; BLM, Prineville District, 541/416-6700; ODFW, Prineville,

541/447-5111; Crook County Parks and Recreation, 541/447-1209; Prineville Reservoir State Park, 541/447-4363; Prineville Reservoir Resort, 541/447-7468; R&R Grocery and Sporting Goods, 541/447-7231; Sun Rocks RV Park and Campground, 541/447-6540; Numb-butt Fly Shop and Outfitters, 888/248-8309; Patient Angler Fly Shop, 541/389-6208; Deschutes River Anglers, 541/617-1571; Cent Wise Sporting Goods, 541/548-4422.

🖸🖸 NORTH FORK JOHN DAY RIVER

east of Kimberly

Map 4.7, page 247

The North Fork of the John Day River is a 113-mile tributary of the John Day River that provides critical habitat for spawning steelhead and salmon. The North Fork originates on the Elkhorn Ridge of the Blue Mountains, picks up the Middle Fork near Monument, and joins the main river at Kimberly; it runs through a matrix of private property, wilderness areas, and BLM and Forest Service lands. A Prineville District BLM map or Forest Service map for the Umatilla National Forest showing the North Fork will assist you in finding good public-access points and navigating the winding, dead-end roads. The North Fork is well known for producing good catches of steelhead and smallmouth bass it its lower sections and wild and hatchery trout in the headwaters. Salmon are present during their spawning times, but the river has been closed to salmon fishing since 1977.

No single road follows the river its entire length. The first 28 miles of river from the mouth headed east is accessible by good roads from Kimberly to Birch Creek, 12 miles southeast of Monument. At Birch Creek the road dead-ends, and there is no access for 11 miles to Potamus Creek because of private property. North of Potamus Creek, river access returns through Dale and into the headwaters. From Dale to the headwaters you will need to drive on a series of Forest Service roads for 11 miles, then walk on a hiking trail.

The North Fork's primary draw for anglers is the presence of smallmouth bass and summer steelhead, which arrive in early winter and spring. Some trout fishing exists, but it is better sought in the river above Dale, where stocking practices have helped improve the populations. The river around Monument, and the confluence of the Middle Fork, hold the most promising water for steelhead and bass fishing, and may be reached by bank or boat. A popular set of pools exists at the confluence with the Middle Fork. Steelhead fishing from the mouth to the Highway 395 bridge is open for hatchery fish January 1–April 15 and September 1–December 31. Bank anglers can fish around Monument at the Monument River Access; consult a Prineville District BLM map showing the North Fork for specific access points on public lands. Boaters have the advantage in this stretch, with put-ins at Wall Creek, above Monument, and in Monument itself. The drift from Wall Creek to Monument is approximately six miles, and it's another 15 miles to the mouth at Kimberly. Numerous Class II and III rapids exist along this stretch, so boaters should be prepared before venturing into these waters. Further opportunities can be had by floating from one of the North Fork put-ins to the John Day River and pulling out at one of the take-outs below Kimberly.

The fishing in this lower section is characterized by large runs suitable for flies and drift fishing. Drift anglers targeting steelhead may want to try Spin-N-Glows or salmon eggs rigged with slinky weights to get on the bottom. Float fishing is not commonly practiced but may hold promise for those adept at its techniques. Fly anglers can employ a variety of techniques, including streamers, nymphs, and skating flies. Look for good holding/resting water indicated by rocks, drop-offs, or ledges. The deeper runs are good for both nymphs and drift gear fished close to the river bottom. For bass, anglers can use poppers or shallow diving crankbaits in the slower water, pools and back eddies.

The upper river from Dale to the headwaters

remains low-gradient and provides good opportunities to catch wild and hatchery trout in a scenic environment. Steelhead may be fished for below the Highway 395 bridge, accessible in part by Highway 395 to the west. Again, private property will prove a hindrance in these areas, and a Prineville District BLM map showing the location of the North Fork will prove useful for identifying access points.

The river above the 395 bridge to the headwaters is limited to catch-and-release trout fishing for wild and hatchery fish; steelhead fishing is prohibited. Only artificial flies and bait may be used, no lures, and all bait hooks must have single-point barbs no larger than one-quarter inch. Above the Forest Service roads, anglers must use hiking trails to get higher up in the watershed.

Species: Trout, smallmouth bass, hatchery and wild steelhead, whitefish.

Facilities: Unimproved boat launch sites, suitable only for drift boats and rafts, are available at the mouth of Wall Creek and Monument and can be used for free. There is fee camping near Kimberly at Lone Pine Campground and Big Bend Campground. There is additional fee camping around Dale and closer to the headwaters at Ukiah Dale State Park, Toll Bridge, Trough Creek, Gold Dredge, and Orient Creek. Supplies and accommodations can be had in Kimberly, Monument, and Dale.

Directions: To reach the lower river from Kimberly, head east on Hwy. 402 (Kimberly–Long Creek Hwy.), following the river for 15 miles to Monument. Wall Creek Rd. north out of Monument will take you three more miles upriver to Birch Creek before dead-ending into a roadless area. The upper river is accessible from Dale.

West of Dale, Hwy. 395 follows the north bank of the river for four miles; when 395 turns north and away from the river, continue west on gravel Forest Rd. 3961 for 10 miles to its dead-end at Potamus Creek. Above Dale, Forest Rd. 55 and Forest Rd. 5506 will take you east along the river for 14 miles into the headwaters. To reach the headwaters take Forest Rd. 55 east out of Dale and drive four miles before turning southeast on Forest Rd. 5506. Follow Forest Rd. 5506 along the river for 10 miles to Trailhead No. 3022. The trail will take you farther into the upper headwaters.

Contact: Grant County Chamber of Commerce, 800/769-5664; Malheur National Forest, 541/575-3000; Blue Mountain Ranger District, 541/575-3000; BLM, Vale District, 541/473-3144; ODFW, John Day, 541/575-1167; John Day Parks and Recreation, 541/575-0110.

39 MIDDLE FORK JOHN DAY RIVER

south of Dale

Map 4.7, page 247

The Middle Fork is a tributary of the John Day River originating in the Malheur National Forest near Prairie City. For 75 miles it winds through high desert to join the North Fork just north of Monument. Most of the river, except for the lower nine miles, is accessible by good roads. Anglers will still find it difficult to reach much of the river because of private property.

As on the North Fork, the Middle Fork's primary draw is a late-arriving run of summer steelhead. The best fishing occurs in late winter or early spring. Most of the fishing takes place in the 20-mile stretch from the mouth to the steelhead fishing deadline at the Highway 395 bridge, 11 miles southeast of Ritter. Boating is not an option on this small water, so anglers will have to scout for public access points. Landowners in this area have been known to be generous in granting access to anglers. Highway 15 (Long Creek–Ritter Hwy.) follows the river northwest a few miles past Ritter toward the mouth and southeast up to the Highway 395 bridge. Steelhead fishing is open January 1–April 15 and September 1–December 31.

Steelhead anglers can use a variety of techniques to catch fish in this water. Keep in mind that the river doesn't have the large, sweeping runs of its parent river or other forks. The water is faster and consists of pools and chutes. For this reason it will be important to allow your tackle to reach the bottom behind boulders, logs, and drop-offs. Nymphs and drift gear rigged with weighted flies or lead will facilitate getting to where the fish hold. Move locations often to cover as much water as possible and ensure good dead drifts through each of the holes.

The river above Highway 395 to the headwaters presents a fair fishery for wild and planted trout and whitefish, as well as catch-and-release fishing for bull trout. Highway 20 (Middle Fork Rd.) off Highway 395 follows the river past the towns of Galena and Bates and the Austin Junction exit into the headwaters. Access is generally good, but watch for No Trespassing signs. Buying a good BLM or Forest Service map for the Malheur National Forest showing the Middle Fork will prove helpful in identifying public access points. This upper section of river is restricted to artificial flies and bait with single-point barbs no larger than one-quarter inch. Lures are prohibited. Again, focus on areas where trout may be holding for either cover or food supplies. Moving often and covering water thoroughly will improve your chances for success.

Species: Trout, bull trout, hatchery and wild steelhead, whitefish.

Facilities: There are two campgrounds on the river near Austin at Middle Fork Campground and Deer Horn Campground. Dixie Campground is approximately 10 miles west of the Austin Junction exit on Hwy. 26. Ritter Springs General Store provides supplies and access to a hot springs. Supplies can be bought in Ritter, Susanville, and Austin.

Directions: From Dale, drive 13 miles south on Hwy. 395 to where the highway crosses the river. From the Hwy. 395 bridge, can either drive northwest (downriver) or southeast (upriver). To reach points downriver, drive northwest along Long Creek–Ritter Rd., which is on the northwest side of Hwy. 395 near the bridge. Long Creek– Ritter Rd. follows the

river for 11 miles, past Ritter to a dead-end, and the beginning of a roadless area. To reach the river above Hwy. 395, drive southeast on Middle Fork Rd., which can be found on the northeast side of the highway near the bridge. Middle Fork Rd. will lead you along the river and into the headwaters past the towns of Galena (23 miles) and Austin (38 miles).

Contact: Grant County Chamber of Commerce, 800/769-5664; Malheur National Forest, 541/575-3000; Blue Mountain Ranger District, 541/575-3000; BLM, Vale District, 541/473-3144; ODFW, John Day, 541/575-1167; John Day Parks and Recreation, 541/575-0110.

⁴⁰ JOHN DAY RIVER: KIMBERLY TO SERVICE CREEK

east of The Dalles

Map 4.7, page 247

The John Day River flows here through country equally as magnificent as other parts of the John Day with narrow canyon gorges and steep mountainsides. Bank access is extremely limited because of private property that borders the river, requiring most anglers to fish from a boat. There are several single- or multiday floats available in this stretch. The best starting point is at the put-in at Kimberly Creek. From here, anglers can float east, downriver to the take-out at Spray (12 miles) or Service Creek (27 miles). Boats can also be launched at Spray and floated to Service Creek (15 miles). Bank access is limited to the boat ramps in Kimberly, Spray, and Service Creek.

Both steelhead and smallmouth bass are present in good numbers and the occasional trout can be found between Kimberly and Spray, 12 miles above Service Creek. Salmon are present in the spring, but fishing is prohibited. All methods of fishing are permitted, including bait. Trout season is May 27–October 31. Steelhead and smallmouth bass fishing is open year-round from Kimberly to Service

Creek; a steelhead season comes into effect above Kimberly. Bass may be retained up to five fish per day, and only three fish may be over 15 inches. Two hatchery steelhead may be kept per day, no more than 20 per year. Five trout may be kept per day with only one over 20 inches.

Bass become most active in the spring, beginning in April, after the waters have warmed to 60°F or more. This area is not as densely populated with bass, and anglers wishing for better bass fishing should consider the river below Service Creek. Bass average 12–13 inches. Larger bass up to 18 inches are more rare in this section compared to the river below Service Creek. Early-season bass anglers will need to fish deeper in the water with weighted nymphs and diving crankbaits. Later in the summer, July–September, anglers can fish the top water with poppers and Rapalas for some exciting surface action.

Steelhead fishing is good in this stretch late October–February or March. John Day steelhead tend to be on the small side, averaging 5–7 pounds with some larger fish possible. Most traditional fishing techniques work in the river for catching steelhead. Side drifting, drift fishing, float fishing, flies, lures, and drift rigs are all productive. Look for runs where boulders and current meet and create pockets for resting steelhead. The John Day attracts many fly anglers who hope to catch a large steelhead swinging dry flies or streamers.

Trout fishing is limited in this section, but they are present. Anglers can catch trout on nymphs and dry flies as well Rooster Tail spinners and bait such as night crawlers. When searching for trout, focus on areas of water in riffles, around rocks, and other river obstructions.

Species: Smallmouth bass, steelhead, trout.
Facilities: Free riverside camping is available along the river at natural campsites from Kimberly to Service Creek. Because the riverbank is composed of a mix of both public and private lands, boaters need to carry either a Prineville District BLM map showing the section of river or use a river guidebook to identify publicly accessible lands. The BLM requires no-trace camping at all boat-in campsites, including packing out garbage and solid human waste. Fires are not allowed during summer. BLM in Prineville can provide you all the updated regulations regarding boating, camping, and river use. Free boat ramps are available in Kimberly, Spray, and Service Creek. Fee camping is available at Service Creek and one mile east at Muleshoe. Fee camping is available near Kimberly at Big Bend and Lone Pine campgrounds. Supplies can be had in Kimberly.

Directions: From The Dalles drive 20 miles east on I-84 to Biggs Junction (Exit 104). From the base of the I-84 off-ramp turn south onto Hwy. 97. Drive southeast on Hwy 97, eight miles to the Hwy. 206 junction. Turn east onto Hwy. 206, passing through Wasco and crossing the John Day River near Cottonwood, and follow the highway for another 50 miles to Condon. From Condon, turn south on Hwy. 19, headed toward Fossil and Service Creek. Highway 19 reaches Service Creek in approximately 42 miles. From Service Creek, you can drive east along the river on Hwy. 19 through the towns of Spray (12 miles) and Kimberly (27 miles).

Contact: Grant County Chamber of Commerce, 800/769-5664; Wheeler County Chamber of Commerce, 541/763-2698; BLM, Prineville District, 541/416-6700; ODFW, John Day, 541/575-1167; River flow information: U.S. Department of Commerce, River Service Center, 503/261-9246, www.oregon.wr.usgs.gov; John Day Fossil Beds Information Line, 541/987-2333 or 541/987-2333; Wheeler County Visitor Information, 541/763-2355; Shuttle information: Wheeler County Visitor Information, 541/763-2355; J&Z Shuttles, 541/468-2182 or 541/468-2447; Fishing Guides: Marty Sheppard, 503/622-1870, littlecreekjd@earthlink.net; Gorge Fly Shop, 541/386-6977, gorgeflyshop@gorgeflyshop.com.

41 JOHN DAY RIVER: KIMBERLY TO HEADWATERS

southeast of Kimberly

Map 4.7, page 247

The John Day River's headwaters begin approximately 86 miles southeast of Kimberly, in the Strawberry Mountains of the Malheur National Forest. The river makes only a short eight-mile run north out of the National Forest before emerging into farmlands; it turns west at Prairie City into a preponderance of private property and agricultural farmlands 22 miles east of John Day. From John Day the river continues its westerly flow 28 miles, passing through Mount Vernon and Dayville and picking up the Middle Fork near Dayville. Past Dayville the river turns northward, finally reaching Kimberly and the North Fork in 26 miles.

Except for the section of river that flows through the National Forest, and a few feeder creeks above the headwaters such as Summit Creek, access to most of the river is scarce, limited to a few parks and roadside pullouts around towns and parks. Fishing is equally marginal, except for trout in the headwaters. Most of the steelhead passing through this section are reaching spawning conditions and become less than desirable. Smallmouth bass fishing begins to taper off around Kimberly and is nonexistent above Dayville. From Dayville to the headwaters, trout are the main attraction, but because of irrigation uses and farming practices the river does not support a very healthy population. Anglers hoping for better fishing should concentrate on the river below Kimberly or consider one of the river forks.

This section of the John Day is a bank fishery and does not contain any boat ramps. The headwaters is the best prospect for trout fishing and is followed by Highway 62 for all of its length. Fishing in the headwaters is unlimited from roadside pullouts as long as you're in National Forest. Two campgrounds in the headwaters, Trout Farm and Crescent, give additional river access. Further bank access can be had lower in the river from various roadside turnouts along Highway 19, which follows the river west of Dayville, and Highway 26, which follows the river east and west of John Day. One of the few parks along this stretch of river is Clyde Holliday State Park near Mount Vernon. Here anglers can walk up and down the river to find good holding water for both trout and steelhead. If you risk fishing the river from highway points, pay close attention and watch for No Trespassing signs. Acquiring a BLM map for the Prineville District showing this part of the river can help anglers navigate between private property and public access along Highways 26 and 19.

Bass, where present, can be fished for year-round and bag limits are limited to five per day with only three fish over 15 inches. Above the confluence of the North Fork in Kimberly, steelheading is open to the steelhead deadline at Indian Creek, near Prairie City, January 1–April 15 and September 1–December 31. There is a two-fish limit per day of hatchery steelhead and 20 per year. All wild fish must be released unharmed. John Day steelhead tend to be on the small side, averaging 5–7 pounds. Steelhead begin to show at the river mouth in late August and begin moving upriver in September. October and January tend to be the best months, when water temperatures cool and river flows increase. Fish runs can be delayed until December or January if river flows are not up to par.

A population of wild redband trout and planted rainbow trout are available in the upper section of the main river from Kimberly to the headwaters. Trout fishing is open May 27–October 31. There is a limit of two trout per day and all trout over 20 inches are considered steelhead and can be retained only under steelhead regulations. Flies, lures, and bait all work. Focus on shady areas along the bank or behind structures such as logs, rocks, or in rapids.

The John Day does get a modest run of chinook salmon, but they are off-limits to sportfishing. Chinook are in the river from early spring until they spawn in the upper river in September. If you hook a salmon it must be released unharmed.

Species: Smallmouth bass, steelhead, wild redband and stocked rainbow trout. Closed to salmon.

Facilities: Several archaeological and paleontological sites are in the area around Dayville, such as the John Day Fossil Beds National Monument and Picture Gorge. Fee camping is available in the headwaters along Hwy. 62 at Trout Farm and Crescent campgrounds. Fee camping is also available in Prairie City at Depot Park, Mount Vernon at Clyde Holiday Park, and outside Kimberly on the North Fork at Lone Pine and Big Bend. Supplies and other accommodations can be had in Kimberly, Dayville, Mount Vernon, John Day, and Prairie City.

Directions: To reach the river above Kimberly, drive south on Hwy. 19 from Kimberly for 19 miles to the Hwy. 26 junction. Turning east on Hwy. 26 will take you to Dayville (seven miles), Mount Vernon (29 miles), John Day (37 miles), and Prairie City (52 miles). To reach the headwaters from Prairie City, turn south on Hwy. 62 to reach the campgrounds at Trout Farm (14 miles) and Crescent (16 miles).

Contact: Grant County Chamber of Commerce, 800/769-5664; Wheeler County Chamber of Commerce, 541/763-2698; BLM, Prineville District, 541/416-6700; ODFW, John Day, 541/575-1167; John Day Fossil Beds Information Line, 541/987-2333 or 541/987-2333.

42 SOUTH FORK JOHN DAY RIVER

south of Dayville

Map 4.7, page 247

The South Fork of the John Day River originates on the slopes of Sugarloaf Mountain in the Snow Mountain area and runs 60 miles to join the main John Day River in Dayville. The

South Fork includes fast, plunging water in its upper reaches and slow, broad currents in the middle and lower stretches. It is closed to all salmon and steelhead fishing, but it is a good destination for catching wild redband trout and mountain whitefish. The fishing here is all bank access and wading, no boating. The river is open May 27–October 31.

The recipient of concentrated habitat restoration plans, the South Fork is a testament to what can be accomplished with proper stream management. Trout populations have risen greatly in the last few years and anglers are beginning to catch larger fish up to 15 inches. The presence of mountain whitefish is a bonus and can always be counted on to take a fly or lure, especially when redbands are not feeding. River access is very good from roads and campgrounds for most of its length and all but the first four miles of river near the mouth flow through publicly accessible lands. Anglers wishing to fish these first four miles must get permission from local landowners. The South Fork Road, unimproved at times, follows the river most of the way, providing easy access from the car via roadside turnouts or from unimproved campsites. The trout are not large, but they are plentiful. Expect to catch fish averaging 15 inches, with some a bit larger. A good place to begin fishing is 15 miles south of Dayville in the Philip W. Schneider Wildlife Management Area (also called Murderer's Creek).

Small stream fish are not typically difficult to catch. Concentrate on areas behind rocks or logs and in runs of faster water—any water you suspect may be holding a resting or feeding trout. Anglers can employ any form of tackle; flies, spinners, and bait all work. Don't ignore dry–fly-fishing opportunities. With or without a hatch, this is a great place to practice your skills with a size 12 Adams or Royal Wulff.

Species: Wild redband trout, mountain whitefish.

Facilities: Pine Tree Campground is about eight miles upriver from Dayville. Primitive camping is available in nearby Black Canyon Wilderness and at Wolf Creek and Sugar Creek campgrounds in the Ochoco National Forest, and in the Philip W. Schneider Management Wildlife Area. Limited supplies are available in Dayville and Mount Vernon.

Directions: From Dayville drive south on County Rd. 42 (South Fork Rd.) to follow the river 60 miles into the headwaters. South Fork Rd. turns into Izee Rd. approximately 25 miles upriver from Dayville. Above Izee, the river is followed another 20 miles on County Hwy. 68, which turns into County Hwy. 47. Where Forest Rd. 3750 intersects County Hwy. 47, the river ends by branching into smaller forks.

Contact: Grant County Chamber of Commerce, 800/769-5664; Malheur National Forest, 541/575-3000; Blue Mountain Ranger District, 541/575-3000; BLM, Vale District, 541/473-3144; ODFW, John Day, 541/575-1167; John Day Parks and Recreation, 541/575-0110.

43 ANTHONY LAKE
west of North Powder in the
Wallowa-Whitman National Forest

Map 4.8, page 248

Situated at 7,100 feet in the Elkhorn Mountains of southern Wallowa–Whitman National Forest, Anthony Lake is a must-see for the visiting angler and a great place for families, providing scenic, isolated campsites and a wilderness experience. Surrounded by granite peaks, pristine forests, and numerous hiking trails, the 23-acre lake averages 12 feet in depth; the deepest point (30 feet) is in the middle. Anthony Lake is easily accessible for both the boater and bank angler. Bank anglers will relish the scouting possibilities made easy by the mile-long hiking trail around the lake. Boaters and float tubers can safely launch their nonmotorized craft from the concrete ramp near the campground. Anthony Lake may be open all year, but most anglers can't get to the lake before ice-out, which occurs in the first week of July. If you are headed to this lake during the early season, it always pays to check with the local Forest Service before making the trek.

Regular stocking begins with smaller fish, 8–10 inches, and larger trout, 14 inches or more, are available in fall. Numerous trophy-size trout are stocked in April or May, early in the season, and some of these can reach 17 inches or larger. Brook trout are also stocked, but there is also a healthy native population because, unlike the rainbows, they spawn in the tributaries. Brook trout run smaller, the average being 10 inches. All methods of angling are permitted and productive at Anthony Lake. Bait and artificial lures can make fishing attractive for both the novice and the advanced angler. Five fish may be kept per day with only one over 20 inches. Typical approaches include casting small spinners and bait or trolling in the deeper waters. Fly-fishing is popular at this lake, particularly at the southwest corner. Fly anglers can begin by prospecting with small leech patterns or nymphs stripped back from the bank at various speeds until you hit on the right tactic. During summer, watch for hatching insects during the warmest parts of the day and tie on a Parachute Adams or emerger pattern.

Species: Rainbow and brook trout.

Facilities: Anthony Lake is a perfect jumping-off point to reach other alpine lakes such as Van Patten and Hoffer. A good Forest Service map can reveal small, hidden lakes in the Anthony Lakes area. Fee camping, drinking water, restrooms, hiking trails, and a concrete boat ramp are all available. There is no fee to launch a boat or day use of the lake. Supplies and accommodations can be had in North Powder or Baker City.

Directions: From North Powder drive west on North Powder River Ln. for three miles. Turn south on Ellis Rd. for one mile until you reach the junction of Anthony Lakes Hwy. Turn west on Anthony Lakes Hwy., which becomes Anthony Lakes Rd. and the Elkhorn National Scenic Byway. Drive for approximately 15 miles on the Byway to reach Anthony Lake. The campground and parking are on the south side of the highway.

Contact: Baker City Chamber of Commerce, 800/523-1235; Wallowa–Whitman National Forest, 541/523-6391; ODFW, Baker, 541/523-5832; York's Grocery and Sporting Goods, Baker City, 541/523-2577; Four Seasons Fly Shoppe, La Grande, 541/963-8420.

44 PHILLIPS LAKE
southwest of Baker City on the Powder River
Map 4.8, page 248

Set beautifully against the Elkhorn Mountains, Phillips is a 2,235-acre reservoir with 11.5 miles of shoreline on the Powder River 15 miles west of Baker City. The reservoir's average depth is 45 feet, and it is 125 feet at its deepest point near Mason Dam. The reservoir is open year-round and all methods of fishing are permissible; there are no boating restrictions. Numerous cold- and warm-water species coexist, making this an attractive option for just about any angler. Rainbow trout, crappie, perch, channel catfish, and smallmouth and largemouth bass are all present in good numbers. All methods of fishing are permitted on this year-round fishing lake. Rainbow trout average 10–14 inches but have been known to get to trophy size. The most popular area to fish is around the dam, where boaters troll the depths for larger trout and channel catfish. The shorelines are well populated with debris and underwater obstructions, creating good holding water for bass, perch, and crappie. Effective bass lures for this water are crankbaits and spinnerbaits, used to cover large areas of water in search of fish. Once the fish have been found, you can switch to plastic worms trolled slowly through the water. Vary the colors of your lures until you hit on a productive shade. Perch, incidentally, have become something of a problem at Phillips. Overpopulated, they tend to be the first species to grab your bait, sometimes making it difficult to catch the larger fish.

Species: Rainbow trout, crappie, perch, channel catfish, smallmouth and largemouth bass.

Facilities: Three campgrounds are on the lake, Union Creek on the north shore and Millers Lane and Southwest Shore on the south shore. Millers Lane is free and has no drinking water (May–Nov.), Southwest Shore also has no drinking water (May–Nov.), and Union Creek has shower and concessions (Apr–Sept.). There are also two picnic areas, Mason Dam Picnic Area near the dam and Mowich Picnic Area at the northwest corner of the lake off Hwy. 7. Drinking water, restrooms, RV hookups, and hiking trails are all available. Three free boat ramps service the lake. Supplies and accommodations can be had in Baker City. Anglers and families wishing for a little diversion can visit the historic mining town of Sumpter, 10 miles west on Hwy. 7.

Directions: From Baker City follow Hwy. 7 west for 15 miles to reach the lake and Mason Dam Picnic Area, which will appear to the south of the highway. Union Creek Campground and boat launch and Mowich Picnic Area can be found two and four miles west of Mason Dam Picnic Area on Hwy. 7. To reach the south shore campgrounds, drive five miles west on Hwy. 7 from the Mason Dam picnic srea and turn south on Hudspeth Rd. Follow Hudspeth for 1.5 miles until you're forced to make a turn east on an unnamed road at the locked Forest Service gate. Southwest Shore will appear immediately to the north and Miller Lane can be had two miles down this road.

Contact: Baker City Chamber of Commerce, 800/523-1235; Wallowa–Whitman National Forest, 541/523-6391; ODFW, Baker, 541/523-5832; York's Grocery and Sporting Goods, Baker City, 541/523-2577; Old Pine Market, 541/742-4366; Four Seasons Fly Shoppe, La Grande, 541/963-8420.

45 BURNT RIVER FORKS
southwest of Baker City
Map 4.8, page 248

The Burnt River has three forks (South, Middle and North), all of which feed Unity Reservoir. All three forks are small rivers, appropriate for bank angling but not boating. The South Fork originates in the Blue Mountains and provides the best fishing in the area. The Middle and North forks also provide fishing access, but irrigation draws create an unstable environment for good fishing. Avoid fishing the Middle Fork until some stream rehabilitation plans are employed. All forks have good access roads through forest lands and provide anglers unlimited opportunities to explore the region. The Burnt River forks are open April 22–October 31. Five fish per day may be retained and the use of all fishing methods is permitted, including bait.

The South Fork is about 12 miles long and is by far the most developed fishery in the area, boasting spring-fed waters that run cold and stable throughout the year, making this a good bet for the entire fishing season fishery. Trout are not large, but they are plentiful with a mixed stock of wild and hatchery fish. Bait fishing is allowed and quite popular, making this a perfect river for novice anglers to get their feet wet. Fly and spin anglers will enjoy the challenge of fishing pocket water in search of that elusive bigger trout. The shaded pine forest offers relief from the summer heat and there are four primitive campgrounds.

The longer North Fork (25 miles) also contains good populations of planted and native trout in the 10–12-inch range. The North Fork originates in the Wallowa–Whitman National Forest and is followed closely by good county and Forest Service roads. The river improves in habitat and water condition above Whitney. The same fishing techniques work on either fork. Bait, spinners, and flies are all productive.

Species: Rainbow trout.

Facilities: There are four primitive campgrounds on the South Fork: South Fork, Stevens Creek, Elk Creek, and Mammoth Springs. All are near the headwaters off Forest Rd. 6005. There is a well-developed state park with fee camping options at Unity Reservoir. Buy supplies in Unity and Bates.

Directions: From Baker City drive south six

miles on Hwy. 7 to the Hwy. 245 junction. Turn south on Hwy. 245 and drive 21 miles through Hereford to the south end of Unity Reservoir. To reach South Fork, from Unity Reservoir drive south on Hwy. 254 for five miles to Hwy. 26. Turn west on Hwy. 26 and drive approximately two miles. Turn south on County Rd. 537. County Rd. 537 will change to Forest Rd. 6005 and leads into the headwaters in approximately seven miles. Look for the South Fork, Stevens Creek, Elk Creek, and Mammoth Springs campgrounds (in that order) along Forest Rd. 6005. To reach North Fork, from Unity Reservoir drive east on Hwy. 245 two miles to County Rd. 535, five miles west of Hereford. Turn north on to County Rd. 535, which eventually turns into County Rd. 529 and leads to Whitney in approximately 12 miles. From Whitney, drive west on Hwy. 7 approximately four miles to County Rd. 503. Turn northwest onto County Rd. 503, which reaches the headwaters in approximately four miles.

Contact: Baker City Chamber of Commerce, 800/523-1235; Wallowa–Whitman National Forest, 541/523-6391; Grant County Chamber of Commerce, 800/769-5664; BLM, Vale District, 541/473-3144; ODFW, Baker, 541/523-5832; Oregon Parks and Recreation Department, 800/452-5687; Unity Lake State Park, 800/551-6949, www.oregonstateparks.org; York's Grocery and Sporting Goods in Baker City, 541/523-2577; Old Pine Market, 541/742-4366; Kiger Fly Shop, 541/573-1329.

46 UNITY RESERVOIR

north of Unity

Map 4.8, page 248

Five miles north of Unity on Highway 245 sits this large, high-desert, 1,000-acre irrigation reservoir fed by the Middle, South, and North forks of the Burnt River. The outlet at Highway 245 forms the Burnt River proper. Unity has an elevation of 3,800 feet, an average depth of 27 feet, and a maximum depth of 50 feet by the dam. There are 12.7 miles of shoreline accessible by foot or from a boat. Unity is a multiuse reservoir, and anglers will share its waters with recreational boaters, water-skiers, and waterfowl hunters (in the fall), and it is a popular ice-fishing spot in winter. The reservoir's drawdown occurs July–October, but good fishing can be had at this year-round fishery even in low-water conditions. All methods of fishing are permitted, including bait, and there are no special restriction on bag limits.

Unity is best fished in the early season beginning in April with higher water levels and cooler temperatures. Summer and fall also provide good fishing, but anglers will need to search the deeper water by the dam and from a boat to catch sizable trout. Rainbow trout thrive in Unity's cold waters and average 9–12 inches with larger fish near 16 inches. Warm-water species such as bass and crappie are present, but the persistent cold-water conditions keep their sizes small. Bass average 11–12 inches and perch are 6–7 inches. Trolling and bait fishing are by far the most popular and productive method of fishing. Bait such as worms or grubs suspended under a bobber should produce good results. Spinners such as Rooster Tails should be used in smaller sizes and trolled with various speeds and depths. Fly anglers will be challenged on this large body of water. For the best results, always start with good searching patterns such as a Woolly Bugger in white, pink, or black, or a small nymph stripped at various retrieves. Look for hatches of insects emerging during the day near the banks. Trout tend to forage in shallower water during the low-light conditions of morning and evening.

Species: Rainbow trout, smallmouth bass, crappie, perch.

Facilities: Unity Lake State Park (May 1–Sept. 30) is perfect for families looking for comfortable desert camping. It provides fee campsites, RV hookups, tepee rentals, fire pits, showers, drinking water, restrooms, hiking trails, nature center, and a free boat ramp. Families may also enjoy a few side trips to the mining town of Sumpter and the wilderness areas of Monument Rock, Strawberry Mountain, and North Fork John Day. Some historical artifacts exist in the park, such as an old mining dredge that is open to visitors during normal operation hours. Supplies can be had in the nearby town of Unity.

Directions: From Unity follow Hwy. 26 north about two miles, merging onto Hwy. 245. Drive three miles to reach the reservoir.

Contact: Grant County Chamber of Commerce, 800/769-5664; Wallowa–Whitman National Forest, 541/523-6391; BLM, Vale District, 541/473-3144; ODFW, Baker, 541/523-5832; Oregon Parks and Recreation Department, 800/452-5687; Unity Lake State Park, 800/551-6949, www.oregonstateparks.org; York's Grocery and Sporting Goods, 541/523-2577; Old Pine Market, 541/742-4366; Kiger Fly Shop, 541/573-1329.

47 CANYON CREEK

south of John Day

Map 4.8, page 248

Formed on the slopes of the Strawberry Mountain Wilderness, Canyon Creek is a small year-round trout stream with good bank fishing for west slope cutthroat, brook trout, and redband trout. Canyon Creek Meadows Reservoir dams part of the river and provides good fishing in early spring. The brook trout, escapees from the reservoir, are found below the dam The river itself is approximately 27 miles long, forming a few miles above the dam and emptying into the upper John Day River near John Day. Both the upper and lower sections of the river are easily accessible by roads following most of its course.

Trout are not large, averaging 12–13 inches, but they're plentiful and good practice for beginners. In the lower river, the best places to fish are right below the reservoir in the summer, and along Highway 395 in winter and fall. The upper river above the reservoir holds small trout, but the river is small, faster-flowing, and not very productive. Bait, small lures, and flies are all permissible and work well all year. Typically, small fish in small rivers are not choosy about what they eat, so one can expect to catch a lot of fish on whatever is thrown out. Bait such as worms and PowerBait are effective in the small pools. Lures such as Rooster Tails should be kept small to match the size of the fish. Small rivers always present good opportunities to practice dry–fly-fishing. Using a small Parachute Adams, Royal Wulff, or Humpy will most certainly get you lots of strikes. When scouting the river, pay attention to pools and pocket water. Pay particular attention to areas around obstacles such as rocks or logs and in the deeper pools at the end of tail-outs.

Species: Wild west slope cutthroat, redband and brook trout.

Facilities: Several fee campsites service the area along the highway to the headwaters: J Bar L Guest Ranch and Starr Campground on Hwy. 395, Wickiup Campground on Canyon Creek Ln. (Forest Rd. 15), and Canyon Meadows campground on Canyon Meadows Reservoir. There is a boat ramp at the Canyon Meadows campground. Buy supplies in John Day.

Directions: The river is accessible by roads all the way into its headwaters. From John Day take Hwy. 395 south, following the river for 10 miles to Canyon Creek Rd. (Forest Rd. 15). Turn east on Canyon Creek Rd., again following the river for 10 miles until you reach Forest Rd. 1520. Follow the Forest Service road three miles to reach the reservoir. Anglers can park at the Canyon Meadows Reservoir boat ramp and walk down to the river below the dam. Driving past the reservoir and onto logging roads will enable you to reach the headwaters. A good Forest Service map for the Malheur National Forest showing the river will help you navigate this area.

Contact: Grant County Chamber of Commerce, 800/769-5664; Malheur National Forest, 541/575-3000; Blue Mountain Ranger District, 541/575-3000; BLM, Vale District, 541/473-3144; ODFW, John Day, 541/575-1167; John Day Parks and Recreation, 541/575-0110; J Bar L Guest Ranch, 541/575-2517; Kiger Fly Shop, 541/573-1329.

48 CANYON CREEK MEADOWS RESERVOIR

south of John Day

Map 4.8, page 248

This 32-acre man-made reservoir, also known as Canyon Meadows Lake, is situated in a scenic valley and fed by Canyon Creek, which provides good year-round trout fishing for native redband, cutthroat, and brook trout. Rainbow trout make an occasional appearance because of previous stocking programs, but no current stocking program exists. Retained by a rubble dam constructed in the early 1960s for recreation, the reservoir has been plagued with leaks since its inception and consequently rarely holds water for an entire fishing season. Past attempts to fix the leaks have failed, and there are no plans for additional repairs or trapping water by closing the floodgates. All species of fish run small since they have only a short time to develop. All methods of fishing are permitted, including bait. There are no boating restrictions, but one doesn't need more than a float tube or canoe to get at the fish. Bank access is good around most of the reservoir.

If you do plan to fish here, make your trip early in the spring, just after ice-out, sometime in March. By July the reservoir is dry or too low to hold a decent population of fish. During very wet years the reservoir may retain enough water to be fishable into summer and fall. It is advisable to check with the ODFW for water levels before planning a trip. If the snowpack doesn't get to be an obstacle, ice fishing can be good in the winter—December–February or until the ice gets too thin.

Species: Cutthroat, rainbow, redband, and brook trout.

Facilities: The nice West Side Campground provides fee camping and facilities such as restrooms, drinking water, and a free boat ramp. Supplies and accommodations can be had in John Day and Burns.

Directions: From John Day, take Hwy. 395 south for 10 miles to Canyon Creek Rd. Turn east onto Canyon Creek Rd. and drive for another 10 miles to Forest Rd. 1520. Drive east on Forest Rd. 1520 and drive three miles to where the road dead-ends at the reservoir and West Side Campground. Parking is available in the campground.

Contact: Grant County Chamber of Commerce, 800/769-5664; Malheur National Forest, 541/575-3000; Blue Mountain Ranger District, 541/575-3000; BLM, Vale District, 541/473-3144; ODFW, John Day, 541/575-1167; John Day Parks and Recreation, 541/575-0110; Kiger Fly Shop, 541/573-1329.

49 POWDER RIVER

east of Baker City

Map 4.9, page 249

The Powder River stretches more than 140 miles, running east from the Blue Mountains east of Sumpter to the Snake River at Brownlee Reservoir on the Oregon/Idaho border. Two dams capture the river, forming Thief Valley Reservoir near North Powder and Phillips Reservoir southwest of Baker City. The lower 10 miles of river east of Richland make up the Powder River Arm of Brownlee Reservoir. It was once a great trout fishery, but dams and agricultural and mining practices have reduced the river's capacity to produce consistent populations of fish. That said, there are good tail-water bank fisheries below each of the two reservoirs and anglers have good opportunities to catch stocked rainbow trout that can reach 20 inches plus, and small wild redband trout. Boating is not practiced on any section of the river.

The most productive fishing on the river for larger trout is below Thief Valley Reservoir Dam, where there are two access points. The first access point is directly below the dam. Because of private property most of this section is inaccessible but a quarter mile of river access on the northeast side of the river has been granted for angler use by a generous landowner. The second section of river is along Highway 86 northwest of Huntington. This area, also called the Powder River Canyon, offers anglers 12 miles of river between Colvard Station, 24 miles below the dam, to Huntington. Fishing is spotty in this section but does hold larger fish in the deep water. Anglers should focus on riffle water and pools, identifiable from the highway, and use roadside pullouts to scramble down the banks to the river. All this water below Thief Valley Reservoir is open for fishing upstream from the Huntington–Richland Road Bridge in Huntington to Hughes Lane, above the Thief Valley Dam near Baker City, April 22–October 31. Use of bait is allowed and a bag limit of five fish, with only one fish over 20 inches, is permitted. The best time to fish any of this water is just after opening day and again in fall. This is the favorite water of fly anglers employing streamers such as Woolly Buggers and Zonkers in the deeper runs to catch the largest trout. Dry–fly-fishing is also good and the river produces good hatches of caddis. Spinners such as Rooster Tails and bait such as night crawlers and PowerBait also work.

The other area of productive fishing on the river is directly below Mason Dam, which sits at the east end of Phillips Lake. The trout in this section are smaller, under 16 inches, but it is heavily stocked with rainbow trout. The river here is accessible directly below Mason Dam and along Highway 7 south out of Baker City. Again, the best times to fish this section of river is during spring and early fall because irrigation draws during summer can severely reduce the water flows. This section of river is open from Hughes Lane Bridge in Baker City to Mason Dam January 1–April 21 and November 1–December 31 and is limited to catch-and-release fishing with artificial lures and flies. Bait fishing is allowed in this section April 22–October 31. Night crawlers and PowerBait are both productive. Fly anglers in particular will find good hatches of caddis flies and terrestrials during the summer. Streamer fishing with Woolly Buggers and Zonkers can produce the biggest catches. Spin anglers should use small Rooster Tails or similar spinners to fish pools and runs.

Species: Rainbow and redband trout.

Facilities: Fee camping is available at Thief Valley Reservoir, Phillips Reservoir, and at the Hewitt Park Campground near Richland. There are two improved public access points below Phillips Reservoir along Hwy. 7 with restrooms, parking lots, and wheelchair-accessible hiking trails. Supplies and accommodations can be had in Richland, North Powder, and Baker.

Directions: From Baker City, reach the river below Phillips Reservoir by following Hwy. 7 west 15 miles, passing through Salisbury after eight miles. Parking is available at the Mason Dam Picnic Area or along Hwy. 7 just below the dam. Other access points are available along Hwy. 7 west of Salisbury. Look for roadside pullouts along productive water.

From North Powder, reach the river directly below Thief Valley Reservoir by driving northeast on Hwy. 237 for five miles to Government Gulch Rd. Turn south on Government Gulch Rd. and drive two miles to Telocaset Rd. Turn southeast onto Telocaset Rd. and follow it approximately five miles to Thief Valley Rd. Turn southwest on Thief Valley Rd. Drive one mile and begin to look for a rough unnamed dirt road to the southeast. A Vale District BLM map showing the location of the reservoir would be helpful to negotiate these unnamed roads. Turn southeast on the dirt road and drive approximately three miles to the base of the dam and to roadside parking. This is where the public access begins, from the dam to 0.25 mile downriver. Signs or markers may or may not be present to indicate these boundaries so use caution not to trespass.

To reach the river northwest of Richland, drive on Hwy. 86 west out of Richland. Follow the highway west for approximately five miles,

at which point the river will appear to your south. From this point 12 miles northwest on Hwy. 86 to Colvard Station, the river is accessible from roadside pullouts.

Contact: Baker City Chamber of Commerce, 800/523-1235; BLM, Vale District, 541/473-3144; ODFW, Baker, 541/523-5832; Whitman Unit Pine Ranger District, 541/742-7511; Hells Canyon Chamber of Commerce, 541/742-4222, www.hellscanyonchamber.com.

50 POWDER RIVER ARM

Brownlee Reservoir

Map 4.9, page 249

Of the two river arms on Brownlee Reservoir, Powder and Burnt, the Powder River Arm is by far the most productive and popular with three good boat ramps and one campground. The Powder River Arm of Brownlee Reservoir is six miles long, extending from Richland east to Brownlee Reservoir. It is formed by the Powder River's being backed up by Brownlee Reservoir. Fishing the arm is productive all year from the bank or boat. Good bank fishing can be had at any of the three boat ramps or along Snake River Road on the south side of the river arm.

Of the fisheries available in the Powder River Arm, the most popular are largemouth bass, crappie, and channel and brown bullhead catfish, followed by smallmouth bass and bluegill. The largemouth bass fishing is some of the best on Brownlee Reservoir. Anglers fish along the banks around river structure from the vicinity of Hewitt Park to the mouth, six miles downriver. Crappie can be found in shallower water around rocks and other river obstructions. The best crappie fishing occurs in April during the spawning season and slows as summer progresses and the fish move to deeper water. Catfish are abundant and are fished for around Hewitt Park and are caught with every kind of bait, including night crawlers, shrimp, and PowerBait. Also fished for around Hewitt Park are bluegill and what exists of a small population of smallmouth bass.

Species: Largemouth bass, smallmouth bass, crappie, channel and brown bullhead catfish, bluegill.

Facilities: Fee camping is available at Hewitt Park Campground in Richland. Three boat ramps are all within close proximity of each other at Hewitt Park Campground, Hewitt Day Use Area, and Noble Holcomb; all require a fee. Supplies and accommodations can be had in Richland.

Directions: To reach the Powder River Arm from Baker City, drive east on Hwy. 86 for 38 miles to Richland. Continue heading east of Richland on Hwy. 86 for approximately 0.5 mile to Holcomb Lane. Turn south on Holcomb Ln., following signs to Hewitt Park, and drive two miles to the dead-end at Hewitt Park. Parking is available either at the campground or in the day-use area; both require a fee. To reach the south side of the river arm from Richland, turn south on 2nd St. from downtown Richland and drive 1.5 miles to the intersection with Snake River Rd. At this point you're headed west on 2nd St. Turn south on Snake River Rd. The river arm will be to the north. Access can be had from roadside pullouts for two miles.

Contact: Baker City Chamber of Commerce, 800/523-1235; BLM, Vale District, 541/473-3144; ODFW, Baker, 541/523-5832; Whitman Unit Pine Ranger District, 541/742-7511; Hells Canyon Chamber of Commerce, 541/742-4222, www.hellscanyonchamber.com.

51 BURNT RIVER
north of Huntington
Map 4.9, page 249

The Burnt River is formed at the outlet of Unity Reservoir and flows 77 miles to Huntington on the Snake River. On its eastward journey the river cuts through the towns of Bridgeport and Durkee before turning south to parallel I-84 to Huntington. The river at Huntington is backed up to create the Burnt River Arm of Brownlee Reservoir. Between Bridgeport and Durkee the river passes through scenic Burnt River Canyon. Although much of the river is followed by good roads, access is a problem because of private property and because there is no boating on the river. Fishing season on the Burnt River is open April 22–October 31 upstream from the Huntington–Richland Bridge below Huntington near the Snake River and year-round from the bridge to the Snake River.

Fishing on the Burnt River below the reservoir has in the past provided good fishing for sizable rainbow trout. But in the last few years, this part of the river has been hard-hit by low water in Unity Reservoir, thereby limiting water releases to support the river and trout populations. In fact, Unity Reservoir has gone dry in the years before 2006, causing the Burnt River to run at a trickle. According to the ODFW, it's possible that very few fish survived. After low-water years the fish usually need a couple of years to recuperate with better water conditions. Be sure to check with ODFW before making a trek to this area.

In good water years the best trout fishing is right below Unity Reservoir and is accessible by Highway 245. Public access can be found from roadside turnouts and around bridges. Watch for No Trespassing signs and ask landowners for permission to use their property. Burnt River Canyon upstream from Durkee in I-84 is an option for anglers who want to fish the river closer to the dam for rainbow trout. This area is not as affected by the water releases from Unity Reservoir. But again, pay attention to No Trespassing signs. Since most of this land is on BLM property, a Vale District BLM map showing this area will assist you in finding publicly accessible lands leading to the river.

Species: Rainbow trout, crappie, smallmouth bass, perch, channel catfish.

Facilities: Camping is available at Farewell Bend Recreation Area on Brownlee Reservoir and at Unity Lake State Park on Unity Reservoir. There are a few primitive campgrounds on the South Fork of the Burnt River. Supplies and accommodations can be had in Unity, Durkee, and Huntington.

Directions: From Huntington near the Snake River, drive north on business Rte. 30, following the river for 20 miles to Durkee. At Durkee, drive two miles north on business Rte. 30 to Burnt River Canyon Rd. Turn west on Burnt River Canyon Rd. and follow the river another 18 miles before the road turns south just before reaching Bridgeport. Approximately 0.25 mile before entering Bridgeport, turn west onto Bridgeport Dr. and drive four miles to the Hwy. 245 junction. Drive west on Hwy. 245, again following the river, to reach Unity Reservoir in approximately 18 miles. There is plenty of roadside parking below the dam.

Contact: Baker City Chamber of Commerce, 800/523-1235; Wallowa–Whitman National Forest, 541/523-6391; BLM, Vale District, 541/473-3144; ODFW, Baker, 541/523-5832; Farewell Bend State Recreation Area, 800/452-5687; Oasis RV Park and Campground, 541/262-3504; Unity Lake State Park, 800/551-6949, www.oregonstateparks.org.

52 BURNT RIVER ARM
Brownlee Reservoir in Huntington
Map 4.9, page 249

The Burnt River Arm of Brownlee Reservoir is two miles long, extending from Huntington east to Blakes Junction on Brownlee Reservoir. It is formed by the Burnt River's being backed up by Brownlee Reservoir. This is a year-round warm-water fishery with bass, channel catfish, crappie, and perch. Fishing the arm is productive all year from the bank or boat. A majority of the fishing is still-water fishing with bait or jigs. The Burnt River Arm of Brownlee Reservoir is closely followed by Snake River Road. Boaters wanting to fish this arm of Brownlee Reservoir must motor up from Brownlee Reservoir. Boats can be launched at either Farewell Bend State Recreation Area or Oasis RV Park and Campground, approximately four and five river miles upriver from Huntington. Bank angling is good from Snake River Road along most of the two miles to Brownlee Reservoir.

Species: Smallmouth bass, channel catfish, crappie and perch.

Facilities: Camping is available at Farewell Bend Recreation Area on Brownlee Reservoir and at Unity Lake State Park on Unity Reservoir. Supplies and accommodations can be had in Huntington.

Directions: From Huntington drive east on Snake River Rd. Snake River Rd. follows the Burnt River Arm for two miles to Blakes Junction.

Contact: Baker City Chamber of Commerce, 800/523-1235; Wallowa–Whitman National Forest, 541/523-6391; BLM, Vale District, 541/473-3144; ODFW, Baker, 541/523-5832; Farewell Bend State Recreation Area, 800/452-5687; Oasis RV Park and Campground, 541/262-3504; Unity Lake State Park, 800/551-6949, www.oregonstateparks.org.

53 MALHEUR RESERVOIR
southeast of Unity
Map 4.9, page 249

Malheur Reservoir was a well-known, year-round, high-desert fishery especially popular with the float tube, fly-angling crowd wishing to catch large rainbow trout. Sadly, this reservoir has been dry since 2002, and all fish have been lost. As of 2005, the reservoir still had not accumulated any water and all stocking ceased. (The snowpack in 2005 was one of the lowest on record, and the reservoir will not fill again until conditions permit.) With that said, future years hold promise that this once-great fishery will return to its former glory and reputation for churning out large rainbow and redband trout. Check with the ODFW's website to get current reports on the fishing conditions. Malheur Reservoir sits at an elevation of 3,350 feet, surrounded by sagebrush, hills, and very little shade. When full, it comprises 1,300 acres with an average depth of 40 feet and a maximum depth of 105 feet near the dam. There are 12.5 miles of shoreline, all accessible to the angler by either foot or boat. The reservoir is privately owned but sits on public lands, and access has graciously been granted for public use. Take care to obey all No Trespassing signs and clean up after yourself. The reservoir is serviced by two boat ramps on the north side of the lake near the dam. Some limited, primitive camping and restrooms are available around the boat ramps and access roads. There are no boating restrictions.

Species: Redband and rainbow trout.

Facilities: Limited primitive campsites are at boat ramps and along access roads. Restrooms are available at boat ramps. Supplies can be had in Ironside or Unity.

Directions: From Unity drive 18 miles east on Hwy. 26 to the Willow Creek Rd. junction near Ironside. Turn north onto Willow Creek Rd. You will reach the southeast side of the reservoir in approximately 14 miles.

Contact: Grant County Chamber of Commerce, 800/769-5664; Wallowa–Whitman National Forest, 541/523-6391; BLM, Vale District, 541/473-3144; ODFW, Baker, 541/523-5832; York's Grocery and Sporting Goods, 541/523-2577; Old Pine Market, 541/742-4366; Kiger Fly Shop, 541/573-1329.

54 OXBOW RESERVOIR
northeast of Baker City
Map 4.10, page 250

Oxbow Reservoir is a 12-mile impoundment between Oxbow Dam and Brownlee Dam. The reservoir has a well-developed fishery for smallmouth bass and crappie, but you can also catch trout, channel catfish, and flathead catfish. Highway 86 follows the river on the Oregon side from Oxbow Dam to Brownlee Dam, allowing bank anglers to stop anywhere and fish or even launch a small boat at numerous unofficial ramps (the only developed boat ramp is at McCormick Park, below Brownlee Dam, on the Idaho side). To boat the reservoir, scout the unimproved ramps along the Oregon side for feasibility. Boats longer than 20 feet are not recommended. Water levels can drop as much as four feet during the evenings, so use caution when mooring your boat for the night.

Together with Brownlee Reservoir, Oxbow boasts a nationally recognized trophy smallmouth bass fishery. Bass season is open all year, and there is a limit of two bass per day. All fish 12–16 inches must be released unharmed. January 1–June 30 there is a catch-and-release restriction to help protect spawning fish. Unlike largemouth bass, smallmouth bass like cooler, deeper water. You can catch bass on the surface more readily in the spring and on cooler overcast days than in the summer. To catch the bigger fish, most anglers troll the deeper waters around rock piles or other underwater obstructions, which can be identified on depth finders. Keep your bait or lure close to the bottom and allow a pause now and then to imitate a struggling baitfish. Lures such as crawfish imitations, jigs, pork rinds, spinners, minnows, surface plugs, and worms all work. During the summer, fly anglers can catch large numbers of smaller bass by casting poppers to the bank or around rocky points. Vary the speed of your retrieves using erratic pauses to imitate a struggling frog or mouse.

Crappie fishing provides the other main attraction at Oxbow. Crappie can show up anywhere in the reservoir, but they almost always hang out in schools. On calm days you can take crappie closer to the surface around rocks, brush, and other structure such as dam walls. On windy days you'll have to go deeper to undisturbed waters. If you are unsure about where the crappie may be lying, you can always troll a small jig, occasionally moving the rod tip up and down to get their attention. When you find one crappie, stay put and fish the entire area because there are probably more. Light tackle will help you detect strikes. Ultraresponsive lightweight spinning rods rigged with 4-pound test should do the trick. Keep your jigs small or use small pieces of worm or minnows for bait.

Both channel and flathead catfish are present in Oxbow. Channel cats can reach 15 pounds, and flatheads have been known to tip the scales at 28 pounds or more. More often than not, these are bottom-loving fish that love mud, deep channels, and pools—

wherever there is an abundance of live and dead food. Channel cats can be ultrasensitive to environmental changes such as wind, low-pressure systems, and weather. Bait choices include cut baits, worms, liver, crawfish, shrimp, and clams. Larger hook sizes such as 2/0 will help ensure a good hook set.

During the spring and early summer, anglers can find good populations of trout in larger sizes. Fish the shorelines, especially in the early morning and evenings. Inlets around small tributaries or rivers are always good places to find trout. Nymphs and dry flies work when there are insect hatches; otherwise, try trolling with small baitfish patterns such as Woolly Buggers, Zonkers, and small Marabou Leech patterns.

Species: Trout, smallmouth bass, crappie, channel and flathead catfish.

Facilities: Fishing licenses from either state are valid on the Snake River when angling from a floating device or launching watercraft. You must buy the required state license when fishing tributaries or landforms within either state. Primitive campgrounds are on the Oregon shores, and there are two developed campgrounds below Brownlee Dam at Mc-Cormick Park in Idaho and Copperfield Park in Copperfield. Primitive boat ramps, all free, are available on the Oregon side along Hwy. 86 with the only developed boat ramp (free) at Mc-Cormick Park. Supplies and accommodations can be had in Copperfield and Baker City.

Directions: From Baker City drive east on Hwy. 86 for 75 miles to Copperfield. From Copperfield, stay on Hwy. 86, which turns south and follows the river for another 11 miles before crossing the river just below Brownlee Dam. Primitive boat ramps can be found along Hwy. 86 south of Copperfield at approximately four, nine, and 10 miles. McCormick Park ramp is immediately to the north of Brownlee Dam on the Idaho side of the river.

Contact: Wallowa County Chamber of Commerce (Troy, Joseph, Enterprise), 800/585-4121; Hells Canyon National Recreation Area managed by the Wallowa–Whitman National Forest, 541/523-6391; BLM, Vale District, 541/473-3144; ODFW, La Grande, 541/963-2138; Wallowa Mountains Visitors Center, 541/426-5546; Hells Canyon Chamber of Commerce, 541/742-4222, www. hellscanyonchamber.com; McCormick Park and Woodhead Park Information, 541/785-3323; Idaho Power's Recreation Information Line, 800/422-3143; Rapid River Outfitters, 208/628-3862; Brownlee Reservoir Charters, 208/257-3703; Joseph Fly Shoppe, 541/432-4343, www.josephflyshoppe.com; Oxbow Boat Dock, 541/785-3323; Scotty's Hells Canyon Outdoor Supply, 800/785-3358; Hells Canyon Shuttle Service, 800/785-3358, float@hellscanyonshuttle.com.

55 BROWNLEE RESERVOIR

east of Richland

Map 4.10, page 250 **BEST (**

Brownlee Reservoir is nationally recognized for its smallmouth bass and channel catfish populations and is the largest reservoir on the Snake River. Brownlee Reservoir backs up 57 miles of the Snake River from Brownlee Dam, south, to Farewell Bend Recreation Area. The lower section of the reservoir is accessible from roads that follow the river from Brownlee Dam to Woodhead Park, Idaho. The middle and upper sections of the reservoir, 27 miles of river, are accessible from Richland, Oregon, to the south end of the reservoir at Farewell Bend Recreation Area. The reservoir also backs up two major tributaries in Oregon, creating the Powder River Arm and Burnt River Arm of Brownlee Reservoir.

Brownlee Reservoir is open year-round for all species of fish. Bag limits exist only for bass, which can be kept at five per day, none under 12 inches. A word of caution to anglers who keep fish: Both Oregon and Washington have issued fish-consumption advisories for Brownlee Reservoir because of high levels of mercury. Species identified as being affected by mercury in the water are perch, crappie, bass, and catfish. Do not keep and eat larger fish, as they have a greater chance of accumulating high levels of toxins.

Though this is a wonderful fishery, there are precious few boat-launching facilities and excessive drops in water levels can render all existing ramps useless. When water levels do drop, stay in the main channels to avoid shallow rocky shorelines. During high water, the main channels can get rough, especially if the wind picks up. In these instances most anglers fish the shallower shorelines and around islands for protection. The most developed boat ramps are at Woodhead Park in Idaho (the only boat launch on the lower river), and Spring Recreation Site near Huntington. You can find other ramps at Hewitt Park Campground, Hewitt Day Use Area, and Noble Holcomb in Richland on the Powder River Arm of Brownlee Reservoir; south of Richland along Snake River Road at Swede's Landing; and at Farewell Bend Recreation Area south of Huntington. Be sure to scout all boat ramps before launch and call the Idaho Power Information Line to get the latest on reservoir water levels.

Bank access on the reservoir is good, but it is limited to parks, day-use areas, and roadside pullouts on the Oregon side. The only bank access on the lower reservoir is upstream from the Highway 71 crossing at Brownlee Dam. Bank anglers can fish either from Brownlee Dam on the Idaho side or along Highway 71 headed south to Woodhead Park (both sites require a Idaho state fishing license). The other area with good bank access is on the Oregon side, 16 miles south of Brownlee Dam outside Richland. From Richland, anglers can drive 24 miles along the river headed south on Snake River Road, which dead-ends at the Burnt River Arm of Brownlee Reservoir near Huntington. Bank access can be had along Snake River Road wherever a car can be parked along the roadside and anglers can walk down to the river, or from two boat ramps. The two boat ramps are at Swede's Landing, eight miles south of Richland, and Spring Recreation Site, 14 miles south of Richland.

Smallmouth Bass: Smallmouth bass are abundant in the reservoir, as evidenced by the hosting of major bass-fishing tournaments throughout the year. Unlike largemouth bass, smallmouth bass seek out cooler water wherever it can be found. Spring is the best time of year to catch keeper-size bass of 12 inches or more without a lot of trolling. Bass spawn in the spring, and you can find good populations of larger bass in the shallows when the water is cooler. In summer, when the water temperatures begin to warm, larger bass move into water 30–75 feet deep. To find these larger bass in the summer you can troll bait or plugs in the deeper channels. Smaller bass are available all year around rocky outcroppings and shorelines, and they can generally be taken on surface baits such as poppers and crankbaits. During the summer, anglers should look for shaded areas and fish mostly during the morning and late evening. Other favorite smallmouth lures and bait include crawfish imitations, jigs, pork rinds, spinners, minnows, surface plugs, and worms.

Crappie: Crappie are plentiful here. Good places to look are around steep banks, brush, rocks, and submerged structures. Sometimes you'll find a school out in the middle of the lake, or some large singles while trolling. A good rule of thumb is to fish wherever the water is least disturbed. During inclement weather or windy days anglers should focus on protected areas such as deeper water or around structures such as docks. Crappie hit with very light taps that require ultralight tackle to detect strikes. Small lures baited with pieces of worm, shrimp, or minnows are productive. The most popular methods include fishing jigs straight under the angler, moving the tip of the rod in a slow up-and-down motion. There's good crappie bank fishing near Brownlee Dam and Hewitt Park.

Catfish: Brownlee Reservoir is home to the current state record-breaking flathead catfish, a 45-pounder caught in 1994. Catfish aficionados tend to congregate around the Powder River Arm and the area between Burnt River Arm and Farewell Bend. Bank anglers can find good catfish areas around the campground at Spring

Recreation Site. Anglers use all sorts of bait to catch catfish, some of the most popular being bloody baits, cut baits, worms, spoiled shrimp, cheese, grasshoppers, liver, crawfish, and shrimp. Night fishing is very popular, as it capitalizes on catfish instincts to feed in the dark. While catfish are commonly caught in deeper water during the summer, change tactics to surface methods in the spring when the fish feed on carp fry. It is often unnecessary to go more than three feet deep during these times. The only trick is finding schools of small carp fry, which can be accomplished with a depth finder.

Trout: Trout are stocked in the reservoir in spring and average 10–14 inches, though trout up to three pounds are also available. Spring is the best time to fish for trout. Focus on the shallow areas around shorelines, islands, and shallow rocky areas and around stream inlets where moving water keeps the waters cool. Swede's Landing is a good place to find a lot of these small-stream inlets. During summer larger trout can be taken by trolling the deeper water in the main channels.

Sturgeon: Sturgeon are present, but in dwindling numbers and don't provide much sport here. Sturgeon do not spawn in the Snake River reservoirs and will continue to decline.

Species: Trout, smallmouth bass, perch, bluegill, crappie, channel catfish, sturgeon.

Facilities: Fishing licenses from either state are valid on the Snake River when angling from a floating device or launching watercraft. You must buy the required state license when fishing tributaries or landforms within either state. Fee camping is available at Woodhead Park in Idaho and at Hewitt Park Campground and Farewell Bend State Recreation Area in Oregon. Free boat ramps are available at Woodhead Park in Idaho; Hewitt Park Campground, Hewitt Day Use Area, and Noble Holcomb in Richland on the Powder River Arm of Brownlee Reservoir; Swede's Landing and Spring Recreation Site south of Richland along Snake River Rd.; and near Huntington at Farewell Bend. Supplies and accommodations can be had in the nearby towns of Richland and Huntington.

Directions: To reach the middle and upper reservoir from Richland, turn south on 2nd St. from downtown Richland and drive 1.5 miles to the intersection with Snake River Rd. You are now heading west on 2nd St. Turn south on Snake River Rd. You will reach the river and the first boat ramp at Swede's Landing in approximately 10 miles. Snake River Rd. follows the river for another 21 miles, crossing the Burnt River, and dead-ending at the Huntington Hwy. (Business Rte. 30) in Huntington. Turn south on Huntington Hwy. and drive another four miles to Farewell Bend State Recreation Area. The entrance to Farewell Bend State Recreation Area will appear on the east side of the road. Free parking is available in the park.

To get to lower Brownlee, from Baker City drive east on Hwy. 86 for 75 miles to Copperfield. From Copperfield, stay on Hwy. 86, which turns south and follows the river for another 11 miles before crossing the river just below Brownlee Dam. Crossing the river puts you into Idaho and Hwy. 86 turns into Hwy. 71. Drive south on Hwy. 71 four miles to reach Woodhead Park Campground.

Contact: Wallowa County Chamber of Commerce (Troy, Joseph, Enterprise), 800/585-4121; Hells Canyon National Recreation Area managed by the Wallowa–Whitman National Forest, 541/523-6391; BLM, Vale District, 541/473-3144; ODFW, La Grande, 541/963-2138; Wallowa Mountains Visitors Center, 541/426-5546; Hells Canyon Chamber of Commerce, 541/742-4222, www.hellscanyonchamber.com; McCormick Park and Woodhead Park Information, 541/785-3323; Farewell Bend State Recreation Area, 800/452-5687; Idaho Power's Recreation Information Line, 800/422-3143; Rapid River Outfitters, 208/628-3862; Joseph Fly Shoppe, 541/432-4343, www.josephflyshoppe.com; Brownlee Reservoir Charters, 208/257-3703; Scotty's Hells Canyon Outdoor Supply, 800/785-3358.

SOUTHERN CASCADES

© CRAIG SCHUHMANN

BEST FISHING SPOTS

❰ Brown Trout
Middle Deschutes River, **page 332**
Wickiup Reservoir, **page 359**
Paulina Lake, **page 363**
Wood River, **page 388**

❰ Rainbow Trout
Upper Metolius River, **page 330**
Upper Rogue River, **page 379**
Lower Williamson River, **page 389**
Klamath River: Keno Dam to Topsy Reservoir,
    page 392

❰ Steelhead
Middle North Umpqua River, **page 346**
Upper Rogue River, **page 379**

❰ Family Fishing
Upper Metolius River, **page 330**
Wickiup Reservoir, **page 359**
Upper Klamath Lake, **page 381**

❰ Places to Teach Kids to Fish
Upper Rogue River, **page 379**

❰ Most Accessible for Disabled Anglers
Upper Rogue River, **page 379**
Wood River, **page 388**

The Southern Cascades is rich in lakes and rivers

for rainbow trout, steelhead, and several unique species such as Atlantic salmon, mackinaw, Upper Klamath Lake rainbows, and steelhead half-pounders. Many of this region's best spots feature either trophy rainbow or brown trout, but they also include family areas, access for those with disabilities, one world-class smallmouth bass fishery, and two world-class steelhead rivers. Most of these destination fisheries lie within a few hours' drive of each other. Along the way are great opportunities to visit quaint towns, natural wonders, and Crater Lake, Oregon's only national park.

The Deschutes forms the major drainage on the east side of the Cascades. The Middle Deschutes, famous for its early-season and winter brown trout fishing, is just 25 miles from another great winter fishery, the Metolius, a spring-fed river running through ponderosa pine forests, where anglers can chase lunker rainbows and bull trout. Worth a stop between them is the town of Sisters, famous for rodeos, spectacular views of the Three Sisters, and big milkshakes at the town's drive-in. Slip over the Cascades on Highway 20 to fish the upper Santiam or McKenzie Rivers and other area tributaries for seasonal trout. Still-water anglers can stop off at Suttle Lake, Clear Lake, Smith River Reservoir, and Blue River Reservoir to catch both brook and rainbow trout.

No still-water angler in Oregon should miss an opportunity to fish the area around La Pine, Bend, and the Cascade Lakes Basin. This is a mecca for big-trout anglers who desire something more than stocked trout. East and Paulina Lakes both are top producers for state record brown and rainbow trout, plus large numbers of kokanee and landlocked Atlantic salmon. Three of the best mackinaw fisheries are here at Cultus, Crescent, and Odell lakes. Crane Prairie Reservoir, a fine fishery for big rainbows, may be the best spot for families and anglers to enjoy a plethora of opportunities. Fish blue-ribbon lakes such as Davis for more Klamath redbands; Wickiup for rainbows, bass, and kokanee; Hosmer for landlocked Atlantic salmon; and Lava, Twin Lakes, Little Cultus, and Elk for bigger trout and more kokanee. All these lakes are within minutes of each other in a scenic basin surrounded by the southern Cascades peaks. Enjoy an all-day excursion to Newberry National Volcanic Monument to view geological wonders such as obsidian flows, lava caves, and the crater lakes of Paulina and East Lakes.

The three upper forks of the Willamette River – the Middle Fork and North Fork of the Middle Fork of the Willamette and the Coast Fork–are superb trout streams and appear nothing like the much slower Willamette that runs into Portland. These forks rival some of the best fisheries in the state and are beautiful to boot. Some of the best steelhead fishing in Oregon can be found on the nearby North Umpqua, a river that remains a frontier for many steelhead anglers to this day. People have been known to quit their jobs, sell their possessions, and leave their families just to live and fish this river; I know, I've met a few. Both the North and South Umpqua produce fantastic runs of steelhead that challenge the best anglers in Oregon. The smallmouth bass fishing at the confluence of the two forks is fast becoming a world-class fishery of its own.

A stone's throw from the Umpqua lie the Middle and Upper Rogue, year-round rivers that always have something going on: summer and winter steelhead, spring and fall chinook, coho, trout, sea-run cutthroat, and half-pounders. While not for everyone, the Rogue is a giant when it comes to destination fisheries and is very challenging for newcomers. The Applegate River, a tributary of the Rogue, is no slouch either when it comes to winter steelhead and catch-and-release fishing for wild rainbows.

Those who are culturally inclined, need a bed-and-breakfast, or have the sudden urge to see a play should head over to Ashland. From Ashland, drive over the hill on Highway 66 to the Klamath Basin, stopping along the way to fish Howard Prairie and Hyatt Reservoirs, both well-known producers of big rainbows and largemouth bass. The Klamath Basin provides great water in a region with a lot of private property, but anglers can drive to more than a handful of waters famous for big Upper Klamath Lake redband trout. Nearby Crater Lake is a breathtaking place for nonfishing fun.

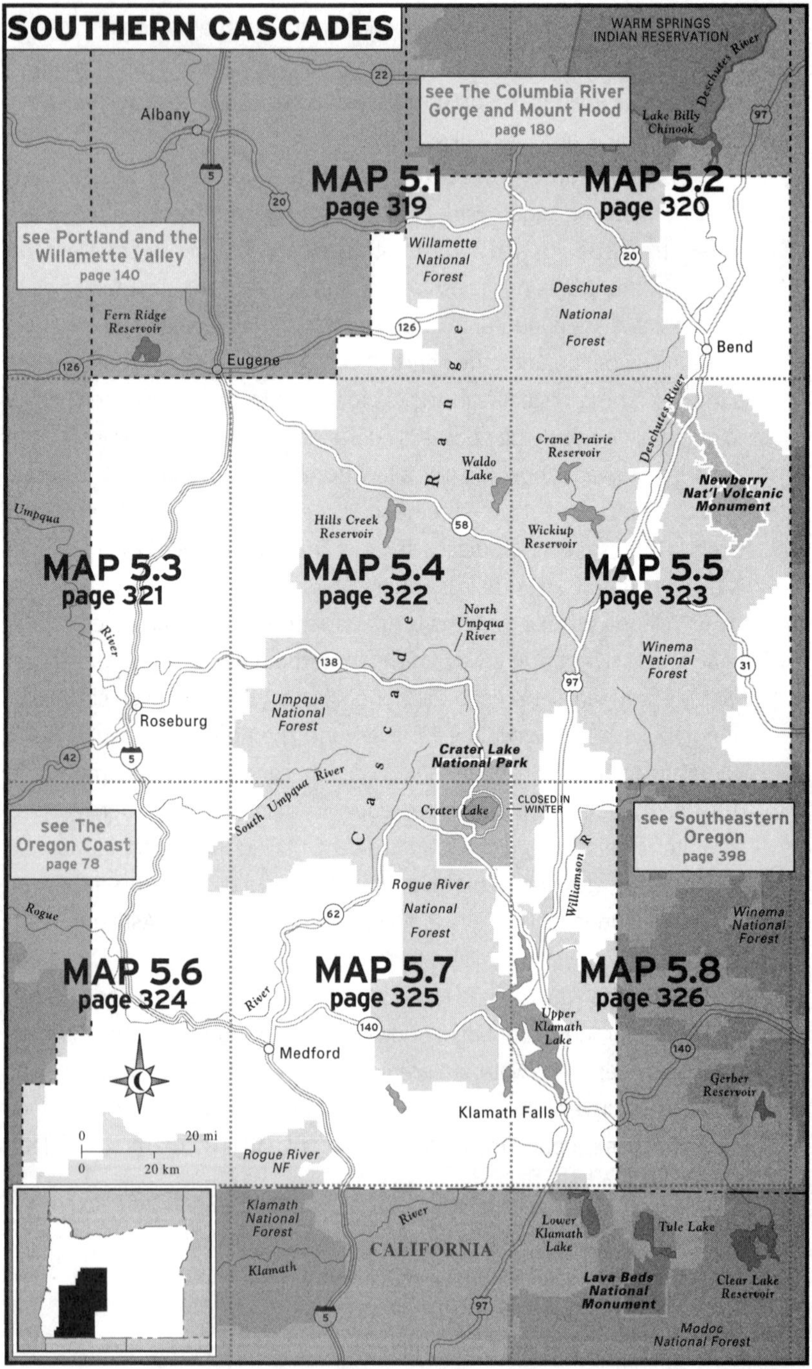

SOUTHERN CASCADES

WARM SPRINGS
INDIAN RESERVATION

Deschutes River

Albany

22

Lake Billy
Chinook

97

see The Columbia River
Gorge and Mount Hood
page 180

20

MAP 5.1
page 319

MAP 5.2
page 320

see Portland and the
Willamette Valley
page 140

*Willamette
National
Forest*

20

*Deschutes
National
Forest*

Bend

Fern Ridge
Reservoir

126

126

Eugene

R
a
n
g
e

Crane Prairie
Reservoir

Deschutes River

Umpqua

Waldo
Lake

*Newberry
Nat'l Volcanic
Monument*

Hills Creek
Reservoir

58

Wickiup
Reservoir

MAP 5.3
page 321

MAP 5.4
page 322

MAP 5.5
page 323

River

North
Umpqua
River

138

97

*Winema
National
Forest*

31

Roseburg

*Umpqua
National
Forest*

C
a
s
c
a
d
e

42

5

South Umpqua River

*Crater Lake
National Park*

Crater Lake

CLOSED IN
WINTER

see The
Oregon Coast
page 78

see Southeastern
Oregon
page 398

Rogue

*Rogue River
National
Forest*

Williamson R

*Winema
National
Forest*

62

MAP 5.6
page 324

MAP 5.7
page 325

MAP 5.8
page 326

River

140

0   20 mi
0   20 km

Medford

*Upper
Klamath
Lake*

140

Gerber
Reservoir

Klamath Falls

Rogue River
NF

*Klamath
National
Forest*

River

Lower
Klamath
Lake

Tule Lake

Clear Lake
Reservoir

CALIFORNIA

Klamath

*Lava Beds
National
Monument*

*Modoc
National Forest*

5

97

Map 5.1

Sites 1-3
Pages 327-328

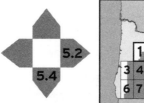

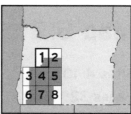

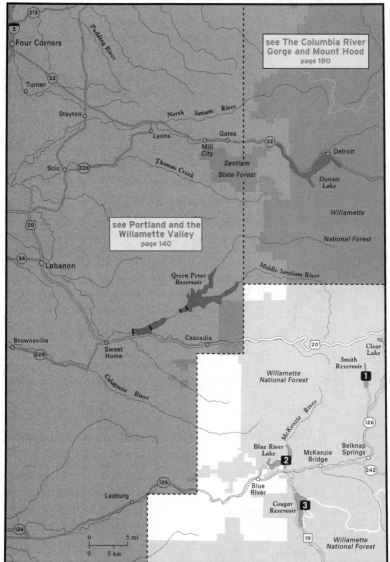

see The Columbia River Gorge and Mount Hood
page 180

see Portland and the Willamette Valley
page 140

© AVALON TRAVEL PUBLISHING, INC.

Map 5.2

Sites 4-10
Pages 329-335

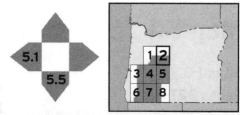

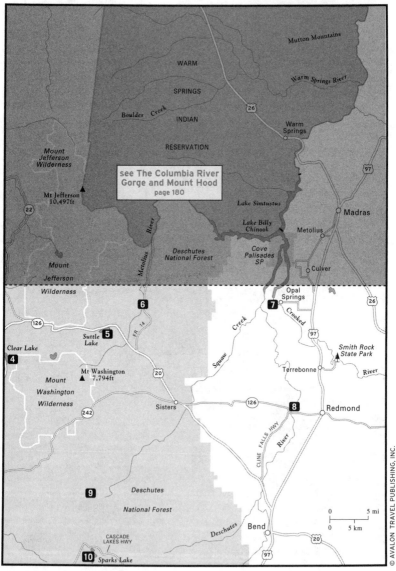

see The Columbia River Gorge and Mount Hood page 180

© AVALON TRAVEL PUBLISHING, INC.

Map 5.3

Sites 11-14
Pages 336-338

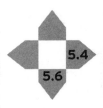

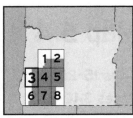

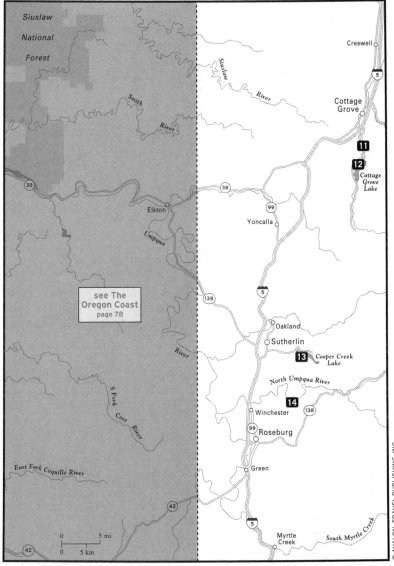

Map 5.4

Sites 15-25
Pages 340-350

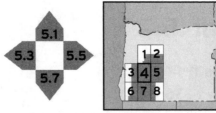

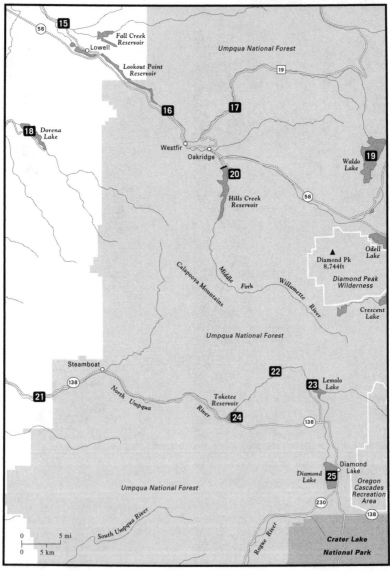

© AVALON TRAVEL PUBLISHING, INC.

Map 5.5

Sites 26-45
Pages 350-369

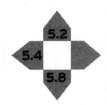

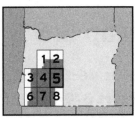

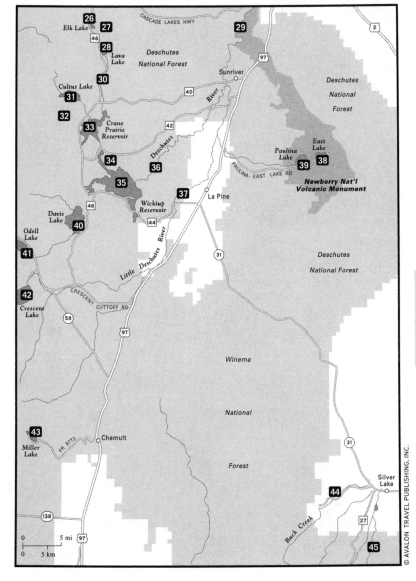

Map 5.6

Sites 46-51
Pages 370-376

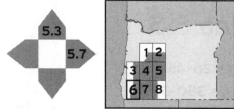

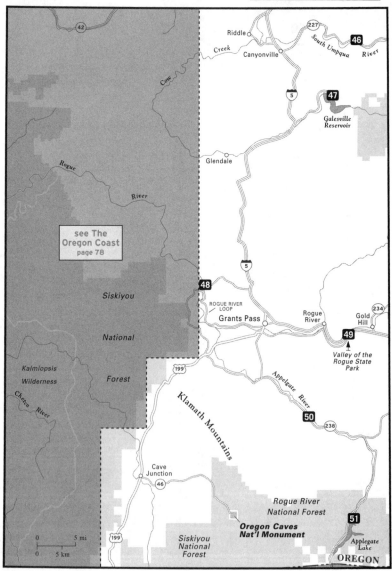

Map 5.7

Sites 52-61
Pages 378-386

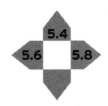

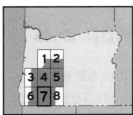

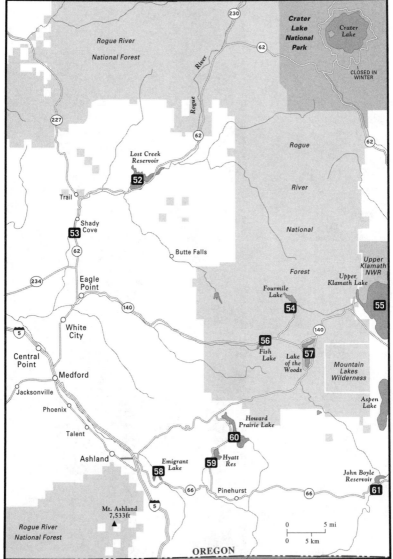

Map 5.8

Sites 62-65
Pages 388-392

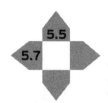

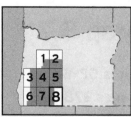

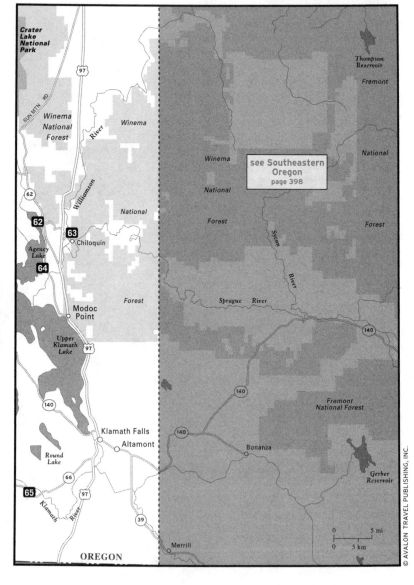

◱ SMITH RIVER RESERVOIR

east of McKenzie Bridge in the
McKenzie watershed

Map 5.1, page 319

Smith is a cigar-shaped reservoir with four miles of shoreline on 175 acres. The maximum depth is 200 feet, and the average is 90 feet. The shallowest areas are at the north end near the Lakes End Campground, which has a ramp. Smith offers good fishing for average-size stocked trout in a richly forested setting of Douglas fir. Most anglers troll Rooster Tails, Mepps Spinners, or gold and silver spoons. Still, fishing with bait is popular with night crawlers and PowerBait. Flies, nymphs, streamers, and dries are effective in the shallower northern end. Trollers will do best if they stay close to shore where there is more food and cover. Steep banks limit bank angling to campgrounds. Boats are allowed, but there is a 10 mph speed limit. The lake is open year-round.

Species: Brook and rainbow trout.

Facilities: There is a free, unimproved ramp at the dam, on the lake's southern end; it has parking and restrooms. Lakes End Campground, at the northern end of the lake, is accessible by boat only. It has 17 tent-only sites and no drinking water. The campground at Trail Bridge Reservoir has 46 sites, 19 for RVs, with drinking water, flush toilets, and fire rings. Supplies can be had in Springfield.

Directions: From McKenzie Bridge, travel 13 miles east on Hwy. 126 to Forest Rd. 732. Follow Rd. 732 west one mile to Rd. 730, passing Trail Bridge Reservoir in the meantime. Smith Reservoir is two miles ahead, at the end of Forest Rd. 730.

Contact: McKenzie Chamber of Commerce, 800/318-8819; McKenzie River Ranger District, 541/822-3381; ODFW, Salem, 503/378-6295.

◲ BLUE LAKE RESERVOIR

east of Blue River in the McKenzie watershed

Map 5.1, page 319

Blue Lake Reservoir could be a good fishery if it were managed for fishing, but it's really used as a holding tank for flood control, and it suffers from extreme summer drawdowns. Because of these water fluctuations, the lake offers only fair to good springtime fishing for stocked rainbow trout 8–14 inches. The lake is narrow and scenic, with thick stands of fir, rolling hills, and steep banks. Five river tributaries come into the lake on its west and east ends. Blue River Reservoir is 6.4 miles long and covers 1,420 acres. The reservoir is open year-round, and there are no special restrictions. Bait, flies, and lures all work. Bank angling is limited to campgrounds because of the steep shorelines. Most fish are caught from a boat or float tube. Boaters should be aware of lots of shallow obstructions such as submerged stumps, logs, and rocks near the shore. The wind blows regularly, generating good-size whitecaps. It is a good idea to call ahead to the Blue River information line to check water levels for safe boating.

Good starting places are at Mona and Lookout campgrounds at the east end of the lake. Here you will find several tributaries that attract good populations of trout in the spring and fall. Trolling is good with spinners and spoons. Also, fish with bait such as PowerBait and night crawlers. Fly anglers can fish along the banks and may run into the occasional caddis hatch for good dry–fly-fishing.

Species: Stocked rainbow trout.

Facilities: Saddle Dam boat launch (Apr.–Sept., $3 per vehicle) offers a vault toilet and unimproved boat ramp, although the water sometimes isn't high enough to launch boats here. It also honors the Northwest Forest Pass ($5 per day; $30 annually), which is available from most sporting goods or outdoors shops or from Nature of the Northwest in Portland. Lookout Campground also has a floating dock and boat ramp ($5 per vehicle or Northwest Forest Pass); the campground has 20 sites, restrooms, and drinking water. Mona Campground has 23 sites, along with restrooms and drinking water. Buy supplies in Springfield.

Directions: From Blue River, travel three miles east on Hwy. 126 to Forest Rd. 15. Turn left (north) on Rd. 15, which goes to Saddle Dam boat launch in 0.8 mile and then wraps around the eastern shore of the lake, leading to Lookout Campground in three miles and Mona Campground in 3.8 miles.

Contact: McKenzie Chamber of Commerce, 541/822-3381 or 800/318-8819; ODFW, Salem, 503/378-6295; McKenzie River Ranger District, 541/822-3381; Blue River Reservoir Information, 541/822-3317; Nature of the Northwest, 503/872-2750, www.naturenw.org.

❸ SOUTH FORK McKENZIE RIVER

east of Springfield

Map 5.1, page 319

The South Fork of the McKenzie offers fair to good catch-and-release fishing for wild redside, cutthroat, and bull trout. Its final three miles starts at the Cougar Reservoir outlet and enters the main-stem McKenzie a few miles east of Blue River. Cougar Reservoir breaks up the river for five miles, and above it are 12 more miles of river. The headwaters are formed by a series of smaller tributaries flowing from the flanks of Roaring River Ridge (Roaring River) and the Mink Lakes Basin in the Three Sisters Wilderness. Good roads follow this scenic little river both below and above the reservoir. The river is open for fishing April 22–October 31 and is restricted to artificial flies and lures only. Expect small-stream fishing for fish 10–14 inches. Basic light tackle is appropriate in the form of 3–4-weight rods. Attractor dry flies such as Elk Hair Caddis, Humpies, and Royal Wulffs will work all summer in the small plunge pools and riffles. Nymphs fished under an indicator will pick up even more fish than dry flies. Experiment with basic spinners such as Rooster Tails and Mepps in various colors.

Species: Redside, cutthroat, and bull trout.

Facilities: Six campgrounds are in the area, three of them at Cougar Reservoir. At Cougar, Slide Creek Campground has a boat ramp and 16 sites with fire rings, tables, restrooms, and a bathhouse. It is an 800-foot walk to the drinking water. Cougar Crossing has seasonal portable toilets, no drinking water, and 12 sites—as well as a free boat ramp. Sunnyside has vault toilets, no water, and 13 sites. The three campgrounds along the South Fork above Cougar are French Pete with drinking water and 17 sites; Homestead seven sites, no water; and Frissell Crossing 12 sites, restrooms, and water. Buy supplies in Springfield.

Directions: From Springfield follow Hwy. 126 east for 33 miles to Aufderheide Dr. (Forest Rd. 19), four miles past Blue River. Continue on Aufderheide Dr. for 9.5 miles to Cougar Crossing Campground. To reach the other two Cougar Reservoir campgrounds, turn left on Forest Rd. 1900–500; you'll reach Sunnyside in 0.2 mile and Slide Creek Campground in 1.5 miles. The three South Fork campgrounds are farther along Aufderheide Dr.: French Pete is 1.5 miles past Cougar, Homestead is 8 miles past it, and Frissell Crossing is in 12 miles.

The river below Cougar Reservoir is followed closely by Forest Rd. 410, which leads to the base of the dam on the east bank, and Hwy. 19, leading to Cougar Reservoir, on the west bank. Highway 19 will take you into the upper river above Cougar Reservoir, to the confluence with the Roaring River. From here, Forest Rd. 1964 will take you upriver a few more miles, at which point you will need to get on hiking trails to reach the headwaters in the wilderness.

Contact: Convention and Visitors Association of Lane County, 541/484-5307; Oregon Parks and Recreation Department, 800/551-6949; Willamette National Forest McKenzie River Ranger District, 541/822-3381; ODFW, Salem, 503/378-6295; BLM Salem, 503/375-5646; The Caddis Fly Angling Shop, 541/342-7005, www.thecaddisfly.com.

4 CLEAR LAKE

east of Eugene in the McKenzie watershed

Map 5.2, page 320

Clear Lake, the source of the McKenzie River, is high in the beautiful Willamette National Forest, southwest of Santiam Junction. The lake holds fair numbers of stocked brook and rainbow trout and is popular for its particular geological and lake-bottom features. Clear Lake was formed when a lava flow blocked the McKenzie, filling a valley and burying a still visible forest 100 feet deep. This 148-acre lake is deep, 175 feet near the southern end, and maintains an annual temperature of 34–38°F. The extremely cold water means all species of fish remain small, only 9–14 inches. Fishing is primarily done by trolling streamers such as Rooster Tails, small spoons, or bait such as night crawlers, PowerBait, and eggs. Fly-fishing can be good along the shorelines, where some hatches may occur and bring fish to the surface. Otherwise, fly anglers can use streamers or small nymphs. The north shore near Clear Lake Resort has some of the shallowest water and is a good place to start. Boats are allowed, but not motors. The lake is open year-round, when weather permits, and there are no bait restrictions. Bank fishing is excellent from most points around the lake on good hiking trails.

Species: Stocked brook and rainbow trout.

Facilities: Clear Lake Resort offers cabins, RV sites without hookups, along with a café, groceries, fishing supplies, and rowboat rentals. The public can also launch their own boats ($5). The Forest Service's Cold Water Cove Campground has 35 sites for tents and RVs, as well as a boat ramp, drinking water, vault toilets, and fire rings.

Directions: From Eugene, drive east on Hwy. 126, the McKenzie River Hwy., for 44 miles to McKenzie Bridge, and then another 17 miles to Clear Lake.

Contact: McKenzie Chamber of Commerce, 800/318-8819; McKenzie River Ranger District, 541/822-3381; ODFW, Salem, 503/378-6295; Clear Lake Resort, 541/258-3729, www.clearlakeresort-oregon.org; Santiam Fish and Game Association, 541/967-5030.

5 SUTTLE LAKE

west of Sisters

Map 5.2, page 320

Scenic Suttle Lake is set in a deeply wooded area of ponderosa pine and Douglas fir just off Highway 20. This popular multiuse lake is notable for good catches of kokanee and big brown trout. Suttle, a popular winter fishery, has five boat ramps, is open year-round, and fishing is good all year. The lake's average depth is 45 feet, and the deepest point is 75 feet. There are 3.5 miles of shoreline, all accessible by good hiking trails. Brown trout average 14–18 inches but can run as big as 10 pounds; 3–4-pound browns are common. Five trout per day may be retained, with only one longer than 20 inches. Kokanee average 9–10 inches and fight with every bit of their strength. Twenty-five kokanee may be kept per day in addition to the trout limit. All methods of fishing are permitted, including bait. Boats are the most convenient way to fish, but equal opportunities exist for float tubers and bank anglers.

The most popular way to fish Suttle for brown trout is by trolling small baitfish patterns such as Rainbow Spinners, Rapalas, and streamer flies. Brown trout are predators and feed voraciously on small kokanee smolts. Kokanee are taken most often on jigs and bait such as eggs and night crawlers fished under the boat. Early in the season (May and June) anglers stick close to the shore for both species. Later in the season the fish move to deeper areas of the lake in search of cooler water. Anglers need to go quite a bit deeper with spinners, flashers, and bait in the summer. The most productive areas are around the resort at the east end of the lake, where the water averages 70 feet deep. Bank anglers can fish for kokanee from the shore around the resort. Fly anglers should be on the lookout for insect hatches, which will draw the fish back to the shore in the evenings and early mornings. Dry flies such as a Griffith Gnat or small Adams will work a majority of the time. Nymphs and streamers are useful when stripped in slowly.

Species: Brown trout, kokanee.

Facilities: Five boat ramps, three Forest Service campgrounds, and a resort with cabins provide good accommodations for anglers and their families; hiking, waterskiing, boat rentals, and sailing are just a few of the amenities available. Campsites at South Shore, Link Creek, and Blue Bay campgrounds are available for tents and RVs up to 50 feet. All three also have day-use areas with boat ramps; parking at these areas requires a Northwest Forest Pass ($5 per day; $30 annually), which is available from most sporting goods or outdoors shops or from Nature of the Northwest in Portland. The Camp Sherman Store is open year-round and offers fishing tackle, deli, general store, gas station, trailer storage, and post office.

Directions: From Sisters, drive northwest on Hwy. 20 for 14 miles, and then turn left (south) into the lake area on Forest Rd. 2070. The Forest Service campgrounds are all along this road: Blue Bay in one mile, South Shore in 1.5 miles, Link Creek in 2.3 miles.

Contact: Sisters Area Chamber of Commerce, 541/549-0251; ODFW, Bend, 541/388-6363; Sisters Ranger District, 541/549-7700; The Lodge at Suttle Lake, 541/595-2628; Nature of the Northwest, 503/872-2750, www.naturenw.org; The Fisher's Place in Sisters, 541/549-3474.

6 UPPER METOLIUS RIVER
near Sisters in Deschutes National Forest

Map 5.2, page 320　　　　**BEST (**

Anglers either love the Metolius and quickly adopt it as their home water, or they reject it altogether as impossible and a waste of effort. The former—many of whom drive all the way from Portland—have to display a manic degree of patience, persistence, and stubborn determination; the latter, common sense. But I have never met an angler who would disagree that this is one of the most beautiful and alluring rivers in all of Oregon.

The upper 10 miles of river between the headwaters and Lower Bridge (also known as Bridge 99) near the Warm Springs Reservation Boundary is housed in a diverse setting of ponderosa pine forests, deep basalt canyons, and meadows. The river forms as a gentle, unpretentious spring bubbling out from under Black Butte and runs for its first two miles through open meadows. Then, as the river picks up numerous tributaries and is channeled near Camp Sherman, it loses its spring creek character and becomes more like a large freestone river, complete with Class IV and V rapids, deep pools, exceedingly fast runs, and surprisingly little pocket water. In fact, this may be one of the most difficult rivers to find fish on, simply because its water is so hard to read. Bank vegetation is often dense, with high willows making river access difficult and casting frustrating. Wading in the wrong spots can be treacherous, perhaps fatal, and cold spring waters make wet wading virtually impossible. Anglers should know that the Metolius offers challenges that go beyond catching fish.

This stretch of the Metolius is for fly-fishing only, and all fish must be released unharmed; however, artificial lures may be used below Bridge 99. The river is open year-round, except above Allingham Bridge (one mile north of Camp Sherman), which is closed January 1–May 26 and November 1–December 31. Barbless hooks are required, and no external weight such as split shot may be used. Barring serious winter weather, the Metolius is an excellent winter trout stream, but it fishes well all year because of the water's constant temperature of 46°F.

The Metolius is noted for producing large wild rainbows, bull trout, and, to a lesser degree, brown trout. A run of kokanee arrives from Lake Billy Chinook in September. Though trout-stocking programs were discontinued in 1996, the river is once again producing good numbers of rainbow trout. Average catches range 10–14 inches, but 16–20-inch fish are common. (Trout can get as big as seven or eight pounds, but fish that size are rare and extremely difficult to catch.) Bull trout are a huge attraction, often overshadowing rainbows because of their size and numbers. Bull trout average 5–6 pounds, and 15-pounders are common. Brown trout are rare, but a weekend of fishing usually produces one or two.

Bank angling is excellent in the most important water and easily accessible from roads that follow the river, as well as from hiking trails and campgrounds. Below Lower Bridge, the river's west bank is entirely within the Warms Springs Reservation, and angling is prohibited from this side. Boating is suitable only for white-water rafts and kayakers. Begin fishing from the campgrounds north of Camp Sherman to Allingham Bridge. Here, streamside vegetation is limited, and the river maintains some of its gentler character with shallow water and slower flows. This is also the place where beginners and young children have the best opportunities to catch fish. Below Allingham Bridge to Wizard Falls Fish Hatchery, the river becomes more difficult to reach and is recommended for intermediate and advanced anglers only. Some easier access can be had at campgrounds (Smiling River and Pine Rest), but for the most part the river is swift and deep, and its banks are lined with brush, meaning you'll have to wade. An exceedingly difficult gorge section extends from the Gorge Campground to the hatchery. The area between Wizard Falls Fish Hatchery and Lower Bridge is accessible by two campgrounds (Allen Springs and Pioneer Ford) or on good hiking trails on both sides of the river, but again this section should be fished by advanced anglers only.

The Metolius offers good opportunities to catch large fish on nymphs, dry flies, and streamers. Dry-fly anglers can either choose to "match the hatch" or use attractor patterns such as Royal Wulffs or Humpies. Mayfly hatches include blue-wing olives, pale morning/evening duns, and an odd assortment of other less-typical insects throughout the summer. Green drakes are a highlight in May and June, followed by golden stone flies and caddis. Green drakes are an elusive and sparse

hatch, but when they are present they never fail to draw bigger fish to the surface. Search for green drake hatches below Wizard Falls and Lower Bridge, wherever large boulders and fast flows dominate. Nymphs are often fished under a strike indicator, two at a time, weighted and on the bottom. It's important to keep flies on the bottom of the river in a dead-drift presentation; this can be difficult to achieve with fast swirling currents, and it requires quite a bit of mending to keep flies in the zone. Try patterns such as Golden Stone Flies, Hare's Ears, Pheasant Tails, and the ever-popular Prince Nymph and Copper Johns.

Streamer fishing on the Metolius is an art form, and its practitioners catch a lot of fish when nymph and dry-fly anglers go fishless. Perhaps the most productive pattern is a weighted Egg Sucking Leech in sizes 4 to 6. Most anglers use an upstream presentation, mending furiously through the drift to get the streamer on the bottom, and wait for the strike at the end of the drift or through the swing. Dropping a small nymph or egg pattern off the bend of the streamer can prove especially productive in fall when the kokanee are spawning.

Guiding is restricted on the river at House on the Metolius above Canyon Creek Campground, and only one guide (John Judy) has permission to fish it. If you really want to learn about the Metolius, this is the place to go and the man to go with. (Read his books before the trip, and ask that the trip be structured as a technical fishing lesson.)

Species: Wild rainbow, brown, and bull trout, kokanee.

Facilities: Eight campgrounds operated by the Sisters Ranger District of Deschutes National Forest lie along the river above Bridge 99. The following are above the bridge (in order along the road): Camp Sherman, tent-only Riverside, Allingham, Smiling River, tent-only Pine Rest, Gorge, Canyon Creek (no drinking water), Allen Springs, Pioneer Ford, and Lower Bridge. Candle Creek (no drinking water) is below the bridge. The Camp Sherman Store is open year-round and offers fishing tackle, deli, general store, gas station, trailer storage, and post office.

Directions: From Sisters, drive west on Hwy. 20 for 9.7 miles, and then turn right (north) on Forest Rd. 14 (Camp Sherman Rd.), which leads five miles to Camp Sherman. In Camp Sherman, pick up Forest Rd. 900 to the campgrounds above the bridge: Camp Sherman in 0.5 mile, Allingham and Smiling River in one mile, Pine Rest in two miles, Gorge in 2.5 miles, Allen Springs in nine miles, Pioneer Ford in 11 miles, and Lower Bridge in 12 miles.

Contact: Sisters Area Chamber of Commerce, 541/549-0251; ODFW, Bend, 541/388-6363; Sisters Ranger District, 541/549-7700; Metolius Recreation Association, www.metoliusriver. com; House on the Metolius, 541/595-6620; Cold Springs Resort and RV Park, 541/595-6271; Lake Creek Lodge, 800/797-6331; Metolius River Lodges, 800/595-6290; Kokanee Café, 541/595-6420; Camp Sherman Store and Fly Shop, 541/595-6711, www.campshermanstore.com; The Fisher's Place in Sisters, 541/549-3474; John Judy Fly-Fishing, 541/595-2073, www.johnjudyflyfishing.com.

7 LOWER CROOKED RIVER
north of Redmond

Map 5.2, page 320

The lower section of the Crooked River flows approximately 30 miles from Prineville to Lake Billy Chinook, passing through the scenic Smith Rocks Recreation Area and the Crooked River Gorge. Both the gorge and Smith Rocks are spectacularly scenic and arid. Smith Rocks is a popular rock-climbing area with large cliffs; the gorge is a deep canyon with vertical basalt rocks, sagebrush, knarled junipers, and scree hillsides.

All of the river between Prineville and Smith Rocks is private property and inaccessible. Between Smith Rocks and Lake Billy Chinook Reservoir, the river opens again; this is below Highway 97, which crosses the

river north of Terrebonne. Access into Smith Rocks is easy; several miles of river are accessible, and fishing is fair for average trout 8–12 inches. Below Highway 97, the best access is at Opal Springs hydroelectric facility southwest of Culver. Here you have to park at a gated road and walk two miles down a steep grade. Fishing at Opal Springs can be as good as that below the dam near Prineville but anglers have to leave the premises by 4:30 P.M. A kiosk at the bottom of the hill explains where fishing is allowed and not, and also about the timing issues. Fish average 10–14 inches, with some bigger fish present. Bull trout migrate up this part of the river to the Opal Springs Dam from Lake Billy Chinook.

Species: Rainbow trout, bull trout.

Facilities: There are primitive, walk-in campsites at Smith Rock State Park. The park ($3 per vehicle) also has restrooms, hiking trails, and a picnic area. Supplies are available in Redmond.

Directions: From Redmond drive north on Hwy. 97 for 5.5 miles. Turn right (east) on Smith Rock Way and follow it 2.6 miles to Smith Rock State Park. To reach Opal Springs from Redmond, go north on Hwy. 97 for about 10 miles and then turn left (west) onto Monroe Lane. Follow Monroe about three miles to LaSalle Ln., which leads two miles to the gate. From there, it's a two-mile walk down.

Contact: Central Oregon Visitors Association, 541/389-8799; Oregon Parks and Recreation Department, 800/551-6949; BLM, Prineville, 541/416-6700; Smith Rock State Park, 541/548-7501; ODFW, Bend, 541/388-6363; Cent-Wise Sporting Goods, 541/548-4422.

8 MIDDLE DESCHUTES RIVER
from Bend to Lake Billy Chinook

Map 5.2, page 320   **BEST (**

The Middle Deschutes is a good, but varied, trout stream flowing approximately 50 miles from bustling Bend to the remote Lake Billy Chinook. Several falls along this reach

(Steelhead, Big, Odin, and Awbrey) block any significant migration of fish from Lake Billy Chinook, confining most of the fish to their sections of the river. Wild rainbow, brown trout, and whitefish are found throughout the river, and bull trout are available below Steelhead Falls. The river flowing through Bend is placid, surrounded by manicured parks; otherwise, the areas above and below Bend are a mix of arid high-desert vegetation, gentle flows through marshlands, and raging rapids through jagged basalt canyons. All of this river is restricted to artificial lures and flies only, and fishing is not allowed from a floating device.

Except for the areas around Bend, above the North Canal Dam, this is primarily a winter fishery from Bend to Lake Billy Chinook. Significant summer irrigation drawdowns almost wipe out the river in some years. Fish this river in early spring, winter, and late fall when water is restored. Fishing above the North Canal Dam into downtown Bend is good—in some years, great. It's easily accessible from good hiking trails and parks, and it gets significant insect hatches. There are approximately 17 parks along the Deschutes River in the vicinity of Bend. The Deschutes River Trail runs adjacent to the river starting at River Rim Park to the south and Sawyer State Park to the north. Between these two points lies a lot of water, all accessible to the angler. Contact the Bend Metro Parks and Recreation District for a good river and trail map.

The river below Bend receives far more attention from anglers, perhaps because of its remoteness from the city, but also for its bigger fish. Areas around Tumalo State Park and Cline State Park provide good access for average-size rainbows (12–14 inches) and larger brown trout up to several pounds; however, the river gets much more desirable (and harder to reach) from the river crossing at Lower Bridge Road (Borden Beck Access) to Lake Billy Chinook. Here, anglers can fish winter stone-fly hatches in February and salmon flies in June. Several significant mayfly hatches (blue-wing olives and pale morning duns) can be found March–June, before the reduction of flows. Trout, both brown and rainbow, average 12–16 inches, with much bigger fish available.

Lower Bridge at Borden Beck Access offers good, easy bank access and several miles of river trails. The water here is placid and runs through marshlands, cattails, and channels. This is great dry-fly water when stone flies and mayflies are hatching in the winter and spring. Streamers such as Woolly Buggers and nymphs are also productive, as are wet flies. Below Lower Bridge there is great fishing to be had below Big Falls, Steelhead Falls, and near Whychus Creek (formerly Squaw Creek) above Lake Billy Chinook. All of these areas can be reached with a degree of patience, the motivation to hike a few miles, and a good map (they are remote and roads can be rough, tricky, and often unmarked). The reward for getting to these areas is often big fish, and plenty of them, as these areas don't see that many anglers.

Species: Rainbow and brown trout, bull trout, whitefish.

Facilities: All of Bend's parks along the river are free. Harmon Park (1100 N.W. Harmon Rd.) is developed with restrooms, picnic tables, a playground, and river access; 1st St. Rapids Park (N.W. 1st St.) is a primitive trailhead area with portable restrooms, picnic tables, and canoe/kayak launch. Farewell Bend Park (S.W. Reed Market Rd.) has a canoe launch and a hiking trail that connects it to several other river-access points. Sawyer Park (62999 O. B. Riley Rd.) is connected to the Deschutes River Trail by a footbridge and has picnic tables, drinking fountains, and portable restrooms. River Rim Park (River Rim Dr.) has no facilities. Among the state parks, Tumalo (year-round, day-use $3 per vehicle) offers campsites for hiker/bikers without a car, cars with tents, full hookups, and yurts. There are restrooms, picnic tables, and plenty of river access. Cline Falls State Scenic Viewpoint (no fee) is really just a rest area, with restrooms, picnic tables, and river access. Supplies are available in Bend.

Directions: From Bend, travel northwest on Hwy. 20 for 6.3 miles, and then turn right (north) onto Cline Falls Hwy. After 10 miles on this road, turn right (east) onto Hwy. 126. Follow this 0.3 mile and then follow the signs for the rest area, which will lead you north 0.3 mile on S.W. 74th St. to Cline Falls. To reach Tumalo State Park, travel northwest of Bend on Hwy. 20 for 4.3 miles, and then turn left (west) onto Old Bend–Redmond Hwy. After 0.2 mile on this road, turn right (north) on O. B. Riley Rd., which leads 1.2 miles into the park.

Lower Bridge and Borden Beck Park: Take Hwy. 97 north from Bend for 20 miles to the small town of Terrebonne. At the north end of Terrebonne, turn left (west) on Lower Bridge Rd.; a sign here says "Crooked River Ranch." Follow this road six miles to the bridge and park, which is managed by the Central Oregon Parks and Recreation District of Redmond.

Steelhead Falls and the Folley Water: From Hwy. 97, drive west on Lower Bridge Rd. After about 2.5 miles turn north (right) onto 43rd St., which is the main entrance to Crooked River Ranch. Continue for approximately two miles, and then turn west (left) on Chinook Drive. Continue on Chinook Dr. for two miles, then turn west (left) on Badger Rd., which turns into Blacktail Dr. at the bottom of the hill. Take a right at the T-intersection onto Quail Rd. After driving about one mile on Quail Rd., turn west (left) on River Rd. and follow it for a mile to the trailhead. It's a 0.5-mile hike down to Steelhead Falls.

Folley Waters: Follow the same directions as for Steelhead Falls, but after turning left off Quail Rd. onto River Rd., turn left on Folley Waters Dr. and continue for approximately 0.7 mile, past Lone Pine Court. The trailhead is on the left (west) side of the road. The trail is about 0.7 mile long. Construction and changing road names in the Crooked River Ranch development were creating potentially confusing circumstances for finding Folley Waters and Steelhead Falls. Call the development for an up-to-date map, or call the BLM for further access advice.

Contact: Central Oregon Visitors Association, 541/389-8799; Oregon Parks and Recreation Department, 800/551-6949; Bend Metro Parks and Recreation District, 541/389-7275, www.bendparksandrec.org; Central Oregon Park and Recreation District, 541/548-7275; ODFW, Bend, 541/388-6363; BLM, Prineville, 541/416-6700; Crooked River Ranch, 541/548-8939.

9 GREEN LAKES
west of Bend in Three Sisters Wilderness

Map 5.2, page 320

These three high alpine lakes are set on a mountain pass between the Cascade peaks of South Sister (10,358 feet elevation) and Broken Top (9,152 feet elevation). A five-mile hike will lead you into the spectacular Three Sisters Wilderness, complete with meadows, small streams, alpine marshes, and plenty of rock boulders and cliffs. Each of the lakes presents fair to good fishing for small rainbow and brook trout, and, if you're so inclined, the opportunity to climb one or both peaks from lake trailheads.

Though not strictly an angling destination, Green Lakes is a great place to visit if your agenda also includes hiking, backpacking, climbing, or the desire for an alpine experience—and you want to include fishing. Pack that combination spinning/fly rod you have stuffed in the basement, collect a small assortment of streamers, nymphs, dry flies, lures, and/or bait (which is allowed), make sure the trail is clear of snow (mid-July), and head out to this wonderful destination. Then again, if solitude is what you're after, bear in mind that this is perhaps the most-hiked trail in the Deschutes National Forest, so consider calling the Forest Service for suggestions on other places to try.

Of the three lakes, Middle Green is the best and the biggest at 85 acres and a maximum depth of 55 feet. Aside from the average catches of 10–12-inch fish, there is the possibility of hooking something bigger, up to 18 inches. South Green, the first lake you come to on the trail and the only one of the three that is stocked, is eight acres and 26 feet deep. Smaller legal-size rainbow and brook trout dominate. North Green is 10 acres and 20 feet deep and produces even smaller fish, but they are still fun.

Species: Stocked and wild rainbow and brook trout.

Facilities: There are hike-in backpacker campsites at each lake. Camping is limited to designated sites only, and no fires are permitted within a quarter mile of any of the lakes. The nearest place to spend a more civilized night is at Lava Camp Lake Campground, west of Sisters near McKenzie Pass. It has 10 sites and restrooms, but no drinking water. Supplies are available in Bend.

Directions: From Bend, head west 27 miles on Cascade Lakes Hwy., also called Forest Rd. 46, to the trailhead. To reach these lakes, you'll have to hike. Start at the Green Lakes Trailhead near Sparks Lake. Parking at the trailhead requires a Northwest Forest Pass ($5 per day; $30 annually), which is available from most sporting goods or outdoors shops or from Nature of the Northwest in Portland. You'll start out on Trail No. 17 in the Bend–Fort Rock Ranger District but, before reaching the lakes, you'll be on Trail No. 4070 of the Sisters Ranger District. Both are called the Green Lakes Trail. It's just over four miles to the first lake.

Contact: Sisters Area Chamber of Commerce, 541/549-0251; ODFW, Bend, 541/388-6363; Sisters Ranger District, 541/549-7700; Bend–Fort Rock Ranger District, 541/388-5664; Central Oregon Visitors Association, 541/389-8799.

🔟 SPARKS LAKE

west of Bend in Cascade Lakes Basin

Map 5.2, page 320

Sparks, a fly-fishing–only lake, is in a scenic valley behind Mount Bachelor, just three miles beyond the Mount Bachelor Ski Area on the Cascades Lakes Highway. It offers fair to good fishing in the spring for average to larger-size rainbow and brook trout. From the lakeshore one can see Mount Bachelor, the Three Sisters, and Broken Top in all their rugged glory. The lake itself is also beautiful, surrounded by ponderosa forests, meadows, and willows. While you're there, consider fishing some of the small creeks that flow into the lake from the meadow. There are upper and lower sections of the lake, connected by a half-mile channel, making a total of 400 acres. The deepest part of the lake is 10 feet, at the south end of the lower lake. This is where one can find the larger fish, especially as summer progresses. Smaller fish can be caught in the channel between the two halves of the lake. Sparks should be considered a spring fishery only. Summer water losses can make the lake go completely dry in some years because of a faulty natural dam and droughts. Some eager anglers resort to snowshoes and cross-country skis to get the first action of the season just after ice-out.

Sparks Lake can be a challenging place to fish. Shallow, clear water makes for spooky trout, and since this is a popular lake (not only with anglers but also campers and hikers), you can be certain these fish have seen a few people. Tackle restrictions limit anglers to flies and barbless hooks only; pinch your barbed hooks with a pair of forceps. Boating is permitted with motors, but there is a 10 mph speed limit, and motors must be shut off while fishing. Rowboats, canoes, pontoon boats, and float tubes are better options, if for no other reason than for trolling. Look for opportunities to fish dry flies such as an Adams or Griffith Gnat when hatches occur; otherwise, use basic nymphs such as Pheasant Tails and Hare's Ears. Try a leech pattern such as the Seal Bugger or Marabou Leech in olive, maroon, brown, and black mixed with purple or red.

Species: Rainbow and brook trout.

Facilities: Soda Creek Campground has 10

sites of 30 feet or less and no drinking water. The Ray Atkeson Trailhead and Day Use Area (June–Oct.) has parking, a concrete boat ramp, vault toilets, and a hiking trail that explores the southeast shore of the southern (larger) section of the lake. The boat ramp is not usable when the water level is low. Parking at the trailhead requires a Northwest Forest Pass ($5 per day; $30 annually), which is available from most sporting goods or outdoors shops or from Nature of the Northwest in Portland. Supplies are available in Bend.

Directions: From Bend, drive 26.2 miles west on Cascade Lakes Hwy. (Forest Rd. 46). The campground is on Rd. 46; to reach the day-use area, drive one mile south on Forest Rd. 4600–400.

Contact: Central Oregon Visitors Association, 541/389-8799; ODFW, Bend, 541/388-6363; Nature of the Northwest, 503/872-2750, www.naturenw.org; Bend–Fort Rock Ranger District, 541/388-5664.

11 COAST FORK WILLAMETTE
south of Eugene

Map 5.3, page 321

The Coast Fork of the Willamette River begins seven miles above Cottage Grove Reservoir in the Calapooya Mountains. The upper river is captured in Cottage Grove Reservoir and then parallels I-5 from Cottage Grove to its confluence with the Middle Fork and main-stem Willamette River near Springfield. The upper river near the lake is scenically forested in stands of Douglas fir. The lower river lacks visual appeal, since it's so close to I-5. A health advisory has been issued against eating all species of fish from the Coast Fork because of high levels of mercury, PCBs, dioxins, and pesticides. Contact the Oregon Department of Human Services for more information on contaminated waters.

Fishing above the reservoir is fair for wild cutthroat; this is also a popular destination for fly anglers. Catches in the lower river are limited to stocked trout, and fishing is marginal but easy for small fish. Fishing is catch-and-release January 1–April 23 and November 1–December 31; five trout of an eight-inch minimum length can be retained April 24–October 31. Use of bait is allowed April 23–October 31; otherwise the river is restricted to artificial flies and lures only.

River access is spotty from pullouts off London Road in the lower river and a few miles past the reservoir. The inlet arm on Cottage Grove Reservoir is productive and is accessible from a boat for quite a way. Avoid areas of the river where private-property signs are posted.

Species: Wild cutthroat and stocked rainbow trout.

Facilities: Pine Meadows Campground, on the east side of the lake and run by the Corps of Engineers, has restrooms, showers, drinking water, swimming area, campsites, and RV sites with no utilities. There's also a primitive campground one mile north of Pine Meadows on the east shore, with fire rings and drinking water and little else. Supplies are available in Eugene.

Directions: From Eugene, take I-5 south, which parallels the Coast Fork for 19 miles to Cottage Grove Reservoir. Beyond the lake, a total of 22 miles from Eugene, take Exit 172 (Cottage Grove Lake) and turn left onto 6th St. This street turns into London Rd. and follows the upper river for 10 miles to London and beyond.

Contact: ODFW, Corvallis, 541/757-4186; Oregon Department of Human Services, 503/947-5107; Steelheaders West Tackle shop, 541/744-2248; The Caddis Fly Angling Shop, 541/342-7005, www.thecaddisfly.com.

12 COTTAGE GROVE RESERVOIR
south of Cottage Grove

Map 5.3, page 321

Cottage Grove Reservoir is an irrigation impoundment on the Coast Fork of the Willamette River. Anglers can find quite a bit of peace among its scenically forested shorelines and campgrounds. This is a medium-size lake (1,150 acres) suitable for recreational boating and swimming, of which there is quite a bit. Lake depths (30 feet average, 75 feet near the dam) are conducive to good holding water for bigger fish. As in Dorena Reservoir, Copper Creek Lake, and the Coast Fork of the Willamette River below Cottage Grove Reservoir, there has been a health advisory issued against eating all species of fish because of high levels of mercury, PCBs, and pesticides. Contact the Oregon Department of Human Services for more information on contaminated waters.

The primary catches in the reservoir are stocked trout and largemouth bass up to five pounds. During March and April the reservoir is stocked with 12,000 legal-size trout, providing plenty of sport for early-season anglers. Holdover trout from previous years average 16–18 inches. The reservoir is open all year. All fishing methods are permitted, including the use of bait. There is a limit of five trout per day and an eight-inch minimum length for retention. Five bass per day are allowed, but only those smaller than 15 inches in length may be kept.

Anglers can either use a boat or fish from the bank with equal success. A majority of the fish species are found in the southern end of the lake in spring and fall, and near the dam in deeper waters in the summer. A depth finder will help you find fish in the deeper waters. There are two boat ramps, one at the dam and the other near Wilson Creek at the south end. Bank access is good either from the boat-launch areas or from two roads that border the lake, Cottage Grove Reservoir Road on the east shore or London Road on the west shore. Williams Creek on the west shore and Wilson Creek and Sweeney Creek on the east shore provide good river inlet fishing for both bank and boat anglers.

Species: Trout, largemouth bass, brown bull-head catfish.

Facilities: There's a free asphalt ramp with restrooms at Lakeside Park, next to the dam on the northwest shore. There's also an asphalt ramp in Wilson Creek Park, on the southeast shore, as well as a swimming beach, drinking water, restrooms, and picnicking. Pine Meadows Campground on the east side of the lake and run by the Corps of Engineers, has restrooms, showers, drinking water, swimming area, campsites, and RV sites with no utilities. There's also a primitive campground run by the Corps, with fire rings and drinking water and little else. Supplies are available in Cottage Grove.

Directions: From Cottage Grove, follow 6th St. out of town. It will change into London Rd. after 2.1 miles, and 2.8 miles past that it intersects Cottage Grove Reservoir Rd., which loops around the south shore 3.2 miles to Wilson Creek Park, passing Pine Meadows Campground along the way. Following London Rd. toward the north shore will bring you, in 0.2 mile, to the ramp at Lakeside Park.

Contact: Convention and Visitors Association of Lane County, 541/484-5307; Army Corps of Engineers, 541/942-8657; ODFW, Springfield, 541/726-3515; Oregon Department of Human Services, 503/947-5107; Cottage Grove Area Chamber of Commerce, 541/942-2411; Pine Meadows Campground, 541/942-5631; Primitive Campground, 541/942-5631; Village Green Motel and RV Park, 541/942-2491; Happy Eagle Lodge and RV Park, 541/946-1228.

13 COOPER CREEK LAKE

east of Sutherlin in the Umpqua
National Forest

Map 5.3, page 321

Cooper Creek is a beautiful, narrow reservoir nestled in a valley of Douglas fir with steep hillsides that drop to the shoreline. The lake covers 160 acres with five miles of shoreline and numerous arms all accessible from roads, good hiking trails, or boats. Cooper does get some recreational boaters, water-skiers, and Jet Skiers, but their influence is mostly limited to deeper areas around the dam and in the middle

of the lake. Anglers can find a degree of solitude fishing for bass, trout, and panfish at the
southern end and in the arms and coves. Sadly,
Cooper Creek suffers the same fate as Dorena
Reservoir, Cottage Grove Reservoir, and the
Coast Fork of the Willamette River—a health
advisory issued against eating all species of fish
because of high levels of mercury, PCBs, and
pesticides. Contact the Oregon Department
of Human Services for more information on
contaminated waters.

Two good boat ramps with day-use areas
offer access to the lake at the western end near
the dam and on the north shore. Both these
access points will place anglers in the deepest
parts of the lake. In spring and fall, anglers
can find the majority of fish at the southern
end of the lake at the Cooper Creek inlet.
There is a lot of structure in the water here
in the form of tree stumps and underwater
vegetation, making exceptional habitat for
bass and plump bluegill. In the summer most
of the fish seek out cooler water around the
dam and boat ramps. Good bank access can
be had from a trail that surrounds the lake
or from the boat-launch sites. All methods of
fishing are permitted, including bait.

Species: Trout, largemouth bass, bluegill,
brown bullhead catfish.

Facilities: Douglas County operates two free
boat ramps at the lake, one at each end. Both
are concrete and have restrooms. There's no
camping in the area, but accommodations
are available in Sutherlin and in Roseburg.
Nonfishing distractions in the area of Sutherlin include a covered bridges tour, wineries
and vineyards, and the Sutherlin Blackberry
Festival in mid-August. Supplies are available
in Sutherlin.

Directions: From Sutherlin, go east on Non-
pareil Rd. for 1.5 miles, turn right (south) on
Southside Rd., and follow it for two miles to
the ramp at the west (dam) end of the lake.
Turn left (east) on Cooper Creek Rd. for 1.4
miles to the eastern ramp.

Contact: Sutherlin Chamber of Commerce
and Sutherlin Visitor Information Center,

541/459-5829; Cooper Creek Reservoir,
541/459-2703; ODFW, Corvallis, 541/757-
4186; Oregon Department of Human Services, 503/947-5107.

14 LOWER NORTH UMPQUA RIVER
confluence to Rock Creek
Map 5.3, page 321

This section of the lower North Umpqua runs
from Rock Creek in Idleyld Park to the river
confluence with the main-stem Umpqua at
River Forks Park. Above Rock Creek the river
is open to fly-fishing only. This is blue-ribbon
water for winter and summer steelhead, fall
and winter chinook, coho, and trout. From
Rock Creek the river flows 31.5 miles through
the towns of Idleyld, Glide, and Winchester.
The upper section maintains the wild, forested
feel of the upper river, with tight chutes and
canyons. A few miles downriver from Idleyld
the river begins to open up into pasture lands,
rolling hills, and large gravel bars typical of a
valley river. All methods of fishing are permitted, making this water especially attractive
to traditional gear anglers employing bait,
spinners, and drift-fishing techniques. Drift
boating is the preferred method of access; also,
some bank fishing is available, especially above
Winchester Dam.

The Umpqua is well known for its mixed
run of wild and hatchery summer steelhead
May–October, with peak runs July–September. September can be a difficult time to fish
because of warm water, but fishing resumes in
October. Winter steelhead, the largest steelhead to enter the river, are composed entirely
of wild stock and run January–April with peak
fishing in February and March. Spring chinook are in the river April–July, with the peak
run occurring in June. Fall chinook and coho
enter the river together September–December
with peak runs in October. Drift fishing with
bait or corkies and casting spinners, spoons,
and plugs are the most popular methods of
fishing for all species. Fly-fishing is also popu-

lar, but most fly anglers head upriver to the fly-fishing–only section above Idleyld.

Regulations are broad and changing, so be sure to check for updated river closures. There is no fishing from a floating device upstream of Lone Rock boat ramp, east of Glide. The river is closed to all fishing from Old Highway 99, near I-5, upstream to Winchester Dam. All trout fishing is catch-and-release to protect sea-run cutthroat. Steelhead fishing is open all year, and hatchery fish may be retained anytime. Wild steelhead may be kept at one per day, or five per year January 1–April 30. The coho fishing season is August 1–December 31; the chinook season extends January 1–July 31.

Boaters can float above Winchester Dam starting at Lone Rock, the highest put-in for anglers fishing from a boat. From here you can float to Colliding Rivers (2.5 miles), Whistler Bend Park (8.5 miles), Winchester (22 miles), or put in or pull out at any of these spots. Class II and III rapids can make this water challenging. Below Winchester Dam, anglers can launch a boat at Amacher Park and float to Hestness Landing (three miles) or River Forks Park (6.5 miles). Most of this water can be run with a jet sled, and they are more commonly used below Winchester Dam. While boating offers the easiest access to the river, some good bank access can be had at the boat-launch sites, parks, and roadsides, along Old Glide Road off Highway 138, Colliding Rivers Viewpoint in Glider, and from Narrows Park in Idleyld Park to Rock Creek at Stillwater Park and the fly-fishing–only deadline.

Species: Summer and winter steelhead, fall and spring chinook, coho, trout.

Facilities: These boat access points appear in order going upstream from the confluence:

- **River Forks County Park,** with improved ramp, picnicking, developed beach access (no fee).
- **Hestness Landing,** with improved ramp, parking, restrooms.
- **Amacher County Park,** with improved ramp, parking, restrooms.
- **Winchester,** with pole slide, no other facilities.
- **Whistler's Bend,** with improved ramp, parking, restrooms.
- **Colliding Rivers,** with improved ramp, parking, restrooms.
- **Lone Rock,** with pole slide, parking, restrooms.

There's also bank access in Idleyld Park at The Narrows, a small park with a picnic table and vault toilet. Camping options include Amacher Park and Whistler's Bend, which has showers. This is a great family recreation area with a lot of nonangling activities such as hiking, biking, camping, rafting, mushroom picking, and sightseeing. One can also spend a nice afternoon touring 25 waterfalls around Tokeetee, Susan Creek, Fall Creek, and Watson Creek. Waterfall tour maps and other resources can be had from the local tourist or Forest Service field office. Supplies are available in Winchester.

Directions: From Winchester, travel north on Hwy. 99 for 0.4 mile, then turn left (west) onto County Rd. 115/Del Rio Rd. Follow this road for four miles to Hestness Landing. To keep going to River Forks Park, turn right (west) onto County Rd. 31D/Garden Valley Rd. Follow that road 1.3 miles, turn left (south) onto Old Garden Valley Rd., and after 0.5 mile turn right (west) onto River Forks Park Rd. This will lead you 0.5 mile into the park. Amacher Park is in Winchester, just west of I-5. The Winchester ramp is on the east end of town; follow Page Rd. for approximately two miles. The other sites are all east of Winchester, and are best reached by following Hwy. 138 east from Roseburg.

Contact: ODFW, Roseburg, 541/440-3353; BLM, Roseburg, 541/440-4930; Umpqua National Forest, 541/672-6601; North Umpqua Ranger District, 541/496-3532; Colliding Rivers Information Center, 541/672-6601; Roseburg Visitors and Convention Bureau, 800/444-9584; Douglas County Park Department, 541/957-7001; Amacher Park,

541/957-7001; Whistler's Bend Park, 541/673-4863; River Forks Park, 541/673-6935; Dry Creek Store, 541/498-2215; Lemolo Resort, 541/496-0900; Steamboat Inn, 800/840-8825, www.thesteamboatinn.com; Elk Haven RV Resort, 888/552-0166; Blue Heron Fly Shop, 541/496-0448; Big 5 Sporting Goods, Roseburg, 541/440-8954; Waldron's Outdoor Sports, 541/672-8992; Lamm's Guide Service, 541/440-0558; Doug's Guide Service (Doug Warren), 541/679-0599, www.loganet.net/dougsguideservice; Bill Conner (Drift Boat Guide), 541/496-0309.

15 LOWER MIDDLE FORK WILLAMETTE

from Dexter Reservoir to Willamette River

Map 5.4, page 322

The lower Middle Fork of the Willamette flows primarily through about 20 miles of agricultural lands in the Willamette Valley from Dexter Dam to the confluence with the Coast Fork to form the main stem of the Willamette River. Unlike the main Willamette, the river here is more like a freestone river with fast-flowing water, runs, riffles, and deep holes. The riverbanks are often bordered by scenic stands of cottonwoods and conifers. Good fishing can be had for summer steelhead, spring chinook, and some trout.

Both hatchery and spring chinook fishing are open all year, and all methods of fishing are permitted, including bait. Spring chinook enter the river April–July, with peak catches in mid-May and June. Most chinook are taken by casting spinners, or trolling and back-bouncing plugs such as Kwikfish and Flatfish, or bait in the form of large clusters of salmon roe. Bank anglers find the best success plunking with salmon roe. Bait can be suspended under a float or simply weighted with lead and allowed to bounce off the bottom. Steelhead make a slow showing in March with peak catches June–September. Spoons, plugs, and drift fishing are popular either from the boat or bank. Float fishing with bait such

as salmon roe or sand shrimp is becoming increasingly popular. Trout are present all year and present in every part of the river. Fishing is catch-and-release January 1–April 23 and November 1–December 31; five trout of an eight-inch minimum length can be retained April 24–October 31. Summer is a good time to fish caddis hatches; otherwise attractor dry flies, nymphs, and streamers will work well along the banks and around structure such as rocks.

Appropriate boats for this stretch are drift boats or rafts, but some anglers use canoes or kayaks when fishing for trout. There are four boat ramps in the upper section and one on the main Willamette at Island Park in Springfield. Most of the fish are caught in the three-mile stretch between Dexter Park at the dam and Pengra Access. There is a five-mile stretch below this point to Jasper Bridge, but boating can sometimes be hazardous because of log jams. The local sheriff's office can alert you to any boating dangers in this stretch. Bank fishing is good from each of the five boat ramps, and a good starting place is at Dexter Park right at the dam. From Dexter Park anglers can walk downstream on trails and find good water along the bank. From the dam 400 feet downstream to river markers, there is no bank angling from the north shore, from a floating devise, or while wading.

Species: Summer steelhead, spring chinook, trout.

Facilities: Island Park (6 A.M.–10 P.M. year-round) in Springfield (Willamalene Parks District) has a concrete ramp, restrooms, shelters, electric outlets, and hiking trails. The next site upstream is Clearwater Landing (6 A.M.–10 P.M. year-round), part of Willamalene District's Clearwater Park. It has an asphalt ramp, parking, and restrooms. A few miles upstream is Jasper Bridge ramp, near Jasper, with a gravel ramp and no other facilities. Pengra Access, three miles below the dam, is part of Elijah Bristow State Park (picnicking, restrooms, and hiking trails along the river). The boat ramp is on the north shore, opposite the main part of the park. It's concrete and has restrooms onsite. Camping is available on Dexter Reservoir at Dexter Shores RV Park, which also has laundry and Internet. Supplies are available in Eugene.

Directions: From Springfield, reach Island Park at the west end of B St. downtown. To reach Clearwater Park from downtown, head south on A St. for 2.2 miles, then turn right (west) on S. 32nd St. Follow this road for 1.8 miles; it will turn into Jasper Rd. and take you to Clearwater Lane. Turn right (south) here and enter the park. For Jasper Bridge, stay on Jasper Rd. for 5.2 miles, then turn right (south) onto Parkway Rd., which crosses Jasper Bridge in 0.1 mile. The boat ramp is on the far side. And for Bristow Park and its Pengra ramp, take I-5 south from Springfield for one mile, then pick up Hwy. 58 east toward Oakridge. Follow this road for 13.5 miles, then turn left (north) on Pioneer St., which crosses Dexter Reservoir and enters Lowell after 0.6 mile. From Lowell, go west on North Shore Dr., which becomes Old Pengra Rd. and, after 2.4 miles, intersects Pengra Access Rd. on the left. Follow this road south for 0.1 mile to the ramp.

Contact: Springfield Area Chamber of Commerce, 541/746-1651; Convention and Visitors Association of Lane County, 541/484-5307; Oregon Parks and Recreation Department, 800/551-6949; Willamalene Park District of Springfield, 541/736-4104; ODFW, Corvallis, 541/757-4186; Lane County Sheriff's Office, 541/682-4150; Dexter Shores RV Park, 541/937-3711; Steelheaders West Tackle Shop, 541/744-2248; The Caddis Fly Angling Shop, 541/342-7005, www.thecaddisfly.com.

16 MIDDLE FORK WILLAMETTE RIVER

Middle Fork above Lookout Point Reservoir

Map 5.4, page 322

The Middle Fork of the Willamette originates from several small lakes and tributaries high in the Cascades south of Diamond Peak Wilderness. Then, as it makes its westward journey to the main stem of the Willamette, it passes through three reservoirs, Hills Creek near Oakridge and Lookout Point and Dexter east of Springfield. Between Hills Creek Reservoir and Lookout Point Reservoir there are approximately 14 miles of river managed as a good wild trout stream for rainbows and cutthroat. These are not big fish, but they are plentiful. Fishing is open year-round and permitted with artificial flies and lures only; all wild fish must be returned to the river unharmed. Average fish is 9–14 inches with a few bigger fish up to 18 inches possible. Starting in May and throughout the summer, there are good hatches of caddis, stone flies, and assorted mayflies. Winter hatches keep the action going with blue-wing olives and midges. The river is followed closely by Highway 58 on the south bank and Forest Road 5821 on the north bank to the confluence with the North Fork Middle Fork. Above the North Fork confluence, follow Highway 58 on the north bank and Forest Road 5852 on the south bank to Hills Creek Reservoir. All of this water is available from roadside turnouts or from Black Canyon Shady Dell campgrounds or Greenwater and Ferrin Parks near Oakridge.

Boating is possible through this stretch, but there is only one concrete ramp at Black Canyon Campground near Lookout Point Reservoir, and a pole slide at Greenwater Park. Unofficial ramps can be had a mile below the reservoir at the bridge crossing off Forest Road 5852 and again from a gravel bar at the confluence of the Middle and North Middle Forks off Westfir-Oakridge Road. It is a good idea to scout both the rapids and put-ins and takeouts before committing yourself to a drift. Some Class III rapids exist in this section.

Above Hills Creek Reservoir, fair fishing can be had for hatchery rainbow and cutthroat trout and bull trout. The angling season runs April 22–October 31, and only artificial flies and lures are permitted. The river is followed closely by Highway 21, and there are several smaller primitive campgrounds. Access is un-limited along roadside turnouts.

Species: Wild and stocked rainbow and cut-throat trout, bull trout.

Facilities: There are eight Forest Service campgrounds along the Middle Fork. Middle Fork Willamette Trail connects all of these campgrounds, and then some, in its 27-mile course along the river. It starts in Sand Prairie Campground at Hills Creek Reservoir and winds up all the way above Indigo Springs Campground. Hampton Campground on Lookout Point Reservoir has only four sites with water and toilets; there's also a boat ramp onto the reservoir in its day-use area, where parking requires a Northwest Forest Pass ($5 per day; $30 annually), which is available from most sporting goods or outdoors shops or from Nature of the Northwest in Portland. Black Canyon Campground on the Middle Fork above Lookout Point Reservoir is a full-service affair, with 72 sites, drinking water, and fire rings. Its ramp is also in day-use area, which also requires the Forest Pass. Packard Creek Campground has 35 sites (some with their own docks), vault toilets, drinking water, and fire rings. Its day-use area has a year-round ramp and a fishing dock; Forest Pass is re-quired. Sand Prairie Campground at Hills Creek Reservoir is the small option; it has 21 sites, toilets, and water. Four sites are stretched along the Middle Fork above Hills Creek Res-ervoir. Secret Campground has only six sites and no water. Campers Flat has five sites and water. Sacandaga has 17 sites and water. And Indigo Springs has three tent-only sites and no water. Supplies are available in Springfield.

Directions: Hampton and Black Canyon campgrounds are west of Oakridge; Hampton is nine miles west, and Black Canyon about seven. The rest are east of Oakridge. Follow Hwy. 58 east for two miles to Kitson Springs Rd. (Forest Rd. 23) and turn right (south). Proceed on Kitson Springs Rd. for 0.5 mile to Forest Rd. 21, and follow that road six miles to Packard Creek Campground. Sand Prairie Campground is five miles farther on Rd. 21,

and Secret Campground is eight miles past that. Campers Flat and Sacandaga are one and five miles past Secret, respectively, and Indigo Springs is three miles past Sacandaga.

Contact: Springfield Area Chamber of Com-merce, 541/746-1651; Convention and Visitors Association of Lane County, 541/484-5307; Middle Fork Ranger District, 541/782-2283; ODFW, Corvallis, 541/757-4186; Lane County Sheriff's Office, 541/682-4150; Na-ture of the Northwest, 503/872-2750, www.naturenw.org; The Caddis Fly Angling Shop, 541/342-7005, www.thecaddisfly.com.

17 NORTH FORK OF THE MIDDLE FORK WILLAMETTE RIVER

east of Springfield near Oakridge

Map 5.4, page 322

This beautiful little river joins the Middle Fork of the Willamette approximately 35 miles east of Springfield. This 40-mile-long river is man-aged exclusively for wild cutthroat and redband trout. It heads in the pristine waters of Waldo Lake, high in the Cascade Mountains, and fol-lows dense forests of Douglas fir all the way to its confluence. In 1988, it received the honor of being designated a Wild and Scenic River. Because this is a wild trout stream, only artificial flies and lures may be used. Its wild redband and cutthroat both average 9–13 inches but can get as big as 20 inches. The lower 10 miles of river is more popular and a better producer of fish than the upper waters. The river is followed by Highway 19 (North Fork Rd.) for most of its length to the Waldo Lake Wilderness Boundary, approximately eight miles below Waldo Lake. The remainder of the river can be fished from hiking trails. Unlimited bank access can be had both from the roads and the wilderness hik-ing trails. This is not a boating river. Summer hatches of caddis and small mayflies is usually good; otherwise, nymphs will always produce in the holes and pocket water. Any small lures such as a Rooster Tail or Mepps will catch fish.

Species: Wild redband and cutthroat trout.

Facilities: There is one campground along this river: Kihanie Campground has 19 sites, water, and restrooms. There are plenty of other options on the nearby Middle Fork. There is a hiking trail (North Fork Segment Trail, No. 3666) along the north bank of the southern section of the river, across from Rd. 19 about two miles out of Oakridge. The Shale Ridge Trail (No. 3567) leaves the end of Rd. 19 and follows the river for about three miles before climbing away from it. Supplies are available in Oakridge.

Directions: From Oakridge, follow Westfir–Oakridge Rd. north, then turn north onto Forest Rd. 19. The lower trailhead is about one mile ahead on the left. Rd. 19 continues to follow the river, reaching Kihanie Campground in 20 miles and the trailhead at its end in 30 miles.

Contact: Springfield Area Chamber of Commerce, 541/746-1651; Middle Fork Ranger District, 541/782-2283; Convention and Visitors Association of Lane County, 541/484-5307; ODFW, Corvallis, 541/757-4186; Lane County Sheriff's Office, 541/682-4150; The Caddis Fly Angling Shop, 541/342-7005, www.thecaddisfly.com.

18 DORENA LAKE

east of Cottage Grove in the Umpqua National Forest

Map 5.4, page 322

Good bass fishing can be had in this scenically forested reservoir of 1,840 acres in the foothills of the Umpqua National Forest. There are 13 miles of shoreline, most of which is accessible from good roads. The area near the dam is the deepest part of the lake at 100 feet. Average depths are 45 feet and get shallower the closer you get to the Row River Inlet. A health advisory against eating all species of fish has been issued for the lower river because of high levels of mercury, PCBs, dioxins, and pesticides. Contact the Oregon Department of Human Services for more information on contaminated waters.

Dorena Lake is subject to summer drawdowns that move all fish from the cooler waters near the Row River inlet to the deeper waters near the dam in summer. Spring is the best time to fish shallower water for largemouth bass up to eight pounds. There is an abundance of submerged logs and vegetation perfect for big bass habitat. For bass use Rapalas, bass crankbaits, plastic worms, and jigs. Surface poppers work well when the water starts to warm. Only bass smaller than 15 inches in length may be taken. Trout are found in similar locations as bass and are caught by trolling lures or using bait such as night crawlers and PowerBait. Bluegill, crappie, and brown bullhead catfish can all be found around the lake's edges, inlets, or deeper water.

Boat access is good from two boat ramps on the north and south shores near the dam. The ramp at Baker Bay Park has boat rental; motors may be used. Bank access is good at the dam, the Row River inlet, along the north shore on Row River Rd., and at the two boat ramps.

Good trout fishing can be had on the Row River both above and below the reservoir, but access is very poor because of private property. The best places to reach the river are by walking upriver from the lake inlet and at Schwartz Park at the dam.

Species: Rainbow and cutthroat trout, largemouth bass, bluegill, brown bullhead, crappie.

Facilities: The Army Corps of Engineers operates two parks at the lake. Schwartz Park, at the base of Dorena Dam on the banks of the Row River, has a primitive boat ramp, restrooms, showers, campsites, and RV sites with no utilities. Harms Park (day-use only), on the north shore, has a gravel ramp and restrooms. Baker Bay Park (day-use May 1–Sept. 30, $3), operated by Lane County, has 49 campsites, showers, restrooms, and an asphalt boat ramp. Other diversions include a tour of six covered bridges in the Cottage Grove area. Supplies are available in Cottage Grove.

Directions: From Cottage Grove, drive east

on Row River Rd. for three miles, then follow Government Rd. to the right (east) another 1.2 miles to the lake. Schwartz Park is on the left just past the dam, and Baker Bay Park is two miles farther along. To reach Harms Park, stay on Row River Rd. for three miles past Government Rd. to the ramp on the right.

Contact: ODFW, Corvallis, 541/757-4186; Cottage Grove Area Chamber of Commerce, 541/942-2411; Oregon Department of Human Services, 503/947-5107; Schwarz Park, 541/942-5631; Baker Bay Park, 541/942-7669; Village Green Motel and RV Park, 541/942-2491; Happy Eagle Lodge and RV Park, 541/946-1228.

19 WALDO LAKE

east of Oakridge in Willamette National Forest

Map 5.4, page 322

Waldo Lake—the second-largest and second-deepest lake in Oregon—is rated as having some of the purest water in the world. There are marginal populations of brook trout and kokanee, some of which can reach five pounds. Not many anglers fish Waldo because the lake is virtually sterile and the small populations of fish are very difficult to find; kokanee are extremely sparse, making brook trout the primary catches. Your best bet is to fish the shallow shoals around Rhododendron Island, Shadow Lake, and North Waldo campgrounds. Trolling small gold and silver spinners and lures is effective and the best way to catch brookies. Streamers, dry flies, and bait will work along the bank evenings and mornings or any time there may be a hatch of insects. Boating is a near necessity since most of the 22 miles of shoreline are too dense with brush for easy access. There are three boat ramps on the most productive parts of the lake. While the lake is open year-round, the lake's high elevation (5,400 feet) almost ensures that there will be a heavy snowfall that will prevent access until the first part of July; the recreational season is usually over by mid-October.

Species: Brook trout, rainbow trout, cutthroat trout, kokanee.

Facilities: North Waldo Campground has 58 sites, drinking water, and restrooms. The boat ramp is in the day-use area, where parking requires a Northwest Forest Pass ($5 per day; $30 annually), which is available from most sporting goods or outdoors shops or from Nature of the Northwest in Portland. Islet Campground, also at the north end of the lake, has 55 sites, drinking water, and restrooms, but no ramp. Shadow Bay Campground, at the south end of the lake, has 92 sites, water and restrooms, and a boat ramp. The ramp is in a day-use area that's open June–October and also requires the Northwest Forest Pass. There is also a hike-in or boat-in day-use area on Rhododendron Island, where there are no facilities but a great show of rhodies in early summer. Several hiking trails offer access into the Waldo Lake Wilderness backcountry and more remote areas of the lake. One section of the Waldo Shoreline Trail (No. 3590.1) starts at the North Waldo boat ramp and heads south, along the lakeshore and through Islet Campground, for three miles. Another section goes north from the ramp for one mile, after which it joins the main Waldo Lake Trail (No. 3590). The 3590 trail, which encircles the lake for a total of 19.6 miles, is also accessible from the Shadow Bay Campground. A good Forest Service map will show you other hiking options from the 3590 to numerous lakes in the local backcountry. Supplies are available in Oakridge.

Directions: From Oakridge, follow Hwy. 58 east for 25 miles to Waldo Lake Rd. (Forest Rd. 5897). Turn left (north) onto Rd. 5897. For Shadow Bay Campground, drive 6.5 miles on Rd. 5897, then turn left (west) onto Rd. 5896, which leads two miles to the campground. For Islet and North Waldo campgrounds, stay on Waldo Lake Rd. for 11 miles, then turn left (northwest) onto Rd. 5898. When the road splits after about a mile, North Waldo is on your right, and Islet is on your left, both about one mile away.

Contact: Central Oregon Visitors Association, 541/389-8799; ODFW, Bend, 541/388-6363; Middle Fork Ranger District, 541/782-2283.

20 HILLS CREEK RESERVOIR
near Oakridge in Willamette National Forest
Map 5.4, page 322

Forested Hills Creek Reservoir is a 2,735-acre irrigation impoundment on the Middle Fork of the Willamette with excellent angling for legal-size rainbow trout and a mix of warm-water species such as largemouth bass, crappie, and brown bullhead catfish. The reservoir is characterized by deep waters, 300 and 100 feet from the dam throughout the body of the lake, and shallower arms where the majority of the fishing takes place. These arms include Hills Creek, Larison Creek, Packard Creek, Bull Creek, and Modoc Creek. The most popular arm is Hills Creek at the northern end of the lake.

Hills Creek is open for all methods of angling, including bait, year-round; however, its tributaries are open for fishing only during the regular trout season. Trout do tend to run small (8–12 inches), but they are abundant because of generous stocking programs. Larger trout (up to 20 inches) are present and challenge the more experienced angler. Warm-water species are most active and therefore more readily caught during summer, when the waters have receded because of irrigation. Bull trout are present but must be released unharmed. Trolling is best for crappie and trout, and still-water fishing will catch both species as well as catfish. Bank access is best from hiking trails extending from the campgrounds and day-use areas. Good bank access can also be had by driving along Highway 21, which follows the entire west shore. Forest Rd. 2118 follows the entire east shore. Power boating is allowed, but there is a 5 mph speed limit in certain posted areas.

Species: Stocked rainbow trout, largemouth bass, crappie, brown bullhead catfish, bull trout.

Facilities: The forested setting is popular for a variety of activities (canoeing, sailing, sailboarding, water-skiing, camping, picnicking, swimming, and wildlife-viewing) that make this a good place for families. Packard Creek Campground has 35 sites (some with their own docks), vault toilets, drinking water, and fire rings. Its day-use area has a year-round ramp and a fishing dock. Parking in the day-use area requires a Northwest Forest Pass ($5 per day; $30 annually), which is available from most sporting goods or outdoors shops. Sand Prairie Campground has 21 sites, toilets, and water. Larison Cove Campground on Larison Cove is canoe-in only; you'll need a Forest Pass to park at any of the boat ramps. In addition to the ramp at Packard Creek, there are ramps at CT Beach on the east side and Bingham on its south end, as well as picnic areas at Larison Cove and Cline-Clark. Each of these sites has a restroom and requires a Forest Pass for parking. Supplies are available in Oakridge.

Directions: From Oakridge, follow Hwy. 58 east for two miles to Kitson Springs Rd. (Forest Rd. 23) and turn right (south). Proceed on Kitson Springs Rd. for 0.5 mile to Forest Rd. 21, and follow that road six miles to Packard Creek Campground. Sand Prairie Campground is five miles farther on Rd. 21. Along the way, you will pass Larison Cove and Cline Creek picnic areas. To reach Bingham ramp, follow Rd. 21 to Sand Prairie Campground at the lake's southern end, then turn left (north) on Rd. 2118, which follows the lake's eastern shore for three miles to the north. To reach the ramp at CT Beach, stay on Kitson Springs Rd. for three miles instead of turning onto Rd. 21.

Contact: Springfield Area Chamber of Commerce, 541/746-1651; Middle Fork Ranger District, 541/782-2283; Convention and Visitors Association of Lane County, 541/484-5307; ODFW, Corvallis, 541/757-4186; Lane County Sheriff's Office, 541/682-4150; The Caddis Fly Angling Shop, 541/342-7005, www.thecaddisfly.com.

21 MIDDLE NORTH UMPQUA RIVER

Rock Creek to Soda Springs Dam

Map 5.4, page 322   BEST (

This 35-mile section of North Umpqua River is designated fly-fishing–only water, and it is some of the most beautiful and challenging steelhead fishing in Oregon. This river is stunning, with emerald-green waters flowing through deep, rugged basalt canyons lined with Douglas fir, hemlock, and cedar. The allure of this river, and its history as a decades-old fly-fishing river, is captured by the names given to its most productive water: Camp Water above Steamboat Inn; Boat Hole; Kitchen Pool; Upper, Middle and Lower Mott; Glory Hole; Gordon; Takahashi; and many others. Fortunately, these holes are easy to find because the river is totally accessible, albeit with some scrambling, from Highway 138 on the north bank and the Umpqua River Trail on the south bank.

While anglers can expect some great fishing on the North Umpqua, they also have to be aware of its many challenges. Wading is downright treacherous and anglers should come prepared with gear to handle slippery rocks, fast water, and deep holes on the edge of shallow rock ledges. Waders, wading belts, wading staffs, and cleated boots are all highly recommended. Also, prepare for some strenuous hiking. Although the road may be only a couple of hundred yards away, hiking to the riverbank requires getting around huge boulders, fallen trees, thick brush, and steep hillsides. Last, fish shadows will not be the only shadows you'll be chasing. Set your alarm clock (and the coffeemaker) early and get to your intended water at first light or during the last hours of the day. Fish each hole and move to the next one before light reaches the water; many anglers call this "chasing the shadows." You can catch fish all day, but not like they can be early in the morning. It's a good idea to spend an afternoon scouting potential fishing sites so you can move directly to productive water during fishing hours.

The most productive fishing on the river is from the confluence of Steamboat Creek, at Steamboat Inn, downriver to the fly-fishing deadline at Rock Creek. Anglers can either drive along the river's north side on Highway 138, looking for pullouts on the side of the road, or hike the Umpqua River Trail on the south side. A trail map can be acquired from the Forest Service office in Glide showing various access points along this 77-mile trail, which follows the river from Idleyld Park to Maidu Lake. More established access points are available at numerous campgrounds that dot the highway. Some of the better campgrounds for good water access are the Susan Creek boat ramp and Bogus Creek Campground.

Summer steelhead fishing is by far the most popular time to fish the river. Summer runs usually number 8,000–10,000 fish per season, usually a mix of native and hatchery fish. They enter the river as early as May, and July–September are the peak fishing times. The winter run is composed mostly of wild fish, and an average year will see as many as 4,500–6,000 returning fish. Salmon are present but not allowed to be targeted. Trout are available throughout the river in good numbers, and there's a tiny run of sea-run cutthroat (fewer than 100 fish over Winchester Dam most years) in the river April–September. All fish under 16 inches on the North Umpqua are considered trout and must be released unharmed.

Aside from the usual difficulties associated with steelhead fishing (timing the runs, finding the fish, and using the right lure), the Umpqua offers a few special ones. During the summer steelhead season, July 1–September 30, angling is restricted to single unweighted barbless hooks. External weight, strike indicators, or any other gear that may be attached to the fly line or leader is prohibited the entire year; sinking lines are legal, though their use is debated among the purists. Most anglers overcome the obstacle of no weight by refusing to fish anything but streamers cast down and across in the runs. Many of the most popular Northwest streamer patterns were developed specifically for this river, such as the Skunk, Umpqua Special, Black Gordon, and Cummins Special. Other common patterns include the Green and Red Butt Skunks, Golden Demons, Purple Perils, Brad's Brats, Silver Hiltons, and Steelhead Muddlers. The skated dry fly is used almost as often as streamers for summer fish and can generate explosive strikes. Popular dry-fly patterns include Bombers, Stimulators, Dry Muddlers, Waller Wakers, and October Caddis. If nymphs are used they are usually very lightly dressed to facilitate quick sinking and fished with a series of mends to reduce tension on the fly.

Winter steelhead fishing uses similar techniques, but sinking lines are more often employed, and the flies can be considerably bigger. Hook sizes from 1/0 to 4/0 are common. Many of these flies are tied spey style and dressed in purples, oranges, black, and hot pinks to make some of the most beautiful Northwest flies. John Shewey's Spawning Purple is one such fly, as are Syd Glasso's Orange Heron and Dave McNeese's Light Umpqua Spey and Spawning Spey. Other good winter flies include Popsicles, Egg Sucking Leeches, Starlight Leeches, Articulated Leeches, and anything from the Boss series with orange or red collars.

As with most of the North Umpqua, the regulations are complicated. Fishing for trout is catch-and-release the entire year. Steelhead fishing is open year-round, and hatchery coho can be fished August 1–December 31; January 1–June 31, and again October 1–December 31, fishing is restricted to a single barbless hook but flies may be weighted. There is no angling from a floating device, but it isn't necessary anyway, since river access is unlimited from the main highway and the Umpqua River Trail.

Species: Wild and hatchery summer steelhead, wild winter steelhead, coho, trout, Spring chinook salmon, coho salmon.

Facilities: Eight campgrounds are stretched along this section of river. The first you come to driving upstream from Idleyld Park is Susan Creek, which is operated by the BLM and also includes a raft take-out, drinking water, and showers. The rest of the sites, in order going upstream, are all run by the Forest Service: Bogus Creek has 15 sites and drinking water. Williams Creek has three sites and no water. Island Campground has seven sites and no water. Apple Creek has eight sites, tables, fire pits, and no water. Horseshoe Bend has 22 sites, tables, and drinking water. Eagle Rock has 25 sites, tables, fire rings, and no water. Boulder Flat has 11 sites and no water. Swiftwater County Park, on the south side of the river just east of Idleyld Park, has picnic tables, drinking water, and flush toilets. Just across the river is the BLM's Swiftwater day-use site, with an accessible fishing platform, picnic tables, and restrooms. Cable Crossing Wayside, one mile above Rock Creek Bridge on Hwy. 138, has one picnic unit, no drinking water, and a vault toilet. Supplies are available in Glide and Idleyld Park.

Directions: All of these sites are reached by taking Hwy. 138 east from Glide, home of the Forest Service's Colliding Rivers Information Center. Susan Creek is 12 miles up the road. Bogus Creek is 18 miles. Williams Creek is 21 miles. Swiftwater is 23 miles; turn right (south) on Swiftwater Bridge Rd. and go 0.2 mile. Island is 24 miles on Hwy. 138. Apple Creek is 28 miles. Horseshoe Bend is 30 miles, Eagle Rock is 34, and Boulder Flat is 36 miles.

Contact: ODFW, Roseburg, 541/440-3353; BLM, Roseburg, 541/440-4930; Umpqua National Forest, 541/672-6601; North Umpqua Ranger District, 541/496-3532; Colliding Rivers Information Center, 541/672-6601; Roseburg Visitors and Convention Bureau, 800/444-9584; Dry Creek Store, 541/498-2215; Idleyld Lodge, 541/496-0088; Steelhead Run Lodge, 800/992-8942; Lemolo Resort, 541/496-0900; Steamboat Inn, 800/840-8825, www.thesteamboatinn.com; Elk Haven RV Resort, 888/552-0166; The North Umpqua Foundation, www.northumpqua.org; Blue Heron Fly Shop (Joe Howell),

541/496-0448; Scott Howell Guide Service, 541/608-0403, www.scotthowellfishing.com; Summer Run Guide Service (Tony Wratney), 541/496-3037.

22 UPPER NORTH UMPQUA RIVER

Soda Springs to headwaters

Map 5.4, page 322

The upper reaches of the North Umpqua are small and fast compared to the rest of the river, which grows significantly once it receives numerous tributaries. The upper waters are inhabited by fair numbers of rainbow and brown trout, and the river maintains the scenic beauty of the lower river with deep, clear, cold water flowing through basalt gorges and tall stands of Douglas fir, cedar, and hemlock. The origin of the river is deep within Mount Thielsen Wilderness, and it flows west, passing through Lemolo Lake and Toketee Lake before compounding at Soda Creek Reservoir. The river is open to trout fishing April 22–October 31, and the use of bait is allowed. None of this water is boatable, but bank access is unlimited from access roads. Highway 138 follows the river to Toketee Lake, and then Forest Service roads follow the river past Lemolo Lake. Finally, the headwaters are reached by hiking trails into Mount Thielsen Wilderness.

Species: Wild rainbow and brown trout.

Facilities: There are no campgrounds on this section of river, but plenty of accommodations are available at nearby Lemolo Lake and Diamond Lake. Supplies are available in Glide and Idleyld Park.

Directions: From Glide, take Hwy. 138 east for 42 miles, and turn left (north) onto Forest Rd. 34 (Toketee–Rigdon Rd.). Drive past Toketee Reservoir for two miles, then continue on Rd. 34, following the North Umpqua. After about eight miles, turn right onto Rd. 3400–680; you'll be going south where Rd. 34 turns back to the north, about a mile after you cross Deer Creek. Road 680 follows the river for about 20 winding miles before dead-ending into Rd.

600; turn right here. This road follows the river for about eight more miles to Lemolo Lake. When you get to the dam, stay left onto Rd. 999, which skirts the north side of the lake and then continues upstream. About 10 miles past the dam, it reaches Kelsay Valley Campground and Rd. 1414. Turn right here, and after four miles this road dead-ends into hiking trails that lead up to the river's source at Maidu Lake.

Contact: ODFW, Roseburg, 541/440-3353; BLM, Roseburg, 541/440-4930; Umpqua National Forest, 541/672-6601; North Umpqua Ranger District, 541/496-3532; Diamond Lake Ranger District, 541/498-2531; Colliding Rivers Information Center, 541/672-6601; Roseburg Visitors and Convention Bureau, 800/444-9584; Dry Creek Store, 541/498-2215; Lemolo Resort, 541/496-0900; Elk Haven RV Resort, 888/552-0166; Steamboat Inn, 800/840-8825, www.thesteamboatinn. com; Blue Heron Fly Shop (Joe Howell), 541/496-0448; Scott Howell Guide Service, 541/608-0403, www.scotthowellfishing.com; Summer Run Guide Service (Tony Wratney), 541/496-3037.

23 LEMOLO LAKE

east of Roseburg in the Umpqua watershed

Map 5.4, page 322

Just up the highway from the other impoundment on the North Umpqua, Toketee Lake, Lemolo Lake also offers good year-round fishing for rainbow, big brown trout, brook trout, and some kokanee and landlocked chinook. The setting is unbeatable, surrounded by wilderness high in the Cascades; Mount Thielsen looms in the distance, and forests of lodgepole pine, mountain hemlock, and Shasta red fir populate the lakeshore. Lemolo is managed primarily as a brown trout fishery with additions of stocked rainbow trout. Brook trout, kokanee, and a small population of landlocked chinook may show up in the catches, but their numbers are too small to target. Rainbows are legal-size stocked fish and provide fair action for still-water bait fishing from the shore or a boat. Browns provide the real challenge for experienced anglers, with fish reaching 15 pounds or more. Browns can be taken on bait, but for the big guys you're going to have to go deep with plugs such as Flatfish or spinners. Both Poole Creek and Lemolo Lake Resort have boat ramps that give quick access to the best and deepest water around the dam. Look for trout also around the tributary mouths and in the arms of the North Umpqua at the far east end of the lake and Lake Creek at the far south end. Fly anglers will encounter fish rising to small mayfly hatches and terrestrials in the summer.

Species: Rainbow, brown, and brook trout, kokanee, landlocked chinook.

Facilities: This lake has good family facilities and other diversions such as water-skiing, hiking trails to nearby waterfalls, and the North Umpqua River; Crater Lake is an easy 15-mile drive. With all these amenities plus four campgrounds, a resort, and RV park, this can be a busy place. Lemolo Lake Resort offers gas; a restaurant; showers and laundry; rentals of paddleboats, pontoons, and motorboats; bait; tackle; and a boat ramp. Nearby Poole Creek Campground has 59 campsites and a boat ramp. Use of the boat ramp requires a Northwest Forest Pass ($5 per day; $30 annually), available from most sporting goods or outdoors shops. Three other Forest Service campgrounds are much more rustic: Bunker Hill has eight sites; East Lemolo has no designated sites; and Inlet has 14 sites. All offer vault toilets and picnic tables, but no drinking water.

Directions: From Roseburg, drive 72 miles east on Hwy. 138 and turn north on Forest Rd. 2610 (Bird's Point Rd.). For East Lemolo and Inlet campgrounds, continue three miles on Rd. 2610 and turn right onto Rd. 2614. In two miles, turn left onto Rd. 2610–430; East Lemolo is at the end of the road (0.3 mile). For Inlet, stay on Rd. 2614 for another 0.5 mile past the turnoff for Rd. 430. To reach Poole Creek and the resort, drive four miles on Rd. 2610. This will get you to the Poole Creek entrance. In another 0.5 mile, you'll reach the entrance to the resort. And for Bunker Hill, stay on Rd. 2610 for a total of 5.5 miles, crossing the Lemolo Lake Dam, then turn right onto Rd. 2612. The campground is on the north shore of the lake, about one mile east of the dam.

Contact: ODFW, Roseburg, 541/440-3353; BLM, Roseburg, 541/440-3353; Umpqua National Forest, 541/672-6601; Diamond Lake Ranger District, 541/498-2531; Lemolo Lake Resort, 541/643-0750, lemololakeresort.com.

24 TOKETEE RESERVOIR
east of Roseburg in the Umpqua watershed

Map 5.4, page 322

Seventy-five–acre Toketee is a scenically forested reservoir on the upper North Umpqua. It offers good fishing for rainbow and brown trout and is home to an abundance of wildlife such as beaver, otter, great blue heron, kingfishers, ducks, geese, and bald eagles. Fishing the lake is not difficult, either from a boat or shore. The deepest waters are no more than 35 feet and are at the narrow section before the lake opens up near the dam. Bait is allowed, and ample numbers of fish are taken still fishing with night crawlers and PowerBait. Trolling is popular from canoes, rowboats, and float tubes. Fly anglers will find a fair number of rising fish feeding on mayflies and terrestrials in the summer.

Species: Rainbow and brown trout.

Facilities: This is a good place for families, with plenty of nonangling activities such as day trips to Crater Lake, waterfall tours along the North Umpqua, and hiking trails around the lake (2.5 miles), into local wilderness areas (Boulder Creek and Mount Thielsen), and along the North Umpqua River. The Toketee Lake Trail parallels the lake for 0.4 mile; it starts at the northwest corner of the lake. The North Umpqua Trail also passes by the lake, offering access both upstream and downstream, and the Toketee Falls Trail (0.4 mile) offers access to, if not great fishing, at least an amazing waterfall. Toketee Campground has 33 campsites, picnic tables, fireplaces, a boat ramp and vault toilets, but no drinking water. The closest facilities are available at Dry Creek, which offers RV camping, cabins, gasoline, propane, groceries, fishing supplies, and hunting and fishing licenses.

Directions: From Roseburg, drive 60 miles east on Hwy. 138. Turn north onto Forest Rd. 34. Then turn left at the bottom of the hill and cross a concrete bridge on the right. Proceed 1.5 miles to the campground entrance on the right.

Contact: ODFW, Roseburg, 541/440-3353; BLM, Roseburg, 541/440-3353; Umpqua National Forest, 541/672-6601; Diamond Lake Ranger District, 541/498-2531; Dry Creek Store, 541/498-2215.

25 DIAMOND LAKE
north of Crater Lake
Map 5.4, page 322

It would be impossible to write a book about fishing in Oregon without including Diamond Lake. With trout up to 10 pounds and average catches in the 5–6-pound range, Diamond is certainly a trophy trout destination. Were this book written even a year earlier, you would be reading a lengthy listing; however, in the fall of 2006 Diamond Lake was drained and treated with rotenone, completely killing off the fish population and closing the lake for 18 months. The reason for this drastic action was the intrusive populations of chub minnow and blue-green algae. The plans for this process are extensive, well documented, and entirely dependent on available funding. Anglers can keep abreast of the progress on the ODFW website. Stocking programs after 2007 are aggressive and should restore the fishery quickly. What anglers have to look forward to is the return of a remarkable fishery in the years beyond 2008.

Contact: Up-to-date information can be found at www.dfw.state.or.us/fish.

26 ELK LAKE
near Bend in Cascade Lakes Basin
Map 5.5, page 323

Elk is a beautiful, clear-blue, mixed-recreation lake with marvelous scenery amid ponderosa pine forests and views of South Sister, Broken Top, and Mount Bachelor. Fishing is good for medium-size brook trout and fair for kokanee. Elk Lake's total surface area is 405 acres, and it includes several arms and numerous coves. At 5,000 feet in elevation, the summer weather is often cooler than at other places, and there is a persistent wind that blows most of the day, beginning in the late morning or early afternoon. Overall depth is a modest 12 feet, and maximum depth is 62 feet near the southern end. There are 5.1 miles of shoreline surrounded by trails, campgrounds, and some roads. Access is easy and unrestricted for both boaters and bank anglers. Boats may use motors, but there is a 10 mph speed limit. Float tubes, pontoon boats, canoes, and kayaks are all very useful here. Twenty-five kokanee may be kept per day in addition to other fishing limits. All fishing methods are permitted.

Elk Lake is stocked every year with fingerling brook trout, and average catches are 10–12 inches, but 14–18-inch fish are common. Brook trout are scattered throughout the lake, and the best starting places are along the shores in the deeper southern end and in the northeast cove by the Sunset View Picnic Area. Brook trout can be taken on bait such as night crawlers, trolling spinners, or flies. Kokanee are not as abundant as in other lakes and average 7–10 inches. Kokanee are caught almost exclusively in the deepest areas at the lake's south end and nearer the east shore. Kokanee are caught with both bait and by jigging.

Species: Brook trout and kokanee.

Facilities: This is a wonderful place for families: great campgrounds, nice beaches and swimming areas, and a resort with boat and fishing rentals. Sailboarding and sailing are popular. All three Forest Service campsites at the lake have drinking water and a free boat ramp. Elk Lake and Little Fawn both have

23 sites; Point has 10. Elk Lake Resort (year-round, though snow blocks the road Nov–May) has primitive tent camping and rustic cabins. Their limited store (11 A.M.–6 P.M.) offers canoe, kayak and paddleboat rentals. Supplies are available in Bend.

Directions: From Bend, drive southwest on Cascade Lakes Hwy. (Forest Rd. 46). After 33 miles, you'll reach the north end of the lake, home of Elk Lake Campground and the Elk Lake Lodge. Point Campground is one mile farther. To reach Little Fawn Campground, drive 1.5 miles past Point Campground, then 1.7 miles east on Forest Rd. 4625.

Contact: Elk Lake Resort, 541/480-7228; ODFW, Bend, 541/388-6363; Central Oregon Visitors Association, 541/389-8799; Bend–Fort Rock Ranger District, 541/383-4000; Elk Lake Resort, 541/480-7378, elklakeresort.net.

27 HOSMER LAKE
near Bend in Cascade Lakes Basin

Map 5.5, page 323

Catch-and-release fishing for salmon at a high mountain lake in Central Oregon's Cascade Range; how's that for a novel fishing adventure? Actually, it is not quite as strange as it sounds. Hosmer, a premier fly-fishing lake noted for rearing big brook trout, is one of the few places in Oregon you can catch landlocked Atlantic salmon. Hosmer is a place of symphonic beauty, composed of a chorus of alpine meadows and marshes, islands, ponderosa forests, a streamlike channel, wildlife, and views of several majestic Cascade Mountains. Geographically, Hosmer is divided into two pools, north and south, connected by a mile-long channel that runs through Mallard Marsh. The north pool is the biggest but also the shallowest, 3–4 feet deep. The south pool is smaller but has a deeper center up to nine feet. The most popular places to fish are in the deeper south pool and in the channel, but that doesn't mean there are no fish in the north pool. The north pool is fed by several

cold-water streams, such as Quinn Creek, and the mouths of these streams are good places to find fish.

Fishing at Hosmer is restricted to artificial barbless flies only and catch-and-release fishing for Atlantic salmon; brook trout may be retained with no limit to size or numbers. Boats are permitted, including motors, but there is very little need for anything but a float tube, canoe, pontoon boat, or rowboat. Hosmer is 160 acres and is less than nine feet at its deepest point.

Typically, anglers will see far more fish than they will ever catch. The shallow, clear water provides very little structure for fish to hide, so they just cruise around as if anglers were no threat. As a general rule, don't sight fish for the trout you can see. Ignore them, and fish 30–70 feet (depending on how far you can cast) out into the lake, using patience to concentrate on good fishing techniques. Long, 12–18-foot fluorocarbon leaders are your best bet. Floating lines work, but full sinking clear lines are also effective in helping one deliver a fly consistently on the bottom. Begin with a variety of small leech patterns such as Seal Buggers or Mole Hair Leeches in mixed colors of black, brown, maroon, and especially olive. The speed at which you strip in your fly or apply small nuanced twitches is 80 percent of the fishing on Hosmer. You can always switch to nymphs such as Pheasant Tails or Hare's Ears if the leeches are not producing. Also, watch for hatching insects such as caddis, *Callibaetis,* chironomids (midges), and damsels for dry-fly opportunities. Heavy vegetation and marshlands make bank fishing at Hosmer extremely difficult; thus most fishing is accomplished from a boat.

Species: Brook trout, landlocked Atlantic salmon.

Facilities: Both of the campgrounds at the lake—South and Mallard Marsh—have boat launches and restrooms but no drinking water.

Directions: From Bend, drive 35 miles southwest on Cascade Lakes Hwy. (Forest Rd. 46),

then turn east on Forest Rd. 4625. South Campground is 1.2 miles down this road, and Mallard Marsh is 0.1 mile past it.
Contact: ODFW, Bend, 541/388-6363; Central Oregon Visitors Association, 541/389-8799; Bend–Fort Rock Ranger District, 541/388-5664.

28 LAVA LAKE
near Bend in Cascade Lakes Basin
Map 5.5, page 323

It's hard to go wrong when visiting any of these Cascade lakes. They have spectacular beauty and solitude, great fishing, and close proximity to Bend. Lava Lake is no exception. Rainbow and brook trout are the primary catches at Lava Lake. Brook trout are no longer stocked, but they naturally reproduce in sufficient numbers to make this a fair brook trout lake. Brook trout average 12 inches but can run as big as 16–19 inches. Rainbow trout are plentiful because of annual stocking. Average fish run 12–14 inches but get as big as 20–24 inches. Spring is the most popular time to fish here, after the lake thaws and the roads have been cleared. The fishing season runs April 22–October 31. All methods of fishing are permitted, including bait.

Lava is most easily fished from a boat, but some good bank access can be had close to the deeper water on the northeast shore. Bank anglers who decide to fish anywhere other than the campground and resort areas will have to find clearings or rocky outcroppings. A hiking trail skirts the northeast side of the lake and the deepest water, but access is mostly a scramble down hillsides to brushy banks. Boat anglers can launch a craft at the Forest Service campground at the southern end of the lake or at the resort. The best place to begin is by trolling to the north end of the lake along the northeast bank. The deepest area of the lake is the upper two-thirds along the northeast shore, 30–80 feet off the bank.

The most popular methods of fishing include bait and spinners. Cheese seems to be a favorite bait here, as suggested by the nicknamed "Velveeta Point" on the northeast shore. Other baits include night crawlers, eggs, and PowerBait. Bait anglers should use small hooks and clear (camouflage or fluorocarbon) fishing line of 3–4-pound test. Other methods of fishing include spinners such as Rooster Tails and flashers when trolling deeper waters. Flies are effective around the grass-lined banks; use streamer patterns such as Zonkers and Woolly Buggers in olive, maroon, and black, or white.

Species: Stocked rainbow trout and brook trout.

Facilities: Anglers and their families will welcome the serene setting with a good campground and resort amid conifer forests and views of Cascade Range peaks. The Forest Service's Lava Lake campground (Apr.–Oct., $10 per vehicle) has a boat ramp, drinking water, and vault toilet. Lava Lake Lodge has boat rentals, fuel, groceries, and other merchandise, camping with full hookups, showers, and laundry. Supplies are available in Bend.

Directions: From Bend, drive southwest on Cascade Lakes Hwy. (Forest Rd. 46). After 39 miles, turn east onto Lava Lake Rd. Drive east on Lava Lake Rd. approximately one mile to the southern end of the lake. The road dead-ends at Lava Lake Campground. Parking is available at the resort or in the campground.

Contact: Central Oregon Visitors Association, 541/389-8799; Bend–Fort Rock Ranger District, 541/388-5664; ODFW, Bend, 541/388-6363; Lava Lake Lodge, 541/382-9443; Garrison's Fishing Guide Service, 541/593-8394.

29 UPPER DESCHUTES RIVER: SUNRIVER TO BEND
southwest of Bend
Map 5.5, page 323

The Upper Deschutes, 20 miles from the boat launch at Harper Bridge above Sunriver to Bend at River Rim Park, offers good to excellent fishing for large rainbow and brown trout and whitefish. All but the upper six miles of this river are characterized by high gradient flows, dangerous rapids, and deep pools. Much of the river here runs through steep canyons of rimrock, juniper, ponderosa pine, and sagebrush. Below Benham Falls near Sunriver, the river is open all year and restricted to artificial flies and lures only; above Benham Falls to Wickiup Reservoir the river is open May 27–October 31, and use of bait is allowed. Most anglers take trout on lures such as Rooster Tails, Rapalas, or other attractor spinners and bait such as night crawlers or eggs. Fly anglers fish the whole river with a combination of streamers, nymphs, and attractor dry flies. Streamers such as Zonkers and Woolly Buggers are particularly effective on brown trout. Fishing is permitted from a floating device.

Boating this stretch of river is quite popular in rafts and drift boats, but it requires a degree of expertise in all but the topmost section. Good, safe boating can be had from Harper Bridge (or above) downriver to the Benham Falls Campground (approximately six miles). This is an easy float through meadows and slow-moving water, productive for both browns and rainbows. Beyond Benham Falls Campground, for the next 14 miles, lies a series of challenging and often dangerous, even fatal, falls (Benham, Dillon, Big Eddy, Lava Island, and unnamed rapids below). A lot of improved and unimproved take-outs are in this stretch at parks and day-use areas such as Denham Falls, Slough Camp, Dillon Falls Campground, Lava Island Falls, Meadow Camp Picnic Area, and Mount Batchelor Village. This is also very good water to catch large brown and rainbow trout; however, access is limited to bank fishing at the parks, unless you have the experience to negotiate heavy water. Bank fishing is most convenient at the many boat ramps and day-use areas listed above. Most of these places have hiking trails to lead you up and down the river. Be cautious around Sunriver, below Harper Bridge on the east bank, and in the vicinity of Meadows Picnic Area, where private property dominates. In these areas, stick to the river below the high watermark and respect all private-property signs.

Species: Rainbow and brown trout, whitefish.

Facilities: Camping is available at LaPine State Park (year-round, full hookup and tent sites, on the Deschutes just north of La Pine. The park has hot showers and a park store that closes after Labor Day. Sunriver Resort offers a range of accommodations, as well as spas, golf, and the other accoutrements of the luxurious lifestyle. Several boat ramps are in this section. The Harper's Bridge ramp is unimproved and has no facilities, but it is free. The rest of these ramps—Besson, Benham Falls, Slough Camp, and Dillon Falls Camp—all have parking, improved ramps, and restrooms, and each requires a Northwest Forest Pass ($5 per day; $30 annually), which is available from most sporting goods or outdoors shops or from Nature of the Northwest in Portland. Supplies are available in Bend and La Pine.

Directions: From Bend, take Hwy. 97 19 miles south and turn right (west) onto LaPine State Recreation Rd., which leads 3.2 miles to LaPine State Park. As you head upstream, the ramps are, in order: For Dillon, travel 7.9 miles west on Cascade Lakes Hwy., then 2.6 miles south on Forest Rd. 41, 0.5 mile east on Rd. 4120, and one mile south on Rd. 4120–100. Slough is 0.7 mile farther along on the road. For the rest, take Hwy. 97 south from Bend. For Benham Falls, go 10.9 miles on Hwy. 97, then follow Forest Rd. 9702 west for four miles to the ramp. For Harper's Bridge and Besson, stay on Hwy. 97 for a total of 14 miles, then turn right (west) onto Century Dr., following signs for Sunriver. After two miles on Century Dr., turn right (west) onto Harper's Bridge Rd., which leads two miles to the bridge. To reach Besson ramp, drive across the bridge, go 0.5 mile, and turn right (north) on Besson Rd., which leads one mile to the ramp.

Contact: Central Oregon Visitors Association,

541/389-8799; Oregon Parks and Recreation Department, 800/551-6949; ODFW, Bend, 541/388-6363; Sunriver Resort, 800/801-8765; Bend–Fort Rock Ranger District, 541/388-5664.

30 UPPER DESCHUTES RIVER: LITTLE LAVA LAKE TO WICKIUP RESERVOIR

southwest of Bend

Map 5.5, page 323

The Deschutes originates at Little Lava Lake in the Deschutes National Forest, runs seven miles to Crane Prairie Reservoir, exits Crane Prairie, and flows another three miles into Wickiup Reservoir. The outlet of Wickiup forms the upper Deschutes. Keeping in character with the mountainous regions of Central Oregon, most of this water is lined with a mix of conifers and pines, meadows, and banks of tall grasses and wildflowers. The water runs cool and clear, and the riverbeds are gravel-lined, perfect for spawning habitat. Both sections of the river are small and easily waded, so neither requires a boat.

Rainbow trout throughout this stretch range 8–12 inches but get as big as 18 inches. Brook trout are small, 10 inches, but feisty. The river below Little Lava Lake produced the state record brook trout of nine pounds, six ounces, but this is considered an anomaly and not what anglers should expect. Brown trout are present, especially between Crane Prairie and Wickiup, and they average 12–14 inches but get as big as 18 inches. Both stretches of river are restricted to artificial flies and lures only, but each has different seasons and retention limits. The area between Wickiup and Crane Prairie is open for fishing May 27–August 31 and has the standard limit of two fish per day. The upper reach between Little Lava Lake and Crane Prairie is open May 27–September 30 and is catch-and-release only.

There is no need to get fancy on this water. Simple dry flies such as an Adams and Humpy will take smaller fish all day. Nymphs and streamers are always productive, especially the latter if you want to catch the bigger browns that inhabit the river. Streamers such as Zonkers and Woolly Buggers will imitate small baitfish. Lures such as Rooster Tails in various colors, especially reds and white, are very effective.

Because the river is flowing through Forest Service lands, access is unlimited but not well organized. Bushwhacking from roads is perhaps your best option, but there are a few campground access points on both stretches. The upper section between Little Lava Lake and Crane Prairie is accessible from the Lava Lake Outlet, Mile Camp, Deschutes Bridge on Forest Rd. 4270, and at Cow Meadow Campground near Crane Prairie. Forest Rd. 46 parallels the river, and anglers can park on the side of the road and bushwhack their way to the river. The river between Crane Prairie and Wickiup is accessible along Forest Rd. 42 and at Sheep Bridge Campground.

Species: Rainbow, brown, and brook trout.

Facilities: Four Forest Service campgrounds lie along this stretch of the river, three of which also have boat ramps onto reservoirs. Little Lava Lake (Apr.–Oct., $8 per vehicle) has 12 sites and a boat ramp. Deschutes Bridge (Aug–Oct., $5 per vehicle) has 12 sites and drinking water. Cow Meadow (May–Oct., $5 per vehicle), on Crane Prairie Reservoir, has 21 sites and a boat ramp. Sheep Bridge is on Wickiup Reservoir and has a ramp and 23 sites. Despite its name, Mile Camp isn't a camp. It's a free picnic area with restrooms along the river. Supplies are available in Bend and La Pine.

Directions: From Bend, drive southwest on the Cascade Lakes Hwy., also known as Forest Rd. 46. For Little Lava Lake, go 38.4 miles on Rd. 46, then 0.7 mile east on Rd. 4600–500 and 0.4 mile east on Rd. 4600–520. For Mile Camp, go 40.4 miles on Rd. 46. For Deschutes Bridge, travel 41.1 miles on Rd. 46. And for Cow Meadow, drive 44.7 miles on Rd. 46, then 0.4 mile east on Forest Rd. 40 and two miles south on Rd. 4000–970.

For Sheep Bridge, go 26.8 miles south from Bend on Hwy. 97 to Wickiup Junction, then 11 miles west on Forest Rd. 43. Turn west on Rd. 42 for 4.6 miles, then go 0.8 mile south on Rd. 4260.

Contact: Central Oregon Visitors Association, 541/389-8799; Bend–Fort Rock Ranger District, 541/388-5664; ODFW, Bend, 541/388-6363.

🕱 CULTUS LAKE
near Bend in the Cascade Lakes Basin
Map 5.5, page 323

When Oregon anglers want to catch big mackinaw or lake trout, one of the places they go is Cultus Lake, 50 miles southwest of Bend. Scenic Cultus, with its sparking blue waters sprawled amid the deeply forested Cascade Mountains, is a 791-acre lake with depths to 200 feet. It sits higher than most lakes in the basin, at an elevation of 4,688 feet. Few anglers will dispute either the scenic or fishing quality of Cultus. Cultus is known for its mackinaw lake trout, which grow to anywhere from 12 inches to 20 pounds, but it also has decent populations of both wild and stocked rainbow and brook trout. Rainbow and brook trout average on the small side at 8–12 inches, but there are plenty of bigger fish up to 20 inches. The lake is open all year, barring heavy snows that can block passage. All methods of fishing are permitted, including bait.

Cultus is best fished starting in May, a few weeks after it thaws. Boat anglers try to catch the larger mackinaw in shallower water along shorelines and the edges of any remaining ice. This is also a good time to fish for the larger rainbows with small leech and baitfish patterns. Starting in July, mackinaw retreat to the colder depths in the deepest parts of the lake, 125–200 feet of water. Typical methods for getting deep include either weighted lead-core line or downriggers. The best lures are those representing baitfish such as a Flatfish, and a flasher or dodger. Jigs fished directly on top of fish have also been known to work. The abundant stocked rainbows are fun to catch in the lake's shallower water, around shorelines, with flies, spinners, and bait. Boats are useful for trout fishing, but good catches can be made from shore and from float tubes, canoes, and kayaks.

Two boat ramps are available on the southeast shore in the vicinity of the lake's most popular water, the 200-foot lake trout holes. Cultus Lake Resort sits at the south end of the deepest trolling water. From here, anglers move northwest toward the mouth of the big bay on the north side of the lake. There are three campgrounds, all hike- or boat-in, supplying adequate bank access. A good hiking trail can be caught at Cultus Lake Campground; it follows the lake's most productive northern shoreline.

Species: Rainbow and brook trout, mackinaw.

Facilities: Cultus hosts some recreational boating and waterskiing. Families will enjoy the nice campgrounds, resort, and easy boating and fishing opportunities. Cultus Lake Resort has a lodge, restaurant, boat rentals, fuel, and store. The Forest Service operates the Cultus Lake Campground and day-use area (May–Sept., $12 per vehicle) at the southeast corner of the lake. The campground has 55 sites for tents, trailers, and RVs. The boat ramp is in the day-use area, which also has picnic tables. Parking in this area requires a Northwest Forest Pass ($5 per day; $30 annually), which is available from most sporting goods or outdoors shops or from Nature of the Northwest in Portland. The North Shore Coves and West Cultus campgrounds are accessible by boat or hiking trails, but parking requires a Northwest Forest Pass. Access is via the Winopee Lake Trail (No. 16), which runs along the north shore of the lake from Cultus Lake Campground. Supplies are available in Bend and La Pine.

Directions: From Bend, drive 46 miles south on the Cascade Lakes Hwy., also known as Forest Rd. 46. Turn west on Forest Rd. 4635, following a sign for the lake. Cultus Lake Resort is 1.8 miles down this road, and Cultus Lake Campground is 0.2 mile past it.

Contact: Central Oregon Visitors Association, 541/389-8799; Bend–Fort Rock Ranger District, 541/388-5664; ODFW, Bend, 541/388-6363; Cultus Lake Resort, 541/389-3230, www.cultuslakeresort.com.

32 LITTLE CULTUS LAKE
near Bend in the Cascade Lakes Basin
Map 5.5, page 323

Little Cultus Lake is a fair to good fishery for stocked rainbow and brook trout, and it offers an element of seclusion among more popular basin lakes such as Cultus Lake. Its beauty is similar to that of all the basin lakes, with dense conifer forests and mountain views. Little Cultus is open year-round, but fishing is best in spring and snow may deny access until then. It has 175 surface acres, and the deepest part of the lake, near the center, is 60 feet. All methods of fishing are permitted, including bait. Boating is popular, as is the use of float tubes, canoes, and kayaks. Boat anglers can launch at Little Cultus Campground on the south shore and troll in the lake's deep center or around the shorelines. Bank angling is good around the campgrounds and boat ramps. Other areas of the lake are very accessible, if off the beaten path. Most of the shoreline can be easily waded on shallow shoals extending into the lake.

Stocked rainbows average 8–12 inches, with some bigger fish up to 16 inches available. Brook trout populations are small, since they are no longer stocked, but anglers can still catch fish up to 16 inches. All methods of fishing work with bait such as night crawlers, eggs, and PowerBait being the most productive. Fish all bait close to the lake bottom. Trolling is also popular with flashers, lures, and flies. Use weighted lines or spit shot to achieve deeper levels. Fly anglers may stumble across the occasional mayfly or damsel hatch near the shorelines. Terrestrial patterns such as ants and grasshoppers can be fished against the bank during summer. Fish Woolly Buggers or other small leech or damsel patterns

on clear sinking line in deep water around the center of the lake.

Species: Stocked rainbow and brook trout.

Facilities: This is a good place for families with children who have the option of staying in an established campground or moving to one of the primitive sites around the southern end of the lake. The Forest Service campground here has 20 sites. It also offers a boat ramp, drinking water, and restrooms. Supplies are available in Bend and La Pine.

Directions: From Bend, drive 46 miles southwest on Cascade Lakes Hwy. (Forest Rd. 46). Turn west on Forest Rd. 4635 and go 0.8 mile, then go 1.7 miles south on Rd. 4630 and one mile west on Rd. 4636.

Contact: Central Oregon Visitors Association, 541/389-8799; Bend–Fort Rock Ranger District, 541/388-5664; ODFW, Bend, 541/388-6363; Cultus Lake Resort, 541/389-3230, www.cultuslakeresort.com.

33 CRANE PRAIRIE RESERVOIR
southwest of Bend in Cascade Lakes Basin
Map 5.5, page 323

Scenic Crane Prairie is surrounded by the spectacular sights and sounds of nature: vast, wide vistas of the central Cascade Mountains; rolling, forested foothills; abundant birdlife such as osprey, herons, bald eagles, and assorted waterfowl; and interesting lake features such as old forests emerging from the water. But amid the gentle breezes and distant cries of hawks, there stirs the restlessness of anglers not content with idyllic wanderings but with more serious pursuits in mind, namely, catching big trout. Crane Prairie can get busy. Crane Prairie is not a deep lake; it averages only 11 feet for most of its 4,161 surface acres and 22.3 miles of shoreline. There are some deeper holes, 20 feet or more, in isolated spots. The reservoir sits at almost 4,500 feet elevation and is fed by both natural springs and several significant tributaries, some of which create the many arms of the reservoir (Quinn

River, Rock Creek, Cultus, and Deschutes). The combination of creeks and springs means there's a generous supply of cold water favored by trout later in the season. The outlet of Crane Prairie forms the Deschutes River, which runs to Wickiup Reservoir.

Crane Prairie is open for fishing April 22– October 31, and all methods are permitted. Fishing must cease from one hour after sunset to one hour before sunrise. Trout are stocked annually in large numbers and they grow to tremendous size—five pounds or more—very quickly. Trout average 10–16 inches; 18-inch fish are caught regularly, and fish up to 10 pounds are taken every year. Brook trout, no longer stocked, are not common but can show up in catches and have been known to reach five pounds or more. Largemouth bass, 3–5 pounds, are present in thriving numbers. Kokanee are present and well established and best fished for in spring and fall around tributary mouths such as the Deschutes.

Boaters have a much easier time than bank anglers, with the latter being restricted to campgrounds and boat launches. Boats can be launched from four ramps. Float tubes are a good option if you don't have to paddle much to get into productive water. Float tubers should launch at Quinn River, Rock Creek, or near the resort for the best and quickest fishing opportunities. Canoes are a popular, effective, and peaceful method of moving around the lake. Those with serious intentions and wishing to escape crowds altogether can do so with a small outboard. Boats with motors are allowed, but there is a 10 mph speed limit.

Some of the best and most popular fishing times are in April, just after the lake opens, barring heavy snowfalls that may prevent passage. Early in the season the trout are fairly spread out, so good fishing can be found almost anywhere, except in the colder river channels. Fishing the grassy areas or shorelines with cast-and-retrieve tactics is especially effective. As the summer progresses and the lake water warms, fish will congregate around springs and in old river channels, where the water is considerably cooler. Most of the fishing this time of year takes place in the eastern and northeastern parts of the lake around the Rock Creek Channel, Quinn Channel, Cultus Creek and River channels, and the Deschutes Arm. A lot of these places are denoted by old timber stands sticking out of the water. Fishing is often good in these areas, as they provide safe habitat and an abundance of insects and baitfish for trout to feed on.

Aquatic insects such as scuds, damsels, dragonfly and mayfly nymphs, caddis leeches, water beetles, as well as small baitfish all make up a trout's diet. Fly anglers have the advantage of imitating many of these food forms with dry flies, nymphs, and streamers. Standard fishing techniques include Woolly Buggers or Seal Buggers in various shades; olive, brown, red (maroon), and black with mixed colors are best and can be fished exclusively most of the time. Nymphs such as Pheasant Tails and Hare's Ears work well but require a little more patience to draw a reaction from a passing fish. Dry flies should not be overlooked, especially during hatches of *Callibaetis,* caddis, and damsel flies. The largemouth bass fishery should also not be ignored, and good action can be had with surface poppers. Spin and bait anglers do very well on Crane Prairie. Because of the shallow lake depths, trolling is not popular; instead, anglers will cast and retrieve Rooster Tails, Panther Martins, Rapalas, and other baitfish-type lures. Bait anglers do best with night crawlers, grubs, and PowerBait fished under a float and kept off the bottom. Fish the same areas as fly anglers, amid the forest remnants and around the creek channels. Fish for bass with surface lures, crankbaits, or plastic worms.

Species: Rainbow and brook trout, largemouth bass, kokanee.

Facilities: There are four Forest Service campgrounds, a resort, and a total of six ramps that service Crane Prairie Reservoir—all of them operated by the Forest Service, except for Crane Prairie Resort. The full-service Crane

Prairie Resort (Apr.–Oct.) has boat rentals, fuel, a store with fishing tackle, camping, and an RV park. Its showers and laundry are open to the public. Crane Prairie Campground has 146 sites and a boat ramp. The ramp is in a day-use area and requires a Northwest Forest Pass ($5 per day; $30 annually), available from most sporting goods or outdoors shops or from Nature of the Northwest in Portland. Quinn River has 41 sites, drinking water, and restrooms. A Northwest Forest Pass is required. Rock Creek has 31 sites, drinking water, and restrooms. A Northwest Forest Pass is required. Cow Meadow Campground has 21 sites and a free boat ramp. Brown's Mountain (no fee) day-use area has a ramp, parking, and restrooms.

Directions: From Bend, drive southwest on Cascade Lakes Hwy. (Forest Rd. 46). To reach Crane Prairie Resort and Crane Prairie Campground, turn left (east) after 40 miles onto Century Dr. and follow it seven miles to Forest Rd. 4270, which leads 3.4 miles south to the lake. Quinn River is on Rd. 46, 48 miles from Bend. Rock Creek is on Rd. 46, 50 miles from Bend. For Cow Meadow campground, travel 45 miles on Rd. 46, then turn left (east) on Forest Rd. 40. Follow Rd. 40 for 0.4 mile, then turn right (south) onto Rd. 4000–970, which leads two miles to the campground. For the Brown's Mountain ramp, travel three miles past Rock Creek Campground (or 53 miles from Bend) to Rd. 42, then follow it east for four miles to Brown Mountain Rd., which leads one mile north to the ramp.

Contact: Central Oregon Visitors Association, 541/389-8799; Bend–Fort Rock Ranger District, 541/388-5664; ODFW, Bend, 541/388-6363; Crane Prairie Resort, 541/383-3939, www.crane-prairie-resort-guides.com.

34 TWIN LAKES
near Bend in Cascade Lakes Basin
Map 5.5, page 323

As the name implies, these are two almost identical lakes that sit adjacent to each other a half mile from Wickiup Reservoir. North Twin, the less developed and popular of the two, is 130 acres and offers fair fishing for rainbow trout 8–12 inches. South Twin offers slightly bigger catches, 10–14 inches, with 18-inch fish common; fish up to 13 pounds have been recorded. South Twin also has two campgrounds and a small resort with boat rentals and cabins. Both lakes have a maximum depth of 60 feet, deep enough to house bigger trout, and both offer a degree of solitude amid ponderosa pine forests away from the angling pressure on Wickiup. The twins are also good places to retreat to when the winds start picking up. North Twin is open all year, and South Twin is open April 22–October 31. All methods of fishing are permitted. Boats are permitted, but not motors. Anything more than a small rowboat, canoe, pontoon boat, or float tube is not necessary.

Flies, bait, and lures all work with equal success. Both lakes produce an abundance of insects, including scuds, mayflies, damsel and dragonflies, and caddis. Patterns to match any of these insects in either nymph or adult stages are productive. There are perhaps even better opportunities to use terrestrial patterns such as ants, beetles, and grasshoppers. Spin anglers can use Rooster Tails cast and retrieved or trolled. Best baits are night crawlers and PowerBait floated off the bottom with a float. South Twin's deeper areas lie at the south end. Anglers can also troll the weed beds along the north shore. North Twin's deepest waters are on the west shore, and this gets most of the attention from trollers and bank anglers. Both lakes offer unlimited bank access and can be easily walked, especially in summer when water levels decline. A short hiking trail connects the two lakes. Both lakes are great for families with small children learning how to fish.

Species: Stocked rainbow trout.

Facilities: The Forest Service operates three campgrounds at Twin Lakes. The North Twin campground has 19 sites and a free boat ramp, but no drinking water. South Twin Campground has restrooms, drinking water, and 26 sites. Its boat ramp is in the day-use area, where parking requires a Northwest Forest Pass ($5 per day; $30 annually), available from most sporting goods or outdoors shops or from Nature of the Northwest in Portland. West South Twin Campground also has a boat ramp, but it leads onto Wickiup Reservoir. It has 24 campsites, restrooms, and drinking water. Twin Lakes Resort, on South Twin Lake, has a lodge, store, restaurant, cabins, fuel, boat rentals, showers, RV park with full hookups, and laundry. South Twin Lake also has developed hiking and mountain-biking trails. Supplies are available in Bend and La Pine.

Directions: From Bend, drive 26.8 miles south on Hwy. 97 to Wickiup Junction, then turn west on Forest Rd. 43 for 11 miles. Turn west onto Forest Rd. 42 and follow it 4.6 miles, then turn south on Rd. 4260. You'll reach North Twin Campground in 0.2 mile and the two South Twin campgrounds in two miles.

Contact: Central Oregon Visitors Association, 541/389-8799; Bend-Fort Rock Ranger District, 541/388-5664; ODFW, Bend, 541/388-6363; Twin Lakes Resort, 541/593-6526.

35 WICKIUP RESERVOIR
near Bend in Cascade Lakes Basin

Map 5.5, page 323   BEST (

Wickiup, the largest of the Cascade Basin Lakes, comprises 10,000 surface acres and 51 miles of shoreline. It offers good fishing for kokanee and trophy brown trout and, to a lesser extent, rainbow trout, large whitefish, and largemouth bass. There is much to behold here, with scenic vistas of the Cascades, rolling hills of ponderosa pine forests, and much birdlife such as bald eagles, blue herons, and sandhill cranes. The average lake depth is a manageable 25 feet, and the deepest point is 70 feet near the center and the dam. The lake is made up of one large body of water and two significant arms, the Davis and Deschutes. The arms emerge from the west shore and converge at the lake's center, where they push to

the dam. This area between the convergence (difficult to identify without a depth finder) and the dam is the deepest part of the lake. The outflow at the dam on the east shore forms the highly productive and beautiful Upper Deschutes.

The reservoir is home to record-size brown trout and holds the former state record at 24 pounds, 14 ounces. Average catches are considerably smaller at 16–20 inches, but five- and six-pound fish are quite common. Popular lures for brown trout are small baitfish patterns such as Rapalas and flies, especially big streamers such as Muddlers. Kokanee are abundant and attract many anglers who troll the deepest waters with spinner or still fish with bait and jigs. Average catches range 12–18 inches. Rainbows are also available and often show up among anglers fishing for kokanee and brown trout; average catches of rainbows can be 2–7 pounds, or bigger. Whitefish run exceedingly large, 3–4 pounds, as do brook trout, which can reach five pounds. Bigmouth bass, increasing in popularity, are more common at the south end of the lake near Goose Island and run up to five pounds. Wickiup is open to all methods of fishing April 22–October 31. The Deschutes River Arm north of the South Twin boat ramp, at the ODFW marker, is closed to bait fishing and has a two-trout limit July 15–October 31. It is closed to all fishing September 1–October 31. Kokanee may be kept at 25 fish per day. Boats are allowed, but limited to 10 mph in the reservoir arms; there is no speed limit on the main body of the lake.

Wickiup is big and admittedly a hard place to find fish. Seasonal changes such as water temperatures, water levels, and spawning insects have a pronounced influence on where fish hold. Spring usually finds fish spread out through the entire lake. Likely holding spots can be anywhere, but the easiest to find are those around structure, shorelines, tributary mouths, or changes in the lake bottom. As summer progresses, fish will seek cool and/ or deeper water on the Deschutes and Davis channels, or in the lake arms. Spawning, a fall and early winter affair, also pushes fish up into the channels and is the reason for some of the closures in the Deschutes Arm. Rainbow trout are more prevalent in the Davis Arm than anywhere else. A majority of the brown trout and kokanee spawn in the Deschutes Arm. This is primarily a boat fishery, with some good opportunities for bank fishing around the dam, boat launches, channels, and campgrounds. In spring and fall, bank fishing is good at Gull Point and along the Deschutes channel across from South Twin Lake. The dam also has good fishing most of the year. Bait is the best option when fishing in the main lake anywhere from the bank. Flies and lures can be effective in the Deschutes and Davis river channels.

Species: Brown and rainbow trout, kokanee, whitefish, largemouth bass.

Facilities: Families can take advantage of nice campgrounds, a resort with boat and fishing-supply rentals, and nice drives into the surrounding areas for glimpses of mountain summits and smaller lakes and rivers. Six campgrounds, each with a boat ramp and restrooms, service this large lake: Wickiup Butte with eight sites, no drinking water; Gull Point with 81 sites; West South Twin Campground 24 sites; Sheep Bridge has 23 sites; North Davis Creek has 15 sites; and Reservoir has 28 sites and no drinking water.

Directions: From Bend, take Hwy. 97 south 27 miles to Wickiup Junction, then turn west on Forest Rd. 43. To reach Wickiup Butte, travel 10.4 miles west on Rd. 43, then 3.6 miles south on Forest Rd. 4380, and then east on Rd. 4260 for three miles. For Gull Point, West South Twin, and Sheep Bridge, go 11 miles on Rd. 43 to Rd. 42, then travel west on Rd. 42 for 4.6 miles. Turn south on Rd. 4260, and you'll reach Sheep Bridge in 0.8 mile, West South Twin in two miles, and Gull Point in three miles. For North Davis Creek and Reservoir, it's best to follow Cascade Lakes Hwy. (Forest Rd. 46) southwest from Bend. North Davis Creek is on that highway in 56

miles. For Reservoir, go 58 miles on Rd. 46, then 1.7 miles east on Forest Rd. 44.

Contact: Central Oregon Visitors Association, 541/389-8799; Bend–Fort Rock Ranger District, 541/388-5664; ODFW, Bend, 541/388-6363.

36 UPPER DESCHUTES RIVER: WICKIUP RESERVOIR TO SUNRIVER

southwest of Bend

Map 5.5, page 323

This is some of the most productive and scenic water on the upper Deschutes. The river here is idyllic, composed of gentle, meandering currents slipping through soft, green meadows, shady forests of ponderosa pine, and scenic backdrops of mountains and hills. The scene is even more exciting when one considers there are lunker brown trout, 15 pounds plus, lurking under cut banks. Even average catches of browns here are impressive, ranging 14–18 inches and more. Rainbows occasionally get big, but seem stunted (10–14 inches) compared to the brown trout. Trout season is open May 27–October 31, and there is a five-trout limit, of which two can be wild and non–fin-clipped. All methods of fishing are permitted, including bait. Fishing from a floating device is allowed. Motors may be used but are unnecessary, and there is a 5 mph speed limit. The most suitable craft here are drift boats, canoes, and kayaks.

The first eight miles of river below Wickiup Dam flows through public lands and offers excellent opportunities to catch large brown trout and average rainbows. Both sides of the river are accessible from dirt roads, Forest Road 4370 on the west bank and Forest Road 600 on the east. Don't expect to do too much wading here, as the deeply undercut banks fall off sharply into deep water. Walking in this area is a problem without waders or hip boots to get through swampy areas. Fish are equally scattered throughout the river. Fish from shore with streamers and nymphs or dry flies if there is an insect hatch. To catch the big browns use minnow pattern flies or lures such as Woolly Buggers and Zonkers or Rainbow Rooster Tails. Fish them deep and on the swing. Try stripping your flies or lures back up the bank. Bait such as grubs or night crawlers work when cast and drifted down currents and along the edges of shorelines.

Tenino boating ramp is two miles downstream from the dam on the east bank and is the highest official put-in. Smaller cartop boats may also be launched from below the dam and add 1.5 miles to the drift. From Tenino, anglers can float downriver to takeouts at Bull Bend Campground (5.5 miles) and Wyeth Campground (6.5 miles). Before you reach Wyeth Campground there are signs warning of the upcoming Pringle Falls, a short distance below Wyeth Campground. Do not attempt Pringle Falls; instead, pull out at Wyeth. Likewise, drift boats should avoid the water between Pringle Falls and Tetherow Logjam, four miles downriver, but smaller craft capable of being portaged around the logjam are OK. Drift boats can launch again below the Tetherow Logjam.

Two popular floats are from Tetherow to Big River Campground (12 miles) and from Big River to Harper's Bridge near Sunriver (11 miles). Fall River and Little Deschutes flow into each of these stretches. Some anglers will stop and fish the mouths of these two rivers or even push up them a way with electric motors or by rowing. These two lower floats are particularly easy and popular with both enthusiasts and Bend/Sunriver fishing guides.

Species: Rainbow and brown trout.

Facilities: Camping is available at LaPine State Park, on the Deschutes just north of La Pine. The park has hot showers and a park store that closes after Labor Day. The Deschutes National Forest also operates four campgrounds in the area. Bull Bend has 12 sites and a boat ramp; Wyeth has three sites and a ramp; Pringle Falls has six sites and no ramp; Big River has six sites and a ramp, but no drinking water. Sunriver Resort offers a range of accommodations, as well as spas and golf. Both the Tenino and Tetherow ramps are improved and have

free parking and restrooms. Supplies are available in Bend and La Pine.

Directions: From Bend, head 17.3 miles south on Hwy. 97, then 7.9 miles west on Forest Rd. 42 to Big River Campground. For Harper's Bridge, take Hwy. 97 for 14 miles, turn right onto Century Dr., following signs for Sunriver. After two miles on Century Dr., turn right onto Harper's Bridge Rd., which leads two miles to the bridge. For Tetherow, head 26.8 miles south on Hwy. 97 to Wickiup Junction, then turn west on Rd. 43. Go 5.2 miles west on Rd. 43, then 2.6 miles north on Rd. 4330 and a mile north on Rd. 4330–600.

Contact: Central Oregon Visitors Association, 541/389-8799; Oregon Parks and Recreation Department, 800/551-6949; Nature of the Northwest, 503/872-2750, www.naturenw.org; Bend–Fort Rock Ranger District, 541/388-5664; ODFW, Bend, 541/388-6363.

37 LITTLE DESCHUTES
south of Bend

Map 5.5, page 323

The Little Deschutes is a very long, slow, meandering tributary of the Deschutes originating near Crescent Lake and flowing 100 miles, much of it through lush willow valleys, to its confluence. While the river holds good populations of rainbow, brook, and brown trout, there are a few drawbacks. Ninety percent of the river is on private property, limiting access to the uppermost reaches, road crossings, or requiring permission from local landowners. The river also gets dangerously low below Crescent from summer irrigation draws. The river is open May 27–October 31 and all methods of fishing are permitted, including bait. The two best access points are at Rosland Recreation Area a few miles north of La Pine near Highway 97. The river is also accessible on Forest Service lands above Crescent, and at a small parcel of BLM land on State Park Road, which leads from Highway 97 to LaPine State Park. Forest Road 5825 follows the river between Crescent Cutoff Road west of Crescent and

Highway 58. The river crossings at Crescent and at Highway 58 offer more access from the roadside, and Forest Road 300 will take you into the headwaters above Highway 58. While the river is legally floatable, there are no put-in or take-out points within reasonable distance of each other.

Species: Rainbow, brown, and brook trout.

Facilities: Contact the La Pine Parks and Recreation District for an update on the Rosland Recreation Area, which may include camping when reopened.

Directions: From Bend, follow Hwy. 97 south for 27 miles to Wickiup Junction, then travel west on Burgess Rd. about two miles to where it crosses the Little Deschutes. Rosland Recreation Area is on the west bank, south of the road. To reach the upper stretches of the river, take Hwy. 97 south of La Pine for 17 miles to Crescent. Travel west on Crescent Cutoff Rd. (which crosses the river at Crescent). After 0.5 mile, turn south on Forest Rd. 11, which loops along the river for about three miles and then back to Crescent Cutoff Rd. Following this road just under five miles west of Crescent, you'll come to unpaved Rd. 5825 heading south along the river to Hwy. 58, a drive of about six miles. South of Hwy. 58, Rd. 5825 roughly parallels the river for 1.5 miles to the tiny community of Mowich. From there, stay on Rd. 5825 for approximately 0.5 mile to Rd. 100, or Two Rivers Rd. Follow Two Rivers Rd. into the headwaters.

Contact: Central Oregon Visitors Association, 541/389-8799; Bend–Fort Rock Ranger District, 541/388-5664; La Pine Parks and Recreation District, 541/536-2223; ODFW, Bend, 541/388-6363.

38 EAST LAKE
southeast of Bend in Newberry National Volcanic Monument

Map 5.5, page 323

The national monument is home to two large, deep, and sumptuous lakes with great fishing, East and Paulina; both are situated in the Newberry Crater. East Lake offers some of the best fishing in Central Oregon, and the catches are the stuff of legend. Rainbow and brown trout, Atlantic salmon, and kokanee are all present in good numbers. Both brown and rainbow trout grow big here; some can span 20 inches or more, though average catches range 10–16 inches. The largest recorded brown trout caught here weighed 22 pounds, 8 ounces. Sister Lake Paulina holds the state record for biggest German brown at 28 pounds, 5 ounces.

East Lake covers 1,044 acres when full and has an average depth of 65 feet. The deepest point (180 feet) is at the lake's center and extends toward the north shore. There are 5.9 miles of shoreline, all accessible from good hiking trails. The season runs April 23–October 31. Anglers may keep a standard five fish per day, with only one being longer than 20 inches. Bait, flies, and lures are all allowed, as is boating with gas or electric motors.

The lake attracts a lot of fly anglers, and for good reasons. Float tubing and bank fishing are equally productive, and good starting places are around boat ramps and campgrounds. The areas around East Lake Resort and Hot Springs Campground both have good wading, float tubing, and bank access. The northwest corner of the lake also holds good populations of trout, and access can be had from either hiking trails or a boat. Anglers can wade into the chilly waters or use a float tube and cast out along shelves and drop-offs for most species except kokanee. During summer there are dependable hatches of *Callibaetis,* chironomids, and caddis. Match any of these insects with the appropriate dry fly, emerger, or nymph pattern. Wet flies such as Soft Hackles are good to fish under the hatch; strip line and raise your rod tip to imitate an emerging adult. Concentrate your fishing around shorelines and woody structure or wherever fish are rising. During off times when fish are not feeding on the surface, try full sinking lines with streamers such as Woolly Buggers, leeches, and Zonkers. Strip your streamers fast or slow, depending on what produces strikes. Anglers may need to fish streamers a bit deeper than expected during bright sunny days.

For brown trout, focus around woody structure, rocks, or places with deep shade, any place you think these shelter-loving fish may be hiding. Rainbows and Atlantic salmon are more commonly found in open waters, on flats and shelves, or cruising along the banks in search of food. Fish for Atlantic salmon the same way you fish for rainbows. Kokanee are a bit more difficult to catch on a fly, because they hang out in depths of 50–60 feet or more.

Bait and lure anglers can have a field day trolling the depths for all species of fish, especially kokanee. To fish for kokanee use either a downrigger setup or lots of weight to get deep. Some of the best areas to begin are near the north bank across from East Lake Campground. Anglers can start trolling at the rock cliffs and encircle the deeper water from east to west. A depth finder will help you discover pods of fish. Fish the south and east shores for brown trout near East Lake Resort and Hot Springs Campground. Stay a couple of hundred feet offshore when trolling, and fish the banks when casting. Cast gold and silver spinners and Rapalas close to the bank during low-light hours and around structure and in deep water during the day. Rainbows take a variety of lures and attractor setups. Fish lures such as Rooster Tails or Mepps with a little color; work the shorelines or troll your lures behind the boat. Attractor setups with Ford Fenders, Dodgers, and Jack-O-Diamonds are good, but use a long leader (four feet or more) and a smaller lure in the clear waters. Fishing with bait is productive and popular, especially with kids. Try worms, cheese, or PowerBait for good results, and keep the bait suspended just off the bottom under a bobber. Some depth adjustment may be necessary for catching different species.

A health advisory has been issued for East Lake Reservoir because of very high levels of mercury. Contact the Oregon Department of Human Services for more information.

Species: Rainbow and brown trout, Atlantic salmon, and kokanee.

Facilities: There is a plethora of attractions and activities in the park: geological wonders such as Big Obsidian Flow and Lava River Cave, self-guided tours on hiking trails, numerous waterfalls, mountain peaks, and smaller rivers, as well as mountain-biking, hiking, sightseeing, and wildlife-viewing. Camping and boat ramps are available at East Lake, Hot Springs, East Lake Resort, and Cinder Hill campgrounds. Facilities include restrooms, drinking water, day-use areas, and picnic grounds. A general store at Paulina Lake Resort (three miles west on Forest Rd. 21) provides limited supplies and fishing guides. Supplies, accommodations, fly shops, and sporting goods stores can be had in Bend, La Pine, and Sunriver.

Directions: From Bend, drive 20 miles south on Hwy. 97 to the Newberry Crater turnoff. Turn east on paved Forest Rd. 21 and drive 17 miles, passing the entrance to Paulina Lake, to any one of the campgrounds along East Lake.

Contact: La Pine Chamber of Commerce, 541/536-9771; Bend Chamber of Commerce, 541/382-3221; Deschutes National Forest, 541/383-5300; ODFW, Bend, 541/388-6363; Oregon Department of Human Services, 503/731-4012; Lava Lands Visitor Center, 541/593-2421; The Hook in Sunriver, 541/593-2358; Numb-butt Fly Shop, 888/248-8309; Big 5 Sporting Goods, 541/385-3091; G.I. Joe's, Bend, 541/388-3770; Fly and Field Outfitters, 541/318-1616.

39 PAULINA LAKE

southeast of Bend in Newberry National Volcanic Monument

Map 5.5, page 323   BEST (

Paulina Lake shares the volcanic caldera with the equally productive East Lake. Both lakes are capable of growing trophy species of trout and kokanee that will challenge even the most seasoned of anglers. Paulina Lake has held state-record catches of brown trout since 1965. The last record catch was made in 2002 when a 28-pound, 5-ounce behemoth was successfully landed. Other record catches here include kokanee, the last of which was 4 pounds, 2 ounces; that record has since been superseded by another fishery. There have been no record catches of rainbows, but fish up to 12 pounds are common. Catching record-size fish says very little about an angler's skill, but it says a lot about their luck and the amount of time they spend on the water. There are very few well-known anglers with record catches under their belts, so there is always the chance that you could be the next one. For regular anglers who wear the occasional hip boot or Gore-Tex wader, even average catches at Paulina are impressive. Rainbow and brown trout run big. Kokanee catches average 12–18 inches, but 24-inch fish are common. Rainbows and browns are caught anywhere 12–30 inches and as fat as 10 pounds. The cold, deep, rich waters of Paulina enable fish to reach such impressive size. The lake covers approximately 1,300 acres and is 250 feet deep near its center. Average depths are an impressive 170 feet, almost 2.5 times the average depth of East Lake. There are seven miles of shoreline, all accessible by good hiking trails and some boat-in-only campgrounds. Paulina adheres to the regular fishing season and is open April 23–October 31. Five fish may be kept per day, only one longer than 20 inches.

Fishing at Paulina adheres to two main rules: Fish shallow in the cool months and deeper in the hot months. Most spring and fall angling takes place around the edges of the lake, where fish tend to congregate along weed beds around the lake perimeter. Fishing within 35 feet of the bank is all that's required for catching most species. In the summer, fish move into the deeper waters (30–60 feet) during the day and return to shallower waters during evening and morning times. The only exception is kokanee, which tend to hang out in the deepest parts of the lake most of the summer. A good depth finder can be a real asset for finding schools of fish, taking out the guesswork required on such a large body of water.

Trolling with flashers is by far the most popular way to fish Paulina. Fishing with bait and flies is also popular but those methods don't catch the numbers of big fish that trollers get. Fly anglers will have a difficult time and are better off traveling over to East Lake for better opportunities. Still, Paulina does hold some promise for fly anglers in the shallower waters around the resort, at Paulina Lake Campground, and near the north and northeast shores. Dry flies are effective during hatches of *Callibaetis,* midges, and damsels. Nymphs and streamers are effective around weed beds and structure. Scuds, leeches, water beetles, minnows, and mayfly nymphs all make up the diet of Paulina trout. Bait anglers can fish the same waters as the fly anglers and have better opportunities from a boat along the edges of the shore. Worms, PowerBait, and cheese all work. Fish with a weighted rig that keeps the bait a foot or two off the bottom, or suspend the bait under a bobber.

Species: Rainbow trout, brown trout, kokanee.

Facilities: Camping and boat ramps can be had on the south shore at Paulina Lake Resort, Paulina Campground, and Little Crater Campground. Two hike-in or boat-in campgrounds are on the north shore at Warm Springs and North Cove. Newberry Group Campground on the south shore is available by reservation only. A horse camp is available at Chief Paulina Campground. A general store provides limited supplies and fishing guides at Paulina Lake Resort. More supplies, accommodations, fly shops, and sporting goods stores can be had in Bend, La Pine, and Sunriver.

Directions: From Bend, drive 20 miles south on Hwy. 97 to the Newberry Crater turnoff. Turn east on paved Forest Rd. 21 and drive 14 miles to the first of many campgrounds. To reach East Lake, continue driving east three miles on the forest road.

Contact: La Pine Chamber of Commerce, 541/536-9771; Bend Chamber of Commerce, 541/382-3221; Deschutes National Forest, 541/383-5300; ODFW, Bend, 541/388-6363; Lava Lands Visitor Center, 541/593-2421; The Hook in Sunriver, 541/593-2358; Numb-butt Fly Shop, 888/248-8309; Big 5 Sporting Goods, 541/385-3091; G.I. Joe's, Bend, 541/388-3770; Fly and Field Outfitters, 541/318-1616.

40 DAVIS LAKE

west of Crescent in Cascades Lakes Basin

Map 5.5, page 323

Davis Lake, a fly-fishing–only destination, has in years past been considered one of Oregon's premier trophy trout waters. In the last two decades it has been hit with droughts, fires, and intrusive populations of chub minnows, but is once again fishing well with good water years and the introduction of the Klamath strain of rainbows. Davis sits on the edge of the Cascade Lakes Basin, surrounded by scenic forests and vistas of the Cascade Mountains 10 miles south of Crane Prairie Reservoir. It is composed of 3,900 acres and has an average depth of nine feet. The deepest area of the lake is on the northeast shore near the lava flows. This is a good place for families, with excellent campgrounds and two boat ramps.

Davis is best fished from a boat, float tube, pontoon boat, or canoe to reach the most productive waters. Motors are allowed and make trolling a good option. Some good bank angling can be had near the deeper waters adjacent to the lava flows on the east shore, and around the Odell Creek Arm on the south shore; otherwise most shorelines are too shallow to fish from the bank. Barbless hooks are required on all flies.

Davis's Klamath rainbows are known for their size, and 5–6-pound fish are quite common. Klamath rainbows love to forage around tules, eating dragonfly nymphs, leeches, and small baitfish. They are also known to take advantage of most insect hatches, and there are plenty here. *Callibaetis* and caddis are present, as are other minor mayfly hatches. Anglers heading to Davis in May and June should have an assortment of dragonfly and damsel dry flies, both of which hatch in abundance around grassy areas. Streamers such as Seal Buggers and Zonkers are good go-to flies almost anytime of year, with black, brown, maroon, and olive being the best colors.

The fish in Davis Lake tend to move around, seeking warmer water in the spring and cooler water in the summer. Klamath rainbows in particular are very consistent when it comes to seeking cooler water in the summer and will be almost absent from colder areas early in the season. Before the summer heat you will find rainbows scattered throughout the lake, particularly along shallow shorelines and among tules. Early in the season start fishing along the banks west and east of Odell Creek. Concentrate your fishing around patches of aquatic grasses. When casting in grassy areas get as close to the edge as possible—even in the grass; landing your fly with a thud is sometimes productive. In most cases start stripping immediately, and if there is a fish in the vicinity it should strike within the first few strips. A few feet off the bank can make a difference between fish and no fish. When the hot weather sets in, focus on the inlets and springs around tributaries such as Odell Creek at the southernmost end, and Ranger and Moore creeks along the west shore. Also try the deeper waters near the lava flow on the northeast bank. Davis also has a reputation for producing big largemouth bass, up to six pounds, which can be found in the coves and bays or anywhere structure is present. Flies and surface poppers can induce violent strikes.

Species: Klamath rainbows, largemouth bass.

Facilities: East Davis Campground has drinking water, toilets, an unimproved ramp, and 30 sites. South Lava Flow Campground has six sites and vault toilets but neither drinking water nor garbage service. As of 2006, North Lava Flow Campground was still in a primitive state (six no-fee sites with a pit toilet but no drinking water or garbage service); the Forest Service hopes to redevelop it in 2007, so call the Crescent Ranger District for up-to-date information. The West Davis boat ramp is free.

Directions: From Crescent, travel 8.8 miles west on County Rd. 61 (Crescent Cutoff Rd.), then turn north on Forest Rd. 46 for 7.7 miles to Rd. 4600–850. North Lava Campground is 0.2 mile down this road; South Lava Campground is 1.8 miles; East Davis is 2.6 miles. For the West Davis boat ramp, leave Rd. 46 after just 3.4 miles, heading west on Forest Rd. 4660. After three miles on Rd. 4660, go north on Forest Rd. 4669 for two miles.

Contact: ODFW, Bend, 541/388-6363; Central Oregon Visitors Association, 541/389-8799; Crescent Ranger District, 541/433-3200.

41 ODELL LAKE

west of Crescent in Deschutes National Forest

Map 5.5, page 323

Odell is managed as a trophy fishery for mackinaw and draws anglers from all over the state to take a shot at catching the next state record (Odell holds the current record at 40 pounds, 8 ounces, from 1984). You'll need three tools when visiting Odell Lake: a boat, a depth finder, and a downrigger. This is a big, deep lake, with 3,582 surface acres, 13 miles of shoreline, and an average depth of 120 feet. The deepest part of the lake is in the southern half. The shorelines are composed of thick mixed conifer forests and dense underbrush; this provides scenic interest, but it makes bank fishing very difficult anywhere but at the resort and campgrounds. Mackinaw are predators; as such they are caught on lures that imitate small baitfish, rainbow trout, kokanee, and whitefish. Most anglers troll Flatfish and Rapala-type lures using downrigger setups to get to depths of 100

to 200 feet. Popular starting points are almost always alongside the deeper waters in the southern half of the lake. Boat launches at Princess Creek and the Odell Lake Resort are convenient places to begin trolling the edges of deeper water on the northeast and southwest shores.

Aside from the gigantic mackinaw (8–9 pounds), Odell offers decent catches of kokanee and rainbow trout. Kokanee average 10–12 inches but have been known to reach 20 inches or more. Successful kokanee fishing usually requires knowing where the fish are and at what depth. The north shore above Princess Creek Campground is the most productive area. Anglers use jigs or troll with flashers trailing a small bit of corn or small bait such as worms or grubs. Early spring will find fish in shallower water, 12–35 feet, and in the summer they'll be around 100 feet. In fall, September, kokanee begin to move into shallower water for their annual spawn and can be fished before they move into the tributaries. All tributaries into Odell are off-limits to fishing.

Rainbow trout average 12–16 inches, and fish longer than 20 inches are caught every year. While they can be found scattered all over the lake, a few good starting places are near the resort and the start of Odell Creek and to the north and south of Pebble Bay Campground along the shorelines. Trolling is effective, as are spinners such as Rooster Tails and basic flies such as Woolly Buggers, Zonkers, and other baitfish or leech-type patterns. The best bank fishing is around the Odell Lake Lodge and at each of the campgrounds and boat ramps.

Odell is open for fishing April 22–October 31. All methods of fishing are permitted, including bait. Bull trout cannot be targeted and must be released unharmed. Twenty-five kokanee can be retained per day in addition to other fish limits. Fishing is illegal within 200 feet of Trapper Creek. Also, all other tributaries flowing into Odell are closed to fishing. Odell Creek near the Odell Lake Lodge is open to catch-and-release fly-fishing only May 27–October 31 and provides fair fishing for rainbow trout.

Species: Mackinaw, rainbow trout, kokanee, bull trout.

Facilities: Odell Lake Lodge (year-round), at the east end of the lake, has a general store, lodge, restaurant, cabins, fuel, boat rentals, ski rentals, fishing tackle, mountain-bike rentals, boat launch, boat moorage, groomed cross-country skiing trails, and a fishing guide. Shelter Cove Resort (year-round), at the west end, has a general store, cabins, camping, and boat moorage, ramp and rentals. There are four Forest Service campgrounds at Odell, all with drinking water and restrooms. Odell Creek Campground, adjacent to the lodge, has no hookup sites. Princess Creek Campground has 46 sites, but also has no hookups. It does have a boat ramp, for which there's no extra charge. Sunset Cove Campground has a boat ramp and 20 sites (no hookups). Trapper Creek Campground has a boat ramp and 32 sites.

Directions: From Crescent, drive west on County Rd. 61, the Crescent Cutoff Rd. Follow this road 12.2 miles to Hwy. 58 and turn north. After 5.4 miles, follow the East Odell Lake Access Rd. to reach Odell Creek Campground and Odell Lake Lodge. For Sunset Cove Campground, go 6.2 miles north on Hwy. 58, and for Princess Creek go 6.2 miles on Hwy. 58, which in this area rounds the northern shore of Odell Lake. To reach Trapper Creek Campground and Shelter Cove, go 10.4 miles on Hwy. 58 (starting at County Rd. 61) and turn south on Forest Rd. 5810 (West Odell Lake Access Rd.). Trapper Creek is 1.9 miles down this road, and Shelter Cove is 2.2 miles.

Contact: Central Oregon Visitors Association, 541/389-8799; Odell Lake Lodge, 800/434-2540, www.odelllakeresort.com; Shelter Cove Resort, 800/647-2729, www.sheltercoveresort.com; Crescent Ranger District, 541/433-3200; ODFW, Bend, 541/388-6363.

42 CRESCENT LAKE

near Crescent in Deschutes National Forest

Map 5.5, page 323

Crescent Lake, along with Odell and Cultus lakes, is one of the most popular lakes in Oregon for trophy mackinaw that can reach up to 20 pounds or more. There are also good populations of kokanee and large brown trout, and some rainbows. Crescent is also popular with recreational boaters. With more than 4,500 surface acres and 12.4 miles of shoreline, there is room to accommodate everyone's needs. As with all lakes in this area, the shorelines are heavily forested, meaning they are scenic and peaceful but they also make bank access difficult except at campground and resort clearings.

Crescent Lake is open year-round, and there are no limits on fishing methods. Only one mackinaw of 30 inches or more may be retained. Crescent Lake runs deepest, approximately 265 feet, in the center. Average depths are 124 feet, and even the shorelines drop off quickly to 40 feet or more. A majority of the fishing takes place at the north end of the lake near the resort and along the southwest and southeast shores. This water is perfect for most of the popular species because of the multiple depths alongside the deepest water. Launching boats at Crescent Lake Campground, Crescent Lake Lodge, and Simax Campground will immediately put you in good water.

Mackinaw, the primary attraction at Crescent, average 5–10 pounds with some fish reaching 30 pounds. In the spring, these large predatory fish can be found in shallow water, 8–10 feet, near any remaining winter ice, and particularly near the resort at the north end of the lake. In summer, anglers have to begin trolling the edge of the deeper waters on the northwest shore near the summer homes. Ideal depths range 80–130 feet. Depth finders will assist greatly in finding lake-bottom features and fish. Some mackinaw fishing is also found on the southern shore between Rainbow Point and Contorta Flat Campground. Most mackinaw anglers troll baitfish patterns such as Flatfish and Rapalas colored to represent small whitefish, kokanee, or brown trout.

Kokanee, also a deep, cool-water dweller, average 12–14 inches but can reach 20 inches. Jig or troll waters 30–60 feet deep with small spinners or flashers and bait such as worms. Popular areas are just inside the best macki-naw water at the north end of the lake, out in front of the summer homes southwest of the resort, and on the southeast shore near the Simax Beach Campground. Rainbow and brown trout are present in respectable numbers and can grow to good size. Both are popular sport among fly anglers in float tubes fishing the shorelines and spin anglers fishing from the bank. Early season is a good time to catch trout on bait such as eggs, night crawlers, and PowerBait from the many campgrounds and boat ramps.

Species: Mackinaw, rainbow and brown trout, kokanee, whitefish.

Facilities: Crescent Lake Lodge and Resort (year-round) offers fishing tackle, mountain-bike rentals, general store, a restaurant, boat rentals, fuel, boat moorage, and fishing guide service. The Crescent Ranger District of De-schutes National Forest runs three campgrounds at the lake. Crescent Lake Campground also has a boat ramp, drinking water, and restrooms; its 47 sites each have fire pits and tables. Spring Campground also has a ramp, but there's a $3 day-use fee to use it; it has 68 sites, none with hookups. Contorta Flat Campground has 18 sites but no drinking water. There is also an unimproved boat ramp at Tranquil Cove, one of several day-use areas around the lake. This is the best ramp to use when the water level is low. It has restrooms but no drinking water, and there's no fee to use it.

Directions: From Crescent, drive 12.2 miles west on Rd. 61, then 3.5 miles north on Hwy. 58. Turn west onto Rd. 60. For the lodge and resort, go 2.2 miles west on Rd. 60, then turn left and go 0.2 mile south on Rd. 6005. For Crescent Lake Campground, go a total of 2.6 miles west on Rd. 60. Tranquil Cove

day-use area is 6.4 miles on Rd. 60, Spring Campground is 8.1 miles, and Contorta Flat Campground is 9.9 miles.

Contact: Central Oregon Visitors Association, 541/389-8799; ODFW, Bend, 541/388-6363; Crescent Ranger District, 541/433-3200; Crescent Lake Lodge and Resort, 541/433-2505, www.crescentlakeresort.com.

43 MILLER LAKE
west of Chemult
Map 5.5, page 323

On the eastern slope of the Cascades, scenic Miller Lake is situated among pleasant pine forests, high rolling hills, and steep banks. Miller is probably best known for its quantity of sizable brown trout, and it has been popular with southern Oregon fly anglers for many years. A little out of the way from most fishing destinations in the area, Miller is a worthwhile side trip if you want to catch big brown trout, plus rainbow and kokanee.

The lake is 500 surface acres with an aver-age depth of 75 feet (the maximum depth is 150 feet near the center and north end). Most anglers use traditional streamer patterns such a Royal Coachman, Matuka, Muddler Min-now, and Woolly Bugger. Browns can average 16–18 inches, and there are quite a few fish up to 30 inches. Fall is a favorite time here, when the brown trout are getting ready to spawn and can be found around tributary mouths. The water is cold and clear, and there is a lot of underwater structure in the form of logs to create good cover. The shallower east end of the lake receives the most angler attention. This is also a good area to catch kokanee with jigs and trolling. Focus on the deeper water in the middle and toward the north end. Twenty-five kokanee may be kept per day. Boaters take the majority of fish here. Small outboards, float tubes, rafts, and canoes are all productive means of getting around. Bank angling is good in the vicinity of Digit Point Campground, but most of the lakeshore is too steep for reasonable bank access.

Species: Rainbow and brown trout, kokanee.
Facilities: Digit Point Campground has a boat ramp and dock, drinking water, restrooms, and 64 tent and RV sites with a dump station. There's also a 2.5-mile, round-the-lake hiking trail that takes off from each end of the campground. Supplies are available in Chemult.
Directions: From Chemult, travel one mile north on Hwy. 97, then 12 miles west on Miller Lake Rd. (Forest Rd. 9772).
Contact: Central Oregon Visitors Association, 541/389-8799; ODFW, Bend, 541/388-6363; Chemult Ranger District (Winema National Forest), 541/365-7001.

44 BUCK CREEK
south of Silver Lake
Map 5.5, page 323

Buck Creek is one of a handful of creeks (along with Bridge Creek and Silver Creek) that flows out of the Fremont National Forest into Paulina Marsh. For the most part, these are modest fisheries holding some bass and small (10–12-inch) trout. Originating in the Yamsi Mountain Recreation Area, Buck Creek flows 20 miles into Paulina Marsh west of Silver Lake. A section of the river flows through the Cabin Lake–Fort Rock Wildlife Area, which is accessible from hiking trails at Lower Buck Campground. The river is crossed by Highway 31 about three miles west of Silver Lake. Buck Creek is followed by good highways in the lower section and logging roads into the headwaters. The upper river is quite small and holds only a marginal population of small fish. The lower section of river, where it widens and deepens, holds bigger and more abundant trout.

All forms of fishing work, including bait, spinners, and flies. Buck Creek is more conducive to fly-fishing because of its size, so anglers will do well with small nymphs and dry flies in the summer. Bait and spinners can be used in the small pools. Children may especially enjoy catching lots of small trout around the campgrounds.

Species: Redband trout, brook trout, bass.
Facilities: Camping can be had at Lower Buck and Upper Buck campgrounds on Forest Rds. 2804 and 038. Additional camping can be had at natural campsites in the Fremont National Forest. A popular chuckwagon barbecue restaurant, the Cowboy Dinner Tree, can be found on Hwy. 28 near Silver Lake.
Directions: From Silver Lake, take Hwy. 31 west of Summer Lake one mile to the Bear Flat Rd. turnoff. Take Bear Flat Rd. six miles to Forest Rd. 2804. The Cabin Lake–Fort Rock Wildlife Area will be to your east. Look for Lower Buck and Upper Buck campgrounds along this road. To reach the headwaters stay on Forest Rd. 2804, which turns into Forest Rds. 038 and 039. The river will be to your east.
Contact: Christmas Valley Chamber of Commerce, 541/576-2166; Fremont–Winema National Forest, 541/947-2151; Silver Lake Ranger District, 541/576-2107; ODFW, Summer Lake, 541/943-3324; BLM Lakeview District, 541/947-2177; Cowboy Dinner Tree (reservations required), 541/576-2426.

45 SILVER CREEK
south of Silver Lake
Map 5.5, page 323

Silver Creek (not to be confused with the world-famous spring creek in Idaho) is a fair bass and trout stream that forms the outlet of Thompson Valley Reservoir. A short river at just under 16 miles, it flows through arid grasslands and ponderosa forests to Paulina Marsh just south of Silver Lake, where it is crossed by Highway 31. An equally productive West Fork flows out of the Fremont National Forest and joins the main river about four miles up from Silver Lake. Though not a destination fishery, it makes a nice diversion on your way to other waters.

Trout are generally small (6–10 inches), but bass run a little bigger at a pound or more. Anglers have a few options for access to the river. The confluence of the main river and West Fork is accessible via logging roads from Highways 28 and 27. There is a campground at Bunyard Crossing on the main river about midway between the reservoir and Silver Lake on Forest Rd. 2917. Anglers can walk up- and downstream in this section for good catches of bass and trout. Continuing southwest on Forest Rd. 2917 will take anglers along the productive West Fork, where there is a small campground at Silver Creek Marsh about five miles from Bunyard. The area below the reservoir is accessible by walking trails from Thompson Reservoir Campground. Spring flows after heavy runoff is the best time of year to fish this stretch. More access can be had from small logging roads off Highways 28 and 27, both of which parallel the river. Buy a good Forest Service map to find details for access to these small roads.

Species: Rainbow trout, largemouth bass.

Facilities: Primitive campgrounds are available at Bunyard Crossing, Silver Creek Marsh, and Thompson Valley Reservoir. Some supplies are available in Silver Lake, but campers should be well equipped before their arrival. A popular chuckwagon barbecue restaurant, the Cowboy Dinner Tree, can be found on Hwy. 28 near Silver Lake.

Directions: From Silver Lake drive south eight miles on Hwy. 27 to follow the West Fork and reach Silver Creek Marsh. Stay on Hwy. 27 for another five miles to reach Thompson Valley Reservoir Campground and for access to the upper main river. For Bunyard Campground, follow Hwy. 28 south out of Silver Lake eight miles to Forest Rd. 2917. Turn west on the forest road and drive one mile to Bunyard Campground. Access to the lower river can be had from numerous side roads off Hwy. 28. Consult a good Forest Service map to navigate this area.

Contact: Christmas Valley Chamber of Commerce, 541/576-2166; Fremont–Winema National Forest, 541/947-2151; Silver Lake Ranger District, 541/576-2107; ODFW, Summer Lake, 541/943-3324; BLM, Lakeview District,

541/947-2177; Cowboy Dinner Tree (reservations required), 541/576-2426.

46 SOUTH UMPQUA RIVER
near Roseburg in the Umpqua watershed

Map 5.6, page 324

The South Umpqua flows 95 miles from the Rogue–Umpqua Divide Wilderness to its confluence with the main-stem Umpqua at The Forks. This is a good but underfished river, compared to local giants such as the Rogue, Umpqua, and North Umpqua Rivers. Its attraction is smallmouth bass in the lower river and winter steelhead higher up. The river cuts through the towns of Tiller, Milo, Canyonville, Myrtle Creek, Winston, and Roseburg and picks up countless tributaries that are important rearing streams for migrating salmon and steelhead. The most famous of these tributaries is Cow Creek. The upper South Umpqua runs through scenic forests and canyons, while the lower river loses its wilderness setting, flowing through towns and agricultural lands.

Steelhead fishing on the South Umpqua is open January 1–April 30 and again December 1–December 31. All methods of angling are permitted, including bait. Winter steelhead arrive in two waves, November–December and then again January–April. Except for the fish that arrive in November, these times coincide with the regulated season. There is a steelhead fishing deadline at Jackson Creek Bridge five miles north of Tiller.

Trout are available throughout the whole river for catch-and-release fishing May 27–September 15. Trout fishing is restricted to artificial flies and lures above Jackson Creek Bridge. The best smallmouth bass fishing takes place from the confluence at The Forks to Canyonville, May–September, or when the water hits 65°F. Salmon are present but are off-limits to angling. The river between the mouth and the fishing deadline at Jackson Creek is closed to all fishing September 16–November 30.

Spring and winter, or times of high water, offer the only opportunities to drift the river, which otherwise gets too low in the summer. Numerous boat ramps are between the towns of Roseburg and Milo, but the only drift-boat water is between Days Creek, approximately six miles upstream from Canyonville, and the confluence with the Umpqua. From the gravel ramp at the Days Creek Bridge, one can float downriver to Stanton County Park in Canyonville, Lawson Bar, Boomer Hill, and four other ramps before reaching the main Umpqua. Bank fishing is available at the boat ramps and at public parks, including the mouth of Myrtle Creek in Myrtle Creek, the mouth of Lookingglass Creek near Winston, the fairgrounds in Roseburg, and near the confluence at Singleton Park.

Species: Winter steelhead, trout, smallmouth bass.

Facilities: From upstream from the confluence: Douglas County Fairgrounds has a boat ramp and an RV park with 50 sites 30 feet and up. At Happy Valley, the ramp is improved, with no other facilities. Weigle Landing is an unimproved ramp with no other facilities. Stanton County Park, sometimes called Canyonville Park, has a boat ramp, restrooms, and campsites, some with hookups. At Three C Creek, the ramp is unimproved and has no facilities. The Forest Service has three campgrounds farther upstream along the South Umpqua. All have vault toilets and restrooms. Dumont Creek has three sites and no drinking water; Boulder Creek has eight sites with fire pits and drinking water; Camp Comfort has eight sites and fire pits, no drinking water. Supplies are available in Canyonville.

Directions: In Roseburg, Douglas County Fairgrounds is off Exit 123 from I-5. For Happy Valley, from Roseburg, head south four miles on Hwy. 99 to Green, then follow Happy Valley Rd. west for about two miles to the river. The Happy Valley ramp is on the north side of the road. For Weigle Landing, take I-5 south from Roseburg

five miles to Exit 119, then follow Hwy. 99 south for right miles to where it crosses the South Umpqua. Just past the bridge, look for a road headed (left) north along the river; Weigle Landing is two miles up the road. For Stanton County Park, from Canyonville, take I-5 to Exit 98, then turn left (east) on Canyonville–Riddle Rd. and left again onto Hwy. 227. Follow this road east for 1.1 miles and turn left (north) onto Canyonville Park Rd., which leads 0.2 mile to Stanton Park. For Three C Creek, from Canyonville, head 23 miles east on Hwy. 227 to where it intersects County Rd. 46 (South Umpqua Rd.). Follow this road northeast for about seven miles to the Three C Creek ramp on the right. To reach the Forest Service campgrounds, from I-5 at Canyonville take Hwy. 227 east 23 miles to Tiller. Follow County Rd. 46 for eight miles to its intersection with Forest Rd. 28. Follow Rd. 28 northeast, and you'll reach Dumont (11 miles), Boulder Creek (14 miles), and Camp Comfort (26 miles).

Contact: Douglas County Parks Department, 541/957-7001; Stanton County Park, 541/839-4483; ODFW, Roseburg, 541/440-3353; BLM, Roseburg, 541/440-3353; Umpqua National Forest, Tiller District, 541/825-3201; Northwest Outdoors (Tackle Shop), 541/440-3042; Waldron's Outdoor Sports, 541/672-8992; Wildlife Safari RV Park, 541/679-6761; Douglas County Fairgrounds RV Park, 541/957-7010; Twin Rivers RV Park, 541/673-3811; All Hooked-Up Guide Service (Rusty Preston), 541/281-7756, www.allhookedupguideservice.net; Doug's Guide Service (Doug Warren), 541/679-0599, www.loganet.net/dougsguideservice.

47 GALESVILLE RESERVOIR

east of Azalea in the Umpqua watershed

Map 5.6, page 324

Galesville Reservoir, on upper Cow Creek, is managed for both rainbow trout and largemouth bass, and it provides good fishing for both. The reservoir is four miles east of Azalea and I-5. It sits in a scenic, timbered valley surrounded by high Cascade foothills and is popular for other water sports. A health advisory has been issued for this reservoir because of high mercury levels, and fish are general considered to be unsafe for eating. Consult either the Department of Human Services or the ODFW Regulations Booklet for more information.

When the reservoir was created, some forethought was given to the potential fishery here, and trees were left standing in the flood area to provide improved fish habitat. It must have worked, because both trout and bass flourished. Other species that can be found in smaller numbers include bluegill, crappie, smallmouth bass, and landlocked coho. The reservoir is subject to summer drawdown but it's not drastic enough to discourage fishing. The lake is open year-round and allows for all methods of fishing. All bass 12–15 inches must be released, and only one fish longer than 15 inches may be retained. Landlocked salmon are to be included in the bag limit for trout. Boating is preferred, but bank angling is unlimited and good. There are two paved boat ramps on the eastern shore.

The best place to begin fishing is around the old stands of trees. To catch bass use poppers, crankbaits, Rapalas, or any other favorite bass lure. Trout can be taken with bait and casting rigs, flies, or spinners in the same areas. Most of the other species are in very small numbers and don't afford much sport but may show up in some of the catches. Some anglers will troll the deeper parts of the lake for 15-inch landlocked coho. Trolling techniques are similar to kokanee fishing.

Species: Largemouth bass, rainbow trout, bluegill, crappie, smallmouth bass, coho.

Facilities: The ramp in Chief Miwaleta County Park (7 A.M.–dark) is four lanes and paved; the park also has picnic sites, drinking water, flush toilets, play equipment, and hiking trails. The upper ramp, at Cow Creek,

is also paved and has restrooms and parking. Supplies are available in Canyonville.

Directions: From Azalea (Exit 88 on I-5), follow County Rd. 36 (Upper Cow Creek Rd.) northeast for five miles to the Galesville Dam, then one more mile to the park.

Contact: Galesville Reservoir (Douglas County Parks), 541/837-3302; ODFW, Roseburg, 541/440-3353; BLM, Roseburg, 541/440-3353; Umpqua National Forest, 541/672-6601; Northwest Outdoors (Tackle Shop), 541/440-3042; Waldron's Outdoor Sports, 541/672-8992; Department of Human Services, 503/731-4021; Azalea General Store, 541/837-3798.

48 LOWER MIDDLE ROGUE
Savage Rapids Dam to Grave Creek Landing
Map 5.6, page 324

The Lower Middle Rogue encompasses approximately 45 miles of river between Savage Rapids Dam and Grave Creek, the start of the Wild and Scenic roadless section. The river here is more urban, though still scenic, surrounded by forested lands that buffer views into the urban areas of Grants Pass. River access is highly developed, with no fewer than 20 parks, boat ramps, and numerous bank fisheries; several good river maps show the extensive access points. Popular waters are the lower sections below Grants Pass from Hog Creek, through the Hellsgate Canyon to Galice, and below Galice to Grave Creek. Because of difficult white water in this section, obtain a boater's river guidebook before attempting these runs.

Because fish runs are so extensive, varied, and overlapping throughout the year, there is no bad time to be in the river, but some times are better than others. Winter steelhead are available January–April, with some fish showing as early as November–December; February and March are the peak runs. Summer steelhead and their smaller cousins, half-pounders, are available August–December with October being the peak season; both can be picked up into January and February. Fall chinook are present in peak numbers September–November, but not in the same impressive numbers as spring chinook. "Springers" are a major highlight on the Rogue and peak just before the arrival of fall chinook in June and July. A very small run of coho is present in September and October. Rainbow trout are present all year but are most active May–July when insect activity is the strongest. Sea-run cutthroat, a surprisingly feisty fish and usually caught by steelheaders, are in the river July–November.

All of this water can be fished with flies or traditional tackle, including bait. The most popular methods of catching salmon from a boat include back-trolling or back-bouncing with bait, plugs, or divers and bait. Back-trolling is especially popular with large Kwikfish or Flatfish with attached strips of herring. Salmon will most often be found in the deeper pools of slower water or wherever deep holes can hold their enormous bulk; this includes some very fast water at times. Bank anglers use a variety of techniques, including plunking with salmon roe, spoons and spinners, and drift fishing. Fly anglers do not generally target salmon.

Steelhead can be caught with similar techniques used for salmon, albeit smaller lures, but float and drift fishing are far more popular. Guide Rusty Preston has his clients side drift for steelhead using a very simple combination of a hook, night crawlers, and small foam bead. He claims it looks like an Egg Sucking Leech, a popular fly pattern. The worm is slid over the shank of the hook and up the leader; a small foam bead is then slid over the point of the hook to help keep the night crawlers from sliding off the hook. Other drift-fishing techniques include yarn, corkies, and salmon roe. The most effective places to fish these techniques are along the banks in deeper water (referred to as "buckets" by some guides) or in the softer currents and behind rocks in fast water. Some of the most popular water for drift boats is the flat between Galice and the pullout at Grave Creek

Landing. Pullouts along this stretch such as Rand Access, Almeda Park, and Argo Access can make for shorter or longer day floats.

Fly anglers can use any number of methods to catch steelhead, from swinging flies to nymphing. Swinging flies is effective using floating or sinking lines and patterns such as Egg Sucking Leeches, Rogue River Specials, Juicy Bugs, Silver Hiltons, and Green Butt Skunks. Effective nymphs include Golden Stones, October Caddis, and steelhead-size Copper Johns and Copper Swans. The best fly water is near current seams: runs where fast and slow current meet in about 4–6 feet of water. Some good fly water exists between Grants Pass and Hog Creek and is accessible from several parks, including Schroeder, Whitehorse, Matson, Griffin, and Hog Landing. Trout fishing is straightforward and is productive with small lures such as Rooster Tails and drifting PowerBait or night crawlers or using flies. Sea-run cutthroat and half-pounders tend to like a fast swinging bright lure or fly.

Fishing for steelhead is open year-round. Trout fishing is limited to the regular fishing season. Half-pounders are treated as trout and do not require a steelhead tag. Salmon seasons shift from year to year, and sometimes week to week. Regulations are complex and subject to frequent changes, and the angler is responsible for knowing them. Check the local newspapers and call or visit the ODFW website.

Species: Winter and summer steelhead, half-pounders, fall and spring chinook, coho, rainbow, and sea-run cutthroat.

Facilities: There are five campgrounds (four with boat ramps), and four boat ramps around Galice:

- **Schroeder Park:** The campground has showers and 51 campsites, some with hookups and two yurts. The day-use area ($2 fee) has an ADA fishing platform and restroom, a boat ramp, and a large parking area. Supplies are available in Grants Pass.
- **Whitehorse Park:** There are 42 campsites, most for tents, one yurt, and showers. The day-use area ($2) has a boat ramp.

•**Griffin Park:** There are 19 sites, most with hookups, and one yurt. Memorial Day–Labor Day you can pitch a tent on a gravel bar in the river here. The day-use area ($2) has a boat ramp.

•**Indian Mary Park:** There are 108 campsites, some with hookups, and two yurts, as well as showers.

•**Almeda Park:** There are 34 campsites, none with hookups, one yurt, and a vault toilet. The day-use area ($2) has a boat ramp.

The Robertson Bridge, Grave Creek Landing, and Galice Landing ramps are all paved, with restrooms and parking. Galice also has a store. The ramp at Argo is unimproved but has restrooms.

Directions: From the junction of Hwys. 99 and 199 in Grants Pass, head west 0.7 mile on Hwy. 199. Turn right (west) on Redwood Ave. and travel 1.5 miles to Willow Ln. Turn right (north) and Willow turns into Schroeder Ln., reaching Schroeder Park in 0.9 mile. For Whitehorse Park, take G St. west from Grants Pass; G St. turns into Upper River Rd. reaching the park in six miles. For Griffin Park, go south on Hwy. 199 for seven miles, then turn right (north) on the Rogue River Loop Hwy. (also signed as Riverbanks Rd.) and continue for 6.2 miles. Turn right (east) on Griffin Rd. and follow it 0.5 mile to the park.

The Indian Mary, Almeda, Robertson Bridge, Grave Creek Landing, Galice Landing, and Argo boat ramps are all around Galice, northwest of Grants Pass. From Grants Pass, go north on I-5 for five miles to Exit 61 (Merlin). Turn west on Merlin–Galice Rd. and follow it 3.5 miles. Continue left (west) on Galice Rd. and follow it five miles to Hog Creek Landing, seven miles to Indian Mary Park, 11 miles to Galice, 15 miles to Almeda, 17 miles to Argo Landing, and 23 miles to Grave Creek.

Contact: Grants Pass/Josephine County Chamber of Commerce, 800/547-5927; Josephine County Parks Department, 541/474-5285; ODFW, Central Point, 541/826-8774; BLM, Medford, 541/6182400; Rogue River National Forest, Galice District, 541/471-6500; Native Run Fly Shop, 541/474-0090; The Fishin' Hole in Shady Cove, 541/878-4000; McKenzie River Outfitters, 541/773-5145; Big R-Medford, 541/830-3713; Doug's Guide Service (Doug Warren), 541/679-0599, www.loganet.net/dougsguideservice; Roe Outfitters, 877/943-5700, www.roeoutfitters.com; All Hooked-Up Guide Service (Rusty Preston), 541/281-7756, www.allhookedup-guideservice.net.

49 UPPER MIDDLE ROGUE
Gold Ray Dam to Savage Rapids Dam
Map 5.6, page 324

Like the lower river running through Grants Pass, this section is very urban, flowing through the towns of Gold Hill, Rogue River, and along sections of I-5. The river is still scenic, bordered by a mix of cottonwoods, conifers, and willows, but one has the feeling that civilization lies just beyond the banks. Regardless, the fishing is great for salmon and steelhead and is popular when the fish have not quite made it over the Gold Ray Dam or when the upper river is limited to fishing with flies in the fall. There is a lot of private property, but five boat ramps and several parks along this stretch allow good access to both boaters and bank anglers. Fisher's Ferry below Gold Ray Dam is a popular launch for jet sleds and drift boats with motors. Here, anglers will troll up to the heads of runs, fish down, and then repeat the process sometimes 4–5 times. If it's salmon anglers are after, they are most likely back-trolling Flatfish and Kwikfish rigged with herring. Steelhead anglers will be drift-fishing bait such as night crawlers and salmon roe.

The Gold Nugget Recreation Area five miles below Gold Ray Dam has some dangerous rapids and is a good bank fishery, but it is not often floated by anglers. Other good bank fishing can be had at Gold Hill Park, downriver at Sardine Creek, and Rocky Point Bridge. Other popular floats begin at Valley of the Rogue State Park, where anglers can drift 2.5 miles downriver to Coyote Evans Wayside or another few miles to the Savage Rapids take-out. Good bank access can be had at any of these launch sites, plus at Ben Hur Lampman State Wayside.

Winter steelhead are available January–April with some fish showing as early as November–December; February and March are the peak runs. Summer steelhead and their smaller cousins, half-pounders, are available August–December with October being the peak season; both can be picked up into January and February. Fall chinook are present in peak numbers September–November but not in the same impressive numbers as spring chinook. Springers are a major highlight on the Rogue and peak in June and July, just before the arrival of fall chinook. A very small run of coho is present in September and October. Rainbow trout are present all year but are most active May–July when insect activity is the strongest. Sea-run cutthroat, a surprisingly feisty fish usually caught by steelheaders, are in the river July–November.

Regulations are complex and subject to frequent changes, and the angler is responsible for knowing them. Check local newspapers and call the ODFW or visit its website. Fishing for steelhead is open year-round. Trout fishing is limited to the regular fishing season. Salmon seasons shift from year to year, and sometimes week to week.

Species: Winter and summer steelhead, half-pounders, fall and spring chinook, coho, rainbow, and sea-run cutthroat.

Facilities: Valley of the Rogue State Park has 69 campsites, some with hookups, six yurts, and a day-use area ($3) with a boat ramp. Additional camping is available downstream in the parks along the Savage Rapids to Grave Creek section. The boat ramps at Fisher's Ferry, Gold Hill, Savage Rapids, and Coyote Evans Wayside are paved with parking and restrooms. Gold Hill and Savage Rapids each charge a day-use fee of $3. Supplies are available in Gold Beach and Shady Cove.

Directions: From Grants Pass, take I-5 south

for seven miles to Exit 48 (Rogue River). Turn left onto Depot St., then an immediate right onto Classic Drive. After 0.4 mile, turn right onto North River Rd. and follow it 1.4 miles to the Valley of the Rogue State Park.

For the boat ramps: For Savage Rapids Dam, from Grants Pass head south on Hwy. 99 for six miles. For Coyote Evans Wayside, continue on Hwy. 99 for four miles. To reach the Gold Hill ramp, take I-5 south to Exit 40 (Gold Hill), then follow Hwy. 234 left (north) across the river and into town. When Hwys. 234 and 99 split, follow 224 right (east) for 0.2 mile into Gold Hill Recreation Park. For the Fishers Ferry ramp follow the directions as above, but just before Hwy. 234 crosses the Rogue east of Gold Hill, turn right (north) onto Upper River Rd. and follow it along the south bank of the river for about five miles to the ramp.

Contact: Grants Pass/Josephine County Chamber of Commerce, 800/547-5927; Oregon Parks and Recreation Department, 800/551-6949; Valley of the Rogue State Park, 541/582-1118; Jackson County Parks, 541/774-8183; City of Rogue River, 541/582-4401; City of Gold Hill, 541/855-1525; ODFW, Central Point, 541/826-8774; BLM, Medford, 541/618-2400; Rogue River National Forest, Ashland, 541/552-2900; Native Run Fly Shop, 541/474-0090; The Fishin' Hole in Shady Cove, 541/878-4000; McKenzie River Outfitters, 541/773-5145; Big R-Medford, 541/830-3713; All Hooked-Up Guide Service (Rusty Preston), 541/281-7756, www.allhookedupguideservice.net; Roe Outfitters, 877/943-5700, www.roeoutfitters.com; Doug's Guide Service (Doug Warren), 541/679-0599, www.loganet.net/dougsguideservice.

50 APPLEGATE RIVER
near Grants Pass in Siskiyou National Forest

Map 5.6, page 324

For Oregon anglers, the Applegate begins at the outflow of Applegate Reservoir, one mile north of the California border; it flows into the Rogue River west of Grants Pass near

Whitehorse Park. The river is bordered by cottonwoods, willows, and some conifers and feels a lot like a wilder cousin to the river bottomlands one might expect in the Willamette Valley. This is a gravelly river, and parts of it tend to fan out and thin around islands, becoming very low in summer. The Applegate is composed entirely of bank fishing with no boat ramps. Access is good from parks and roadsides between sections of private property. Depending on the size of returning runs, this is a fair to good winter steelhead river and summer trout fishery.

Steelhead arrive in two runs: a run of hatchery fish at the start of the season in January and a wild run February–April. Most of the steelheading takes place between the mouth and the Little Applegate River, approximately 2.5 miles above Ruch. A highway map or river guide can direct you to good public access points. Highway 238 (Jacksonville Hwy.) follows the river's southwest bank from Murphy to Ruch, and the North Applegate Road follows the northeast bank. From Ruch, access to good steelhead water can be had upriver at Cantrall–Buckley Campground and downriver at the Thompson Creek bridge crossing. Further roadside access can be had along the North Applegate Road above and below Murphy. The best access below Murphy is along Fish Hatchery Road at the Fish Hatchery Parks on both the south and north banks, Turtle Park, and Fish Hatchery Bridge at the junction of Fish Hatchery Road and South Side Road. There are numerous good public access points above and below the bridge crossing at Highway 199 near the intersection of Highway 99 and Fish Hatchery Road. Trout fishing is best in the upper river with access limited primarily to road crossings off Applegate Road, McKee Covered Bridge eight miles below the dam, and Jackson Park, four miles below the dam.

Species: Hatchery wild and winter steelhead, trout.

Facilities: Cantrall–Buckley County Park has almost two miles of riverfront and several campsites, some with hookups. The Forest Service's Jackson Campground has 10 tent sites and drinking water in summer only. Supplies are available in Grants Pass.

Directions: Highway 199 crosses the Applegate eight miles south of Grants Pass. From Grants Pass head south on Hwy. 238; turn right (west) on New Hope Rd. just as you leave town. Follow this road for three miles, then turn right (west) onto Fish Hatchery Rd. The road crosses the river in about two miles, then parallels the southern bank for several miles downstream. To reach the bridge at Thompson Creek, follow Hwy. 238 for 18 miles south of Grants Pass, to where it crosses the river in Applegate. To reach Cantrall–Buckley County Park, take Hwy. 238 six miles past Applegate (24 miles south of Grants Pass) and turn right (south) onto Hamilton Rd., which leads one mile to the park. And to reach Jackson Campground and points upstream, stay on Hamilton Rd. for another mile past the county park, then turn right (south) onto Upper Applegate Rd., which goes all the way up the river to the dam. Eight miles from Hamilton Rd. (one mile past McKee Bridge), turn right onto Palmer Creek Rd., which leads one mile to the campground.

Contact: Grants Pass/Josephine County Chamber of Commerce, 800/547-5927; Josephine County Parks Department, 541/474-5285; Applegate Ranger District, 541/899-3800; ODFW, Central Point, 541/826-8774; BLM, Medford, 541/618-2400; Rogue River National Forest, Applegate, 541/899-3800; Native Run Fly Shop, 541/474-0090; McKee Bridge Restaurant and Store, 541/899-1101; Applegate River Lodge and Restaurant, 541/846-6690.

51 APPLEGATE RESERVOIR
southwest of Jacksonville in Siskiyou National Forest

Map 5.6, page 324

Applegate is a 950-acre reservoir managed primarily for fishing that produces good catches of stocked rainbow trout, landlocked chinook, bass, and crappie. The reservoir is scenically situated in a remote wilderness setting. The 10 mph boat speed limit ensures anglers are not disturbed by water-skiers and Jet Skis. Applegate is heavily stocked with both legal-size rainbow trout and chinook fingerlings. Trout average 8–10 inches in spring and 14–16 inches by fall. Spring trout fishing can be very good with the combination of winter holdovers and plantings of lunker-size trout in April. Chinook average 8–16 inches and are included in the daily trout limit of five fish per day. Chinook are caught in deeper water, the same as kokanee. Most of the deepest water (100–200 feet) is at the dam and in the middle for three-quarters of the lake's length.

Fishing for bass, largemouth and smallmouth, and crappie improves as the weather warms in summer; they're often found in the shallower areas in one of the four arms. The French Glen and Squaw Creek arms at the northern end and the Carberry Arm at the south end all provide good habitat for bass in the form of submerged structure and thick bank vegetation. Bass from 12–15 inches must be released unharmed. Landlocked chinook count as trout. All forms of fishing are allowed, including bait. Boats are permitted, but a 10 mph speed limit has been imposed on the entire lake. Three good ramps, two at the north end and one at the south, provide access. Bank fishing is good from all six campgrounds and from hiking trails and roads that surround the lake on each side to the dam. Some deeper water can be reached from the bank; Hart-tish campground is a good place to start.

Species: Stocked trout, landlocked chinook, large and smallmouth bass, crappie.

Facilities: Some facilities are being closed in rotation for renovations; boat ramps may not be available if the water is particularly low. Call the Applegate District for information. Supplies are available in Grants Pass.

•**French Gulch Trailhead and Ramp:** Gravel ramp, two campsites, vault toilets, and a trailhead parking area that requires a Northwest Forest Pass ($5 per day; $30 annually), which is available from most sporting goods or outdoors shops or from Nature of the Northwest in Portland. The following lists available facilities:

•**Harr Point:** Boat in or hike via Payette Trail (No. 970). Five sites, no other facilities (year-round).

•**Tipsu Tyee:** Boat in or hike via Payette Trail (No. 970). Five sites, vault toilets, picnic tables (year-round).

•**Hart-tish:** Five walk-in tent sites, parking for self-contained RVs, water, toilets, and a boat ramp ($5).

•**Cooper Ramp:** Has a paved ramp (free), and no facilities.

•**Watkins Campground:** Fourteen sites, vault toilets, and fire rings.

•**Carberry Campground:** Ten tent sites, vault toilets, and water.

•**Seattle Bar:** Day-use trailhead area only; requires a Northwest Forest Pass.

Directions: From Jacksonville, go 6.5 miles south on Hwy. 238 to Ruch, then turn south on Upper Applegate Rd. Follow this road 15 miles to the lake.

For the boat ramps: For French Gulch and the Payette Trail to the hike-in campsites, turn left on County Rd. 1075, crossing the dam. French Gulch ramp and trailhead is one mile down this road. Two miles further on Road 1075, turn right onto Forest Service Rd. 100 and follow it 0.5 mile to the Squaw Arm Parking Area. From here, take the Payette Trail about 0.25 mile to the Harr Point Campground, and a mile past that to Tispu Tyee.

The rest of the sites are accessed by staying right at the dam and driving along the west side of the lake. Hart-tish is a little over a mile ahead, on the left; Copper Ramp is two miles past it. Watkins Campground is 0.5 mile past Cooper, and for Carberry Campground, go one mile past Watkins and turn right (north) onto County Rd. 777 for 0.3 mile. Go the other way on Road 777 for one mile to Seattle Bar.

Contact: Medford/Jackson County Chamber of Commerce, 541/779-4847; Applegate Ranger District, 541/899-3800; Nature of the Northwest, 503/872-2750, www.naturenw. org; ODFW, Central Point, 541/826-8774; BLM, Medford, 541/618-2400; McKee Bridge Restaurant and Store, 541/899-1101; Applegate River Lodge and Restaurant, 541/846-6690; McKenzie River Outfitters, 541/773-5145; Trophy Waters Fly Shop, 541/734-2278; Big R-Medford, 541/830-3713.

52 LOST CREEK RESERVOIR
east of Medford in Rogue River
National Forest

Map 5.7, page 325

Lost Creek Reservoir is a large flood-control impoundment that sits in a scenic, mountainous valley. Two forks of the Rogue—South and Middle—and numerous other tributaries converge to form 3,430 acres of coves and tributary arms. Anglers can fish a healthy population of stocked trout and warm-water species such as crappie, perch, and largemouth and smallmouth bass. There are 31.5 miles of shoreline, and the average depth is 136 feet. The deepest water is near the dam at 325 feet. Bank fishing is good from several campgrounds and picnic areas. Boat fishing is very productive, especially for access to the areas around the dam and up into the tributary arms at the northeast and northwest corners of the lake. All methods of boating and fishing are permitted.

Smallmouth bass fishing is very good and generates a lot of attention from anglers. Search for smallmouth around the dam and rocky outcroppings around the southwest shorelines and in the coves. Largemouth bass can be found in the north shore coves around underwater structure between Fire Glen Camp and the Lost Creek Arm. An abundance of trout are stocked annually and are easily caught using still-water bait methods from shore. Fish for crappie, bluegill, perch, and brown bullhead in the shallower water along the south and west shores later in the year beginning in July when the water warms.

Species: Rainbow and brown trout, small and largemouth bass, crappie, perch, bluegill, brown bullhead catfish.

Facilities: This is a good family vacation spot with a resort and plenty of nonfishing activities such boating, hiking, biking, swimming, waterskiing, and kayaking. Joseph Stewart State Park has 201 campsites, showers, and hiking trails along the lakeshore. Lost Creek Marina is in the park's day-use area, with a restaurant, boat rentals, and a ramp. The Corps of Engineers operates Takelma Park on the northwest side of the lake just north of the dam, with a paved ramp, dock, and restrooms. Fire Glen Camp and Four Corners Camp are both hike- or boat-in sites with garbage containers, tables, fire rings, and vault toilets; no drinking water or docks. After early July water levels drop to the point where each of these sites is up to 100 yards from the shore. Supplies are available in Shady Cove.

Directions: From Medford, travel 29 miles north on Hwy. 62 to the dam. To reach Takelma Park, turn north on Takelma Dr. and follow it approximately two miles; a hiking trail will take you one mile along the lakeshore to Four Corners Camp. To reach Stewart State Park and Lost Creek Marina, stay on Hwy. 62, follow it around the south side of the lake, four miles past the dam, to the park on the left. To reach Fire Glen Camp, follow Lewis Rd. 1.5 miles to a trailhead parking area, then hike a mile down the shoreline.

Contact: Medford/Jackson County Chamber of Commerce, 541/779-4847; Oregon Parks and Recreation Department, 800/551-6949; James H. Stewart State Park, 541/460-3334; Lost Creek Marina, 541/560-3646; Army Corps of Engineers, 541/878-2255; ODFW, Central Point, 541/826-8774; BLM, Medford, 541/618-2400; Rogue River National Forest, Ashland, 541/552-2900; The Fishin' Hole in Shady Cove, 541/878-4000; McKenzie River Outfitters, 541/773-5145; Pat's Hand Tied

Flies and Bait Shop, 541/878-2338; Big R-Medford, 541/830-3713; Lost Creek Marina, 541/560-3646.

53 UPPER ROGUE RIVER
Lost Creek Dam to Tou Velle State Park
Map 5.7, page 325   **BEST (**

The upper Rogue from McGregor Park is one of the most popular fisheries on the river for salmon, steelhead, and trout. The area is also fishy with anglers, so consider this an immersion experience for older kids to witness firsthand the excitement, energy, and buzz that often surround a destination fishery. The river flows through nicely forested and undeveloped land for 10–12 miles above Shady Cove before opening up in the valley floor, where the land becomes developed with riverfront homes and agricultural lands. Even this lower section flows through a corridor of cottonwood trees and dense bank vegetation, affording a degree of solitude from civilization. A majority of this water is easy to row from a boat, but there are a few trouble spots such as Rattlesnake Rapids that could cause an inexperienced oarsperson some difficulty.

A distinctive fly-fishing–only trout fishery can be had in the so-called "Holy Water" between Cole M. Rivers fish hatchery and Lost Creek Dam. Just three-quarters of a mile, the Holy Water is a bank fishery for 16–20-inch rainbows and is catch-and-release fishing. Good hatches of caddis, mayflies, and large salmon flies (May–June) occur every year in spring and summer.

Drift boating is a mainstay on this part of the river, especially popular with fly anglers, and is the most productive way to fish the river. Among the more popular drifts are a mix and match of the following: McGregor Park to Rogue Elk (five miles), Rogue Elk to Shady Cove (eight miles), Shady Cove to Dodge Bridge (8.5 miles), and Dodge Bridge to Tou Velle State Park (eight miles). Boaters do not want to drift beyond Tou Velle Park, as there are no take-outs and the water is extremely dangerous.

Many anglers will make much longer drifts, for example Shady Cove to Tou Velle State Park or Rogue Elk to Dodge Park, simply to cover a lot of water. Jet sleds can be launched at Tou Velle and run either upstream or downstream to good fishing water. Bank fishing is good from all these launch points and parks.

Winter steelhead are available January–April with some fish showing as early as November and December; February and March are the peak runs. Summer steelhead and their smaller cousins, half-pounders, are available August–December with October being the peak season; both can be picked up into January and February. Fall chinook are present in peak numbers September–November but not in the same impressive numbers as spring chinook. Springers are a major highlight on the Rogue and peak in June and July, just before the arrival of fall chinook. A very small run of coho is present in September and October. Rainbow trout are present all year but are most active May–July when insect activity is the strongest. Sea-run cutthroat, a surprisingly feisty fish usually caught by steelheaders, are in the river July–November.

Regulations are complex and subject to frequent changes, and the angler is responsible for knowing them. Check local newspapers and call the ODFW or visit its website. Fishing for steelhead is open year-round. Trout fishing is limited to the regular fishing season. Salmon seasons shift from year to year, and sometimes week to week.

Because the water in the upper Rogue is colder than average most of the year, popular steelhead fishing techniques tend to be those that deliver the fly, bait, or lure deep in the water to reach the fish. Swinging flies and casting spinners and spoons are not practiced as much as nymphing, side and drift fishing, and back-trolling bait and plugs. These latter techniques tend to get tackle deep, right where the fish live. Still, success is not guaranteed, and it will take time to learn where fish hide in this river. The most likely starting places are around rocks in riffles, along the bank in pockets of deeper water, along ledges and underwater boulders, and in any soft-water seams where fast and slow water meet in 4–6 feet of water. It's common for anglers to hit a fish in a pocket one foot off the bank in what appears to be shallow water but, upon inspection, is a two-foot hole.

Salmon are most often caught in the deep slots and in pools at the ends of bigger runs. Back-trolling Kwikfish rigged with bait is the most popular technique, next to back-bouncing bait such as large chunks of salmon roe. The latter technique often requires large weights to keep the bait on the bottom.

Species: Winter and summer steelhead, half-pounders, fall and spring chinook, coho, rainbows, and sea-run cutthroat, spring and fall chinook salmon, coho salmon.

Facilities: Most areas include fishing piers and wheelchair access to restrooms and hiking trails. Many more sites are planned, but right now you have your choice of Dodge Bridge, Takelma Park, Upper Rogue Regional Park, Casey State Park, and McGregor Park. The following sites are listed in order, going upstream from White City. Supplies are available in Shady Cove and Medford.

• **Tou Velle State Recreation Area:** Tou Velle has picnicking, a paved boat ramp, hiking trails, and restrooms.

• **Dodge Bridge and Takelma County Parks:** Each park has a third of a mile of river frontage, restrooms, a fishing platform, and a paved ramp.

• **Upper Rogue Regional Park:** In Shady Cove (formerly known as simply Shady Cove Park), this park has the same amenities as Dodge Bridge and Takelma.

• **Rogue Elk County Park:** The same amenties as above, but with the only camping on this stretch of river. The campground has 15 sites, some with hookups; the day-use fee is $3.

• **Casey State Park:** Casey has picnicking, a paved boat ramp (no fee), and restrooms.

• **McGregor Park:** Operated by the Corps of Engineers, this park has a paved ramp, park-

ing, and restrooms, and was designed to accommodate visitors with disabilities.

Directions: From White City, five miles north of I-5 on Hwy. 62, head west on Ave. G, which turns into Pacific Ave. After 0.4 mile, turn right (west) onto Kirtland Rd. Go 0.2 mile, turn right (north) onto Table Rock Rd., and follow that 0.3 mile to the Tou Velle Park.

For the remaining boat ramps: For Dodge Bridge Park, take Hwy. 62 north from White City 6.4 miles to Hwy. 234. Head west on Hwy. 234 for 1.3 miles to the park. For Takelma Park, go 0.1 mile past Dodge Bridge Park, turn right (north) on Rogue River Dr., and follow that five miles to the park. To reach the rest of the boat ramps, continue north on Hwy. 62, past Hwy. 234. Rogue Elk Park is 18 miles from White City, Casey State Park is four miles past that, and McGregor Park is one mile past Casey.

Contact: Medford/Jackson County Chamber of Commerce, 541/779-4847; Oregon Parks and Recreation Department, 800/551-6949; Jackson County Parks, 541/774-8183; Army Corps of Engineers Rogue River Basin Project, 541/878-2255; ODFW, Central Point, 541/826-8774; BLM, Medford, 541/6182400; Rogue River National Forest, Ashland, 541/552-2900; Trophy Waters Fly Shop, 541/734-2278; The Fishin' Hole in Shady Cove, 541/878-4000; McKenzie River Outfitters, 541/773-5145; Pat's Hand Tied Flies and Bait Shop, 541/878-2338; Big R-Medford, 541/830-3713; All Hooked-Up Guide Service (Rusty Preston), 541/281-7756, www.allhookedupguideservice.net; Roe Outfitters, 877/943-5700, www.roe-outfitters.com; Doug's Guide Service (Doug Warren), 541/679-0599, www.loganet.net/dougsguideservice.

54 FOURMILE LAKE
east of Medford in Winema National Forest
Map 5.7, page 325

Southern Cascade lakes are wonderful for their remoteness and their often stunning beauty and Fourmile (which is actually closer to three miles) is no exception. Fourmile sits at the base of the majestic Mount McLoughlin (9,495 feet elevation) and is known for producing bigger-than-average rainbows and abundant populations of kokanee. The 763-acre lake sits at an elevation of 6,000 feet and views of the mountain from the lake are picturesque. There are seven miles of shoreline, but don't expect to do too much bank fishing; most of the banks are littered with fallen trees, making access to the water difficult. Instead, bring some kind of floating device or motorized boat for the best access. The lake is also deep, close to 150 feet near the center and 50–60 feet along the shoreline. While these depths are not conducive to wading, they are excellent for trolling close to the shore for most species; this can be helpful when the winds start to howl in the afternoons, creating whitecaps on the water. The abundance of underwater debris creates good habitat, especially for the solitude-loving brown trout. Kokanee can be found along both the west and east shore, close to the banks. Rainbow trout can be found at one of many inlets at the lake's northern end, which is spring-fed and remains cold even during summer.

Kokanee 6–10 inches are abundant, as indicated by the 25-per-day limit. Rainbows are stocked annually in abundance and average 12–16 inches, but they run as big as 22 inches. Brook trout grow larger than average for a high mountain lake and are caught in sizes 12–19 inches. Brown trout remain somewhat stunted at 10–14 inches. The lake is open year-round but is not accessible until the spring thaw, sometime around late June or early July. All methods of fishing are permitted. Boating is permitted without restrictions.

Species: Rainbow, brown and brook trout, kokanee.

Facilities: Fourmile Lake Campground, operated by the Forest Service, has 25 sites, picnic tables, water, and vault toilets. Supplies are available in Medford and Klamath Falls.

Directions: From Medford, go northeast on Hwy. 62 for five miles to Exit 30, then follow Hwy. 140 east for 40 miles to Forest Rd. 3661. Turn north and drive six miles to the campground.

Contact: Klamath Falls Chamber of Commerce, 541/884-5193; ODFW, Klamath Falls District, 541/883-5732; BLM, Klamath Falls Area, 541/883-6916; Freemont–Winema National Forest, 541/885-3400; The Ledge (Mountain Sports and Fly Shop), 541/882-5586; Parker's Rod and Gun Rack, 541/883-3726; Roe Outfitters, 541/884-3825.

55 UPPER KLAMATH LAKE
north of Klamath Falls

Map 5.7, page 325   BEST

Upper Klamath Lake is an enormous body of water, covering 96 square miles in the expansive Klamath Basin. Upon seeing this lake most anglers give up all hopes of fishing, not knowing where to start on such a big lake—and without some knowledge of the fishing, their reaction may well be justified. There is great fishing on Upper Klamath Lake, but it is spotty and seasonal. The strain of redband rainbow trout contained in the lake are extremely intolerant of warm water and very quickly seek cooler water when summer arrives.

All rainbows are wild. Bait fishing is allowed, and only one trout may be kept per day. Trout average 4–6 pounds, and fish up to 12 pounds are common. Water conditions on Klamath Lake are imperative for productive fishing, and since most of the lake averages seven feet deep and is plagued with algae problems, by midspring or early summer the water has sufficiently warmed to push almost all the fish into cooler coves, channels, rivers, and inlets, leaving most of the lake barren. Anglers can ignore most of what they see from the highway and concentrate on a few key areas. During winter and spring, most of the fish congregate at the lake's southern outlet, near Pelican Marina and Moore Park. Boats can be launched from either location, and good fishing is immediately available from the Lakeshore Bridge Crossing out into the bay.

Most anglers slow-troll spinners, spoons, and flies just about anywhere to great effect. Bait anglers can cast night crawlers and PowerBait suspended under floats. Fly anglers and spin casters will find the most success casting flies such as Woolly Buggers, Zonkers, and spinners such as Rooster Tails to the shorelines and making a slow retrieve back to the boat.

Starting in midspring or early summer, water temperatures begin to warm, and algae blooms all but destroy water quality in most of the lake's southern half. The fish retreat to the northern parts of the lake, along the west shore around Eagle Point, Howard Bay, Sholewater Bay, Rocky Point, and Agency Lake. There are two areas on the east shore where fish can be found: the mouth of the Williamson River and the waters around Hagelstein Park on Highway 97. Fish are attracted to these areas by either the presence of deeper water or natural cold-water springs. With the exception of the mouth of the Williamson, boat ramps exist at all these locations, and fishing grounds are rather easy to spot by the presence of other boats. Access to the mouth of the Williamson can be had from the Sportsman River Retreat three miles up the Williamson River off Modoc Point Road or from Henzel Park on Agency Lake. From Henzel Park it is a long eight-mile boat ride to the mouth. Trolling flies and lures remains the most effective way to fish all these areas. Popular flies are those that represent leeches or small baitfish such as Woolly Buggers, Zonkers, and Denny Rickard's Seal Buggers. Popular lures are those that represent baitfish such as Rapalas, Rebels, Little Cleos, and Rooster Tails.

Almost all the fishing on Klamath Lake requires a boat. There are a few springtime bank fisheries, but they are limited and often crowded. Pelican Bay is a good bank fishery in the spring from Moore Park. Howard Bay can be fished from roadside turnouts along Highway 140. Eagle Ridge Road will take you out to Sholewater Bay, Ball Bay, and Eagle Point. Odessa Recreation Site and Campground provides some additional bank access.

Rocky Point is a unique area for fly anglers for its concentration of freshwater springs and spring creeks. Both Recreation and Crystal creeks flow into the bay and can be fished from a pontoon boat, canoe, or drift boat; float tubes would require a lot of kicking. Areas out in front of, and to the south of, the Rocky Point boat launch contain freshwater springs and are productive for big trout.

Species: Wild Upper Klamath Lake redband rainbow trout.

Facilities: Pelican Marina in Klamath Falls has a paved ramp, docks, and a full-service boating store. The city's Moore Park has two marinas, each with paved ramps, restrooms, and docks. Area attractions include Crater Lake, Oregon's only national park, a pleasant dinner cruise on the *Klamath Belle* paddle wheel, and extensive bird- and wildlife-watching. Other boat ramps include:

- **Howard Bay:** Klamath County's ramp (also known as Wocus Bay) is paved and has parking and restrooms.
- **Eagle Ridge Park:** The park has a paved ramp and restrooms.
- **Odessa Campground:** Operated by the Forest Service, the campground has an unimproved ramp, five sites (no fee), and no water.
- **Rocky Point Boat Launch:** This has a paved ramp and restrooms. Rocky Point Resort is on the same, far-northwest corner of Upper Klamath Lake, with a lodge, restaurant, tent sites, RV hookup sites, cabins, and guest rooms.
- **Hagelstein County Park:** This park has a paved ramp, water, restrooms, and 10 campsites.

Directions: Moore Park and Pelican Marina are both in Klamath Falls. The boat ramps along the west shore include the Howard Bay ramp (go three miles south on Hwy. 97, then 12 miles west on Hwy. 140); Odessa Campground (17 miles on Hwy. 140, then one mile north on Forest Service Rd. 3639); Eagle Ridge Park (20 miles on Hwy. 140, then five miles east on Eagle Ridge Rd.); Rocky Point Resort (24 miles on Hwy. 140, then 2.1 miles north on Rocky Point Rd.); and Rocky Point Boat Ramp (five miles further up Rocky Point Rd.). Along the east side of the lake, follow Hwy. 97 north from Klamath Falls for 12 miles to Hagelstein Park.

Contact: Klamath Falls Chamber of Commerce, 541/884-5193; Klamath County Tourism Department, 541/884-0666; ODFW, Klamath Falls District, 541/883-5732; BLM, Klamath Falls District, 541/883-6916; Fremont–Winema National Forest, 541/885-3400; Crater Lake Information, 541/830-8700; Crystal Wood Lodge, 541/381-2322; Roe Cabin at Rocky Point, 541/884-3825; Rocky Point Resort, 541/356-2287; *Klamath Belle* Paddle Wheel, 541/883-4622; Sportsman River Retreat, 541/783-3857; Klamath Wing Watchers, 541/883-5732; Klamath Basin Audubon Society, 800/445-6728; The Ledge (Mountain Sports and Fly Shop), 541/882-5586; Parker's Rod and Gun Rack, 541/883-3726; Big R-Klamath Falls, 541/882-5549; Pelican Marina, 541/882-5834; Guides: Denny Rickards, 541/381-2218; Tight-Line Troutfitters (Bryan Carpenter), 541/882-6610; Darren Roe, 541/884-3825.

56 FISH LAKE
east of Medford in the Rogue River National Forest

Map 5.7, page 325

Fish Lake is in a remote part of the Cascades, surrounded by scenic views and old-growth Douglas fir. This is a quiet but popular setting for valley anglers wishing to escape the heat of Medford. The lake comprises 480 acres, open year-round, and is popular for good catches of large rainbows and brook trout. Annual stocking of trout exceeds 20,000 fish per year, and there are some notable bigger fish exceeding eight pounds. Steelhead smolts are also stocked annually and reach 22 inches in length. Brook trout are naturally reproducing and abundant, averaging 10–12 inches. Trolling flies and lures are the most popular methods of fishing. Still-fishing with bait is

equally productive, with PowerBait and night crawlers being favorites. Boats are the most effective way to fish, but float tubes and canoes also do well. A majority of the fishing takes place at the west end, near the dam, and out front of the resort. Good bank angling can be had along hiking trails on the west bank between the campgrounds and the dam.

Species: Stocked rainbow and brook trout.

Facilities: Families will enjoy the nice campgrounds and resort (May–Oct.). Fish Lake Resort has a boat ramp, six tent sites and 45 RV sites, cabins, plus restrooms, showers, a recreation hall, store, café, and laundry rooms. Fish Lake Campground has a ramp, 19 sites, water, toilets, and bike and boat rentals. Doe Point Campground has 30 sites (five of them walk-in tent sites), water, and toilets. Supplies are available in Medford and Klamath Falls.

Directions: From Medford, go northeast on Hwy. 62 for five miles to Exit 30, then follow Hwy. 140 and go east 30 miles to Fish Lake. All three campgrounds are within a mile of each other on the right side of the road.

Contact: Ashland Chamber of Commerce, 541/482-3486; ODFW, Central Point, 541/826-8774; BLM, Medford, 541/618-2400; Rogue River National Forest, Ashland, 541/552-2900; Rogue Angler, 800/949-5163; The Ashland Outdoor Store, 541/488-1202; G.I. Joe's, Medford, 541/772-9779.

57 LAKE OF THE WOODS
northwest of Klamath Falls in Winema National Forest

Map 5.7, page 325

Lake of the Woods is a large (1,146 acres) natural lake surrounded by forests, and if it were not for the resort, lakeshore homes, motorboats, and water-skiers, it would provide a great wilderness experience. Still, despite the lake's congestion, this is a nice place—possibly too busy for the quiet family vacation but a good place to rent a boat and spend half a day trying to catch large brown trout, kokanee, or perch. Anglers will certainly find the lake less disturbed in the spring and fall, but winter comes fairly quickly here at almost 5,000 feet elevation, and you may get some exceedingly cold weather by late August. (Lake of the Woods is a popular ice-fishing spot.)

Traditionally, Lake of the Woods has been a great producer of large brown trout, which are stocked every year, and kokanee. Today, anglers also have the opportunity to catch illegally introduced bass, perch, crappie, and brown bullhead catfish. Largemouth bass range in size 2–5 pounds, and one fish longer than 15 inches may be kept. Brown trout obtain lunker size with all the available smolts and baitfish, and catches over six pounds are frequent. Since these voracious feeders are most active at night, the lake is kept open for fishing 24 hours a day. Kokanee average 8–12 inches and may be retained at 25 per day. All methods of angling are permitted, including bait.

The lake's west shore has steep lake-bottom drop-offs and is the most popular area for trolling, especially for kokanee in the spring. Otherwise, fishing is open and good on the entire lake. Fishing for bass and other warm-water species gets better as summer progresses. Fish for browns in the low-light hours or at night near the shorelines.

Species: Brown trout, kokanee, bass, perch, crappie, and brown bullhead catfish.

Facilities: Lake of the Woods Resort (year-round) has 27 campsites and eight cabins, plus restrooms, showers, laundry, a café, a lounge, boat ramp, and marina with boat rentals. Supplies are available at the marina. The Forest Service has two campgrounds at the lake: Aspen Point Campground has 60 sites with picnic tables, water, restrooms, and a boat ramp; Sunset Campground has 67 sites, tables, water, a boat ramp, and docks.

Directions: From Klamath Falls, take Hwy. 140 west for 32 miles. For Sunset Campground, turn left (south) on Dead Indian Rd. for two miles. For Aspen Point, go another mile west on Hwy. 140, then turn left (south)

on Forest Rd. 3704 for one mile. The resort is 0.5 mile south of Aspen Point.

Contact: Klamath Falls Chamber of Commerce, 541/884-5193; ODFW, Klamath Falls, 541/883-5732; BLM, Klamath Falls, 541/883-6916; Fremont–Winema National Forest, 541/885-3400; Lake of the Woods Cabins, 541/949-8300; Lake of the Woods Resort, 866/201-4194; The Ledge (Mountain Sports and Fly Shop), 541/882-5586; Parker's Rod and Gun Rack, 541/883-3726; Roe Outfitters, 541/884-3825.

58 EMIGRANT RESERVOIR
southeast of Ashland

Map 5.7, page 325

This 878-acre irrigation reservoir offers fair to good fishing for stocked trout and warm-water species. The reservoir is very popular with recreationalists, water-skiers, and Jet Skiers, and while it has an urban feel, it is surrounded by grass and forested foothills. Emigrant is fairly narrow and spread out between two major arms: Emigrant Creek and Hill Creek. It is fed by numerous other tributaries, and this is where the coolest water can be found most of the year. There is a fair amount of submerged structure and vegetation, creating good habitat for bass, crappie, bluegill, and brown bullhead.

Because the reservoir is subject to irrigation draws, the best trout fishing takes place in the spring and fall. Most successful fishing occurs in the two arms, Emigrant Creek and Hill Creek. Both arms contain numerous small tributaries that attract trout with cooler waters. Warm-water fishing is better in summer, and a lot of anglers focus on the areas around the dam and also in the arms. Landlocked chinook can be fished for in the reservoir's deeper waters near the dam. To catch these small 16-inch salmon, use kokanee fishing techniques. Emigrant Reservoir is open year-round and allows all fishing methods, including bait. Boating is good from three ramps at Emigrant Lake Recreation Area at the northern end of the lake and Songer Wayside at the south end of the Emigrant Arm. Bank fishing is limited to the recreation area and boat ramps.

Species: Stocked rainbow trout; large and smallmouth bass, crappie, bluegill, brown bullhead catfish, landlocked chinook.

Facilities: Emigrant Lake Recreation Area (day-use $3), operated by Jackson County, has 32 hookup sites, 42 tent sites, showers, and two boat ramps; a 280-foot waterslide is open Memorial Day–Labor Day. The ramp at Songer Wayside is unimproved but has restrooms. The nearby city of Ashland is a mecca for culture-hungry residents in southern Oregon and provides interesting amenities in the form of bed-and-breakfasts, gourmet restaurants, shopping, and theater at the internationally renowned Shakespeare Festival. Supplies are available in Ashland.

Directions: From Ashland, travel east on Main St., which is also Hwy. 66. Follow the highway 7.2 miles to the entrance for the recreation area. To reach Songer Wayside, keep going on Hwy. 66 another five miles, around the west and south shores of the lake.

Contact: Ashland Chamber of Commerce, 541/482-3486; Jackson County Parks, 541/774-8183; ODFW, Central Point, 541/826-8774; BLM, Medford, 541/618-2400; Rogue River National Forest, Ashland, 541/552-2900; Oregon Shakespeare Festival, 541/482-4331; Rogue Angler, 800/949-5163; The Ashland Outdoor Store, 541/488-1202; G.I. Joe's, Medford, 541/772-9779.

59 HYATT RESERVOIR
east of Ashland

Map 5.7, page 325

Hyatt is another large irrigation reservoir popular for good catches of larger rainbow trout and largemouth bass. If you're approaching from Ashland, the winding drive on Highway 66 is not one you'll soon forget. In 10 short miles you'll gain almost 3,000 feet of elevation, most of it on tight switchbacks that give stunning views of the

valley below. Once at the lake you'll find a refreshing mountain atmosphere, surrounded by the forested hills of the Rogue National Forest. Families will enjoy the quiet solitude and easy fishing this lake offers. The lake is open to fishing April 22–October 31. All methods of fishing are permitted, including bait. As many as 250,000 trout are stocked per season, and they grow quite quickly. Twenty-inch fish are common, and average catches are 14–16 inches. Most trout are caught by trolling or casting spinners and flies along the bank. Search for tributary mouths along the west shore to find cooler water. Bass and other warm-water fish are best caught in summer when the water has warmed. Best catches occur along the shorelines and around structure. There are three coves at the north end of the lake that are quite productive for bass.

Species: Rainbow trout, largemouth bass, crappie, bluegill, brown bullhead catfish.

Facilities: Hyatt Lake Resort (Apr.–Oct.) has a small tackle shop, a boat ramp, and 35 campsites, 22 of them with full hookups. Cabins are also available. The larger BLM campground has 47 sites and a boat ramp. Camper's Cove, for RVs only, has 23 sites and also a restaurant, bar, store, ramp, and docks. The Pacific Crest Trail runs parallel to the southeast shore of the lake.

Directions: From Ashland, drive east on Hwy. 66 for 17 miles to East Hyatt Lake Rd. Turn north and drive three miles; you'll see here the entrance to the BLM campground. You can also turn left here on Hyatt Prairie Rd. and drive one mile to the Hyatt Lake Resort, or turn right on Hyatt Prairie Rd. and drive 2.5 miles to Campers Cove.

Contact: Ashland Chamber of Commerce, 541/482-3486; ODFW, Central Point, 541/826-8774; BLM, Medford, 541/618-2400; Rogue River National Forest, Ashland, 541/552-2900; Hyatt Lake Resort, 541/482-3331; Hyatt Lake BLM Campground, 541/482-2031; Camper's Cove 541/482-1201; Rogue Angler, 800/949-5163; The Ashland

Outdoor Store, 541/488-1202; G.I. Joe's, Medford, 541/772-9779.

60 HOWARD PRAIRIE RESERVOIR

east of Ashland

Map 5.7, page 325

This popular 1,990-acre irrigation impoundment is surrounded by the pine and fir forests of the Cascade Mountains and is a welcome escape from the heat of the valleys around Ashland and Medford. Howard Prairie is open April 22–October 31 and all methods of fishing are permitted, including bait. Boats can be launched from four different ramps, and seven campgrounds dot the lake shore. A majority of the lake is accessible on foot from surrounding roads and hiking trails, but the campgrounds provide the best access. Good places to start are at the lake's south end, where deeper water is liable to hold bigger trout.

The reservoir is stocked with literally hundreds of thousands of fingerling trout every year. With so much stocking, catching trout is all but expected, and some trout run big, up to five pounds or more. The most popular methods of fishing are still fishing with bait such as PowerBait, night crawlers, and grubs. Trolling spinners and flies will pick up a fair share of fish. The south end of the lake contains the deepest water and consequently attracts most of the anglers, who troll the shorelines on the edges of deeper water. Though the lake is managed exclusively for trout, some dissatisfied anglers decided it might make a better warm-water fishery and so illegally introduced largemouth and smallmouth bass. Since that time their numbers have flourished—to the satisfaction, no doubt, of these rogue fish stockers.

Species: Rainbow trout, large and smallmouth bass.

Facilities: Besides fishing, the area is popular for waterskiing, Jet Skiing, sailing, hiking, and family camping. Howard Prairie Recreation Area (Apr.–Oct.), managed by Jackson County, is a sprawling site with more than 1.5 miles of lake frontage; four campgrounds totaling nearly 350 campsites; three boat ramps; and Howard Prairie Resort, with 300 sites, a restaurant, store, marina, and boat rentals. Grizzly Campground is relatively quiet, with only 21 sites; Willow Point has 40 sites; and Klum Landing has 30 sites and showers. The day-use fee for each ramp at the lake is $3. Supplies are available in Ashland.

Directions: From Ashland, follow Hwy. 66 east for one mile, then turn left (north) on Dead Indian Rd. and follow it 17 miles to Howard Prairie Rd. Turn right (south) and drive three miles to Grizzly Campground, four miles to the resort, seven miles to Willow Point, and 12 miles to Klum Landing.

Contact: Ashland Chamber of Commerce, 541/482-3486; Howard Prairie Lake Resort, 541/482-1979; ODFW, Central Point, 541/826-8774; BLM, Medford, 541/618-2400; Rogue River National Forest, Ashland, 541/552-2900; Rogue Angler, 800/949-5163; The Ashland Outdoor Store, 541/488-1202; G.I. Joe's, Medford, 541/772-9779.

61 KLAMATH RIVER: BELOW JOHN C. BOYLE DAM

southwest of Klamath Falls

Map 5.7, page 325

Another section of the Klamath River is available to anglers and provides great dry–fly-fishing in the summer for small trout. (This section is also part of the Wild and Scenic network of rivers in Oregon.) Much of the river here flows through scenic but remote, rugged canyons, forested in pine and fir. The banks are often dense with willows, and walking rarely takes a direct path along the river, instead requiring navigation around boulders and thick brush. Waders will greatly ease the task of walking through brush or trying to wade the river, and they afford some protection against rattlesnakes.

There are approximately five miles of river between John C. Boyle Dam and the powerhouse downstream. The river here is small because of water diversions, but the fishing is good for 8–12-inch trout, which seem to have a real taste for dry flies. What makes this stretch of water a favorite for many anglers is the fact that dry flies work so well. Flies that consistently take fish are a size 12–14 Adams, Yellow Humpy, Elk Hair Caddis, or Royal Wulff. Access through this stretch is unlimited from roads that follow the river. Fishing around the dam is easier than attempting to fish from the road below the dam, where the road rises above the river and anglers are forced to walk into a steep canyon with no hiking trails. Even wading around the dam can be treacherous, as the area here is composed of the same rocks and grass found in the Keno Stretch of this river.

Below the powerhouse, the river regains its original flow levels and becomes something of a monster with big white water. The fish are more plentiful in this section and slightly bigger, 12–16 inches, and occasionally 18 inches. River flows are highly variable because of water releases from the power station and can present a potential hazard to anglers when the water rises suddenly, gaining a foot or more. It is advisable to call the Pacific Power hotline to learn when water will be released and avoid those times. Roads follow this section, but they are rough and slow going, and four-wheel drives are recommended. Some anglers float this section of river in drift boats, but it is extremely hazardous and should be attempted only by experts. Roe Outfitters (eight miles east of Klamath Falls in Midway) holds a special permit to guide on this section of river. Clients who book fishing trips on this river are often treated to amazing dry–fly-fishing and 60-fish days.

The Klamath produces a lot of insects. Salmon flies and golden stones begin to appear in June and make for some of the best fishing of the season. Caddis hatches are thick during summer, as are assorted mayflies. Grasshoppers and other terrestrials such as ants and beetles work well during the heat of summer.

Patterns to match any of these hatches will prove successful, such as Stimulator, Elk Hair Caddis, Adams, Yellow Humpies. Nymphs such as Hare's Ears, Pheasant Tails, and Stony Fly Nymphs also work great. Effective streamers include Woolly Buggers, Zonkers, and leech patterns.

Fishing is restricted to artificial files and lures and is open year-round. One fish may be kept per day, except June 16–September 30, when the river turns catch-and-release.

Species: Rainbow trout.

Facilities: The only developed campground in the area is a BLM site on Topsy Reservoir. It has 13 sites, picnic tables, vault toilets, and drinking water. The site also has a boat ramp onto the reservoir. Primitive camping is available throughout the area. Supplies are available in Klamath Falls and Keno.

Directions: From Klamath Falls, follow U.S. 97 south for 1.7 miles, then turn right (west) onto Oregon Hwy. 66. Continue nine miles to Keno. From Keno drive west for eight miles on Hwy. 66 to where the highway crosses Topsy Reservoir. To reach the southern bank (river left), turn left (south) on Topsy Grade Rd. on the eastern shore of the reservoir, following signs for Topsy Recreation Site, one mile south on the reservoir. Keep driving on Topsy Grade Rd., which is a four-wheel drive road. After about eight miles, the first time this road drops to river level, you'll see Dorris Rd. coming in from the left (southeast). Stay with Topsy Grade Rd., which now drops into the canyon. After one mile, look for an even smaller road cutting back to the right, into a large flat area that's the home of historic Frain Ranch, now owned by the Pacificorps electric company. Once you're down in this flat, you'll find a two-track road going up- and downstream for two miles, as well as numerous primitive campsites.

To reach the northern bank (river right) and the powerhouse area, continue on Hwy. 66 until it crosses the reservoir, then go another two miles and turn left (south) onto an unnamed road with signs to Boyle Powerhouse.

All along this road, which leads six miles to the powerhouse, you'll have rough hike-in access to the river. Beyond the powerhouse, the road goes from two-lane gravel to one-lane, four-wheel drive with pullouts, and essentially follows the river all the way to the California border.

Contact: Klamath Falls Chamber of Commerce, 541/884-5193; ODFW, Klamath Falls, 541/883-5732; BLM, Klamath Falls, 541/883-6916; Freemont–Winema National Forest, 541/885-3400; Pacific Power Hotline, 800/547-1501; Keno Store, 541/884-4944; The Ledge (Mountain Sports and Fly Shop), 541/882-5586; Parker's Rod and Gun Rack, 541/883-3726; Roe Outfitters (Darren Roe), 541/884-3825.

62 WOOD RIVER
west of Chiloquin

Map 5.8, page 326   **BEST (**

The Wood River is one of the premier brown trout and migratory rainbow rivers in Oregon. It flows 30 exceedingly windy miles from the spring-fed headwaters at Kimball State Park to Agency Lake near Petric Park. Along the way it collects two significant spring creek tributaries, Crooked Creek and Fort Creek. The river flows through a valley of scenic pasture lands and ranch property, and it is surrounded by the mountains of the Winema National Forest. The rim of Crater Lake can be seen at the north end of the valley. Ducks, geese, eagles, owls, hawks, and many more birds are abundant.

Fishing is open April 22–October 31 and is catch-and-release only with artificial flies and lures. The Wood River is rich in aquatic insects, producing many significant hatches of mayflies, caddis, stone flies, damsels, dragonflies, and midges. Summer grasshopper hatches produce some explosive fishing, and other terrestrials, such as ants and beetles, also work. Fishing is often difficult and technical. Success depends on presentation and keeping your presence hidden, which can be difficult when walking over undercut banks. The river is mostly composed of smooth, winding surfaces interspaced with shallow riffles, deep pools, and severely undercut banks. Wood and other debris is abundant in the river and accounts for the loss of a lot of tackle. Dry flies are effective in the mornings and early afternoons, and rising fish are a frequent sight. Otherwise nymphs and streamers are the best way to attract big browns and migratory rainbows. All presentations should be downstream, regardless of the fly being used, to hide your presence from the fish.

Access to the river is limited. Ninety-nine percent of the river is on private property, a frustrating fact for many anglers. There are four access points for bank anglers: Kimball State Park at the headwaters, Kimball Day Use Area a mile downstream, the Loosley Road crossing, and the Petric Park Dike. With the exception of Loosley Road, these are all public access points, the best being Kimball Day Use Area. This area is managed for anglers and provides about 1.5 miles of access on the east bank. There is a lot of good water here, and the patient, observing angler will be well rewarded for due diligence. The Loosley Road crossing is private property that a generous landowner has opened for the public to use. Access is through a gate and down the east side of the river only. Access here is unlimited as far as you can walk. Don't walk close to the bank unless you want to scare fish; wait for rising fish if you see none; make all presentations downstream; resort to streamers and nymphs when there is no surface activity.

Kimball State Park is not very good fishing. The water here is so cold that it is sterile and holds no fish. The river improves about 600 yards below the headwaters, but the only way to reach this water is by canoe or kayak. The Petric Park access requires a 0.5-mile walk along a dike to an area just above the mouth. Fishing can be very good here, especially with casting spinners and flies. A lot of fish stage in this section, waiting to go up the river. Float tubing is especially popular in this section and in the canal leading to the boat ramp.

Species: Wild migratory Upper Klamath Lake redband rainbow trout, brown trout.

Facilities: Kimball State Park (year-round) has 1.5 miles of paved trails, numerous fishing platforms, restrooms, and 10 campsites but no drinking water. Additional camping is available at Agency Lake Resort. Petric County Park (Apr.–Oct.) has a boat ramp and restrooms. Supplies are available in Fort Klamath and Chiloquin.

Directions: From Chiloquin, go north on Hwy. 97 for two miles, then turn left (west) onto Chiloquin Hwy. Follow this about five miles and turn left (south) on Modoc Point Rd., which you'll reach 0.1 mile after crossing Hwy. 62. Petric Park is two miles south on Modoc Point Rd. To reach Kimball State Park, turn north on Hwy. 62 instead, traveling eight miles to Fort Klamath Junction. Highway 62 turns west; to reach Kimball Park, continue north on Sun Mountain Rd. for three miles to the park. The Loosley Rd. crossing is a mile west of Hwy. 62; turn west about three miles south of the Fort Klamath Junction. Occasionally, roads in and around Fort Klamath and the Wood River are halted when cowboys drive cattle down the road to new pasture lands.

Contact: Klamath Falls Chamber of Commerce, 541/884-5193; ODFW, Klamath Falls, 541/883-5732; BLM, Klamath Falls, 541/883-6916; Fremont–Winema National Forest, 541/885-3400; Crystal Wood Lodge, 541/381-2322; Horseshoe Ranch, Fort Klamath, 866/658-5933; Crater Lake Resort, 541/381-2349; The Ledge (Mountain Sports and Fly Shop), 541/882-5586; Parker's Rod and Gun Rack, 541/883-3726; Fort Klamath General Store, 541/381-2263; Guides: Tight-Line Troutfitters (Bryan Carpenter), 541/882-6610; Sid Mathis, 541/884-3222; Miranda Guide Service, 888/810-0618; Marlin Rampy, 541/660-3780; Roe Outfitters (Darren Roe), 541/884-3825; Craig Schuhmann, crsscs@hotmail.com.

63 LOWER WILLIAMSON RIVER

north of Klamath Falls

Map 5.8, page 326   BEST (

The lower Williamson forms at the southern end of Klamath Marsh and runs south approximately 26 miles to Upper Klamath Lake near Modoc Point Road. Along its route it flows through the Williamson River Recreation Area and Collier State Park, where it picks up Spring Creek before running through Chiloquin. Below Chiloquin the river increases in volume after picking up the Sprague River. Five miles below the confluence with the Sprague, it is crossed by Highway 97 and carries on another six miles to the lake. The river is beautiful, with gin-clear water flowing through corridors of aspens and pines and surrounded by the hills of Winema National Forest.

The primary catches here are for large Upper Klamath Lake redband trout and some brown trout. Average catches range 4–6 pounds, and a two-fish day is pretty good. Catches up to 15 pounds and more are available, and 10-pounders are common. The river produces several notable hatches, including salmon flies, caddis, yellow "sally" stone flies, trios, *Callibaetis*, October caddis, and blue-wing olives. The most famous hatch is the *Hexagenia*, a large yellow mayfly that emerges the last week of June–the first of August. *Hexagenia* can be fished with some success around Collier State Park and down below the Waterwheel Campground; otherwise it takes a boat to reach most of the "Hex" water.

Upper Klamath Lake redband trout have two important traits. First, they are the progeny of landlocked steelhead and as such, they behave like steelhead when they move from the lake to the river. This means that the fish may or may not be present in the river. Likewise, their locations change from day to day as the run moves through, and they might go back out to the lake. This is one of the greatest misunderstandings about this river and why a lot of anglers have such a difficult time catching fish here: The fish move. Resident trout populations on the Williamson are generally thought to be much smaller in size, and these are the fish most often caught by visiting anglers.

Second, unlike steelhead, redbands are aggressive feeders and love to chase down a good meal. Big streamers (4s–6s) and smaller ones (12s, 14s, 16s) work equally well. Drawing a strike from these fish is 90 percent presentation, whether it's a small Soft Hackle or a giant Zonker, and the key is how you move the fly in the water. Don't be afraid to twitch your fly as it swings through the run. Skated dry flies have been known to take a lot of fish. Nymphs will work in the faster pocket water, but there aren't a lot of nymphing areas on the river. The best streamers are Black Flash Buggers, maroon, gold, and black/purple Seal Buggers, Zonkers, and any leech pattern such as a Mole Hair Leech or Mini-Leech.

The larger fish tend to hold best in what is typically identified as steelhead-type water—passage or resting water alongside fast runs, deep in channels, around ledges and big obstructions, and in shallower resting water on the edges of pools. While some fish may be caught in riffle water, this is not where the big fish hold. Catching big fish in the Williamson means going deep in medium to medium-fast runs. Six-weight rods with full sinking clear intermediate lines are standard equipment throughout the summer for streamer fishing. Type II and III full sinking lines are useful when the water is high in spring. Fluorocarbon leaders are a must.

Traditional gear anglers do well on Rooster Tails, Rainbow Spinners, and Rapalas. Again, the key is to fish the good water, deeper runs with faster current, and vary your retrieves imparting some jerking motion with the rod tip. Use slightly heavier rods than you would normaly use for trout and six-pound fluorocarbon line.

Above the Williamson River Recreation Area, the river is quite small and flows through canyons. Access is good, but difficult, and should be considered more for exploration than quality fishing. Access points include Kirk Bridge off Forest Road 9740 and downstream, above the recreation area off Forest Road 9730 where the road crosses the river. Here, the west bank is open to public access. Though big fish do inhabit the upper river toward October, most of this river contains smaller fish. Kirk Bridge to the headwaters is open April 22–October 31. Below Kirk Bridge to the river mouth the river is open May 27–October 31.

A majority of the fishing for big rainbows begins at Collier State Park, where several miles of river up and down the west bank are accessible to anglers. The confluence of Spring Creek and the Williamson in the park is a popular hole for nymph and dry–fly-fishing. Below the confluence, anglers can walk on the west bank on a good trail to spot holes where fish may be lying. A lot of this water is very thin and shallow, and holding water is difficult to identify. Most anglers have the best luck casting to the east bank with streamers and letting them swing down in the runs. A mile down from Collier, private property is identified by signs and fences and is the end of access unless you stay in the water. The river above Chiloquin is mostly private with no boat ramps. Angling from a floating device is prohibited. About the only means of floating this river is with a canoe or kayak to the bridge in Chiloquin.

The next access is at Chiloquin County Park across from the airport and just below the confluence with the Sprague River. Here the river becomes much bigger and is composed of riffles, deep holes, and rock ledges. Anglers can fish the west bank with ease from the boat ramp down one mile to where the river bends at the highway. Alternatively, carefully cross the river above the first set of riffles and walk up the east bank to the Sprague River confluence. This is also the only place to launch a drift boat or pontoon boat and float five miles downriver to the take-out at the Waterwheel Campground below the Highway 97 crossing.

Or, you can float another two miles downriver to the Sportsman River Retreat Park. Below the Waterwheel Campground the river slows considerably, and the fishing is difficult.

Species: Upper Klamath Lake redband rainbow trout, brown trout.

Facilities: The Williamson River Recreation Area is operated by Winema National Forest and includes three tent sites and seven RV sites, as well as picnic tables, vault toilets, and drinking water. Collier State Park has 18 tent sites and 50 hookup sites, showers, water, picnicking, and, for what it's worth, a logging museum and logging movies on summer weekend nights. Waterwheel Campground has six tent sites and 28 RV sites, as well as drinking water, showers, laundry, and a store. The ramp at Chiloquin is unimproved but does have restrooms. Supplies are available in Chiloquin.

Directions: From Klamath Falls, start by driving north on Hwy. 97. You'll cross the river at Waterwheel Campground in 16 miles. Six miles farther north, you'll come to Hwy. 422/Chiloquin Hwy. Turn right (northeast) here, and immediately on the right you'll see Chiloquin boat ramp. For Collier State Park, stay on Hwy. 97; it's 28 miles north from Klamath Falls, about six miles north of Chiloquin. From here, go northeast on Forest Rd. 9730 for one mile to Williamson River Recreation Area. Road 9730 crosses the Williamson about 1.5 miles north of here.

Contact: Klamath Falls Chamber of Commerce, 541/884-5193; City of Chiloquin, 541/783-2717; ODFW, Klamath Falls, 541/883-5732; BLM, Klamath Falls, 541/883-6916; Fremont–Winema National Forest, Chiloquin, 541/783-4001; Melitas Motel and Café, 541/783-2401; Crystal Wood Lodge, 541/381-2322; Lonesome Duck, 800/367-2540; Water Wheel Campground, 541/783-2738; Collier Memorial State Park, 541/783-2471; The Ledge (Mountain Sports and Fly Shop), 541/882-5586; Parker's Rod and Gun Rack, 541/883-3726; Guides: Tight-Line Troutfitters (Bryan Carpenter), 541/882-

6610; Sid Mathis, 541/884-3222; Miranda Guide Service, 888/810-0618; Marlin Rampy, 541/660-3780; Roe Outfitters (Darren Roe), 541/884-3825; Craig Schuhmann, crsscs@hotmail.com.

64 AGENCY LAKE
north of Klamath Falls

Map 5.8, page 326

Agency and Upper Klamath Lakes are essentially the same body of water, separated by a small channel; Agency sits to the north of Upper Klamath. Large redband trout from Upper Klamath migrate into Agency seeking cool waters that come from the mouths of the Wood River and other spring-fed creeks such as Seven-Mile. There is a higher concentration of brown trout in Agency than in Upper Klamath; most of them migrate up the Wood River, the Seven-Mile, and other spring creeks.

Rainbow trout in Agency Lake average 4–6 pounds, but 10-pound fish are common, and 15-pound fish are caught every year. This is exclusively a boat fishery with no bank access to productive water. There are three boat ramps, one at Petric Park on the Wood River and two on Agency Lake at Henzel County Park and the Agency Lake Resort. The put-in at Petric Park requires a 1.5-mile row or motor out to the lake through the Wood River Canal.

This is a year-round fishery, but the best fishing occurs June–fall. A majority of the fishing during these times occurs between the river mouths of the Wood River and Seven-Mile Creek, both in the north end of the lake, and in the canal between Agency and Upper Klamath lakes. Trolling flies and lures is best most of the year. A common practice is something called wind drifting, in which anglers will cast out their tackle and let the wind push the boat, trailing the lures behind. Special catch-and-release, no-bait restrictions apply around the mouth of the Wood River.

Popular flies for trolling include Zonkers, Woolly Buggers, and Seal Buggers. Lures that represent baitfish are most productive and include Rapalas, Rooster Tails, and spoons. Bait is always effective, the favorites being night crawlers and PowerBait.

Species: Wild brown trout, Upper Klamath Lake redband rainbow trout.

Facilities: Agency Lake Resort has tent and RV sites as well as a paved ramp, boat rentals, and moorage. Henzel and Petric county parks (Apr.–Sept.) both have a paved ramp and restrooms. Supplies are available in Chiloquin.

Directions: From Klamath Falls, drive north on Hwy. 97 for 17 miles, then turn left (west) onto Modoc Point Rd. You'll reach Henzel Park in seven miles, Agency Lake Resort in 10, and Petric Park in 14 miles.

Contact: Klamath Falls Chamber of Commerce, 541/884-5193; Klamath County Parks, 541/883-5121; ODFW, 541/883-5732; BLM, 541/883-6916; Fremont–Winema National Forest, 541/885-3400; Crystal Wood Lodge, 541/381-2322; Agency Lake Resort, 541/783-2489; *Klamath Belle* Paddle Wheel, 541/883-4622; The Ledge (Mountain Sports and Fly Shop), 541/882-5586; Parker's Rod and Gun Rack, 541/883-3726; Guides: Denny Rickards, 541/381-2218; Tight-Line Troutfitters (Bryan Carpenter), 541/882-6610; Roe Outfitters (Darren Roe), 541/884-3825.

65 KLAMATH RIVER: KENO DAM TO TOPSY RESERVOIR

below Keno Dam

Map 5.8, page 326   **BEST (**

The six miles of river between Keno Dam and Topsy Reservoir (also known as Doyle Reservoir) is "big fish" water, holding many of the same fish found in the Williamson River and Klamath Lake. Average catches are much smaller, 16–18 inches, but many fish here go over 10 pounds. The river flows through timbered, rocky canyons for its whole length, and though scenic and accessible, it is very difficult and dangerous wading. Don't let the muddy

water deter your expectations; the river runs dirty all year.

The best place for access to the river is below Keno Dam, via unimproved roads from Keno. Most anglers park at the end of this road and hike up- or downriver. The water is composed of deep holes and big boulders and is best avoided unless you're very sure-footed and in good physical condition. Walking the bank is not easy over grass-covered boulders, and it can be quite exhausting. Other access points include the power-line crossing on Highway 66, three miles west of Keno, and Sportsman's Park five miles west of Keno. At the power-line crossing, park by the road and walk down into the canyon. Sportsman's Park is an easy drive to the river and offers access to the water below the canyon. The fish are smaller in this section, but just as prolific.

Effective flies include most nymphs, but also big streamers such as Muddler Minnows, Zonkers, Zoo Cougars, and Woolly Buggers to imitate the high population of chub minnows, a primary food source for big trout. Bigger streamers seem to work better. Streamers can be cast down and across, and when that's not working try an upstream approach; cast upriver and let the fly swim downriver. There are prolific hatches of caddis and other insects, but it's not often one sees fish feeding on the surface. At these times you might try a Skated Elk Hair Caddis or Stimulator. Spin anglers can use baitfish patterns such as Rapalas, Crayfish Plugs, Rooster Tails, and spoons such as a Little Cleo. Keep the lures deep, especially through the deeper runs. Vary retrieves, imparting some jerks with the rod tip.

The river is closed to bait fishing, and only one trout may be retained per day. The river is open to fishing January 1–June 15 and October 1–December 31. Fishing is good whenever the river is open and can be quite popular.

Species: Upper Klamath Lake redband trout.

Facilities: Keno Dam Recreation Site (Memorial Day–Labor Day), operated by Pacificorps electric company, has 25 campsites, toilets, and a boat ramp onto Keno Reservoir. Sportsman's

Park doesn't offer any fishing-related activities; its archery ranges, offroad biking, and so on are just something to drive by to get to the river. Supplies are available in Keno and Klamath Falls.

Directions: From the west end of Keno, follow signs for Keno Dam Recreation Site; it's about 1.5 miles north of Hwy. 66. The power-line crossing is about three miles west of town on Hwy. 66. For Sportsman's Park, drive west of Keno on Hwy. 66 about seven miles and turn north at a sign for the park; if you reach Topsy Reservoir, you missed it by about 0.6 mile. Drive one mile north to the park, then skirt the eastern edge of it, making your way upstream and toward the canyon. You can also get to the far side of the reservoir. Continue west on Hwy. 66 until it crosses the reservoir,

then turn right (north) onto Keno Access Rd. (about 0.1 mile west of the reservoir), then right (east) on Hall Rd., which leads past Spencer Creek and, after about a mile, to an area where you can hike up into the canyon. All roads, other than Hwy. 66 and the developed access roads, are rough, essentially four-wheel drive; always carry extra water, fuel, and a BLM map.

Contact: Klamath Falls Chamber of Commerce, 541/884-5193; ODFW, Klamath Falls, 541/883-5732; BLM, Klamath Falls, 541/883-6916; Fremont–Winema National Forest, 541/885-3400; Keno Store, 541/884-4944; The Ledge (Mountain Sports and Fly Shop), 541/882-5586; Parker's Rod and Gun Rack, 541/883-3726; Roe Outfitters, 541/884-3825.

SOUTHEASTERN OREGON

© CRAIG SCHUHMANN

BEST FISHING SPOTS

❰ **Brown Trout**
Lower Owyhee River, page 416

❰ **Smallmouth Bass**
Warm Springs Reservoir, page 415

❰ **Hike-In Fisheries**
Donner und Blitzen River, page 439

❰ **Places to Teach Kids to Fish**
Chickahominy Reservoir, page 410

Spend some time in this mainly arid region and

you may be reminded of the badlands of South Dakota or Nebraska: a hot, desert landscape with wide-open vistas and long straight roads that seem to lead nowhere. Not all areas are dry and devoid of forests, though. Pine forests and grasslands surround the drier areas of the Central Basin and Range. The Sycan, Sprague, and Chewaucan Rivers are in pleasant forests and green meadowlands that make great retreats from the summer heat. What's particularly appealing about the desert lakes and rivers in this region is the strong contrast between the stark landscape, where little seems to thrive, and the potentially big, hard-fishing trout that inhabit these waters.

Unlike in most of Oregon, fishable bodies of water in the Southeastern region are not within a half-hour's drive of each other – roads are circuitous, rarely running in directions you want to go. Fishing waters such as Mann Lake and the Donner und Blitzen and Owyhee Rivers in the region's far corner are 50-100 miles apart, with roads traversing mountain ranges much like switchbacks on a hiking trail. Anglers may end up driving through parts of Nevada they never knew existed (sorry, no casinos).

What anglers may be surprised by are the great distances one has to travel to get to fish that may not exist because the reservoir has gone dry or the river has evaporated. A large part of Southeastern Oregon lies in the Oregon Closed Basin. All the area's mountain runoff and precipitation collects in reservoirs and lakes, where it remains until it evaporates or gets used. This type of watershed is unique in Oregon. Other watersheds are dynamic: They have a steady supply of water from mountainous areas and moist climates that feed lakes and rivers that then return it to a larger water source to repeat the cycle. Not so in most of Southeastern Oregon, where rivers often run at trickles and reservoirs are precious sources of water for farmers and ranchers.

The problems of distance are further compounded by remoteness and weather. Towns are few, as are gas stations and supply points, and roads can be rough and dangerous, especially when wet. Because so many of these waters are best fished in the spring and fall – when water quality is best or fishing pressure has decreased – chances of running into sudden bad weather and muddy roads are better than 70 percent. If you choose to go in summer, be prepared for all sorts of nasty weather – and blazing hot temperatures. Freak thunderstorms are common in summer, as are snowstorms and howling windstorms. There are some fine fisheries in the perimeter, but they are solitary and remote; travel to these areas should not be undertaken lightly and should be attempted only in small expeditions. Self-sufficiency is key and anglers need to come prepared with four-wheel drives, good tire jacks, spare tires, plenty of water, sunscreen, and a set of clothes for all types of weather.

Though fisheries come second to farming, the BLM and ODFW make an effort to ensure quality fisheries in the region. Stocking programs have vigilantly kept fish in Chickahominy, Mann, Moon, and Krumbo Reservoirs. Special species, such as Mann Lake cutthroats, brown trout, hybrid bass, Alvord cutthroat, Lahontan cutthroat, and Goose Lake redbands have been restored or introduced to withstand the grueling climatic changes and harsh environments of high alkaline lakes. Stocking has also improved warm-water fisheries, including prize catches of perch, crappie, and smallmouth bass. And habitat restoration and protection through such watershed-management vehicles as the Wild and Scenic River designations have greatly improved water quality to support stable fish populations.

As visitors whose sole purpose is recreation, be mindful that sometimes the fish will not be where you want them to be. Note those fisheries that are susceptible to fluctuating water conditions and use the included references to call ahead and plan trips accordingly. The BLM, Forest Service, and ODFW are invaluable resources that are also extremely generous and knowledgeable about local fishing and stocking programs – many of them are anglers just like you. If you plan your trip well, and ignore what your mind might tell you about the perceived lack of water around you, you can have a truly memorable fishing experience in the deserts of Southeastern Oregon.

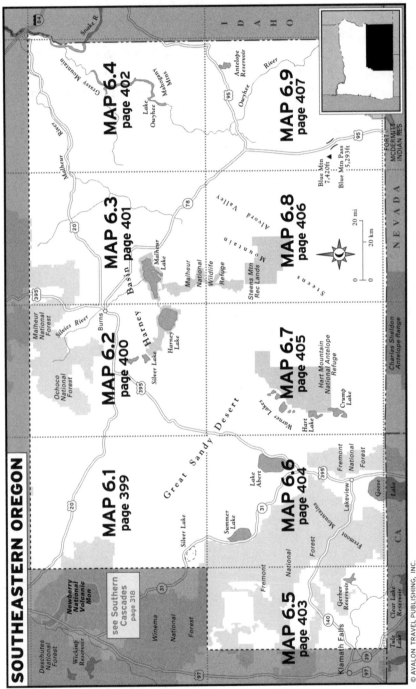

SOUTHEASTERN OREGON

MAP 6.1 page 399

MAP 6.2 page 400

MAP 6.3 Basin page 401

MAP 6.4 page 402

MAP 6.5 page 403

MAP 6.6 page 404

MAP 6.7 page 405

MAP 6.8 page 406

MAP 6.9 page 407

see Southern Cascades page 318

Deschutes National Forest

Newberry National Volcanic Mon

Wickiup Reservoir

Winema National Forest

Fremont National Forest

Klamath Falls

Tule Lake

Clear Lake Reservoir

Gerber Reservoir

Goose Lake

Lakeview

Fremont Mountains

Summer Lake

Silver Lake

Lake Abert

Great Sandy Desert

Warner Lakes

Hart Lake

Crump Lake

Hart Mountain National Antelope Refuge

Fremont National Forest

Ochoco National Forest

Malheur National Forest

Silver Lake

Silvies River

Burns

Harney Lake

Harney

Malheur Lake

Malheur National Wildlife Refuge

Alvord Valley

Steens Mtn Rec Lands

Steens Mountain

Charles Sheldon Antelope Range

Blue Mtn 7,420ft ▲

Blue Mtn Pass 5,293ft

McDERMITT INDIAN RES

N E V A D A

C A

Malheur River

Grassy Mountain

Lake Owyhee

Mahogue Mtns

Antelope Reservoir

Owyhee River

Snake R.

I D A H O

20 mi
20 km

© AVALON TRAVEL PUBLISHING, INC.

Map 6.1

Sites 1-2
Page 408

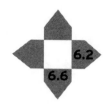

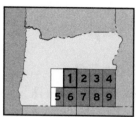

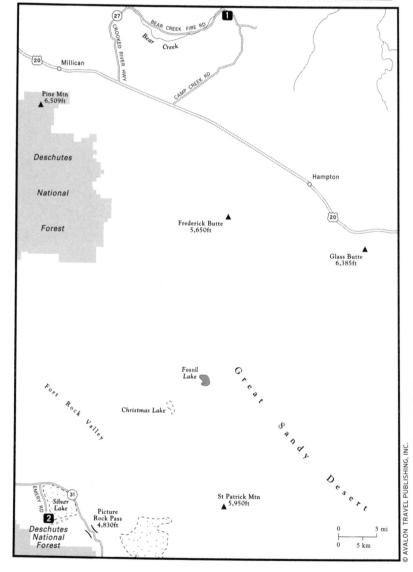

© AVALON TRAVEL PUBLISHING, INC.

Map 6.2

Sites 3-7
Pages 409-411

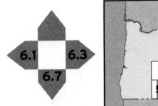

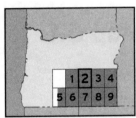

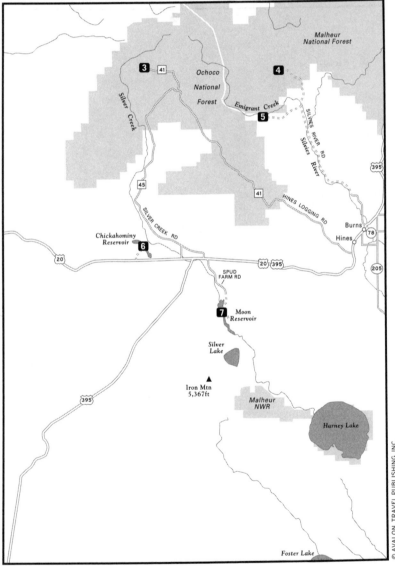

Map 6.3

Sites 8-12
Pages 412-416

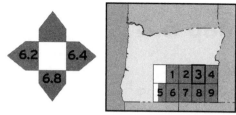

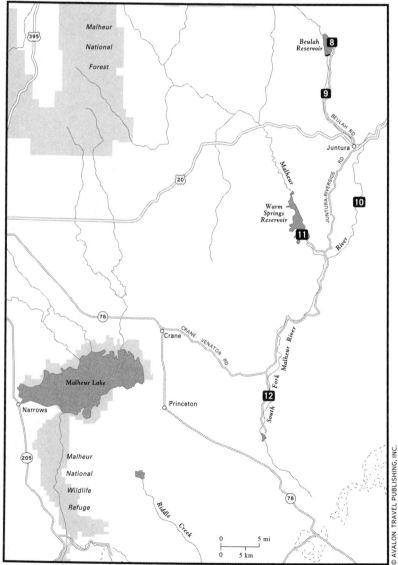

Map 6.4

Sites 13-15
Pages 416-419

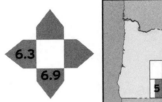

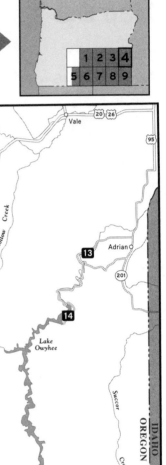

Map 6.5

Sites 16-21
Pages 419-424

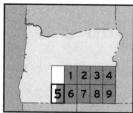

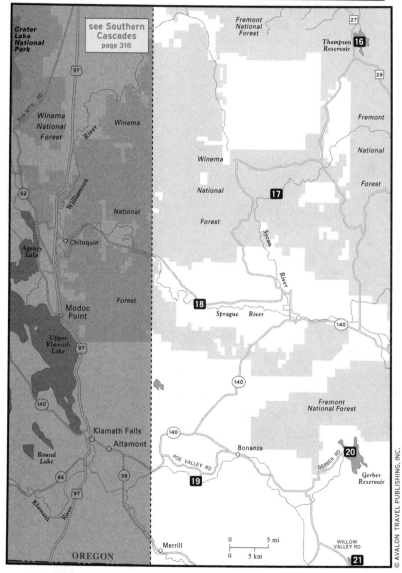

© AVALON TRAVEL PUBLISHING, INC.

Map 6.6

Sites 22-38
Pages 424-436

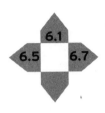

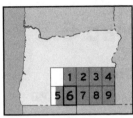

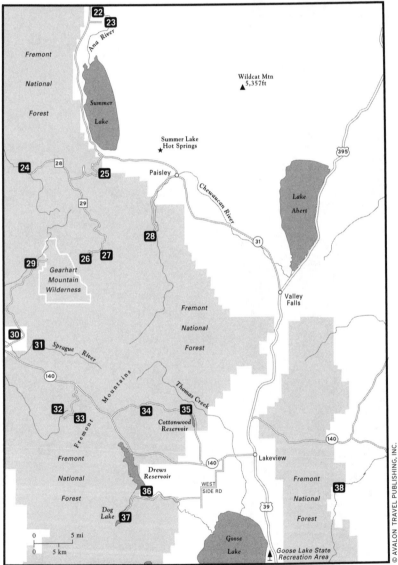

Map 6.7

Sites 39-40
Pages 437-438

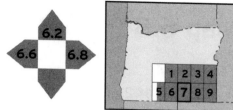

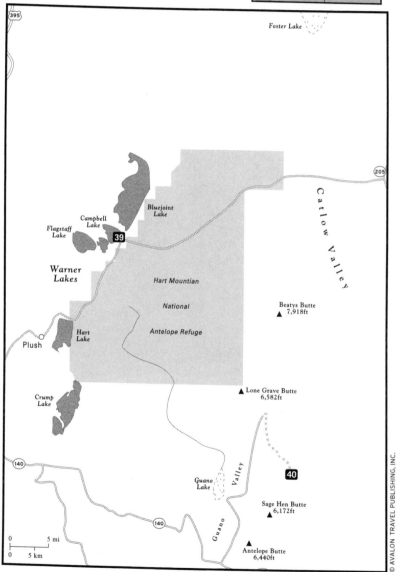

Map 6.8

Sites 41-44
Pages 439-442

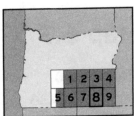

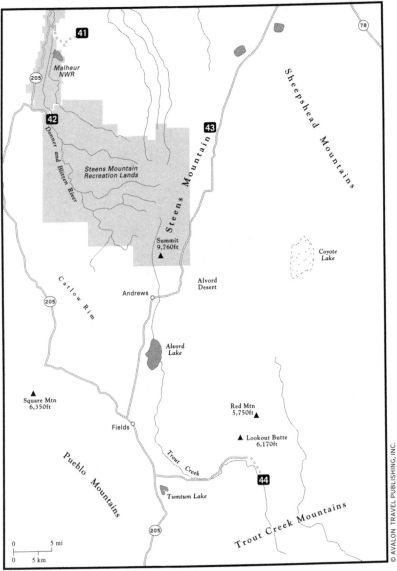

Map 6.9

Sites 45-46
Pages 442-443

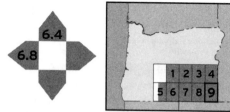

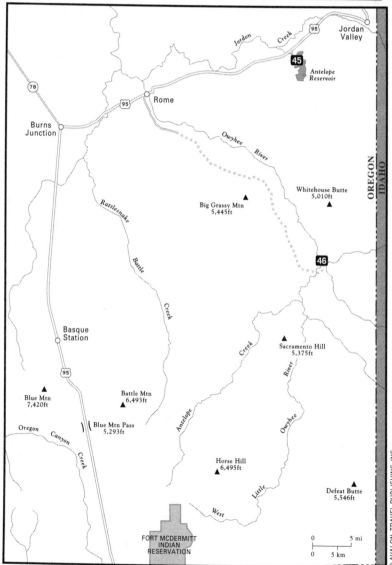

1 ANTELOPE FLATS RESERVOIR

in the Ochoco National Forest
south of Prineville

Map 6.1, page 399

A somewhat remote and high-elevation lake, Antelope Flats Reservoir has pleasant scenery and higher-than-average rainfall for the area. The lake covers less than 170 acres and has an average depth of 15 feet. It provides fair to good fishing for stocked rainbow trout in the 10-inch range and winter holdovers that can reach several pounds. The best time to fish is spring, when the roads clear and the lake thaws. Bank angling is good, but a boat really helps here. Bank anglers can fish with few obstructions from the boat launch to the dam. Trollers generally use flies such as leech patterns or baitfish imitations. Spinners and bait also work. When trolling, look for transition points in the lake bottom, rocky areas, points of land, or weed beds. The deepest parts of the lake are around the dam at the west end. Trolling the shoreline anywhere 15–20 feet off the bank from west to east is a good way to start. If you're spooking fish, stop trolling and start casting lures or flies with sinking line. The east end of the lake tends to be shallow near the creek inlet.

Species: Stocked rainbow trout.

Facilities: Camping is available at the lake and includes a boat ramp, picnic tables, and fire rings—but no drinking water. Buy supplies ahead of time; Prineville is the most convenient place for this.

Directions: To reach the lake from Prineville drive southeast on Hwy. 380 (Paulina Hwy.) 32 miles to County Rd. 17. Turn south and drive approximately nine miles to the lake.

Contact: Bend Chamber of Commerce, 541/382-3221; Ochoco National Forest, 541/416-6500; ODFW, Prineville, 541/447-5111.

2 DUNCAN RESERVOIR

south of Silver Lake

Map 6.1, page 399

Duncan Reservoir, a 33-acre irrigation impoundment two miles east of Silver Lake, is managed for stocked rainbow trout and is open all year. Rich waters tend to grow trout fast, to 20 inches or more by fall. Some holdovers from the previous season will be lurking in spring. Duncan Reservoir Access provides a boat ramp and small primitive campground with restrooms. With all the good fishing in the area, Duncan Reservoir is not a first choice, but it is a possible overnight option. Anglers will generally not be disappointed if they arrive in the spring or fall and launch a small boat or float tube. One can spend a relaxing morning or evening fishing for larger trout in the deeper waters and against the bank. Flies, bait, and spinners are all allowed. Fly anglers should pay attention to possible insect hatches for some dry-fly or emerger fishing. Small leech patterns and nymphs trolled back to the angler are sure to provide some results. A small outlet provides fishing in the early spring before it dries up completely in the summer. Those wishing to catch brown bullhead catfish can twitch small nymph patterns off the bottom or use bait such as worms or cheese.

Species: Trout, brown bullheads, stocked rainbows.

Facilities: Camping, a boat ramp, and restrooms are all provided at the lake. Supplies can be had in Silver Lake, but anglers should come well prepared. A popular chuck-wagon barbecue restaurant, the Cowboy Dinner Tree, can be found on Hwy. 28 near Silver Lake.

Directions: From Silver Lake take Hwy. 31 east six miles to Emery Rd. Turn south on Emery Rd. and make another quick right on Forest Rd. 6197. Follow the forest road four miles to the lake, where it dead-ends into Duncan Reservoir Access.

Contact: Christmas Valley Chamber of Commerce, 541/576-2166; Fremont–Winema National Forest, 541/947-2151; Silver Lake Ranger District, 541/576-2107; ODFW, Summer Lake, 541/943-3324; BLM, Lakeview District, 541/947-2177; Cowboy Dinner Tree (reservations required), 541/576-2426.

3 DELINTMENT LAKE
in the Ochoco National Forest
northwest of Burns

Map 6.2, page 400

Delintment is a high mountain lake (elevation 5,536 feet) situated in a refreshing pine forest in the Ochoco National Forest. Anglers will find this a nice change of scenery from the stark and windswept beauty of most of Southeastern Oregon's desert reservoirs and streams. This 50-acre lake was created for recreation by damming Delintment Creek. It is stocked every spring, and holdovers from the previous years can get up to 3–4 pounds; average catches range 10–14 inches. Because of the lake's shallow depth (15 feet) it is susceptible to winterkills that can completely wipe out the fish populations; 2003 was such a year. The rich waters grow fish quickly, and fingerlings planted in the spring reach legal size by fall.

From ice-out in the spring to fall, the lake fishes well all year. This is a great place for families who want to introduce small children to fishing; the fishing is not difficult, and a worm and bobber fished from the bank will catch fish all day. Flies and lures also work. Small insect hatches will keep dry-fly anglers happy during summer, and a float tube is a great way to fish the shorelines. Boats are allowed on the lake with a five mph speed limit, and anglers can troll deeper waters for larger trout.

Species: Rainbow trout.

Facilities: There is a nice Forest Service campground on the lake along with a boat ramp, day-use area, and wheelchair-accessible pier. The closest towns for supplies are Hines and Burns.

Directions: From Burns, drive two miles west on Hwy. 20 to Hines. Look for Hines Logging Rd. (County Rd. 47) to the east of town. Turn north on Hines Logging Rd. and drive for 12 miles to County Rd. 41. Turn west on County Rd. 41 and drive 35 miles to the lake.

Contact: Harney County Chamber of Commerce Burns, Oregon 541/573-2636; Ochoco National Forest, 541/416-6500; ODFW, Hines, 541/573-6582; Kiger Fly Shop, 541/573-1329, www.oregonvos.net/~rwassom/kigercreek.html.

4 YELLOW JACKET RESERVOIR
in the Malheur National Forest
northwest of Burns

Map 6.2, page 400

Family-friendly Yellow Jacket is a small but quaint 35-acre lake surrounded by pine forests at the base of Sugarloaf Mountain. A small inlet feeds the lake at the north end, and the southern outlet forms Yellow Jacket Creek, a tributary of the inaccessible Silvies River. The lake offers fair to good fishing for rainbow trout year-round, with the best fishing occurring in the spring and fall; winter access is often limited by snowfall. Average catches are 8–12 inches with some bigger fish present. Bait, flies, and lures are all allowed and work well on these stocked trout. With good bank access, hiking trails, and a campground, young anglers can cast worms and bobbers all day to catch small pan-size trout. Fly anglers can troll or strip streamers from a float tube or from the bank and fish small insect hatches during the day. Spinners such as black, red, and gold Rooster Tails in smaller sizes are always productive. When fishing from a boat, keep to the center of the lake and close to the earthen dam where the waters are the deepest. Both the south and north ends tend to be shallow and marshy.

Species: Stocked rainbow trout.

Facilities: Camping is available at the lake with a small boat ramp, restrooms, tables, pit barbecues, and drinking water. The lake will accommodate only small, nonmotorized boats and float tubes.

Directions: From Burns, drive two miles west

on Hwy. 20 to Hines. Look for Hines Logging Rd. (County Rd. 47) to the east of town. Turn north on Hines Logging Rd. and drive for 30 miles into the Malheur National Forest until you hit County Rd. 37. Turn east, and in approximately two miles turn south on Forest Rd. 3745. The lake will appear through the trees. Supplies are available in Burns.

Contact: Harney County Chamber of Commerce Burns, Oregon 541/573-2636; Malheur National Forest, 541/575-3000; Emigrant Creek Ranger District, 541/573-4300; ODFW, Hines, 541/573-6582; Kiger Fly Shop, 541/573-1329, www.oregonvos.net/~rwassom/kigercreek.html.

5 EMIGRANT CREEK
northwest of Burns

Map 6.2, page 400

Emigrant Creek is a tributary of the inaccessible Silvies River. It originates in the Ochoco National Forest and runs 30 miles, gathering a handful of smaller streams, before making its confluence with the Silvies. Anglers have good access on Forest Service lands in the upper and middle sections and limited access to the lower river because of private property. Fishing is best in the spring and in the fall. Emigrant Creek offers better than average fishing for 8–10-inch trout. The water here runs in pockets and pools. Anglers can enjoy a nice walk in the woods while looking for that perfect holding spot where larger trout lie. Small nymphs, attractor dry flies, and a selection of small spinners is all an angler needs here. Use lighter-weight rods, 3- and 4-weights in six- and seven-foot lengths to be able to cast among the brush into small pocket water. Emigrant Creek may also be a good introduction for young anglers learning how to fish rivers, read water, and identify fish lies.

Species: Rainbow trout.

Facilities: Camping is available at natural campsites in the forest and at two primitive campgrounds near the headwaters, Falls and Emigrant. Camping can also be had at Yellow Jacket and Delintment Lakes. The closest towns for supplies are in Hines and Burns.

Directions: From Burns, drive two miles west on Hwy. 20 to Hines. Look for Hines Logging Rd. (County Rd. 47) to the east of town. Turn north on Hines Logging Rd. and drive for 25 miles into the Malheur National Forest until you hit County Rd. 43 (Emigrant Creek Rd.). Turn east and follow the river along the middle section of the river for 15 miles to Forest Rd. 4360. Follow the forest road to the right to reach the headwaters.

Contact: Harney County Chamber of Commerce, Burns, 541/573-2636; Ochoco National Forest, 541/416-6500; Emigrant Creek Ranger District, 541/573-4300; ODFW, Hines, 541/573-6582; Kiger Fly Shop, 541/573-1329, www.oregonvos.net/~rwassom/kigercreek.html.

6 CHICKAHOMINY RESERVOIR
west of Burns

Map 6.2, page 400   BEST (

Reservoir comebacks are always a thing to cheer in Southeastern Oregon, and Chickahominy has come back from years of being plagued by low water and an intrusive population of goldfish. The reservoir was drained in 2003 but has since been restocked, and the fish populations are starting to blossom again. Chickahominy (590 acres) is managed exclusively for anglers by the BLM and has a devoted following of both fly and bait anglers—a sometimes contentious combination. The reservoir is open all year and has a standard five-fish limit; one fish over 20 inches may be kept. Trout grow fast and big in these rich waters by feeding on scuds, leeches, minnows, snails, water beetles, and nymphs. Up to 100,000 trout fingerlings are planted each spring, and by the third year they can reach 20 inches or more. Average catches are 14–16 inches—not bad for a remote desert reservoir. The average lake depth is shallow (12 feet), with the deepest point being around the dam (24 feet). Chickahominy is narrow and runs northwest to southeast, and some of the best fishing takes place in the numerous coves near the middle and northern parts. The narrowest section is referred to appropriately as "the narrows" and is a popular place for trolling spinners and flies.

Weather is always an issue here (and may be a problem for anglers under 10 years old); it's usually too hot, cold, windy, or wet. The best times to fish are during the spring and fall. Starting early in the morning, or later in the evening, will almost certainly promise some relief from the ever-present winds. The coves are also good places to escape the winds, and they can lend a degree of solitude to your fishing.

Both bank fishing and boating are popular, and each results in good catches. Bank anglers can walk or drive around the lake, stopping at attractive spots in the protected coves or near the narrows. Float tubes and waders are often seen lining the banks. Wind drifting, a popular technique practiced by float tubers, involves letting the wind do the work by pushing the boat and letting the flies or lures trail behind. Hatches of midges, *Callibaetis,* and damsel flies are common in the spring and provide good dry–fly-fishing. Pay particular attention to the weedy areas. Aquatic weed beds are the supermarkets of lakes, and trout will congregate in these areas to feed on all forms of aquatic insects such as scuds, snails, and water beetles and small minnows. Boats are most commonly launched at the paved boat ramp, but other more primitive launches can be had around the lake. Bait and spin anglers are particularly successful at Chickahominy. Bait anglers can use roe, worms, PowerBait, or just about any other bait. Since the lake is not very deep, keep your weights light and your bait just off the bottom. Weeds may pose a problem in the summer. Spinners such as small Rooster Tails in black, purple, and white are good when cast and retrieved or trolled through the water.

Access roads have been improved, with paved roads leading across the dam to the south parking lot and boat ramp. The access road along the northeast side of the lake has also been improved, and there are also several developed angler access points along the road. Other access roads are dirt and often rutted, requiring a four-wheel-drive vehicle. Driving on these unimproved roads is not recommended when they are wet, and every year some poor angler has to be pulled out of a mud hole.

Species: Stocked rainbow trout.

Facilities: Camping is available at 25 developed sites that include paved roadways, drinking water, and restrooms. Unimproved camping sites are also available at various locations around lake, but without water, restrooms, paved access, or campground markers. The paved area around the dam has a boat ramp and also functions as a day-use area with picnic tables and shade covers. Supplies and accommodations can be had in Burns. The general store and gas station in Riley offer limited supplies and gas.

Directions: From Burns, drive east on Hwy. 20 approximately 30 miles to the Chickahominy Reservoir turnoff. A paved road will take you across the dam and into a large parking lot with restrooms, a boat ramp, and drinking water. Very little shade exists anywhere on the lake. Camping is available at 25 developed sites with drinking water and restrooms. Unimproved camping sites can be had from dirt access around the lake.

Contact: Harney County Chamber of Commerce, Burns, 541/573-2636; ODFW, Hines, 541/573-6582; BLM, Burns District, 541/573-4400; Kiger Fly Shop, 541/573-1329, www.oregonvos.net/~rwassom/kigercreek.html.

⑦ MOON RESERVOIR
west of Burns
Map 6.2, page 400

Similar in many respects to Chickahominy Reservoir—year-round fishing, stark landscape, hot summers, perpetual winds, and big trout—Moon Reservoir offers the addition of warm-water species such as largemouth bass, crappie, and bluegill. Moon Reservoir is moderately sized at just over 600 acres when full, and summer drawdowns for irrigation can reduce its size significantly and even dry it up in some years. When it does go dry it takes a few years for the fish populations to rebuild. The lake went dry in 2003, and it was stocked in 2004 with trout fingerlings and warm-water fish that reached legal size by fall. Future years hold promise for big trout if water levels maintain stability. The warm-water fishery should bounce back by 2007.

In good years, bank fishing and boating are both productive. The north end of the reservoir comprises shallow silted waters and is not very good habitat, so most anglers concentrate their efforts in the southern half around the dam and rock cliffs. Bank anglers have good access to deeper waters around the dam and along the Silver Creek inlet, and to the rest of the lake on dirt access roads. Crappie fishing is good along canyon walls with minnow imitations and jigs. There is a lot of habitat for bass around submerged structure, brush, and lava outcroppings. Bass anglers do best fishing the deeper waters during the day and the shallows during evening and morning. Surface poppers, bass crankbaits, and Rapalas all work. Boaters do have an advantage when it comes to trolling in the deeper channels and around the dam for trout and crappie.

Species: Trout, largemouth bass, bluegill, crappie.

Facilities: There is no camping at the lake. The nearest camping is at Chickahominy Reservoir, 15 miles to the north on Hwy. 20 and six miles past Riley. A small primitive boat ramp and restrooms are at the dam. Supplies and accommodations can be had in Burns, but anglers should come equipped to be self-sufficient. The general store and gas station in Riley offer limited supplies and gas.

Directions: From Burns, drive 20 miles east on Hwy. 20 and turn south on Spud Farm Rd., two miles east of Riley. This is an ungraveled dirt road that can be slippery in the wet months. Follow Spud Farm Rd. nine miles to the access road. Four-wheel-drive vehicles are recommended on the access roads around the lake.

Contact: Harney County Chamber of Commerce, Burns, 541/573-2636; ODFW, Hines, 541/573-6582; BLM, Burns District, 541/573-4400; Kiger Fly Shop, 541/573-1329, www.oregonvos.net/~rwassom/kigercreek.html.

8 BEULAH RESERVOIR
north of Juntura

Map 6.3, page 401

Beulah Reservoir, on the North Fork of the Malheur River, is well known among Oregon anglers as a big-trout lake. Waters rich in aquatic life grow hatchery rainbow quickly to 20 inches or more in good years. Even average catches are above average at 14–18 inches. All methods of fishing are permissible, including bait, lures, and flies. Harvest limits are standard at five fish per day, and high catch rates do much to promote Beulah's popularity.

Most great fisheries are tainted by some drawbacks: Fish are often hard to catch, access may be difficult or expensive, and there is often competition among anglers for good water. While Beulah does suffer from some of these issues, what really plagues the reservoir is a history of low-water conditions and droughts that have wiped out the fishery. Since 2003, the reservoir has been drained every year, and no fish have been stocked since then. In 2005, the reservoir was drained, and what remains in store is anybody's guess. Once fish are stocked, it takes approximately 3–4 years for a recovery to occur if water levels remain stable. In good years anglers can look forward to 14–20-inch hatchery fish that feed on scuds, snails, leeches, baitfish, and mayfly populations. The best times to fish are spring and fall, when anglers can take fish from shallower water without relying too much on trolling or searching. Whitefish and bull trout are also present. Whitefish can prove something of a nuisance to anglers who don't appreciate them as a game species. Bull trout need to be released unharmed.

Species: Trout, whitefish, bull trout.

Facilities: Unimproved camping is available at the lake, as are restrooms and a boat ramp. You can buy supplies in Juntura and Burns, but anglers are advised to bring their own and plenty of them.

Directions: From Juntura drive north on Beulah Rd. 15 miles to reach the north end of the reservoir. Beulah Rd. can be reached at either end of town.

Contact: Ontario Chamber of Commerce, 888/889-8012; ODFW, Ontario, 541/889-6975; BLM, Vale District, 541/473-3144; Kiger Fly Shop, 541/573-1329, www.oregonvos.net/~rwassom/kigercreek.html.

9 NORTH FORK MALHEUR RIVER

north of Juntura

Map 6.3, page 401

The North Fork of the Malheur River originates in the Blue Mountains, runs south to Beulah Reservoir and then continues south to the confluence with the Malheur River just below Juntura. All fishing access to this river is by foot; there is no boating. The upper North Fork is designated Wild and Scenic and produces trout up to 20 inches. The North Fork Malheur Campground and Elk Creek off of Forest Service Road 13 provide the best access points; good hiking trails follow the river up- and downstream. Below Beulah Reservoir there is one access point through the gatekeepers drive at Agency Valley Dam. Fish in this section also run up to 20 inches and are best taken on big nymphs and streamers fished through the deeper holes. Trout populations below Beulah have suffered in recent years due to the lack of water in the reservoir. Check with the local ODFW for latest status.

Species: Wild redband rainbow trout.

Facilities: Camping is available at the North Fork Malheur Campground and Elk Creek Campground; each has five free sites and no drinking water. Camping is also available at Beulah Reservoir and Warm Springs Reservoir (see separate listings). Supplies and accommodations can be had in Burns or Juntura.

Directions: To get to the North Fork: From Juntura drive north on Beulah Rd., following the river for 15 miles to reach the north end of Beulah Reservoir and the junction of several roads. Turn west on Beal Ranch Rd. Beal Ranch Rd. dead-ends after 13 miles and only accesses the lower portion of river above the reservoir.

To reach the upper section of the North Fork: From Juntura drive 16 miles west on Hwy. 20 to Drewsey Rd. and turn north (purchase a good Forest Service Map to help direct you from this point). You will reach the town of Drewsey in approximately 2 miles and the junction of Hwy. 304 (Otis Valley Rd.). Turn east on Otis Valley Rd., which turns into Forest Service Rd. 1663 in approximately 19 miles. Keep driving 14 miles to the north, winding through a confusing series of spur roads, to the junction of Hwy. 16 near the Crane Prairie Forest Service Station. Turn east on Hwy. 16 and follow it 12 miles to Elk Creek Campground. From Elk Creek you can turn south on Forest Service Rd. 1675 to get to the North Fork Malheur Campground (2 miles) or Crane Crossing (3 miles). Staying north on Hwy. 16 will take you to the headwaters and Elk Flat Trailhead (4 miles).

Contact: Grant County Chamber of Commerce, 800/769-5664; Malheur National Forest, 541/575-3000; Blue Mountain Ranger District, 541/575-3000; Prairie City Ranger District, 541/820-3311; BLM Vale District, 541/473-3144; ODFW John Day, 541/575-1167; John Day Parks & Recreation, 541/575-0110; Kiger Fly Shop, 541/573-1329, www.oregonvos.net/~rwassom/kigercreek.html; The Idaho Angler, 208/389-9957.

Chapter 6

10 MALHEUR RIVER
west of Vale

Map 6.3, page 401

The Malheur is a sweeping river drainage that gathers waters from three forks and two containment reservoirs, making a 55-mile journey to Gold Creek near Ontario. Like most rivers in this region, the lower section of the Malheur is mostly bordered by private property or by public lands with little road access. Further, its waters are relied on for irrigation, making the fishery less than predictable. The best fisheries in the area are those directly below the dams at Beulah Reservoir and Warm Springs Reservoir and a good distance above both reservoirs in the Malheur National Forest. Trout average 15–20 inches in many places with some larger fish available. The Malheur is popular in both late fall and early spring, when the water is at its peak in flow and clarity. Summer angling is spotty, and air temperatures can get as high as 112°F with very little shade or water resources. Don't expect the clear cool waters of a spring creek; this river runs muddy most of the year and green in the summer during irrigation releases. Late fall is your best opportunity to find any clearer water.

The Malheur River from Warms Springs Reservoir downstream to Juntura is one of the best trout fisheries in the area. Trout grow large in this water, 20-plus inches to six pounds. This is classic fly-fishing water, complete with insect hatches for anglers wishing to match the hatch. *Callibaetis* and caddis hatches come off in the early summer and blue-wing olives hatch in the fall and winter. Other insect populations include damselflies, scuds, leeches, and terrestrials such as grasshoppers. Leech and minnow patterns work very well in the deeper pools. This is all publicly accessible land, but access requires some effort as there are very few roads. You can reach this area from two points: downstream from Riverside at the Riverside Management Area, and upstream from Juntura at the Allen Diversion Dam. A few anglers choose to boat this area during high-water months. There are two boat launches: one near the Riverside Management Area and one near the South Fork confluence on Riverside–Juntura Road. The take-outs can be had at the Allen Diversion Dam or four miles downstream from Juntura at Twin Bridges.

Below Juntura the river flows into a deep, scenic canyon before flattening out into farmlands surrounding Vale. Highway 20 out of Juntura follows the river for most of its length, providing access from roadside pullouts. Private property does predominate here, so use caution when crossing lands and ask landowner permission. Fishing is fair in this section, and anglers will be happy with the abundant pools and runs, but the fish are much smaller than their upstream relatives.

Another area worthy of an angler's consideration is the upper Middle Fork above Warm Springs Reservoir near the headwaters in Logan Valley. Designated Wild and Scenic for its first 10 miles, the river here is accessible by good roads and hiking trails from Big Creek Campground and Malheur Ford. The fishing in this section is best during summer and fall. Trout can average 6–12 inches with some larger fish present up to 16 inches. Again, fly anglers tend to dominate this water, attracted by spring stone-fly hatches and a productive late-season grasshopper hatch. Streamers such as Woolly Buggers and Zonkers work well in the deeper pools and runs. Nymphs are a good bet any time of year.

Species: Wild redband rainbow trout.

Facilities: Camping is available at the North Fork Malheur Campground and Elk Creek Campground; each has five free sites and no drinking water. On the Middle Fork camping can be had at Big Creek (water, fee) and Murray (no water, free) campgrounds. Camping is also available at Beulah Reservoir and Warm Springs Reservoir. Supplies and accommodations can be had in Burns or Juntura.

Directions: To reach the lower river: From Vale drive 56 miles west on Hwy. 20, following the river for most of its length to Juntura. From Juntura you can reach the upper river and forks quite easily but a good Forest Service map would be helpful to navigate the spur roads.

To reach the upper section of the North Fork: From Juntura drive 16 miles west on Hwy. 20 to Drewsey Rd. and turn north (buy a good Forest Service map to help direct you from this point). You will reach Drewsey in approximately two miles and the junction of Hwy. 304 (Otis Valley Rd.). Turn east on Otis Valley Rd., which turns into Forest Rd. 1663 in approximately 19 miles. Keep driving 14 miles to the north, winding through a confusing series of spur roads, to the junction of Hwy. 16 near the Crane Prairie Forest Service Station. Turn east on Hwy. 16 and follow it 12 miles to Elk Creek Campground. From Elk Creek you can turn south on Forest Rd. 1675 to get to the North Fork Malheur Campground (two miles) or Crane Crossing (three miles). Staying north on Hwy. 16 will take you to the headwaters and Elk Flat Trailhead (four miles).

To reach the Malheur River below Warm Springs Reservoir: From Juntura drive west on Hwy. 20 0.25 mile to Juntura–Riverside Road. Turn southwest on this road and drive 17 miles to the junction at Warm Springs Rd. (follow unmarked roads to the east of this highway to reach the canyon). At Warm Springs Rd. you can go in two directions. Staying south on Juntura–Riverside Rd. will take you past Riverside Campground to the ranch site of Riverside (1.5 miles), where you will find a small access road below the town leading into the canyon. Turning west onto Warm Springs Rd. will take you to a fork and two access roads. The road to the north will take you to the dam and access to the river below the dam. The road to the west traverses the south side of the lake, passing a boat ramp and leading you to the north end at Warm Springs Landing Campground.

To reach the upper Malheur: From Juntura drive 16 miles west on Hwy. 20 to Drewsey Rd. and turn north (buy a good Forest Service map to help direct you from this point). You will reach Drewsey in approximately two miles and the junction of Hwy. 307 (Drewsey Mar-

ket Rd.). Turn west on Hwy. 307 and follow the river 13 miles to Hwy. 310. Turn north on Hwy. 310, merging onto Hwy. 306 in about five miles. Follow Hwy. 306 for eight miles to Forest Rd. 1630 and turn northeast to the junction at Forest Rd. 114 (eight miles). From here you will have lots of options for getting to the river and a good Forest Service map will help you navigate the roads. Malheur National Scenic Trail can be reached from driving east on Forest Rd. 114 (eight miles); Hog Flat is accessible to the east on Forest Rds. 114 and then south on 1643 and 143 (12 miles).

Contact: Grant County Chamber of Commerce, 800/769-5664; Malheur National Forest, 541/575-3000; Blue Mountain Ranger District, 541/575-3000; Prairie City Ranger District, 541/820-3311; BLM, Vale District, 541/473-3144; ODFW, John Day, 541/575-1167; John Day Parks and Recreation, 541/575-0110; Kiger Fly Shop, 541/573-1329, www.oregonvos.net/~rwassom/kigercreek. html; The Idaho Angler, 208/389-9957.

🔟 WARM SPRINGS RESERVOIR

southwest of Juntura

Map 6.3, page 401   BEST (

Warm Springs Reservoir sits on the Middle Fork of the Malheur River south of Juntura. At 4,500 acres, this is a big, sprawling body of water in the middle of the desert. It is home mostly to sagebrush, but there are also large smallmouth bass (up to four pounds) and trout, and good populations of warm-water species. Like most reservoirs in this region, Warm Springs is susceptible to irrigation draws that create low water during the summer, even drying up the lake at times. This is a trolling fishery, and anglers should plan to fish from a boat for the best success. Depth finders will assist anglers in finding schools of fish. Boat ramps service the lake's north and south ends. Some bank fishing occurs at the campground and on road-access points, but the fish here tend to hide out in the deeper water, especially the trout. Bass fishing, on the other hand, is best around structure anywhere you can find it, and there is plenty.

Species: Trout, smallmouth bass, catfish, crappie, perch.

Facilities: Warm Springs Landing Campground provides primitive camping and a boat ramp at the north end of the lake. Camping is also available at the lake in primitive natural sites. A second boat ramp can be found along the south side of the lake. Buy supplies ahead of time, including plenty of water. The nearest towns are Juntura (17 miles) and Burns (54 miles).

Directions: To reach the reservoir from Juntura drive west on Hwy. 20 0.25 mile to Juntura–Riverside Rd. Turn east on this road and drive 17 miles to the junction at Warm Springs Rd. Turn west on Warm Springs Rd. and drive one mile to where the road splits. The road to the north will take you to the dam, and the road to the west traverses the south side of the lake, passing a boat ramp and leading you to the north end at Warms Spring Landing Campground.

Contact: Ontario Chamber of Commerce, 888/889-8012; ODFW, Ontario, 541/889-6975; BLM, Vale District, 541/473-3144; Kiger Fly Shop, 541/573-1329, www.oregonvos.net/~rwassom/kigercreek.html.

12 SOUTH FORK MALHEUR RIVER
south of Juntura

Map 6.3, page 401

The South Fork, flowing from the Malheur Cave area to Riverside, is probably the least productive fork and the most difficult to access due to private property. The river is not stocked, but there is a small population of wild redband trout in most of the river and a small population of smallmouth bass near the mouth near Riverside Campround. In summer, the river is heavily drawn upon for irrigation purposes, thus reducing its flow considerably. April and May hold some promise, but on the whole this is not

a destination that holds much attraction for anglers, and it can be bypassed without much loss. Good roads follow most of the river, but anglers must ask farmers for access. There are some accessible state lands near the headwaters above the community of Venator.

Species: Wild redband rainbow trout, smallmouth bass.

Facilities: The closest camping is available at Beulah Reservoir and Warm Springs Reservoir (see separate listings). Supplies and accommodations can be had in the towns of Burns or Juntura.

Directions: For road access to the river, start in Juntura and follow Juntura-Riverside Rd. for 18 miles southwest to the confluence of the South Fork at Riverside. Just after crossing the mainstem of the river, a road leads right (southwest) across the South Fork and then along the west side of the river for about two miles. Juntura-Riverside Rd. continues along the east bank for another six miles to South Fork Mahleur Rd., which heads west and across the river in 0.3 mile. A good Forest Service map is helpful to navigate this area.

Contact: Grant County Chamber of Commerce, 800/769-5664; Malheur National Forest, 541/575-3000; Blue Mountain Ranger District, 541/575-3000; Prairie City Ranger District, 541/820-3311; BLM, Vale District, 541/473-3144; ODFW, John Day, 541/575-1167; John Day Parks & Recreation, 541/575-0110; Kiger Fly Shop, 541/573-1329, www.oregonvos.net/~rwassom/kigercreek.html; The Idaho Angler, 208/389-9957

13 LOWER OWYHEE RIVER
south of Nyssa

Map 6.4, page 402   BEST (

The majority of anglers who want to fish the Owyhee come here for rainbow and sizable brown trout. From the Owyhee Reservoir to the Oregon–Idaho border, the river flows through agricultural lands. In 1990, brown trout were introduced into the Owyhee River downstream of Owyhee Dam with greater-than-expected success. Most trout fishing takes place in the first 10 miles downstream of the dam. This section offers unlimited access from a good paved road. The river below this point is inaccessible.

Angling is best in early spring just before irrigation flows are turned on and again in the fall just after irrigation flows are turned off. Summer provides good action, but not what anglers have come to expect from the early spring and fall. The river normally runs off-color, so don't let that discourage you from thinking the fish won't bite. Winter fishing can be excellent and attracts a solid group of hard-core anglers from both Idaho and Oregon. Rainbows are stocked every year (13,000–40,000 fish). Brown trout reproduce naturally though some introductions do occur infrequently. Bait, flies, and lures are all allowed. There is a five-fish limit per day for rainbows, and all brown trout must be released unharmed. The presence of brown trout has increased angler participation, and the Owyhee has exploded in the last few years as a destination fishery exclusively for brown trout. Catch rates for browns are almost as good as for rainbows. The potential size of brown trout in the Owyhee is still up for speculation; average catches are quite a bit smaller at 4–6 pounds, but catches up to 12 pounds have been confirmed.

Brown trout over 12 inches differ from rainbow trout in many key ways. Browns are most active in the mornings and evenings and on cloudy days. They are more tolerant of warm, slow-moving water and absolutely love to hide in the darkest sections of the river. Undercut banks, river snags, deeper slow-moving pools, and overhanging brush are classic brown trout lies. Brown trout are also more predatory than rainbows. While they do feed on insects, their preferred diet includes crayfish, mollusks, salamanders, frogs, rodents, and baitfish, so put some meat on the line. Large Bunny Streamers, Woolly Buggers, Zonkers, Muddlers, crayfish imitations, and Zoo Cougars are just a few of the patterns used. Black, yellow, white, burnt orange, and especially purple are all great colors. Large terrestrial patterns such

as Chernobyl Ants, grasshoppers, and Madam Xs are good for top-water presentations early and late in the day. Floating lines are most the most useful—try a clear sinking line or sink tips to get down deep. Sections of the Owyhee are not very deep, so use unweighted flies with the sinking lines.

Rainbow trout also grow big here. Fish average 14–16 inches, but fish up to six pounds are common. Rainbows will take streamers with aggression but are far more inclined to eat floating insects and nymphs. Search for rainbows in faster runs where the water is cool. Larger attractor dry flies such as Stimulators, Humpies, Royal Wulffs, Elk Hair Caddis, and Madam Xs will work all day long. If you do see a hatch you can try to match the insect in size, shape, and color. Emergers and Soft Hackles are particularly effective when fish appear to be taking insects below the surface. Generally, rainbows and browns don't coexist in the same pools, so move around if you want one species or another, and focus on different kinds of water.

Species: Rainbow and brown trout.

Facilities: Camping is allowed near the river in natural campsites. Snively Hot Springs has a nice campground, as does the north end of Lake Owyhee at Government Camp and Owyhee Lake State Park.

Directions: From Nyssa drive south approximately seven miles on Hwy. 201 to Owyhee. Turn west on Owyhee Ave. and drive four miles to Owyhee Lake Rd. Turn south on Owyhee Lake Rd. and follow the river 15 miles past Snively Hot Springs to the headwaters below the dam.

Contact: Ontario Chamber of Commerce, 888/889-8012; ODFW, Ontario, 541/889-6975; BLM, Vale District, 541/473-3144; Lake Owyhee State Park, 800/452-3687; Lake Owyhee Resort, 541/339-2331, www.lakeowyheeresort.com; Tight Lines Fishing and Rafting, 541/896-3219, www.tightlinesfishing.com; Kiger Fly Shop, 541/573-1329, www.oregonvos.net/~rwassom/kigercreek.html; The Riverkeeper Fly Shop, 208/344-3838; The Idaho Angler, 208/389-9957.

14 LAKE OWYHEE

southwest of Nyssa

Map 6.4, page 402

Lake Owyhee is the largest reservoir in Oregon, spanning 52 miles through deeply carved canyons that rival any place in the state for scenic beauty. Lake Owyhee is remote and offers very few facilities other than a few primitive campgrounds and an airstrip. The most popular section is at the dam, where there are several well-developed campgrounds. Travel in this country should be taken seriously, and four-wheel drives are recommended. Come prepared to rough it with plenty of food, water, and shelter. There is very little cover to protect anglers from the unrelenting winds and summer heat. Bank fishing is mostly limited to various campgrounds. Owyhee is a boater's paradise with many miles of coves, arms, and stream inlets; however, boaters need to come prepared for remote access and sometimes hazardous weather conditions. Wind is a constant factor on the reservoir, and waters can get rough. Wildlife and scenic beauty are abundant in the splendid, deeply gorged canyons that line the reservoir.

Largemouth bass are the main attraction at Owyhee. Average catches range 1–2 pounds, with five-pound fish possible. The best fishing occurs in the spring and early summer in coves and around stream inlets. Most methods work for catching bass, from surface poppers to deeper diving plugs. During summer the fish move into the deep waters. Black crappie are everywhere and can be taken on bait and jigs. Smallmouth bass are available in the upper reaches of the reservoir and tend to follow the cooler water cycles. Spring fishing for smallmouth bass is good along shorelines and at stream inlets. During summer, anglers should move to deeper waters. Although scattered and no longer stocked, trout are available. Larger trout can make for a nice surprise. Fish the river inlets in the spring for best opportunities.

A health advisory has been issued for Owyhee Reservoir because of very high levels of mercury due to past mining practices. ODHS recommends women of childbearing age, children under six, and people with liver and kidney damage should avoid eating fish from these waters. Healthy adults should eat no more than one eight-ounce meal per month. For more information, check with the Oregon Department of Human Services.

Species: Trout, largemouth bass, smallmouth bass, catfish, crappie.

Facilities: Lake Owyhee Resort operates two campgrounds, McCormack and Indian Creek, with boat ramps, tent sites, and full RV hookups. Two other campgrounds and boat ramps can be had in the same area at Government Camp and Owyhee Lake State Park. Camping and a boat ramp are available on the north end of the reservoir at Slocum Creek Campground, but conditions are primitive. Camping can also be had inland at Succor Creek State Natural Area. Camping is available for boaters at natural campsites anywhere on the lake. Supplies and other accommodations are available in Nyssa and Ontario.

Directions: From Nyssa drive south approximately seven miles on Hwy. 201 to Owyhee. Turn west on Owyhee Ave. and drive four miles to Owyhee Lake Rd. Turn south on Owyhee Lake Rd. and follow the river 15 miles past Snively Hot Springs to the dam. The road dead-ends at Lake Owyhee Resort at the north end of the reservoir. Government Camp and Owyhee Lake State Park are in the same area. To reach Slocum Creek at Leslie Gulch, from Adrian drive south on Hwy. 201 10 miles to Succor Creek Rd. Follow Succor Creek Rd. south 30 miles to the Leslie Gulch Rd. cutoff. From the turn-off turn west and drive 15 more miles to the campground.

Contact: Ontario Chamber of Commerce, 888/889-8012; ODFW, Ontario, 541/889-6975; BLM, Vale District, 541/473-3144; Lake Owyhee State Park, 800/452-3687; Lake Owyhee Resort, 541/339-2331, www.lakeowyheeresort.com; Owyhee Reservoir Airstrip, 503/378-4880.

15 COW LAKES
northwest of Jordan Valley in the Jordan Craters Geological Area

Map 6.4, page 402

Stark, scenic surroundings and unspectacular warm-water fishing are available at Cow Lakes. The two lakes, Upper and Lower, total approximately 1,000 acres and sprawl in a marsh flatland that attracts numerous waterfowl and shore birds. Low water reveals numerous mudflats that extend into the lake. The lakes were formed when the Jordon Craters lava flow to the east blocked stream flows on Cow Creek. Cow Creek, originating in the mountains of Nevada, is now impounded by the lakes before carrying on to the Owyhee River. Recent low-water years may have affected the populations of fish here, but a quick recovery is expected when water levels rise. Upper Cow provides the best fishing opportunities for brown bullhead catfish, crappie, and largemouth bass. Spring is the only time to fish this area because the weather is comfortable, water levels are at their maximum, and weeds haven't begun to choke the waters. During the summer large mudflats turn the lakes into puddles.

Species: Brown bullhead, crappie, largemouth bass.

Facilities: The BLM manages a small primitive campground and boat ramp on Upper Cow Lake. Few facilities exist here other than natural tent sites. Little shade, wind, and summer heat can prove trying, especially when catch rates are low. Supplies are available in Jordan Valley.

Directions: From Jordan Valley drive west on Hwy. 95 five miles to Lower Cow Creek Rd. Keep following the road west and then northwest for 15 miles until you reach the lakes.

Contact: Ontario Chamber of Commerce, 888/889-8012; ODFW, Ontario, 541/889-6975; BLM, Vale District, 541/473-3144.

16 THOMPSON VALLEY RESERVOIR
south of Silver Lake

Map 6.5, page 403

Approximately 40 miles north of Dead Horse and Campbell lakes along the top of Winter Ridge sits the popular Thompson Valley Reservoir, a sprawling 2,500-acre impoundment close to Silver Lake. Surrounded by mountain ridges, ponderosa pine forests, and large meadows, Thomson Valley is a scenic, if weather-beaten, recreation area. Families enjoy the environment for easy and fun fishing, but weather conditions are unpredictable at best; come prepared for all sorts of inclement conditions, varying from thunderstorms and high winds to freak summer snow showers. The Thompson Reservoir and East Bay campgrounds both have boat ramps and are on the north and east side of the reservoir. Access to the reservoir is limited to summer and fall because of heavy snowfall, though some ice fishing is practiced. In fall, be prepared to meet lots of deer and elk hunters who use the reservoir's campgrounds and surrounding meadows as base camps. Cold weather and snow can begin as early as October, with ice-out occurring in late spring.

The reservoir is fed at one end by Squaw Creek and numerous other smaller tributaries, all of which hold small rainbow and brook trout. The reservoir outlet near the dam forms Silver Creek, a fair trout fishery that runs down into the Silver Lake Valley. Once a great trout fishery producing large fish of 20 inches or more, it has since changed because of the illegal introduction of largemouth bass and the prolific tui chub minnow. Trout are still present, and a few fish can be caught in the 20–24-inch range, but their numbers have dropped significantly. Think of this reservoir as a good largemouth bass fishery and plan your trip and gear accordingly.

Thomson Reservoir has an average depth of 30 feet and nutrient-rich waters that account for its larger trout. Irrigation draws can lower the reservoir's waters drastically in the summer, making late spring and fall the best times of year to fish. During low-water times, boat ramps may require a four-wheel drive. Rocky shorelines, tree stumps, and aquatic grasses create good habitat for trout and especially bass. Look for good insect hatches and lots of rising fish just off the boat ramp at Thompson Reservoir Campground. Search for trout and bass in the channels between the aquatic grasses and near rocky points of land. Trolling with spinners and streamers such as Woolly Buggers is effective almost anywhere. Bass poppers can be used around stumps and ledges to good effect. Bait such as worms, fished under a bobber and near the bottom, is always effective.

Species: Rainbow and brook trout, largemouth bass.

Facilities: The reservoir is serviced by two campgrounds, Thompson Reservoir and East Bay, both of which provide restrooms and boat ramps. Some supplies can be had in Silver Lake, but come prepared. A popular chuck-wagon barbecue restaurant, the Cowboy Dinner Tree, can be found on Hwy. 28 near Silver Lake.

Directions: From Silver Lake drive 18 miles south on Hwy. 28 to reach the East Bay Campground, or south 14 miles on Hwy. 29 to reach the Thompson Valley Reservoir Campground. The roads parallel each other and are connected at the south end of the reservoir by Forest Rd. 3142.

Contact: Christmas Valley Chamber of Commerce, 541/576-2166; Fremont–Winema National Forest, 541/947-2151; Silver Lake Ranger District, 541/576-2107; ODFW, Summer lake, 541/943-3324; BLM, Lakeview District, 541/947-2177; Cowboy Dinner Tree (reservations required), 541/576-2426.

17 LOWER SYCAN RIVER
north of Beatty

Map 6.5, page 403

The lower Sycan is a charming trout stream that holds good populations of both wild rainbow and brown trout. From the marsh, the river runs 30 miles south through forest lands to the confluence with the Sprague River north of Beatty. Access is not always easy, and this can be inhospitable country, especially during the summer heat, but the fish can run big, especially in fall.

The only angling opportunities in the lower river are below the privately owned Sycan Marsh to approximately 12 miles above Beatty. Here, the river bears little resemblance to the freestone character and high gradient flows of the upper Sycan; the lower river is a meandering stream of willows, undercut banks, and pools. Warm weather and irrigation draws can take their toll on the lower river in mid- to late summer, making it tough for both fish and anglers. The best fishing usually occurs in June and October. Brown trout are common here, as are bull trout and some rainbows; however bull trout are off limits to fishing and must be returned to the river unharmed. Average catches of rainbow and brown trout will range 10–14 inches, with the occasional 20-inch fish. Mayfly hatches occur regularly in the softer currents, but streamers are the ticket to lure out the big browns hiding under banks and brush. Wooly Buggers, Seal Buggers, and Zonkers should be thrown down and across the stream and retrieved through deeper holes. Patience is a virtue with this kind of fishing; try various techniques like letting a streamer or nymph hang down in a hole for as long as possible, then begin a short jerky retrieve up the bank. Move often in this kind of water making sure to cover all good lies thoroughly.

The lower river can be floated from the crossing at Forest Service Road 27 near the marsh, 12 miles downstream to below Teddy Powers Meadows at Forest Service Road 347. The lower 12 miles of river flow through private lands, and access is prohibited without permission. A Fremont National Forest map is indispensable to navigate the area.

Species: Wild redband rainbow trout, brown trout, brook trout.

Facilities: Camping is available above the marsh at Pikes Crossing and Rock Creek (see *Upper Sycan River*). Supplies can be bought in Beatty and Klamath Falls.

Directions: From Beatty head east on Hwy. 140 for eight miles to Forest Rd. 30; turn north and follow it 12 miles to Forest Rd. 27. Turn left (west) onto 27 and follow it 12 miles to the river crossing. To get to the lower river boat take-out at Teddy Powers Meadows, take Godowa Springs Rd. north from Beatty 2.5 miles to Forest Service Rd. 3462. Stay on Forest Service Rd. 3462 for approximately 7.5 miles to the junction with Forest Service Rd. 347. Take Forest Service Rd. 347 northwest five miles to the river crossing below Teddy Powers Meadows.

Contact: Klamath Falls Chamber of Commerce, 541/884-5193; Fremont-Winema National Forest, 541/947-2151; Chiloquin Ranger District, 541/783-4001; Bly Ranger Station, 541/353-2427; ODFW, Klamath Falls, 541/883-5732; BLM, Klamath District, 541/883-6916; The Ledge Fly Shop and Outdoor Store, 541/882-5586; Parkers Rod and Gun Rack, 541/883-3726; Roe Outfitters, 541/884-3825.

18 SPRAGUE RIVER

east of Klamath Falls

Map 6.5, page 403

The Sprague runs 100 miles through ponderosa pine forests and farmlands and then returns to the forest near its confluence with the Williamson River in Chiloquin. Two river forks form the upper waters and come together east of Beatty. The South Fork begins by gathering several smaller streams off Coleman Rim near Quartz Mountain Pass on the way to Lakeview. The North Fork originates in the Gearhart Mountain Wilderness northwest of Dead Horse and Campbell lakes.

The main stem of the Sprague forms at the meeting of the two forks east of Beatty and flows through Sprague River Valley and the towns of Sprague River, Lone Pine, and Bray-

mill before meeting the Williamson River near Chiloquin. The confluence can be reached from a boat launch at Sprague River Park, but it's a good eight miles downstream. Most of this river from Braymill to Beatty is bordered by private property and not accessible except in the lower five miles from the confluence with the Williamson River to Braymill. There are a few miles of access along the roadside west of Lone Pine.

The Sprague is a river of mixed terrains and fish. In Sprague River Valley, the area between Beatty and Braymill is slow and meandering and gets quite warm in the summer; bass, catfish, and brown trout predominate. The lower five miles of river, from Braymill to the mouth, is faster-flowing, composed of riffles and runs, and it hosts early- and late-season migratory redband trout from the Williamson River. Spring and fall are the best times to fish the Sprague for trout. The mouth can be reached from Chiloquin near the high school or by rowing up the Williamson River from Williamson County Park. A short section of the river, from the dam in Chiloquin to the mouth, is closed to bait fishing. From the dam upstream the river flows through the national forest and is accessible to bank anglers from Chiloquin Ridge Road east of town. Bass fishing in the Sprague River Valley is mostly a topwater affair. Poppers and crankbaits will work in the deep, slower-moving water. Flies such as streamers and mouse and frog imitations will also work. Catfish are primarily taken on worms fished close to the bottom.

Species: Redband trout, brown trout, largemouth bass, catfish.

Facilities: Camping is available on the North Fork at Sandhill Crossing and Lee Thomas Meadows. Williamson River Campground (May–Nov.) and Waterwheel Campground (year-round) are near Chiloquin off Hwy. 97. Supplies can be had in Klamath Falls, Chiloquin, Beatty, and Bly.

Directions: From Chiloquin head north on Chiloquin Rd., which becomes Sprague River Hwy. a couple miles out of town. Follow

Sprague River Hwy. five miles to Chiloquin Ridge Rd. The turn-off is at the Pacific Power substation. Follow Chiloquin Ridge Rd. less than a mile until it begins to turn from the river. Park and walk downstream.

To reach the campgrounds on the mainstem: From Chiloquin go south on Oregon Hwy. 422 for one mile, then south on U.S. 97 for three miles to the Waterwheel Campground. For the Williamson River Campground, go north on U.S. 97 for 5.5 miles, then turn right (northeast) on Forest Rd. 9730, which leads to the camp in one mile.

Contact: Klamath Falls Chamber of Commerce, 541/884-5193; Fremont–Winema National Forest, 541/947-2151; Chiloquin Ranger District, 541/783-4001; Bly Ranger Station, 541/353-2427; ODFW, Klamath Falls, 541/883-5732; BLM, Klamath District, 541/883-6916; The Ledge Fly Shop and Outdoor Store, 541/882-5586; Parkers Rod and Gun Rack, 541/883-3726; Roe Outfitters, 541/884-3825.

19 LOST RIVER
southeast of Klamath Falls
Map 6.5, page 403

Today, this river is a sleepy, slow-moving, warm-water fishery that belies the secrets of its bloody past. The river and its basin have a long and storied history of Native American civilizations (Modoc tribe), Indian wars (the 1872 Battle of Lost River), controversial river-management practices, and recent restoration efforts to restore the Klamath Basin watershed. The Lost River is an enclosed river sub-basin of the Upper Klamath Basin near Klamath Falls. It originates at Clear Lake Reservoir in California and flows 70 miles north and then west, hijacking Oregon farmlands though the towns of Bonanza, Olene, and Merrill before returning to California and the wildlife refuge at Tule Lake.

Upon seeing this river for the first time, anglers will hunger to get on the water and fish the slow, gentle currents and tule-lined bends.

So inviting is the appearance of this river, flowing through fertile Oregon valleys, that any angler can be excused for thinking about all the fish that will be caught. However, while it was once perhaps a great trout river, the Lost River today is a victim of yearly agricultural runoff, river diversions, and farming practices that have made its waters uninhabitable to anything but a marginal (though improving) supply of warm-water species such as bass, brown bullheads, crappie, perch, sunfish, and Sacramento perch. The Oregon state record Sacramento perch was caught here in 1998, weighing 11.2 ounces. The Lost also produced the state record black crappie in 1978, but that four-pound mark has since been superseded elsewhere. Anglers may stumble across the occasional trout, but they are rare.

If you do decide to fish this river, angling is open all year, but spring is the best time, before warm waters and aquatic growth of summer chokes the currents. Summer catches are possible, but prepare for hot weather, little to no shade, and dense river weed growth. Access is not great, because most of the river flows through private agricultural lands. Still, there are a few access points in Bonanza and Olene. There is a county park in Bonanza, and anglers can walk the bank for a short distance. Just east of Olene on Highway 140, there is a day-use area and limited bank access. Crystal Springs Park south of Olene on Crystal Springs Road offers more bank access and a boat launch. Boaters can use small watercraft and electric motors to navigate both up- and downstream. Bass will be the main species, and they can grow big, 6–7 pounds. To fish for bass, cast plugs, spinners, or plastic worms to the shorelines and downstream into deep holes. The Lost River, neither deep nor wide, is conducive to good fly angling. Cast streamers such as Woolly Buggers or Zonkers downstream or against the bank and make a gentle but erratic retrieve back. Other warm-water species can be taken on bait such as worms drifted through deeper water and along shorelines.

Species: Trout, bass, brown bullhead, crappie, sunfish, perch.

Facilities: No camping is available on the river or in the vicinity. RV parks can be had in Klamath Falls and north on the Williamson River. Crystal Springs Park is a day-use area with restrooms, boat launch, and a parking area. Supplies can be had in the nearby town of Klamath Falls.

Directions: From Klamath Falls drive south on Hwy. 97 to the south end of town and take the Hwy. 39 exit toward Lakeview. You will reach Olene in approximately five miles. Look for a rest area and Crystal Springs Rd. on the south side of the highway after you pass through Olene. Take Crystal Springs Rd. approximately five miles to the park. To reach Bonanza, stay on Hwy. 39 east and look for signs to Bonanza. It's about 17 miles from Olene to Bonanza.

Contact: Klamath Falls Chamber of Commerce, 541/884-5193; ODFW, Klamath Falls, 541/883-5732; BLM, Klamath District, 541/883-6916; The Ledge Fly Shop and Outdoor Store, 541/882-5586; Parkers Rod and Gun Rack, 541/883-3726; Roe Outfitters, 541/884-3825.

20 GERBER RESERVOIR
east of Klamath Falls

Map 6.5, page 403

Gerber Reservoir is a large, remote, high-desert reservoir managed for both recreation and irrigation. Rough roads approach the lake, which is surrounded by publicly owned BLM lands on the edge of the Fremont National Forest. The reservoir sits in a valley surrounded by a mix of ponderosa pine forests, hills, and arid grasslands. The reservoir itself contains numerous coves and arms, deep holding water near the dam, and plenty of islands and rocky shorelines. Fed by Miller Creek, the reservoir comprises 3,950 acres, with an average depth of 30 feet and maximum depth of 70 feet. There are campgrounds, hiking trails, and 29 miles of shoreline, most of which is accessible by dirt roads. Bald eagles, golden eagles, prairie falcons, osprey, american kestrels, and sandhill cranes inhabit the area.

Gerber is primarily a warm-water fishery and perhaps one of the best prospects for catching record-size perch and crappie in Southeastern Oregon. The state record white crappie came from here in 1967, weighing 4 pounds, 12 ounces. Other catches include largemouth bass, brown bullhead, and pumpkinseed. Trout, holdovers from previous stocking programs, are occasionally caught but shouldn't be expected. Crappie fishing is generally at its best April–May. Find the shallow water along the bank or around creeks and islands. Beginning in June, or when the weather gets hot and surface temperatures begin to warm, fish hide in the deepest waters around the dam. Jigs are by far the most popular method of fishing, but bait such as worms also works. Perch fishing is best in July and August, after crappie move to deeper water. Anglers can fish near the banks and around obstructions most of the summer with good results. Small jigs, worms, and perch meat are all good lures for perch. Try trolling along the shoreline in 5–10 feet of water or in the deeper channels. While fishing for perch try casting plastic worms and spinnerbaits for bass in the same shallow waters up against the bank, around island points or near brush.

Species: Yellow perch, white and black crappie, largemouth bass, brown bullhead, pumpkinseed, trout.

Facilities: There are three fee campgrounds at the lake, all with boat ramps, tent sites, drinking water, and restrooms. Supplies and accommodations can be had in Klamath Falls or Lakeview.

Directions: From Klamath Falls, take Hwy. 140 east 19 miles to Dairy. Turn south and drive 17 miles on Hwy. 70 to Bonanza. From Bonanza, continue east on East Langell Valley Rd. for 11 miles. Turn onto Gerber Rd. at the junction and drive east for 8.5 miles. The reservoir will appear on the east side of the road.

Contact: Klamath Falls Chamber of Commerce, 541/884-5193; ODFW, Klamath Falls, 541/883-5732; Bly Ranger Station, 541/353-2427; BLM, Klamath District, 541/883-6916; The Ledge Fly Shop and Outdoor Store, 541/882-5586; Parkers Rod and Gun Rack, 541/883-3726.

21 WILLOW VALLEY RESERVOIR

southeast of Klamath Falls

Map 6.5, page 403

Willow Valley Reservoir is situated on a remote section of the Oregon–California border; in fact, the southern end of the lake is in California. A branch of the Lost River flows from the southwest side of the lake. Willow Valley Reservoir covers about 500 acres in a good water year, but it can be reduced significantly during drought years. Bank fishing is good, but boats are the best way to fish the various arms and channels found through the reservoir.

Willow Valley is one of the few reservoirs in Oregon to stock Lahontan cutthroat trout, a beautiful, speckled trout that comes from well-known fish stocks out of Pyramid Lake in Nevada. Rumors of these fish reaching 60-plus pounds may be a truth lost in another era, but these fish can still get big at 20 inches or more. Slightly sluggish compared to most species of trout, they are quite beautiful and strike with fierce determination. Other species of fish found in Willow Valley Reservoir are largemouth bass, crappie, and bluegill.

To fish for the legendary Lahontan cutthroat, try using black Woolly Buggers in size 10s and 12s or Chironomids in black, red or green. Concentrate on fishing in shallower water in the morning and evenings and the deeper water during the day. Trolling spinners along the shorelines and around rocky points can be productive. Bass can be caught around most structures such as sunken junipers, logs, or along rocky shorelines. Crankbaits, Rapalas, and poppers will all work for catching

bass. Jig for crappies in the shallower water during cool months and in deeper water during the summer.

Species: Stocked Lahontan cutthroat trout, largemouth bass, crappie, bluegill.

Facilities: Willow Valley Reservoir provides a boat ramp. Camping is allowed at the reservoir at natural campsites where posted. More camping is available at Gerber Reservoir to the north. Buy supplies in Klamath Falls or Lakeview.

Directions: To get to Willow Valley Reservoir from Klamath Falls take Hwy. 140 east 14 miles to Dairy. Turn south on Hwy. 70 and drive seven more miles to Bonanza. From Bonanza drive east on Langell Valley Rd. for 27 miles to Willow Valley Rd. Turn east on Willow Valley Rd. and drive another eight miles to reach the lake and boat ramp.

Contact: Lakeview Chamber of Commerce, 541/947-6040; Fremont–Winema National Forest, 541/947-2151; Lakeview Ranger District, 541/947-3334; ODFW, Lakeview, 541/947-2950; BLM, Lakeview District, 541/947-2177.

22 ANA RESERVOIR

north of Summer Lake

Map 6.6, page 404

The Ana is a spring-fed reservoir of 60 acres that sits in the middle of the desert. The primary attractions are large hybrid bass (a sterile cross between striped bass and white bass) and legal-size planted rainbows that can reach 18 inches or more. The ever-present, bait-stealing chub minnow serves as a nuisance to bait anglers, but they also provide the main food source for the hybrid bass. The state record fish was caught here in 2002, weighing 18 pounds, 8 ounces—and they get bigger.

The reservoir is open all year, stays at an even level, and avoids freezing over thanks to springs that keep the waters at a constant temperature of 58°F. Despite the cold winters and hot summers, fishing remains good all year; however, most anglers fish in the cooler seasons. There is no structure in the water, only a bottom and steep banks. A small dock provides wheelchair access and is not a bad place to start fishing. Boats can be launched from a small ramp.

Anglers wishing to catch hybrid bass need to find the deepest waters, which means most of the lake, and keep their tackle near the bottom or in schools of chub minnows. Slow trolling is effective, as is casting from the bank and making slow retrieves back. Bank anglers prove just as successful as boat anglers. Spinners, flies, and bait are all legal and effective. No bass under 16 inches can be kept, and only one bass may be kept in a 24-hour period. Trout are taken closer to the surface. Casting and retrieving spinners or flies without much pause should find success. Bait anglers can float a worm or other bait at medium depths under a bobber.

Species: Hybrid bass, rainbow trout.

Facilities: Primitive camping is available around the reservoir at natural campsites. A boat launch and wheelchair-accessible dock are provided for angler access. A general store and gas station are available in Summer Lake. The next-closest town is Paisley, 29 miles to the south on Hwy. 31. Buy food, supplies, and water ahead of time. The Summer Lake Lodge offers nice accommodations and private fishing for big trout in its ponds.

Directions: From Summer Lake drive north on Hwy. 31 five miles to the Ana Reservoir turnoff. Turn east on the access road and drive 0.25 mile to the reservoir. Dirt roads will take you around the reservoir and to the outlet, which is the beginning of the Ana River.

Contact: Christmas Valley Chamber of Commerce, 541/576-2166; Fremont–Winema National Forest, 541/947-2151; Silver Lake Ranger District, 541/576-2107; ODFW, Summer Lake, 541/943-3324; Summer Lake Wildlife Refuge, 541/943-3152; BLM, Lakeview District, 541/947-2177; Summer Lake Lodge, 541/943-3994, www.thelodge atsummerlake.com.

23 ANA RIVER
east of Summer Lake
Map 6.6, page 404

Every angler has his or her idea about what makes the perfect trout stream, and the Ana comes very close to my ideal: spring-fed waters rich in aquatic insects; remote location; stark, unpretentious surroundings; and challenging rainbows sipping small mayflies off the surface in the dead of winter. It's no wonder this small desert stream remained in obscurity for so long, known only to a handful of anglers living in Central Oregon.

This is a small enough river that a good long jumper could clear its banks in most places. It's also deep enough that there is no place to cross without having to swim. And it's murky, a characteristic it gets from the surrounding lime that covers the banks. The river originates from Ana Reservoir via a corrugated irrigation pipe and maintains a constant temperature of 50–60 degrees. The river's headwaters are shallow and small, flowing through a crumbly limestone canyon. It fairly quickly comes into its own, with deep, slow currents, 90-degree bends, and brush-lined banks of cattails and tules. From the headwaters to its mouth at Summer Lake, the Ana covers about 12 miles. Bait, flies, and lures are all allowed, and a limit of five fish per day has been set; however, the Ana reflects the spirit of fly anglers and those who practice catch-and-release fishing.

The Ana is accessible from either Ana Reservoir or from River Ranch Road about 2.5 miles downriver. Anglers can walk upriver on either side from the crossing at River Ranch Road or drive along the river's west bank from an entrance just above the crossing. Use caution when driving through the soft limestone landscape; four-wheel drives are recommended. The access at River Ranch Road will also allow you to walk downstream through the Summer Lake Wildlife area on either side of the river. Some anglers carry float tubes up to the headwaters and float down to the road crossing or below.

Anglers can expect small fish, 10–14

inches, in the upper river with bigger fish down below in the deeper water. There is no shortage of small fish in the entire river, but the five-pound lunkers maintain a fairly low position in the river. Insect hatches occur most of the year, and anglers can match the hatch accordingly. Dry flies always work when sized for the naturals, but don't ignore wet flies and emerger patterns. Blue-winged olives and midges emerge in the coldest months, during the warmest parts of the day, November–June. Beginning in early spring, pale morning duns start hatching, followed by *Callibaetis,* tricos, and an assortment of other mayflies and caddis. Hatches can be heavy and complex at times. During the summer, anglers need to be on the water close to sunrise, patiently awaiting the morning emergences as soon as the sun warms the air. By 10–11 A.M. the hatches are generally over, and the fish seem unwilling to take a fly. Spring and fall are the most comfortable times of year for anglers and provide the longest fishing days, stretching well into the afternoons. When the fish are not rising, anglers can spend time throwing weighted streamers and wet flies into the deeper pools and runs. Most hits on a streamer are hard and fast, and they occur when the fly is in the deepest part of the swing or being stripped back. An angler friend has dubbed these fish Jordan trout for the way they constantly leap out of the water when hooked.

When fishing, approach the water carefully; stalking is the name of the game on the Ana. Walking up to the bank is the surest way to put down fish. If you do walk up to the bank, sit down and wait 10–15 minutes, and most likely the smaller fish will come back and start feeding; the bigger fish will have fled. One can also find a hill or high bank and watch the river through a pair of binoculars to spot fish in the distance. Also, listen! The Ana is very quiet, and there is no mistaking the sound of a fish rise from way off in the distance. However you decide to approach the fish, from upstream or down, stay way back from the bank and deliver a good, drag-free drift.

Float tubing is a mixed bag. On the pro side it gets you to more water because you're on the inside of the tules and cattails; you can spot fish way downriver and plan your approach if you keep your wits about you; you can deliver a great downstream cast without worry about your back cast; and it's a peaceful way to get intimate with the river. On the con side, you make waves when you float, and that puts down fish. It may be possible that more opportunities are lost by floating the river, but you'll have to decide that for yourself.

Species: Redband trout.

Facilities: Camping is available at Ana Reservoir, along the river in designated areas, and in the Summer Lake Wildlife Refuge. Twenty-four miles east on Hwy. 31 near Paisley, you can camp and soak in mineral baths at Summer Lake Hot Springs. Supplies and some limited accommodations are available in Summer Lake and Paisley, but anglers should come prepared. The Summer Lake Lodge offers nice accommodations and private fishing for big trout in its ponds.

Directions: To reach the reservoir and the beginning of the Ana River from Summer Lake, drive north on Hwy. 31 five miles to the Ana Reservoir turnoff. Turn east on the access road and drive 0.25 mile to the reservoir. Dirt roads will take you around the reservoir and to the outlet and the beginning of the Ana River. To reach the river crossing on River Ranch Rd., drive into Summer Lake on Hwy. 31 and turn east at the old church across the street from the general store. Follow the road for approximately four miles to reach the river.

Contact: Christmas Valley Chamber of Commerce, 541/576-2166; Fremont–Winema National Forest, 541/947-2151; Silver Lake Ranger District, 541/576-2107; ODFW, Summer Lake, 541/943-3324; Summer Lake Wildlife Refuge, 541/943-3152; BLM, Lakeview District, 541/947-2177; Summer Lake Lodge, 541/943-3994, www.thelodge atsummerlake.com.

24 UPPER SYCAN RIVER

west of Paisley

Map 6.6, page 404

The Sycan River originates on Winter Ridge in the Fremont National Forest east of Summer Lake. The upper river flows approximately 25 miles through heavily wooded forests and meadows into the expansive and privately owned Sycan Marsh. From the marsh, the river continues another 30 miles south through forest lands to the confluence with the Sprague River north of Beatty. Relatively underfished because of its remote location and difficult access, the Sycan offers excellent trout fishing for wild rainbow trout.

The upper river is all accessible—though not easily—by good Forest Service roads and is characterized by rough-and-tumble water through basalt canyons. This is small-stream fishing for some surprisingly large trout (20 inches or more), though average catches will be 12–14 inches. A couple of campgrounds at Pikes Crossing and Rock Creek service the area. Roads abound, but very few take anglers close to the river; a good Forest Service map is highly recommended to navigate this country. Other than the areas directly around the campgrounds, anglers will have to hike through forest property to reach most of the river. Forest Roads 3239, 019, and 018 will get you close to the river between Pikes Crossing Camp and the marsh. Forest Road 3239 crosses the river near the marsh and is a good access point to fish a gentler section of river.

Small rivers generally mean small tackle, and the upper Sycan is no exception. After the spring runoff in June, the river fishes well throughout the summer and fall. Short rods and an assortment of small spinners and flies will make for a successful trip. The Sycan is especially attractive to fly anglers. Dry flies such as Elk Hair Caddis, Stimulators, and terrestrial patterns (ants, beetles, grasshoppers) all work during the summer. Nymphs and streamers can be fished in the deeper holes for a chance at bigger fish.

Species: Wild redband rainbow trout.

Facilities: Camping is available above the marsh at Pikes Crossing and Rock Creek. Buy supplies in Beatty and Klamath Falls.

Directions: From Paisley, head north on Oregon Hwy. 31. After 11 miles, turn left (west) onto Forest Rd. 29 (government Harvey Rd.). Go 10 miles to the junction with Forest Rd. 2901 and the Summer Lake Viewpoint. Stay on Forest Rd. 29 for two more miles then, at a paved-T junction with Forest Rd. 28, turn left and look for Rock Creek Camp in 0.5 mile. The next three miles of road also offer access to the Sycan River. At the intersection of Forest Rds. 29 and 28, stay to the right to reach the Pikes Crossing Camp. Go 3.6 miles to a junction with Forest Rd. 30 and stay left at the paved "Y" intersection. After three miles on Forest Rd. 30, take a turnoff signed Pike's Crossing Recreation Area.

Contact: Klamath Falls Chamber of Commerce, 541/884-5193; Fremont–Winema National Forest, 541/947-2151; Chiloquin Ranger District, 541/783-4001; Bly Ranger Station, 541/353-2427; ODFW, Klamath Falls, 541/883-5732; BLM, Klamath District, 541/883-6916; The Ledge Fly Shop and Outdoor Store, 541/882-5586; Parkers Rod and Gun Rack, 541/883-3726; Roe Outfitters, 541/884-3825.

25 SLIDE LAKE

southwest of Paisley

Map 6.6, page 404

Slide Lake is a three-acre lake at the southern end of Winter Ridge. It offers fair fishing for small planted rainbow and brook trout in a nice wilderness setting that offers a refreshing contrast to the warm valley in Summer Lake. Steep switchback roads lead drivers up to the trailhead, where a half-mile trail leads to the lake. Four-wheel drive will help you navigate these roads. The lake is situated in a bowl at the base of Slide Mountain, whose summit is visible from the lakeshore. Tall mountains and dense forests surround the lake, forming a scenic backdrop. The lake water is gin clear, and numerous logs that extend from the bank make good fishing platforms. Some anglers pack in float tubes or small inflatable boats.

Slide Lake contains illegally introduced brook trout and stocked rainbow trout. Fish size is on the small side at 8–10 inches. Flies, bait, and lures can all be used effectively. Small insect hatches occur during the summer, making this an effective dry–fly-fishing spot. Leeches and small nymphs can be trolled from a float tube or stripped back to the bank. Fly anglers will have a more difficult time casting very far because of dense bank vegetation. Spin casters have the advantage here because they can cast out into the deeper holes. Spinners such as Rooster Tails and Mepps work great all summer. Bait such as worms can be floated under a bobber to catch the rogue brook trout.

Species: Rainbow and brook trout.

Facilities: Camping is available at natural campsites around the lake and at Summer Lake Hot Springs in the valley. You can buy supplies in Paisley or Lakeview, but campers are well advised to be prepared before starting their trip. The Summer Lake Lodge offers nice accommodations and private fishing for big trout in its ponds.

Directions: From Paisley follow Hwy. 31 north 12 miles and turn south on Forest Rd. 29. Follow Forest Rd. 29 for four miles until you get to Forest Rd. 017 and see signs for Slide Mount Geological Area. The lake trailhead is three miles down Rd. 017.

Contact: Christmas Valley Chamber of Commerce, 541/576-2166; Fremont–Winema National Forest, 541/947-2151; Paisley Ranger District, 541/943-3114; ODFW, Summer Lake, 541/943-3324; Paisley Ranger District, 541/943-3114; BLM, Lakeview District, 541/947-2177; Summer Lake Lodge, 541/943-3994, www.thelodgeatsummerlake.com.

26 DEAD HORSE LAKE
north of Bly

Map 6.6, page 404

Dead Horse and Campbell lakes are often spoken of in the same breath because they are just half a mile from each other. The Lakes Loop hiking trail connects the two lakes with good walking trails. Dead Horse Lake sits in a scenic, forested high-alpine setting at 7,372 feet. On Dead Horse Rim in the Winter Ridge Area, it is easily accessible by good roads from Paisley to the east or Bly to the south. Winter Ridge is notorious for having short summers and long winters. If you're going to fish this area, do so July–October. Roads are not usually clear from snow until late spring. A quick check with the local Forest Service in Bly or Paisley will let you know if road and weather conditions are safe.

Dead Horse is approximately 20 acres and well stocked with rainbow and brook trout. Boats or float tubes can be launched from a good boat ramp at the day-use area. Boats can be equipped with electric motors only, which makes for good trolling. Bank fishing is very good from all points around the lake. Campground sites are scattered along the road that encircles the lake. Average catches of trout range 10–14 inches, with some bigger trout present. Bait, lures, and flies are legal, with bait being the best choice, especially for kids. Trolling is popular along several miles of shoreline and in the deeper water near the middle. Structure is usually a good indicator for fish presence, but the whole lake fishes well. Fly anglers can watch for rising fish during the summer or troll streamers from a float tube.

Species: Stocked rainbow and brook trout.

Facilities: This is a perfect place to bring the family for a few days of fishing, solitude, and other diversionary activities such as hiking, biking, wildlife-viewing, and collecting pine cones. Day outings to the Chewaucan, Sprague, and Ana Rivers are all easy drives. Summer Lake Hot Springs east of Paisley, with its curious birdhouses and eclectic decor, offers mineral bath soaks in a large pool and limited accommodations and tent camping. Camping is available at the lake, as are a boat ramp and restrooms. Buy supplies in Bly, Beatty, or Paisley.

Directions: To get to Dead Horse Lake from Bly, take Hwy. 140 east out of Bly one mile to the Campbell Rd. turnoff. In 0.25 mile, turn east on Hwy. 34 and drive 24 miles to the Hwy. 28 junction. Turn north on Hwy. 28 and drive seven miles to Forest Rd. 033. You will reach Dead Horse Lake approximately three miles down the forest road.

Contact: Christmas Valley Chamber of Commerce, 541/576-2166; Fremont–Winema National Forest in Paisley, 541/943-3114; Bly Ranger Station, 541/353-2427; ODFW, Klamath Falls, 541/883-5732; BLM, Lakeview District, 541/947-2177.

27 CAMPBELL LAKE
north of Bly

Map 6.6, page 404

Sister lake to Dead Horse and connected by good hiking trails, Campbell is another high alpine lake situated among scenic ponderosa pine forests on Dead Horse Rim. Almost identical to Dead Horse's 20 acres, Campbell provides good fishing for stocked rainbow and brook trout and the occasional trophy fish of 20 inches or more. Good campgrounds surround the lake, and a boat ramp allows anglers to launch nonmotorized craft (electric motors are allowed). Access times are similar to those of Dead Horse, with July–October being the best months for weather. Late snowmelts will prohibit travel to this area well into June. Check with the local Forest Service offices in Bly or Paisley for weather and road conditions.

Bait, lures and flies all work, with no single approach being better. Trolling with small lures is popular and catches a lot of fish. Float tubers can spend time fishing the shorelines and deeper areas in the middle of the lake, while watching for the occasional insect hatch and surface-feeding fish. Kids can have fun with bobber and worm casting from any point on the shore.

Species: Stocked rainbow and brook trout.

Facilities: Great for families with children, Campbell provides all sorts of recreation other than fishing, such as hiking, biking, and wildlife-watching. Day trips can be had to other area rivers such as the Chewaucan, Sprague, or Ana Rivers. Summer Lake Hot Springs east of Paisley provides mineral baths and some accommodations. Camping, a boat ramp, and restrooms are available at sites around the lake and at Dead Horse Lake. Buy supplies in Paisley, Bly, and Beatty.

Directions: To get to Campbell Lake from Bly, take Hwy. 140 east out of Bly one mile to the Campbell Rd. turnoff. In 0.25 mile turn east on Hwy. 34 and drive 24 miles to the Hwy. 28 junction. Turn north on Hwy. 28 and drive seven miles to Forest Rd. 033. You will reach Campbell Lake approximately two miles down the forest road.

Contact: Christmas Valley Chamber of Commerce, 541/576-2166; Fremont–Winema National Forest, 541/947-2151; Bly Ranger Station, 541/353-2427; ODFW, Klamath Falls, 541/883-5732; BLM, Lakeview District, 541/947-2177.

28 CHEWAUCAN RIVER
south of Paisley

Map 6.6, page 404

The Chewaucan (chew-WA-can) is a fair trout stream with a troubled past due to irrigation practices in the lower marshes. The future looks brighter thanks to efforts to restore a run of large trout from the privately owned River's End Reservoir near Lake Albert (restoring river channels through the marsh and removing a dam that blocks the upstream migration of fish). This could make the Chewaucan a trophy trout fishery, as the fish below the marsh in inaccessible River's End Reservoir can reach lengths of 24 inches or more. Time will tell if this plan comes to fruition, but target dates for implementation were set for 2007.

The Chewaucan River is about 50 miles long, originating in the Fremont National Forest at the south end of Winter Ridge above Paisley. The headwaters are situated in a large meadow flatland where about a dozen smaller streams come together to form the river. A little lower in the river, Coffee Pot Creek enters the river, forming the topmost section of the canyon. All these smaller creeks, especially Dairy, have fair fishing for wild rainbows with artificial flies and lures only. From the upper meadows the Chewaucan flows into a rough-and-tumble canyon before emerging into the Summer Lake Valley near Paisley. Below Paisley the river is collected in two marshes, Upper and Lower, before finally emptying into the privately held River's End Reservoir and Lake Albert. The lower river below Highway 31 is open May 28–October 31 and allows bait fishing, but access is completely blocked by private property. The best stretch of water for anglers has been the lower 12 miles of river through the canyon between Paisley and Coffee Pot Creek. All 12 miles of river are accessible from a good highway and three campgrounds. Above Coffee Pot Creek the river flows through private ranch lands and is inaccessible. Trout are generally small, 10–14 inches, with an occasional stocked trophy trout available. Both stocked and wild fish are present.

The best times to fish the river are after spring runoff until the arrival of snow in the mountains. Heavier than normal winters and summer rainstorms can keep waters high and off-color for longer periods. The river above Highway 31 is open all year and restricted to artificial flies and lures. Caddis, stone flies, and some green drakes start their emergences in summer after flows have subsided, followed by grasshoppers in late summer. There is not much need to match the hatch on this river, because any reasonable attractor pattern such as Stimulators, Royal Wulffs, Humpies, and terrestrial patterns such as ants and beetles all work. Nymphs in these same patterns can be used by themselves or attached under a larger

dry fly with a piece of short tippet. Small spinners in silver and gold will work when cast behind rocks and through deeper slicks.

Species: Wild and stocked rainbow trout.

Facilities: Camping is available on the river about 12 miles east of Paisley on Hwy. 33 at Masters Spring, Chewaucan Crossing Group, and Jones Crossing. Traveling another 12 miles south on Hwy. 33 will put you in the vicinity of Dairy Creek, where several more campgrounds are available. Buy supplies ahead of time in Lakeview or Klamath Falls. You can buy limited supplies in Paisley. Accommodations and mineral baths are available at Summer Lake Hot Springs. The Summer Lake Lodge offers nice accommodations and private fishing for big trout in its ponds.

Directions: From Paisley, drive west on Hwy. 33. The river will be on the south side of the highway for 12 miles as it flows through the canyon. The highway departs the river at Coffee Pot Creek but continues up into the headwaters and the start of Dairy Creek. Look for campgrounds on Hwy. 33 starting about road mile eight.

Contact: Christmas Valley Chamber of Commerce, 541/576-2166; Fremont–Winema National Forest, 541/947-2151; Paisley Ranger District, 541/943-3114; ODFW, Summer Lake, 541/943-3324; BLM, Lakeview District, 541/947-2177; Summer Lake Lodge, 541/943-3994, www.thelodgeatsummerlake.com.

29 NORTH FORK SPRAGUE RIVER
northeast of Bly

Map 6.6, page 404

The North Fork of the Sprague was, at one time, a tightly guarded secret of southeastern Oregon anglers, but has since seen it's share of publicity. As the recipient of both spring and fall migrations of redband rainbows and brown trout out of the lower Sprague and Williamson Rivers, this small river can hold some very large trout; browns up to five pounds or more are not unheard of.

The North Fork is best fished in the summer months after the run-off season. Good hatches of golden stones come off in the early season followed by caddis in the summer. Roads follow the river to its headwaters, 10 miles of which are Wild and Scenic, and the Sandhill and Lee Thomas Meadows campgrounds. Sandhill offers especially good river access and anglers can get very remote with some hiking. There is good access to the lower river along Forest Service Road 335 where the road makes a 180-degree bend. Park on either side of the road and walk upstream through the Fremont National Forest. The river here is small and fast (no boats) and composed of dense streamside vegetation with large boulders and downed trees. It is almost impossible to fish from the bank; get in the river with waders and walk upstream in cold, often waist-deep water.

Robert West, a long-time North Fork angler, mastered this river with a two-fly nymphing technique and he swears he landed five-pound browns out of this section. The basic set-up is two flies, a heavy Golden Stone, and a smaller nymph dropped 6–8 inches off the bend of the first fly. A strike indicator is used. Using a short rod (7 feet is adequate) walk up the middle of the stream and cast your nymphs into the pocket water or into the throat of small fast runs. Fast stripping is required to keep the nymphs dead-drifting through productive water. When the strike indicator goes down, set the hook and move through holes quickly—two or three casts per section. The big fish hold in the deeper holes, chest deep in places, so bring a good pair of chest waders. A majority of the fish will be in the 10–14-inch range. The occasional spit shot can be added to get your flies deeper in the holes. This is strenuous fishing at best and not for beginners. Take your time, carry a good supply of water and food, and watch for poison oak that grows around the river banks. Brook, rainbow, and brown trout are all waiting for you.

Species: Wild redband rainbow trout, brown trout and brook trout.

Facilities: Camping is available on the North Fork at Sandhill Crossing and Lee Thomas Meadows; both have five sites, tables, fire pits, and water (June 1–Oct. 30). Williamson River Campground and Waterwheel Campground are near Chiloquin off of Hwy. 97 (see *Sprague River* listing). Supplies are in Klamath Falls, Chiloquin, Beatty and Bly.

Directions: From Bly travel one mile east and turn north on Campbell Rd. Campbell Rd. connects to Forest Service Rd. 3411 in about three miles. Stay on Forest Service Rd. 3411 for about three more miles and turn north on Forest Service Rd. 335. Follow Forest Service Rd. 335 five miles to Forest Service Rd. 3411. Turn east and follow the North Fork seven miles to Sandhill Campground and a little further to Lee Thomas Meadows.

Contact: Klamath Falls Chamber of Commerce, 541/884-5193; Fremont-Winema National Forest, 541/947-2151; Chiloquin Ranger District, 541/783-4001; Bly Ranger Station, 541/353-2427; ODFW, Klamath Falls, 541/883-5732; BLM, Klamath District, 541/883-6916; The Ledge Fly Shop and Outdoor Store, 541/882-5586; Parkers Rod and Gun Rack, 541/883-3726; Roe Outfitters, 541/884-3825.

30 CAMPBELL RESERVOIR
northeast of Bly

Map 6.6, page 404

Campbell Reservoir is a 200-acre high-desert irrigation impoundment. The terrain is a mix of distant hills, arid grasslands, and sparsely populated ponderosa forests. Red cinder forest roads offer access to most of this region. As in other reservoirs in this area, water-management practices favor farmers for irrigation, meaning the reservoir can go dry from year to year without a thought for the fish populations. Some stocking takes place during good water years, but this is hardly ideal conditions for a stable, long-term fishery. When fish are present they can grow big, quite fast. Both trout and bass are stocked and available to anglers from a small piece of publicly owned BLM land at the southeast corner. Drive by the reservoir to see if the water levels can support fish; spring will be the best time of year, before irrigation draws.

Species: Redband trout, largemouth bass.

Facilities: Camping is allowed where posted on BLM lands. More camping can be had on the North Fork of the Sprague, Dairy Creek, and Dead Horse and Campbell lakes. Buy supplies ahead of time in Klamath Falls. Limited supplies are available in Bly and Beatty.

Directions: From Bly drive one mile east on Hwy. 140 to Campbell Rd. Turn north on Campbell Rd., drive 0.25 mile, and take a left at Hwy. 34. Drive on Hwy. 34 for approximately five miles. The reservoir and access road will be on the west side of the road.

Contact: Lakeview Chamber of Commerce, 541/947-6040; Fremont–Winema National Forest, 541/947-2151; Bly Ranger Station, 541/353-2427; ODFW, Lakeview, 541/947-2950; BLM, Lakeview District, 541/947-2177.

31 SOUTH FORK SPRAGUE RIVER

east of Bly

Map 6.6, page 404

The South Fork is followed by Highway 140 from Sprague River Park to the confluence with the North Fork east of Beatty. It begins as a tumbling river in its upper reaches but quickly hits the valley floor to become slow and meandering. The better fishing on this river occurs in its lower portions east of Bly. Sprague River Park, two miles east of Bly, offers both bank access and a boat launch. Bank angling is limited, but boaters can use a small electric motor and travel both up- and downriver. The Sprague is met by Fishhole Creek one mile downriver, which creates a set of channels flowing into the main river. It's worth your time to spend a little effort navigating these channels for trout lies, casting tightly against the bank or straight up-stream

with nymphs, streamers, and spinners. A common practice is to motor upstream from the boat launch three or four miles and float down to the take-out. Look for rising fish during the day, but streamers and spinners cast downstream to the bank are far more effective.

Species: Wild redband rainbow trout, brown trout, and brook trout.

Facilities: Camping is available on the North Fork at Sandhill Crossing and Lee Thomas Meadows (see *North Fork Sprague River* listing). Williamson River Campground and Waterwheel Campground are near the town of Chiloquin off of Hwy. 97 (see *Sprague River* listing). Supplies are in Klamath Falls, Chiloquin, Beatty and Bly.

Directions: From Bly travel two miles east on Hwy. 140. Sprague River Park in on the north side of the highway; it's indicated by a sign and dirt road.

Contact: Klamath Falls Chamber of Commerce, 541/884-5193; Fremont-Winema National Forest, 541/947-2151; Chiloquin Ranger District, 541/783-4001; Bly Ranger Station, 541/353-2427; ODFW, Klamath Falls, 541/883-5732; BLM, Klamath District, 541/883-6916; The Ledge Fly Shop and Outdoor Store, 541/882-5586; Parkers Rod and Gun Rack, 541/883-3726; Roe Outfitters, 541/884-3825.

32 HOLBROOK RESERVOIR

west of Lakeview

Map 6.6, page 404

Holbrook Reservoir is in the Fish Hole Lake Area one mile west of Lofton Reservoir and consists of 40 acres surrounded by scenic pine forests and grassy meadowlands. Holbrook is great for families who desire easy, fun fishing, camping, and other diversionary recreation. Watch the skies for bald eagles, golden eagles, and other predatory and fishing birds. The waters of Holbrook are clear and deep. The trout in Holbrook are often plump from the abundance of insect life that populates the water. Trout can exceed 20 inches, and average catches are fat and range 12–14 inches. Bait, flies, and lures are all allowed, and there are no fish-harvest restrictions. Fly anglers will have opportunities in the summer to fish good hatches of chironomids, *Callibaetis,* and damsel flies. Simple dry flies such as a Parachute Adams or Griffith Gnat will work in most cases. Ants, beetles, and grasshopper patterns can prove effective when fished with a small twitch in the shallows and against the bank around trees and shrubs. Small leech patterns and nymphs such as scuds, water boatman, water beetles, or Pheasant Tails can be fished on or near the bottom or stripped in the top water with good results. Bait such as small worms and grubs fished under a bobber will catch fish all day. Spinners should be small; gold and silver are best, or something with small feathers such as a Rooster Tail can be trolled or cast from the bank and retrieved fast or slow.

Though it's surrounded by private lands, the landowner has graciously given special permission to allow public access. There is a good campground and boat ramp for anglers to launch small craft such as rowboats and float tubes.

Species: Fat rainbow trout.

Facilities: Holbrook is great for diversionary recreation such as hiking, bike riding, and bird-watching. Simple campgrounds and a boat ramp are available at the lake. Other campgrounds are close by at Hart Lake and Lofton Reservoir. Supplies and accommodations can be had in Lakeview.

Directions: From Lakeview drive west on Hwy. 140 for 20 miles to the Quartz Mountain Rest Area, then turn south on Forest Rd. 3715. It is approximately 6.5 miles to the Holbrook Reservoir turnoff. A short access road will lead you to the lake campground. Other lakes in the area are accessible either by unimproved roads or hiking trails off Forest Rd. 3715. Use a good Forest Service map to navigate smaller logging roads and hiking trails.

Contact: Lakeview Chamber of Commerce, 541/947-6040; Fremont–Winema National Forest, 541/947-2151; Lakeview Ranger District, 541/947-3334; ODFW, Lakeview, 541/947-2950; BLM, Lakeview District, 541/947-2177.

33 LOFTON RESERVOIR
west of Lakeview
Map 6.6, page 404

Lofton Reservoir, in a valley on the west side of Barnes Ridge, is a fair to good fishery for stocked rainbow trout. It is accessible from a good road east of Quartz Mountain Pass, 20 miles west of Lakeview. Pine forests and arid meadowland surround this scenic 40-acre lake popular for its larger trout and nice Forest Service campground. This is a good getaway for families, providing easy and productive bank fishing with good hiking trails surrounding the lake. Boating is allowed and popular, and it gives better access to the deeper areas of the lake. Small crafts such as float tubes or rowboats equipped with an electric motor are all that is necessary. Stocking occurs in the spring, and trout can grow to two pounds or more by the end of summer. Average catches will be 8–12 inches, the perfect size for a tasty trout dinner. Bait, flies, and lures are productive year-round. Aquatic growth can take over parts of the reservoir in summer, making flies and lures a better option than bait. During the summer, fly anglers should be on the lookout for insect hatches of various small mayflies. Kids will enjoy casting a worm and bobber from the bank or boat for good catches of smaller trout. Trolling the deeper waters with streamer flies and lures might dredge up some of the lake's larger trout.

Species: Stocked rainbow trout.

Facilities: Simple campgrounds are available at the lake. Other campgrounds are close by at Hart Lake and Holbrook Reservoir. Supplies and accommodations can be had in Lakeview.

Directions: To reach Lofton Reservoir from Lakeview, drive west on Hwy. 140 for 20 miles to the Quartz Mountain Rest Area and turn south on Forest Rd. 3715. It is approximately seven miles to the Lofton Reservoir turnoff. A short access road will lead you to the lake campground. Other lakes in the area are accessible either by unimproved roads or hiking trails off Forest Rd. 3715. A good Forest Service map will help you navigate the smaller logging roads and hiking trails.

Contact: Lakeview Chamber of Commerce, 541/947-6040; Fremont–Winema National Forest, 541/947-2151; Lakeview Ranger District, 541/947-3334; ODFW, Lakeview, 541/947-2950; BLM, Lakeview District, 541/947-2177.

34 COTTONWOOD MEADOWS LAKE

northwest of Lakeview in the Fremont National Forest

Map 6.6, page 404

Cottonwood Meadows Lake is a 45-acre natural lake nestled in an aspen grove. What this lake lacks in fish size it more than makes up for in scenery. Fall is an especially beautiful time to listen to the aspens, admire the fall colors, and fish the lake with small dry flies. Good hatches of mayflies can occur in fall, and streamers in rust or burgundy can be killers; try an Adams or rust-colored Seal Bugger for best results. Stocked rainbow and brook trout average 10–16 inches with some bigger fish available. The lake fishes well all year, from ice-out to the first snows. Boats are allowed with electric motors, but float tubes are just as effective to reach deeper waters and brushy shorelines. Summer aquatic growth can pose a problem in shallower areas. All methods of fishing are allowed, including bait, flies, and lures.

Species: Stocked and wild rainbow trout and brook trout.

Facilities: The lake is serviced by two campgrounds, Cottonwood Meadows Lake Campground and Cottonwood Recreation Area, and two concrete boat ramps. Supplies can be had in Lakeview.

Directions: From Lakeview drive seven miles west on Hwy. 140 to Obegaard Rd. (County Rd. 1–20). Turn north on Obegaard Rd. (which turns into Forest Rd. 3870) and drive approximately 14 miles, passing Cottonwood Reservoir to the south, to the Cottonwood Meadows Lake Campground.

Contact: Lakeview Chamber of Commerce, 541/947-6040; Fremont–Winema National Forest, 541/947-2151; Lakeview Ranger District, 541/947-3334; ODFW, Lakeview, 541/947-2950; BLM, Lakeview District, 541/947-2177.

35 COTTONWOOD RESERVOIR

northwest of Lakeview

Map 6.6, page 404

Cottonwood Reservoir—not to be confused with much smaller Cottonwood Meadows Lake—is a scenic, 900-acre irrigation reservoir on Lower Cottonwood Creek. It was closed to fishing after its demise in the 1990s, but it is once again a fine fishery. The main attraction is trophy-size Goose Lake redband trout, a unique, hardy, and thoroughly studied subspecies of migratory trout from a stock of wild fish in Goose Lake. Average catches will be 14–18 inches, with plenty of fish available up to six pounds or more. All fish in Cottonwood Reservoir are wild.

The reservoir is open all year to all methods of fishing, including bait, lures, and flies; two trout per day may be retained. Fishing is best in spring and summer, before irrigation drawdowns, but it's discouraged during low-water years to alleviate the stress on the native fish populations. Cottonwood is rich in aquatic insects and is a good place to troll the banks in a float tube looking for rising fish. Use a small Adams or other attractor mayfly pattern for best results. Leech and streamer patterns will work well in both shallow and deeper water. Fly anglers may want to use a clear sinking line (also called a slime line) to get deep in the water. Spinners such as Rooster

Tails and bait such as worms are good choices for spin anglers.

Although the lake is surrounded by private property, generous landowners have granted special use for anglers. Good bank access and a boat ramp can be found at the north end of the lake near the dam. Additional bank access is available from the Forest Service road on the north shore and from hiking trails on the south side.

Species: Native Goose Lake redband trout.

Facilities: A campground and boat ramp are available at the lake. Supplies and accommodations can be had in Lakeview.

Directions: From Lakeview drive seven miles west on Hwy. 140 to Obegaard Rd. (County Rd. 1–20). Turn north on Obegaard Rd. (which turns into Forest Rd. 3870) and drive approximately five miles to reach the east shore of the lake.

Contact: Lakeview Chamber of Commerce, 541/947-6040; Fremont–Winema National Forest, 541/947-2151; Lakeview Ranger District, 541/947-3334; ODFW, Lakeview, 541/947-2950; BLM, Lakeview District, 541/947-2177.

36 DREWS RESERVOIR
west of Lakeview

Map 6.6, page 404

This 5,000-acre irrigation reservoir is a productive warm-water fishery supporting good populations of crappie, brown bullhead, perch, and a few rainbow trout. Most notable is the presence of a healthy population of large channel catfish that can reach 18 pounds or more. The entire reservoir has good angler access from dirt roads that encircle the lake. As with most reservoirs in the area, Drews receives only marginal fishing pressure from local anglers. Chances are you won't have the lake all to yourself, but a generous amount of solitude is afforded in the numerous arms and bays. Reservoir drawdowns for irrigation needs can be extreme during the summer, making this primarily an early-season fishery. Boats are

allowed and provide the best access, especially when fishing for channel catfish.

Fishing methods for channel catfish vary from location to location, and they are known to be picky about what they bite. In general, fish flat areas above deeper channels, muddy bottoms, deep holes, and sometimes river shallows. Baits can include bloody baits, cut baits, worms, stink baits, cheese, grasshoppers, liver, crawfish, shrimp, and clams. Hook sizes should be bigger (2–6/0) to ensure a good hook set. There are no particular best times of year to catch channel catfish, but abrupt changes in water conditions can put them off the bite. Night fishing is quite popular and productive during the summer. Crappie and perch are generally found in shallower water and river inlets during spring spawning times and in deep, cooler water in the summer. Largemouth bass can be found around structure and along the lakeshore; they become most active when water temperatures warm in the late spring and summer.

Species: Redband trout, channel catfish, crappie, brown bullhead, perch, bass.

Facilities: There are a good boat ramp and campground at Drews Creek at the south end of the lake. More campgrounds can be had at Dog Lake to the south and Cottonwood and Juniper reservoirs on the north side of Hwy. 140. Supplies and accommodations can be had in Lakeview.

Directions: From Lakeview drive west on Hwy. 140 for nine miles to West Side Tunnel Hill Rd. (County Rd. 1–13). Turn south on West Side Tunnel Hill Rd. and drive four miles to Dog Lake Rd. Turn west on Dog Lake Rd. and drive approximately seven miles to get to Drews Creek Campground. Two miles west of there, you'll be at Drews Reservoir Picnic Area.

Contact: Lakeview Chamber of Commerce, 541/947-6040; Fremont–Winema National Forest, 541/947-2151; Lakeview Ranger District, 541/947-3334; ODFW, Lakeview, 541/947-2950; BLM, Lakeview District, 541/947-2177.

37 DOG LAKE

southwest of Lakeview

Map 6.6, page 404

A noted warm-water fishery 5,197 feet above sea level, Dog Lake provides high-elevation fishing on 500 acres of water in remote and scenic forested lands. It is home to numerous species of warm-water fish, including perch, brown bullhead, crappie, bluegill, and a few largemouth bass. The best fishing times are in the spring and early summer, when the reservoir is least affected by irrigation drawdowns and fish are more inclined to feed in the shallower waters. Fishing can be good throughout the summer, but anglers will have more of a challenge finding fish in deeper waters.

There are a campground, concrete boat ramp, and plenty of hiking trails for good bank access. Dog Lake has an inordinate amount of submerged structure and vegetation, providing good fishing habitat for most species. Boating is allowed and may be the best way to get to the fish in low-water years. Float tubes and small kick boats are also helpful to get away from bank vegetation. Bait, lures, and flies all work with equal success.

Species: Perch, brown bullhead, crappie, bluegill, largemouth bass.

Facilities: Camping and a boat ramp are all available at the lake. Supplies and accommodations can be had in Lakeview.

Directions: From Lakeview drive west on Hwy. 140 for nine miles to West Side Tunnel Hill Rd. (County Rd. 1–13). Turn south on West Side Tunnel Hill Rd. and drive four miles to Dog Lake Rd. Turn west on Dog Lake Rd. and drive 18 miles to get to Dog Lake Campground. You will pass Drews Reservoir on the way to Dog Lake.

Contact: Lakeview Chamber of Commerce, 541/947-6040; Fremont–Winema National Forest, 541/947-2151; Lakeview Ranger District, 541/947-3334; ODFW, Lakeview, 541/947-2950; BLM, Lakeview District, 541/947-2177.

38 DEEP CREEK

east of Lakeview

Map 6.6, page 404

Deep Creek is a modest-size trout stream originating in the Crane Mountain Recreation Area of the Warner Mountains southeast of Lakeview. Among the smaller streams that form the river are Dismal, Willow, and Burnt creeks, all of which have populations of small trout. The river flows through Big Valley and then falls into a roadless canyon for a few miles, picking up a few more tributaries (Sage Hen, Camas, and Parsnip creeks) before emerging along Highway 140 west of Adel. The river follows Highway 140 for a few miles through Adel but then takes a northerly turn and terminates at Crump Lake in Warner Valley.

Anglers can reach the river in three distinct sections. Whichever section you fish, be very careful of high populations of rattlesnakes—a bite you'd rather not tap into. Waders, hip boots, or high-top hiking boots and tough jeans can offer good defense against rattlesnake attacks; leave the shorts and flip-flops in the car. The lower river, parallel to Highway 140 on the way to Adel, receives the most attention from anglers because of its proximity and easy access from the highway. Still in a canyon, the river comprises pools and riffles that form around large rocks. Fish will range 10–16 inches. Since water levels can fluctuate with the increase of warm weather, the best time to fish this section would be in the early summer after the spring runoff. Water levels in this lower section can be reduced to a trickle in the late summer and fall, and anglers are better off moving to the headwaters in the Crane Mountain Recreation Area or in the canyon reach.

The headwaters are small but productive for trout in the 10–14-inch range, with some bigger trout available. Deep Creek Campground provides a good access point. Anglers can also fish other small creeks in the area for chances at similar-size fish. From the campground at Dismal Creek, anglers can fish the confluence of Dismal Creek and Deep Creek.

Are you tough? Sure you are, and you will need to be to fish the third and best section of river in the roadless canyon between Burnt Creek and Parsnip Creek. Fish in this section are the biggest in the river at 18 inches-plus. Anglers can reach this area from small dirt roads off Forest Road 3910. A good BLM map such as the *South Half Lakeview Resource Area Recreation Guide* will make your trip into this area more productive and enjoyable. Prepare for rough roads and quite a bit of hiking to get to the river and watch for rattlesnakes. Carry plenty of water and snacks into this remote area. Very few anglers venture into this region because of the difficult access, but your efforts should be well rewarded with the opportunity to catch larger fish.

Species: Redband trout.

Facilities: Primitive campgrounds abound near the headwaters at Deep Creek and Dismal Creek off Forest Rd. 3915. Other area camping can be had on the way to the headwaters at Willow Creek and Twin Springs. Some camping exists farther south on Forest Rd. 3915 at Lilly Lake. Supplies and other accommodations can be had in Lakeview.

Directions: To reach the headwaters from Lakeview drive on Hwy. 140 east 6.5 miles and turn south onto Forest Rd. 3915. Follow Road 3915 20 miles to Dismal Creek Campground at the confluence of Deep Creek and Dismal Creek. Deep Creek Campground is a short distance west of Dismal Creek Campground on Forest Rd. 4015. To reach the lower section of river around Adel, drive east 22 miles on Hwy. 140 until you see the river to the south side of the highway. The spot where the highway converges with the river is also the spot where two creeks—Drake and Parsnip—empty into Deep Creek. Follow Hwy. 140 approximately five miles to Adel, and fish anywhere along the roadside. To reach the roadless canyon, drive south three miles on Forest Rd. 3915 to Forest Rd. 3910. Turn east and follow the road until it starts to make a sweep back to the north. Armed with a good BLM map, you

should be able to find small spur roads that will lead you close to the river.

Contact: Lakeview Chamber of Commerce, 541/947-6040; Lakeview Ranger District, 541/947-3334; BLM, Lakeview District, 541/947-2177; ODFW, Lakeview, 541/947-2950.

39 WARNER VALLEY LAKES
north of Adel

Map 6.7, page 405

Warner Valley is an expansive desert region with a series of large lakes running south to north adjacent to the Hart Mountain National Antelope Refuge. From north to south they are Blue Joint, Stone Corral, Lower Campbell, Upper Campbell, Flagstaff, Swamp, Jones, Anderson, Hart, Crump, and Pelican. All 11 lakes in Warner Valley are alkaline and support populations of warm-water fish (brown bullhead, crappie, largemouth bass) and some trout. Trout have had a tough time in this area and are generally confined to the lower lakes and inlets. During high-water years the lakes are connected by a series of channels. All the lakes are shallow, no more than 10 feet deep, and in low-water years and times of drought have dried up completely. The last drought occurred 1988–1992, but the area has recovered since 1993 and again supports good populations of fish. Still, even in moderate-rain years the upper lakes have a tendency to drop to nonsustainable levels.

Pelican, Crump, and Hart lakes, the lowermost lakes in the basin, are considered to have the best fishing for perch and bass because they provide the most consistent water conditions to promote fish growth. Farther north the lakes get less likely to hold sustainable levels of water. Boat ramps service all three lakes, but a majority of fishing takes place from the bank. Shallow water, dense aquatic growth, and high winds can make boating hazardous. Other notable lakes for good crappie fishing include Upper Campbell and Campbell lake at the far north end.

Anglers need nothing more than a few jigs, bass poppers, and bait such as worms to catch perch, brown bullhead, and bass. Fly anglers may also do well on small leech patterns and nymphs stripped with erratic retrieves. Change water often until you find a good cache of fish. Inlets around channels are always a good bet for finding most fish species, especially in spring when fish are looking for spawning grounds.

There's very little shade in the valley, so be sure to take plenty of water and sunscreen. All the lakes are accessible by good roads from numerous points, but the easiest access is from Adel on the north side of Highway 140.

Species: Redband trout, brown bullhead, crappie, largemouth bass, perch.

Facilities: There are no developed campsites, but camping is allowed in natural campsites and where posted. Restrooms and a small boat launch are available at the Warner Valley Day Use Area on Stone Corral Lake. Hart Mountain, Warner Peak, and Poker Jim Ridge make up the majority of landmarks to the east and offer numerous activities such as hunting, wildlife-viewing, and natural-history exhibits at the Hart Mountain National Antelope Refuge Headquarters and Information Center. There is a rustic hot springs south of the refuge headquarters. Supplies are available in Lakeview.

Directions: From Adel drive north on Hogback Rd. (County Rd. 3–10). It is approximately five miles to Crump Lake, 10 miles to Hart Lake, and 20 miles to Plush. To get to the upper lakes, start from Plush and drive east on Hart Mountain Rd. In approximately 17 miles you will reach Warner Valley Overlook. Smaller roads will lead you from the overlook to Flagstaff and Campbell lakes. Stay east on Hart Mountain Rd. and drive five miles to Hart Mountain National Antelope Refuge Headquarters and Information Center.

Contact: Lakeview Chamber of Commerce, 541/947-6040; Lakeview Ranger District, 541/947-3334; BLM, Lakeview District, 541/947-2177; ODFW, Lakeview, 541/947-2950; Hart Mountain National Antelope Ref-uge, 541/947-3315; for information on birds in Warner Valley, www.npwrc.usgs.gov/resource/othrdata/chekbird/r1/hartmtn.htm.

40 SPALDING RESERVOIR
northeast of Adel

Map 6.7, page 405

Anything east of Lakeview is remote, and this 20-acre irrigation impoundment is no exception. Chances are that on any given day you will have the whole reservoir to yourself. What makes Spalding worth the drive is big trout of 20 inches or more. The reservoir went dry in 2003, but fresh stocks of fingerlings were planted in 2004; fishing prospects for 2007 are hopeful. Thanks to the rich waters, the trout in Spalding can grow about an inch a month. Spalding does grow them big, but anglers need to come prepared for roughing it. There are no constructed campgrounds, drinking water facilities, or boat ramps; very little cover is available to shade anglers from the summer heat and strong desert winds; freak snowstorms can arrive in early summer, turning this area into a winter wonderland. Thunderstorms are no small threat in this area, and Spalding can be a spooky place to be when there is little cover and no place to go except the car. Oh! The lengths one will go to catch big trout.

Spalding fishes well with bait, lures, and flies from ice-out to the first snowfall. Spring and fall are probably the most comfortable times to be here, when cooler weather doesn't wash out the afternoon and make you feel as if you're in an oven. Float tubes and small boats are not necessary but offer some advantage to tracking down fish, especially in the deeper water. Bank fishing is equally productive, and access is good around the whole lake. Fly anglers can use an assortment of small streamers, nymphs, and dry flies. Spin anglers should use smaller lures in gold and silver and Rooster Tails in red, white, and black. Any type of bait will work, but worms are probably the best choice.

Species: Rainbow trout.

Facilities: Natural campsites can be had at the

lake. You can buy supplies in Lakeview, but anglers should come prepared with water and supplies. Also, make sure there is plenty of gas in the tank, a good tire jack in the trunk, and an inflated spare tire.

Directions: To get to the reservoir from Adel drive east 20 miles on Hwy. 140 to Beatty Butte Rd. (Forest Rd. 6176), a washboard-infested dirt road. Drive north on Beatty Butte Rd. 14 miles to Forest Rd. 6176M. Turn east and drive another five miles to reach the reservoir.

Contact: Lakeview Chamber of Commerce, 541/947-6040; Lakeview Ranger District, 541/947-3334; ODFW, Lakeview, 541/947-2950; BLM, Lakeview District, 541/947-2177.

41 KRUMBO RESERVOIR
southeast of Burns in the
Malheur Wildlife Refuge

Map 6.8, page 406

Krumbo is a popular desert reservoir. Stark but beautiful, the reservoir covers 150 surface acres and averages 20 feet deep. Most anglers come for the trout, which can reach 20 inches or more, but it is also a good largemouth bass fishery. Fish tend to congregate around aquatic weed beds where insects are more concentrated. Boats are popular, but float tubes are better, and bank fishing is also productive. Popular starting points for boats and float tubes are in the cove near the boat ramp, out in the lake on the south shore around weed beds, and at the inlet of Krumbo Creek. The creek below the reservoir is closed to all fishing. Bank anglers can walk from the boat ramp to two rocky points and fish the deeper water.

Flies, lures, and bait are allowed in the reservoir and in Krumbo Creek above the reservoir. The reservoir is open April 23–October 31, but these dates change from year to year. Five fish may be taken per day with an eight-inch minimum length; only one trout over 20 inches may be kept per day. Fly anglers have the opportunity to fish over several insect hatches, including *Callibaetis* and chironomids. Leeches, minnows, scuds, and snails are present as food sources for trout and bass. Small streamers such as Woolly Buggers or Seal Buggers trolled or stripped near the bank or weed beds is very effective. Nymphs and scud patterns can be fished in the weed beds. Lure anglers can use gold and silver spinners and small Rooster Tails in black, yellow, and white, cast against the bank or trolled in deeper water. Bass should be targeted with surface poppers or Rapalas around structure at the boat ramp or along the bank during low-light hours.

Species: Rainbow trout, largemouth bass.

Facilities: There is no camping at the lake. The closest camping can be had at Page Springs on the Donner und Blitzen River. There is a single-lane boat ramp and wheelchair-accessible fishing pier at the south end of the lake. Boats may use electric motors only. Accommodations are available in Frenchglen and Diamond. Supplies are available in Burns.

Directions: From Burns drive east on Hwy. 20 one mile to Hwy. 205. Drive south on Hwy. 205 approximately 40 miles to Krumbo Reservoir Rd. (marked by signs). Turn east; the reservoir is about 3.5 miles down Krumbo Reservoir Rd.

Contact: Harney County Chamber of Commerce, Burns, 541/573-2636; ODFW, Hines, 541/573-6582; BLM, Burns District, 541/573-4400; Malheur National Wildlife Refuge, 541/493-2612; Frenchglen Hotel, 541/493-2825; Diamond Hotel, 541/493-1898; McCoy Creek Inn, 541/493-2131; B&B Sporting Goods, 541/573-6200; Kiger Fly Shop, 541/573-1329, www.oregonvos.net/~rwassom/kigercreek.html.

42 DONNER UND BLITZEN RIVER
southeast of Burns

Map 6.8, page 406   **BEST (**

The Donner und Blitzen (German for Thunder and Lightning) is a wonderful, small trout stream near Frenchglen, 60 miles southeast of Burns. It flows 40 miles from Steens Mountain Loop Road, through the Malheur Wildlife Refuge, and into Malheur Lake. The upper river originates from an expansive network of important tributaries that include Fish Creek, Dry Creek, the Little Blitzen, and Indian Creek. The main river and most of its tributaries have been classified Wild and Scenic and form 86 miles of protected waters. Typical of most desert streams, fishing is best in early summer after the spring runoff and again in fall. Mid- to late summer the river loses much of its flow, and the fish tend to pool up in pockets and deeper runs. Summer is also the time for frequent and sudden thunderstorms and unpleasantly hot weather. All trout in the Donner are wild redbands and average 12–14 inches. Larger fish are present and can reach an impressive 20–24 inches. Two fish may be kept per day, none over 20 inches, May 28–October 31. January 1–May 27 and November 1–December 31 the river is catch-and-release only. Fishing is closed from Bridge Creek, two miles downstream from the campground, to Malheur Lake.

The most popular and productive area to fish is upriver from Page Springs Campground. Here you will find a fairly gentle river composed of deep pools, riffles, runs, and pocket water. The river is lined with tall grasses and overhanging trees, creating perfect habitat for the larger trout. Anglers can walk on a good, but rocky, hiking trail from the campground about four miles upriver to Fish Creek. Be prepared to ford the river in several places. Beyond Fish Creek there are no formal trails, and you'll need to scramble over boulders through the canyon. To avoid crowds, start fishing up higher in the river, about a three-mile walk from the campground. Use caution when hiking in this area as rattlesnakes are present. Waders or at least hip boots can make walking through grass and water more comfortable and lends an element of protection against snakes. Mosquitoes plague summer so take plenty of insect repellent and wear a long-sleeved, lightweight shirt.

Fishing techniques for this river include nymphs, dry flies, streamers, and lures. Bait fishing is not allowed. Anglers will find the most success fishing small nymphs under an indicator and attractor dry flies in the faster runs, pocket water, and up against the bank under overhanging brush. Streamers such as small Woolly Buggers or Seal Buggers work great when cast under trees or along the bank in broad, deep pools. Don't ignore the use of small Soft Hackles such as a Partridge and orange or yellow Hare's Ear. You can use Soft Hackles as a dropper on streamers or nymphs, letting them swing through the bottom of runs and imparting a slight twitch to the line. Small lures in gold or silver, or Rooster Tails in black or yellow, can be fished in the deeper, slower runs.

Species: Wild redband trout.

Facilities: Camping is available at Page Spring Campground and provides nice grassy areas, shade trees, RV sites, and drinking water. Supplies, accommodations, gas, and frozen treats are available in Frenchglen and Burns, but anglers should come prepared to be self-sufficient. Frenchglen Hotel is a historic landmark, good for breakfast, lunch, and dinner with B&B accommodations.

Directions: From Burns drive east on Hwy. 205, which you will reach one mile east of Burns on Hwy. 20. Drive south approximately 60 miles on Hwy. 205 to Frenchglen. Drive through Frenchglen to the south side of town and look for signs to Steens Mountain Loop Rd. and Page Springs. Drive down a gravel access road approximately two miles to the campground. The trailhead at the campground is at the far southern end. Parking and restrooms are available. To reach the headwaters from Frenchglen, continue south eight miles on Hwy. 205 to Steens Mountain Loop Rd. Turn east on Steens Mountain Loop Rd. and drive approximately 17 miles to the river crossing at Blitzen Crossing. Park at the river crossing to hike either up- or downriver.

Contact: Harney County Chamber of Commerce, Burns, 541/573-2636; ODFW, Hines, 541/573-6582; BLM, Burns District, 541/573-4400; Malheur National Wildlife Refuge, 541/493-2612; Frenchglen Hotel, 541/493-2825; Diamond Hotel, 541/493-1898; McCoy Creek Inn, 541/493-2131; B&B Sporting Goods, 541/573-6200; Kiger Fly Shop, 541/573-1329, www.oregonvos.net/~rwassom/kigercreek.html.

🔢 MANN LAKE

north of Fields

Map 6.8, page 406

Few lakes in Oregon shoulder the level of angler devotion and respect of Mann Lake. Perhaps it's because anglers have to drive so far to fish here that some justification is needed; or that Mann Lake is so stunningly scenic and powerful in its stark beauty that anglers cannot resist bathing in its splendor; or enchantment at the thought of catching Mann Lake cutthroats. Mann is as good as they say, and anglers who make the long trek to this area are well rewarded—barring the worst winds and cold you can imagine. Anglers should come prepared for just about all kinds of weather; cover of any kind is nonexistent, and the winds can blow hard and cold off Steens Mountain. Snowstorms are frequent in the early summer and fall.

Mann Lake is situated in a sagebrush valley north of the Alvord Desert at the base of stunning Steens Mountain. Steens Mountain looms large over the lake at an elevation of 9,773 feet and creates a picture-postcard backdrop for anglers working the water with leeches, nymphs, and dry flies. Modestly sized at 275 acres, Mann is susceptible to seasonal summer drawdowns and serious winter freezes. Oddly, this is one of the first places devoted anglers look to kick off the fishing season. In the spring, Internet posting boards are filled with seemingly minute-by-minute reports of the lake's thaw, baiting the anticipation of those in the know. Spring and fall are the most popular times to fish the lake and generate the

best action from the fish. In spring expect to see quite a few anglers.

Since the lake is relatively shallow with an average depth of eight feet (15 feet at its deepest point) and lacks structure of any kind, anglers can wade or float in a tube anywhere on the lake and cast in all directions for trout. Fish tend to cruise here, swimming up and down the banks feeding on insects such as leeches, scuds, damsels, snails, and chironomids in the rich waters. Hatches of damsels and extra-large chironomids take place in the spring.

Mann Lake cutthroats are genetically related to Lahontan cutthroat trout, a legendary fish originating in Pyramid Lake, Nevada. Rumors of the original stock of fish reaching 60-plus pounds may be a truth lost in another era, but these fish can still get big at 20–24 inches. Slightly sluggish compared to redband trout, Mann Lake cutthroats have a beautiful speckled look and strike with a fierce determination sure to send a shock to the hands of any angler. All fish in Mann Lake are stocked. No other fish species exists except illegally introduced goldfish. Check the local ODFW field office before venturing to the lake in the coming years to make sure ODFW hasn't killed off the lake to get rid of the goldfish.

Species: Mann Lake cutthroat.

Facilities: Camping and a boat ramp are available at the lake. You should buy supplies and water ahead of time, but limited supplies are available in Fields. Supplies and other accommodations can also be had in Frenchglen and Burns. Alvord Hot Springs to the south affords a nice respite from the cold weather.

Directions: To get to Mann Lake from Fields drive north on the Fields–Denio Rd. one mile to the junction with Catlow Valley Rd. Stay north on Fields–Denio Rd. (also known as the Steens Mountain Rd.) and drive 39 miles to Mann Lake. Mann Lake will be marked by signs on the west side of the road.

Contact: Harney County Chamber of Commerce, Burns, 541/573-2636; ODFW, Hines, 541/573-6582; BLM, Burns District, 541/573-4400; Alvord Inn, 541/493-2441.

44 TROUT CREEK
southeast of Fields

Map 6.8, page 406

Anglers must love the remoteness of southeastern Oregon to even consider driving to this river. The 175-mile drive from Lakeview—including 75 miles in Nevada—ensures this is no day trip. The endurance this drive requires is compounded by the need to navigate a series of primitive roads into the headwaters; four-wheel drives are recommended. What's the attraction? You're within spitting distance of Mann Lake, a great Lahontan cutthroat fishery at the base of Steens Mountain. The Owyhee and Donner und Blitzen Rivers are close and provide equally good fishing for redband trout. Finally, anglers get an opportunity to catch a special breed of trout, a hybridized form of the speckled Alvord cutthroat (pure Alvord cutthroat trout are thought to be extinct) and perhaps appreciate an area of Oregon few Oregonians ever get to see. These trout are hybridized with coastal rainbow.

Trout Creek is about 30 miles long and originates in the Trout Creek Mountains on the Nevada border east of Denio, Nevada. Only the upper sections of the river near the headwaters are available to the angler; carry a good BLM map to navigate the roads. The lower river flows through private property and is inaccessible. Spring is the best time of year to be on the stream. The headwaters run at a very low flow, and most of the trout are small; expect average catches 8–10 inches. During the summer, dry flies and small nymphs will catch fish all day, as will spinners. For some, Trout Creek represents what the spirit of fishing is all about: solitude, exploration, and catching fish, no matter the size.

Species: Alvord cutthroat.

Facilities: There are no constructed campgrounds, but anglers can pitch a tent anywhere on BLM lands. The closest towns are Denio, Nevada, and Fields, Oregon. Both towns have gas stations and frozen ice-cream treats. You should buy supplies, and plenty of them, before the trip. Along the way to the creek you will pass a nice hot springs in the Alvord Desert, which no angler should pass up if your passions include soaking in boiling water under the blazing hot summer sun; try an evening or early morning soak.

Directions: To get to Trout Creek from Fields drive nine miles south on the Fields–Denio Hwy. to Whitehorse Ranch Rd. Turn east on Whitehorse Ranch Rd. (Hwy. 203) and drive five miles to the junction at Cottonwood Ranch Rd. (Hwy. 205). Cross Cottonwood Ranch Rd. and stay east on Whitehorse Ranch Rd. for eight more miles until Whitehorse Ranch Rd. begins to turn north. Look for Trout Creek Mountain Rd. to the east. Turn east onto Trout Creek Mountain Rd. and drive approximately 14 miles, following Little Trout Creek to the west. Where the road begins to turn west, Trout Creek will appear to your south and follow the river for approximately two miles. Here you can hike down into the canyon or use your BLM map to discover logging roads that will take you downstream.

Contact: Harney County Chamber of Commerce, Burns, 541/573-2636; ODFW, Hines 541/573-6582; BLM, Vale District, 541/473-3144; Alvord Inn, 541/493-2441.

45 ANTELOPE RESERVOIR
near Jordan Valley in the Owyhee Basin east of Burns Junction

Map 6.9, page 407

Antelope Reservoir is a remote high-desert lake (elevation 4,318 feet). It covers approximately 3,285 acres when full and is subject to summer drawdowns. Once known as a great fishery for producing large redband trout, the lake has since fallen on hard times with a leaky dam, very high levels of mercury, no stocking program since 1989, and an overpopulation of brown bullhead catfish. Tough fishing is in store for anglers trying to catch the few remaining, but potentially very large, trout. Anglers coming here should be well prepared with plenty of food and water as well as protection from the sun and high winds.

In good years, bait, flies, and lures are all allowed and work equally well. Irrigation draws make this a better place to fish in the spring. Bank access is good, and a majority of the fishing is done from shore, but small boats and float tubes can be launched for access to deeper waters near the middle of the lake. A health advisory has been issued for Antelope Reservoir because of very high levels of mercury due to past mining practices. ODHS recommends women of childbearing age, children under six, and people with liver and kidney damage should avoid eating fish from these waters. Healthy adults should eat no more than one eight-ounce meal per month. Check with the Oregon Department of Human Services for more information.

Species: Redband trout, brown bullheads,

Facilities: There are 25 family camping sites, an outhouse, and an unimproved boat ramp at the lake. Buy supplies in Jordan Valley or Rome.

Directions: From Jordan Valley drive southwest on Hwy. 95 about 11 miles to the Antelope Reservoir Rd. Turn south on Antelope Reservoir Rd., a dirt road, and drive two miles to the reservoir.

Contact: Harney County Chamber of Commerce, Burns, 541/573-2636; ODFW, Hines, 541/573-6582; BLM, Vale District, 541/473-3144; Oregon Department of Human Services, 503/731-4012; Rome RV and Café, 541/586-2294.

46 UPPER OWYHEE RIVER
south of Jordan Valley

Map 6.9, page 407

The Upper Owyhee flows out of the Independence Mountains of northern Nevada and unceremoniously enters a remote southeast corner of Oregon. On its 186-mile route from the Oregon border to Lake Owyhee, it receives three forks and numerous tributaries while flowing through the rugged Owyhee Canyon. The West Little Fork meets the main river south of Three Forks; the North Fork,

Middle Fork, and main Owyhee all meet in Three Forks. From here the river continues through the Owyhee Canyon past Rome and into to Lake Owyhee. Below Lake Owyhee, a 52-mile impoundment and the longest reservoir in Oregon, the lower river continues a 20-mile run before entering the Snake River on the Oregon–Idaho border, five miles south of Nyssa. Four sections (129 miles) of the 186 miles of upper river have been designated Wild and Scenic: Three Forks downstream to China Gulch, Crooked Creek to the Owyhee Reservoir, the South Fork from the Idaho–Oregon border downstream to Three Forks, and the North Fork from the Oregon–Idaho state line to its confluence with the Owyhee River.

Fishing in the upper river is rated fair to good, but it takes a back seat to most other recreation. The best fishery here is for smallmouth bass, some of which can reach four pounds or more. Because of the lack of roads, most fishing access is by boat on the float from Three Forks to Rome (37 miles) or Leslie Gulch at Lake Owyhee (66.5 miles). Guides or experienced boaters are recommended for these stretches, since they contain numerous Class III, IV, and V rapids, and one Class VII. All the floats through this section are multiday, and because of their remoteness should be considered as major river expeditions. Good river guidebooks can give you mile-by-mile instructions about how to run the river.

The upper sections of the river and its forks provide very little fishing. There are some redbands in West Little Owyhee, Cow Creek, and North and Middle forks of the Owyhee, but the fish are mainly high up in Idaho. And it's said that there are also some redbands in catchable numbers in Dry Creek, which enters Owyhee Reservoir. Jordan Creek in Oregon is 99 percent private. The North Fork at Three Forks provides the best opportunity for bass and trout, when high water pushes the fish lower in the river. The Middle Fork also experiences some of this during high water. Five miles of the North Fork are accessible by foot from the mouth or by walking down a steep

Chapter 6

500-foot canyon near the top. There are no hiking trails, so walking is tough. The only true headwater that can be reached in Oregon is on the West Little Owyhee.

Species: Trout, smallmouth bass, catfish.

Facilities: The main attractions in this section of river are white-water rafting, remote hot springs, wildlife-viewing, scenic beauty, hiking, and mountain biking. Camping is available on BLM lands anywhere you can pitch a tent. Nearest towns for supplies are in Jordan Valley and Rome, so take plenty of gas and supplies. Three Forks is not a community.

Directions: From Jordan Valley drive west 11 miles on Hwy. 95 to Three Forks Rd. Turn south on Three Forks Rd. and drive 36 miles on gravel roads to Three Forks. From Three Forks use a good BLM map to navigate smaller roads into the headwaters of the North Fork, Middle Fork, and main stem of the river. Travel into this area should not be taken lightly, and four-wheel drives are highly recommended. Cell phone service is doubtful.

Contact: Ontario Chamber of Commerce, 888/889-8012; ODFW, Ontario, 541/889-6975; BLM, Vale District, 541/473-3144; Rome RV and Café, 541/586-2294; River Shuttles, 541/586-2352; Tight Lines Fishing and Rafting, 541/896-3219, www.tight-linesfishing.com; Oregon River Experiences, 800/827-1358, www.oregonriver.com; Destination Wilderness, 800/423-8868, www.wildernesstrips.com; The Riverkeeper Fly Shop, 208/344-3838.

RESOURCES

OREGON DEPARTMENT OF FISH AND WILDLIFE

Northwest Region
Astoria Field Office, 503/325-2462
Mapleton Satellite Office, 541/991-7838
Newport Field Office, 541/867-4741
North Coast District (Tillamook),
　503/842-2741
North Willamette District (Regional
　Office, Clackamas), 503/657-2000
Salem Field Office, 503/378-6925
Sauvie Island Wildlife Area, 503/621-3488
South Willamette District (Corvallis),
　541/757-4186
Springfield Field Office, 541/726-3515

Southwest Region
Charleston Field Office, 541/888-5515
Gold Beach Field Office, 541/247-7605
Rogue District (Central Point),
　541/826-8774
Umpqua District (Regional Office,
　Roseburg), 541/440-3353

Northeast Region
Baker City Field Office, 541/523-5832
Enterprise Field Office, 541/426-3279
Grande Ronde District (Regional Office, La
　Grande), 541/963-2138
Heppner Field Office, 541/676-5230
John Day District (Pendleton),
　541/276-2344
John Day Field Office, 541/575-1167

Central and Southeast Region (High Desert Regional Offices)
Deschutes District (Regional Office, Bend),
　541/388-6363
Klamath District, 541/883-5732
Lakeview Field Office, 541/947-2950
Madras-Trout Creek Field Station,
　541/475-2183

Malheur District (Hines), 541/573-6582
Ontario Field Office, 541/889-6975
Prineville Field Office, 541/447-5111
Summer Lake Field Station, 541/943-3324
The Dalles Field Office, 541/296-4628

NATIONAL FORESTS

Columbia River Gorge National Scenic Area
902 Wasco Avenue, Suite 200
Hood River, OR 97031
541/308-1700
www.fs.fed.us/r6/columbia/forest

Deschutes National Forest
1001 S.W. Emkay Drive
Bend, OR 97702
541/383-5300
www.fs.fed.us/r6/centraloregon

Bend-Fort Rock District
1230 NE 3rd Street, Suite A-262
Bend, OR 97701
541/383-4000

Crescent District
P.O. Box 208
136471 Highway 97 N.
Crescent, OR 97733
541/433-3200

Sisters District
P.O. Box 249
Pine Street & Highway 20
Sisters, OR 97759
541/549-7700

Fremont-Winema National Forests
1301 South G Street
Lakeview, OR 97630
541/947-2151
www.fs.fed.us/r6/frewin/

Bly District
Highway 140
P.O. Box 25
Bly, OR 97622
541/353-2427

Chemult District
P.O. Box 150
Chemult, OR 97731
541/365-7001

Chiloquin District
38500 Highway 97 North
Chiloquin, OR 97624
541/783-4001

Klamath District
2819 Dahlia Street
Klamath Falls, OR 97601
541/885-3400

Lakeview District
Highway 395 N.
HC 64 Box 60
Lakeview, OR 97630
541/947-3334

Paisley District
Highway 31
P.O. Box 67
Paisley, OR 97636
541/943-3114

Silver Lake District
Highway 31
P.O. Box 129
Silver Lake, OR 97638
541/576-2107

Hells Canyon National Recreation Area
88401 Highway 82
Enterprise, OR 97828
541/426-4978
www.fs.fed.us/hellscanyon/

Clarkston Field Office (WA)
2535 Riverside Drive
Clarkston, WA 99403
509/758-0616

Riggins Field Office (ID)
189 Highway 95
Riggins, ID 83549
208/628-3916

Malheur National Forest
431 Patterson Bridge Road
John Day, OR 97845
541/575-3000
www.fs.fed.us/r6/malheur/

Blue Mountain District
P.O. Box 909
John Day, OR 97845
541/575-3000

Emigrant Creek District
265 Highway 20 South
Hines, OR 97738
541/573-4300

Prairie City District
P.O. Box 337
Prairie City, OR 97869
541/820-3800

Mount Hood National Forest
16400 Champion Way
Sandy, OR 97055
503/668-1700
TTY: 503/668-1431
www.fs.fed.us/r6/mthood/

Barlow District
780 N.E. Court Street
Dufur, Oregon 97021
541/467-2291
TTY: 541/467-5170

Clackamas River District
595 N.W. Industrial Way
Estacada, OR 97023
503/630-6861

Hood River District
6780 Highway 35
Parkdale, OR 97041
541/352-6002

Zigzag District
70220 E. Highway 26
Zigzag, OR 97049
503/622-3191

Ochoco National Forest
3160 N.E. 3rd Street
Prineville, OR 97754
541/416-6500
www.fs.fed.us/r6/centraloregon/

Lookout Mountain District
3160 N.E. 3rd Street
Prineville, OR 97754
541/416-6500

Paulina District
7803 Beaver Creek Road
Paulina, OR 97751-9706
541/477-6900

Rogue River-Siskiyou National Forest
PO Box 520
333 West 8th Street
Medford, OR 97501
541/858-2200
TTY: 866/296-3823
www.fs.fed.us/r6/rogue-siskiyou/

Applegate District
6941 Upper Applegate Road
Jacksonville, OR 97530-9314
541/899-3800

Ashland District
645 Washington Street
Ashland, OR 97520-1402
541/552-2900

Butte Falls District
730 Laurel Street
Butte Falls, OR 97522
541/865-2700

Chetco District
P.O. Box 4580
539 Chetco Avenue
Brookings, OR 97415
541/412-6000

Galice District
2164 N.E. Spalding Avenue
Grants Pass, OR 97526
541/471-6500

Gold Beach District
29279 Ellensburg Avenue
Gold Beach, OR 97444
541/247-3600

Illinois Valley District
26568 Redwood Highway
Cave Junction, OR 97523
541/592-4000

Powers District
42861 Highway 242
Powers OR 97466
541/439-6200

Prospect District
47201 Highway 62
Prospect, OR 97536-9724
541/560-3400

Siuslaw National Forest
4077 S.W. Research Way
P.O. Box 1148
Corvallis, OR 97339
541/750-7000
www.fs.fed.us/r6/siuslaw/

Florence Office
4480 Highway 101, Bldg. G
Florence, OR 97439
541/902-8526

Hebo District
31525 Highway 22
P.O. Box 235
Hebo, OR 97122
503/392-3161

Waldport Station
1094 S.W. Pacific Highway
Waldport, OR 97394
541/563-3211

Umatilla National Forest
2517 S.W. Hailey Avenue
Pendleton, OR 97801
541/278-3716
www.fs.fed.us/r6/uma/

Heppner District
P.O. Box 7
Heppner, OR 97836
541/676-9187

North Fork John Day District
P.O. Box 158
Ukiah, OR 97880
541/427-3231

Pomeroy District (WA)
71 West Main
Pomeroy, WA 99347
509/843-1891

Walla Walla District (WA)
1415 West Rose Street
Walla Walla, WA 99362
509/522-6290

Umpqua National Forest
2900 N.W. Stewart Pkwy.
Roseburg, OR 97470
541/672-6601
www.fs.fed.us/r6/umpqua/

Cottage Grove District
78405 Cedar Park Road
Cottage Grove, OR 97424
541/767-5000

Diamond Lake District
2020 Toketee RS Road
Idleyld Park, OR 97447
541/498-2531

Diamond Lake Visitor Center
541/793-3310

North Umpqua District
18782 N. Umpqua Highway
Glide, OR 97443
541/496-3532

Tiller Station
27812 Tiller Trail Highway
Tiller, OR 97484
541/825-3201

Wallowa-Whitman National Forest
P.O. Box 907
1550 Dewey Avenue
Baker City, OR 97814
541/523-6391
TDD 541/523-1405
www.fs.fed.us/r6/w-w/

Baker District
3285 11th Street
P. O. Box 947
Baker City, OR 97814
541/523-4476

Eagle Cap District
88401 Highway 82
Enterprise, OR 97828
541/426-4978

La Grande District
3502 Highway 30
La Grande, OR 97850
541/963-7186

Pine District
38470 Pine Town Lane
Halfway, OR 97834
541/742-7511

Unity District
214 Main Street
P.O. Box 39
Unity, OR 97884
541/446-3351

Wallowa Mountains Visitor Center
88401 Highway 82
Enterprise, OR 97828
541/426-4978

Wallowa Valley District
88401 Highway 82
Enterprise, OR 97828
541/426-4978

Willamette National Forest
211 East 7th Avenue
Eugene, OR 97401
541/225-6300
www.fs.fed.us/r6/willamette/

Detroit District
HC73, Box 320
Mill City, OR 97360
503/854-3366

McKenzie River District
57600 McKenzie Highway
McKenzie Bridge, OR 97413
541/822-3381

Middle Fork District
46375 Highway 58
Westfir, OR 97492
541/782-2283

Middle Fork District (Lowell Office)
60 South Pioneer Street
Lowell, OR 97452
541/937-2129

Sweet Home District
4431 Highway 20
Sweet Home, OR 97386
541/367-5168

BUREAU OF LAND MANAGEMENT

BLM Oregon/Washington
333 SW 1st Avenue
Portland, OR 97204
503/808-6002
TDD: 503/808-6372
www.blm.gov/or/index.htm

Burns District
28910 Highway 20 West
Hines, OR 97738-9424
541/573-4400

Coos Bay
1300 Airport Lane
North Bend, OR 97459-2023
541/756-0100

Eugene District
2890 Chad Drive, P.O. Box 10226
Eugene, OR 97440
541/683-6600

Lakeview District
1301 South G Street
Lakeview, OR 97630
541/947-2177

Medford District
3040 Biddle Road
Medford, OR 97504
541/618-2200

Prineville District
3050 N.E. 3rd Street
Prineville, OR 97754
541/416-6700

Roseburg District
777 N.W. Garden Valley Boulevard
Roseburg, OR 97470
541/440-4930

Salem District
1717 Fabry Road, S.E.
Salem, OR 97306
503/375-5646

Vale District
100 Oregon Street
Vale, OR 97918
541/473-3144

MAPS
Forest Service

For each National Forest, the Forest Service prints one general map of the entire forest, one more detailed map of each Ranger District, and one of any wilderness or other special areas on that forest. Each name on this list represents the name of a map that is available. Each Forest office has its own maps available in the office or by phone, and Nature of the Northwest in Portland (run in part by the Forest Service) has a wide selection, as well.

Columbia River Gorge National Scenic Area
Trails of Columbia Gorge

Deschutes National Forest
Bend Ranger District
Crescent Ranger District
Diamond Peak Wilderness

Fort Rock Ranger District
Sisters Ranger District

Fremont National Forest
Bly Ranger District
Gearhart Mountain Wilderness
Lakeview Ranger District
Paisley Ranger District
Silver Lake Ranger District

Malheur National Forest
Bear Valley Ranger District
Burns East Ranger District
Burns West Ranger District
Long Creek Ranger District
Prairie City Ranger District
Strawberry Mountain Wilderness/
    Monument Rock Wilderness

Mount Hood National Forest
Barlow Ranger District
Bull of the Woods/Salmon
    Huckleberry Wilderness
Clackamas River Ranger District
Hatfield/Badger Creek Wilderness
Hood River Ranger District
Mount Hood Wilderness/Columbia Gorge
Olallie Scenic Area
Zigzag Ranger District

Nature of the Northwest
800 N.E. Oregon Street, Suite 177
Portland, OR 97232
503/872-2750
TDD: 503/872-2752
www.naturenw.org

Ochoco National Forest
Lookout Mountain
Paulina Ranger District
Prineville Ranger District
Snow Mountain Ranger District

Rogue River-Siskiyou National Forest
Applegate Ranger District
Ashland Ranger District
Butte Falls Ranger District

Chetco Ranger District
Galice Ranger District
Gold Beach Ranger District
Illinois Valley Ranger District
Kalmiopsis & Wild Rogue Wilderness
Powers Ranger District
Red Buttes Wilderness
Rogue River Float Guide
Sky Lakes Wilderness

Siuslaw National Forest
Cummins Creek Wilderness & Cape
    Perpetua Scenic Area
Drift Creek Wilderness
Hebo Ranger District
Mapleton Ranger District (North)
Mapleton Ranger District (South)
Oregon Dunes National Recreation Area
Waldport Ranger District (East)
Waldport Ranger District (West)

Umatilla National Forest
Heppner Ranger District
North Fork John Day
    Ranger District (East)
North Fork John Day
    Ranger District (West)
Wenaha-Tucannon Wilderness

Umpqua National Forest
Cottage Grove Ranger District
Diamond Lake Ranger District
North Umpqua Ranger District
Tiller Ranger District

Wallowa-Whitman National Forest
Baker Ranger District
Eagle Cap Ranger District
Eagle Cap Wilderness
Hells Canyon National Recreation Area
La Grande Ranger District
Pine Ranger District
Unity Ranger District
Wild and Scenic Snake River

Willamette National Forest
Detroit Ranger District

McKenzie Pass/Santiam Pass
    Scenic Byway
McKenzie River National
    Recreation Area Trails
McKenzie River Ranger District
Menagerie Wilderness &
    Middle Santiam Wilderness
Middle Fork Ranger District
Mount Jefferson Wilderness
Mount Washington Wilderness
Sweet Home Ranger District
Three Sisters Wilderness
Waldo Lake Wilderness

Winema National Forest
Chemult Ranger District
Chiloquin Ranger District
Klamath Ranger District
Mountain Lakes Wilderness

BLM Recreation Maps

Contact the appropriate BLM agency to acquire any of these maps. Many are also available at Portland's Nature of the Northwest (see above), a cooperative effort of the Forest Service and the Oregon Department of Geology.

Burns District, North Half
Burns District, South Half
Central Oregon
Coos Bay District
Eugene District
Klamath Falls Resource Area
Lakeview District/Resource Area,
    North Half
Lakeview District/Resource Area,
    South Half
Lower Deschutes River
Lower John Day River
Medford District
Roseburg District
Salem District Eastside
Salem District Westside
Upper John Day River

Vale District, Baker Resource Area/South
   Area
Vale District, Malheur Resource Area

NON-PROFIT FISHING CLUBS

Bass and Warm-Water Fish
Cascade Bass Masters
www.geocities.com/cascadebass

Oregon Bass and Panfish Club
www.obpc.tripod.com

Umpqua Valley Bassmasters
www.umpquavalleybassmasters.com

Fly-Fishing
Cascade Family Flyfishers (Eugene)
www.cascadefamilyflyfishers.com

Central Oregon Flyfishers (Bend)
www.coflyfishers.org

Columbia Gorge Flyfisheres (The Dalles)
www.community.gorge.net/cgflyfishers

McKenzie Flyfishers (Eugene)
www.mckenzieflyfishers.org

Oregon Council Federation of Flyfishers
www.oregonfff.org

Oregon Trout
www.ortrout.org

Rainland Fly Casters (Astoria)
www.rainlandflycasters.homestead.com

Rogue Fly Casters (Medford)
www.rogueflyfishers.org

Santiam Fly Casters (Salem)
www.santiamflycasters.com

Steamboaters (Roseburg)
www.steamboaters.org

Trout Unlimited Oregon Council
www.tuoregon.org

Steelhead
The Association of Northwest Steelheaders
www.nwsteelheaders.org

Volunteer Programs
STEP: Salmon and Trout Enhancement
   Program
3406 Cherry Avenue N.E.
Salem, OR 97303
503/947-6000 or 800/720-ODFW (6339)
www.dfw.state.or.us/STEP

Women's Fishing Clubs
Damsel Flies
P.O. Box 3932
Eugene, OR 97402
email: oregondamselflies@hotmail.com

The Lady Anglers Fishing Society
   (Portland Chapter)
17084 S. Monroe
Mulino, OR 97042

Stonefly Maidens
P.O. Box 82412
Portland, OR 97282-0412
www.stoneflymaidens.org

FISHING WITH KIDS

The Oregon Department of Fish and Wildlife's Youth Angling Enhancement Program offers many resources and events for fishing with children. Each year, at stocked ponds across the state, ODFW schedules Youth Fishing Events, during which they furnish rods and reels, bait and lures, and volunteers to help out with instruction. The events are free for kids 13 and under; anglers aged 14–17 need a juvenile fishing license. A schedule and announcements regarding these events is on the ODFW website (www.dfw.state.or.us). The department also offers a Free Fishing Weekend each year, usually the second weekend in June;

licenses and tags are not required for this weekend, but all other regulations and daily catch limits must be followed. As for where to take kids fishing…

The Oregon Coast
Alsea Bay
Cape Meares Lake
Cleawox Lake
Devil's Lake
Hebo Lake
Sand Lake
Siltcoos Lake
Tahkenitch Lake
Yaquina Bay

Portland and the Willamette Valley
Blue Lake
Butte Creek
Cooper Creek Lake
Dorena Lake
Foster Reservoir
Green Peter Lake
Henry Hagg Lake
St. Louis Ponds
Sturgeon Lake
Tualatin River

The Columbia River Gorge and Mount Hood
Detroit Lake
Frog Lake
Harriet Lake
Kingsley Reservoir
Laurance Lake
Lost Lake
North Fork Reservoir (Clackamas River)
Olallie Lake
Pine Hollow Reservoir
Rock Creek Reservoir
Trillium Lake

Northeastern Oregon
Anthony Lake
Jubilee Reservoir
Ochoco Reservoir
Phillips Lake

Prineville Reservoir
Unity Reservoir
Walton Lake
Willow Creek Reservoir

Southern Cascades
Applegate Reservoir
Crescent Lake
Cultus Lake
Elk Lake
Emigrant Reservoir
Fish Lake
Hills Creek Reservoir
Howard Prairie Reservoir
Hyatt Reservoir
Lake of the Woods
Lemolo Lake
Lost Creek Reservoir
Suttle Lake
Toketee Reservoir
Twin Lakes
Wickiup Reservoir

Southeastern Oregon
Campbell Lake
Chickahominy Reservoir
Cottonwood Meadows Lake
Dead Horse Lake
Delintment Lake
Emigrant Creek
Krumbo Reservoir
Lofton Reservoir
Moon Reservoir
Yellow Jacket Reservoir

ACCESS FOR DISABLED ANGLERS

Each site listed is, according to the Oregon Department of Fish and Wildlife, "accessible to most person with disabilities." Sites designated as "ADA" meet Americans with Disabilities Act requirements. More detailed information and a booklet, *Access Oregon: A Guide to Accessible Outdoor Recreation Areas Throughout the State*, are available directly through the ODFW website (www.dfw.state.or.us).

Deschutes Watershed
Blue Hole Recreation Site (ADA)
Fall River Hatchery
Prineville Reservoir
White River Wildlife Area
Wizard Falls Hatchery

Grande Ronde Watershed
Wallowa Hatchery

John Day Watershed
Irrigon Hatchery
Umatilla Hatchery

Klamath Watershed
Collier Memorial State Park
Summer Lake Wildlife Area
Topsy Recreation Site (ADA)

Malheur Watershed
Chickahominy Reservoir
Delintment Lake
Farewell Bend State Park
Fish Lake
Yellow Jacket Lake

North Coast
Alsea Hatchery
Devil's Lake State Park
Lytle Lake
Nehalem Hatchery (ADA)
Salmon River Hatchery

North Willamette Watershed
Blue Lake Regional Park
Bonneville Hatchery
Oxbow Hatchery (ADA)
Sandy Hatchery
Sauvie Island Wildlife Area (ADA)

Rogue Watershed
Butte Falls Hatchery
Dodge Bridge (ADA)
Kenneth Denman Wildlife Area

South Willamette Watershed
Brown-Minto Island (ADA)

Cascade-Gateway Park
Detroit Lake State Park
E. E. Wilson Wildlife Area
Fern Ridge Reservoir
Junction City Pond
Marion Forks Hatchery
McKenzie Hatchery
Roaring River Hatchery
South Santiam Hatchery
Willamette Hatchery

Umpqua Watershed
Loon Lake Recreation Area (ADA)
William M. Tugman State Park (ADA)

VISITOR INFORMATION
Chambers of Commerce
The local Chamber of Commerce or Visitor Information Center is always a good place to start planning a visit. Following is an alphabetical list of all communities listed in the book.

Albany
541/926-1517
www.albanyvisitors.com

Ashland
541/482-3486
www.southernoregon.org

Astoria/Warrenton
800/875-6807
www.oldoregon.com

Baker City
800/523-1235
www.visitbaker.com

Bandon
541/347-9616
www.bandon.com

Bend
541/382-3221
www.visitbend.com

Brookings
800/535-9469
www.brookingsor.com

Central Oregon
541/389-8799
www.visitcentraloregon.com/

Christmas Valley
541/576-2216
www.christmasvalley.org

Clackamas County/Wilsonville
800/647-3843
www.wilsonvillechamber.com

North Clackamas County
503/654-7777
www.yourchamber.com

Coos Bay
800/824-8486
www.oregonsbayareachamber.com

Coquille
541/396-4314
www.coquillechamber.org

Corvallis
800/334-8118
www.visitcorvallis.com

Cottage Grove
541/942-2411
www.cgchamber.com

Elgin
541/437-3456

Estacada/Clackamas River
503/630-3483
www.estacadachamber.org

Eugene/Lane County
800/547-5445
www.visitlanecounty.org

Fairview
503/665-7929

Florence
541/997-3128
www.florencechamber.com

Gold Beach
800/525-2334
www.goldbeach.org

Grant County
800/769-5664
www.grantcounty.cc

Grants Pass/Josephine County
800/547-5927
www.visitgrantspass.org

Harney County
541/573-2636

Hells Canyon
541/742-4222

Heppner
541/676-5536

Hermiston
541/567-6151

Hood River County
541/386-2000
www.hoodriver.org

Jacksonville
541/899-8118
www.jacksonvilleoregon.org

Joseph
541/432-1015

Josephine County
800/547-5927

Klamath Falls
541/884-5193

La Grande/Union County
800/848-9969
www.unioncountychamber.org

La Pine
541/536-9771
www.lapine.org

Lakeview/Lake County
541/947-6040
www.lakecountychamber.org

Lava Lands
541/593-2421

Lincoln City
541/994-3070
www.oregoncoast.org

Madras/Jefferson County
800/967-3564
www.madras.net

Maupin
541/395-2599
www.maupinoregon.com

McKenzie River
800/318-8819
www.el.com/to/mckenzierivervalley

Medford/Jackson County
541/779-4847
www.visitmedford.org

Metolius River
541/595-6117

Milton-Freewater
541/938-5563
www.mfchamber.com

Molalla
503/829-6941
www.molallachamber.com

Monmouth
503/838-4268
www.open.org/micc

Mount Angel
503/845-9440

Mount Hood Region
888/622-4822
www.mthood.info

Nehalem Bay
877/368-5100
www.ohwy.com/or/n/nehalem.htm

Nestucca Valley
503/392-3456

Newberg/Chehalem Valley
503/538-2014
www.newberg.org

Newport
541/265-8801
www.newportchamber.org

North Santiam Area
503/897-2865

Ontario
888/889-8012
www.ontariochamber.com

Pendleton
800/547-8911
www.pendleton-oregon.org

Port Orford
541/332-8055
www.discoverportorford.com

Portland
503/275-9750
www.travelportland.com

Prineville-Crook County
541/447-6304
www.visitprineville.com

Reedsport/Winchester Bay
800/247-2155
www.reedsportcc.org

Rogue River
541/582-0242
www.rogueriverchamber.com

Roseburg
800/444-9584
www.visitroseburg.com

St. Helens/Scappoose
503/397-0685

Salem
503/581-1466
www.travelsalem.com

Sandy
503/668-4006
www.sandyoregonchamber.org

Seaside
800/444-6740
www.seasideor.com

Silverton
503/873-5615
www.silvertonchamber.org

Sisters
541/549-0251
www.sisterschamber.com

Springfield
541/746-1651

Sunriver
541/593-8149
www.sunriver-direct.com

Sutherlin
541/459-5829

Sweet Home
541/367-6186
www.sweethomechamber.org

The Dalles
541/296-2231
www.thedalleschamber.com

Tillamook
503/842-7225
www.tillamookchamber.org

Toledo
541/336-3183

Umatilla
541/922-4825

Union County
541/963-8588

Vale
541/473-3800

Waldport
541/563-2133

Wallowa County
800/585-4121
www.wallowacountychamber.com

Wallowa Mountains
541/426-5546

Washington County
503/644-5555
www.wcva.org

West Columbia Gorge
503/669-7473

Wheeler County
541/763-2355

Yachats
800/929-0477
www.yachats.org

Yamhill Valley
503/883-7770
www.yamhillvalley.org

Internet Resources
Big Fish
www.bigfishtackle.com

Fly-Fishing the State of Jefferson
www.flyfishjefferson.com

The Guide Shop
www.guideshop.com

IFISH
www.ifish.net

Quality Fishing
www.qualityfishing.net

The Guide's Forecast
www.theguidesforecast.com

Westfly
www.westfly.com

Suggested Reading

There is so much good literature on the market about fishing in Oregon that I could not possibly list them all here and still give a short annotation. Instead, I offer a few choice selections in the areas of fishing journals, magazines and periodicals, river guidebooks, maps and atlases, fly-fishing, traditional fishing methods, local literature, and a short list of other highly respected books. For the rest, you will have to discover those on your own.

Fishing Journals

Fong, Michael. *The Inside Angler: The Newsletter of the Informed Angler.* California: The Inside Angler. A series of newsletters published privately by a renowned Northern California fly angler. Dispenses a lot of useful and hard to get information on the Williamson and Wood Rivers plus other Oregon destinations such as the Sandy, Deschutes, Rogue, Owyhee Rivers and the Crane Prairie Reservoir. Good technical information, where to go and how to fish, as well as travel information. Back issues are available from the Inside Angler at www.insideangler.com or 415/586-7668.

River Journal Series. Oregon: Frank Amato Publications, Inc. A series of large softbound journals designed to help anglers better understand a particular river or lake. Each is written by recognized outdoor writers and fishing experts, and each includes discussions of history, fish, ecology, and fishing strategies. Often include maps and, in the case of rivers, boating guides. Only complaint is these books are not updated very often and are frequently out-of-date. Titles for Oregon include: *McKenzie River,* by Deke Meyer; *Crane Prairie: Deschutes*

Headwaters and the *Rogue River,* both by Scott Richmond; and the *Sandy River,* by Mark Bachman.

Fly-Fishing

Johnson, Les. *Fly-Fishing Coastal Cutthroat Trout: Flies, Techniques, Conservation.* Oregon: Amato Books, 2004. A much needed and anticipated update to Johnson's 1971 classic *Sea-Run Cutthroat Trout.* There is a profound shortage of information on the progress of restoring this once declining sportfish which is on the rebound thanks to conservation efforts; this book fills that need. Highly recommended for interested readers.

Judy, John. *Slack Line Fishing.* Pennsylvania: Stackpole Books, 2002.

———. Seasons of the Metolius. California Bill's Automotive Handbooks, 2002. No book has ever been written about how to fish the Metolius, but these two books come as close as anything ever could, and they were written by a passionate angler who has made the river his life and love. Slack Line Fishing is a technical fly-fishing book detailing John's unique approach to fishing difficult water. Seasons on the Metolius is a natural history guide to the area, but it includes a lot of useful fishing information. Both books are very highly recommended.

Rickards, Denny. *Fly-Fishing Stillwaters for Trophy Trout.* Oregon: A Stillwater Productions Publication, 1998. Denny makes his home in the Klamath Basin and conducts most of his research on Klamath Lake and surrounding still waters. Denny's scientific approach makes his theories complex and difficult to apply, yet the general material and analysis of trout behavior make this book an indispensable guide for understanding stillwater fishing. Denny offers a number of seminars every year in the Klamath Basin. Highly recommended for scientifically minded anglers.

Schollmeyer, Jim. *Hatch Guide for Western Streams*. Oregon: Frank Amato Publications, 1997. Highly recommended for anglers wanting to know more about insect hatches on any western river. Good pictures of each type of insect, matching fly patterns and advice on how and when to use each pattern, plus a lot of helpful fishing information. Excellent resource/reference book.

General

Allen, Melinda. *Floating & Fishing Oregon's Wilderness River Canyons*. Oregon: Frank Amato Publications, 2005. Include the Deschutes, John Day, Grand Ronde, Wallowa, Rogue and Owyhee Rivers.

Combs, Trey. *Steelhead Fly-Fishing*. New York: The Lyons Press, 1999. A must-have for steelhead anglers.

Gerald, Paul. *60 Hikes within 60 Miles of Portland*. Alabama: Manasha Press, 2007. A superbly written hiking guidebook with listings that lead to many of the Mount Hood and coastal waters listed in this book. Highly recommended.

Hughes, Dave. *Taking Trout: Good, Solid, Practical Advice for Fly-Fishing Streams and Still Waters*. Pennsylvania: Stackpole Books, 2002. Good beginner guide.

Meyer, Deke. *Advanced Fly-Fishing for Steelhead: Flies and Technique*. Oregon: Frank Amato Publications, 1992. Excellent practical information.

Richmond, Scott. *Fishing in Oregon's Endless Season*. Oregon: Flying Pencil Publications, 1997. A collection of essays from a gifted writer and angler telling what it is like to fish in Oregon through all twelve seasons. Out of print but worth locating a used copy.

Local Fishing Literature

Lesley, Craig. *Winterkill*. Boston: Houghton Mifflin, 1984.

———. *Riversong*. Boston: Houghton Mifflin, 1989. These two novels are of historical interest to anglers wanting to know more about Native American culture around the Pendleton/Hermiston/Deschutes areas. *Winterkill* devotes a good deal of space to the closing of Celilo Falls, the tribal fishing grounds on the Columbia River. The sequel, *Riversong*, takes place on the Warm Springs Indian Reservation and the Deschutes.

Lesson, Ted. *The Habit of Rivers: Reflections on Trout Streams and Fly-Fishing*. New York: Lyons & Burford, 1994. Naturalist, humorist, intellectual, philosopher, angler: Lesson's writing refuses to fit neatly into any one of these categories, but includes them all. A collection of essays that should be read by every angler as an introduction to fishing in Oregon—written, of course, by an East Coast transplant. Topics include drift boats, steelhead rivers, trout rivers, fly tying, entomology, and much, much more. Highest recommendation!

Magazines and Periodicals

Northwest Fly-Fishing. Quarterly. Northwest Fly-Fishing, LLC, Seattle, Washington. Reads more like a journal with better than average articles by the Northwest's leading anglers. Each edition includes destination articles profiling six northwest rivers, helpful fishing tips, conservation news, product reviews, fly tying instructions, fly tier profiles, and literary contributions. Highly recommended as one of the best periodicals for fly-fishing information.

Oregon Hunting and Fishing News. Weekly. Outdoor Empire Publishing, Inc., Bothell, WA. Good weekly publication with fishing reports from around the state. Helpful information regarding fish migration times for salmon and steelhead. Includes helpful fishing tips, best fishing spots for the week and month. Articles are inclusive of all fishing methods with a bias towards bait and traditional gear. Does tend to lack truly original information; stock articles seem to get regurgitated every so often. Recommended for general information.

Salmon, Trout, Steelheader. Monthly. Frank Amato Publications, Portland, Oregon. Detailed and often technical articles concerning Northwest fishing. Unbiased coverage of all types of fishing methods including bait, spinner, float, and fly-fishing. Recommended!

Maps and Atlases

Oregon River Maps & Fishing Guide. 2nd Printing. Oregon: Frank Amato Publications, 2004. A good overview of 37 steelhead and salmon rivers in Oregon covering both traditional and fly-fishing information. Nicely drawn maps include access points such as roads and boat ramps. Additional charts specify types of fish species present in each body of water, hatch charts, best gear to use and fish run times. A nice companion alongside an atlas or road map. The second printing corrects errors found in the first printing, however "Second Printing" is not indicated on the guide. To determine whether you're buying a second edition, look for Harpham Flat launch point (Deschutes River, page 43) to be included.

Middle Rogue Steelhead Chapter Trout Unlimited: River Collections: Rogue, Applegate, Illinois Area and Access Maps. Oregon: Middle Rogue Steelhead Chapter Trout Unlimited, 2003. A handy guide with hand-drawn maps indicating public access points, boat launches, day use areas, notable river features, local outfitters, and fishing shops. The only drawbacks are no

mention of river mileage points and very little commentary, otherwise a worthwhile investment at $4.

Oregon Atlas & Gazetteer. 3rd ed. Maine: DeLorme, 1998. Very detailed categories including bicycle routes, boat ramps, fishing, campgrounds, hiking, historic sites, museums, hunting, oar/paddle trips, parks, forests, wilderness areas, scenic drives, and unique natural features. Well thought out, very useful and highly recommended!

Shewey, John. *The Lower Deschutes River Fishing Map.* Oregon: Frank Amato Publications, 1999. A laminated foldout map detailing the lower 100 miles of river, written by one of the master fly anglers on the Deschutes. Includes insect hatches, fly patterns shown in color for both steelhead and trout, fly-fishing techniques and tackle, campsites, roads, boat launches, and rapids. Very useful as a general guide, but not really a boaters' guide. Presents a good overview of the river and highlights some of the boating hazards.

Streamtime, Inc. *Rogue River: StreamTime Fishing Access and Accommodations Maps.* California: Streamtime, Inc., 1993.
———. *Klamath River: StreamTime Fishing Access and Accommodations Maps.* California: Streamtime, Inc., 1995.
———. *Chetco River: StreamTime Fishing Access and Accommodations Maps.* California: Streamtime, Inc., 2006. An excellent map series designed for anglers. Includes river mileages, fishing spots, hiking trails, road and bank access, boat ramps, whitewater hazards, camping, lodging, and guide services. Maybe the most important feature is river mileage for calculating distances between floats and commentary highlighting dangerous rapids. Limited selection of maps for Oregon. Available in some fishing stores, over the phone (415/461-3882), or through www.streamtime.com.

River Guidebooks

Bureau of Land Management. *Deschutes River-Boaters Guide*. Oregon: Bureau of Land Management, 2001. This waterproof guide is designed to provide an overview of the Lower Deschutes River. It includes comprehensive maps with recreation, fishing and boating information. River safety, rules and history are also included. Limited mile-by-mile commentary. Lacks detail and commentary about how to approach rapids and avoid dangers. Good general information.

Oregon Parks and Recreation Department. *Willamette River Recreation Guide*. Oregon: Oregon State Park publications, 1998. Detailed river maps, river mileage points, timed floats, recreation guide, historical and wildlife information, state parks guide, Available at www.oregonstateparks.org/publications.phpor, or through the Oregon Parks and Recreation Department (800/551-6949). Free is a good price for so much information. Suitable to boaters and anglers.

Quinn, James W. and King, James G. *The Handbook to the Deschutes River Canyon*. 3rd ed. Oregon: Frank Amato Publications, Inc., 1979. Still in print and at one time the best and most popular guide for boating the Deschutes with mile-by-mile descriptions, suggestions for approaching rapids, campground locations and historical anecdotes. Sadly, this book is outdated with recent flood-induced changes to the river and should only be used as a supplement with newer guides (see Scott Richmond, below).

Richmond, Scott. *Fishing In Oregon's Deschutes River*. 2nd ed. Oregon: 4Rivers, 2004.

Written for fly anglers, but one of the few updated guides to boating the river. Good general information for any angler, including hatch charts, fishing tips, detailed boating descriptions and directions to more than 150 camping and recreation sites. The best river guide to come out in years. This is just one of many good books Scott has written on fly-fishing in Oregon.

Willamette Kayak & Canoe Club. *Soggy Sneakers: A Guide to Oregon Rivers*. 3rd ed. Seattle: Mountaineers Books, 1994. Geared towards whitewater enthusiasts, this is an essential boaters' guide covering all the major rivers in Oregon. Details river hazards, access points, driving directions, river mileages and area facilities. Little to no fishing information, but highly recommended.

Traditional Angling Methods

Butler, Jim. *Steelhead Float Fishing*. Oregon: Frank Amato Publications, 2005. Good guide for an exciting new technique in steelhead fishing.

Davis, Jed. *Spinner Fishing for Steelhead, Salmon and Trout*. Oregon: Frank Amato Publications, 1989. Classic reading for anyone who wants to advance their spinner fishing to new levels. Highly recommended!

Herzog, Bill. *Color Guide to Steelhead Drift Fishing*. Oregon: Frank Amato Publications, 1994. Easy to understand basic guide detailing gear selection and techniques for catching steelhead in all conditions.

Oregon State Fishing Records

COLD WATER

SPECIES	LBS	OZ	YEAR	LOCATION	ANGLER
Salmon, Chinook	83	0	1910	Umpqua River	Ernie St Claire
Salmon, Chum	23	0	1990	Kilchis River	Roger Nelson
Salmon, Coho	25	5.25	1966	Siltcoos Lake	Ed Martin
Salmon, Kokanee	6	12	2001	Wallowa Lake	Pamella Fahey
Shad	6	6	2004	Willamette River	Larry Arendt
Sturgeon*	-	-	-	-	-
Trout, Brook	9	6	1980	Deschutes River	Burt Westbrook
Trout, Brown	28	5	2002	Paulina Lake	Ronald Lane
Trout, Bull	23	2	1989	Lake Billy Chinook	Don Yow
Trout, Cutthroat	9	8	1986	Malheur River	Phillip Grove
Trout, Golden	7	10	1987	Eagle Cap Wilderness	Douglas White
Trout, Mackinaw	40	8	1984	Odell Lake	H V Hannon
Trout, Rainbow	28	0	1982	Rogue River	Mike McGonagle
Trout, Steelhead	35	8	1970	Columbia River	Berdell Todd
Whitefish	4	0	1974	McKenzie River	Todd Fisher

*There is no state record information for sturgeon in Oregon because the maximum size limit is 60". It is unlawful to remove an oversized sturgeon from the water.

WARM WATER

SPECIES	LBS	OZ	YEAR	LOCATION	ANGLER
Bass, Hybrid	18	8	2002	Ana Reservoir	Justin C. Marks
Bass, Largemouth	12	1.6	2002	Ballenger Pond, Springfield	B. Adam Hastings
Bass, Smallmouth	8	1.76	2000	Henry Hagg Lake	Nick Rubeo
Bass, Striped	68	0	1973	Umpqua River	Beryl Bliss
Bluegill	2	5.5	1981	Farm Pond	Wayne Elmore
Catfish, Bullhead	3	7	2001	Henry Hagg Lake	Bob Junkins
Catfish, Channel	36	8	1980	McKay Reservoir	Boone Haddock
Catfish, Flathead	42	0	1994	Snake River	Joshua Kralicek
Catfish, White	15	0	1989	Tualatin River	Wayne Welch
Crappie, Black	4	6.1	1995	Corvallis	John Doss
Crappie, White	4	12	1967	Gerber Reservoir	Jim Duckett
Perch, Sacramento	0	11.2	1998	Lost River	Jonathan Cogley
Perch, Yellow	2	2	1971	Brownsmead	Ernie Affolter III
Sunfish, Green	0	11	1991	Umpqua River	John Baker
Sunfish, Pumpkinseed	0	7.68	1996	Lake Oswego	Linda Mar
Sunfish, Redear	1	15.5	1992	Reynolds Pond	Terence Bice
Walleye	19	15.3	1990	Columbia River	Arnold Berg
Warmouth	1	14.2	1975	Columbia Slough	Jess Newell
Whitefish	4	14	1994	Crane Prairie Reservoir	Roger Massey

Index

Acknowledgments

This book is dedicated to my father Robert N. Schuhmann, whose presence, love, and influence permeates these pages. And to my wife, Suvendrini, and our daughter Camille. Without their constant encouragement and support this book would have never been written. And to the Brotherhood of Anglers, may our efforts always mingle with the fire, passion, and creativity of the one who put us here.

Many people provided valuable assistance to make this book happen. My assistant, Paul Gerald, provided invaluable assistance over the course of many months in both the editing and research. This book would not have been possible with Paul's diligence, commitment, and hard work.

All the personnel and staff at the ODFW and BLM for their patience, direction, and guidance through the process of writing this book. Specifically, Greg Currie of the BLM in Prineville, Tim Walters of the ODFW in Hines, Kristeen Volpa and Wayne Hunt of the ODFW Salem, and Grant Weidenbach of BLM in Klamath Falls.

I'd like to offer my special appreciation to all the hard-working fishing guides who took the time to answer my questions: Chris Vertopoulos of the northern Oregon coast, Brent Lamm and Chris Young of the southern Oregon Coast, Doug Warren of the South Umpqua, Marty Sheppard of the Sandy and John Day Rivers, Dave Flynn of the Grande Ronde. Thank you to Ron Wassom of Kiger Creek Fly Shop for his feedback on the *Southeastern Oregon* chapter; Oregon outdoors writer Scott Richmond for providing a great source of fishing information at his website (www.westfly.com) and for providing valuable feedback on the suggested reading list. Thomas and Thomas fly rods for their generous support.

Thank you to all my friends who helped me discover the many rivers and lakes listed in this book, making me a better angler in the process: Ken Stockton, Robert West, Keith Young, John Hyde, Mike Benedict, Dennis Mahoney, Dr. Carl Wenner, Jeff Hanson, and Joey Hurt. Thank you to Mike, Jerry, Grover, and all the customers at The Ledge for having faith in me; Darren Roe of Roe Outfitters for making me a better fishing guide; all the guides in the Klamath Basin for their support; Liz and Peggy at Crystal Wood Lodge for their support, humor, and great food; all my fishing clients over the last two years who taught me more about fishing than any single source.

A heartfelt thanks and wish-you-well to Dr. Brian Darnell without whose assistance and companionship over the last year and a half, the Klamath Basin would still remain a mystery. Thank you to Corky Corcoran, my guide and friend, who taught me that anything worth having in this life can't be earned, but is a byproduct of our efforts.

Most especially, thank you to all the outdoors writers living in Oregon whose efforts and presence constantly enrich our sport: John Shewey, Madelynne Sheehan, Gary Lewis, Scott Richmond, Ted Leeson, Deke Meyer, Trey Combs, Dave Hughes, John Judy, Jim Schollmeyer, Rick Hafele, Frank Amato, Denny Rickards, and Les Johnson, to name a few.

Thanks also to the folks at Avalon: Sabrina Young, Ellie Behrstock, Nicole Schultz, Kevin Anglin, Darren Alessi, and to copy editor Karen Bleske.

Notes

Notes

Notes

Notes

Notes

Notes

www.moon.com

For helpful advice on planning a trip, visit www.moon.com for the **TRAVEL PLANNER** and get access to useful travel strategies and valuable information about great places to visit. When you travel with Moon, expect an experience that is uncommon and truly unique.